Beyond the Nation-State

Beyond the Nation-State

Functionalism and International Organization

Ernst B. Haas

Stanford University Press
Stanford, California

Stanford University Press
Stanford, California
© 1964 by the Board of Trustees of the
Leland Stanford Junior University
Printed in the United States of America
Cloth ISBN 0-8047-0186-5
Paper ISBN 0-8047-0187-3
Original edition 1964
Last figure below indicates year of this printing:
81 80 79 78 77 76 75 74 73 72

To Hil and Peter

Preface

This book is self-consciously eclectic. It is neither a theory, nor a model, nor yet a case study. Yet it contains elements of all these appurtenances of the scholarly doxology. It is not a theory because even though it advances logically interrelated propositions, these do not suffice to explain the nature and predict the behavior of international organizations; nor can it claim that all relevant empirical experience is subsumed under it, or that it is proof against contrary empirical discoveries. It is not a model because it deliberately attempts to remain very closely identified with the empirical material, seeking to induce findings from it rather than deduce propositions from a tightly and logically drawn abstract scheme. However, it is not a case study either, because it shamelessly manipulates the experience of the International Labor Organization, on which it draws very heavily, in order to explore the nature of international integration. The results may well shock the officials of that organization, who do not and need not see their work in the context in which I have cast it.

The eclectic nature of the book is patent as soon as I state the question to which I have addressed myself and describe the way in which I sought to discover the answers. These are the questions: (1) How can the *normal* aims and expectations of nations be related to a process of growing mutual deference and institutional mingling; and, in particular, what can political sociology and sociological political thought contribute to the exploration of this process? (2) What kind of international organization is required in order to maximize a process of international integration as defined in the first question? (3) Is the International Labor Organization such an entity?

Political theory is prominent in my effort to answer the first question even though the result is not a theory. Prominence is assured to pre-behavioral political theory because I draw heavily upon it in order to state the fundamental assumptions that I accept as "the truth" about politics, while using it at the same time as a critical tool for quarreling with the views of those who see this "truth" differently. I depend particularly upon political theory to explore what the hope and aspiration of international integration is, and what can reasonably be expected within the confines of "the truth" as I see it. But I use political theory in a more strictly behavioral sense as well. In a methodological manner developed from the basic principles I have assumed, I draw on the actual history and conduct of a variety of international organizations in order to operationalize the assumptions about politics with which I begin. My survey of political theory and political sociology, therefore, combines a search for intellectual continuity with an empirical effort to use only those aspects of past theory that appear to have a human counterpart in the actual life histories of international organizations. The result of my attempt is a series of propositions concerning the relationship between integration, systems theory, and functional analysis. They owe an abiding debt to scholars who merit the label of "theorist," whose work I have recklessly exploited.

When I turn to answering my second question—what kind of international organization is required to give life in the future to these propositions—a "model" of sorts is the immediate result. The properties found to be necessary in such organizations have much in common with those enumerated in certain abstract efforts at rendering models of sustained cooperative behavior, conflict resolution, and the definition of new common tasks. Here, too, I am deeply indebted to a number of scholars who have directly addressed themselves to these problems in the fields of sociology, management science, and industrial relations, though I have found it necessary to reformulate aspects of their work in order to make it fit the facts of international relations.

In setting up this model I have observed certain methodological maxims that require statement. I have eschewed logical rigor and perfect internal consistency in favor of a more loosely structured design, which remains close to the Weberian ideal type. This choice was dictated by a prior commitment to what has been called "contextual analysis," an approach that tries to bridge the epistemological chasm between those who want to derive general-deductive "laws" on the one hand and those who prefer to concentrate on the painstaking narration of discrete, if related, events on the other. Contextual analysis is more ambitious than historical narration and more modest than the effort at deductive "science." It seeks the general within the more confined context of a given historical, regional, or functional setting. It sees the phenomenon under investigation as a part of a "whole," but defines this "whole" in relatively modest and easily observable terms.

The "whole" can also be described as "reality," the specific reality of time, place, and circumstance that is implicit in the hopes and frustrations of the political actors who build or destroy international organizations. Our ideal type, then, is not so much a general statement of a number of attributes present in diverse concrete types. It is a statement of attributes considered necessary for the realization of what is "ideally" postulated, the process of integration by way of international organization. But these attributes, in turn, are derived from "reality," from the "wholeness" of the historical context as reflected in the predominating aims and motives of actual political actors. I am concerned with making clear that the perception of this reality is not a matter of artistic intuition, of some mystical *Verstehen*. To be sure, it may involve a largely qualitative exercise in observing, sorting, and arranging the "facts" of actor conduct that make up reality. But this qualitative act is intuitive only insofar as it rests on the observer's capacity to identify himself with human motives that all of us accept as "real" and relevant to the study of politics. Since this capacity is fairly widely encountered in professional circles, it is capable of replication and cannot be called intuitive in any rigorous sense of the term.

But even such a "real" context is a distortion of history because it is selective in terms of the events, aims, and circumstances posited for attention and emphasis in the model. The point could become crucial when we turn to our third and final question: Is the International Labor Organization the kind of entity most likely to advance international integration? If we were to give a negative answer, could this not be blamed on an unrealistic definition of the "whole" context? Hence I argue that the criteria of relevance adopted for the design of the model of an international organization comprise more than the observer's whim and prejudice. I submit that they are derived from the "whole" context, culled from the study of a variety of other efforts and organizations, induced from the reality of successful and unsuccessful integration in a "field" of standard human motives and expectations. These criteria of relevance are not derived from a sample of cases; they stem from the total—but numerically small—population, from the activities of most modern international organizations.

This brings us to the choice of the International Labor Organization as the empirical whetstone on which our model was sharpened. The ILO is in no sense typical of the genus "international organization," and an analysis of its dynamic cannot be justified as a case study of something typical, from which generalizations about the whole population can then be hazarded. In other words, I am not attempting a general theory on the basis of a single case study; I am sketching the outline of an eclectic theory of integration and then ask myself to what extent a real organization meets its requisites. But why the ILO? First, the organization is almost a half-century old, one of the very few international organizations with a lengthy and unbroken history. Second, in terms of program and structure the ILO, *ex hypothesi*, fits the requirements of the model very closely: its task concerns the general welfare demands of modern man, and its structure permits the participation of voluntary groups. These attributes characterize the most successful integration efforts at the regional level. Hence they constitute two central criteria for the study of the process on a global scale.

My purpose here is not to attack or defend the International Labor Organization, to expose its shortcomings or praise its services, but to inquire whether its structure, tasks, and achievements meet the desiderata posed by my first and second questions, problems not of immediate relevance to those who originated and perpetuated the ILO. My findings, moreover, are important not so much for the light they may throw on the international protection of labor standards as for what they may suggest with respect to the adequacy of functional international organizations in contributing to integration along lines indicated by functional sociology.

Basic to the formulation of my questions is the work of the Functionalists, notably David Mitrany, who was good enough to comment on my first chapters in manuscript. Although I do not agree with certain aspects of their approach, I believe that it has done more to cast the study of international organization in a dynamic and comprehensive context than most other approaches. Yet the Functionalists are no more responsible for the results of my eclectic meandering among theories and models than the few theorists and model-builders on whom I have relied so heavily for inspiration and guidance.

This book was written with the help of grants received from the Rockefeller Foundation, the Social Science Research Council, and the Institute of International Studies of the University of California (Berkeley). It could not have been written without the generous indulgence of many officials of the International Labor Organization in Geneva, who, however, bear no responsibility whatever for any of my conclusions. I profited greatly from the comments of Dwight Waldo, Philip Selznick, Stanley Hoffmann, John Fried, and Glenn Snyder. Kurt Vogel, Robert Diamond, Xavier Vela, Ajit Singh, Ellen Levine, Laurel Weinstein, and Sharon Pucker aided my labors in Berkeley, and Mlles. Durin, Mardon, and Frank performed research assistance in Geneva. Without their help and criticism the progress of the work would have been a great deal slower. Finally, I should like to acknowledge with gratitude and deep pleasure the stimulation I received from colleagues working in this field with whom I had the privilege to be associated when they studied at Berkeley: James P. Sewell, Leon N. Lindberg, Wolfram Hanrieder, Stuart A. Scheingold, and Philippe C. Schmitter.

E. B. H.

Berkeley, California
June 1964

Contents

Abbreviations

AFL	American Federation of Labor
CIO	Congress of Industrial Organizations (U.S.)
ECE	United Nations Economic Commission for Europe
ECLA	United Nations Economic Commission for Latin America
ECOSOC	United Nations Economic and Social Council
FAO	Food and Agriculture Organization of the United Nations
IAEA	International Atomic Energy Agency
IBRD	International Bank for Reconstruction and Development
ICA	International Cooperative Alliance
ICAO	International Civil Aviation Organization
ICCTU	International Confederation of Christian Trade Unions
ICFTU	International Confederation of Free Trade Unions
ICJ	International Court of Justice
IFTU	International Federation of Trade Unions
ILO	International Labor Organization
IMF	International Monetary Fund
IOE	International Organization of Employers
ITF	International Transport Workers Federation
ITO	International Trade Organization
ITS	International Trade Secretariat
JMC	Joint Maritime Commission (ILO)
NATO	North Atlantic Treaty Organization
OAS	Organization of American States
PCIJ	Permanent Court of International Justice
TAB	United Nations Technical Assistance Board
UN	United Nations
UNESCO	United Nations Educational Scientific and Cultural Organization
UNRRA	United Nations Relief and Rehabilitation Administration
WFTU	World Federation of Trade Unions
WHO	World Health Organization
WMA	World Medical Association

PART I

Functionalism and the Theory of Integration

1. *Functionalism*

The tyranny of words is only slightly less absolute than that of men; but whereas elections, revolutions, or just the dreary passage of time can do away with human tyranny, patient analysis and redefinition are required to remedy the linguistic affliction. The tyranny exercised by the word "function" is a case in point.

As the "functionalist" Robert Merton admits, "the large assembly of terms used indifferently and almost synonymously with 'function' presently includes use, utility, purpose, motive, intention, aim, consequences."[1] To make matters worse, almost all these terms are vital to orderly political discussion and analysis, they can all be used in several senses, and yet each of them can also express a single concept. On the other hand, in the history of science the word "function" has had a variety of conceptual meanings, all of which crop up in contemporary analysis and overlap with the seven terms just enumerated. These conceptual meanings include "occupation," the typical behavior pattern associated with a particular political office, the causal interrelations between mathematical (and social) variables, and the more specifically anthropological usage in which "function" is considered a necessary contribution to the structural-organic unity of some social entity.[2] Matters are further complicated by the fact that in Malinowski and Radcliffe-Brown, for example, this last usage is apparently an adaptation of the mathematical formulation. As our final observation on linguistic obfuscation, let it be noted that social scientists today disagree about whether semantic clarity can be achieved in "functional" analysis, or indeed whether such an effort would be worth our while.[3]

Students of international relations could shrug off the entire issue as irrelevant to their concern if a species of "functionalism" were not one of the most promising modes of analysis available to them, even though this approach seems to have developed quite independently of the larger concern with "functionalism" in social anthropology and sociology.

At one extreme we may note the hegemony of the functional vocabulary as an aspect of international systems theory, albeit a species of systems theory not entirely free from ambiguity. Semantic interest may be aroused by the fact that a *systemic* rendering of established historical relationships here follows in the chronological footsteps of earlier attempts at rendering the same phenomenon in terms of the *balance of power*. Let us permit a typical passage to speak for itself:

The classical nation-state system as it emerged out of the European complex also developed certain mechanisms for preserving its own stability and identity. In effect, the nation-state system sought to ensure that all non-states and all societies which could not meet the qualifications of sovereignty were so controlled and regulated as not to disrupt the effective operation of the nation-states. Viewed from the perspective of the system as a whole, it is possible to identify colonialism as the chief mechanism by which the nation-state system protected itself from the intrusion of influences which for the preservation of the system had to be considered as disruptive, random, and irresponsible. Colonialism functioned to regulate and control societies that had not achieved the capacity to be full states and operate according to the standards of state behavior.

A second function of colonialism in the classical nation-scale system was to provide a mechanism for facilitating the diffusion of culture and technology while preventing the more explosive consequences of social change from disrupting the system. Under the auspices of colonial authorities, 'primitive' people could experience the inevitably painful process of modernizing all phases of their life without dislocating the entire world order.[4]

A prime source of tension for the international system in the next decade is the conflict between the need of the underdeveloped countries to modernize their societies and hence undergo dislocating and even explosive social change and the need for the international system to maximize stability and hence control disruptive influences. These two conflicting developments were traditionally controlled by colonialism. In the post-colonial era, new methods must be found for facilitating the spread of modern culture and for protecting the international system as a whole from the disruptions of such change.[5]

Apparently, then, we have an "international" or "nation-state" system. Who are its members? Does the system "protect" itself, or do the members as actors? Apparently, colonialism was a "function" (i.e. task, purpose, need, consequence?) of the "system," which met certain systemic "needs" (i.e. tasks, etc.?) in the past; but since it does so no longer, "functional" equivalents must be found to meet the same needs. Did the actors engage in colonialism in order to maintain the system and to socialize Africans and Asians to its norms? Or did the system, quite apart from the wills and purposes of the actors, have the "result" (i.e. the function?) of maintenance and socialization?

If carried far enough this type of treatment will, of course, imbue the "system" with an autonomous will that determines in considerable detail the behavior of the actors. The functions of the system will then become patterned processes in which politicians merely act out, in an eternal dance, the self-maintenance needs of the total entity.[6] Everything that actually occurs "must" occur because of some systemic need. What interests us here is whether the "functions" involved refer to the *results* of an action, the implicit *needs* leading to the action, or the explicit *purposes* underlying the action in the minds of the actors.

Not many generations ago the notion of the international actor was rendered by the term "weight," and that of the system by the notion of "balance" or "equilibrium." The patterned relationships among the weights were considered deterministic, i.e. functional. When the weights were in balance, stability—or peace—was said to prevail. Were conditions of imbalance, then, to be considered "dysfunctional," and equilibrium "eufunctional" (i.e. useful and desirable?)? As long as our terminology is no more precise than this, the concepts wrapped up in the terms leave something to be desired. One is tempted to agree with R. L. Schanck that the history of science is a story of "dominant metaphors," each borrowed from some field other than the one to which it was to be applied. If the dominant metaphor in the era of the balance-of-power theory was borrowed from mechanics, that of modern systems theory seems to owe its parentage to homeostatic physiology.[7] Even if the metaphor is just another heuristic device, it appears to suggest deductive answers that had best be avoided. If a dominant metaphor becomes more than a figure of speech, more than an illuminating literary excursion, it runs the grave risk of reifying relationships, so that an initially purely empirical model or system becomes, willy-nilly, a conceptual scheme distorting the real world by imputing laws of behavior deduced from its presumed workings. Unless we make the improbable assumption that the actors will start to behave in accordance with the metaphor, the result may well be demonstrations that reinforce the conceptual system at the risk of further and further alienation from the real.

But what if the notion of "function" could be divorced from its own verbal ambiguity and from its links with systems theory? In fact, the school of political scientists who call themselves Functionalists acknowledges no direct tie to functional analysis in sociology.* Since it is the work

* For purposes of clarity I shall refer to the exponents of the particular school of thought that deals with questions of international organization in "functional" terms as Functionalists, using the lower-case "f" for other writers and modes of thought referred to as "functionalist" in sociology.

of these people, in the realm of the evolution of international institutions and the development of political community at the international level, that will preoccupy this study, I must stress their more modest use of these terms, leaving aside for the moment the question of the finality of their divorce from functional sociology.

Functionalists, in the specific sense of the term, are interested in identifying those aspects of human needs and desires that exist and clamor for attention outside the realm of the political. They believe in the possibility of specifying technical and "non-controversial" aspects of governmental conduct, and of weaving an ever-spreading web of international institutional relationships on the basis of meeting such needs. They would concentrate on commonly experienced needs initially, expecting the circle of the non-controversial to expand at the expense of the political, as practical cooperation became coterminous with the totality of interstate relations. At that point a true world community will have arisen.

The philosophical reasoning underlying this program does not at the moment concern us. What matters is the notion of function: it is, according to the explicit intent of the Functionalist writers, equivalent in meaning to "organizational task." The function of the Food and Agriculture Organization is to increase agricultural productivity and the world food supply; the function of the Universal Postal Union is to speed the world's mail; the function of the International Labor Organization is to raise and equalize the living standards of workers throughout the world. Apparently, there are no half-hidden relationships to systems and models, no intended or unintended consequences: function means task. Functionalism, then, becomes both an analytical tool for criticizing the deplorable present and an ideological prescription for ushering in a better future. The question next arises: Is it possible to reformulate the sociologist's notion of functionalism, to strip it of its ambiguities, so that a purified version can then be applied to the study of international institutions?

Certain awkward questions had best be faced at the outset. Does not the Functionalist notion of function also carry the connotation of cognitively perceived need on the part of the actor, leading to the creation of an organizational task designed to meet the need? If so, cannot the implementation of the task carry with it consequences not planned or intended by the actor, which may then somehow transform both the organization and the actor's initial perceptions? The task may be carried out to fulfill the initial need, but once implemented, it may create an entirely new situation, setting up novel relationships affecting the total context in which action takes place. In that event, has the notion of function not been linked again, however involuntarily, to a system of some kind?

This complication may be illustrated by two statements from the leading contemporary Functionalist writer, David Mitrany: "The truth is that by its very nature the constitutional approach [to world peace and unity] emphasizes the individual index of power; the functional approach emphasizes the common index of need."⁸ And again: "[The functional approach] . . . should help shift the emphasis from political issues which divide to those social issues in which the interest of the peoples is plainly akin and collective; to shift the emphasis from power to problem and purpose."⁹ Now "function" acquires the meanings of need and purpose, in addition to task. "Task" could be considered merely to imply the legal mandate imposed on an organization, or the program that exists in the minds of its officers and executives. But "need" is a more general notion, a concept with vague societal implications, and hence a concept that relates the organization to its environment. If "purpose" refers merely to the task as explicitly conceived by the executive of the organization, we have no terminological or operational problem; but if it is thought to relate to the more general notion of need, the problem of operationalization does arise. Do we look for the impulse generating organizational action in the organization itself or in the environmental forces? As soon as some structured relationship between organization and environment is postulated, as soon as "task" ceases to be some simple practical objective in the mind of a manager, we are faced with the notion of system.

It appears, therefore, that not even our hope of arriving at an unambiguous Functionalism free from methodological issues can be realized. The brooding omnipresence of some species of system simply cannot be banished. What, then, do we mean by system? Following in the footsteps of Nadel, a writer who is dedicated to avoiding the pitfalls of the functionalist vocabulary, I conceive of a system as a second-level body of abstractions, a network of relationships among relationships, leaving the concrete actors one step below: "We arrive at the structure of a society through abstracting from the concrete population and its behavior pattern or network (or 'system') of relationships obtaining 'between actors in their capacity of playing roles relative to one another.' "¹⁰

Whether we wish it or not, such an orientation involves us in political theory, the theory of analyzing *and* prescribing for the international society. This prescriptive intent is central to Functionalist theory: the Functionalists claim to possess a theoretical apparatus capable of analyzing existing society and of pinpointing the causes of its undesirable aspects; they claim, further, to know the way in which a normatively superior state of affairs can be created. Such, however, is not my theoretical intent. To quote Nadel once more, I am interested in functional theory as "a body of propositions (still interconnected) which serve to *map out* the problem area and thus prepare the ground for its empirical investigation by appropriate methods. More precisely, the propositions serve to classify phenomena, to analyze them into relevant units or indicate their interconnections,

and to define 'rules of procedure' and 'schemes of interpretation.' 'Theory'
here equals conceptual scheme or logical framework."[11] Thus armed, let
us leave the semantic aspect and address ourselves to the reconciliation of
Functionalism and functionalism.

INTERNATIONAL FUNCTIONALISM AS REFORMIST IDEOLOGY

Functionalism has no single prophet, no scriptures, and no dogma. As an
ideology seeking to reform the form and substance of international life it
has had a variety of spokesmen since the 1870's. But far from constituting
a coherent body of militants, these people are united only by a vague and
shifting syndrome of common attitudes and propositions: in fact, it is of
the essence of Functionalism to avoid rigidity and dogma. Those qualify-
ing to be called Functionalist have been considered to include Paul S.
Reinsch, Leonard Woolf, G. D. H. Cole, H. R. G. Greaves, Pitman Potter,
Edgar Saveney, and a host of lesser-known writers preparing blueprints for
the brave new world that was to arise at the end of World War II. The chief
exponent of Functionalism, however, is undoubtedly David Mitrany; yet
it should be borne in mind that no one work of his contains the Functionalist gospel, but that the component parts are to be found scattered in books,
articles, and speeches.[12] Nor do all Functionalists agree on all points or
maintain consistency in their emphases over a generation of writing.
Aspects of the Functionalist argument singled out by me as crucial have
not necessarily been so treated by all Functionalist writers. Yet when I
was convinced that a proposition was implicit in the Functionalist case,
even though not necessarily given prominence by an author, I have felt
free to incorporate it in the mainstream of the argument.

My summary will be as eclectic as the Functionalist approach, though
not inaccurate, I trust. It will take up, in turn, the Functionalists' view of
the human condition, their criticism of the nation-state in relation to individual fulfillment and international conflict, their theory of change, and
their program of reform.

Guild Socialism and Pluralism furnished the criteria for diagnosing the
human condition. Man is by nature good, rational, and devoted to the
common weal; when society is organized so as to bring out man's tendency
to mobilize his energies for the general welfare, the forces of peace and
harmony rule. This happy state of affairs is approximated whenever a
maximum of authority is exercised by technicians and administrators dedicated to the common weal, working in close conjunction with the voluntary professional groups that form part of any modern industrial society.
But, cautions Mitrany, "In all societies there are both harmonies and disharmonies. It is largely within our choice which we pick out and further.
. . . We must begin anew, therefore, with a clear sense that the nations

an be bound together into a world community only if we link them up by
hat unites, not by what divides."[13]

Disharmonies and conflict prevail in a society in which authority is exer-
ised by politicians rather than technicians, by parliaments rather than
oluntary groups.* Power, instead of the common good, then determines
olicy, and irrational behavior follows. Like Saint-Simon and Lenin, the
unctionalist would hold that the human condition will improve only when
the government of men" is replaced by "the administration of things";
ut whereas the Liberal will assume merely a quantitative distinction be-
ween politics and administration and recognize their mutual dependencies,
he Functionalist will insist on a rigorous qualitative difference. Politics
s identified with the pursuit of power and with residual infantile behavior
aits, and technical management with a mature mind and a healthy so-
iety.[14] Preaching the administration and construction of the common
ood is itself part of the therapy for a disharmonious society. This is all
he more urgent because technological and industrial progress makes the
ttainment of the general welfare an immediately realizable goal. A healthy
ociety would control the forces of progress for the benefit of mankind; a
ower-oriented society would let the opportunity escape. When men's loyal-
ies are penned up within the territorial confines of the exclusivist nation-
tate, there is little hope of working for the general welfare. However,
hese loyalties, once freed from the shackles of national insecurity and
llowed to identify with humanity at large, will achieve the true common
ood.

This diagnosis brings into focus the distorting role of the modern state
ith respect to the possibilities of human fulfillment. Here again the Guild
ocialist heritage of the Functionalist approach is manifest. Pre-industrial
nd pre-national primary occupational groups were the true focuses for
uman happiness because they afforded a sense of participation in the
olution of practical problems. The rise of the territorially bounded, omni-
ompetent national state changed all that. Group spontaneity was lost, the
endency of man to identify with his occupational colleague elsewhere was
hoked off, the search for national security became the focus of life in the
tate. Even the administration of general welfare measures, such as social
ecurity legislation, took place within the depersonalized context of the
tate structure. The unnatural state took the place of natural society, a
act that was merely codified by the rules of nineteenth-century interational law. According to Mitrany, "Our social activities are cut off
rbitrarily at the limit of the state and, if at all, are allowed to be linked

---

The distinction between "politicians" (concerned with doctrine and ideology) and "tech-
icians" or "experts" (concerned with doing practical tasks) is implicit or explicit in most
unctional writing. Mitrany, however, prefers to distinguish between *a priori* ideology and
n *a priori* setting of social purpose, with the second the more desirable.

to the same activities across the border only by means of uncertain an
cramping political ligatures."[15]

Lack of fulfillment, of course, is closely linked to the element of huma
and group creativity. For the Functionalist a cooperative national effor
aiming only at the negative goal of security is uncreative. So is the minima
program of assuring law and order. True creativity must be tied to th
positive goals identified with the modern service state, "an instrument c
life and not merely an order."[16] The definition of new rights flowing from
an expanding welfare concept is a creative task still possible to the state
provided it once again makes available to voluntary groups channels c
creative participation. Hence the recurrence of the terms "work" an
"working" in the Functionalist vocabulary. Creative work aims at a gen
eral good that normally tends to be obscured by centralization, powe
drives, and uncreative preoccupation with force and national militar
security.

As long as the state remains unreformed with respect to human fulfill
ment internally, its international role will hardly be more reassuring. Whil
the Functionalist is interested in peace, of course, he stresses the element
of creativity and work, of replacing the negatively political in internationa
affairs with the positively functional:

The task that is facing us is how to build up the reality of a common interest i
peace. . . . *Not a peace that would keep the nations quietly apart, but a peac
that would bring them actively together; not the old static and strategic vien
of peace, but a social view of it.* . . . We must put our faith not in a pro
tected but in a working peace; it would indeed be nothing more nor less tha
the idea and aspiration of social security taken in its widest range.*

This passage from Mitrany bears rereading: it contains the essence of th
Functionalist diagnosis of the negative existing order and the germ for it
positive successor. The peace of statesmen, of collective security, of dis
armament negotiations, of conferences of parliamentarians, of sweepin;
constitutional attempts at federation, all this is uncreative. It is so mucl
power instead of creative work. The reintroduction of man, united in
natural occupational groupings that ignore territorial boundaries, func
tioning through voluntary associations dedicated to welfare measures or
which there is general agreement, this is the creative solution. The practi
cal implication, naturally enough, is that working peace-making effort

---

* Mitrany, *A Working Peace System*, p. 51 (italics mine). Mitrany (in 1963) felt that no
even a major relaxation in international tensions would invalidate this dictum: even if a
rededication to welfare policies at the national level took place, as would be made possibl
by saving resources previously devoted to armaments, this would still be a competitive an
uncreative process *because* undertaken by the nation-state.

hould address themselves first and foremost to economic and social reform: o the joint management of scarce resources, unemployment, commodity rice fluctuations, labor standards, and public health. This would have the esult not only of correcting the faults of existing society, but of removing conomic causes of war and international insecurity.

But at this point Functionalist thought must be sharply distinguished rom simple internationalism of the "one world" variety. The Functionalsts' emphasis on social and economic primacy in the elements of a future nternational order is combined with a recognition that group loyalty and ational attachments are more real than vague international good will. If lomestic harmony can be mobilized by engaging the common aspirations f men with respect to tasks that unite them—welfare rather than order— hen the same would be true internationally. By tackling global conflict ead-on, a direct political approach rather than an indirect welfare one, xisting nationalisms are merely triggered into explosive action; in seeking olutions through political international gestures and institutions, man's emoteness from modern life is exacerbated.

International conflict is best tamed by entrusting the work of increasing uman welfare to experts, technical specialists, and their professional assoiations. Being interested in tasks rather than power, they can be expected o achieve agreement where statesmen will fail. They will be unconcerned vith "rightful" authorities and jurisdictions; rightful ends, proper funcions to be performed, are their concern. Further, conflict is simply sidetepped if the territorial principle of representation is abandoned. Tasks vill be entrusted to agencies possessing functional jurisdiction, i.e. conerning themselves with a specific welfare task; they will be staffed by pecialists free from territorial referents. A supreme political authority vould be as impossible as it is unnecessary. An ever-widening mesh of ask-oriented welfare agencies would come to pre-empt the work now done y some governments, leading eventually to the creation of a universal welare orientation. Since men in many nations already share certain welare aims, this process could be set in motion without involving political ources of friction, thus sidestepping the still blazing national loyalties. 'National problems would then appear, and would be treated, as what they re, the local segments of general problems."[17]

Naturally, existing international organizations devoted to welfare meaures could be used for this purpose. If they also feature the principle of unctional representation, they become ideal candidates in the indirect pproach to community-building. It is for this reason that the International _abor Organization is of particular importance in Functionalist thought.[18] And so, among nations as well as within each, conflict resolution and negaive problems of law and order might eventually become no more than an

aspect of politics, falling "to a subordinate place in the scheme of inte
national things, while we would turn to what are the real tasks of ov
common society—the conquest of poverty and of disease and of ign
rance."[19]

The reform of the state and of interstate relations in the direction «
human welfare can bring with it a new type of world only if the Functiona
ist is able to indicate *how* the new world will supersede the old: if he ha
an explicit or implicit theory of change. To this problem we must no
turn—not an easy subject for investigation, since on this vital theoretic;
(rather than ideological) issue the Functionalist theses are somewh;
vague.

Put in the starkest and most abstract terms, the theory of change seem
to be a purely systemic one. If the nations take full advantage of wha
initially, are merely converging technical interests, eventually these inte
ests will become fused. "In the end," wrote one early Functionalist, "th
nations would find themselves federated, after a fashion, by the very forc
of things."[20] This choice of words suggests an automatic process of chang
once the initial carving out of converging task contexts has taken plac«
Further, there is a dialectical quality to the automaticity. Since the Fun«
tionalist admits that national loyalties are too powerful to be overcom
merely by appealing to the symbols of One World, he also stresses th;
world government cannot come into existence until the sentiment of worl
community has come to flourish. Such a feeling, however, can evolve onl
gradually on the basis of joint tasks of equal interest to all. Thus, the thesi
of national exclusiveness can be outflanked by the antithesis of creativ
work dedicated to welfare, yielding the eventual synthesis of world con
munity. To cap off this conception it must be stressed that the Functionali:
not only assumes an automatic and dialectical process of change, but put
his faith into action rather than advance planning of necessary steps, actioi
as creative endeavor and as an index of the degree to which the dialecti
"force of things" has gotten the better of the status quo: "Promissory Cov
enants and Charters may remain a headstone to unfulfilled good intentions
but the functional way is action itself, and therefore an inescapable tes
of where we stand and how far we are willing to go in building up a nev
international society."[21]

In other contexts, however, a more human notion of change emerges ir
the Functionalist literature, resulting in a doctrine of attitudinal reorienta
tion on the basis of "learning." A necessary presupposition is the distinc
tion between "technical" and "political" modes of thought. Change car
be introduced by maximizing the responsibility of the expert and th«
manager: he is committed to performing his task for the benefit of all
conversely, he is indifferent to representing specific (power-infused?) inter
ests. Functional agencies, suggests Mitrany, might be based on "equality

nonrepresentation."* The differentiation seems to be the Rousseauan
ne between the General Will and the Will of All: the manager stands for
e General Will, whereas the politician represents merely the Will of All,
. the interests of his constituents, which are by definition selfish and
erefore not necessarily geared to transforming the system. The General
ill is strengthened by isolating an ever larger slice (Mitrany often refers
"layers of action and of peace") of technical matters, which will be
ministered so as to extend the range of the technical still further.

Yet the problem remains: Do people "learn" to think in non-national
rms merely because of a pattern of technical cooperation? This is indeed
e central issue in the Functionalist theory of change. At first, it seems
be only the experts and managers who learn. They become habituated
consulting with their opposite numbers from other nations about tech-
cal problems, and eventually they come to see all problems from the per-
ective of mankind as a whole. Thus the answer to maximizing the
arning process lies in extending the range of participation in practical
oblem-solving. In the end, others besides experts, managers, and civil
rvants will participate and undergo the same process, particularly by
ay of greatly increased work and responsibility on the part of interational voluntary groups. Learning becomes a species of group therapy.[22]

The practical Functionalist program is implied in its theoretical position.
stead of attacking nationalism and sovereignty frontally, the Functional-
t aims at solving these problems by simply ignoring them and relying on
stemic forces and a learning process for eventually transcending, rather
an defeating, the old order. An increasing number of institutions of
obal scope dedicated to social service, administered for the benefit of
l, manned by technical experts, and supported by the voluntary participa-
on of non-political groups would do the job. The result would be first a
orld community of sentiment, followed by a world government, some-
ing Mitrany once called "federalism by installments." The necessary
yalties of sentiment would develop naturally as people's expectations
adually came to be focused on these new social welfare agencies rather
an on the present nations. Existing international bodies consisting of
ke-minded professional and occupational groups provide logical building
locks for the new structure of society. We cannot improve on Engle's
mmary of the Functional program: "These three features—a reliance
redominantly upon functional units, an expectation of an eventual sys-
m of government made up primarily of interlocking functional units, and

---

* As quoted in Engle, p. 85. In private correspondence with me (1963), Mitrany seems to
sassociate himself from this formulation. He now grants that central guidance would have
be given by a government, a provision that would obviate an ultimate clash between the
olitical and the technical principles of action. He denies any affinity with the syndicalist
rains of thought apparent in my summary of Functionalism.

the assumption that in functional cooperation certain dynamic behavior
mechanisms of an 'institution-building' and a 'consensus-building' natur
are at work—constitute, then, the ideal type of the functionalist theory a
the international level."[23]

FUNCTIONALIST IDEOLOGY AND HISTORY:
TWO CASE STUDIES

In principle, any of the myriad "technical" activities of internationa
organizations provide the case study material for investigating the validit
of the Functionalist ideology. For the reformulation of this ideology t
which we proceed in the next chapter, many of these cases did in fa
furnish the historical basis. Here our purpose is more modest. Withou
attempting a critique of the ideology, we shall review the growth of "func
tional" preoccupations in two specific cases, seeking to highlight, first, th
rival roles of experts and diplomats, and, second, the distinction betwee
power-infused and welfare-dominated aspirations. A superficial view o
these cases may well suggest that the Functional perspective is remarkabl
accurate, and the ideology firmly grounded in historical experience;
second view, however, shows that extensive reformulation is needed.

Our first case deals with the growth of international measures for th
control of contagious diseases, beginning with the pioneering health con
ferences of the nineteenth century and ending with establishment of th
World Health Organization. What were the chief issues? All Europea
governments seemed agreed that the Moslem pilgrim traffic was responsibl
for the recurrent plague and cholera epidemics that threatened the world
but here agreement ended. The medical profession was divided into tw
major schools of thought: those who held that these diseases were sprea
by contagion, and those who felt that they originated in unsanitary atmos
pheric, housing, sewerage, and food conditions. The profession was fur
ther divided in its evaluation of the effectiveness of quarantine, with th
environmentalists generally arguing that the isolation of patients and in
fected vessels was of no avail. Finally, there was dispute on where cholera
in particular, originated. Most medical people were convinced that it wa
in Bengal, but British physicians tended to deny this. Let us note tw
salient features: the experts were sharply divided on the technical issue
involved, and the respective technical positions that they embraced cor
responded strikingly with the political positions espoused by their govern
ments. All the major maritime nations, notably Britain, defended the
environmentalist position, ridiculed quarantine, and continually stressed
the hardships that international quarantine regulations would impose on
commerce and shipping! Britain refused to initiate quarantine measures
to isolate Mecca-bound pilgrims in the Egyptian facilities over which she
assumed control after 1881.[24] Turkey denied that environmental conditions

territories under her sway contributed to disease conditions. Persia de-
ied the efficacy of quarantines. The British medical profession even
pposed the creation of an expert commission to study the diffusion of
idemics.

Between 1850 and 1903 no less than nine international conferences were
nvened to arrive at common measures to deal with these diseases. They
ere attended by national delegations composed either entirely of medical
en or of medical men assisted by lay delegates. Although the lay delegates
ade constant efforts to persuade the medical men to compromise the rival
iews of contagionists and environmentalists, progress was very slow.
ome headway was made after several severe outbreaks of cholera and
lague during the half-century, but until the 1890's the conventions for
uarantines, ship inspections, bills of health, and expert studies were so
oorly ratified and implemented by the participating states that even so
non-controversial" a field as public health showed all the marks of major
olitical conflict. Apparently it was the severe epidemics of 1893 and 1897
at eventually brought success. By joining the two rival medical views,
e major maritime powers were able to come to terms: they agreed to re-
stitute quarantines, disinfect ships, impose standardized inspection of
essels, and notify all other governments when cases of plague were discov-
red. Turkey and Persia, despite their objection to these measures as in-
ringing the rights of Moslems, were compelled to ratify. The edifice was
ompleted in 1907 with the creation of the International Office of Public
ealth, which was entrusted with the task of conducting scientific studies,
arrying out epidemiological intelligence, and suggesting to member states
ew control devices as the older ones proved inadequate. However, the
urisdiction of the Office was limited to the five major contagious diseases.

The record is far from "proving" whether extended contacts among
edical experts were the factor that caused eventual success. It certainly
ook a long time for the pure welfare component of the health activities to
e recognized. But it seems clear that the interest of all in common action
nd rules was directly influenced by the dangers posed by given epidemics.
nce the breakthrough had been scored, so to speak, international health
fforts were not only sustained but intensified. The League of Nations
reated a new health organization staffed entirely by uninstructed experts,
hich carried out the same activities as the International Office for diseases
ot covered by the Office, as well as initiating the first international tech-
ical assistance operations by training national public health officials and
ncouraging them to keep in touch with each other. From then on the de-
iberate, expert-dominated standardization of national public health regu-
ations proceeded quite smoothly. Goodman, for one, attributes this new
neasure of agreement to constantly growing medical knowledge. As inocu-
ations and uniformly administered health certificates took the place of

cruder inspections and quarantines, the commercial and political sting wa
taken out of the "function." But does this demonstrate the growing no
controversiality of health? Since the original issue was, in effect, sid
stepped, no clear answer can be given. Still, it should be noted that as th
epidemics grew more perilous, objections to international regulations pr
viously drafted or recommended at the many conferences died down; in
sense, then, the opinions of experts were implemented as a common sens
of danger and need gripped governments and the medical profession alik

It seems incontestable, however, that since the advent of the Worl
Health Organization in 1948, the consolidation of power in the expert ha
been as complete as the separation of welfare from politics. And the scop
of WHO operations has expanded accordingly. Even though medical su|
plies are not distributed, they are supplied for demonstration purpose
Instead of merely conducting epidemiological intelligence, WHO seeks t
eradicate diseases. Far from merely standardizing public health pr
cedures, WHO assumes responsibility for inoculations in emergencie
Further, "action to meet emergencies is giving place to programme
planned in advance, for a period of years; projects to bring about a pa
ticular advance are giving place to educational work from which genera
advance may come; and emergency action to control communicable di
eases is giving place to investigation of their fundamental causes, and t
work for the eradication of some."[25] WHO possesses some legislative powe
in the very area in which the conferences of the nineteenth century coul
find so little agreement. The major initial decisions of the Organizatior
were made by well-known national public health officials, selected for thei
competence and not for their national allegiance.[26] And in subsequent ac
tivities rigorous professionalism ruled, a consistent desire to limit partici
pation to qualified (if nationally appointed) physicians, nurses, therapists
and public health administrators. The program of the Organization wa
consciously geared to strengthening the competence and autonomy of na
tional and local professional bodies, which were conceived in so strict a
medical context that no thought of "political" involvement could occur to
anyone.[27]

Or could it? Compared with the pre-1945 scope of responsibilities of
international health organizations, the program and powers of WHO point
clearly to that inevitable expansion of function that Mitrany predicts on
the basis of minimizing power and maximizing welfare.[28] But did power
shrink at the expense of advancing welfare? It could well be argued that
the very professionalism of the experts who rule WHO defeats further
inroads on the realm of power and politics. True, American physicians,
despite their fixation on free enterprise, have so far refrained from attacking WHO and have joined in the general professional support of its work.
But they have done so because WHO undertook to stay away from the field

of "socialized medicine," thus giving the World Medical Association a target in the ILO's social security program instead. WHO's efforts to relate health development programs to such politically infused (but welfare-dominated) activities as rural sanitation and control of water resources have been less successful. And suggestions that population control relates to world health have been met by threats of withdrawal on the part of Belgium, Ireland, and several Latin American countries. Perhaps WHO's very success is due to a professionalism that resists the temptation to push back the boundary of power and politics.

Our second case study concerns the participation of scientists in the negotiations aimed at producing a nuclear test ban. Here, the issue between expert and diplomat, between the demands of science and technology on behalf of the welfare of all mankind and selfish national interest, was drawn much more sharply than in the case of health. One school of American scientists, as early as the Baruch Plan, took the clearly Functional position that if everyone's common interest was the prevention of nuclear war, then all reasonable men would arrive at identical conclusions on the purely "technical" matter of *how* to disarm. The "logic of the facts" would dictate the right political formula. Further, they believed that this orientation implied no more and no less than the application of the scientific method to politics, thus "rationalizing" politics since they hoped to apply their mode of analysis in the matter of disarmament to politics in general. Science would push back the boundary of power. Controversy would cease because every political measure would be a logical consequence of first principles accepted by all.

The failure of the Soviet Union to accept the Baruch Plan persuaded some of these scientists that if their vision of peace could not be realized by means of a physicists' theocracy, then the only alternative was unrelenting nuclear rearmament by the United States, leading to eventual victory over the Soviet Union as the irrational political obstacle. Other members of the scientific community, however, felt that if only disarmament negotiations were left to scientists, who would concentrate on the technical merits of the issue, rather than to power-blinded diplomats, then the millennium, if not actually at hand, could at least be reached by stages. Crucial in this calculus were two further Functional assumptions: such negotiations would have to rest on direct contacts with Soviet scientists, who would be expected to be similarly motivated, and some dramatic "first step" would have to be taken to demonstrate to the world the feasibility of progress toward disarmament.[29]

Considerable support for this viewpoint existed within the American government in 1958, although the President's advisers on disarmament disagreed among themselves—as did the scientists, despite their expertise. This support eventually took the form of American participation in the

Geneva Conference of Experts, which was called to explore the possibility of policing a test ban agreement. The American delegation was composed entirely of scientists with no previous experience in diplomacy. Apparently they were neither briefed nor instructed by the political arms of the government, with the exception of the basic mandate to seek agreement with the Soviets on "*a number of systems* with varying characteristics, capabilities, and limitations which would then be presented for consideration to their respective governments."[30] The Functional expectation is best summarized in the words of Eugene Rabinowitch:

> The success of the Geneva conference of scientists . . . has confirmed the belief of scientists that once an international problem has been formulated in scientifically significant terms, scientists from all countries, despite their different political or ideological backgrounds, will be able to find a common language and arrive at an agreed solution. . . . This new approach to the fundamental problems of the arms race and world security, using the criterion of what is technically the most feasible approach to a common aim, instead of what will satisfy the national interests, may be a more radical innovation than the political leadership of the major nations is now willing to contemplate, despite the disastrous experience of traditional diplomacy in the last ten years.[31]

Not only were these hopes unfulfilled, but subsequent events proved that the reasoning behind them was fallacious. For one thing, the Soviet delegation was not composed exclusively of scientists, but was headed by a seasoned atomic diplomat, Semyon Tsarapkin. For another, it at all times enjoyed the help and participation of professional legal and diplomatic advisers. Finally, its instructions were different from those of the American delegation, and, what is more, were firmly linked to pre-existing Soviet policy in the field of disarmament.[32] The fact was that the Soviet scientists were instructed to obtain agreement on a *single* detection system with a minimum of detection stations. Consequently, on the purely "technical" issues of the capability of specific pieces of detection equipment and the detectability of various types of blasts, the Soviet experts consistently took very different positions from their American and British counterparts: what was hard to detect for the West seemed pleasantly simple for the Soviets, who could therefore advocate reducing to a minimum control posts, samples of radiation obtained by airplane flights, and on-site inspections. In other words, the Soviet delegation made no effort to separate the political from the technical, the role of the expert from that of the diplomat, and argued a wholly political position.

The Western delegations eventually interpreted their instructions to permit them to compromise with the Soviet Union, but compromise in such a way that the essence of the Soviet position emerged as the final recommendation. There is no reason to doubt the acquiescence of the two Western governments in this step. But the point is that the purity of the experts'

ledication to the technical issue was violated in such a fashion as to put
n question the very possibility of separating the two approaches in the
irst place. The American experts, in their eagerness to bring home results,
o phrased the final recommendations as to safeguard their "technical"
iccuracy at the expense of specificity in terms of the extent, type, and en-
orceability of controls. James Fiske, the head of the American delegation,
ecognized this himself:

The technical content of arms control negotiations is likely to be very high but
experience in the nuclear test and surprise attack negotiations has shown that
echnical and political arguments cannot be separated completely or for long.
For example, in the nuclear test business the questions of "threshold" and prob-
ability of detection and identification have both technical and political matters
deeply intermixed; if the technical people talk of a 1 kt, 5 kt or 20 kt "threshold" there are important political overtones; whether they talk of 10% prob-
ability or 50% or 90% is largely a political matter—or is it technical? . . . I
hink the Soviets recognized this interplay from the beginning.[33]

If we had analyzed the conference held in 1851 for the control of pilgrims infected with cholera in as stringent terms as those just applied to
the Geneva Conference of Experts, we would probably have reached a
conclusion similar to this one of Fiske's: that dispassionate decisions by
experts are not possible. Yet the field of world health shows an undeniable
functional expansion at the expense of formerly national and political competences. Is it inevitable that the nuclear stalemate must continue? Or is it
implicit in the Functionalist ideology that it must eventually yield to the
same forces that undermined the rigid positions of national public health
officials?

It would be false to answer that health is of immediate concern to everyone, whereas arms control is limited to arousing ideological emotion; certain aspects of health suffer from this defect, too. Nor can it be argued that
political or selfish motives are less likely to be present: at one time even
British officials, now so welfare-minded, were more interested in profits
than health. The question, rather, must be this: Is the Functionalist ideology adequate to explain the undeniable growth of international powers in
certain fields? Is it the role of experts that is crucial? Can power be separated from welfare? The equivocal nature of our two case studies suggests
that it cannot. Or can it? To gain some insight into these matters we must
now turn to a theoretical (as opposed to ideological) examination of
Functionalism.

THE THEORETICAL COMPONENTS OF FUNCTIONALISM

What are the major strands of political theory reflected in Functionalism?
The very obliqueness of the Functionalist approach indicates its eclecti-
cism: in addition to Guild Socialism, we find traces of Marxism, Pragma-

tism, and Liberalism both of the Utilitarian strain and of the psychotherapeutic kind associated with group theory in the tradition of Kurt Lewin. However, the Functionalist emphasis on voluntary action and group participation seems to owe very little to contemporary American Group Theory following the wake of Bentley.

The Marxist component is manifest only in the implied theory of war. Social inequality, linked to unequal distribution of economic benefits, is held to be the chief cause of interstate conflict. Once the inequalities are removed by means of international Functional programs bypassing the state, the creative energies of man will be harnessed to banning war. If the state is incapable of achieving such an end for its own citizens, it is certainly unable to join with other states in constructive programs.

Pragmatism plays a larger part in Functionalism, and is evident in the Functionalists' deliberate avoidance of a constitutional approach to a better world. Step-by-step schemes of material cooperation, evolving in an unplanned fashion, will eventually work themselves out in the direction of a worldwide system of cooperation, for which a constitution will merely be a symbolic crown, recognizing officially what has been true in fact for some time.

All this is based essentially on a utilitarian calculus: man will seek his rational advantage in maximizing his physical welfare by cooperating with other men when necessary. The Functionalists, however, differ from the Utilitarians by stressing the necessity of service rather than the benefits of competition. Advantage is maximized by pooling efforts, by joining in common creative tasks, by stressing what unites men, groups, and nations. This, in turn, implies a theory of conflict at variance with the Utilitarians'. Social conflict is not considered natural and inevitable by the Functionalists if and when there is an abundance of economic resources; only scarcity begets conflict. If intergroup and international conflict prevails even in the presence of material abundance, the reason must be found in some "devil" who perversely sidetracks man from the natural. H. G. Wells discovered this devil to inhabit the diplomatic services and the foreign offices of the Powers; Mitrany, more circumspectly, found it in the frustrations and anxieties of modern man compelled to live in the uncreative nation-state, which conditions him to confuse genuine national differences with nationalistic prejudices and the fears they produce.[34] Service rather than social conflict, then, is the natural condition of man.

Like the modern group therapist, the Functionalist rejects the notion that group conflict is inevitable. Conflicts can be creatively transcended without self-conscious sacrifice. Politics need not be envisaged as the crude clash of interests, each rationally conceived and defended, but may yield to problem-solving. Interests need not be "reconciled" if they can be "integrated" at a higher level of perception by engaging the actor in a "working" effort. This conception opens up possibilities of international integration that are nowhere spelled out in detail by the Functionalists. But it is vital to note that the future structure of international relations would be qualitatively different from the old, precisely because a new moral component—integration rather than conflict—would be its central pillar. To this theme we will return later.

The Functionalist's critique of other theories of international order consists of disputing the validity of a series of propositions fundamental to the so-called Realist school of thought. He hopes to arrive at a totally different conception of world order simply by challenging these assumptions, and since his critique hinges on *separating* notions held to be one by Realists, I shall approach it as a series of "separability" propositions.

We find four propositions. (1) The Functionalist separates power from welfare. Both are thought of as representing types of human and state aims; great insistence is placed upon the distinction, and a great many programmatic points follow from it.

(2) The Functionalist further separates various governmental tasks into discrete elements, even if only temporarily. But he insists on completely separating military-defense (power-oriented) task from economic-abundance (welfare-oriented) tasks, in addition to isolating various kinds of welfare tasks. However, through the learning process he predicates, the Functionalist eventually gathers these tasks together again into one, at which point all governmental activities are coterminous with the achievement of welfare. An important corollary of the separation of functional spheres is the notion of transferability of lessons. Integrative lessons learned in one functional context will later be applied by the actor in new contexts until the dichotomy between functional contexts is overcome. Unlimited learning and transferability are apparently assumed.

(3) A still finer separation occurs in the crucial distinction between the political and the technical, the work of the politician and that of the expert. Again a series of practical consequences follow from this distinction, leading to the conquest, at the hand of the welfare-oriented expert, of the political by the economic. Closely related is the distinction between the wholesome work of the voluntary group and the suspect activities of the government. This brings up the question of whether an expert can contribute to international integration by serving a government rather than a private group, a point on which Functionalist writing is silent.*

(4) A final, but equally crucial, separation occurs between the loyalties imputed to the political actor. Functionalists, along with many social scientists, hold that any one person can entertain a variety of loyalties to a

---

* Mitrany now prefers to weaken this separation by stressing that in the context of a specific task, such as nuclear energy or health, public and private agencies and experts can work creatively together.

number of focuses, whether hierarchically arranged or not; but unlike many others, they also assume that loyalties are created by functions, and that the transfer of functions can produce shifts in loyalty. A plurality of loyalties in any one nation is produced by the variety of functions carried out by various focuses for the person in question. The Functionalist, on the basis of this separation, hopes to transfer loyalties to international focuses carrying out functions. In doing so he seems to deny any existing hierarchical supremacy of nationalism, even though in other contexts he seems to deplore this supremacy.

Functionalists, as I emphasized before, do not think in explicitly functional-systemic terms. Existing needs give rise to appropriate tasks which, by virtue of the theoretical propositions outlined, are expected to give rise to a new and more wholesome international configuration of relationships. The end product of the process is a world federation emerging from an indefinite number of task-oriented agencies that overlie the sovereign state and detach man's loyalty from it. The redirection of loyalties is crucial here because it is expected to yield a *community* of sentiments and loyalties, which, in turn, is conceived as a psychological prerequisite for political federation. Functionalists, then, work with a terminal concept of immanent community much as Marxists use the notion of the classless society. What are the properties of the community concept?

Mitrany defines political community as the sum of the functions carried out by its members. At other times he speaks of it as the commitment to the common good of the members, the common good being the realization of welfare for all.[35] This formulation leaves in doubt whether the "members" are individuals, voluntary groups, or functional agencies, and begs the question of the nature of the functions involved, for Mitrany surely cannot mean all the functions, including waging war, that at present are within the scope of political communities. Finally, the notion of the common good cannot be readily accepted unless one also grants as valid the nature of the learning process and the transferability concept advanced by Functionalists. Otherwise the common good can be no more than the sum of individual group wills. Despite the emotional language used, however, the essentially mechanistic nature of the community stands revealed. It is immanent in man's present condition because of the universality of needs and tasks; the fulfillment of these needs leads naturally to its emergence.

Have we not, in effect, now squared the circle? Is not an immanent community a system in disguise? Are not needs and tasks "functions" in terms of their contribution to the development of the system? The fact that the Functionalists have not faced this apparent theoretical convergence does not mean we should be equally negligent. Suggestive as the convergence may be, it cannot be explored and restated until we have examined Functionalist theory critically.

A CRITIQUE OF FUNCTIONALISM

We can easily summarize the criticism leveled at Functionalism by writers in the Realist tradition: they merely assert the primacy of the political and take for granted the presumed hard outer shell of the sovereign nation-state. Further, they minimize the chances of penetrating or softening the elephantine epidermis.[36] More to the point is the criticism made by Claude, Sewell, and Engle, none of whom is *a priori* committed to the Realist approach. Yet they reject the theoretical assumptions of Functionalism in no uncertain terms simply by denying the adequacy of the separability propositions to sum up the potentialities of human development. Engle arrives at this conclusion on the basis of a study of the European Coal and Steel Community; Claude bases himself on the activities of the specialized agencies of the United Nations; and Sewell's analysis is centered on the International Bank for Reconstruction and Development. Their indictment runs as follows.

Power and welfare are far from separable. Indeed, commitment to welfare activities arises only within the confines of purely political decisions, which are made largely on the basis of power considerations. Specific functional contexts cannot be separated from general concerns. Overall economic decisions must be made before any one functional sector can be expected to show the kind of integrative evolution that the Functionalist describes. Lessons learned in one functional context cannot be expected to be readily transferred to new contexts; success in one functional sphere does not set up a corresponding motion in other spheres: on the contrary, it may fail to develop and be forgotten. The distinction between the political and the technical, between the politician and the expert, simply does not hold because issues were made technical by a prior political decision. Hence voluntary groups are most unlikely to have the salutary effect on international relations that the Functionalist predicts. Most important, both Claude and Engle deny that loyalties develop from the satisfaction of needs, can be separated and rearranged so as to ignore the nation.* "There is room for doubt that functionalists have found the key which infallibly opens the doors that keep human loyalties piled up in sovereign warehouses, thereby permitting those loyalties to spill out into the receptacles of internationalism."[37]

Certainly Functionalism provides no infallible key. But I submit that even if the separability propositions, which are the heart of Functionalist

* Mitrany, in line with his weakening of the distinction between the political and the technical, has recently concurred in the need for central politico-economic decisions to be made before problems are handed over to Functional agencies. Sewell's analysis of Functionalism goes considerably beyond these points in attacking the "liberal" and "pluralist" dreams implicit in Functionalist thought. *Ibid.*, Chapters 6 and 7.

theory, are not accepted in full, there remains considerable hope that they may be revised and refined so as to get us beyond the blind alley of Realist analysis. Anyone who uses the distinction between *kratos* and *ethos* as an analytical device will raise the same objections to Functionalist theory as the Realists do. Even the Functionalists, since they accept the dichotomy as fundamental in their distinction between power and welfare, are in a weak position. Conceding the "reality" of both orientations in international life, they must themselves put up with an unsatisfactory Manichean struggle, and hope for the best. The genuine Realist can then come back and agree to the epic struggle, and confidently predict the victory of *kratos*. Or, better, he can argue, as does Kenneth W. Thompson, that "men seem obstinately to reject the view that state behavior at some point is not a fit subject for moral judgment. One sign that this principle is accepted as relevant is the apparent compulsion of political actors to justify their needs in moral terms. Hypocrisy is the tribute vice pays to virtue."[38] Thompson goes on to point out that expediency and morality move dialectically in international politics, so that a position taken by a government purely for reasons of expediency but extolling some moral principle may come to bind that government in some future situation merely because, by repetition, the principle has been accepted by other governments in the meantime. "On some points at least the practical and moral march hand in hand."[39]

The paradox is now complete: by granting the existence of a power orientation, the Functionalist approaches the Realist; by modifying the absolute victory of power, some Realists join hands with the Functionalists. Those, like Claude and Engle, who deny the first separability proposition are then forced to a subordination of Functionalism to Realism without really investigating the empirical scope of the remaining notions of separation. And the bulk of Functionalist theory goes unexamined.

It is precisely the merit of Functionalism that it broke away from the clichés of Realist political theory. Its fault lies in not having broken radically enough. The separability propositions point the way toward a rapprochement between international relations theory and the rest of the social sciences, specifically political sociology and the empirical study of politics —though they do not point clearly enough in their present form. Our first task, then, must be a refinement of these propositions in the light of social science theory and contemporary empirical studies.

When we have achieved such a refinement, the road of analysis will lead us back to the subject of systems and functions. In our effort to relate Functionalism to a general theory of international integration, the refined separability doctrines will then be put into the framework of systems theory. We must ask ourselves what portions of structural-functional analysis are appropriate to our studies at the international level, what kind of system is presupposed by the sociological functionalist, and to what extent it can be squared with the immanent system dimly perceived by the Functionalists. Let us be frank about this operation: Mitrany sees his system as a concrete set of relationships in which actors participate consciously; to Merton, as to Nadel, a functional system refers to "observable objective consequences" of action *from the standpoint of the observer*.[40] Juxtaposing these two viewpoints, therefore, involves a merger of concrete and analytic systems. After accomplishing this feat, we hope to apply the resulting scheme to organizational theory and thus to be armed for the functional analysis of the International Labor Organization.

2. Functionalism Refined

FUNCTIONALISM AND INTEGRATION

In our opening discussion of the semantics of functionalism, we immediately became involved in further terminological difficulties with the notions of system and integration. Let us now make a brief excursion into the semantics of integration. We shall grapple with systems in the next chapter.

If one could claim that functional cooperation in international relations is not necessarily related to integration, this excursion could be eliminated. If integration is held to be linked to the notion of "community," in the sense of Tönnies' *Gemeinschaft*, and functional cooperation confined to commonly perceived interests that produce ad hoc and asymmetrical relations, then Functionalism is merely the international application of *Gesellschaft*.[1] Hence functional activities need not be related to community-building, and the Functionalist ideology is implicitly cut down in size. However, this approach deprives us of the possibility of viewing international relations in evolutionary terms, and condemns us to a conceptual and empirical straitjacket. It is precisely our hope that functionalist sociology can show how *Gesellschaft* can develop into *Gemeinschaft*. For Mitrany, community is immanent in the evolutionary logic of his action process and hence a notion of integration is implicitly part of his theory. For the sociologist, mutually supporting inputs into a social system tend to be associated with growth of structure, expansion of functions, development equilibrium—in short, a process summed up as "integration."[2] If we want to use Functionalism as an analytical tool for the study of international organization, we cannot sidestep the definition of integration.

The root of the trouble is that scholars disagree about whether the term "integration" refers to a *process*, a *condition*, or both. To make matters worse, many writers vary the sense according to the context. At least a certain simplicity is maintained by those who use the term to describe a condition in which nations are tied together by organized institutions and written rules. The mere fact of the existence of international law and the United Nations, for example, is sometimes held to constitute evidence of integration among nations. One sociologist goes beyond this minimal definition but retains the notion of integration as a condition, which is established empirically when among several states one agency disposes of a monopoly over the means of violence, occupies the center in decision-making, and constitutes the central focus for the emotional identification of the population of the several states.[3]

More commonly, and more confusingly, scholars—wishing to have their cake and eat it—vary the meaning they ascribe to the term. This is particularly true of those who identify integration with a flow of transactions across the boundaries of whatever units are to be integrated. Economists, for example, define integration as the absence of rules that discriminate against trade or movement of factors; but they also use the word to refer to the steps whereby this condition is approximated. The same economists equate integration with the pursuit of certain economic policies designed to achieve equitable distribution of welfare benefits; but the process of adopting such policies also constitutes integration.[4] An advocate of international scientific cooperation equates integration with "international understanding."[5] Understanding, however, is believed to result from the universal dissemination of scientific truth. Therefore, the attainment of understanding, as well as the process of scientific communication, is held to constitute integration.*

The leading exponent of the transactional approach to integration is Karl Deutsch. The flow of transactions in terms of volume—i.e., a process —constitutes one dimension of his analysis. But at the same time Deutsch defines integration as a condition under which "integrated" states have forgone the use of violence as a means of settling their differences. Thus some of the indicators by which the final condition can be identified also serve as a definition of the process; ranges of transactions as well as the presumed result of the transactions constitute integration.[6] This manner of conceptualizing the phenomenon makes it exceedingly difficult to isolate cause and effect.†

---

* This terminological confusion is not confined to the English-language literature. For a survey of French and German usage of "integration," which adds the meaning of an "ideal future condition" to the two connotations found in English, see Dusan Sidjanski, *Dimensions européennes de la science politique* (Paris: Pichon et Durand-Auzias, 1963), pp. 13–19.
† Ranges of transactions can also be treated as pure data designed to assess the degree of unity and compatibility among political or social units. In this context the end product is sharply differentiated from the process, with transactional evidence being merely a tool for accurate observation. Such a differentiation is clearly made by Werner S. Landecker, "Integration and Group Structure: An Area for Research," *Social Forces*, XXX (1952), 395. Landecker establishes ranges of transactions for observing the degree of cultural, normative,

All transactional modes of analysis fuse and confuse the aspects of process and condition. In functional sociology, however, we find a conception of integration that makes the fusion a deliberate tool of analysis. Integration here acquires the meaning of systemic equilibrium. Talcott Parsons conceives of integration either as a static condition of complementarity between systemic components, which thus maintain equilibrium; or as a changing or "moving equilibrium," which modifies the system but maintains its uniqueness.[7] Process and result are one, subordinated to the notion of self-maintenance.

The extreme form of the identification of integration with equilibrium is that employed by Malinowski. Each cultural trait or belief is imputed with functional indispensability for the maintenance of the whole; each meets a vital need for the society. Further, each cultural trait is necessary for the performance of the *specific* function with which it is paired. Merton has restated these postulates in more moderate terms: not every social trait needs to contribute to the survival of the system; nor does the survival of a trait necessarily prove its functional significance. In the place of Malinowski's extreme formulation, he suggests the principle of the "net balance of functional consequences" and the notion of functional-structural equivalents. Yet the tendency of Merton's analysis is still the maintenance of the system in equilibrium. Events (i.e. processes) are therefore evaluated as integrative or disintegrative, eufunctional or dysfunctional, depending on their presumed contribution to the equilibrium (i.e. condition) of the whole.[8]

A concern with uniqueness and self-maintenance is the dominant feature, too, of the Parsonian concept of the "moving equilibrium." A much more flexible construct than Malinowski's, it deliberately allows for the kind of substitutions spelled out by Merton, but does so by focusing attention upon the maintenance of the system at the expense of the environment, rather than dealing with feedbacks into the environment and adaptations by it. In short, the notion of the moving equilibrium seems useful only if the survival of a system is the central matter of interest, not the subtle interaction between system and environment that may lead to slow changes in both without implying sharp qualitative progressions.

This orientation gives us a clue to why some social scientists are impatient with modern international organizations. Because of their presumed liberal parentage these organizations have become associated with an approach to international relations that seems to exaggerate out of all proportion man's freedom of will to change his environment. Critics of

---

communicative, and functional (i.e., the exchange of services) "integration" prevailing at any one time. Deutsch's work is an elaboration and application of this suggestion, though it implies very strongly that cultural, normative, and communicative integration *follow* the functional variety, and depend on it causally.

the United Nations in the realist tradition have never tired of pointing to the presumed dependence of global peace-making bodies on the eternal laws of power. But—for different reasons—sociologists addicted to structural-functional-requisite analysis are also unable to appreciate the significance of modern international organizations. They identify the United Nations as a functional expression of the structural requisites of maintaining the system of sovereign nation-states. Hence the acquisition by the United Nations of some kind of supranational powers would do violence to these requisites by challenging the system and threatening to supplant it with another. Since systems are presumed to be in, or tending toward, equilibrium, this state of affairs seems unreal.[9] Commitment, then, to this kind of systems theory brings with it either an acceptance of the nation-state system or a demand for its radical transformation into a species of world federation. It precludes appreciation and analysis of the existing concrete system as a means of facilitating gradual transitions that depend on a moderate determinism. In part, at least, the sociologist's use of the notion of integration is responsible for this blind spot.

We must avoid the reification of an analytical system. Hence I conceive of integration as referring *exclusively* to a process that links a given concrete international system with a dimly discernible future concrete system. If the present international scene is conceived of as a series of interacting and mingling national environments, and in terms of their participation in international organizations, then integration would describe the process of *increasing* the interaction and the mingling so as to obscure the boundaries between the system of international organizations and the environment provided by their nation-state members. Since such a process involves, obviously, the actions and perceptions of a variety of actors, and since these actions are described in a particularly striking way by the Functionalist approach, sociological functionalism retains its relevance for refining our understanding of integration. Transactional and institutional criteria are helpful, too; but they must be rigorously subordinated to this more limited conception of what international integration means.[10]

The Functionalist approach avoids not only the analytical rigor of assuming the existence of some systemic equilibrium, but also the trap of assuming complete freedom of the will. Transitions between systems are loosely deterministic in the sense that the functional commitments of one generation, one epoch, one set of environmental conditions, set the limits and indicate the direction for the integrative choices leading to the next system. The approach, then, is within the confines of historical sociology, in which systems are always concrete and always defined by the concerns of the epoch's actors. What is assumed is the typicality of actor motives, not the typicality of any one structure or organization in which the motives impinge upon each other. The context is the typical interplay of typical aspirations; the wholeness of the situation analyzed is provided by its predominant hopes, fears, and styles of conduct. Given cases, decisions, or institutions are never "typical," but the motives of the actors prominent in them are. Hopefully, functional sociology will enable us to project their concerns into the future.[11]

Such an aim demands that we undertake a constructive critique of Functionalism. First, we must revise the theory of interest that the Functionalist uses, a theory that apparently misreads through the eyes of nineteenth-century Liberals the intent of the founders of modern Western Liberalism. Next, we must strip the utopian elements from the group theory of the Functionalists and amend their separation of expert and politician, state and society, so as to reflect the integrative potential of actual modern practices. This, in turn, requires the insertion into Functionalist thought of a more highly structured theory of law than is now present. We hope to emerge with a revised series of separability doctrines that portray international organizations as a species of institutionalized interest politics, capable, on the basis of an analysis adapted from structural-functional sociology and empirical systems theory, of transforming the international system.

INTEREST, PROGRESS, AND TECHNOCRACY

One reason why the Functional approach arouses suspicion is the fuzzy manner in which progress toward world community is related to the leadership of the expert. In particular, Functionalists leave themselves open to the charge that their concept of interest and interest politics is either hopelessly utopian or rigorously mechanical. Yet without the link provided by a theory of interest politics, Functionalists cannot hope to explain why experts, whether working through the medium of voluntary groups or governments, are going to introduce us to the blessed state of world community.

The impression of utopianism is created by the Functionalists' pluralist heritage and their inarticulate dependence on the Durkheimian notion that only voluntary groups can " 'drag' isolated individuals 'into the general torrent of social life.' "[12] If such groups represent what is both good and real about society, dependence on their activities will not only overcome the anomie experienced by modern man as an individual, but result in creative work toward the common good, or, in short, the realization of the General Will. This formulation presupposes some natural harmony of interests nationally and internationally. Functionalists hold this harmony to be immanent in an underlying common concern with welfare—and its advent constitutes progress—while also insisting on the therapeutic magic of creative participation. The theory of interest politics here implied begs a number of questions that require further analysis.

But first let us examine the opposite charge, that the linkage between interest, progress, and technocracy is a purely mechanical contrivance. Suppose we agree with the Functionalists, as many liberal internationalists today seem to do, that there is a universal concern for the advancement of welfare and the protection of democratic human rights. Suppose we agree further that all political systems, with the exception of the fascist, can subscribe to this order of values. A simple mechanical translation of these values into the interests defended by national policy in the United Nations would then beget policy priorities sharply at variance with the Functionalist emphasis on physical welfare. For this priority would subordinate the economic and social good to the political. In order to realize these values, international political and military security must be established *first*, because nations will not dedicate themselves to working for human rights and physical welfare until their military security is assured. Further, unless that security is assured, the holocaust may overtake us before democracy is established in Upper Volta, Samoa, or Bolivia.[13] Since the Functionalist has no articulate interest theory, he leaves himself open to this interpretation and to the consequent reversal of his causative emphasis.

To return to the implications of the utopian interpretation, the Functionalist's emphasis on the role of the expert puts him squarely in the camp of contemporary theories of technocracy and managerial leadership. If he postulates a natural harmony of interests, we must sharply disagree with him, and dispute the ability of his theory to lead to an understanding of international integration. If, however, he remains faithful to managerial theory, he has an apparent way out by falling back on the manipulation of the members of voluntary groups or governments by their expert-leaders. To be sure, he starts out by postulating the wholesome organic unity of society, of which professional groups and their leaders are merely a part, and in which group interests represent, not a divisive clamor, but an affirmation of the common good. But he soon identifies with the managerial emphasis upon the spontaneous realization of individual creativity within the confines of an *organization* rather than in society in the abstract, and he therefore grants the importance of organizational personality and mystique. Although the individual may profit from this therapeutically, he also exposes himself to the artifice of those who arrange and preach the purposes and values of specific organizations. If, therefore, divisive tendencies should appear in intergroup relations, the manipulators of organizational ideology, by "creative statemanship" and the "establishment" of consensus, will see to it that the common dedication wins out. As Philip Selznick puts it "the aspirations of individuals and groups are so stimulated and controlled . . . as to produce the desired balance of forces."*

* *Leadership in Administration*, pp. 14, 100; as cited in Wolin, *Politics and Vision*, p. 429. A variant of the technocratic thesis is found in the writings of some social scientists who

But why should we grant any more validity to the notion of a natural harmony of interests, a consensus, among the manipulating experts than to the existence of such a tendency among their followers? Demonstrably, experts do not agree, and rival sets of organizational leaders see far from eye to eye. Hence the connection between groups, interests, experts, and progress still remains obscure in relation to international integration, unless we can specify a more adequate theory of interest politics.†

Like so many of us, Functionalists have apparently misread the intent of the classical British liberals. If they had paid more attention to the socio-political assumptions and formulations of Adam Smith, Bentham, the Mills, and even Spencer, instead of being repelled by their economic doctrines, they might have found a theory of interest politics that would serve the needs of international integration. To this material let us now turn.[14]

First of all, Functionalists share the basic preference of classical Liberals for "society." Mitrany like Mill regards the state and government as something suspect, and elevates society to the place of honor in the hierarchy of human institutions. Since the Functionalist accepts the vital importance of day-to-day economic and social pursuits, and of the voluntary action associated with them, he might well have gone all the way in also adopting the theory of interest politics that the classical Liberals obtained from their sublimation of society.

To the Liberal, each individual's pursuit of his economic interest is the first social fact of political relevance. Each man alone is regarded as understanding what is good for him individually, and since no other agency can or should make his economic decisions for him, social justice becomes the equivalent of man's unrestricted effort to maximize his economic interest. Political equality was the natural corollary, for "to be able to vote was to be in a better position to defend one's interests."[15] Although Liberals also

---

would make the lessons of social science a cardinal point in political education, thereby hoping to supplant outworn political ideologies of the nineteenth century that still linger on in contemporary party politics. See, for example, J. P. Corbett, *Europe and the Social Order* (Leyden: Sythoff, 1959), who argues that these surviving ideologies are not up to the dominant European task of accommodating, explaining, and controlling the "systematic" structural innovation that has gone on for two hundred years; but social science is considered capable of doing this:

"The day of speculative social doctrines is now done. Providence and natural law, progress and historical necessity, the invisible hand of the market and the invisible will of the sovereign people, the very intellectual impetus to find and to impose such theoretical constructions, are all so much detritus of the human past. What is then left of philosophical endeavour is to demolish such illusions and steadily to bring our social questions down into a form in which a patient, piecemeal, empirical analysis of social fact can handle them." (Corbett, p. 188.)

† At this stage of the argument we are using the terms "expert," "leader," and "manager" interchangeably to denote the "technocrat" as distinguished from the politician and parliamentarian.

stressed the confining, if not conformity-imposing, aspects of society while lauding absolute *economic* autonomy, this is a refinement irrelevant to our argument.

By abstracting the pursuit of economic interest from any imputed concern with general welfare, systemic equilibrium, or social order, the Liberal opens the door to a theory of naked interest politics, in which the natural and opposing interaction of interests in an impersonal market determines the shape and evolution of the social system. To Herbert Spencer this state of affairs was even "democratic," an attitude that bears some resemblance to Mitrany's concern with the "equality of non-representation" in a governmental system in which decisions are made by experts on the basis of maximizing welfare. The beauty of this Liberal conception lies in the fact that it does not seek harmony and it does not presuppose selfless human motives. Order can develop from chaos; the general good can emerge from the compounding of ruthless egoism. Human actors can be accommodated in the system without any utopian assumptions. Yet the interconnections need *not* develop automatically in the direction of the historically determined utopia of the Marxist, who makes the same assumptions about individual interests. Automatic progress is not implied by the Liberal theory of interest politics, a refinement Functionalists should also heed. Nor did the theory rely on a "true" or "objective" interest: what men felt to be their interest was good enough to make the system work.[16]

A further lesson the Functionalist could have learned from the Liberal is the psychological basis of political conduct: the pervasive role of anxiety. Whereas the Functionalists waver between regarding modern man as "sick," to be cured by group therapy, and holding him equipped to maximize his concern with welfare if given the institutional opportunity, the Liberals were agreed that the basis for man's acquisitive conduct and ruthless pursuit of interest was his emotional uncertainty, his dependence on irrational drives, his inability to be at peace with nature. As Wolin reminds us, we should take literally the famous Liberal "pursuit of happiness" precisely because happiness was so difficult to capture and retain. If we assume anxiety and its modern variant, status insecurity, to be fixed features of social life, the pitiless pursuit of interest becomes a natural corollary designed to yield a modicum of certainty.[17] "Smith's famous 'unseen hand,' which so many commentators have interpreted as a symbol of the convergence of rational plans, individually conceived, into a rational good for the whole society, was exactly the same as Smith's theory of individual moral behavior: both the moral good of society and its material-well being had their origins in instinct, desire, and passion; and neither was the result of action intended to advance the good of society as a whole."[18]

In Smith, therefore, the common good was an unforeseen consequence, a "function," of unplanned, uncoordinated, diversely if not perversely conceived individual "purposes." To assume more for an interest theory of politics is to ask more of man than he is likely to deliver: he may, indeed, be selfless to the point of demanding public action on the basis of some notion of public interest or the general good; but it is safer to assume that more immediate considerations take precedence in the daily play of politics. A Functionalist theory of converging but separate purposes, partaking of some general notion of welfare individually conceived and elaborated, would ring truer than a utopian vision of technocratic progress based on identical interests. Somehow it seems more modest, but also more accurate, to conclude with Harrington that "as Man is sinful, but yet the world is perfect, so may the Citizen bee sinful, and yet the Commonwealth bee perfect."[19]

Having acknowledged our intellectual debts, we are now in a position to restate the elements in an interest theory of politics that we hold to be germane to an acceptable and useful Functionalism. We banish from our construct the notion that individual actors, groups, or elites regularly and predictably engage in political pursuits for unselfish reasons. All political action is purposively linked with individual or group perception of interest. While the unseen hand may somehow hold a system of opposing perceptions and clashing interests together, we reject the notion of any natural harmony of interests based on purposive, calculated behavior. We further reject the notion of conscience, good will, dedication to the common good, or subservience to a socially manipulated consensus on welfare questions, as possessing little consistent reality in living politics. Cooperation among groups is thus the result of convergences of separate perceptions of interest and not a spontaneous surrender to the myth of the common good.

But when it comes to defining more precisely what "interest" means, we must part company with the classical Liberal tradition as well as with its more simple-minded contemporary heirs. The Utilitarians differentiated man's legitimate and autonomous *economic* interest from his general subservience to the civilizing and restraining force of *society,* which would balance self-reliance and private initiative with a conformist pattern. "Interest" here would seem to mean "economic claims and demands"; thus the balance among opposing *economic* interests would conduce to the general economic good. I postulate a more extended meaning for the notion of interest, one that encompasses every kind of group-backed demand that enters the marketplace of political competition. Any claim made upon the community on behalf of the values dear to some group represents an interest, even though substantively it may refer to religious education, residential zoning, reforestation, or the prevention of cruelty to animals. But this expansion in the scope of the interest concept implies also a certain rigidity, a certain determinism: since values tend to remain stable over considerable periods of time, the interests flowing from them cannot be expected to change readily. Therefore, this conception of interest politics rejects, essentially, the notion of extensive freedom of the will. Modern liberals who expect to reform the world by simply "changing men's minds" with respect to what they hold to be the prevalence of "false" interests will be no happier with my formulation than Smith or Bentham would be. My application of Functionalism thus discards any belief in the immanence of progress as flowing from a natural harmony of economic interests, and minimizes the possibility of relying on man's free will to change the sluggish law of group-based interest perception.

How, then, can there be international integration? At this point the essence of Functionalism reasserts its analytical vigor: certain kinds of organizational tasks most intimately related to group and national aspirations can be expected to result in integration *even though* the actors responsible for this development may not deliberately work toward such an end. These organizational tasks rest on the perception of certain interests by the actors initiating them, and Functionalism has offered some very shrewd insights into the nature of these interests. Our revised interest theory can thus point the way toward the identification of group aims and the resulting interaction of aims at the international level, an interaction that may give rise to integration based on the unwilled, or imperfectly willed, separate demands and claims that enter the arena.

Thus viewed, integration is conceptualized as resulting from an institutionalized pattern of interest politics, played out within existing international organizations. Far from considering "power politics" the central demon who propels the universal engine along a path of uneasy give-and-take within the United Nations, we should, it appears, regard the type and intensity of organizational compromise as being directly related to the type of demands that are made, the variety of concessions that are exchanged, and the degree of delegation of authority to new central institutions that imposes itself in order to make the compromise workable. But just as Functionalism helps to illuminate the actual pattern of institutionalized interest politics at the international level, it also discredits the Wilsonian notion that peace and cooperation follow from a common dedication to a common good. There is no common good other than that perceived through the interest-tinted lenses worn by the international actors. But international interest politics causes the tinting to fall into converging patterns, and Functionalism sensitizes us to spotting the tasks responsible for the pattern. To do this, however, we must first explain our position with respect to the group theory of politics.

GROUPS, INTEGRATION, AND FUNCTIONAL ANALYSIS

Mitrany's reliance on voluntary associations, apart from its striking ethical implications in preferring "society" to the "state," has the obvious merit for the social scientist of giving him an empirical starting point for studies of integration: groups seem so nice and real, so alive and so readily inter-viewable. To accept even the non-normative aspects of Functionalist theory here would be to avoid coming to grips with the vigorous criticisms that American political scientists have leveled at group theories of politics.

As far as the normative point is concerned, it is simply irrelevant to our quest. It may or may not be preferable in terms of our values to rely on group as opposed to state action. Personally, I am often tempted to trust the impersonal and bureaucratized state apparatus more than the appeals of my neighbors or the claims of my professional association. The question remains irrelevant. If groups can be demonstrated to exist and to make their influence felt politically—and nobody denies this much—their actions may indeed prove relevant to national and international integration.

Groups as analytical points of reference are therefore of the essence of Functionalism even if we reject their ethical value. But this refinement of Mitrany will take us only part of the way. We may regard groups as "real" *and* as the single most important feature of the polity, the building blocks of a theory of politics. In this sense "reality" has the double aspect of postu-lating the existence of the units and of construing the ultimate meaning of political life as resulting from the interaction of the units. Contemporary group theorists in the tradition of Bentley use the notion of groups in precisely this fashion.

If Functionalists distort the ethical meaning of voluntary groups, group theorists reify them analytically. Roy Macridis puts the matter succinctly:

Group theory claims that it is more "comprehensive" and "operational" in that it directs the student to the study of concrete and observable entities—the groups—and leads him immediately to the promised heaven of data-accumula-tion and explanation. When the real test of the utility of the theory comes, how-ever—field work—groups prove to be just as stubborn in yielding their secrets as other structures and units of the system. Their pulsating reality often proves to be nothing but a ghost that haunts the field worker from one interest group office and organization to another, from one interest group publication to another. In some cases, especially in the underdeveloped systems where interest articulation is weak, the office may be vacant. Even where interest articulation and interest groups pulsate with life and vigor the student soon discovers that the "interest universe" overlaps with the political universe; that it is indeed enmeshed with the political universe in which tradition, values, habits, styles and patterns of leadership and governmental organization must be carefully studied before we begin to understand the system as a whole.[20]

This sweeping attack justly castigates group theory for mistaking the part for the whole; it could equally well be directed against the Functionalists for writing off the formal structure of the state and the state-system in favor of voluntary groups. But there is another, and perhaps more serious, criticism. The logical consistency of its propositions, and their ability to explain what they seek to explain, are also thrown into doubt when the effort is made to subsume all of politics under group organization and struggle. Thus Stanley Rothman accuses David Truman of bringing in such concepts as role and status, as well as the residual category "potential group," to explain what cannot be rendered clearly in terms of pure group competition.[21] He questions whether the reality of group existence should be identified with the "reality" of a universe made up of squabbling and overlapping purveyors of limited interests.

This perspective enables us to specify a third way of dealing with voluntary groups and to rescue them for use in integration theory. After all, why cannot groups be "real without constituting the whole or even the central part of a theory? Why can we not treat groups—which we know to exist and to influence politics—as analytical carriers of the integration process along with numerous other carriers and within a larger system of related factors? If they are important in national politics, we are certainly entitled to treat them as at least potentially important in an international process as well. And to the extent that critics of Functionalism deny even this role of voluntary groups they overstate their case.

The species of systems theory that is beginning to flourish in studies of comparative politics puts to work this more limited conception of groups.[22] Groups are here represented as societal structures that *articulate* interests, as distinguished from aggregating them or translating them into policy; their overall systemic role is thus confined to functioning alongside political, and their life is subordinated to the dominant "style" and "culture" of the system. This way of looking at the phenomenon of groups facilitates their use as building blocks in a theory that seeks to specify a process of integration or disintegration, whether at the national or the international level.

Whereas Mitrany speaks merely of "groups" and "experts" and Truman confines himself to treating "actual" and "potential interest" groups, the systems theorist immediately proceeds to establish a typology of groups whose relationship to integration is not assumed to be the same. Almond and Coleman distinguish between institutional, non-associational, anomic, and associational interest groups, whereas the Functional theory of integration, apparently, had in view only the associational variety that is familiar to the Western political tradition. Hence Functionalists are unable to predicate their international integration process on any pattern other than an international system made up of pluralistic-industrial-democratic nations, each characterized by an associational group structure. But what if the international scene is in fact not dominated by such nations, as indeed it is not today?[23]

Specificity with respect to types of groups, and with respect to systems of aggregation in terms of a typology of party structures, thus provides an important corrective to Functionalist group theory. Member states of contemporary international organizations possess party systems ranging from totalitarian to the competitive multiparty structure familiar to the Functionalist, covering a continuum of degrees of authoritarianism in between. Each party system hides a different system of groups. Clearly, not all can be equally relevant to a unilinear or even a dialectic process of international integration. At a later point, therefore, we must specify which types of groups and parties can be expected to enter the process.

One more point demands clarification in our restatement of Functionalist group theory. Mitrany avoids the oft-repeated charge that group theories overlook the common interest, the general will, or the national interest in their preoccupation with discrete demands and ideologies. He does so by positing the notion of an immanent commnunity of aspirations arising, phoenix-like, from the ashes of separate group aspirations toward welfare. But he begs the question with respect to the compatibility of the various conceptions of welfare, and since he neglects the role of law in providing a normative procedure for settling differences among rival welfare conceptions, we are hardly the wiser for his demonstration. However, unless we are willing to equate the common good or the general welfare with systemic equilibrium, functional analysis is not able to meet the charge any better. If we persist in denying the adequacy of these formulations but continue to doubt—with the group theorists—that there is such a thing as a common interest in operational terms, we are compelled to settle for an *unwilled* and even *accidental* consensus on the common good arising from the competition of group goods.*

* Certain "advanced" systems of industrial relations, e.g., in the Netherlands, might cast some doubt on the finality of this formulation. There, since the end of World War II, the incidence of strikes has been sharply reduced. In the words of one commentator: "This is not to say that there is no conflict in industrial relations in the Netherlands. The struggle, however, does not take place in the factories or on the docks but around . . . the 'mahogany table.' It is carried on with the weapons of persuasion, scientific calculations and piercing argument." (W. G. De Gaay Fortman, "Industrial Relations in the Netherlands Today," *Delta*, III (1960), 2.) The very firmness and intractability of ideological and confessional voluntary associations in the economy—implying that no single voluntary group could hope to win control of the state—gave rise to a consciousness of permanent negotiation among the parties through which the collective bargaining process is carried on. To prevent the two major parties from imposing an anti-consumer compromise on the nation, the government participates in the negotiations, thus holding out the "general interest" to the major parties. All this is achieved through a hierarchy of social and economic councils, combining mutual threats, continuous conciliation by the government, and appeal to economic trends on the basis of economic analysis carried on by employers, workers, and the government. Thus, while the groups retain their rival ideological commitments, they also accept a "general" commitment that is the result of their continuous interaction.

As of now the success of this system is not yet assured, and it remains confined to one country. If it were to be universally accepted, it would enable us to posit a theory of general consensus on the general welfare—thus vitiating Mitrany. But it may well be that the success

I do not deny that men, on occasion, may agree on the common good. Nor do I wish to belittle the manipulative devices of society in persuading men that they must agree to certain conceptions as constituting the common good. I wish to stress merely that these convergences of opinion cannot be relied upon to operate all the time or even with reasonable frequency. Since societies and organizations, however, show a capacity for survival even in the absence of a demonstrable and continuous devotion to a generally accepted common good, we must posit a more basic consensual tie than such agreement. This tie I find in a conception of *Gemeinschaft* which differs from that of Mitrany and that of Tönnies. A modern political community tends to lack the warmth and devotion we associate with ascriptive ties and communities based on primary contacts or loyalties: yet it is no less a community for being based on abstract symbols and vicarious identification. Like the Functionalist, then, we may think of modern nation-states as communities whose basic consensus is restricted to agreement on the *procedure* for maintaining order and settling disputes among groups, for carrying out well-understood functions. Unlike that of the Functionalist, this conception presupposes agreement merely on the *means* for achieving welfare, but not on the content of laws and policies, not on the substance of the functions.

The modern nation-state, then, is a *Gemeinschaft* that looks and acts much like the *Gesellschaft* we associate with our international system. Instead of being intimate and cozy, it functions like a large-scale bureaucratic organization. Its tasks may involve the maximization of the welfare of its citizens, but not necessarily in the sense of aggregating all their demands and hopes into a general consensus. International organizations and national states thus share many of the characteristics of a society; they differ in that the national state also enjoys the procedural dedication of its members, who identify with it vicariously. Far from assuming any realization

---

of such a system would depend on all or some of these conditions: assurance of considerable and regular economic growth; reconciliation to the thought that one's own ideology will never achieve complete victory; dedication to a powerful ideology of service permitting the postponement of material rewards; continuation of an authoritarian legitimacy pattern in which the lower classes do not persist in challenging the judgment of their governors.

The one condition we cannot postulate is a predisposition among the parties to agree with each other: this is a possible result but certainly not a prior condition. According to industrial relations specialists, however, the Dutch pattern may become the dominant mode of settling economic group conflict in all societies that have achieved a certain level of industrialization, an argument that isolates advanced industrialism as the crucial factor. This argument holds, too, that labor dissatisfaction tends to be a constant factor in all early phases of industrialism, which will be overcome by a restrained kind of pluralism blossoming within a highly bureaucratized and manipulated economic system as industrialism achieves its logical apex. This tendency is thought to prevail in *all* political systems, irrespective of ideological professions or variations in the kind of elites initially active in the industrialization process. See the monographs in the Inter-University Study of Labor Problems in Economic Development, as summarized by Clark Kerr *et al.*, "Industrialism and Industrial Man," *International Labour Review,* LXXXII (1960).

of the common good, we merely postulate the compatibility of the multi-
group competitive national society with an agreement on the means of
resolving internal conflict by peaceful methods. To the extent that the
international system does not even enjoy this much cohesion, it falls short
of our revised concept of the political community.

A FUNCTIONAL THEORY OF LAW

In his concern with process and with becoming, it is understandable that
the Functionalist should devote little attention to law, and indeed should
minimize its role in the gradual unveiling of the immanent world community. Even though we predicate such developments on conflict and compromise borne by such disharmonious forces as interest-motivated groups,
it would be unpardonable if we neglected to spell out the norm-generating
aspects of these actions. If Functionalists rightly feel that traditional international law, whether monist or dualist, positivist or natural, is of little
avail in such a quest, we have all the more reason to search out areas of
international jurisprudence that promise some help.

Increasingly, thoughtful legal scholars have ceased simply to assert the
existence of a supreme set of international norms and have tired of castigating the states which, in their conduct, belie that existence. Julius Stone,
for instance, frankly dropped the famous distinction between law and
force, between power politics and politics based on some rule of law. He
argues instead that all politics involves the use of force. But he continues
to think of the law as a whole cloth, subject to common principles: what is
required to give us a world rule of law is a change in the social substructure
of the law so that "those who wield supreme power share certain common
ethical convictions as to the basic principles of decency between man and
man."[24] The basis of a true international law is thus a consensus on values
among national elites—a very tall order. Arguing along similar lines, Judge
Charles de Visscher condemned international legal thinking that postulated the rule of specific norms on the existence of an international community of shared values, and found the absence of such law to be caused
by the non-existence of such values. The task, then, must be the creation
of a world moral order. De Visscher would advance toward this aim by
elevating the aspirations of the individual human being at the expense of
the state and its sovereignty, would make the attainment of the common
good of *individuals* the purpose of international action. Hence the repeated
invocation of basic human rights by international organizations and documents, even though of no immediate legal or practical significance, can be
expected slowly to erode preoccupation with the state and to focus attention on the only values truly capable of being shared.[25]

Despite their admirable willingness to see the modern world as it really
is, these scholars still adopt sociological patterns of reasoning that would

condemn international law to continued futility simply because their demands are too formal and too high. Generalized agreement on values among national elites is probably the most elusive way of conceiving consensus, especially if the rights of the individual are selected as a focus: the claims upon clashing ideologies, social structures, and conflicting policies are gargantuan. It is precisely the virtue of Functionalism that it permits us to set our sights at a more modest level and still remain true to the actual nature of our world. Under varying labels this has been attempted by two legal scholars deeply impressed with the potential impact of non-political international organizations.

Thus C. Wilfred Jenks has singled out United Nations specialized agencies and their work as the source of a new kind of law, which he calls the "common law of mankind." Institutionally, this law differs from the old because it is made by organizations rather than by states, with the participation of private experts and interest group representatives rather than purely of diplomats. Substantively, it is a dynamic and human law because it is concerned, not with the rights of states and their territorial jurisdictions, but with the welfare of individuals. It complements, at the international level, the scope and purpose of the welfare state.[26] However, Jenks tends to overstate the universality of this "law" by minimizing unique regional factors that make for its development, and by evaluating ringing declarations more highly than they deserve. Furthermore he fails to make clear whether this new law is different from the old in terms of its binding quality, its interpretation, or its manner of being amended; and he therefore predicts its almost unlimited expansion "functionally" without committing himself on whether this involves the *de facto* advent of a world welfare-oriented, legal (and political) community.

Under the label of "co-operative international law," however, W. Friedmann has no hesitation in postulating the emergence of true international communities on the basis of the same type of reasoning.[27] With respect to public health, communications facilities, and safety in transportation, he feels that the problem of shared values is secondary: as long as states are assumed to be competent to act in these fields, their differing internal ideologies and social structures remain as irrelevant to the evolution of this type of law as they were during the nineteenth century. But with regard to all other aspects of law relating to welfare, this is not the case. Unlike Jenks, Friedmann demonstrates the erosion of international consensus in a large array of economic fields with respect to the norms that once governed there. He therefore feels that regional efforts and organizations hold the key to the creation of genuine political communities in terms of dedication to welfare aims shared widely and deeply, because they are also capable of generating political institutions that depart from the accepted intergovernmental character. And these in turn rest on previously shared common value commitments. Neither Friedmann nor Jenks tells us *how* new value commitments with legal consequences can arise; they are content to point to an already existing commitment to welfare policies at all national levels as the internationally generating force. More important still, neither tells us in any detail how a welfare-oriented "new" law differs qualitatively from the old international law in terms of the very factors which cast doubt on the "legal" character of that law.

All these formulations have the enormous merit of directing our attention to the impact of welfare politics on international legal relations and thus detracting from the dominant concern with state rights, peaceful settlement, and diplomatic protocol. If Stone and de Visscher go too far in their realism, Jenks and Friedmann fail to go quite far enough: one has the feeling that, in their eagerness to demonstrate the obsolescence of the bulk of international legal concepts, they are merely substituting new labels for established ways of conceptualizing a legal evolution. For a different kind of attempt, one which aims at legal concepts that are capable of facilitating integrative evolution and yet rest on a demonstrable and modest consensus, we must turn to a self-consciously "functional" theory of law.

What properties should we expect such a theory to possess? Contemporary obsolescent international law exists in opposition to the prevalent practices of states, not in symbiosis with them. Its norms are invoked to restrain, not an occasional and isolated violator, but the bulk of the membership of the international society at any one time. Its rules serve not as a device to admonish evil-doers but as weapons in a verbal armory with which the violators fight one another. A meaningful theory of international law would have to posit norms and procedures that both describe and guide the actual conduct of members, a law that both corresponds to practice and permits the projection and planning of new practices.

In short, the basis of this type of law is some version of sociological jurisprudence, an orientation shared by the pioneering legal scholars whose work was reviewed above. However, the degree of sociological precision here required is not adequately met by these formulations. Léon Duguit, one of the founders of international sociological jurisprudence, could write that "the rule of law appears when among the mass of individuals there appears a consciousness in which [an] economic or moral rule is of importance for intersocial relations, that the sanction of this rule of law must necessarily be organized, and when, at the same time, sentiment imposes on the mass of minds that it is just that this sanction should be organized."[28] No doubt; but what kind of intersocial relations create this sentiment? Whose sentiment is crucial? What does "necessarily" convey in terms of structured social processes? It is a great step forward to separate the evolution of legal norms from the notions of sovereign will, inherent rights, and similar mythical beings, and to stress the "intersocial norm" as the true basis of a law that seeks to regulate an expanding socio-economic scene. But the theory must seek to specify the nature of society in addition.

"Social" and "intersocial" norms can mean only needs experienced in common by participants in international politics regardless of their different national contexts. If we were to make a restrictive assumption, we would have to give up all hope of constructing a theory of international law with universal scope. It must refer to rules of conduct accepted or acceptable not only at the verbal or documentary levels, but in the practice of states, so as to unite in deference to a common scheme communists and free enterprise advocates, democrats and totalitarians, feudal landowners and trade union leaders, *ulama* and commissars. Further, it must do so by spelling out what it is in the nature of each of these varying social systems that creates the need for common "intersocial" norms, both at the articulate and purposive levels of policy and in the hidden byways of unintended consequences of organized action. What, in short, is it in the teleologically explicit aims underlying the norms demanded by disparate social systems that may lead them to the teleologically submerged but implicit consequences involving international integration? The task of this type of legal theory, then, is not merely the explanation of how, why, and owing to whose action norms are accepted in a general sociological context; it also involves an explanation of how, why, and owing to whose purposive or unintended action the norm expands and eventually integrates the disparate social systems into a more closely knit whole. This is the task faced by the self-consciously "functional" approach to international law pioneered by Gerhard Niemeyer.[29]

Based on assumptions reminiscent of the Functionalists', this type of law is seen as flowing almost automatically from social and economic interaction, which is brought about by organizational necessity and "immanent need." The law is therefore non-formal, non-legislative, and devoid of any general and abstract rules. While it need not dovetail with the power aspirations of states, neither is it contradictory to them: it coexists with them. International conflict prevents the emergence of norms based on general consent; therefore this type of law "just grows" because the antagonists experience a need for it despite—or because of—their antagonism. Society is pictured everywhere as no longer directed toward individualism and the defense of individual autonomy, but toward the fostering of coordinate man, man organized with others for the achievement of specific ends.

Consequently functional law refers above all to the ends of social relationships, thus fostering in the individual a consciousness of the functional coordination of his conduct. It strives to bring about in individuals the inner orientation toward the ends of social relationships as such, by virtue of which individuals can immediately experience the immanent "fittingness" or "unfittingness" of their behavior. The ultimate criterion of value in functional law is to be found in the inner necessity, by which, in a given cultural and historical situation, individuals empirically feel compelled to acknowledge certain social ends and to select the means thereto.[30]

If Mitrany was able to link his approach to Kurt Lewin, it becomes apparent why Niemeyer is able to fall back on *Gestalt* psychology for conceptual legitimacy. But just as Gestaltism lacks neatness and structure in its eagerness to comprehend total phenomena conceived in dynamic flux, functional law lacks a sense of orderly process. The merit of functional law lies in its ability to comprehend a multitude of diverse national social systems and aims, and still find a consensus; and to predict the rough outlines of how such a consensus may grow. Niemeyer contrasts the established "personalist" law with the functional variety in these terms:[31]

Personalistic Law	*Functional Law*
1. Idea of Social Reality	
The independent existence of separate persons.	The coordinate behavior of individuals.
2. The Will of Legal Subjects	
Free subjective will.	Individual wills governed by the necessities of reciprocal understanding and functional coordination.
3. Idea of Social Relationships	
Determined by the subjective interests of the separate persons.	Determined by the transpersonal ends which constitute the meaning of each relationship or institution.
4. Idea of Legal Order	
Objective limitation on the free action of the various subjective interests.	The element of orderliness which is inherent in actual coordinate behavior of individuals.
5. Legal Valuation	
Value standards conceived abstractly and in opposition to social reality.	Value standards derived from the functional "directedness" of concrete relationships.
6. Materialization of Legal Order	
Authoritative commands imposing standards of abstract values upon individual wills.	Promoting the individual's consciousness of law by pointing out ends and suggesting means of social relations.

In this form, functional law is still somewhat too elusive to suit our purpose of equipping a functional theory of international integration with an appropriate concept of law. Further, it includes a number of assumptions which, since I do not accept them, must first be discarded. The national state appears as a willful organism spontaneously performing common services for its pluralistic membership. These services are dictated by physical, cultural, demographic, and economic "necessity"—a form of super-teleological analysis that defies a more earth-bound understanding of the political process. This necessity, immanent as it is held to be within the framework of a pluralistic, divided, but welfare-oriented society, is artfully manipulated by the state, which no longer merely responds to the demands of society but now tells society what to demand. Bureaucratic organization, in short, is responsible for creating, defining, and meeting necessity. This picture results in an overemphasis on the state, just as other sociological jurists overemphasized the supposedly automatic, norm-generating capacity of society.[32] The reality of the manipulative state in many actual contemporary settings becomes the organizing image for the total concept of functional law. If this is so, how can the functionalist lawyer also expect presumably unmanipulated social efforts to result in the generation of new international norms? This could happen only with the connivance of the state. This view of functionalism would therefore exclude the possibility of unintended normative consequences by staking everything on "coordinate," articulate, and explicit ends.

But we need not accept this assumption of the nature of the state in order to profit from the functional approach to law. Experience shows that there *are* ends professed in common by antagonistic social systems, and that the norms regulating these ends *do* grow without formal legislation and in the absence of sanctions. If by "orderliness inherent in actual coordinate behavior" Niemeyer conceives unintended consequences flowing from the legal regulation of initially explicit ends, this also can be demonstrated to have occurred in the realm of international economic law. We may postulate, therefore, a notion of law that is based on the existence of common aspirations among contending states, primarily in the fields of health, safety, and communications, but also in the area of economic development and increasingly in fields imbued with military importance, in particular outer-space activity, which constitutes a danger shared by all. Commitments here, devoid of meaningful sanctions though they normally are, may lead to further commitments as the attainment of the original common end is demonstrated to be impossible.

The common sentiments involved range from the fear of war to the dread of epidemics, from the desire for speedy mail service to the hope for safety at airports. They involve, not masses of people, but small articulate elite groups whose expectations of a fruitful life are associated with the creation of specific conditions conducive to the attainment of that life. And, almost universally, economic groups seem to be in the forefront of those who clamor for the recognition of common needs. The "state" is an abstraction in this context: but its bureaucratic servants in ministries of economics and defense, postmasters and civil aviation specialists, surgeons-general and directors of social security, make themselves heard just the same. The actors who articulate the needs that result in norms, then, are not "society" or the "state," but groups with specific interests, whether associational or institutional, motivated by the desire for profit or the drive to improve the services they are called upon to administer. Put into this sociological perspective, the functional process of generating norms can be accepted and made part of a general Functional theory of international integration.

This manner of viewing the legal process is implicitly apolitical and non-directive. It is apolitical in the sense that it declines to postulate some specifically "political" public quality and assumes politically relevant norms to flow from the total *Gestalt* of need-inspired policy. It is non-directive because no effort is made to create or identify a supreme legislative or political "authority" that acts as the source of norms. As such, this approach differs sharply from a more popular vision of international integration, that of the federalist.

Federalists, especially in the Western European setting, do emphasize the distinction between the economic and the political, between the humdrum satisfaction of economic needs by regional agencies and the creative breakthrough implicit in the creation of a genuine political community. Hence they do not believe that the multiplication of "functional" agencies will result in the birth of a new system. The distinction corresponds to de Jouvenel's *action de forme politique*, which may have accidental political consequences inspired by specific task-oriented cooperative behavior, and his *politique pure*, in which the realization of a community becomes an end in itself. In a kindred conception, Pierre Duclos postulates the "threshold of politicization" as the crucial indicator marking the advent of the true political community, the nobler aim sanctifying integration. Partial integration efforts based on socio-economic perceptions of need, apparently, cannot approach or cross this threshold. These conceptions condemn the Functional approach to eternal failure of fulfillment.[33]

In part this critique is inspired by ethical considerations, and in part it relies on some ephemeral myth of "the political." Let us contrast it with Mitrany's conception of "the political":

Because all public action is *ipso facto political* action, and because it is spreading ever more—in Communist states or other such systems to the virtual exclusion of any private group or individual choice—I want to see "functional" organization

1. to rescue as much as possible within each state the element of democratic government; and

2. to provide internationally as wide as possible a basis for cooperative peace, because every relation between countries and peoples having become political, as it is controlled by the State, the area of possible friction and conflict between States gets extended to the same degree.[34]

FUNCTIONALISM REFINED

On the basis of this critique we can now restate the Functionalist separability doctrines. It should be made clear that the restatement rests not only on the theoretical and conceptual points made above—many of them in the realm of assumptions about politics—but also on the empirical evidence that has accumulated about the actual behavior of international organizations and governments participating in them.[35]

1. *Power is separate from welfare.* This proposition is clearly false in fact and misleading in its implications. Unless we assume the Hobbesian *homo homini lupus* as our model, neither organized men nor organized states ever make "power" their aim. Power is merely a convenient term for describing violence-laden means used for the realization of welfare aims. The crucial question is: whose welfare is being realized by what means? The welfare of groups within states, of entire states, of groups of states, or of the whole world? The ambiguity of the proposition is manifest when we consider that organizational tasks inspired by aims of military security can have consequences that promote both welfare and international integration. By way of example it should suffice to point to the experience of the North Atlantic Treaty Organization in the field of multinational defense contracting and to the increasing powers of the UN Secretary-General in mounting pacification campaigns. Every policy at least aims at the satisfaction of someone's welfare, and many policies have consequences consistent with welfare aims even if inspired by other considerations.

Yet the proposition does clarify a point confused by realists who wish to subsume all of international relations to the search for national military security. Organizational programs tied to the totality of all aspects of all national foreign policies never seem to enjoy implementation, whereas well-defined narrow programs conforming to parts of policies or certain states fare much better. In short, we can say that *functionally specific international programs, if organizationally separated from diffuse orientations, maximize both welfare and integration.* Functionally specific programs give rise to international organizations whose powers and competences gradually grow in line with the expansion of the conscious task, or in proportion to the development of unintended consequences arising from earlier task conceptions. Such organizations develop their own norms and their own accepted procedures for dealing with conflict over these norms. But these norms and procedures remain "coordinate" with each other rather than being unified in a general international code.

2. *Through the process of learning, initially power-oriented governmen-*

tal pursuits evolve into welfare-oriented action. Since there is no such thing
as purely power-oriented governmental action, this proposition must also
be stated differently. Further, the notion of "learning" must be understood
in terms of what was said above concerning group behavior, unintended
consequences, and the role of new norms. Learning is based on the perceptions of self-interest displayed by the actors. When actors realize that their
interest would best be achieved by adopting new approaches, and if these
approaches involve commitment to larger organizations, then and only
then does "learning" contribute to integration. Learning, further, often
involves the redefinition of an earlier conception of self-interest concerning welfare as a result of exposure to a new situation. As new alternatives
for action become apparent to the actor, his original notion of his welfare
may undergo some change. In this sense, initially unintended consequences
of organizational action are assimilated into the perceptive equipment of
the actor—in other words, he "learns." The accumulation of such experiences may then give rise to the evolution of new rules of conduct, rules
tailored to the specific pursuits and postulated aims of the action context.
In this sense, "needs" may really give rise to a functionally specific law.

   *Corollary: Integrative lessons learned in one functional context will be
applied in others, thus eventually supplanting international politics.* Put
so generally, this derivative proposition is as misleading as its parent. The
contemporary lessons of the functionally specific European regional organizations show that functional contexts tend to be autonomous; lessons
learned in one organization are *not* generally and automatically applied in
others, or even by the same group in a later phase of its life. We may restate
the corollary of the proposition on learning as follows: if the actors, on the
basis of their interest-inspired perceptions, *desire* to adapt integrative lessons learned in one context to a new situation, the lesson will be generalized.
This formulation presupposes clarity of purpose among the actors. But it
is also true that when actors are united only on a procedural consensus
learned from an earlier integrative experience, this consensus will perform
the role of an unintended consequence in enabling them to achieve integrative behavior with reference to a new situation. It should be recalled
that such a result is possible even when the actors are by no means agreed
on the substantive welfare content of the new step. Finally, it may be said
that to the extent that the initial functional task contained its own expansive
logic—i.e., could not be satisfied on the basis of an initial grant of powers—
it possesses an ad hoc norm-generating capacity redounding to the advantage of the organization and diminishing the powers of the member states.

   3. *Dedication to the welfare orientation is achieved most readily by
leaving the work of international integration to experts and/or voluntary
groups.* This proposition is subject to two qualifications, one pertaining to
the size and the other to the kind of group and expert participation. It is
also subject to severe clarification as to who the experts might be.

The matter of size is merely an aspect of the differing thrusts of regional nd universal organizations. Voluntary groups coming from a regional set-ing are much more likely to achieve integration than an organization con-isting of representatives from the entire globe. Regionalism may foster n underlying homogeneity of values and expectations, and is therefore rucial with respect to the accuracy of the proposition. Group-designated xperts are unlikely to act much differently from their governments if the ocus of action and representation is universal. Further, the groups repre-ented must be roughly symmetrical in membership, belief, strength, and osition in their home societies. An institutional or a non-associational roup speaking for employers is not similar in these respects to an associ-tional employers' federation. Activity by an organization in which group epresentation is both universal and asymmetrical is most unlikely to yield mpressive integrative results.

Finally, the nature of the experts must be specified. In some functional ontexts, high civil servants wholly loyal to their governments may produce lecisions of an integrative nature: witness the NATO air defense system, he Universal Postal Union, or the Permanent Representatives Committee of the European Economic Community. In other contexts, respected ex-perts responsible to nobody may see their recommendations ignored pre-cisely because they are responsible only to themselves—their thoughts may be irrelevant to concrete political demands for specific benefits. Experts chosen by, and loosely responsible to, voluntary groups—in organizations with a membership of democratic nations—do speak for constituencies whose political demands are rarely considered irrelevant. But unless their demands are palatable to governments, integrative consequences of their activity cannot be taken for granted. We have used the notion of "expert" here to include any specialist, whether he works in a public or a private bureaucracy, who participates in the making of some international deci-sion, whether he formally "represents" his home constituency or not. But if this kind of person is simultaneously a leader or manager in his home bureaucracy, his impact on integration is likely to be more pronounced. The most effective carriers of integration, then, are expert-managers of functionally specific bureaucracies at the national level, joined together to meet a common need.

This crucial proposition must therefore be rephrased to read: interna-tional integration is advanced most rapidly by a dedication to welfare, through measures elaborated by experts aware of the political implications of their task and representative of homogeneous and symmetrical social aggregates, public or private.

4. *Personal political loyalties are the result of satisfaction with the per-formance of crucial functions by an agency of government. Since actors can be loyal to several agencies simultaneously, a gradual transfer of loyal-ties to international organizations performing most of the crucial functions*

is likely. Again, with the addition of several qualifications and clarifica
tions, this proposition is both acceptable and enlightening. If what Max
Weber called the "rational" justification for legitimate authority were the
generally prevailing one, we would have no difficulty at all. In a rational
political system, satisfactory performance of functions probably does gen
erate political loyalty. The existence of multiple political loyalties is a
simple empirical fact. Why then should this loyalty not be transferable to
larger units and agencies? Unfortunately for the Functionalists, the limit
ing condition of rationality is not met too frequently.

But there is at least one traditional type of political system that is con
sistent with the proposition. If government is in the hands of some oli
garchy that rules a tranquil and unmobilized people, in which mass
emotions play no part and in which there is no general political participa
tion, spontaneous or manipulated, the logic of the proposition may well
apply. However, the introduction of these qualifications tends to eliminate
from the sweep of the proposition all the world's totalitarian nations, as
well as those nations of Asia, Africa, and Latin America in which oli
garchies now rule peoples rapidly being mobilized and clamoring to par
ticipate in politics—without as yet approaching Weber's model of ration
ality and status based on achievement alone. To the extent, then, that the
integration process is influenced by nations with ascriptive status patterns,
traditional or charismatic leadership, the proposition is unlikely to hold

In the process of indicating whether and how the Functionalist proposi
tions can be meaningfully applied in the study of international integration,
our debt to functionalist sociology has become implicitly obvious. It re
mains now to spell out the intellectual debt explicitly, and thus to make
sociology more clearly a part of international relations studies than it has
hitherto been.

3. *Functionalism and International Systems*

We live in a period exuberantly given to theorizing about social relations of all kinds. International relations seems to have been singled out for especially tender attention, not so much by political scientists and historians, who had a certain tradition to defend in this area, as by social psychologists, political sociologists, mathematical biologists, nuclear physicists, and disillusioned theologians. This influx of interest from disciplines relatively remote from the study of international relations has brought with it the application of analogies and models that had their habitats in their mother disciplines. If one happens to be a political scientist, this feature sometimes proves annoying because the analogies may seem farfetched, the analysis unhistorical, and the consequent prediction chiliastic.[1]

Yet political scientists and historians have too little theory in the study of international relations to permit themselves an unlimited smugness. Even if the models seem irrelevant and the analogies farfetched, the present period of immoderate theorizing is proving exhilarating precisely because it forces a re-examination of traditional tenets. It is true that the specific new propositions and perspectives thrown out to compel self-criticism may not stand the test of time and study. It may well be doubted that we are on the threshold of *the* theory of international relations: we are in a period of desperate self-analysis. The intellectual products of such a search should not be judged merely as correct or incorrect, true or false. Their merits depend on their usefulness in clearing up specific areas of understanding, in serving as building blocks, in delineating defined relationships.

In so construing the task of theory, we are, in effect, parting with one major tradition in international relations. In the past, theory in international relations involved the application of some dogma or doctrine (say, of a Grotius, a Machiavelli, or a Hobbes) to the *description* of an existing state of affairs, and to the *prescription* for getting a ruler, a nation, or the world out of it. Theory was given either a descriptive or a normative task. When, as happened frequently, specific description was deliberately subordinated to advocacy of a given policy or a new order, the total effort was merely propagandistic. The current era of prolific theorizing, no matter what its intellectual antecedents may be, has the enormous merit of catapulting us beyond the range of this branch of apologetics.

One traditional theoretical image stands out in illustrating this use of theory: the image of the balance of power as an organizing concept in explaining all of international relations. The balance of power has been promiscuously and interchangeably used to serve as description, prescription, and propaganda, not merely by governments and their apologists but by scholars as well. Yet, as Cobden so aptly put it, it was never more than a "chimera." In factual historical terms, the mode of state conduct dictated by the balance-of-power theory, since 1789, never actually (i.e., descriptively) prevailed often enough to explain the nature of international relations. Prescriptively, it never consistently guided the conduct of statesmen, and if its norms had been applied, the result would have been unceasing war.[2]

Liberation from the balance-of-power image, if used in this manner, promises a kind of theory that can rise above advocacy, that can order phenomena, explain relationships, isolate trends, and thereby project the future rather than prescribe for it. Systems theory, borrowed though it may be, affords such an opportunity. But is balance-of-power reasoning not merely a species of systems theory, in which state interactions are the inputs, states the units, and the total direction of the international order the outputs? In its most sophisticated form the balance-of-power image is indeed a type of systems theory. If balance-of-power reasoning is used for purposes of *analysis,* and if the balance of power is regarded merely as a way of abstracting recurrent behavior patterns, thus serving as a predictive model, this species of theory remains relevant to the self-critical trend of which this essay is a part. But the continued importance of the image then owes its validity to this more general and more detached way of theorizing about international relations that we associate with systems. And in this context we shall look again at the balance of power, once we have scrutinized some contemporary efforts at rendering international relations in systemic terms.

SYSTEMS THEORY IN INTERNATIONAL RELATIONS

The application of systems theory in international relations is in its infancy. Except for its balance-of-power form, the effort is hardly a decade old; its application to the study of international organizations is younger still.

Hence agreement on terms, propositions, and models is hardly to be expected. This, however, provides all the more reason for rigorously posing the question of the relevance of systems theory to the study of international integration by way of Functionalism. What kinds of systems—apart from their accuracy and internal symmetry or perfection—are *useful* for dealing with integration? Let it be said immediately that approaches deriving from General Systems Theory, of biological lineage, and from efforts to subsume all of science under a general systemic way of analysis have proved far too abstract and tentative to give order to the resolutions of organizations and the policies of nations.[3] Nothing so elaborate is intended here; our concern is at a much more modest level of theorizing, a level at which the concrete activities of observable social units are under review, and on a plane of projection where we will be fortunate if we can foresee the next decade.

Throughout this discussion, the kind of "system" to which we shall address ourselves is the network of relationships among relationships; not merely the relations among nations, but the relations among the abstractions that can be used to summarize the relations among nations; one of these abstractions refers to the national and bloc behavior patterns refracted through the prism of international organizations. Thus the system is not made up of specific trade between Canada and Mexico, war between Cambodia and Thailand, emigration from Greece to Argentina, American-directed subversion in Russia or Russian-directed subversion in America, or any of the other myriad transactions and relationships that have made up international relations. Instead, the system consists of the relationships among the *patterns* of trade, war, migration, and subversion as they impinge upon one another in the confines of international organizations.

Such relationships may or may not be perceived by the statesmen, citizens, soldiers, exporters, or *agents provocateurs* whose actions make up the events from which the systemic abstractions are derived. Systems, then, refer to ways adopted by outside observers to interpret actions: they are analytical devices scholars use to make the real world understandable to themselves and to their fellow scholars.* Systems may stress or slight the empirical world; what matters is that the empirical world need not be aware of the system.

---

* Stanley Hoffmann's definition is similar, though less overtly indebted to sociology: "An international system is a pattern of relations between the basic units of world politics, which is characterized by the scope of the objectives pursued by those units and of the tasks performed among them, as well as by the means used in order to achieve those goals and perform those tasks. This pattern is largely determined by the structure of the world, the nature of the forces which operate across or within the major units, and the capabilities, patterns of power, and political culture of those units." "International Systems and International Law," *World Politics*, Vol. XIV, No. 1 (1961), p. 207. Hoffmann's definition seems preferable to more abstract efforts because it deliberately includes the domestic ideological, social, and constitutional arrangements of the units, i.e., the states, composing the system.

Following Hoffmann for the moment, we can specify the abstractions summarizing the patterns of interaction among the units as (1) objectives sought, (2) tasks performed, and (3) means used. This said, another distinction is immediately in order. A *concrete system* is a pattern of relationships that can be specified with reasonable certainty and accuracy—as defined by the purposes of the scholar or observer—for a given historical period or a given empirical setting. An *analytical system* is a pattern of relationships that may or may not exist in actual life. It is designed by the observer for purposes of projection, or for comparison with actual behavior patterns. Analytical systems can even be used for purposes of prediction if nothing more elaborate and specific is sought than statements of the "if . . . then" variety. While both kinds of systems are heuristic devices, the analytical variety is more abstractly and projectively heuristic than its concrete twin.[4]

But we are interested not primarily in systems, but in the relation between Functionalism and international integration. Of what use is systems theory in the study of integration? Systems theory may be useful for defining the end-states of integration, conceived as a process. Perhaps we can specify a concrete system at a given moment, spell out the functional aspects of its transformation, and project the results of this transformation in terms of an analytic system.[5] Hoffmann seeks to do this by differentiating between discrete historical systems on the basis of three questions: when is there a change in the nature of the units interacting; when do these units have dramatic new means available for fighting; and, given changes in the units and their technologies, what new objectives are these units pursuing?[6]

These questions, if used as indicators, may be appropriate for judging the disintegration of a concrete system, but they do not touch centrally on the issue of tasks tending toward greater integration. They highlight new sources of discord and therefore the disappearance of earlier norms that may have governed behavior patterns. But our concern, based on that of the Functionalists, is to seek out changing relationships and perceptions among actors, even in a system under strain, which may make for the evolution of new tasks, new common interests, and new organizational forms. The disintegration of one concrete historical system—even when it entails a period of revolutionary upheaval—may lead to the perception of new common interests, so that a new order may be created from the ruins of the old system. A Toynbeean time of troubles may not be troublesome on all counts. It is therefore not merely the *goals* and *means* of the acting units that we must scrutinize in focusing on transitions from one system to another, but also the kinds of international *tasks* that derive from these goals and means. Hence we should concentrate on indicators pointing to possible integrative forces present in the demise of a concrete system. And it is in this preoccupation that the refined theory of Functionalism finds its justification. However, if we pursue the argument begun in Chapter 2, the new system toward which functional development may tend, and which we seek to discern in the murky future of international relations, is a system *less* dependent on the goals and means of the acting units, and *more* subservient to the common goals of larger aggregates grouped in international organizations. In formal language, we are on the watch for movement toward relationships that are increasingly system-dominant.

Having stated our expectation of systems theory, we must now summarize some current efforts along these lines in order to examine their suitability for our purpose. Contemporary systems theories in international relations, as David Singer has demonstrated, tend to fall into one of two camps: the "systemic" and the "subsystemic" or "national." Put somewhat differently, "systemic" theory seeks to describe, explain, and predict by examining the totality of relationships from an extraterrestrial pedestal; it also means that the behavior of the actors tends to be subordinated to the norms imputed to the system; phenomenal data relating to the actors becomes irrelevant. The "national" theory, by contrast, tends to focus on the actors—nations, each conceived as being made up of interacting groups, institutions, and individuals—and therefore relies heavily on phenomenal data for purposes of description, explanation, and prediction.[7]

It is important to note that the difference between the two approaches—each perfectly valid, depending on the objective of the observer—is more than the distinction between the study of international relations and the comparative study of foreign policy. One could argue—and indeed the "national" theory tends to argue—that international relations, in their totality, encompass the second-level abstractions culled from the comparative study of foreign policy. The devotee of the "systemic" theory, however, holds that the comparative study of foreign policy will reveal merely what we already suspect to be true on the basis of studying the total system: that national actors tend to behave as the rules of the system dictate. Propositions derived from the two theories are non-additive. "Representing different levels of analysis and couched in different frames of reference, they would defy theoretical integration; one may well be a corollary of the other, but they are not immediately combinable. A prior translation from one level to another must take place."[8] This translation can take only one form, however: if properly fleshed out, the phenomenal approach may be used as a test for the adequacy of systemic propositions. Such fleshing out would call for the inclusion of some kind of decision-making theory in national studies, which could then verify to what extent actors have "internalized" the "rules" of the system of which they are assumed to be a part.[9] By itself, the systemic approach is unlikely to be anything but a huge self-fulfilling prophecy.

We are now armed with two central distinctions: analytical systems as opposed to the concrete variety, and system-oriented approaches as opposed to the phenomenal, "national," or actor-oriented emphasis. Because the usefulness and range of these conceptualizations is constantly being debated, we must examine a representative set of current theories in order to decide which are most appropriate to the study of integration in a functional context.

Following in the strict structural-functional tradition, George Modelski has designed two international systems—"Agraria" and "Industria"—which, though analytical, are held capable of facilitating the comparative study of "all known international systems."[10] The demonstration proceeds by way of assumptions: international relations studies are studies of international systems; international systems are social systems (in Parsons' sense); they have structures; "the same functional requirements are satisfied in all international systems"; and concrete systems are always mixtures of the two analytic types.[11] The purpose of the dichotomous statement of international relations is to discover whether the incidence of war in Industria (the system toward which we are tending) is likely to be as high as in Agraria (the system we left behind), or whether it will be even higher. To spare the reader the anguish of waiting, let me say immediately that Modelski feels that the integrative functions performed by war in Agraria can be performed by other structures in Industria; but he poses the alternative exhilarating possibility that the diffusion of nuclear weapons in Industria will multilateralize the balance of terror.[12]

But our present objective is to illustrate systems theorizing that focuses on the influence of the system itself, as distinguished from its units. In Modelski's two models, integration of the system is held to be accomplished successfully if the actors "play" their international roles in complementary terms, and if this takes place in a context of accepted "beliefs, norms, and values engendered in diplomatic intercourse."[13] The specific aims and motives of actors are completely irrelevant in this perspective because the integration of the system is determined by the overall structure of the societies that it includes—structure interpreted from the top down, so to speak.

But why did Agraria as a system ever decline? Why did it stop being integrated? Agraria was characterized by lack of homogeneity, little international specialization, authority based upon tradition and imperial dominance, integration among the members deriving from family ties among the rulers, and a common culture maintained by the influence of princely courts and their professional retainers. Industria is said to have a highly developed international division of labor, authority based on achievement and diversity of leadership roles, highly diffuse and specialized procedures for maintaining its culture, and integration deriving from "ideological loyalty to an international order."[14] An observer seeking to understand changes in international systems as a component of changes in the objectives, means, and tasks of the units might stress the process of industrialization at the national level. Not so the observer determined to make the system itself supreme: "The transition from one system to the other is not merely a process in which more and more states became industrial, as it were of their own volition; it is a change that is mediated through and powerfully reinforced by the international system, which itself changes in the process."[15] Group aims and perceptions of interest, therefore, can remain with us only if they are understood as quasi-automatic adjustments to systemic forces endowed with a life of their own.

In the work of Morton Kaplan we have a set of six models of the international system that are both analytical and system-oriented.[16] The models are stated with economy and great terminological clarity. However, they are strictly self-maintaining in character; no allowance is made for the perceptions and behavior patterns of individual decision-makers and other actors. The models are predictive, says Kaplan, *if* motivations are taken for granted; and, in the execution of the models, motivations are taken for granted in that they hinge on the preservation of the acting unit through the husbanding of power. But, adds Kaplan, if motivations are left open and the boundary conditions of the system are specified, "the models may be viewed as prescriptions for maximizing certain kinds of objectives."[17] In that case, however, the objectives remain in fact fixed by the boundary conditions defined for each model of the system, which still leaves us with a system-oriented mode of thought. In neither case do we find propositions based on the statement "if the relationships among national motivations are such, then the nature of the international system will be thus."

Kaplan's systems, unlike Modelski's, make no attempt to reflect a given state of technological or social development. Whereas Modelski imputes to his international systems the structural-functional attributes of traditional and modern national societies, respectively, Kaplan is concerned exclusively with the number of units in the system and the nature of their power relations. The systems abstract the patterned relations flowing from numbers and capacities. Retranslated into everyday terms, we have these systems: (1) The balance of power, composed of approximately five large powers and devoid of international organizations with punitive capacity.[18] (2) Bipolarity of two major powers, each with a group of more or less reliable allies, each leader of a bloc of dubious cohesion, with uncommitted nations at the periphery and an international organization in the middle.[19] (3) Bipolarity of two major powers, each leader of a group of allies whom it dominates and controls completely, characterized by the elimination of neutrals and the weakening of international organizations. (4) A federal world state based on mutual tolerance and a universal rule of law. (5) A unitary world state based on conquest by some nation or on a democratic consensus that substitutes functional for territorial constituent units. (6) Multipolarity, in which the system is composed of a very large number of sovereign states, unequal in size and population, but all equal in the sense that each possesses sufficient nuclear striking capacity to achieve deterrent security against every other member unit. The integration of each system is assured by the roles "played" by the members, and to these we must now turn.

In Kaplan's world the notions of "regulation," "stability," "flexibility," and "integration" are almost synonymous. The central definitions are as follows:

Regulation is the process by means of which a system attempts to maintain or preserve its identity over time as it adapts to changing conditions. Integrative and disintegrative actions are also regulatory in character. Integration occurs when units join together or cooperate under conditions which do not appear to permit satisfaction of their system needs in any other way. Thus merging to form a larger unit may seem the only way open to maintain some aspects of the old identity or to satisfy some of the old needs or values. Integration may occur also when one system absorbs other systems in order to satisfy its system needs. Disintegrative activity occurs when subsystems regulate to maintain themselves or to satisfy their system needs at the expense of the system in which they are subsystems. Of course, any of these attempts may turn out to be maladaptive rather than adaptive.[20]

Integration, then, is a species of regulatory activity designed to maintain a given international system. Note that Kaplan implies the system dominance of the formulation: actors will perform the integrative tasks specified if their *system needs* so indicate. The formulation suggests that needs perceived in terms of national politics are not relevant; only needs flowing from the self-maintaining tendency of the international system pertain. Yet the formulation also suggests two kinds of integration: acts that merely maintain the system, as opposed to acts that have the result of transforming it. Disintegration, apparently, is identified with self-centered behavior by states undertaken in disregard of (objective?) system needs. The crucial point, obviously, is the notion of need. If Kaplan treats the transformation of a balance-of-power system into a unitary world dictatorship as an integrative adaptation, this may satisfy the need of the state emerging as the dictator, but probably not that of the rest of the world. The matter is clearly left wide open by the terminological dispute about what constitutes a rival system and what constitutes a subsystem in any analytic context. My interpretation of Kaplan is handicapped by my inability to specify what is system and what is subsystem, i.e., at what level perceptions might be expected to exercise integrative or disintegrative impact. If the ambiguity could be resolved, the statement might still be useful.

In the balance-of-power system, integration was achieved by the balancing nation's playing its proper role, that of balancing the system so as to prevent the hegemony of any one alliance or state. Within the system, one state always had to have the "role function" of balancing; if nobody played the role, the system was transformed because the failures of the international regulatory process were fed back into the national units, which—because of excessive democracy—were unable to play their part properly![21] When this occurs, the balance of power is likely to be turned into a unitary world state or a world federation. In the case of the loose bipolar model, however, the integrative role is played by the neutral nations and the international organization. Integration here usually means mediation and conciliation among the major blocs. Repeated performances of this type will create expectations of permanent integrative role functions, and thus create communications and authority structures strengthening the system. Eventually, the objectives of the international organization acquire legitimacy in the eyes of the member states, as do the processes for settling disputes. When the next crisis occurs, the stage is set for transformation into a world federal system, if the actors respond properly to the "needs" of the system.[22] What is not clear is whether this step is a species of further integration or, rather, evidence of disintegration, since Kaplan implies that if the actors play their roles properly the transformation will not occur.

Because of their wholly speculative character, there is little point in reviewing the integrative role functions associated with the remaining models postulated by Kaplan. It is clear, however, that the process associated with the Loose Bipolar System is a huge advance over other ways of viewing a system-oriented international order, even though this system overstates and misinterprets certain tendencies in the actual behavior of nations in the United Nations context, especially in the realm of collective security.[23] If only we could realistically assume that states truly perceive the needs of a given system, irrespective of their national objectives and means, then the task of international organizations could be specified in trenchant terms and Functionalism could find a niche in the specification. But in order to indicate *which* functions would serve as needs, and *where* they would push the system, we must abandon the system-oriented emphasis and turn to scholarly efforts that stress the phenomenal approach to international systems theory.

It is one of the major virtues of systems theory of the actor-oriented variety that it seeks to combine in one image international and domestic political relationships. This trend derives from the recent renaissance in the field of comparative politics, which has led to the temptation to describe the international system in terms found suitable for the analysis of democratic, totalitarian, or oligarchical polities. Any political system, according to Almond's analysis, performs the same input and output functions:

articulation, aggregation, political socialization, rule-making, rule-appli-
cation, etc. But systems may be differentiated from one another by the
kinds of structures available for the performance of these functions. The
structures, in turn, are abstractions describing roles played by recurrent
types of actors: armies, bureaucracies, various kinds of political parties.
While attention is thus focused on actors, the generalized description of
systemic relations is analytical; whereas the particular pattern of structures
that carry out functions sums up a variety of concrete systems.[24]

Although Almond and Coleman deliberately eschew the use of the concept of integration as fuzzy, the notion crops up in other contexts, as indeed
it always seems to in any systemic rendering of these relationships.[25]
Whether we regard the system as being "integrated," "balanced," "in
equilibrium," "responsive," "sensitive"—the terms used could be multiplied almost indefinitely—makes very little difference. The notion persists
that a given system, by definition, must maintain its boundaries vis-à-vis its
environment; else it ceases to be a discrete system. And in order to do so
it must adequately perform the functions that are its "job" in the view of
the actors who are the member units. Integration, then, is the correct relationship between functional demand and structural capacity to meet the
demands. An integrated system is a successful system.

This conception of integration is a far cry from ours. Yet it is the un-
integrated system that has inspired at least one attempt to comprehend
international relations in an actor-oriented fashion.[26] Fred W. Riggs feels
that the international system is not a system of states because so few of the
members of the United Nations do, in fact, meet Almond's prescription for
successful integration. It is rather a "prismatic system," located at some
point between the functional specificity of a developed state and the functional diffuseness of a traditional agrarian society. Enlightened here by
the metaphorical guide of optometry, Riggs constructs a concrete, actor-
oriented system for the international scene that has the same optical attribute (prism) as a transitional national society. International relations
are thus in a state of flux, an impermanence deduced from what we know
of the properties of transitional societies in the non-Western world. The
system is not integrated and therefore tends toward some new form.[27] But
Riggs hazards no guess as to what the new form might be. He tends to
explain patterns of actor conduct, not on the basis of the "prismatic" attributes of the new states and their leaders, but as flowing from the requirements of the transitional system itself, even though the system was intended
merely to render actor characteristics. Instead of using the transitional
attributes as a constituent of disciplined projections of what will follow the
transition, he turns the transition itself into a system.

Yet this approach has the merit of not assuming the model of the in-
dustrial-pluralistic *Rechtsstaat* as the necessary end-state of the interna-

tional society.[28] A future global system might retain some transitional attributes that might be studied now on the basis of the systemic concepts developed for the study of late-developing nations. This might indeed be illuminating by suggesting future international forms other than the bureaucratic-rational-legal model in the forefront of our minds, as well as adapting for use at the international level diagnostic techniques found useful in the study of national polities. But the suggestion remains tentative. In the meantime, the stress on a transitional "system" enshrines the dominance of system-orientation over actor-orientation.

This shortcoming is skillfully avoided by Stanley Hoffmann in his effort to merge actor-oriented systems theory with concrete models derived from historical sociology.[29] It makes a difference, Hoffmann points out, whether the units of the system are city-states, empires, nation-states, or transnational ideological movements. Their relative technological endowment and the intensity of their intercourse are essential in determining historical periods. Hence different kinds of international law flourish in different international systems: we cannot expect from one kind what we expect from another.* All types of international law deal with these requirements. But overall "stability," a term to which we shall return, determines *which* system will prevail.[30] The stability of the international system, unlike the formulations of our other theorists, is held by Hoffmann to be strictly related to the nature of the actors on the international scene. He is able, therefore, to demonstrate the flourishing or demise of a given kind of international law in terms of international systems that reflect, respectively, a mechanical balance of power (1648–1789), an ideologically contaminated balance of power (1815–1914), and a transitional-revolutionary system, in which actor objectives, means, and tasks bear little similarity to anything experienced before (1919–   ). The difficulty with Hoffmann's image is its inability to explain the transition from a stable to a revolutionary system in terms of what survives, which norms carry over; it can account for the causes of system disintegration, but not for the residual items that live on. Kaplan's systems are too continuous, Hoffmann's too discrete.

We have scrutinized, from the viewpoint of their relationship to integration studies, some current theories regarding the international system. If no single one has weathered all possible criticisms, elements of many of

---

* The types of international law Hoffmann correlates with types of international systems are (1) "the law of the political framework," which regulates major power relations among states and depends minimally on institutionalized third-party settlement or accepted norms; (2) "the law of reciprocity," which regulates the permanent interests that states experience in common, irrespective of their mutual state of hostility, e.g., commerce and the rules of warfare; (3) "the law of community," which deals with scientific and technological concerns best delegated to some autonomous body with independent powers, a law from which all expect to derive benefits.

them remain relevant to our quest. Let it be repeated that systems theories must be judged by their degree of usefulness in explaining a particular set of phenomena, not by their symmetry or truth. But the kind of theory we seek is one which is explicitly and deliberately dynamic in the sense that it seeks to explain transitions. It must be a theory that works with developmental and projective models, models that comprehend change *and* abstract upon what seems to remain constant in the progression of concrete experiences. In Kaplan's models these transitions are deduced from the characteristics of the systems themselves, not from the behavior of the actors. In Hoffmann's the historical contexts set the scene for the behavior of the actors, but transitions to new relationships appear to be idiosyncratic rather than systemic. The happy medium we seek is attained by Charles McClelland in a different context. He seeks to explain when and how international crises become less destructive in various historical situations, and he hopes to find his explanation in the degree of bureaucratic routinization in the collection, diffusion, and digestion of new informational stimuli that tend to characterize all modern national societies.[31] Such an approach focuses both on fixed functional characteristics and on structures variable with the degree of social and economic development; but attention remains concentrated on the behavior of the actors. There may be enough in functional sociology to enable us to construct a system of this kind for the explication of international integration.

OBSCURITIES AND PROBLEMS
IN INTERNATIONAL SYSTEMS THEORY

How do we know when a given system is "useful"? Any system that specifies a number of components, in the context of transition, calling attention to the conduct of certain actors, systemic feedbacks on the actors, and actor feedbacks on the system, and manages to do so without being either platitudinous or tautological will have gone a long way toward satisfying our criterion of usefulness. What, then, are the components to be specified, and how do our systems deal with them?

Definitional clarity, verbal and operational, must obtain with respect to (1) the relationships being abstracted, i.e. the nature of the *inputs* and *outputs*; (2) the *units* of which the system is composed; (3) the *environment* surrounding the system; otherwise the boundaries of the system cannot be ascertained—and without boundaries we have no system; (4) the dominant *attributes* of the system, such as the question of whether the system is supposed to be in movement or in equilibrium, stable or revolutionary, self-maintaining or creatively adaptive; it is especially important here to avoid the quality of pure systemic determinism whereby everything is defined in terms of everything else, so that we end with a gigantic self-fulfilling prophecy that makes it impossible to determine which action and what actors cause a given result;* (5) the *structures* that enable the system to perform; and finally (6) the *functions* the system is supposed to perform; as indicated in Chapter 1, there seems to be some scholarly dispute about whether the notion of function refers to the purposes of actors, the results of their actions, the causes underlying action, or unintended consequences flowing from their actions, which may or may not later reappear as conscious purposes; furthermore, we must come to grips with the notion that functions are roles played by actors within a system.

Definitional Problems of System-oriented Approaches

Working in the Parsonian camp, Modelski identifies the basic components of international systems (as of all social systems) as "a set of objects plus the relationships between these objects and between their attributes." These objects are "international status-roles (examples of these are the roles of a great power, of a United Nations member, or of a neutral)."[32] Now, these "status-roles" are the outputs of the foreign policy processes of the actors; inputs are furnished by the policy demands facing the makers of foreign policy, plus the power they have at their disposal. From the point of view of the system, the policies of the actors—their outputs— is "their international role-playing."[33] So far so good. But who are the actors or units of the system? They can be either states or international organizations. But in that case the outputs of one type of actor would be inputs for the other, and vice versa. Modelski ignores the stricture of specificity in identifying his units. The chief attribute of international systems is self-maintenance, i.e. the preservation of an adequate degree of autonomy for the constituent units.[34] System structures are found in the characteristic responses the system makes in the performance of its functions, including the modes of diplomatic intercourse, institution-building, and war. When we come to the specification of functions, however, real difficulties confront us. The main function of the system is the same as its chief attribute—"the safeguarding of the independence of its members and the maintenance of international order by minimizing conflict and violence"— and the additional term "functional requirement" is then introduced, which must be "solved" in order to attain self-maintenance.[35]

At this point one may justifiably ask what is to be gained if a system

---

* I shall take this opportunity to indicate that, within my criteria of relevance and usefulness, so-called requisite structural-functional systems fall afoul of the strictures expressed. They conceive of society as an autonomous self-maintaining system, and then specify which functions are requisite for self-maintenance and which structures are requisite for the performance of these functions. This conception permits almost no projective analysis of the intersystemic transitional variety that I am attempting to delineate. For examples see Marion J. Levy, Jr., "Some Aspects of 'Structural-Functional' Analysis in Political Science," in R. Young, ed., *Approaches to the Study of Politics* (Evanston: Northwestern University Press, 1958).

is defined as status roles, status roles as an exchange of inputs and outputs at an unspecified level of transaction and with variable hierarchies of actors, attributes as functions, and functions as functional requirements to maintain attributes. Kaplan avoids the unnecessary and confusing recourse to status roles as chief system constituents. Inputs are policy demands of systemic units, outputs are policies produced. But instead of simultaneously using states *and* international organizations as actors or units, he regards both entities as subsystems of the international system—but in different analytical contexts. Thus, in one kind of system, national outputs serve as inputs into the international organizational subsystem. United Nations decisions then become the outputs of the international system. But since his analytical systems assume different kinds of subsystems, he is justified in this usage, so long as not everything is claimed for everything at the same time.[36] As for system attributes, Kaplan distinguishes between stability and ultrastability, the latter allowing for considerable and extensive internal change while maintaining the boundaries of the system vis-à-vis its environment. However, he assumes that the ultrastable adaptive mechanism, though transition-oriented, works in response to systemic stimuli. Further, he does not specify the environment any more concretely than Modelski. Structures, unfortunately, are never clearly identified and tend to be confused with the total system. But his conception of functions is unique. Actor-units in a given political system, instead of carrying out ordinary functions, are endowed with "role functions": they must do certain things regularly and consistently in order to preserve the system; the functional needs of the system are met by the roles played by the actors. As demonstrated above, these role functions must be performed within the "rules" of the system in order to retain stability or ultrastability.[37]

With Kaplan we have gained a measure of conceptual clarity as compared with the Parsonian school of thought. But not very much. Role functions remain purely arbitrary deductions with only occasional resemblance to the volitional conduct of flesh-and-blood actors. The fact remains that the conceptualization of functions as role functions calls attention to the multiple—and not necessarily mutually supporting—activities carried out by certain actors within the confines of a system. As long as the usage merely refers to these activities, classifies them and analyzes them in relation to their contribution to system maintenance, something of value is gained. Once, however, the role function of a given party, group, government, or organization is viewed as a "need" of the system—and the notion of a fixed role to be played in connection with a recurrent function almost begs the imputation of need—we are face to face once more with the problem of teleological reasoning. For this reason I prefer not to think of functions as roles, but as tasks performed by structures.

Role functions are not related by Kaplan to the socio-economic characteristics of any environment because the environment is left unspecified.

We could define the environment as the modes of social, political, and economic relations prevailing within the member states of the system, modes resulting from the values dominant in each state. The inclusion of such factors would go a long way toward infusing the breath of life into the six analytical models of Kaplan. As formulated, these system-oriented conceptions are far too rigidly teleological in their mania for stability, equilibrium, and self-maintenance to serve as dynamic stimuli for projection.

Definitional Problems of Actor-oriented Approaches

The tyranny of *telos* can be considerably reduced if, as is the case in Almond's and Hoffmann's approaches, the emphasis is placed on the actor instead of the pattern of actor relationships. Actors, as the basic unit of our interest, are defined into irrelevance once we mistake them for their status roles; once we impute behavioral characteristics hinging on perceptions of status, we rely on phenomena far too fragile operationally to permit an empirical ordering of actions that can be systemically related. Thus Almond conceives of his analytical system of a national polity as a mechanism for turning inputs (demands by discrete actors) into outputs (policies, laws, decisions). There is no difficulty about identifying the units: they are the interest groups and political parties that recruit people, articulate values, and absorb ideas found in the environment. Whether the governing group, as a systemic structure, is also such an actor is not made quite clear. The notion of structure can, apparently, refer to the habits and institutions peculiar to the government, as well as to the groups that in practice tend to dominate the government. When we come to identifying the system's attributes, we find Almond deliberately avoiding the stability notion and addressing himself instead to the matching of demands with performance: the system need not be stable by definition. This is quite appropriate, since it is Almond's purpose to isolate important behavioral variables among his actors in relation to their effect on the shape of the system. In short, the emphasis is on feedback relations between system and units, imputations of inviolate self-maintenance being avoided.

The terminological difficulty arises when we turn to the functions of the system. They are identified with inputs and outputs, thus being viewed as recurrent activities. We now have the embarrassing question of whether functions are prerequisite *conditions for* a system, recurrent *activities* carried on *in* the system, or, in the case of "output" functions, *results* produced *by* the system. Using the concept loosely to cover all these contingencies hardly helps us. Why could not demands and policies be made to refer to inputs and outputs, and the notion of function reserved for tasks of the system stated at a higher level of abstraction?

It is at this point that the open-ended nature of the Almond and Riggs systems creates difficulties for us. Their approaches are useful for the study of international integration precisely because they do focus on functional processes rather than system attributes. But unless one has some kind of vision concerning probable end-states of transition—of future or alternative systems—great uncertainty remains about *which* processes should be selected for focused attention. To be sure, the end-state need not be the Weberian rational entity; but it might be. The international system may well be transitional and incorporate many processes reminiscent of Peru, Thailand, and Upper Volta; but may this not be a temporary feature of international relations? When Alger deliberately applies the Almond categories to the study of international integration, he leaves unresolved the question of what is system and what is environment. When he lists the "functions" central to his analysis he has little to say about concrete interests. Instead he is concerned largely with the secondary matter of how actors "learn" to abide by the rules of the United Nations. Hence the functions singled out refer to communication, socialization, and recruitment rather than to the more elementary matter of demands and policies.[38]

Hoffmann's approach, of course, sidesteps many of these difficulties. For him, the units of any historical system are the states interacting in it. He avoids the words "input" and "output," their equivalents in the system being provided by the demands of states and the policies deliberately decided upon by international conferences, organizations, or other institutionalized modes of deliberation. The environment is provided by the technological development, the culture, and the values of a given historical period—let it be repeated that here we are dealing with concrete actor-oriented systems—and the structures of the system are the institutions through which intercourse is carried on.[39] The term "function" occurs very rarely, and when it does it has no self-conscious definitional attribute, meaning both "result" and "purpose."[40] Yet Hoffmann agrees with Almond and others in specifying essential "requirements" (i.e. "functions"?) for each system: assuring the survival of the units, obtaining the assent of the units, and providing for peaceful change. The result is a looseness of demonstration that exaggerates the idiosyncratic character of each historical epoch and tends to lose the sense of continuity. One wonders whether historical systems have anything in common at all except for the fact that they are made up of interacting units called states.

Hoffmann's important contribution lies in his distinction between two modal kinds of system attributes. By combining environmental factors, unit size, technological endowment, and unit objectives and values, he arrives at two kinds of systems, stable and revolutionary. "A stable system is one in which the life or the essential values of the basic units are not constantly in question, and the main actors agree on the rules according to which the competition will take place; a revolutionary system is one in which the incompatibility of purposes rules out such an agreement."[41] "Rules" here are the concrete norms and limits governments observe, not systemic abstractions deduced from some *telos* of self-maintenance; "purposes" are the concrete policy aims of governments, not the preservation of prerequisites perceived by none but the scholar. Each type of environment will produce its own kind of stable and revolutionary relationships, depending on the technological capacities and value conflicts that happen to prevail. Hence the balance of power was the expression of stability in an environment without absolute weapons, with limited national government, with substantial sharing of beliefs across national boundaries. A dramatically changed environment can still result in a stable system provided the units are *evenly* differentiated. A revolutionary system, by contrast, will result whenever the units are unevenly differentiated, when they are divided in terms not only of different technological capacities, but of fundamental beliefs and incompatible objectives. Examples of unevenness cited by Hoffmann include the emergence of rulers with unlimited aggressive ambitions, the unequal technological development of rival states, the destruction of transnational beliefs, and the intensification of integral nationalism in some of the units. In terms of propositions that flow from this ordering of the international world, Hoffmann can then demonstrate which of his three kinds of law are likely to flourish in what kind of international system.

Let us try to sum up. The purpose of this examination of the properties of systems was not to engage in semantic exercises, but to investigate which systems—in part or in their totality—are most appropriate for studying international integration in Functional terms. Functionalists rest their case on the recurrent objectives of certain kinds of political actors, on their purposes and aims. System theorists wish to abstract these aims into patterns, in the hope of explaining why certain relationships survive and others perish. Let us remind ourselves that if a certain system is said to disintegrate, we are merely saying that a certain pattern of relationships between actor-units is changing beyond the bounds of what was permissible under the original rules; we are not saying that the actors themselves disintegrate, for they may merely reorder their relationships differently and thus establish a new system. The chief point for our quest is to remember that governments may attempt to create new systems *on purpose*. By all means let us watch for automaticity and unconscious laws of behavior. But let us never forget that "system feedback" *must* show up in terms of phenomenal evidence in the conduct of governments in order to prove its existence.

Hence stress must always be put on the environment that yields policies. There are no "needs" of any system, no "rules," and no "prerequisite functions," except insofar as these are metaphors seeking to describe in abstract terms the interaction of state demands. System-oriented approaches have the merit of focusing our attention on the possibilities of feedback, provided we take them as metaphors and not as real things. The language of structural-functional analysis confuses the picture and adds unnecessary complexity. It cannot illuminate our concern so long as its proponents persist in using circular definitions and reifying into concrete edifices their "purely" analytical models. Thus the marriage of Functionalism and functionalism, which was heralded in Chapter 1, cannot be celebrated under the banns of systems theory in the form in which we have here encountered it.

Can the reconciliation be made under the aegis of the variant called the "balance of power," that analytical device which boasts a longer life in the theory of international relations than any other? As argued above, one form of balance-of-power theorizing is clearly a species of systems theory. Its essential uselessness for dealing with integration remains to be established. Although my concern will be with the balance of power in the context of international integration, I should confess at the outset that my argument is pitched at a level of generality sufficient to demonstrate the overall irrelevance of this mode of analysis.

OBSCURITIES ENSHRINED: THE BALANCE OF POWER AS AN ANALYTICAL CONCEPT

In examining the relevance of balance-of-power theorizing to Functionalism and integration, we must be very clear what form of balance-of-power theory is being scrutinized. In an earlier study, I culled from the historical literature on the balance of power no fewer than eight distinct verbal meanings of the expression, ranging from "distribution" of power to a complex notion that holds the balance to be a "guide" to policy-makers, developing into a "system" of international relations when simultaneously used as a guide by all statesmen. However, in the huge majority of cases, those who used the term "balance of power" apparently sought to convey no more than the actions, conditions, and events that can be described by the terms "power politics" or "distribution of power."

Further, in probing the intentions of the writers, I identified four distinct aims. (1) There is a descriptive intent, in which the term could be used with any of eight verbal meanings isolated, merely in order to circumscribe factually a given international situation. Although, of course, theoretical assumptions enter the descriptive effort here, the overall purpose of the user remains the delineation of a state of affairs. (2) Prescriptive intent emerges when the "guide-and-system" or "universal law of history" meanings of the term are so used as to prescribe for governments the kind of action they ought to take. Here theoretical misconceptions can have more serious consequences. (3) Propagandistic intent is dominant when the various meanings associated with the balance of power are used loosely to justify publicly a given course of action involving the application of power. The term serves here as "ideology," as a legitimating device to cloak state action that may have been decided on for a variety of reasons having nothing to do with balancing. (4) Finally, the intent may be conceptual or analytical: the user applies the "guide-and-system" meaning in order to gain clarity and accuracy in predicting the future course of events. This may or may not lead to prescription; it certainly includes description, but avoids propaganda rigorously.[42] It is this fourth usage that will concern us here.

We shall examine several contemporary versions of balance-of-power theorizing. We shall ask ourselves in each case whether the effort is free from the shortcomings of functional systems theory catalogued above, whether it comprehends a sufficient range of environmental conditions for accuracy, whether it can help in explaining transitions to new dominating relationships, and whether it is free from the dangers of self-maintenance assumptions.

Balance of Power as Eternal Law

In a very sensitive demonstration that draws on the theory of the social contract, Kenneth Waltz argues that a systemic version of the balance of power today retains its explanatory superiority as compared with theories stressing the psychological nature of man or the internal political order of the states that make up international society.[43] Psychological and internal political considerations are not irrelevant; but, argues Waltz, they can be properly understood only if they are placed into the *system* in which they unroll, and that system is the international balance of power, as valid today as it always was—in the absence of a world state with universal law.

The informing image is Rousseau's fable of the stag hunt. A number of hungry hunters agree to stick together until they have shot a stag, a quarry large enough to sustain them all. They have difficulty in finding one. One hunter loses patience and, breaking his agreement with the others, leaves the group to shoot a hare he has seen. As a result the remaining members of the group are not strong enough to attain their original objectives. Is the deserter to be blamed for betraying the general good in favor of his particular short-run advantage? Rousseau answers that, in the state of nature, the short-run decision of the deserter to maximize his individual immediate advantage is rational and to be expected. Since nations live in the state of nature, war is rational and to be expected as long as it is to a nation's immediate advantage. According to Waltz, the system of international relations, which does not provide the security of community and law, imposes the superiority of the short-range rationality of the hare-hunter.

But to emphasize the importance of political structure is not to say that the acts that bring about conflict and lead to the use of force are of no importance. It is the specific acts that are the immediate causes of war, the general structure that permits them to exist and wreak their disasters. To eliminate every vestige of selfishness, perversity, and stupidity in nations would serve to establish perpetual peace, but to try directly to eliminate all the immediate causes of war without altering the structure of the "union of Europe" is utopian.[44]

Waltz then concludes that in international relations of the competitive type "the implication of game theory, which is also the implication of [Rousseau's] image, is . . . that the freedom of choice of any one state is limited by the actions of all the others."[45] Hence, irrespective of morality or governmental intent, as long as survival remains the basic state objective, the system as a whole will determine relationships—and the relationships will be those of power politics. More, power politics will take the form of countervailing coalitions and alliances; hence a "balance" of power describes the system, whether consciously willed by statesmen or automatically introduced by their instinctive reaction to challenges. And this would be equally true even if the leading statesmen, like Cobden, publicly adjured the balance of power and claimed to be acting on different grounds. "In summary, then, it can be said that the balance of power is not so much imposed by statesmen on events as it is imposed by events on statesmen."*

In the state of nature, irrespective of technology, communism, liberalism, space exploration, urbanization, economic development, alienation, or whatever other modern phenomena one may wish to add, the balance of power remains an eternal law permitting institutionally unregulated state behavior. We reject this formulation for the same reason that we reject all system-dominant automaticity. Obviously, any sound analysis has the right to insist that the categories found important in characterizing the conduct of a system need not be overtly recognized by the actors; the very purpose of analysis is to rise above these data and events, and induce conclusions from them at a higher level of abstraction. But this is very different from what we do have the right to demand: that the analytic categories must at all times *be consistent with* the perceptions and motives of the actors. We can assume nothing else if we argue that systems are made up of people, groups, and actions instead of pretending that the reverse is the case. Waltz's treatment of the balance of power as an analytic system, however, is not consistent with the perceptions and motives attributed to actors in an earlier portion of his argument. The balance is merely superimposed on the remainder.

The very image of the stag hunt can yield short-run and practical individual motives—understood and reciprocated, if not shared in identical terms, by others—which will erode the simple picture of power balanced

---

* *Man, the State, and War*, p. 209. Lest Waltz's intentions be distorted, let it be repeated that he considers the balance of power to explain the indirect, the permissive, causes of war. But he grants that immediate and specific causes of given wars must be sought in individual motivation and the internal order of the nations involved (*ibid.*, pp. 232ff).

against power. The Functional logic is wholly compatible with the stag-hunt image; in fact, in its reformulated version, it depends upon it.* If the cooperative hunting of the stag is demonstrated to be impossible, the hunters will make informal rules regulating the separate or cooperative hunting of hares. Obviously, as our reformulated separability doctrines argue, this is not inevitable. But neither is the unflinching balancing of power inevitable in the international state of nature—because, in Functional terms, there really is no state of nature at all. Functionalism calls attention to the variety of motives and relationships that flow from a technologically, economically, and socially diverse environment. The eternal law of the balance of power, as an analytic system, sees only physical survival. But a theory of integration sees much more than that.

Balance of Power as a Temporal, Unidimensional System

Taking as his point of departure Waltz's vision of an analytical system of the balance of power, Arthur Lee Burns set himself the task of stating the limits of the system and sketching the conditions of its transition into something quite new.† International relations, prior to the advent of nuclear weapons, was a "balance-of-power" system, in which the dominant relation-

---

* As Hoffmann shows, this formulation is very different from Rousseau's own conclusions. When Rousseau's occasional excursions into international politics are read together with his focused work on the desirable national polity, it appears that there is an inevitable hiatus between a good national order peopled by good citizens and a corrupt international order. Only if all states lived up to the formula of the *Contrat social* could this hiatus be transcended, a condition Rousseau himself did not expect to materialize. Therefore, even good states are exposed to perpetual international competition; the corrupt properties of the system aggravate—and may even destroy—the life of the virtuous units.

On the other hand, Rousseau had no faith in the possibility of reforming international relations by restructuring national and international institutions. A league of ideal societies would undermine the normal working of the general will because it would take the place of the small polity that was held requisite for its operation. In other words, Rousseau's image was of the "all or nothing" variety that is incompatible with Functionalism. It is possible, however, that my reformulation of the stag-hunt image would fit Kant's adaptation of the Rousseauan approach. Hoffmann, "Rousseau on War and Peace," *American Political Science Review*, LVII (1963), esp. 329–33.

† Arthur L. Burns, "From Balance to Deterrence: A Theoretical Analysis," *World Politics*, Vol. IX (1957). I am citing from the reprinted version in James N. Rosenau, ed., *International Politics and Foreign Policy* (Glencoe, Ill.: The Free Press, 1961). As is his commendable wont, Burns later published another essay in which he scrutinized his earlier argument and found it unsatisfactory. After examining the argument I am about to summarize, he found that "it now seems to me very difficult indeed to construct a useful model for the regular workings of a particular international system: each Power enjoys quite a variety of alternatives, and the sort of considerations which I had thought conclusive for one alternative look less so when one reminds oneself of some of the others. And, turning from theory to history, it would not be easy, working only from a description of the European system after the Peace of Westphalia (1648), to predict its subsequent history until the Peace of Utrecht (1713)." He adds that "a truly general and rigorous theory of power politics is unobtainable. But piecemeal theoretical insights are possible; and those that we have owe much to hints and suggestions derived from both the informal varieties of game theory and

ships between the member states were those of an n-person non-zero-sum game, with the payoff consisting in the ability to remain in the game, i.e. to survive. Therefore, military potential, and especially military technology, is held to be the factor that determines the conduct of the actors, and thus shapes the system. "Relationships of alliance, of pressure or opposition . . . are the relations which constitute the international system."[46] The balance-of-power system will then follow the rules normally stated by those who use this image as a supreme analytical device: the maximization of security, switching of alliances, minimizing of uncertainty, etc. The system is unidimensional because it abstracts only military relationships; it is temporal because it is inherently unstable and cannot last. Unlike Waltz, therefore, Burns concluded that the balance of power as an analytical device is temporally limited in its usefulness. Why is this true?

A balance-of-power system is held to lead to the diminution of the number of its members because the contending blocs or states are perpetually in rivalry; they are therefore unwilling deliberately to build up the additional blocs mathematically necessary to maximize system stability. This, in turn, is held to be true because states and blocs are constantly undergoing changes that are assumed to heighten their sense of rivalry. One set of changes refers to the system itself, because wars reduce the number of participants. But, in addition, changes come about as a result of unsystemic developments of a demographic, industrial, and technological nature in certain member states. When these changes have created a situation in which warfare is certain to destroy completely the enemy's economy but is incapable of destroying his military apparatus, we have attained a "deterrent system," an entirely new species. The advent of nuclear weapons and missiles, therefore, has made the balance of power obsolete. We then have the system made familiar by those who associate global stability with the balance of terror, in which no bloc can move meaningfully.

Two things can be said about this formulation. Contrary to Burns's argument, the deterrent system is still, in analytical terms, a variant of the balance-of-power system. It remains unidimensional and takes no account of environmental factors ("alternatives open to governments," in Burns's afterthoughts) other than the military. It therefore fails to satisfy one of the major needs a system must satisfy for our purposes. Furthermore, as Burns himself argues, the new system is also unstable because it can be upset by military innovations that reintroduce possibilities of local maneu-

---

bargaining theory." "Prospects for a General Theory of International Relations," *World Politics*, XIV (1961), 36 and 45.

Consequently, I shall confine myself to stating and evaluating only that portion of the argument which deals with the recurring influence of the balance of power on contemporary theorizing, and which seems to retain its relevance in the minds of many scholars despite Burns's disavowal of his own formulation.

er and limited war, thus giving small and unaligned states a new lease
n life. Yet the deterrent system is also expected by Burns to increase the
ize and reduce the number of blocs in juxtaposition. Paradoxically, Burns
loses with a backhanded encouragement to the Functional argument in
xpressing the hope that "the international republic of science might
levelop institutions and like-minded relationships cutting across state
overeignties and alliances, and thus create the elements of a concrete
vorld community."[47]

In a sense, these thoughts symbolize the unsatisfactory character of all
nalysis couched in terms of balance-of-power systems. Consequences and
auses are interchangeable. When systemic factors do not seem to yield
cceptable consequences, the authors feel free to bring in considerations
hat their own initial assumptions of military or power primacy should lead
hem to discount. When it suits the argument, system feedback on the
ctors is stressed; when that seems to work hardships on history, actor feed-
ack on the system is singled out instead. The poor empiricist is left rather
ewildered in his search for guiding precepts that would propel him beyond
imple empiricism.

The unidimensional and temporal character of balance-of-power think-
ng has prompted a good deal of soul-searching among scholars addicted
o this mode of analysis. Has the soul-searching resulted in any significant
eformulations germane to our examination? John Herz, in confronting
his question directly, has concluded that the "new" balance of power intro-
luced by nuclear relationships is a mere quantitative—and hence highly
langerous—change over the "classical" power balance. But he also believes
hat the new balance obeys essentially the same systemic rules as the old,
vhich can be rendered less dangerous for survival by strengthening certain
eatures—such as the reliability of signals exchanged by opponents, the
neutralization of territory, limited and symmetrical arms control—which
vere also allegedly part of the classical game. We must conclude that the
analysis and prescription, no matter how appealing on policy grounds,
ntroduce no theoretical refinement.[48]

Unidimensionality, however, is the very factor that stimulates Glenn
Snyder to "update" the balance of power as an analytical concept. Taking
Burns's two balancing systems as his point of departure, Snyder transfers
hem from the plane of analysis to the level of immediate existence: they
coexist now as living superimposed systems. The balance of power refers to
he military relationships of the nations at the level of conventional and
limited war forces, and to the strategies associated with them; the balance
of deterrence, on the other hand, refers to the relationships created by
total nuclear striking capacity, a capacity to deter and destroy, rather than
to defend.[49] Various concrete "balances" are possible, depending on the
nature of the capabilities and forces confronting one another, but none

"mean *matching* the enemy in offensive striking forces or having a slight margin of superiority over the enemy in such forces, as in the traditional concept of balance of power. . . . 'Balancing' means introducing into the enemy's risk calculus a prospect of cost which will be sufficient to offset his prospect of gain, *after* discounting the costs by some factor representing the enemy's doubts about one's willingness to inflict them."[50] Yet these two superimposed systems are said to possess a degree of equilibrium to the extent that the forces are invulnerable.

Now Synder feels that the simple systemic superimposition of the two balances is analytically unsatisfactory, even if descriptively accurate, because it obscures the dependence of one systemic balance upon the other; it also neglects the credibility factor; finally, it fails to specify and predict the degree to which unequal local conventional forces depend on the expected behavior of global deterrent forces, and vice versa. Therefore, for Snyder a truly useful analytical balance-of-power theory must specify not only the balance of military capabilities, but also the "balance of intentions" of the antagonists and the "balance of persuasion" that characterizes their non-military relations. The new balance of power, he demonstrates, does not function in disregard of the intentions of statesmen. Whereas under classical conditions intent and motive could be ignored for analytical purposes, the risks involved in nuclear warfare make the assessment of motivation a vital and autonomous component of the balance.

No doubt we must be grateful that balance-of-power devotees have rediscovered the role of motivation. But does this shift to the motives of actors really help us? In his very eagerness to overcome the unidimensionality of military analysis, Snyder has destroyed the analytical appeal that balance-of-power theorizing has—without justification—exerted. How can one meaningfully speak of a "balance" of intentions or a "balance" of persuasion, as if these relationships were in some state of equilibrium? Certainly, the effect of persuasion must be understood and the intentions of governments ascertained. But does descriptive zeal here have anything to do with a conceptual construct suggesting balanced relationships of a systemic character? The quantitative nature of military considerations contributes to the attraction the "balance" concept has exerted; but we can hardly rescue the theory by adding two wholly different ranges of transaction and perception that make a sum of apples and pears.

Balance of Power as Multidimensional Analysis

There remains another analytical formulation of the balance of power as system, a formulation at once multidimensional and temporal in conception. Military relationships cease to be the dominating consideration, and the historical limits of a world that can be analyzed in balance-of-power terms are made explicit. One such formulation is Morton Kaplan's, which we had occasion to describe in a different context.[51] We may take it as an ideal type of what international actors *should* have done all the time, and—Kaplan feels—*did* do frequently enough to permit the drawing up of the model. Whether they actually did so is a matter of historical dispute and empirical disagreement. Ultimate motives are assumed as constant; actors are either smart or stupid in their practical efforts to realize them, able to internalize the rules or to ignore them at their peril. It is this assumption that renders even this formulation of an analytical balance of power of dubious value to us. If we grant that environments have something to do with the prevalence of certain kinds of motives, we simple cannot hold the intentions of actors constant. Or if we do so, we commit ourselves to a series of assumptions that reduce the analytical relevance of the system.

Hoffmann avoids this difficulty by making the environment the point of departure for his historical mode of reasoning, and thereby commits himself to the actor and his motives as the chief analytical referent. But he, too, sees the eighteenth and nineteenth centuries as a concrete balance-of-power system. Furthermore, it was a stable system because the prevalent intentions, local conditions, and common tasks imposed a moderate style. What were the environmental properties singled out by Hoffmann? The balance was centered in the European core area, with an "uncivilized" frontier under European dominance to serve as a theater for expansive tendencies. (Apparently, the *function* of the colonial world for the *system* was to preserve the European balance.) The major states in the core were roughly equal in power, and the process of industrialization did not give any one of them a striking advantage. Value ties among elite groups persisted across national boundaries despite the growth of nationalism. The limited state was ascendant everywhere, and commercial values enjoyed a high degree of legitimacy.[52] Consequently, state objectives were similar enough to avoid running into serious collision and to yield the "common law of Europe" represented by the Concert system; they were identical enough to permit the growth of a large body of reciprocal obligations permitting ease of commercial intercourse and limiting the incidence of violence; and there were sufficient common commitments to technical tasks that could be performed only by autonomous bodies to result in the creation of the first "Functional" international organizations with their own "Functional" community-type law.[53]

But, alas, the system was temporal, soon to be defeated by the revolutionary system in which we now live. What happened to it? The environment began to be transformed asymmetrically so as to destroy homogeneously changing relationships. As history, this is undoubtedly true, and as analysis, it carries us further than if we were merely to note that the boundaries of the system were breached. As an analysis of the nineteenth century it represents an intelligent and fruitful use of the balance-of-power construct. But it helps us only up to a point. It specifies conditions and relationships resulting in certain organizational tasks. It abstracts from national policies the features which, since they were repeated many times, did tend to create the cumulative kinds of interactions that can justifiably be identified as a "system." What it does not do is tell us which of these features survive to make their appearance in the next system. The tone of Hoffmann's argument would militate against any survival at all, even though history would hardly validate such a conclusion.[54]

Where does that leave us with respect to the analytical usefulness of balance-of-power theorizing? We have rejected the dominant formulations that the literature has to offer because they are either overly system-oriented, or unidimensional, or both. We have accepted the version that stresses multidimensional environmental elements and preserves the creative role of the actors; but we have concluded that it does not carry us far enough along the road of reconciling systems theory with Functionalism. The endless efforts to accommodate the interrelations created by various kinds of nuclear deterrents within a concept of bipolarity—the feature that in fact has given the balance-of-power approach its undeserved new lease on life—are little more than *descriptions* of the *distribution* of military power at any one time. At best they are metaphors, not analysis.* Whatever the merits of these efforts may be on military grounds, the notion of "balance" is a superfluous terminological complication that pretends to give theoretical sophistication to a wholly legitimate descriptive attempt that needs no such aid. Let the balance of power be confined to the setting in which Hoffmann placed it, and let the theorists of deterrence labor in the workshop of missile hardware. As for the balance of power in our age, let it rest in peace.

A FUNCTIONALLY USEFUL SYSTEM

Systems theory is useful only when it facilitates projective thinking based on important abstractions that group and categorize important recurrent events. Hence systems that merely reinforce themselves are not useful for our purposes. It follows that extreme care must be taken not to use analogies

---

* With respect to the use of metaphors as a substitute for theory, Anatol Rapoport said: "Interpreted in a physical context, the metaphor 'conflict of forces' calls for some sort of equilibrium theory. Such a theory can be and has been developed purely metaphorically. The concepts of 'force,' 'pressure,' 'balance of power,' 'leverage,' 'stability,' 'instability,' are mostly terms borrowed from physics. Descriptions of conflict situations in these terms sound like descriptions of physical systems. But of course the analogy is a metaphorical not a logical one, i.e. the similarity is felt intuitively, not derived as a consequence of an isomorphism between the two situations. Therefore metaphorical models of conflict, although they may be valuable for a variety of reasons, cannot be expected to yield logically compelling theorems, let alone theorems translatable into predictions." "Various Meanings of Theory," reprinted in Rosenau, p. 51.

that suggest self-reinforcement. Both the mechanistic and the organismic analogies, explicit or implicit in the majority of systems found in the literature, tempt us perpetually along the well-trod path that ends in a cozy bower called "stability," "equilibrium," or "self-maintenance." A dynamic international system must dispense with these notions and with the analogies from which they are derived. The international system most useful for our purposes is neither a machine nor a body.

A dynamic system capable of linking Functionalism with integration studies is a *concrete, actor-oriented* abstraction on recurrent relationships that can explain its own transformation into a new set of relationships, i.e. into a new system. Such a system has no defined attributes, no "needs," no *telos.* Moreover, the relationships among the units cannot be specified until the actors themselves are identified and the environment sketched in.

The actors in our international system are governments and voluntary associations. The environment consists of the beliefs, institutions, goals, and capacities of the actors. Since in past and present concrete systems international organizations have had little independent capacity, they do not contribute—as yet—to the environment. Governmental policies emanating from the environment are the inputs into the system; collective decisions are the outputs. The outputs then *may* transform the environment by being fed back into it. Whether they actually do is a central empirical question that determines whether the system is being transformed in the long run. The particular relationships which define a given system, then, are the patterns of inputs and outputs that prevail during a given epoch. The structures of the system are its body of law, its organizations, national, regional, and universal. Provisionally, international organizations are treated as structures; as a result of the feedback process, however, they may well acquire the position of an autonomous actor at some future stage. The essential purpose of our analysis is to facilitate predictions about when and how this might happen. The functions of the system are the tasks imposed on the structures by the actors. They will occupy us in greater detail below.

To sum up: the system comprehends a series of relationships that are acted out in a given institutional and legal setting; these relationships are economic, military, humanitarian, and territorial.[55] The system further comprehends the specific behavior pattern of the actors (observed empirically instead of being deduced from system rules), and is particularly interested in the results of that behavior with respect to the structures of the system, which may be transformed. The empirical question of *when* a new system has come into existence we answer in the same terms as Hoffmann did.[56] His indicators are specific enough to make the decision simple.

Certain aspects of systemic rendering I have in mind were suggested by Roger Masters. Feeling that Kaplan's systems lacked concreteness in relation to contemporary world events but impressed with their specificity, Masters designed a multibloc system of international relations in which the actors are cohesive regional groupings of states that have delegated substantial powers to permanent "bloc actors."[57] The specifications are reasonably close to the way in which some actual regional organizations today behave. Masters then asks himself what a world system made up of such units would look like, and what rules would be necessary for self-maintenance. The bulk of the prescription is not much different from Kaplan's balance-of-power system. This effort fails with respect to the requirement we have posited for the explanation of transitions, and it depends too much on military relationships at the expense of the patterns created by the beliefs and goals of the actors. But it illustrates the projective use of incipient concrete structures. It is our task now to set forth explicitly how functions relate to structures, and what we take the term "function" to mean in our system.

The way is prepared by a statement of Dorothy Emmet, to whose perceptive treatment my reconciliation of Functionalism and functional sociology owes a great deal:

For a social system is not, in fact, just a closed or repetitive system, which can be brought back into "equilibrium" by its internal functional mechanisms. Up to a point it can be studied in this way, but only up to a point. A society is a *process* with some systematic characteristics, rather than a closely integrated system, like an organism or a machine. Hence its "stability" is something more complicated than that of a biological or mechanical system. For its elements are mobile individuals with private purpose, conflicts and allegiances. Their behavior can be canalized to some extent into institutional patterns, and this is not only through the compulsory measures of law and government. Indeed, pervasive institutionalized patterns of conduct are necessary if the cohesion imposed by government itself is to be possible. . . . But similarly the cohesion of the institutionalized activities themselves is made possible by the powers of individuals. Thus the "system" so disclosed is something much less consistent and more flexible than the older functional models suggested. There will be conflicts within the system leading to periodic crises; and few societies nowadays can be insulated against change. There will be critical occasions when adjustments, perhaps major adjustments, are called for, and these may depend largely on the initiative and resourcefulness of individuals. And not only on critical occasions. Along the line, in all sorts of social situations, adaptations, innovations and decisions will be made, with more and less success. The coherence of a society is thus not just an "equilibrium" secured by the automatic coming into opposition of countervailing tendencies; it is something more precarious, always needing to be renewed by efforts of will and imagination.[58]

These words constitute much more than a panegyric of individual creativity and resourceful statesmanship; they are the summation of an effort to reconcile systemic determinism with the reality of social change, automatic functional adjustment with willed purpose. Although the context of

Emmet's analysis is the national society, her thought applies to the international setting because of its unflinching determination to separate cognitively willed social action from action that is merely the unwilled consequence of previous choices—and yet to retain both types of action within a system that constantly changes. The crucial terms in the statement are "purpose" and "powers," in addition to "function." Before adapting the formulation to the analysis of international systems, let us follow through on Emmet's demonstration.[59]

Teleology, according to her, simply cannot be banished from functional analysis. The important thing is to be clear about the kinds of ends that are postulated. Function must mean more than that a given action has a given result, more than efficient causation; it has to mean that if a given role or action has a function, it has a result *within* the total system, the maintenance of which depends on the performance of the function. Hence, as in other examples, the preservation of the system seems to be always assumed.

But the ends imputed to various kinds of action simply cannot all be subsumed under one notion of *telos*. We must distinguish between the "blind" teleology that refers to the simple maintenance of the system, or to its adjustment to some new "equilibrium"—the type of teleology I have rejected—and the variety that refers to the end I have posited as mine: integration in the sense of movement toward a more universal type of system. As Emmet says, this would be a "natural end" in the Aristotelian sense, though we must bear in mind that the "naturalness" is posited by the observer. Teleology, then, can be thought of as goal-directed action, the goal in our case being integration.[60]

But what kinds of action would qualify, and what is their relationship to the goal? At this level of analysis it becomes useful to distinguish between "purpose" and "function" more explicitly than we have done so far. In Emmet's analysis, the parts of the system as automatically interacting units have no intent, will, function, or purpose at all. They may engage in action either deliberately or not. Action based on will and intent is linked to the purposes of the acting units; the end of action is then part of the actor's explicit motivation and need not be imputed by the observer. However, action may also be considered functional in the sense of having the result postulated by the observer (e.g. the maintenance of the system), without the actor's being aware of this. The actor's motives—explicit to him—may have an *unintended*—for him—result of interest to the observer. Emmet reserves the term function for this type of action. The end, or goal, unlike the first case, is here stipulated not by the actor but by the observer. Yet, and this is the admirable portion of Emmet's treatment, the actor is never relegated to the position of a self-adjusting part in a servomechanism. He is able to "learn" from the functions; functional results become assimilated into his explicit motives, so that functions transform purposes, and observer-

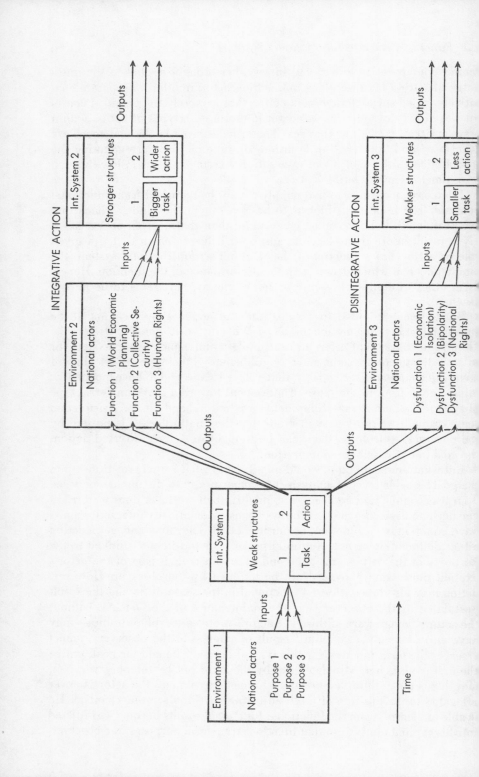

INTEGRATIVE ACTION

Int. System 2

Environment 2

National actors

Function 1 (World Economic Planning)
Function 2 (Collective Security)
Function 3 (Human Rights)

Inputs

Stronger structures

1   2

| Bigger task | Wider action |

Outputs

Int. System 1

Environment 1

National actors

Purpose 1
Purpose 2
Purpose 3

Inputs

Weak structures

1   2

| Task | Action |

Outputs

Outputs

DISINTEGRATIVE ACTION

Int. System 3

Environment 3

National actors

Dysfunction 1 (Economic Isolation)
Dysfunction 2 (Bipolarity)
Dysfunction 3 (National Rights)

Inputs

Weaker structures

1   2

| Smaller task | Less action |

Outputs

Time

posited ends come to influence the ends explicitly formulated by the actor.

This brings us to the concept of "powers." The actor's capacity to learn, to intervene creatively—within the limits of what is possible in the total system—to change his mind, and to seek new ways of attaining his end is summed up by the term "powers." Men, therefore, are not condemned merely to act out a systemic tragedy because, through learning, they are able to change the system itself. Furthermore, the system is then not expected to return to a stable or metastable condition, but to transform itself.[61] What is not clear in Emmet's analysis is whether a transformed system is still the same pattern of relationships that existed before the actors learned, or whether it is something new. Since she is dealing with an image borrowed from the national polity or society, this ambiguity poses no particular problem, for the continuation of the state—albeit with new functions and structures—can be taken as sufficient evidence of the survival of the system. In international relations we have no such simple evidence, and the question can therefore not be dealt with in this fashion. Since the pattern of relationships does, demonstrably, change on the basis of different national policy inputs, and since we experimentally postulate an important transformation of the international structures, we also hold that "learning" results in the creation of a new system. The "powers" would be found in the ability of national governments to learn the art of revising their demands and seeking new ways of satisfying them without destroying themselves in the process.

Let us sum up. Unlike the Functionalists and many functional sociologists we shall reserve the term "purpose" for the action pattern consciously willed by actors in the international system; we shall reserve "function" for the results of these actions, which may bring with them unintended consequences. These may then transform the system by (1) resulting in the kind of learning that is creative in the sense that it enhances the original purposes of the actors, which implies integration; and (2) yielding the kind of learning that forces a re-examination of purposes among the actors such as to involve disintegration. Obviously, integration can be the result of intended or unintended action. Both processes must be kept in mind. But our interest is particularly aroused by the analytical force of *functions* because it enables us to posit a certain kind of international transformation without being discouraged by the prevalence of selfish national motives. The adaptive-transforming force we shall identify with the ability of governments and other actors to recast their purposes in functional terms.[62]

INTERNATIONAL FUNCTIONALISM: SUMMARY

These definitions and relationships are represented on the accompanying diagram. For purposes of clarity it should be remembered that what appear as "functions" in Environment 2 and as "dysfunctions" in Environment 3 become the respective new purposes of the actors, depending on which of the two learning processes postulated happens to be adopted in fact. This conception of the international system in functional terms is greatly in debted to certain types of sociological thought.[63]

But before summing up our sociological-functional system of the inter national world in its relationship to integration, we must face one major question: why, it might well be asked, cast integration into a systemic mold? Why not speak simply of the growing power of international organizations? Instead of worrying about purposes and functions, inputs and outputs environment and feedback, we should be able simply to describe the con ceivable relationships between the growing power of international organi zations—if there be such—and the transformation of the national scene. We could simply state the impact of United Nations policies on the values and habits of the member states after having established the importance of these values on the policies of the United Nations.

To do so would be to commit the error of the Functionalists. Their formu lation, despite its insights and sophistication with respect to the central role of welfare expectations and the trend toward technocracy, remains skewed in the direction of freedom of the will. The Functionalist separability doc trines create an impression of self-evident and automatic progress. The argument seems to say that if we maximize welfare tasks, and if we mini mize purely diplomatic decision-making, then the latent forces making for world community will triumph manifestly. This much free will cannot be accommodated within the conceptions of interest sketched in Chapter 2.[64]

The systemic conceptualization has the virtue of not implying automa ticity or inevitable progress, provided the system used is of the concrete, actor-oriented variety. It gives us a picture of a temporally delimited world that allows for and projects probable evolutionary patterns based on empiri cally established forces. It helps us to imagine the future on the basis of a disciplined view of the past. It sensitizes the observer to search for the con sequences flowing from the established relationships among nations. A discussion of the evolutionary potential of international organizations de void of such a focus runs the risk of assuming unidimensionality; the pro jection of the role of the United Nations seen in the prism of the collective security function is as unreliable as a vision based purely on the welfare function. Only a systemic conceptualization can hope to combine these strands into one sturdy whole.

Concrete actor-oriented systems remain loyal to the historical tradition and owe more to it than to the methods of social psychology. They represent the clinical rather than the statistical mode of reasoning. Incidents of repeated historical experience are examined in the light of both the motives and the mores found to apply in the epoch in which they occurred. Conclu sions are inferred from the cases, even though the cases themselves are analyzed in terms of structured interrelationships previously observed and established.[65] The statistical, as opposed to the historical-clinical, mode deduces trends and verifies hypotheses purely on the basis of quantitative aggregates, without concerning itself with clinical interrelations or historical confluences. The statistical practitioner tends to exhibit wide-eyed wonder concerning the unexpected nature of his conclusions, whereas the historically sensitized observer begins his work with a far more jaded vision.[66]

We are now able to specify the systemic nature of the phenomena to be discussed in the language of functional sociology. The *items* to which functions are imputed in international relations are the policy demands advanced by governments and non-governmental organizations in the forum of international organizations. But, obviously, not all policy demands are important or relevant, a fact that forces us to select "strategic" items, i.e., crucial with respect to telling us something about the transformation of the system. The strategic nature of the items, however, is based on the perceptions of the actors themselves. They, not merely the observer, make claims and counterclaims concerning military security, economic development, human rights, decolonization, and stable trade patterns. These are our strategic policy demands because, in our period of history, governments consider them so.

The *motives* and *purposes* imputed to the actors are derived by studying words *and* actions, verbal pronouncements and demands as well as concrete steps taken, resolutions voted, and treaties ratified. Advocacy in addition to the subsequent steps taken to implement the results of advocacy provide the data for judging motives. When the purposes imputed to the actors include the desire for social transformation leading to system-dominance, i.e. integration, it is unnecessary to introduce the concept of *function*; in that case the overt purposes of the actors are linked to the integrative process. But when this is not the case, functions are those consequences of action noted by the observer that tend toward the integration of the system.

As Merton shows, motives and functions are easily confused. He therefore introduced the distinction between "manifest" and "latent" functions. The former "are those objective consequences contributing to the adjustment or adaptation of the system which are intended *and* recognized by participants in the system," the latter, "correlatively, being those which are *neither* intended *nor* recognized."[67] I find the distinction unnecessary in the international system because I can conceive of no unintended result of purposive action that is not eventually recognized by the actors. Functions, for us, are unintended consequences that may go unrecognized for a while, but not for very long.[68]

Since all functions are understood eventually by the actors, the unin-

tended consequences of their purposes are "learned." Therefore, any func
tion becomes a new purpose at a different systemic level of integration. W
must merely distinguish between learning conducive to integration an
learning that seeks to block the process. The difference is largely one o
perceptions among the actors about which kind of response most nearly ap
proximates the initial purpose.

In contrast with the difficulties encountered in the study of social system
at the national level, the identification of the unit subserved by the func
tion is relatively simple internationally. The *unit* is whoever puts forth de
mands effectively, i.e. is in a position to be heard in the system's structures
This, for the most part, is a position held by governments, though for som
items subject to functional analysis, national and international voluntar
groups must be included. The *mechanism*s through which purposes an
functions must be fulfilled are the central institutional structures of nationa
and international bureaucracies. Chief of these are the division of labo
among discrete units and the delegation of power to expert bodies en
trusted with the implementation of purposes. We should also include
sensitivity to the freedom of maneuver enjoyed by certain individuals witl
respect to the practice of creative innovation.

Suppose some item ceases to have functional significance for the trans
formation of the system. Suppose, indeed, it acquires a dysfunctional sig
nificance. Merton here suggests the concept of the "balance" of functiona
consequences of a given item and the notion of "functional equivalents."
Only clinical study can disclose the existence of such phenomena in the in
ternational system. We may discover that certain items (e.g. demands fo
more highly institutionalized collective security) cease to have functiona
results at a certain time and in the setting of a certain balance of environ
mental conditions (e.g. the inability of revolutionary and conservativ
states to agree on common rules). But we may also find that another iten
(e.g. the demand for financial aid) takes the place of collective securit
in terms of functional consequences. However, it must be realized that th
international system displays a relatively small number of items and thu
restricts the number of functions. In addition the structural context is quit
rigid. Hence the international context probably limits the available equiva
lents as compared with the pluralistic nation-state.

The restricted number of items and functions encountered at the inter
national level actually simplifies the problem of *validation*. We do not a
yet have to worry about locating adequate samples of social systems to b
subjected to functional analysis at the international level; nor do we nee
to concern ourselves with huge numbers of items to be resolved into rep
resentative samples. There are as yet very few international organizations
Their activities hardly overwhelm the observer; entire "populations" o
items can be studied relatively painlessly without having to resort to sam

pling. In recent historical systems the number of states involved has been quite manageable. Existing international structures, such as the United Nations, its specialized agencies, regional blocs and alliances, remain few enough in number to make comparison relatively simple.

A final appeal: the functional analysis of international integration is not necessarily ideologically loaded in favor of "one world." "Functional analysis has no intrinsic commitment to an ideological position," argues Merton. But he continues that "this does not gainsay the fact that particular functional analyses and particular hypotheses advanced by functionalists may have an identifiable ideological role."[69] The ideological bias is exposed by close attention to the end result of functional development postulated by the observer as being desirable. In Mitrany's case we had no difficulty in specifying the end. In rigorous functional studies the "end" (integration, in our case) is clearly postulated. This creates no ideological bias, since the reader can decide for himself whether he likes or dislikes integration. The process, conceived analytically, would exist whether one likes it or not, whether one wishes to aid it or hinder it.

4. *Functionalism and Organizations*

If systems are abstractions invented by the observer to render comprehensible a very complex world, organizations are very concrete entities, made up of living people, divisions, hierarchies, budgets, and programs. Functionalism thrives on organizations; neither the ideological nor the sociological variety of functional thought could live without concrete organizations as a field for projection and empirical study. We must complete our reformulation of Functionalism now by relating it explicitly to the organizations whose conduct we wish to characterize in the context of international integration.

But what is an organization? Some treat it as a system, others as a polity; still others regard it as analogous to a primary group, subject to all the esoteric qualities of group dynamics. Each definition seems to command a body of theory all its own, much as did the versions of systems and functionalism we encountered before. For immediate purposes, let us note that organizations are the entities that are enclosed in boxes in our system diagram (p. 80), the entities that convert purposes into functions or dysfunctions, and evolve the tasks which—if functionally successful—transform the existing international system into something new. Organizations, in this sense, are the flesh-and-blood subsystems of the international system which, through their feedbacks, influence the parent system. But because they are flesh-and-blood they must be treated in far more human terms than the parental relationships we have examined thus far. This, in turn, requires an examination of modern organization theory to determine which of its many formulations will help in our task.

FUNCTIONALISM AND ORGANIZATION THEORY

Let us recapitulate our final objective: we wish to examine one international organization, the ILO, in terms of its contribution to international

integration. But we wish to do so only in order to observe in real life a formal entity of civil servants, experts, governments, and voluntary group representatives that seems to approximate the optimal conditions for integration as defined by functional analysis. This objective, furthermore, is
merely instrumental in positing the *kind* of international organization that
functional imperatives require in order to maximize integration; yet we
also insist that this kind of organization be at least akin to the species represented by the United Nations. We shall examine the current literature of
organization theory because its analytical schemes and empirical conclusions seem, at least in principle, applicable to the international field, which
constitutes a virgin wilderness from the viewpoint of organization theory.
In so doing, of course, I am not proceeding as if the study of international
organization were a *tabula rasa*. My examination of the literature, and my
selection from it, are guided by what I believe to know *already* about the
nature and behavior of international organizations, before having submitted all of them to the test of integrative analysis. I now propose to re-
examine what I think I know within the focus of a model of organizational
behavior; and thus I hope to facilitate the prediction of functions advancing integration.

Novices venture recklessly where the expert fears to tread. Organizations
have been studied "theoretically" by psychologists, sociologists, mathe-
maticians, biologists, and students of business and public administration.
Yet there obviously is no generally recognized "theory" in this area any
more than in the field of systems. Every student, though he draws on the
findings of other students in the realm of data, prefaces his presentation
with his own model, scheme, typology, or "theory." Every basic definition
is matched with a revised but equally basic definition. It may well be that
no science can grow without undergoing this variety of sado-masochistic
self-examination, but for the moment it obviously remains true that every
student is his own theorist.[1] And from this fact the novice draws his courage.

Thus we confront the question, What is an organization? The phenomenon, as Dwight Waldo found, "shades on one side into 'group,' on the other
into 'institution' or 'society,' " depending on whether the vantage point of
the observer is that of psychology or sociology.[2] And his definitional conclusion is incontrovertible: "In view of the inconclusiveness, the diversity,
the amorphousness of the materials put under Organization Theory heading nowadays, one must conclude that, if they all concern the same elephant, it is a *very* large elephant with a generalized elephantiasis."[3]

If "organization theory" is taken to refer to generalizations about any
human collectivity, we cannot seek help from such analytical wedges as
cybernetics, relational mathematics, or decision theory based on the theory
of games. In Waldo's sense, then, we must rather be interested in "theories
of organization," theories whose orientation is at the more mundane level

of *administered* organizations, and whose dominant concern is over degrees of rationality in decision-making and goal articulation, power and hierarchy, instrumental and consummatory ends and means, and the organization in its environment and in its relation to stability or change. But the emphasis on the constraining adjective "administered" may also be misleading for our purpose. To be sure, we wish to exclude primary groups, social institutions, social systems, "bureaucracies" in the abstract, factories, mental hospitals, prisons, parcel delivery services, and the routinized ordering of paper clips. The emphasis on administration is important but not sufficient. Insofar as it delimits scope and focuses attention on a specific structure with fixed internal relations, it certainly narrows the field; but to the extent that it is dominated by *internal* structures, it is likely to make us pay more attention to the management and human relations aspects than is warranted in the international field.

Thus even the notion of "administered organization" includes too many varieties of the species, and excludes a number of analytical features that are of primary empirical relevance in the case of international organizations. Hence I find it very difficult to make use of theories of organization without first specifying the nature of the context in which I wish to generalize.* That context is exceedingly political, imbued with clashing interests, and subject to all the forces we summarized earlier in our schema of the Functionalists' revised separability doctrines. Hence there is every reason to treat our administered organizations as polities that respond to external demands, and that may develop into independent centers of power if the "proper" interaction with those demands is achieved by administering the organization in a certain way. Administration, then, ceases to be an internally directed, management-dominated concern, and becomes a politically adaptive pursuit in which leadership is crucial.[4] If we keep our attention firmly fixed on that political process, most of whose impulses come from the environment in which the organization is active, and if we bear in mind that the majority of these environmental impulses stems from the reasoned demands of governments rather than the subjective needs of bureaucrats, then the outlines of the context are plain. With this understanding we can move back to certain theorists of organization and agree with them on the pivotal role of four aspects common to all organizations: the formal objectives for which the organization was created; the

* "At present organization theory is dealing mainly with general propositions which apply equally well but also equally badly to all organizations. The differences among various organizational types are great; therefore any theory of organizations in general must be highly abstract. It can serve as an important frame for specification, that is, for the development of special theories for the various organizational types, but it cannot substitute for such theories by serving itself as a system model, to be applied directly to the analysis of concrete organization." Amitai Etzioni, "Two Approaches to Organization Analysis: A Critique and a Suggestion," *Administrative Science Quarterly*, V (1960), 270.

actual expectations (as entertained by the organization) on whether and how these objectives can be reached; the actual choices made by the organization toward meeting the expectations; and the measures taken with respect to implementing the choices.[5] Questions of growth, adaptation, and changes in task can then be subsumed under these headings as intended or unintended consequences.

Clearly, therefore, the type of organization theory that proceeds on the basis of psychological emphasis is largely irrelevant to our quest. Psychological models show great concern for the internal efficiency of an organization, and they conceive of efficiency in terms of the happiness of the staff and the perfect adjustment of human means to organizational ends. Now efficiency can be approached in motivational terms; the scholar who works along these lines will then specify optimal arrangements of human work groups, and attain efficiency by way of a utilitarian calculus of happiness.[6] Even though Harry Stack Sullivan and Kurt Lewin tend to replace Bentham and Mill, this type of theory stresses the notion that the life of the organization is internally determined, and thus only secondarily related to the external environment. The approach that focuses on problem-solving and conflict resolution is equally irrelevant because both the theory and the experiments derived from it stem from the study of small-group dynamics. Experiments designed to replicate problem-solving in conflict-dominated situations simply do not help us in the study of international integration as long as the attempt is confined to three-person teams working with artificial problems.[7] International organizations are not small groups, and the conciliation of clashing interests does not proceed on the basis of "interpersonal adjustment."

But even non-psychological approaches to organization that treat efficiency as the central concept do not help much. The organization's objectives, expectations, choices, and administrative actions would remain politically relevant even if an utter disregard for efficiency characterized the men who made these choices.[8] Any public administrative agency operates within a system of values defined by the total political system that it serves; its internal allocation of resources is therefore measured in terms of the satisfaction of its external clients and their values. Efficiency can be used as a concept for the study of public organizations only if we postulate a consensus on values and ends among the groups and individuals who make up the larger political system. Efficiency becomes relevant only if what Dwight Waldo called a "pyramid of values" is perceived by the clients of the organization.[9] Such a consensus rarely exists within a nation, not to mention the international society. Without such a pyramid we cannot speak of an operationally valid notion of authority, and without a concept of systemic authority the concern for efficiency is merely the business of the management consultant.

Perhaps we can obtain guidance if we look upon *growth* as the central concept. Growth theories show a great concern for the environment; they see integration as an aspect of mastering the environment. They have much in common with the Functionalist theory that tasks will expand as society becomes more mindful of its welfare needs. Why are they not the obvious answer?*

Organic growth theory is wholly deterministic and makes no allowance for volitional ambiguities. Organizations are held to expand (in terms of assets, employees, and physical size) in accordance with mathematically ascertainable rates. Momentary departures of actual business firms from the rates were found by Haire to be of a short-run character; the pattern of growth, in the long run, was ultra-stable. These growth rates depend not so much on the wisdom or the neuroses of leaders as on "the geometry of the space within which the organization exists, just as the growth curves tie its growth to the ecological equilibrium between the organization and its environment."[10] Attractive as the dynamism of this conception is for our purposes, it taxes our belief in the metaphysics of an "ecology" that is not operationally meaningful in terms of specific conceptions of objectives, expectations, and choices. Such is the danger of the organic analogy: concern with efficiency leads to neglect of a living and varying environment; but exclusive concern with growth leads to neglect of the rationale underlying the choices of people whose decisions make organizations grow or decline. One approach sacrifices the system to the actors, whereas the other sins in the opposite sense.

Among the most ambitious models of organizations are those that seek to explain organizational development on the basis of the concept of *survival*. Organizations are here treated as subsystems of the larger social system; they are judged in terms of their relationship to the total system in that their activities are either "eufunctional" or "dysfunctional."[11] At the same time, this species of theory is in tune with the tendency of students of public administration to view their subject matter in terms other than those of mechanical efficiency or wholesome primary-group feelings. Organizations are regarded as a species of social system that seek to achieve their

* Thus Mason Haire defends organic growth theory as the proper approach to organization theory in terms the Functionalist should find attractive; he notes that this theory is "focused on the fact that an outstanding characteristic of a social organization is simply that it is a special kind of aggregation of individuals. Many of the problems of organization seem to arise from two facets of this fact—first, that it is made up of individuals and, second, that it is an aggregation of them. From the first comes the problem of conflict between individual and organization, and the organizational necessity of resisting the centrifugal force associated with individuals—each with his own goal and each tending to fly off from the path of the whole. From the second comes the pressure, as the size of the aggregation increases, to provide communication among the parts, integration of the parts into the whole, and the possibility of specialization of function." "Biological Models and Empirical Histories of the Growth of Organizations," in Haire, *Modern Organization Theory*, p. 273.

goals in the context of a larger system. Hence, theoretical constructs dealing with decision-making and bureaucracy are intimately connected with this perspective. It is this type of theory that would appear most germane to our purpose.

According to Talcott Parsons' definition, the survival model of organization is essentially static: if, in the fulfillment of their goals, organizations also perform services that are functional for the system as a whole, they will prosper and survive; if not, they will pass from the scene. In order to make this conception serviceable for our ends, one would have to impute functions to the social system at the global level, an approach rejected in the previous chapter. A similarly static quality is found in the managerial theory of organization developed by Chester Barnard. The function of the manager is to enable his organization to survive in a constantly changing and essentially hostile environment, made more intractable still by the narrow limits imposed on human free will by Barnard's theory of decision-making. A generous range of dynamic qualities is imputed to the executive in working for adaptation; but the overall system is not conceived in dynamic terms.[12] Yet Barnard's approach is of interest to us because of his important distinction between "effectiveness" and "efficiency" in making survival possible. Both qualities must be attained, but they refer to different aspects of organizational behavior. Effectiveness "relates to accomplishment of an objective of the system and is determined with a view to the system's requirements." But efficiency is the capacity of the organization to maintain itself by the individual satisfactions it affords."[13] It would appear, then, that effectiveness refers to relations with the environment, whereas efficiency concerns the commitment and happiness of the staff of the organization in seeking to realize purposes vis-à-vis the environment. Survival, in short, depends on satisfying both clients and staff in a perpetually adaptive manner.

This distinction is utilized by Etzioni in arguing that what may be functional for society, the larger system, may be dysfunctional for the survival of the organization. "The paradox of ineffectiveness" introduces a dynamic dimension: an organization whose objectives clash with its actual expectations, and whose choices do not yield implementation consonant either with its objectives or with its expectations, may be ineffective merely in its own eyes.[14] Still, if the choices and their implementations result in an expanded task that is "functional" from the vantage point of system transformation, the organization is very effective in the context of Functionalism. Basing his concepts on the study of essentially non-political organizations, Etzioni tends to feel that efficiency (in Barnard's sense) will triumph over effectiveness; the organization will adapt by downgrading its goals and purposes in facilitating the survival of its staff and status patterns.[15] Such a conclusion assumes that the founders of the organization are unable to recognize the hiatus between organizational ineffectiveness and functional success. If we, too, were to adopt this assumption, our organizational model would be condemned to the peripheral role that Functionalists assume willy-nilly.

This point demands some elaboration. The traditional Functional approach to the study of international organization tended to equate organizational effectiveness with the task imposed by the international society. International organizations, administrations, and treaties owed their origin to technological and welfare demands that developed "in the national societies of which [they are] composed. The same new inventions, the same intensification and complication of social life have led to a great increase in international regulations which have to do with the relations of States in the economic and social fields and which affect the daily lives of individuals."[16] Hence the approximations to international government that exist are merely a recognition of a universal need, a need imposed by technology and translated into policy by the private groups directly and immediately affected. "International public action in this sense affects the interests and wishes of many individual groups in the nations concerned, just as the laws of a single government affect the interests and wishes of many individuals in a national society."[17] Thus the forms that international organizations take are dictated not by idealism or philosophy, but by the functional demands of whatever need requires regulation. Form rigidly follows function, and function is dictated by the interaction between the demands of technology and welfare. It follows that no dramatic increase in international government can be expected, and that interesting constitutional arrangements have no inherent expansive logic of their own because they remain tied to the context of the original need. This conception, sobering and sane as it is, confines Functionalism to a degree of "effectiveness" that subordinates all possibility of integration to the prevailing perceptions of need, and to the ability of given organizations to meet them. It eliminates the possibility of evolution by way of unintended consequences, dynamic learning, interaction among many clashing objectives and expectations, and a new consensus, at the level of the system, that may condemn to death any given organization which has outlived its usefulness.

To ignore organizational objectives and expectations in favor of the consequences of organizational behavior does damage to what we know about organizations. But to concentrate on these objectives as derived from social need is to relegate our study to the trivial. We need an effectiveness model in which the criterion of success is the *transformation* of the international system to a higher level of integration instead of the survival of the existing system. Possibly, effectiveness for the system may imply ineffectiveness for its constituent organizations, but not necessarily. By stressing the relationship between initial objectives, implementation, consequences for the system, and resulting new objectives—in short, the process of adaptation resulting from functions and dysfunctions as we defined them—we merge the hitherto rival focuses of goals and systemic effectiveness.

We can now state the assumptions on which our model of international organization must rest. Because relations with environmental forces are more important than questions of internal efficiency, we must identify and sort the demands and expectations that flow from the national governments and private groups. We can then safely assert that our "organization theory is only concerned with those aspects of behavior which are determined by organizational structures," not by the psychoanalytic interaction among staff members, bureaus, or sections.[18] The formal objectives of the organization must be related to these demands, and to the structural features introduced by the convictions, the ideology, of the organization's leaders. But since we are aware that these leaders cannot act without reference to the environment, we expect formal objectives to yield to various countervailing pressures; lower-level expectations will come to guide policy choices and to restrict the measures singled out for eventual implementation. Systemic transformation will then be sought in analyzing the results of these measures on the environment.

This view of international organizations fits into the definition of "organization" pioneered by Philip Selznick, with its stress on the political, adaptive qualities that flow from continual conflict.* Functionalists pin their hopes for rational organizational action on the technical and non-controversial character of international welfare activity. I have argued that the process by which a given activity becomes non-controversial is itself a political matter, derived not from initial consensus but from initial conflict, which may shake down to a consensus as a result of national redefinition of "need." If this is true, it follows that a purely rational decision-making model is as inappropriate for a public international organization as it is for any public administrative agency that performs more than routine tasks, such as selling postage stamps or regulating the diameter of telegraph wires.

Broadly speaking, a commitment to advance the welfare of some in-

---

* Philip Selznick, "Foundations of the Theory of Organization," *American Sociological Review*, XIII (1948), 32. Whereas Selznick considers this definition to apply to all kinds of organizations, I prefer to think of it as more nearly appropriate to public administrative agencies. His definition reads as follows: "(1) the concept of organizations as cooperative systems, adaptive social structures, made up of interacting individuals, sub-groups, and informal plus formal relationships; (2) structural-functional analysis, which relates variable aspects of organization (such as goals) to stable needs and self-defensive mechanisms; (3) the concept of recalcitrance as a quality of the tools of social action, involving a break in the continuum of adjustment and defining an environment of constraint, commitment and tension."

ternational clientele may be expected to follow the experience of the Chicago Housing Authority, a study of which was published some years ago.[19] The various private groups interested in and affected by the Authority's formal program (namely, to clear slums and provide new housing) were and remained in disagreement. Various governmental bodies reflected this disagreement and therefore failed to give the Authority unambiguous support. The organization thus became more concerned with preserving its own existence than with stating and implementing firm objectives worked out by its leaders. Therefore, the following propositions can be provisionally made:

1. Serious reflection and firm announcements concerning the objective of an organization tend to destroy the organization by giving the enemies among its clients opportunities for denunciation.

2. Ambiguity in formal organizational objectives facilitates the ability of the leadership to elaborate less ambitious short-range aims reflecting its modest private expectations of success.

3. Commitment to firm objectives prior to the evolution of a reliable clientele undermines the ability of the organization's leaders to develop less ambitious (and less controversial) plans.

4. The making of alternative choices is determined not by overall rationality but by the short-run needs of organizational survival in a hostile environment. Thus, what is ineffective in terms of the objectives of the organization is effective in terms of survival, since it leads to the meeting of lower-level expectations, and eventual system transformation. Effectiveness, in a sense, consists of merely planning enough to survive each crisis as it comes along.

5. Finally, the politics of conflicting interests impose the need for compromise in the making of choices and the manner of program implementation. Hence consistency in programming cannot reasonably be expected.

Is there no way of rising above the plateau of organizational action on which "satisfying" as large a number of clients and groups as possible is the operational maxim, rather than maximizing organizational objectives?[20] Not in the sense of avoiding the constraining environmental and ideological forces to which the organization is subject. However, although the full achievement of initial objectives is perhaps never possible, it is precisely in its manner of adjusting to *new* objectives that the organization displays its integrating powers. Thus formal objectives are "vague platitudes and pious cant" only if they do not undergo some dynamic process of adaptation. For insight into the evolution of objectives, we must turn to the qualities of organizational leadership and ideology as treated by Selznick.[21]

The basic distinction established by Selznick is that between "organization" and "institution." Organizations are entities set up for a narrowly defined technical purpose and confined to that purpose from then on. Their decisions are of a routine character; they call for no self-assessment, no reflection on ultimate values, and no special qualities of administration other than "efficiency." Institutions, however, are entities "stamped by distinctive ways of making decisions or by peculiar commitments to aims, methods, or clienteles. In this way the organization as a technical instrument takes on values. As a vehicle of group integrity it becomes in some degree an end in itself. This process of becoming infused with value is part of what we mean by institutionalization. As this occurs, *organization management* becomes *institutional leadership*. The latter's main responsibility is not so much technical administrative management as the maintenance of institutional integrity."[22]

So conceived, the kind of international organizations able to help "functional" integration must possess the qualities of Selznick's institutions. Mitrany's simple expert bodies dealing with routine affairs would not have the qualities needed for growth. Creative leadership is what enables an organization to adopt new goals, as a change in its internal or external environment makes this necessary. But such adaptive redefinition of goals is often a wholly unplanned, instinctive act by the organizational leadership, adaptive in functional terms, but a matter of common sense as far as the leader is concerned.

The key elements in such a process are (1) administrative ideologies "as conscious and unconscious devices of communication and self-defense," evolved ad hoc or deliberately, accepted spontaneously by the staff or as the result of deliberate managerial manipulation;[23] (2) a special elite to develop and carry on the ideology and to provide future leaders; and (3) contending interest groups, clustering around various aspects of the organization's program and the values it represents, both inside the organization and among its external clients. Organizations that do not develop these characteristics remain routine-bound technical bodies. The organization must "become valued for itself, not as a tool but as an institutional fulfillment of group integrity and aspiration." How do we determine when this occurs? Infusion with value is a quality discerned by the observer rather than by the participants, who may continue to think of themselves as merely "doing their job." It can be identified when staff members and clients exhibit a commitment to the task and the aspirations associated with it, when they consider the organization as somehow vital to their hopes and expectations.[24] The purely technical and instrumental nature of an organization has been transcended when the entity is no longer considered expendable by its clients and staff.

In view of these considerations, it is impossible to place our model clearly and firmly within the categories and classifications of current theorizing about organizations. Our adaptive international organization is obviously not a smoothly functioning machine, a servomechanism; hence it does not fit into the "classical" tradition of theorizing in terms of input-output efficiencies. Nor is it a biological entity, a body that "grows," or an organism of interdependent persons who "interact" so as to maintain equilibrium. While we are sketching an entity that does possess some of the attributes of a survival-oriented social system, our concern with systemic transformations cautions us not to rely too consistently on the propositions associated with such a model. Even though our organization will contain a variety of bureaucratic elements and will rest in some measure on the success of bureaucratic leadership, it cannot be defined in terms of the Weberian bureaucratic ideal type or the authority pattern that goes with it. Even the metaphor of the electromagnetic field that Barnard uses to define the species "organization," though approximating the present need more closely than the notions of machine or organism, suggests greater determinative qualities than I am willing to concede.[25] The eclectic seems condemned to fall between categories, rather than safely repose in them.

Given the likelihood that the recalcitrance of the environment will condition the organization's objectives much as Banfield argues, we must rely on the ability of the organization's leaders to infuse their structure with value commitment as our link with systemic evolution. But leaders work with subordinate officials who must agree with them, and with governments who finance their operations.* They also depend, in the Functional context, on the demands and responses of private groups. As seen by Selznick in the national context, so in the international society effective adaptation demands close attention to the interest groups in the environment, and to their corresponding service departments in the organization. Hence our adaptive international agency must (1) function with special sensitivity in relation to the environment, (2) feature methods of internal conflict resolution that not only effectively compromise hostile environmental inputs, but result in adaptive redefinition of objectives, (3) develop its own dynamic program so as to survive by assuring itself of external support, and (4) so make its choices and push for the implementation of programs that its mission and impact grow in terms of feedback to its clients, whether these be governments or voluntary groups. We now turn to each of these imperatives.

---

* Selznick (*Leadership in Administration*, pp. 26–27, 95) distinguishes between organizational achievement and institutional success as very different results of "leadership" in organizations. Although organizational achievement, in the sense of survival, is a necessary prior condition for institutionalization, it is not the same thing. Institutionalization seems to imply a commitment to expanding values; a leader's mere concern for organizational stability and prestige is necessary but not sufficient in this context. For our purposes it is not essential that we adopt this notion of leadership. Functional implications from organizational action may be discernible without the emphasis on special leadership qualities, even though these would help.

THE DOMINANCE OF THE ENVIRONMENT

International organizations, like other such entities, have formal objectives: these are invariably spelled out in some detail in the opening paragraphs of their constitutions, charters, or constituent treaties. Usually, these objectives violate the postulate of flexibility—or vagueness—because national states do not readily participate in agencies whose goals are not clearly defined. If we are concerned with the redefinition of objectives, as the hostile environment makes the simple implementation of the official program impossible, we must throw into relief the factors that determine such an effort. The nature of the context limits us to two such factors: the government and voluntary groups, which make up the environment, and the organization's own leaders, its bureaucracy.

It is merely a truism to call attention to the ideological heterogeneity of the environment, at least in the case of organizations with a nearly universal membership.* Ideological heterogeneity is manifest in the variety of demands that governments press upon their international organizations. Economic underdevelopment linked with revolutionary-reformist values results in one type of demands; communism carries with it its own variety of inputs; industrialism linked with a free-enterprise doctrine differs in its demands from industrialism subject to welfare doctrines. Dependence on the nature of the national system-making demands, then, is a constraining feature of some weight. Moreover, the prevailing group structure of nations is a crucial and unstable environmental factor. A given organization usually includes member states characterized by the dominance of (1) oligarchies made up of institutional interest groups, such as churches and armies, (2) monolithic single parties subsuming all interest groups, (3) pluralistic groups with specific and limited aims, and (4) anomic "groups" with no predictable demands at all, but continually destabilizing effects on their national polities. Depending on the last election or revolution, each of these national systems poses its own demands on the organization, demands stemming from very different values.

Organizational leadership, if it is true to the imperatives I have sketched, will seek to impose its own values, its organizational ideology, on this cacophony of values. From this welter it will seek to isolate aspirations common to all groups and systems, and deify these on the altar of organi-

---

* The same proposition, however, seems to hold with reference to most regional organizations. Cultural, linguistic, and religious homogeneity among member states is uniformly *less* important in making for the continuity of attachment to formal objectives than economic, military, and political homogeneity. The Arab League, the Organization of American States, the Latin American Free Trade Association, the Nordic Council, and the Council of Europe are telling examples of this truth. On the other hand, the experience of the European Communities demonstrates the proposition that homogeneity in economic and social structure is the single most important background factor making for goal stability.

zational objectives. But which values should be picked? What means shall be chosen to promote them? What services should be offered to whom? Should the choice be based on some minimum common denominator among all possible present and future demands? Or should it aim at some "strategic" value, accompanied by its appropriate strategic means, that will force the opposition in the environment to go along? To answer these questions, we must examine the typical features of the international bureaucracy.

International bureaucracies, typically, are a far cry from the nicely adjusted, self-contained, and hierarchically ordered models of organization theorists. Lest I be accused of arbitrarily ruling out the relevance of management theory to an understanding of international organizations, I adduce the judgment of Gunnar Myrdal, a judgment arrived at as a result of his experiences as Executive Secretary of the United Nations Economic Commission for Europe:[26]

> The basic fictitious notion about inter-governmental organizations, as conveyed by their constitutions, is that they are something more than their component parts, something above the national states in somewhat the same sense as the individual states are above the provincial governments. Their constitutions give them the appearance of being political entities in their own right, following certain political goals, attempting to accomplish certain political changes, in one word: establishing, pursuing and enforcing a collective policy. But it should be clear from the outset that the analogy to the individual sovereign state is a false one. The conference of an inter-governmental organization is not in any real sense comparable with the legislative assembly of a state: the delegates are not elected by people but appointed by governments; they represent nations only indirectly; collectively they do not legislate; there is no supranational government to execute decisions taken, no sanctions can be applied and no taxes levied. . . . In the typical case international organizations are nothing else than instruments for the policies of individual governments, means for the diplomacy of a number of disparate and sovereign national states. When an inter-governmental organization is set up, this implies nothing more than that between the states a limited agreement has been reached upon an institutional form for multilateral conduct of state activity in a certain field. The organization becomes important for the pursuance of national policies precisely to the extent that such a multilateral co-ordination is the real and continuous aim of national governments.

Myrdal rules out any true independent powers for the bureaucracy in making or executing decisions, irrespective of the organization's constitution, because the secretariat remains merely the instrument of governments, and "it is only on the basis of their commonly shared confidence, and with their acquiescence, that the secretariat can move at all in the service of the collectivity of governments."[27] This formulation would seem to suggest that only an organizational ideology incorporating the minimum common denominator among governmental objectives can survive.

Let us assume an organizational leader with almost charismatic qualities and an unmatched political sense in choosing strategies that will attract environmental support and infuse his agency with value commitment. Still, international bureaucracies are staffed with specialists and generalists originating in all the member states; and frequently the governments exercise a heavy hand in selecting the supposedly neutral civil servant who is enjoined not to seek or accept instructions from anyone except his hierarchical chief. The staff thus represents the heterogeneity of ideologies, the cacophony of values. Working with this material, the head of the organization must seek to subject his staff to the organizational ideology he has accepted or even fostered.

These facts make it obvious that the simple application of the Weberian bureaucratic model is out of the question, at least so far as a rigid hierarchical ordering of the staff is concerned. Moreover, Myrdal makes it quite clear that the leadership's relationship to the organization's clients is unlikely to be of a bureaucratic nature. Yet the Weberian model contains so much that might be important to a future international system that we cannot let it go by default.

The engagement of staff exclusively on the basis of professional qualifications, reward and promotion according to merit, close hierarchical supervision, and the employment of sanctions in order to promote detached professional service are of the essence of public bureaucracies in modern industrial states. Weber associated hierarchical staff relations with a clear chain of command downward, with a concept of authority that rests on the *voluntary* submission of subordinates to the imperative will of the superior. This submission is explicable in terms of "charismatic" and "traditional" considerations in some contexts; in the modern state, however, authority rests on the rational perception of legal relationships on the part of all the actors, superiors and subordinates. Imperative command is accepted voluntarily because the subordinate feels it is right and proper that orders be given, a feeling legitimated by the subordinate's understanding and approval of rational-bureaucratic relationships.[28] If this model described the actual authority relationships in contemporary international organizations, integration might proceed far more smoothly than in fact it does. In practice, the so-called "democratic-bureaucratic" model comes closer to describing the truth. Whereas Weber's model, if it prevailed in fact, would enhance integration, the democratic model, because it does prevail in fact, tends to hinder it.[29]

For a concept of bureaucratic authority and structure that combines the best features of the monocratic and the democratic approaches while remaining true to the nature of the present international system, we may take our cue once more from Chester Barnard. "The decision as to whether an order has authority or not," notes Barnard, "lies with the persons to whom it is addressed, and does not reside in 'persons of authority' or those who issue these orders."[30] This formulation sums up the real state of affairs in bureaucratic relationships *within* an international organization. But, what is more important, it also describes the nature of authority between the leadership and the clients, the environmental forces that produce most of the constraints under which international organizations function. In short, hierarchy must prevail as regards hiring, promotion, and the evaluation of work. But orders relating to the formulation and implementation of a policy cannot rest exclusively on a bureaucratic chain of command: they must rest on the staff's voluntary and *non-imperative* acceptance of the values implicit in the policy. And the same is true of the acceptance of "orders" by the governments and voluntary groups who constitute the clients of the organization.

These conceptions of bureaucracy and authority imply certain principles concerning the normal growth of organizations, which are well summarized by Selznick. I paraphrase:

1. After the basic mission is defined, the social base of the organization will be selected, a process that involves the choice of external clientele and supporters, and the identification of competitors and enemies.

2. The institutional core will be built up, which involves choosing personnel motivated by and indoctrinated with the organization's ideology and mission, who will then direct its program to the social base selected. It also involves fostering an elite, inside and outside the organization, capable of giving continuity to the program, and of adjusting it where necessary.

3. Although an organization passing through these steps will at first be characterized by open-ended procedures, personal intervention, and even the suggestion of charismatic leadership, at some stage internal and external administrative procedure must be formalized into legal and constitutional channels, especially as the organization grows in size and complexity. To the extent that this occurs, dynamic leadership will suffer a decline. Hence it is important that formalization does not occur too soon in the history of an organization.[31]

4. Decentralization of staff and program implementation can be successfully undertaken only after the period of central institutional growth has been completed, unless the local personnel is reliably indoctrinated in the organization's ideology, and the lines of authority to the center are unambiguous in the first place. However, in practice these two conditions are rarely met.[32]

5. The organization's viability in future periods will continue to depend on the autonomy of the elite associated with it, its high belief in its own stan-

dards and task, and its "exclusiveness." The organization's specific values must therefore be given an opportunity to mature. This also implies that organization subunits should be permitted to remain autonomous only for as long as may be necessary to permit these values to become firmly established.[33] In short, as long as the values in question are held precariously, central control is crucial.

But all this must take place, in the case of international organizations, in the setting of a very heterogeneous and not necessarily consistently friendly environment. Hence "the leader's job is to *test* the environment to find out which demands can become truly effective threats, to *change* the environment by finding allies and other sources of external support, and to *gird* his organization by creating the means and the will to withstand attacks."[34] This may be a tall order for the Director-General of an international organization whose bosses happen to be also the forces that constitute the environment. But unless he does these things, his organization is bound to remain in the realm of the technical, the routine.

Given this tension between organizational imperatives and environmental realities, we must state what kinds of organizational decisions are most likely to make the organization triumph over its constraints. The leadership must learn *to use a crisis in the tension between organization and environment as an opportunity for self-assessment and self-redefinition*, to profit from critical experience, to undergo growth in character and understanding. To be sure, a "critical" decision cannot always be differentiated from a "routine" one until the outcome is known. The leadership may not consciously know it is making a critical decision. A functional theory of international organization is all the more useful, then, in calling attention to the unintended integrative consequences of decisions made by leaders conscious only of some pressing business. The decision will nevertheless be "critical" if it engenders a new affirmation of organizational objectives under challenge from hostile or conflicting environmental pressures, if it thereby strengthens the sense of purpose of the organization's staff at the expense of environmental ties. But it is crucial to remember that unless the leadership is willing to examine useless old objectives and strike out in new directions with a revalued body of aims, it will merely reaffirm the stale old pattern, it will remain mired in routine.[35]

This approach to the manner in which organizations must advance institutionalization differs fundamentally from Mitrany's. Tasks do not take care of themselves; form does not automatically follow function; institutional goals do not flow naturally from obvious welfare commitments of the clients. It is the task of the organization—the leadership—to define aims *specifically* enough to act as a guide to policy, but *generally* enough to achieve rapport with an articulated body of values. Overspecificity condemns the organization to routine technical tasks (the risk Mitranian Functionalism runs most seriously); but overgenerality results in the platitudinous, if not hypocritical, programming that Banfield takes for granted. For creative leadership, the desire to separate the "military" from the "political" is as fatal as the wish to keep "welfare" insulated from "power," or "administration" from "politics."* The correct balance can be attained only if the organization constantly re-examines its aims in the light of changing environments, and if it avoids early commitment to operating efficiency or a specific technological orientation.[36]

The emphasis is therefore once more on the political. But politics, as we all know, is the art of the possible. Creative decision-making remains constrained by what the environment permits. The leader must develop an organizational ideology, imbue his staff with it, strike the delicate balance between developing self-conscious and committed subelites in his organization and retaining overall hierarchical control, and revalue the whole effort when challenged—all this being combined with the basic aim of extracting organizational functions from the explicit purposes of governments. If he fails, the governments will conclude that the functions are detrimental to their purposes, and will punish the organization by starving it financially, cutting down its task, or bypassing it. The true art of the possible, therefore, does not lies in the Machiavellian practice of deceit through the mouth and pen of the alert international official, but in his ability to persuade governments that the functions are compatible with national purposes, provided the governments reassess their own true aims. Political persuasion, moreover, rests less on golden words than on the sapient construction of coalitions with identical or converging interests. In short, purposes can be turned into functions, with the eventual cooperation of the parties concerned, if the tasks involved are part of the interests of a viable coalition of forces.

But how can leaders both lead and make deals? Will not deals involve sacrifices to organizational objectives? The head of an international organization must simultaneously manipulate not only his external supporters

---

* Organization theory often turns to notions of role-taking and role theory when it reaches the point of seeking to specify who is going to behave how in order to maximize the institutionalization process; and in so doing, it begins to draw heavily on social psychology. Selznick (pp. 82ff) defines role as "a way of behaving associated with a defined position in a social system," and in his discussion of leadership he makes the definition operational by seeking to relate personality characteristics to the particular way of behaving chosen by an organization in implementing its basic purposes (e.g., field action vs. headquarters directives; participation with local clients vs. reliance on officials alone).

Role theory seems of no particular help in the study of international organizations because the personalities of the officials, and the way in which they would go about their work, are less important than their relationship to the environment, the clients, and their demands. Personal styles certainly do differ among officials of international organizations. But since it is difficult to speak of an "international social system," the roles are floating in space rather than anchored to some social point of reference.

and clients, but also those of his own staff specialists who are identified with the environmental groups. In such circumstances, will not all objectives speedily be lost in a practice of making routine decisions aimed no higher than organizational survival? That danger is certainly prominent. Much depends on the manner in which supporting coalitions are constructed and influenced. In a situation in which all groups have equal influence, a form of *immobilisme* may result in which the normal clashes of interest politics, even in international organizations, can be resolved only through bargaining at the level of the lowest common denominator. The result then is descent into the mire of routine, of sheer survival. In situations, however, in which the way groups face each other is not left up to them, but dictated by constitutional rules or shaped by programmatic alternatives presented by the organization itself, minimal bargaining may be replaced with negotiated decisions. Here creative space is reserved for the leader who knows *which* and *whose* interests most closely approach the organizational program.[37] It is the study of national interest politics that furnishes us with the necessary sensitivity.[38]

My emphasis on interest politics and creative manipulation is quite deliberate. Selznick runs the risk of imbuing his creative leader with the attributes of the "heroic administrator," the man uniquely able, because of certain personality traits and gifts of perception, to shape the environment, to fire the imagination of subordinates and the passions of clients. The head of an international agency is seldom a hero, and more rarely still a philosopher-king. Barnard's executive possesses these heroic attributes to an even greater extent. He must lead, not from a sense of duty, but on the basis of a belief that what he does is consonant both with the organization's good and with his personal values. Insincerity, even if temporary, seems not to be permissible. This constitutes the supreme organizational morality, and it determines the life of the organization.[39] My treatment is more modest in its expectations. It accepts as relevant and important the many studies of public administration and policy-making in bureaucratic agencies that show the possibility of combining politics with administration, of proceeding on the basis of negotiation stressing common values between staff and clients, administrative leaders and the public. Administration, instead of appearing in the guise of a heroic ordering of chaos, assumes the form of continuous negotiation attentive to the possibility of maximizing common values.[40]

DECISION-MAKING AND CONFLICT RESOLUTION

For our purposes, "decision-making" and "conflict resolution" are the same thing. Students of administration and of organization prefer the label of decision-making because of their dominant interest in interpersonal and intergroup influence patterns within a bureaucratic structure. A given decision may or may not involve conflict among participants, and therefore the concern over conflict as such need not be central. Students and advocates of pacifism, positive coexistence, unilateral relaxation of international tensions, non-violent action, and systematic negotiation for the elimination of racial, social, or interstate strife prefer to use the term conflict resolution. For them the presence of "conflict"—and its pacification—is the central item of interest.

Let it be repeated that we are concerned with state and organizational action that may have functional consequences for the international system. It is clear, therefore, that we are constrained to focus exclusively on action *within a bureaucratic framework* (be this governmental, intergovernmental, or that of voluntary groups). We are also constrained by the nature of our actors. These are always and exclusively *established power-holders* in national or international structures, or in voluntary groups occupying elite positions with reliable access to public officials. Yet we know, following our assumptions about interest politics and group identification with perceived interests, that every major decision is a choice among conflicting demands and values, and therefore involves the relative victory of one group over another. Hence, in the focus of our concern, "decision-making" and "conflict resolution" are one and the same process. From this formulation two important corollaries follow.

First, organizational decision-making theory that seeks to focus on the effortless and routinized selection of alternatives leading to maximum efficiency of communication is irrelevant. This is true not only because of our previous argument about the functional importance of crisis decisions, but because of the fact that in a setting of interest-informed politics there are no routine decisions in the sense of choices free from group-supported controversy. Second, the suggestive and growing literature on the virtues and possibilities of non-violent action in the resolution of conflicts is equally irrelevant, at least in the way it is usually stated. This is so because all types and historical examples of non-violent political action have always featured efforts by the outsiders, the "weak," those without a foot on the established ladder of power, to bring about a change of some kind.[41] Whether it be Gandhi fighting racial discrimination in South Africa, the Norwegian teachers sabotaging the indoctrination policies of the Nazis, or the Fellowship of Reconciliation protesting nuclear arms—the resolution of conflict involves dedicated but unofficial groups at the periphery of the "establishment." Further, all historical examples of non-violent action (or, often, inaction) have occurred within the structure of one state, often in opposition to an unambiguous body of law. We cannot assume the relevance of the experience to the kind of international action that provides our context. Yet the fact remains that certain non-violent techniques have a strong family resemblance to the doctrines of Functionalism, and to this theme we must return.

Analytical light can be shed on this discussion if we distinguish firmly between the *outcomes* of a decision and the *process* through which it was reached. But we must be concerned with both aspects, especially since decision-making theories concentrate on the latter, and conflict-resolution studies on the former. When we deal with outcomes, we must have in mind the initial preferences of the actors; but when we deal with the process, the actors' notions of causation, of antecedent facts, of scientific data relating to the decision, or of sequences of past events perceived as relevant, are the dominant factor. J. D. Thompson and A. Tuden developed an analytical scheme incorporating these features, assuming that the decision-makers can either agree or disagree with respect to both preferred outcomes and causation. Their scheme gives us this matrix:[42]

Preferred Outcomes

	Actors Agree	Actors Disagree
Actors Agree	COMPUTATION requires BUREAUCRATIC STRUCTURE	COMPROMISE requires BARGAINING IN REPRESENTATIVE STRUCTURE
Actors Disagree	JUDGMENT requires MAJORITY VOTE IN COLLEGIAL STRUCTURE	INSPIRATION requires ANOMIC STRUCTURE AND CHARISMA

Beliefs About Causation

The labels in the matrix describe patterned types of behavior adopted by decision-makers in making choices. The "requirements" in the matrix refer to the structures found appropriate for making choices according to a given strategy. A bureaucratic structure is made up of individual experts with large delegated powers in an administrative hierarchy; a collegium is a body of wise men, inspired by a common purpose, and judiciously able to weigh—and vote on if they cannot agree—the causative factors in dispute; a representative body is a body of less expert delegates from some constituency—i.e., a party, interest group, nation, or region; and the structure for complete disagreement can only be anomic or charismatic. For us, the major difficulty of this formulation is the failure to specify outcome in the sense of the *quality* of final decision in the functional terms necessary for our approach, a point to which we will come back.

To the possibilities of computation, judgment, compromise, and inspiration, current theorizing can add two further ways of resolving conflict. One is random settlement of differences, such as by the flipping of a coin. It is conceivable that a conflict situation characterized not only by enormous destructive consequences for all parties, but also by utter disagreement over causation and complete absence of mutual trust in any possible conciliator, will be resolved randomly. Although in the nexus of interest-informed political action such a situation seems far-fetched, in the armaments field at least, it may not always be.[43] At any rate, this possibility is more remote to our problem than the second suggestion: namely, to consider the dynamics of non-violent conflict resolution in the organizational context. In so doing, we go beyond the context usually chosen for the discussion of *satyagraha* by raising it from the level of non-violent action by a committed group within a state to the setting of decision-making by an international group of experts, wise men, bureaucrats, or delegates.

Compromise, in practice as well as in Western liberal political theory, is prized as a flexible means toward the value-laden end of achieving agreement among clashing groups and interests, a desirable means for the achievement of consensus on ends. Bargains among the participants are common and not inconsistent with liberal theory. Self-interested conduct is taken for granted. As long as the end is good, shady means are easily tolerated. The virtue claimed for *satyagraha*, among the types of non-violent modes of resolving decisional conflict, lies in the reintroduction of means as being value-laden. The analogy is not to Gandhi's salt march but to the procedure of a Quaker meeting. Every participant is inspired and committed by the basic ideal of the group to achieve an outcome consonant with religious values; every participant is expected personally to contribute to consensus; therefore, all means suggesting division must be avoided and only means meeting the consensual and commitment values are permitted; hence discussion is free, and voting is avoided so that there may be neither majority nor minority; when the talking results in agreement a unanimous decision is made; if this does not occur, a decision is postponed. Every decision becomes an exercise in committed problem-solving involving a species of moral conversion to the group's consensus. Since it is the moral quality of the means that is stressed, ends may remain obscure until the last moment. Ends develop creatively from a commitment to ethical means.[44] But the commitment to means, in turn, flows from the conviction of the participant—the *satyagrahi*—that simple compromise among preferences is not acceptable, that the final outcome must be consonant with the basic values of the movement, and that this movement must make positive contributions to the general welfare.

Here is where the family resemblance to Functionalism makes its appearance. Functionalists have neglected the dynamic of means, much as the gloss over the kind of international law that is appropriate to their image. They have blandly assumed that decisions would follow the pattern suggested by the "computation," or, at worst, by the "judgment" box in our matrix. We know that they are wrong, though not perhaps for all time. In the shorter run, then, if the experts and group delegates making up functional boards show a quasi-religious commitment to the general welfare, this could induce the kind of behavior postulated by the Quaker meeting, maximizing means of toleration and participation. Most important, the threat of force would not have to be invoked to constrain a recalcitrant minority defeated in the voting.*

Could Functionalists support such an approach from certain components already present in the international system? The answer depends on whether we interpret international organizations as an expression of Western institutions and practices, i.e. whether we put the stress on voting rules as opposed to norms of accommodation. If we follow the second approach, certain trains of thought deriving from the Asian context would support the non-violent thesis. One example is the insistence by Indian United Nations delegates on the need for unanimous decisions on crucial matters, on the avoidance of voting, on not isolating the opponent—and the consequent need for non-action when no such consensus appears.[45] An example from jurisprudence is provided by the Islamic principle of *solh*, or the reconciliation of hostile parties under religious auspices. Parties do not bind themselves to accept an award, but they must refrain from stipulating conditions and contingencies in submitting to the procedure. A council of reconciliation, composed of respected leaders, is chosen, which then appeals to the parties to compromise their differences on the basis of unshakable unity," and "to preserve the Muslims' solidarity and to ex-

---

* This mode of making decisions, of course, rests on a series of explicit norms that must be part of the decision-makers' basic commitment. They include the dedication to self-realization, to seeking the truth; and in order to enable others to do likewise, the decision-makers practice non-violence. Hence one must act in a given conflict so as to contribute to the long-run reduction of all conflict. Since hostile means beget hostile countermeans, the means chosen to act in a conflict are more important than *immediate* ends (though not the long-run end). From this ensemble results the practical Gandhian program that combines avoiding secrecy, willingness to suffer the consequences of one's acts, making constructive proposals, ascertaining one's moral rightness before acting, and avoiding harm or humiliation to the opponent. For a formal statement of these norms, see Arne Naess, "A Systemization of Gandhian Ethics of Conflict Resolution," *Journal of Conflict Resolution*, II (June 1958), 140–55.

The essence of the approach is to reverse the self-fulfilling prophecy widely attributed to Marxist thinking and Soviet minds. "George F. Kennan once said: 'It is an undeniable privilege of every man to prove himself in the right in the thesis that the world is his enemy; for if he reiterates it frequently enough and makes it the background of his conduct, he is bound eventually to be right.' . . . If for 'enemy' we read 'friend' in this statement, the proposition seems to be equally true but much less believed." Kenneth E. Boulding, "National Images and International System," *ibid.*, III (June 1959), 127.

tirpate the roots of hatred and enmity."[46] Apparently the Council does not advance substantive proposals, and confines itself to evoking Koranic verses imposing such rules as "if two Muslims raise their swords to fight each other, both the killer and the killed shall be doomed to Hell."[47]

My reply to these intriguing versions of conflict resolution in the international setting is to assert their irrelevance. To accept their relevance is to accept some version of "truth," not only as universally valid philosophically, but as acceptable to all parties in international conflict of all kinds. As Joan Bondurant demonstrates, the Gandhian mode is a dialectical one: it postulates a new synthesis, after the conflict is resolved, which is closer to the objectives of the proponent of the antithesis, exactly as is the case in Marxism:

Whatever the subject of a specific conflict, understanding of the nature of conflict in general and of the objective to be attained in the given conflict situation is prerequisite for the [satyagrahi]. The force within any dialectical situation is derived from the clash of opposing elements within that situation. In every case of *satyagraha* the conflict is to be understood in dialectical terms. The immediate objective is a *restructuring of the opposing elements to achieve a situation which is satisfactory to both the original opposing antagonists but in such a way as to present an entirely new total circumstance.* This is, in Hegelian terms, an aiming at synthesis out of the conflict of thesis and antithesis. The claim for *satyagraha* is that through the operation of non-violent action the truth as judged by the fulfillment of human needs will emerge in the form of mutually satisfactory and agreed-upon solution.*

In our matrix, compromise and bargaining involved agreement on the causation of the conflict to be resolved, and disagreement over preferred outcomes. And so it is in most important international disputes involving welfare and the meeting of elementary human needs. Achieving welfare and meeting needs is not enough of an injunction: Welfare with birth control or without? With free enterprise or with planning? With human rights or without? These are the issues. They cannot be defined away by subsuming them to a transcendent or an immanent truth, known initially only to the *satyagrahi*: the yogi as well as the commissar thinks he knows

---

* Bondurant, *Conquest of Violence*, pp. 194–95 (italics mine). This is merely another way of stating the argument that the non-violent effort at synthesis is "right" and "true" because it rests on "justice," whereas the position of the as-yet-unpersuaded opponent does not. The point is made tellingly by the Rev. Martin Luther King, Jr., in "A Letter from Birmingham Jail" (*San Francisco Chronicle*, July 6, 1963, p. 12) :

"You may well ask, 'Why direct action? Why sit-ins, marches, etc.? Isn't negotiation a better path?' You are exactly right in your call for negotiation. Indeed, this is the purpose of direct action. Nonviolent direct action seeks to create such a crisis and establish such creative tension that a community which has constantly refused to negotiate is forced to confront the issue. It seeks so to dramatize the issue that it can no longer be ignored. . . There is a type of constructive nonviolent tension that is necessary for growth."

the truth, and yet they must compromise. And when they compromise, they must scale down their objectives, since we cannot assume that one will persuade the other. This is the lesson rejected by the advocates of non-violence; however, it is precisely this principle that a Western student of administrative accommodation, Mary Parker Follett, found central in her effort to define an approach to conflict resolution that would include the aspirations of all parties. We shall profit from her vision later.

The irrelevance of non-violence can be illustrated by Gandhi's famous rule concerning compromise: "In case of persistent resistance from one of the parties concerned, search for a compromise *without giving up essentials*. That is, search for a compromise affecting limited interests, not basic values."[48] Whose limited interests, and whose basic values? Obviously those of the *satyagrahi*. But what happens if the perception of interests and values is not shared by the antagonists, as is very often the case? We are then forced back to bargaining, and possibly to sordid compromise, which may not have the consequence of a new synthesis favorable to the "truth." Far from being a "no win" policy, non-violent action is a strategy dedicated to "winning over" the antagonist by demonstrating the *satyagrahi*'s moral superiority.

Integration, in a sense, is also a dialectical process. But to be operational it must dispense with assumptions of moral superiority; it must accept the moral relevance of low-level bargaining and compromise without insisting that those who resort to these means also accept the end of world order. To change the environment, the consequences of decisions must remain, in the short run, unintended but consonant with the values of the forces identified with thesis *and* with antithesis. The only way to avoid the neutrality of means associated both with judgmental and with compromise decisions is to resort to "inspiration." Indeed, unkind critics of Gandhi have suggested that his success may be attributable more to his charisma than to his mastery of non-violent technique. But international bureaucracies have had little luck with that type of leadership.

This concern brings us face to face with the possibilities of conflict resolution implicit in the structure of international organizations and bureaucracies. Arguing from experience with international organizations and from general organizational theory, we must ask ourselves *what kind* of conflict over decisions we can expect *where* in the structure. Let us bear in mind the typical structural features we encounter in this field: (1) a formal bureaucracy, "hierarchical" but staffed with specialists who are linked to environmental groups having parallel interests; (2) groups of independent experts who are called upon to make recommendations for programming or examining organizational performance; (3) groups of official experts, subject to instructions by the appointing governments, who do the same; and (4) delegates of governments and of large voluntary organizations rigidly representing the interests of these environmenta[l] structures. Conflict arises within, and sometimes between, all of these. Th[e] normal patterns would be expected to look like this:

1. Bureaucracies	Hierarchical/specialist structure	Computation
2. Independent expert groups	Collegial structure, with occasional voting	Judgment
3. Official expert groups	Collegial structure, with occasional voting	Judgment, shading into compromise
4. Conferences of delegates	Bargaining in representative structure	Compromise

A series of qualifications, however, must be made immediately, in ac[-] cordance with the findings of organizational theory. Bureaucracies, to th[e] extent that they depart from the mythical pure hierarchical-monocrati[c] pattern, *pretend* that internal conflict is resolved by computation. The[y] may even attempt to have recourse to purely non-political techniques. Bu[t] their success in doing so is inversely proportional to the significance o[f] their organization to integration. This is clear if we recall the vital impor[-] tance of organizational objectives, and the role of leadership in articulatin[g] and revaluing them. Organizations with very specific objectives (telecom[-] munications, postal rates, weather information) rarely have the oppor[-] tunity to revalue their objectives, because no state or group in the environ[-] ment questions them. The leadership has no need to resolve conflicts be[-] cause there are none, other than purely technical issues of the kind th[e] Functionalist loves. These are indeed resolved by computation, with th[e] result that the organization cannot grow. Therefore, in organizations tha[t] possess the desirable commitment to general objectives requiring amplifica[-] tion and adaptation in specific fields by the leadership, computation doe[s] not in fact, and should not ideally, dominate decision-making.

Organizations, like all large aggregates, are ruled by oligarchies—includ[-] ing internal elites drawn from each of the four structures listed above: i[n] short, by coalitions of interests depending on mutual accommodation. Bu[t] for purposes of presenting an acceptable "image" to the environment, i[t] is useful that the illusion of computation be maintained. Actual interna[l] consensus, however, can come about only as a result of a judicious mixtur[e] of judgmental with compromise decisions. This, in the instance of conflic[t] between government delegates and independent experts, or—more com[-] monly—the bureaucracy, implies continuous bargaining.[49] The only alter[-] native is charismatic leadership by the bureaucracy, sweeping the othe[r] structures along.

Instead, depending on the institutional structure and the subject matte[r] of the organization, the mixture of judgment and compromise has resulted

1 three recurrent, but qualitatively different, patterns of outcomes. Each attern specifies the degree of integration achieved by a decision. It incorporates antecedent actor conduct concerning causation and preferences, nd permits a qualitative projection of the outcomes. These patterns are:[50]

1. Accommodation on the basis of the minimum common denominator. 'his is the least demanding of the three. Equal bargaining partners gradually reduce their antagonistic demands by exchanging concessions of oughly equal value. Gains and losses are easily identified, but the impact f the transaction never goes beyond what the *least* cooperative bargaining artner wishes to concede. This mode of compromise is typical of classic iplomatic negotiations.

2. Accommodation by "splitting the difference." This carries us a little arther along the path of integration. As before, demands are reduced and oncessions of roughly equal value exchanged among autonomous baraining units. But in this mode of compromise the mediatory services of secretary-general, or an ad hoc international expert study group, may be dmitted by the parties. Conflict is resolved, not on the basis of the will of he least cooperative, but somewhere between the final bargaining positions. This type of compromise is prevalent in the negotiations of interational economic organizations, and in other dealings permitting financial dentification of gains or losses, such as the formulation of a scale of ssessments for members of the United Nations.

3. Accommodation on the basis of deliberately or inadvertently upgrading the common interests of the parties. This comes closest to the peaceful hange procedures typical of a political community with its full legislative nd judicial powers, a condition lacking in international relations. To conuse matters further, this mode of conflict resolution is often identified as 'integration," as by Mary Follett, who writes that, unlike mere compromise, t signifies "that a solution has been found in which both desires have found place, that neither side has had to sacrifice anything."[51] If this is so, it nust mean that the parties succeeded in redefining their conflict so as o work out a solution at a higher level, which almost invariably implies he expansion of the initial mandate or task. In terms of results, this mode f accommodation maximizes what I have elsewhere called the "spill-over" ffect of international decisions: policies made in carrying out an initial ask and grant of power can be made real only if the task itself is expanded, s reflected in the compromises among the states interested in the task. In erms of method, the upgrading of the parties' common interests relies eavily on the services of an institutionalized mediator, whether a single erson or a board of experts, with an autonomous range of powers. It thus ombines intergovernmental negotiation with the participation of independent experts and spokesmen for interest groups, parliaments, and political arties.

One disturbing flaw in our structure of self-reinforcing trends toward international integration stubbornly reappears at every level of analysis. It is this: if we are to assume that governments and voluntary groups in the environment recognize the functional consequences of revalued objectives and expanded programs eventually, no matter on how many constructive compromises they were based, what is to stop them from preventing future compromises, from causing the atrophy of the organization? The organization must, at every step, convince its clients that their interests continue to be served even with new objectives. But this is a purely rational process, and reason, we argued, is no guarantee that states see their objectives in identical or converging terms. In the face of this difficulty, I tentatively suggest that the psychological mechanism of "dissonance" may come to our aid. In the words of Charles Osgood: "When people are made to keep on behaving in ways that are inconsistent with their actual attitudes (e.g., as if they really trusted each other), their attitudes tend to shift into line with their behaviors."[52] Within the bureaucracy, this principle would mean that civil servants hostile or lukewarm to the leadership's professed objectives would gradually change their attitudes to favor the hierarchy because of the bureaucratic compulsion to pretend that they were loyal to the leadership. With respect to governmental delegates, the dissonance principle might imply that a pretended support for such organizational objectives as higher food production, human rights, collective security, or disarmament, when reinforced periodically with new tasks involving more value commitment, would develop into real support. In other words, a functional theory of international integration would look to the dissonance principle as the mechanism for "learning" that the Functionalists treat so cavalierly.[53] This argument, however, should not be carried to the extreme implied by some students of non-violence who regard the unconscious dialectic of conversion to international objectives as operating independently of the rational force of national self-interest. At best, the two forces can be combined in the minds of decision-makers.

But even after we have downgraded computation and inspiration as likely to produce outcomes favorable to integration, a number of difficulties remain in our matrix. Members of an organization do not necessarily agree on identification of issues, as involving long-run or short-run delegations of power or judgmental decisions. Equal constraints on all participants are assumed (e.g., identical perceptions of expertise, hierarchical relations, status). This is usually not true in fact. Further, there may be a cultural lag between formal decision structures and actual needs, so that a new situation may be inappropriately given to an established, routine-bound unit. On the other hand, if a new need is properly assigned to a new unit by way of delegation from the established organ, the act of delegation may be regretted later and the new unit hamstrung. Growing knowledge may make amenable to computation things that had to be treated judgmentally or by compromise before. Conversely, rapid scientific advances in disparate fields may make agreement on the relevance of facts to policy choices more difficult, making judgmental decisions necessary once more.[54]

Yet we continue to assert that organizational action designed to transform the system functionally must rest on an interplay between the perceptions of the governments and the bureaucratic leaders. Wise management recognizes these limitations; it tries to head them off by seeking to arrange, always, a consensus on which procedure is the appropriate one to maximize the leaders' conception of the common objectives. To do this, the leadership must exploit situations in which governmental delegates show no agreement on long-range preferences; it must turn the issue over to expert groups agreed on preferences but divided on their notion of causation. Conflict over preferences can be channeled. But then "causation" must mean more than facts, situations, correlations, or sequences. It must include the ideologies of the decision-makers, since these condition the kinds of facts and the relations between facts that are perceived as relevant. There are, in international organizations, few "pure facts." But where they do occur, their functional relationship to integration is sharply limited unless governments can also agree, *in concert*, to the addition and multiplication of new "pure facts," which would then enlarge the mission of the organization.

PROGRAMMING, SELF-PRESERVATION, EXTERNAL SUPPORT, AND GROWTH

What budgeting is to public administration, programming is to the international organization dedicated to systemic transformation: without a growth-oriented program there will be no impact on the sluggish and unfriendly environment. But even if such a program is the very soul of the organization, it can flourish only within the confines of decisions made by judgment and compromise. In other words, it must evolve within the jaws of the ideological vise that is provided by the heterogeneous environment. Organizational objectives can be initially stated only as the minimum common denominator of these ideologies; they can evolve only within their permissive apathy or tolerance.

This feature imposes several unique needs on programming by international organizations. They cannot simply proceed to feed the world's poor, educate its illiterate, or cure its cripples. The objective of plenty contains, by definition, subgoals involving coffee and wheat, land tenure and tax rates. The objective of education contains subgoals regarding literacy, school construction, teacher placement, and taxes. The subgoals of collective security defy simple enumeration. In order to meet overall objectives, appropriate sections of the bureaucracy must address themselves to programs directed at these subgoals. Subgoals beget specialists with primary interests in subgoals. They also beget alliances between these specialists on the one hand, and groups and governments on the other, these latter being concerned more with the narrow aim than with the broad organizational objective. Can bureaucratic leadership overcome this drag on dynamic programming? Can it subordinate the specialist with his ideological commitment to subgoals? The answer involves the knotty question of consensus, and the danger that programming will become part of a tacit general objective of mere survival.

Even if international organizations, in the sense of relationships among their member governments, are broadly "democratic," their bureaucracies should *not* be. No matter how democratic the organization, its programming must remain hierarchically dominated, or at least manipulated. Consensus must be maintained between leadership and member governments, leadership and expert groups, but not between every official and the Director-General.[55] But if the autonomy of the staff specialist is fully recognized, democracy will destroy the overall objective of the organization.

The possibility that subgoal-dominated programming will degenerate into survival policies calls for some comment on the nature of planning. According to Banfield, planning is to be distinguished from "opportunistic" decision-making by the fact that it subordinates all separate organizational acts to one overarching common purpose; the separate acts, in effect, are to be viewed as means, as instrumental intervening steps toward the achievement of the common purpose. Opportunistic decision-making, however, attaches other than instrumental value to the separate acts. They become ends in their own right and lose touch with what was once a common purpose.[56] It is to be feared that a specialist-dominated organization would lose sight of the common purpose. In order to prevent this, the leadership is called upon to analyze the situation, including the environmental constraints, in which it plans to choose specific intermediate ends, devise means of action to attain them, and then evaluate the consequences. Of course, in view of our earlier argument about the nature of the international environment, such a formulation of programming is as utopian as Banfield argues it to be. One can almost predict the areas in which subgoals will become dominant if specialists and their allies are left to themselves. No leadership can be expected to vanquish all these forces. But as far as the Functionalist is concerned, the opportunistic mode of programming is the desirable one: unwilling or unable to specify institutions and law, satisfied with a concept of immanent community evolving from dedication to welfare, he is quite content to let "functions" develop from an opportunistic approach. We think that he is wrong, even if we grant the utopian nature of wholly rational programming.

Management scientists and Functionalists join forces in advocating de-politicized programming. The Functionalist hopes that more and more issues will become infused with scientific lore and thus lend themselves to routine expert problem-solving. He trusts that issues will move from one decision-making box to another as knowledge grows and delegation of authority becomes reasonable. March and Simon argue that "the prevalence of bargaining is a symptom either that goals are not operational or that they are not shared."[57] They advise the leadership to engage in program-ming in such a way as to maximize reasoning and computation, to eliminate judgment and compromise. Cognitive links between ends and means must be strengthened, intermediate aims must be related to long-range objec-tives. This, they suggest, is very likely to result both in a cognitive strength-ening of subgoals, which are more readily understood and shared, and in a less political process of making decisions on future programming.[58]

Such a prescription, far from advancing integration, is likely to make it stultify. Experts, if left to themselves, do not make critical decisions. They attempt to solve problems once and for all, to deprive them of controversy. If our logic and our insistence on the functional consequences of political choices, however, have any merit, controversy and unfulfillment are essen-tial qualities in begetting new and recurrent critical decisions. Bargaining alone is not the organizational technique to be preferred; but bargaining mixed with judgmental decisions is likely to give us the formula for ever-expansive choices in the evolution of a program that will solve problems only by creating new ones, to be solved in turn.

This carefully manipulated "irrationality" of programming, which we regard as essential to the success of the Functionalist's scheme, remains political precisely because consensus can never be taken for granted. Allies and supporters in the environment must always be found, though it is idle and unnecessary to seek the unanimous support of all environmental forces interested in the organization's objectives. Although self-preserva-tion should never be the sole operational maxim, it remains necessary as an intermediary end, as a means to the larger end of making a contribution to integration. And this requires certain initial programming moves de-signed to assure the organization an initial friendly clientele.

Most international organizations originate in an environment of vague and imperfectly shared objectives. Hence the founders and bureaucratic leaders at first often feel obliged to advance elaborate justification for the appropriateness of the new structure and the importance of its goals. This tends to stress the immediate survival of the organization at the possible expense of later adaptation to new objectives requiring different proce-dures. Further, the multiplicity of organizations creates a certain pressure on the leaders to emphasize, at first, the uniqueness and autonomy of their organization, again contributing to difficulties in adaptation at a later point.

Imperfectly shared objectives, at the outset, result in the leadership's des
perate attempts to find a core of allies and clients in the environment to
assure a precarious survival in the short run. At the same time, vaguenes
of initial objectives, if bolstered by a core of supporters, gives the organiza
tion a better chance for long-run survival on the basis of adaptation, *pro
vided* it can vary its procedures, adapt its goals, and find new supporters.[5]
It follows that while the initial program should be broad enough to attrac
that initial core of clients, it should not be so exclusive as to sacrifice a
change in objectives later on. On the other hand, bureaucracies that ignore
the precariousness of their initial position, that hold out for a dynamic
program immediately although they have few reliable clients, run a desper
ate survival risk.

Expansion in programming, then, can be achieved only on the basis o
coalitions of interests sufficiently stable to enable the leadership to coun
on the persistence of identical or converging subgoals among certain of the
associated governments and voluntary groups. The coalition need not be
composed of the same members for each subgoal or issue: distinct coali
tions can operate in each realm, provided only they last long enough to
assure financial support and produce some impact on the environment. Per
haps no single coalition is attached fully to all of the organization's forma
objectives. But this does not matter so long as the operational subgoals re
main tied to these objectives in the organizational ideology. There is no
way of giving stability to the coalitions other than to "pay them off," to
play the game of interest politics to the hilt. Creative innovations, similarly
must be born from some environmental impulse, some body of demands
The inclusion of the innovation in the program is then interpreted as a
reward by certain members of the supporting coalition.

Now the demands on the perceptiveness of a sensitive leadership become
tremendous. Innovation in the program is subject to certain imbalances
between organization and environment, and these must be guarded against.
At first, of course, objectives, because they are institutionalized to a degree.
will remain acceptable to the initial body of supporters whether actual
achievements are scored or not. The earliest bargains will remain confirmed
for some time. If for some unforeseen environmental reason (e.g., a war
or a depression) achievement suddenly slumps, the "good will" acquired
by the bargain will not be immediately dissipated. Conversely, the organization will be able to make new bargains if some sharp improvement occurs
in the environment, and if this is credited to the organization as an achievement, even though any connection between it and the program may be
tenuous (e.g., the success of the European Common Market and unprece-
dented business prosperity). These slacks and imbalances involve dangers
and opportunities for programming to which the leadership must be very
attentive.[60]

If growth can take place only on the basis of programmatic innovation, the innovation can transform the international system only through its impact on the environment, through its "feedback." If we postulate the possibility of an expansion of international responsibilities along functional lines, and link such a process to the attraction and satisfaction of coalitions of clients, we nevertheless cannot automatically assume that new clients will be found, that old clients will readily adapt to new and more ambitious objectives, that there will be a feedback of sufficient power to generate new demands for organizational action. One objection to the pattern here postulated is the Iron Law of Oligarchy. International organizations, no matter how democratic their charters, tend to be run as oligarchies by groupings of the more influential member states, the chief bureaucrats, and certain selected experts. More important, the very groups in the member nations who are expected to benefit from the organization's program, who are supposed to experience the feedback and thus transform the international environment through new expectations and demands, also tend to be oligarchies. Can they be expected to behave as adaptively as our model specifies?

I submit that bureaucracy and oligarchy in voluntary organizations— pervasive as they certainly are—need not necessarily bar a reconsideration and revaluation of organizational objectives. Western industrial history presents ample examples of group adaptation to changes in economic and political conditions, irrespective of the dominance of bureaucratic structures in the groups concerned.[61] Much depends, then, on the nature of the group. In general, oligarchy does not fatally impede a revaluation of objectives and the emergence of new demands in the case of functionally specific interest groups, groups that articulate demands in an industrial setting. Their response to the integrative logic of international organization programs is optimal for our model. The same is true of governments and political parties aggregating the demands of such groups. However, institutional interest groups are far less adaptive. They tend to predominate in pre-industrial nations, in which a challenge to the group's objectives is also a challenge to the status of the members, a position rightly or wrongly associated with the preservation of a pre-industrial economic and social order. Hence these groups tend to pay lip service to the objectives of international organizations, but carefully refrain from exposing themselves to any feedback influences. The traditional governments in which such groups exercise their power act in much the same manner. Anomic interest groups never flourish long enough to exercise continuing influence; but such non-associational groups as kinship, ethnic, and religious organizations, despite their stability, rarely exhibit enough interest in the programs of international organizations to expose themselves to the feedback mechanism.[62]

The case is different with respect to oligarchic and totalitarian governments committed to industrial and social modernization. These almost invariably, either because of intense nationalism or totalitarian ideology, disapprove of autonomous and powerful international organization on principle. But that does not mean that they oppose each and every program. Frequently they are ardent supporters of subgoals that are consistent both with their own development plans and with the overall objectives of the organizational ideology. Consequently, they do make acceptable coalition partners for programmatic innovation; and they do, willy-nilly, expose themselves to the feedback mechanism.[63] The art of organizational leadership is really taxed when the governments recognize this mechanism, and are tempted to take measures to insulate themselves from it.

The species of human aggregation called "organization" is clearly part of that panorama of evolution of which industrialism, specialization, science, and universalism are also prominent members. In this sense it is undoubtedly true that the advent and growth of international organizations and their programs are a manifestation of the global Westernization of certain values. The functional logic of integration would thus seem clearly rooted in Western experience and modes of perception. Groups and governments characterized by this syndrome are most intimately related to the functional logic, while among pre-modern and non-Western societies those most anxious to emulate the scientific and technological values of the West are also the most closely tied to our model. But this formulation contains its own trick of reason: groups, governments, and societies that are not interested in democracy, organized dissensus, guaranteed human rights, free enterprise, a universalistic law, or any of the other accouterments of a "Western" polity are nevertheless drawn into the western mode of interest politics by virtue of their participation in international organizations. Clearly this does not mean that international organizations are "democratic," or "Western," or demonstrate the advent of a "universal rule of law." But it does imply, for groups attracted by those aspects of the West that have become a universal aspiration, exposure to the feedback implications of programs that derive from the internationalization of interest politics. As subgoals are shared more widely, the mesh of interdependencies grows in proportion to the evolution of programs designed to implement the subgoals. If the leader of an international bureaucracy has true insight, he will manipulate the subgoals in such a way as to make the organizational influence as extensive as possible: he will spread his web of clients as widely as his interpretation of organizational objectives permits. The very fact that he can rely on no homogeneous and stable body of supporters gives him the chance to move and maneuver as the logic of functionalism suggests.

But relatively few heads of international bureaucracies succeed in doing so. Gunnar Myrdal, in line with his restrictive, though wholly realistic, view of the governmental environment, summed up his sobering impressions. Voting resolves no conflicts of a substantive nature, only procedural issues. It may be useful to put occasional pressure on a sensitive government identified with a minority. Since the main purpose of governmental participation in international organization is propaganda, the research function of the bureaucracy acquires real importance, for it enables a government trapped by its own propaganda to see itself as others see it. Governments will accept occasional collective censure, so long as they feel that the damage they suffer will be suffered by others on some later occasion. Institutional autonomy will develop only if and when the organization is used for regular review of national policy; such review must be based on dispassionate research, which can be soberly discussed by high national officials anxious to reach limited agreements among themselves. Then and only then will stable role patterns develop, etiquettes and mutual expectations that no one dares violate because everyone would be expected to suffer. Such an atmosphere can be created by the organizational leadership in technical bodies; in others, a "club" atmosphere of privilege among the participating delegates may do the same. Hence, even on so minimal a basis, organizations do survive. "Even in the absence of any very substantial results in terms of international agreements, it is apparent that practically no government has ever voiced doubt about the general usefulness of the United Nations as a regular means for national diplomacy," and new states invariably regard admission as the crowning symbol of their independence.[64] This minimal prescription provides a frail basis for growth according to the functional logic; yet a more ambitious choice of programs might render inapplicable some of Myrdal's more extreme constraints.

ORGANIZATIONAL IDEOLOGY AND PROGRAMMING: FIVE CASES OF INSPIRATIONAL LEADERSHIP

If an organization is to grow within these constraints, the head of an international bureaucracy must develop the organizational ideology in three distinct but equally necessary ways. First, the ideology must be based on a minimum common denominator of shared goals among the member units; it must then be so construed as to point to the selection of a program that is inherently expansive, but acceptable to some viable coalition among the members. Second, the ideology must be specific enough to act as a reliable guide for the organization's staff in making discrete programmatic proposals to the top policy-making organs, and remain true to the basic objectives. Third, it must point to needs, expectations, and demands in the environment that can be transformed systemically as the program is implemented to meet explicit subgoals.[65] Any organizational ideology that does not satisfy *all* these desiderata will fail to overcome the obstacles experienced by Myrdal. To illustrate this, I shall examine briefly five examples

of ideological dynamism as practiced by the heads of international bureaucracies.*

Gunnar Myrdal and East-West Economic Rapprochement

Myrdal's commitment in the UN Economic Commission for Europe
(ECE) today appears almost quixotic: to maintain the economic unity of
Europe by the rational use and planning of common resources in the face
of ideological and political bloc formation, and thus to triumph over the
logic of political division. The ECE's first effort, in 1947, was to obtain a
mandate for the cooperative planning of the reconstruction of devastated
areas. Its second attempt, in 1948, was to request responsibility for planning the details for implementing the Marshall Plan—on the assumption
of Soviet participation. With the failure of both attempts, the ECE seemed
condemned to a fact-finding role, unlikely to meet Myrdal's central objective. He then sought to "revalue" these objectives by making it the
main business of the ECE to restore East-West trade, despite the confirmation of two hostile blocs. He could draw on the desire of Western European
countries to rely on East European rather than on dollar imports, and on
the wishes of the satellites to retain trade outlets in the West. Converging
national objectives were further reinforced by the Soviet Union's search
for a formula to weaken American-sponsored export controls against the
East. This sufficed for the creation of a trade committee in 1949, which,
prodded by the ECE Secretariat, was to serve as the forum for East-West
trade negotiations. By 1953, a significant revival in East-West trade had
occurred, for which the energetic intervention of the ECE, the availability
of specific negotiating facilities, and the good offices of the Executive Secretary could claim some credit. From then on, it became possible for the
ECE Secretariat to mediate actively in easing payments arrangements,
making long-term trade agreements, and improving commercial arbitration
procedures.[66]

Yet despite Myrdal's partial success in meeting his objective, his efforts
essentially failed: the economic integration of Europe has since become
fixed in the very two camps he sought to bring together. Was the organizational ideology at fault? Myrdal was careful to base his program on shared
and operational goals among the member states. He was mindful of viable

---

* The five examples used obviously do not exhaust the richness of this theme. It has been
argued persuasively, in relation to Eugene Black's leadership in the International Bank for
Reconstruction and Development, in Sewell, "An Evaluation of the Functional Approach."
Similar cases could be made for Raúl Prebisch and the UN Economic Commission for Latin
America, Fiorello La Guardia and UNRRA, Paul Hoffman and the Special Fund, Jean
Monnet and the European Coal and Steel Community, Walter Hallstein and the European
Economic Community, and, of course, Albert Thomas and the ILO. Of these, Monnet, Hall-
stein, and Prebisch probably come closest to having acted consistently on the basis of all
three ideological canons.

coalitions, and sought to choose subgoals with inherent integrative potential—when circumstances permitted. (It was, after all, not the ECE's fault that Washington and Moscow made a truly viable series of coalitions impossible because of their conflicting European policies.) Certainly Myrdal's ideology allowed him to organize a dedicated and energetic staff. Moreover, his policy of associating interest group representatives and a wide variety of unofficial and semi-official experts with the ECE's program could, under other circumstances, have gone a long way toward meeting the ideological canon requiring the transformation of demands in the environment. In short, ideology and program were properly meshed; but the very heterogeneity of the environment Myrdal tried to transform compelled the ECE to operate, eventually, at the level of the lowest common denominator—which found its lasting and visible symbol in the European convention on uniform roadsigns!

Julian Huxley and World Culture

A simpler case is that of the first Director-General of UNESCO, Julian Huxley. Determined that his organization should meet the ringing phrases of its constitutional objectives by developing a generalized intellectual doctrine under which all cultures could find a niche, Huxley advanced his personal philosophy of "scientific humanism" as a proper guide for a specific organizational program.[67] He was also motivated by the urgent need to find some kind of formula for screening and ordering the myriad specific needs and subgoals that were urged by UNESCO's members. Scientific humanism was chosen because it seemed to offer a possibility of uniting the West's belief in human dignity with the Marxist belief in economic welfare—but both under the roof of a materialism that Huxley developed as an analogue of Darwinian evolutionary theory. The proposal was, of course, rejected by UNESCO's General Conference. Huxley resigned soon afterward, and UNESCO quietly forgot about constructing a world culture as a guide to its program.

Which canons of organizational ideology-building did Huxley violate? If his program had been implemented, it would undoubtedly have satisfied the requirement of meeting needs that would lead to new demands transforming the environment. But that is the only canon it satisfied. The ideology was not based on the shared expectations of the member states—indeed one of UNESCO's initial problems was the absence of any shared operational goals—and the program selected was acceptable to no conceivable coalition. Finally, Huxley's own staff was not sufficiently committed to his philosophy to be capable of enthusiastic participation. It is doubtful whether scientific humanism, for all its ingenuity and dynamism, could have carried the day, even if it had not specifically proposed a world birth-control policy and shown a clear anti-religious bias.

John Boyd Orr and World Commodity Markets

The ideological defeat of the first Director-General of the Food and Agriculture Organization (FAO) is more complex. Lord Orr had been identified with a group of Australian agricultural specialists before and during World War II, most prominently Lord Stanley Bruce and F. L. McDougall. These men were eager to bring about "the marriage of health and agriculture" by creating an international structure that would not only dispose of agricultural surpluses, but combat malnutrition at the same time. The same idea was pressed by Orr after he became head of the new FAO: he proposed the creation of a World Food Board that would stabilize prices by buying up surpluses in time of glut, and would dispose of them, subject to health and nutritional standards, in time of famine. Far from being merely an opportunistic plan developed to assure the survival of the FAO in 1945, this approach was part and parcel of a standing agricultural welfare doctrine actually practiced, as national policy, by many states. Yet the FAO turned down the Orr Plan, and the Director-General resigned. Why?

Again, the implementation of the plan would certainly have satisfied the third criterion of ideological need. Possibly it also satisfied the need of engaging the enthusiasm of the organization's staff. It failed with respect to the first criterion. Orr had had plenty of warning at the meeting at which the FAO was set up that the major agricultural exporting nations were not ready to consider an international commodity policy; but he did not heed it. In short, his timing was wrong: a marked decline in world demand and a drop in prices should have been the point at which to propose his plan, not a period of high demand and rising prices. Fortunately for the FAO, the members shared a sufficient number of explicit subgoals to give the organization a very respectable set of objectives despite the defeat of the Orr Plan.[68]

Brock Chisholm and World Health

Huxley's Functionalism led him to believe that the inspired expert could overcome the ideological superstitions of governments. Orr's Functionalism made him feel that a commodity policy tied to a commitment to welfare could overcome the sloth of immediate price calculations. Dr. Brock Chisholm, first Director-General of the World Health Organization (WHO), is also a Functionalist; he holds that the expert in mental health can save the world from the obsolete politician. Chisholm differs from his colleagues in that he also had an operational ideology that enabled him to stress shared subgoals at the expense of the central argument; and he did not have to resign. The reason was his prudent separation of his private ideology from his public programming duties.

The private ideology is easily summarized. Man's scientific evolution now makes possible the total destruction of the race. In the past, the limited potential of destruction made reasonable the accepted attitudes toward war and exclusiveness. This is no longer so; political attitudes of anything less than complete world-mindedness are obsolete, and the politicians, educators, lawyers, and clergymen who adhere to them must be shorn of their power to mislead the generation that is now growing up. Good health demands that man "must take in his ability to function wholly, to function wholly in all circumstances — physical, mental, social."[69] Good mental health demands that nations change their educational policies to make this evolution of world-mindedness inevitable. No other means to survival is apparent, because the politicians' inability to understand the contemporary world merely produces anxieties that tend to be cathartically resolved by violence and verbal aggressiveness. Moreover, ideologies and political systems unmindful of mental health are equally regressive.

But Chisholm apparently recognized that this stricture comprised the bulk of his clients and supporters. He admitted the limitations of international organizations much as did Myrdal—the answer he advances is to change the climate of opinion *at home,* so that it may fall into line with the ringing words of international constitutions and charters. But so far as carrying over the ideology into programming for WHO is concerned, there is almost no trace: more technical assistance, more understanding for underdeveloped societies, and more generous long-term financing for UN agencies—demands bearing little relevance to the fundamental reformism of the ideology.[70] The program of WHO remained geared to subgoals firmly accepted by a stable coalition of members; it concentrated on malaria, maternal and child health, and venereal disease. Mental health remained a stepchild, and when it was discussed, there was no suggestion that Chisholm's ideology had made an impact. He remained firmly mindful of the first ideological canon and did well in meeting the second. But in so doing, he lost sight of the third, and committed WHO to a professionalized and routinized program.[71]

Dag Hammarskjöld and World Peace

The scholarly Swedish economist–civil servant who, in the last two years of his tenure, sought to infuse the UN with a dynamic and expansive ideology arrived at his doctrine gradually and perhaps even reluctantly. Following in the footsteps of a Secretary-General whose efforts at dynamic leadership were marked by failure, Hammarskjöld at first considered himself the neutral and dispassionate servant of the governments making up the UN. Conscious of the negotiated political compromise on which his election had been based, he practiced his now famous "quiet" and "preventive" diplomacy only when encouraged to do so by significant groupings in UN organs. Only when specific military crises arose, crises that were characterized by the absence of any immediate consensus among and within important coalitions of governments, did he intervene on his own initiative and in the name of the United Nations. Only then did he elaborate his organizational ideology. The process began in the Suez Crisis of 1956 and found its practical and doctrinal culmination in the Congo episode of 1960–61. What was this ideology?[72]

The historical purpose of the UN is to encourage the evolution of a world community beyond the minimal level of cooperation represented by a permanent conference of governments; to reach a stage at which the organization can act autonomously for constructive and universal ends—in short, in a more supranational manner than the bare words of the UN Charter suggest. But, true to the first canon of a wise organizational ideology, this can be done only on the basis of what is said or implied by the Charter—as interpreted by the organs of the UN—because the Charter represents the minimal convergence of common interests in the environment Specifically, Hammarskjöld argued that the evolution he wished to encourage must be based on giving increasing reality to the Charter provisions regarding the equality of political rights, equal economic opportunity, and the rule of law. For this purpose it was essential to separate the legitimate from the unlawful use of force, and to encourage all techniques for the peaceful settlement of disputes. Normally, any discrepancy between these minimal "agreed" principles and actual state conduct would be resolved by action of the Security Council or the General Assembly: but, and this is the essence of Hammarskjöld's dynamic ideology, if there is insufficient consensus for meeting the aims of the Charter in a specific instance, it is the clear constitutional duty of the Secretariat and its head to overcome the discrepancy. Thus, the ideology postulates increasing functional scope for the organization on the basis of initial common objectives that have been insufficiently realized in fact. It postulates, further, a doctrine uniting the staff behind its chief in advancing interpretations and programs designed to realize these objectives in fact. And it certainly makes possible the realization of the third ideological canon, the meeting of demands and expectations in the environment that are designed to transform the system. The very scope of the Charter objectives could make this possible, *provided* that general objectives can be transformed into specific operational subgoals on the basis of reliable support by shifting coalitions.

Despite the superficial success of Hammarskjöld's ideology, it is my contention that he ignored this proviso. He abided by the first canon in part only, and thereby deprived himself of reliable support and subgoal spec

---

* My argument is deliberately confined to those aspects of Hammarskjöld's ideology that were publicly advanced and defended by him. It is not yet possible to put the public argument within the full context into which it surely belongs, the private mystical world of the Secretary-General revealed posthumously in his *Vägmärken*.

ficity in terms of the third canon. The Congo crisis exemplifies my argu-ment. Hammarskjöld sought to exploit to the hilt the many and mutually contradictory UN Congo tasks, which had been so laboriously extracted from the process of parliamentary diplomacy, by placing his own interpre-tation of priorities upon them. He also sought to increase the UN's auton-omy, with respect to its environment, by exercising the power to make his own proposals and take his own steps when parliamentary diplomacy pro-duced no consensus and no clear guides for action. But since he invoked the Charter as his ideological scripture, he committed himself to mutually irreconcilable subgoals, which made the growth of a stable supporting coalition an impossibility. He sought at various times to (1) maintain order in the Congo, (2) expel the Belgians, (3) keep other "interested" foreign forces out, (4) unify the Congo, and (5) respect the right of *all* Congo factions to some degree of self-determination, *all without violation of the Charter injunction against intervention.*

The result was, of course, that no stable supporting coalition could be found for any one of these aims, since many conflicted with the national attitudes and purposes of the members. I suggest that if Hammarskjöld had opted for the expulsion of the Belgians, the exclusion of others, and the unification of the Congo, without going out of his way to make an issue over non-intervention, he would have had a stable coalition sup-porting him, including the bulk of the Afro-Asian states, the Soviet bloc, some Europeans, and the United States. He would have had to sacrifice the support of Britain, France, and Belgium—and this he was unwilling to do. Without a stable coalition there can be no continuity in attachment to subgoals and hence no feedback. Since the overall UN objective was not operational in the first place, though it may have been "shared" at a meaningless level of generality, such an ideology is likely to remain a heroic exercise in futility.

5. *Functionalism and the International Labor Organization: A Paradigm*

A PARADIGM OF ORGANIZATIONAL IMPACT

We have indicated the areas within organizational theory that appear relevant to the model of an international organization designed to advance
the indirect transformation of the international system. We have stated requisites derived from the constraints of the environment, specifying types
of bureaucracy, ideology, leadership, conflict resolution, programming,
supporters, and feedbacks. We are now able to restate the properties of the
model in a succinct fashion while remaining true to the marriage of Functionalism with functional sociology.

System and Organization

A given organization may be ineffective with respect to achieving its
explicit objectives; but it is nevertheless effective if it contributes to the
transformation of the system. Such an organization requires a leadership
which

1. is able to redefine organizational objectives "upward" upon realizing
that they have produced systemic consequences not initially intended by
the founding governments;

2. is willing and able to persuade member governments that unintended
consequences may, if viewed properly in terms of certain national goals,
be useful for the governments, and that the objectives of the organization
must therefore be adjusted upward;

3. is able to recognize that the mere implementation of the organization's objectives, through anticipated consequences, is likely to result in
the organization's stultification. (This requisite would not apply in organizations whose basic task rested on objectives that were not only inherently expansive, but shared as well; the trouble is that no such international organization has ever existed.)

Leadership and Ideology

The leadership must develop an organizational ideology which

1. extracts from a heterogeneous and unstable environment a body of shared objectives that are capable of redefinition on functional lines, and are based on definite coalitions of supporters whose subgoals are consistent with the leadership's major ideological premises;

2. binds and fires the organization's staff in support of objectives, and induces the specialists in the bureaucracy so to shape their relations with specific groups of clients as to make the central objectives triumph over disruptive subgoals; self-preservation implies a maximum of autonomy;

3. persuades clients, supporters, and enemies that constantly revalued objectives linked to new demands and new expectations in the environment can be met only by strengthening the organization.

Expert and Political Decisions

Organizational decisions should be such as to reconcile conflicting interests on the basis of upgrading common interests; they should also have the result of extending organizational powers and objectives. Decisions that split the difference among juxtaposed interests are also acceptable; but decisions that have as their outcome the minimum common bargaining denominator of the parties are rarely helpful. Eufunctional decisions should

1. avoid a course of action in which conflict is resolved on the basis of agreement among bureaucrats who hold identical views not only on preferred outcomes, but also on reasoning patterns; such decisions tend to be confined to the routine, and obviate the need of re-examining values;

2. avoid a course of action in which conflict is resolved by majority voting among instructed delegates, and in which there may agreement on reasoning patterns but no identity of preferred outcomes; such decisions are likely to follow the minimum common denominator in the bargaining situation;

3. avoid a course of action in which conflict is resolved by referring it to a body of experts who may agree on preferred outcomes but differ on patterns of reasoning; such decisions tend to be suspect to political leaders, even if functional from the organization's viewpoint;

4. be made by a judicious mixture of bargaining among instructed delegates and judgments rendered by experts; such a procedure maximizes the possibility for defining alternatives that are both sound technically and acceptable politically, since it is difficult to challenge the judgment of the experts while remaining, formally, subject to the will of the politicians; experts selected from official bureaucracies are more useful than independent experts.

Program and Growth

Programming must proceed within the confines of the organizational ideology. Initial objectives must be divided into specific subgoals that appeal to specific groups of clients and supporters in order to assure the survival of the organization in the short run. Subgoals, however, should be defined so as to make operational and accepted the overall objectives. Subgoal dominance must be avoided by

1. making programmatic innovation the responsibility of the top bureaucratic leadership in alliance with appropriate coalitions of clients;
2. keeping in check the autonomy of specialists in the bureaucracy, and preventing the preparation of programs on the basis of simple "problem-solving" by experts.

Planning should not be wholly rational. It must be manipulated politically so as to find tasks that will generate enough controversy to lead to new tasks but not enough controversy to endanger organizational survival. Therefore program plans should

1. feature consultation with clients and the building of variable coalitions, composed differently for each issue;
2. be developed by a mixture of judgment and compromise;
3. avoid extravagant claims for programmatic uniqueness in order not to endanger the legitimation of eventual changes in objectives.

Growth through planning can be achieved only on the basis of stimulating groups and governments in the environment to submit new demands calling for organizational action. Feedbacks that strengthen the organization at the expense of the environment develop most readily among groups exhibiting an industrial-pluralistic-modernizing syndrome of expectations. Such groups are most receptive to the schemes for increasing human welfare and dignity that arise from the unintended consequences of earlier organizational action.

INDICATORS OF GROWTH

This completes the restatement of our desirable organizational model. Living organizations may or may not approximate it. If we wish to predict the transformation of the international system on the basis of organizational contributions, we must examine actual organizations in terms of our paradigm. Taken together, they represent a forum for all major national attitudes, purposes, and ideologies. The manner in which national inputs are reconciled determines the performance of organizations and the direction of systemic change. What, then, are the proper indicators for studying this interplay?

We started with a discussion of international systems and their transformation, and to this point we must now return. We need three different sets of indicators to do justice to the interplay: the characteristics of a given system that are imposed by the environment; the structure and performance of a given international organization in terms of the paradigm; and the transformations—if any—in the system that are attributable to organizational activity.*

System Characteristics Imposed by Environment

What is needed to deal empirically with systems is a set of indicators that will enable us to observe the transformations described in more general terms by Hoffmann.[1] A given system—for instance, that which created the League of Nations in 1919 or the UN in 1945—can be described by the distribution of the types of nationalism that prevail in it. Following the classification of C. H. J. Hayes, this would include liberal, Jacobin, traditional, and integral nationalism. Here we are concerned not with the ontology of various nationalisms, but with the content of national beliefs as representing the totality of values and interests spilling over into the arena of institutionalized world politics. By studying the content of national beliefs, we are choosing a short cut for the creation of a more elaborate typology of various socio-political cultures and their policies. Thus we might specify that in 1945, for instance, x number of states professed a "liberal" nationalism, y number a "Jacobin" variety, and z number an "integral" nationalism. This relationship may then be compared with the ratios obtaining in 1955, for example; and the ideological "field" in which the UN operates might thus be delimited. A UN composed overwhelmingly of "Jacobin" or "integral nationalist" members would seem unlikely to exercise much influence on world affairs.

Further, the political systems that prevail must be sorted by determining the number of democracies, totalitarianisms, traditional oligarchies, and "modernizing" oligarchies that exist. Their degree of economic development and type of social structure is equally relevant as an indicator. I suggest that we distinguish between industrialized, newly industrializing,

---

* Obviously international systems do change and have been transformed as a result of developments having nothing to do with international organizations. Although this was clearly true in past periods, it is less likely to be true in the future because of the universalization of membership, tasks, and values implicit in the phenomenal growth of such organizations since 1945. But it remains a factor of central importance to which due weight must be given in searching for explanations of systemic change. For two dramatically different evaluations of the UN as being central or peripheral to such changes, compare Robert M. MacIver, *The Nations and the United Nations* (New York: Manhattan Publishing Co., 1959), and Maurice Bourquin, *L'Etat souverain et l'organisation internationale* (New York: Manhattan Publishing Co., 1959). The authors used identical source materials, the national studies on the UN prepared under the auspices of the Carnegie Endowment for International Peace. Yet MacIver, following Functional insights, concludes that interaction in the UN has produced an almost universal new consensus on peaceful and constructive tasks, whereas Bourquin holds that the sovereign nation-state remains supreme and merely uses the UN for its selfish aims, without visibly transforming the system.

mature agricultural, and underdeveloped economic-social structures. Finally, we require an indicator concerning the economic doctrines and institutions that prevail, such as free enterprise, welfare statism, communism, or corporatism. Together this would give us sixteen indicators.[2]

Separately they tell us nothing. But they can be combined so as to give us an idea of the "general interest" or "shared aims" that the member governments profess at any one time, and that they seek to impose on the international organization. By doing this we are able to have a point of reference, an anchor, for studying such questions as: Under what conditions is there an increase in the global task? Under what circumstances a diminution? Is contact between global agencies and nationally significant individuals and groups enhanced or reduced through given tasks? Are national loyalties and expectations affected? Or, more generally, in what way is the evolution of the global task connected with the birth of a different international system, more nearly approaching government as we usually understand it?

Each international organization owes its origin to some pattern of shared expectations, the "general interest" that must be specified. One example, chosen from the field of peace and security, would be the nature of the status quo considered appropriate by the founders. Three such conceptions can be historically identified. The "Wilsonian" conception of a status quo is usually summed up as "national self-determination," or giving each nation its state and guaranteeing its frontiers. It predicates the successful functioning of a collective security system on the satisfaction of this minimum of accepted national aims. Opposed to this notion, we find the "Churchillian" status quo, implying the satisfaction of the security aims of the major powers and their obligation to maintain world peace by force, if necessary. Apparently the statesmen of the major powers in 1945 thought they were acting out the Churchillian notion. Finally, there is a "Gandhian" conception of the status quo; it implies a provisional and expediential acceptance of the new rules in order to enable the member states to change them peacefully, by continued participation in the new institutions, while quite frankly disputing their legitimacy. Agriculture would provide its own confluence of aims and its status quo; so would health or labor standards.

Organizational Structure and Performance

The general interest of the founding states becomes the initial set of objectives of the organization. If organizational ideology, leadership, and programming meet the requisites of our model, the organization will transform, deepen, and strengthen these objectives; if it fails to do so, it will merely carry out the initial mandate. But if the system, in effect, transforms itself owing to forces having nothing to do with the organization and its performance, the leadership may never even get a chance to lead or to develop a program. This, for example, is what happened to the collective security aspect of the League of Nations' program.

Our organizational paradigm makes it possible to investigate the performance of the Universal Postal Union, the United Nations, or the Arab League in terms of these three alternatives. The indicators are provided by what was said above about leadership, effectiveness, ideology, decision-making, programming, and feedbacks.

System Transformation and Environmental Change

In the broadest sense, the proof of an organizational impact on the environment lies in the appearance of a new set of general interests that command respect among the members—in short, a new world task. Our first indicator, then, would be the construction of a framework of shared objectives, five, ten, or twenty years after the crystallization of the first notion of a status quo. In doing so, we would merely ascertain, for example, whether there was now a dominant attachment to the protection of human rights as opposed to territorial integrity, to the sharing of resources as opposed to the protection of private property, to conciliation as opposed to enforcement measures.

But to penetrate beneath the surface of a new consensus, more specific indicators must be provided. They are:

1. *Institutional autonomy.* The organization will develop as a result of the changing pattern of aims and expectations, the emergence of a world task, its implementation through new norms, procedures, and institutions, and the reverse influence of these patterns on the expectations and aims of the member nations; but this development can result in a new system only if the organs acquire independent powers of some kind. These powers will differ functionally and will enjoy uneven popularity among member states. They may involve the expansion of the role of the Secretary-General or Director-General, or growing respect for IBRD survey teams, IAEA inspectors, or TAB resident-representatives. But their impact must be summed up conceptually.

2. *Authority and peaceful change.* The outputs of international organizations take the form of resolutions and recommendations that urge a course of action on member governments, but do not bind them to act; conventions and treaties that are binding when ratified; and various kinds of decisions and judicial rulings that are binding unconditionally. The dominant pattern in contemporary international relations, of course, subordinates the use of decisions and legal judgments to the more ambiguous means of negotiated recommendations and conventions.

Yet if the environment is changed at all, the transformation proceeds by virtue of the implementation bestowed on these acts by member governments. Together they constitute what the international lawyer calls "peaceful change": the process of altering established rights and procedures, the status quo, by means of organizational outputs lacking coercive sanctions. A peaceful transformation of the status quo can, in Functional language, proceed only on the basis of "law without force," i.e., on the basis of some degree of consensus with respect to substance and procedure. The history of our organization, in any period, will have yielded evidence of the circumstances and fields in which changes in national policy recommended by the organization have been accepted. Whether acceptance has been brought about by the actions of standing organs, or by the work of special mediatory agencies appointed to deal with highly specific problems does not matter. According to the objectives of the organization, peaceful change can be arranged for boundary problems, national self-determination, minority rights, commodity prices, freedom of the press, compensation of nationalized property, water rights—in the modern pattern of economic and political interdependence, the list is never-ending.

What is important here is that the member states accept the peaceful change procedure as consonant with revised and upgraded purposes. The indicator we label "authority" means merely that member governments and voluntary groups accept the peaceful change procedure by implementing whatever is decided or recommended, *without necessarily agreeing that the decision or recommendation is just and right*. In fact, they may denounce the organization as meddling in domestic matters and stepping outside its declared objectives. This does not matter for present purposes, as long as the protesting governments implement the decision or recommendation anyway. By repeated implementation of "unjust" decisions, then, the peaceful change procedure may effectively influence the environment.* Authority thus becomes an indicator which, through the use of quantitative techniques, provides a simple way of checking on the degree of grudging implementation bestowed on organizational acts.[3]

3. *Legitimacy and value change.* So far our guiding concepts have revolved around policies, not around the attitudes and beliefs of nations, groups, elites, or individuals. The operations of the UN, especially of such specialized agencies and other bodies as have direct contact with individuals rather than governments, *may* influence the beliefs of such persons and groups. If so, rigorous empirical theory requires that the direction of

---

* This formulation of "authority" differs from the Weberian notion of "legitimate authority" in that it does not invoke the sanctions of tradition, charisma, or reason to explain the acceptance of a decision. Tradition may develop as a result of rule internalization eventually; charisma is unlikely to prevail at the international level; reason may be considered the true sanction if we assume that states implement decisions as a result of a calculation of risks and losses attending non-implementation. But this assumption for explaining state behavior contains its own limiting logic: reason may dictate implementation in one set of circumstances but not in another, thus preventing a predictable growth pattern in authority.

such changes be correlated with fields of action, with circumstances, and with institutional powers. Comparative evaluations of various nations and various organizations, based on the historical material, thus become imperative here, too. Information concerning public and elite satisfaction or dissatisfaction with UN policies in various spheres is clearly germane in this context.

It is more than doubtful that the UN system enjoys legitimacy in the minds of member governments in Weber's sense of that term. But the position of the system in the total scheme of national ideologies and international politics could be summed up very convincingly if—at any one time—its legitimacy could be specified and stated. I suggest that a rough measure of legitimacy can be provided by distilling from the historical material the situations in which member states invoke the purposes and principles of the UN to justify some item of national policy, such invocation being at the same time accompanied by an expansion of the global task. The use of UN plebiscite machinery, inspectors, and general resolutions in deciding upon the future of the two Togoland trust territories, in conjunction with the French and British governments, is an example of such invocation-cum-task expansion.

Legitimacy, therefore, provides an indicator of the circumstances under which organizational decisions are implemented, while also specifying whether the values involved in task expansion are somehow internalized by the forces in the environment. Whereas a growth in authority does not guarantee a repetition or expansion of peaceful change procedures, a growth in legitimacy would provide such a presumption. If only we could assume that such a development rested on some overriding national calculus of *Zweckrationalität*, we could invoke the canons of functional sociology without caution or restraint in predicting the transformation of the international system.

FUNCTIONAL HYPOTHESES
AND THE INTERNATIONAL LABOR ORGANIZATION

Armed with a series of functional propositions and a model of organizational requisites, we must now face the problem of assessing the contribution of one of the specialized agencies of the United Nations, the International Labor Organization (ILO), to international integration. Our model and the indicators have been deliberately designed to fit all types of subject matter and objectives entrusted to international organizations. But their application in any one case, clearly, must be subordinated to the specific task of the organization selected for study. The task of the ILO is the world-wide improvement of labor standards. It approaches its task by means of conventions, recommendations, technical assistance, expert studies, discussion among and training of national officials concerned with labor and industrial matters, investigations, and the adjudication of specific complaints alleging violations of established standards. These methods of operation, and the program of which they are a part, developed gradually since the Organization's birth in 1919. The ILO constitutes a particularly fruitful case for the study of the functional logic of integration because, uniquely among UN agencies, it provides for direct participation by representatives of voluntary groups. Further, its elaborate rules governing the reporting and following up of the implementation of earlier decisions make possible a quantitative evaluation of its effectiveness in transforming the international environment.*

Within the context of this task, then, what hypotheses are suggested by our functional setting?

Organizational Objectives and Ideology

1. The initial program is based on the converging interests of the founding governments: the protection of labor standards in industrialized countries and the facilitation of industrialization elsewhere without harm to working-class welfare.

2. The organizational leadership develops an ideology based on this objective, but so construing it as to make the establishment of labor standards a dynamic doctrine of world economic and political progress.

3. In so doing, it lays the basis for claiming new powers and tasks, as the original task founders on spotty implementation by the member governments.

4. The choice of program is dictated by the search for allies among trade unions and the identification of enemies among the employers.

5. Disparate subgoals among trade unions and governments force an expansion and dilution of the program; as a result, the original ideology is strained, and can be restored only by redefinition at a more comprehensive level. The field of standard-setting thereby comes to include technical assistance for labor efficiency, protection of human rights, and modernization of pre-industrial societies.

6. The organizational ideology, confronting a larger task and a greater heterogeneity in the environment, loses specificity and seeks to regain coherence through the leadership's efforts to convince recalcitrant members that, in the long run, everything conduces to their benefit.

---

* Before proceeding with the perusal of integrative hypotheses, the reader is strongly advised to glance at the formal rules under which the ILO operates and at the powers of the major organs, the Governing Body, the International Labor Conference, and the International Labor Office. See Appendix, "The Constitution of the International Labor Organization," pp. 501–16.

International Legislative Effectiveness

1. Within the confines of the ideology, the Organization can agree only on a minimal legislative program for establishing binding labor standards.

2. Labor standards are implemented only by industrial countries with a functionally specific group structure.

3. Labor standards are considered with interest by modernizing oligarchies and by totalitarian countries contemplating specific programs of domestic modernization.

4. Standards established by way of recommendations, rather than conventions, arouse less internal conflict but enjoy less implementation.

5. The integrative effectiveness of the legislative process is manifest not primarily in the implementation of the rules, but in the closer relations established among the groups and governments who meet and discuss desirable standards. Integration of values precedes identical national policies.

International Industrial Cooperation

1. In recognition of its unequal impact on the environment, the Organization will diversify its program by seeking to implant labor standards by means of small-group discussion in specific fields and for a limited number of interested nations.

2. The flexibility of the procedure will result in less stringent rules and even less uniform implementation.

3. Again, the integration of values defined by the functionally specific aims of similar groups of varying nationalities will facilitate eventual harmonization of policies. This, in itself, is an unintended consequence as far as the participants are concerned.

International Adjudication and Trade Union Rights

1. The increase in programmatic scope will result, without this having been intended by the members, in the creation of new machinery with new powers.

2. The recalcitrant members can object to this process only by denying ideological commitments to which they had bound themselves earlier.

3. The "law without force" doctrine entails a new procedure of investigating and resolving specific complaints, a result that is fruitful in transforming the environment because the member states cannot afford openly to block the procedure.

4. Implementation of decisions varies with the stability and self-confidence of the state concerned.

5. Voluntary groups will avail themselves of the procedure in proportion to their striving for a pluralistic-industrial order.

6. The effectiveness of the ILO procedure may lie less in strengthening the autonomy of international institutions than in transforming the attitudes of the Organization's clients. Legitimacy may grow without apparent increase in authority.

International Pressure and Worker Welfare

1. Under the guise of programs of client-determined technical assistance, effective standardization of industrial conditions is advanced, an unintended consequence that the member state cannot resist if it wants technical aid.

2. Taking advantage of programmatic and ideological announcements, clients press on the ILO complaints that are not, technically, subject to its jurisdiction. The leadership will accept these complaints, but seek to resolve them on the basis of general consensus.

3. Subgoal specificity among staff and clients will constantly tend toward the inclusion of new activities in the declared objectives of advancing labor welfare standards.

4. If clients are indifferent or divided, ILO leadership can mobilize its own diplomatic skills to persuade member states to abide by ILO objectives and to submit new fields to its scrutiny and advice.

These hypotheses are obviously not exhaustive. We are directed to them by the assumptions and logic of functional analysis. We can investigate them by submitting them to any or all the indicators that seem applicable in a given case. And to this task we must now turn.

PART II

Functionalism and the International Labor Organization

6. *Organizational Ideology, 1919–48*

If we wish to remain true to the guidelines specified in Part I, we must start our investigation of the International Labor Organization by examining the various environmental backgrounds that provided the inputs for the ILO's program. These did not remain constant during the period since 1919; hence it is essential to retrace the contours of the international environment at various historically strategic moments, and then ask ourselves what kind of inputs were provided by the new forces thrown forward by history. Such an approach would give us four phases in the record of the ILO: (1) 1919–32, the period of origin and the program that evolved from the initial consensus; it so happens that this period coincides with the tenure of the first Director, Albert Thomas; (2) 1933–43, the period of the Great Depression, the fascist challenge, and World War II, a period that covers the exile of the ILO in Montreal and the tenure of three Directors; (3) 1944–48, the period of post-war reassessment and adaptation to the United Nations; and (4) 1948 up to the present, the period dominated by the Cold War, the revolution of rising expectations, and the advent of non-Western states, a period that coincides with the tenure of David A. Morse as the fifth Director-General.

What features shall we isolate and compare during each of these phases, and what environmental characteristics shall we specify at the beginning of each period? We are concerned here with establishing the relationship between environmental background and organizational development, not with organizational impact on the environment. Hence we must relate varying environmental situations with the patterns of ILO leadership, ideology, programming, and possible task expansion. This is our aim in Chapters 6 and 7. However, we must also relate environmental situations to the clients of the Organization, to ties among clients, to organizational power and effectiveness, to conflict resolution, and to decision-making. This constitutes the task of Chapter 8. Chapters 9, 10, 11, and 12 will be devoted to assessing the impact of ILO on the international environment.

The magic words "functionalism" and "functional" will recur with astounding frequency in the pages that follow; but since they will take on a more specific meaning than in the previous discussion, an effort at terminological recapitulation is in order. Thus far we have distinguished between three kinds of "functionalism," not only assigning different and ascending levels of abstraction to each, but conferring a different analytical purpose on each level as well. First, we discussed Functionalism as an ideology of organization and world peace, an ideology that exists in the minds of its advocates but bears no overt relationship to sociological functionalism. Second, we explored the sociological theory of functionalism with reference to maintenance and destruction of discrete social systems. By using this analytical approach and applying it to what we already know empirically about the work of international organizations, we then revised ideological Functionalism in terms of sociological functionalism. Third, we incorporated our "revised Functionalism"—now no longer an ideology but a tool for social analysis—into a systemic theory of organization; the purpose of this theory is to explain how certain conceptions of organizational task and certain organizational programs contribute to the transformation of the international system through the mechanism of initially unintended consequences. For the second and third meanings we continue to reserve the lower-case "f."

We are about to introduce yet a fourth level of meaning. For the sake of clarity it will be referred to as "Official Functionalism." It is the term we shall bestow on the ideology of the ILO staff and client groups, the ideology that they evolved to justify the expansion of the organizational task and program to themselves and to others, the "organizational ideology" *par excellence.* "Official Functionalism," then, is not a researcher's tool: it is the living belief of a group of officials and delegates. It remains the researcher's job to assess Official Functionalism, in all its permutations, in relation to the analytical functionalism selected for the study of system transformation.

ENVIRONMENT AND IDEOLOGY, 1919–32

The origin of the ILO retains few mysteries. In a very real sense, the Organization is the result of the political commitments undertaken by the Allied governments during World War I, commitments that were later endorsed by Imperial Germany and given the quality of an urgent political necessity by the success of the Bolshevik Revolution and the imminence of kindred outbreaks in the West. Between 1914 and 1919, the major American, British, French, and Belgian trade unions had all come out for a detailed international program designed to improve the lot of the worker, to let him share in the benefits of the very democracy for which the war was allegedly being waged, and to cement peace by dedicating governments to social reform. During the same period, no less than twelve international conferences were convened, nine by trade union and socialist organizations, and three by other reformist groups. Similar demands were put forth at all these gatherings.

Nor was this the only impetus for drastic new international action coming from the voluntary-group context. Trade union demands were based on experience with the International Association for Labor Legislation, an unofficial international group of experts established with the approval of several governments in 1901, and subsequently active in doing the research and lobbying that led to the adoption of the pre-war international labor conventions.

Trade union and socialist demands, by 1919, came to agree on these points: national social welfare was to be advanced by joint international action, by way of more international labor conventions; labor should receive a basic "charter" of fundamental rights; and labor should be permanently represented in international agencies charged with the preparation of conventions, as well as in the official delegations assembled to draw up the peace treaties. The Allied governments, in order to reward labor for the support it had given to the war effort and to protect themselves against a further radicalization of the labor movement, complied by generously co-opting labor specialists and representatives into their delegations, instructing them to organize themselves into the Commission on International Labor Legislation of the Peace Conference and to draft an appropriate instrument.[1] Labor had "arrived" on the international scene.

The essence of the labor consensus had been hammered out at the Leeds (1916) and Bern (1919) conferences, both of which stressed the actual post-war program that was desired; yet relatively little attention was paid to the questions of how an international agency should be composed and what powers it should have. However, the American Federation of Labor—speaking through the mouth of Samuel Gompers—did not share even this programmatic consensus. Gompers opposed a labor organization that would institutionalize trade union cooperation with governments and with employers. He also opposed the idea of promoting labor progress through social legislation, preferring collective bargaining and political contests with democratic legislators. And, on constitutional grounds, he had no use for an international organization with anything even smacking of a legislative competence. Even though Gompers presided over the work of the Labor Commission, he never shared its consensus. His reservations were responsible for many of the constitutional weaknesses built into the ILO

Constitution, and the principle of tripartism was adopted over his continuing doubts.

Given the concern of the governments over social unrest, it is hardly surprising that the French and British proposals to the Commission were largely inspired by the Leeds and Bern programs. The bulk of these demands was faithfully reproduced in the Preamble to the Constitution, but not quite so faithfully in the operative sections. The Preamble holds that the ILO should seek to regulate working hours, recruitment of manpower, and unemployment; establish wages sufficient to guarantee minimal welfare; create old-age, sickness-accident, and occupational-disease insurance; protect women, young workers, and migrants; provide trade education; and—perhaps most important—establish the principles of trade union freedom and non-discriminatory wage scales. The chief operative article said nothing about unemployment and manpower recruitment, sidestepped the social security provisions, and watered down the endorsement of trade union freedom, non-discrimination, and minimum wages. It recognized the principle of the eight-hour day, the need to protect women, young workers, and migrants, and added provisions for weekly rest and the creation of labor inspectorates.[2]

Clearly, the specific programmatic consensus was hardly overwhelming in its scope. What is more important, perhaps, is the substratum of ideological conviction on which all the trade union representatives and several of the government delegates did agree. Peace and social justice were indissolubly linked; without social justice there could be no permanent peace. Social justice, moreover, was attainable only by way of progressive labor legislation. But since governments argued that legislation was dependent on the conditions of international economic competition, they were forced to concede that only joint international action was likely to produce *equal* and *uniform* social justice. Thus commitment to the principle of progressive social action, willy-nilly, forced them to accept the derivative principle of joint action.[3] While it almost appears as if the peacemakers of 1919 accepted a version of the Functionalist creed, it would be more correct to argue that they acted in conformity with the functional logic.

Certainly, the members of the Labor Commission were ideologically receptive to the doctrine, but their superiors in the foreign offices and the Supreme Council were scarcely preoccupied with satisfying labor, after they had made their initial major gesture. Their attention was preempted by the pervasive political issues at Paris, not by Part XIII of their treaty, the section dealing with the ILO. If they accepted the draft of the Labor Commission without much debate, it was not because they fully agreed with its ideology or completely shared its programmatic consensus; it was because they were committed to a gesture and had more important things on their minds. Yet it remains true that governmental preoccupation with larger issues permitted the Functionally-motivated members of the Labor Commission to draw up a constitution that was revolutionary for its day in terms of the procedural constraints to which it subjected sovereign governments. To this extent we might be tempted to consider the major statesmen either to have been generous in their prescience, or to have been duped by their agents. Actually neither was the case. The agents were permitted to embark on a radical new departure and develop ingenious constitutional devices because the final power of *action* continued to rest with governments: the consent of the Council of the League of Nations was required to initiate serious sanctions; the League controlled ILO pursestrings; and the acceptance of the new international labor standards remained—as before—a purely voluntary act.

There is, then, some point in treating the evolution of the ILO as an unintended consequence of the very immediate and expediential governmental concern here laid bare. This thesis is strengthened if we bear in mind the origins of the British initiative for the ILO, since it was British thought that translated a generalized trade union unrest into an ongoing international organization. This applies not only to the principle of tripartism, but to the very idea of building labor representation into government at the national and international levels. War production needs provided the initial stimulus. The Lloyd George government, in 1916, sought ways to increase labor productivity and obtain the support of organized labor. Hence it faced the necessity of raising especially low wages in certain plants, reconciling both labor and employers to its policies. For this purpose it became desirable to have a special ministry of labor that would provide the stimulus, permit labor participation, *and* make available expert studies concerning economic and social requirements that would be difficult to challenge inside the government. The establishment of the Ministry of Labor, therefore, was a manipulative step in co-optation. The persons most responsible for this national decision became, two years later, the ones who drafted the British proposals to the Commission on International Labor Legislation. The ILO was conceived as an exercise in co-optation.[4] But the unintended consequences of this decision were not slow in arriving, once the derivative principles of tripartism and convention-drafting were constitutionally established.

These consequences became apparent at the first meeting of the newly created Governing Body. That meeting elected as Director of the ILO Albert Thomas, the dynamic French trade union leader who had headed the French Ministry of Production during part of the war. But the election took place over the opposition of the British government delegate, who sought to obtain the directorship for Harold Butler. Almost immediately the logic of pluralism made itself felt in that Thomas was elected as a result of an ad hoc coalition of worker and employer delegates, opposing the wish of most government delegates to postpone the choice. Some of the employers, further, voted for Thomas for purely anglophobic reasons, rather than from approval or knowledge of his policies. If the first unintended consequence was the election of a strong Director not wanted by the governments, the second was the initiation of a self-consciously dynamic policy on his part. The government delegates, in 1919 and 1920, had few instructions and tended to flounder in meetings of the Governing Body, thus mirroring the lack of foresight and deliberate preparation of any real international social policy on the part of the victor statesmen. Governments, therefore, were in no position to feed demands into the ILO because they had not expected the need for any policy. In this vacuum, Thomas organized his own research staff, the International Labor Office, and *it* speedily became the source of policy demands. Thomas and the Office were able to impose the original ILO conceptions of program and task; governments, because of their lack of initial interest, soon recognized the unintended consequence by using the reports and studies of the Office as a base for the instructions given to their delegates after 1921.[5] What was this ideology?

Thomas's conception of the relationship between social justice and peace is basic here, and this conception was *superficially* identical with the ideology of the peace treaty. There could be no lasting peace without social justice because peace was held to depend on the dominance of democracy; political democracy, however, was unable to serve man and achieve legitimacy unless it first became imbued with social democracy. Social democracy, finally, could not be brought into life unless organized labor was given a permanent place in the polity. Hence the cementing of peace calls for the creation of a strong international stimulus to strengthen labor, give it self-confidence, and make it penetrate the body politic.[6] At this point in the argument the unique role of the ILO becomes apparent. Thomas shared the Functionalists' disdain for diplomats and officials; he favored "living instruments" and opposed the League of Nations because it was "divorced from peoples."[7]

He saw the Organisation not as a mechanism for collaboration but as the collaboration itself in full action. He saw it not in any sense as a Super-state . . . but he saw it as much more than inter-state. He saw it as an organisation of the peoples of the world, an organisation in which cabinets and parliaments, national and colonial civil services, factory and medical inspectorates, associations of workers and employers, and the individuals composing them, ministers, deputies, civil servants, employers and workers, had all their appointed place and function.[8]

If the conception was shapeless, it was nevertheless that of a pluralism wholly consonant with the Functional creed. But here is where the difference from the drafters of Part XIII becomes apparent: Thomas, it seems, was not interested primarily in the legislative *output* of the ILO and gave little serious attention to the actual uniform standardization of labor conditions, though he paid it occasional lip service.[9] He thought of social democracy and worker rights as being introduced through the process of interaction generated at Geneva—"the collaboration itself," the *act* of research, debate, and voting.

This collaboration was conceived dialectically. Workers were the challengers seeking to penetrate the national environment and thereby transform the international scene. Employers opposed this trend, and governments tended to side with them, or at least to assess the process from a purely national vantage point. Hence, it was the duty of a dynamic ILO—in the person of the Director and the Office—to provide the necessary synthesis as a result of which employers and governments would accommodate themselves to the new order and share in it constructively. The ILO would advance the synthesis by always going out of its way to seek the participation of voluntary groups, to strengthen and even create them. The Office would maintain direct and continuing contact with unions at the *national* level through the system of ILO correspondents, and thus strengthen them against their dialectic opposites. Attachment to the kind of international competition in which labor cost factors were eliminated or held constant was merely a cover: the true aim of the ILO was to usher in universal social and industrial democracy.[10] The ILO would act as the coordinator and unifier of national trade unions, compel employers to deal with labor as equals, produce impeccable research and advice that would eliminate the possibility of anti-labor criticism, and seek to convert everyone to the need for social justice. The ILO, in short, would be the medium for organizing a global consensus on justice as well as be the agent for realizing it.

We thus have an organizational ideology based on Functional convictions and giving a central place to the role of bureaucratic leadership allied to one group of clients. What is the program implied by this commitment? Thomas was committed, without much discrimination, to any kind of new norms that would project labor into the polity and increase its share of the national product. He justified Conventions as eliminating competition based on labor cost differentials, when the simple humanitarian argument for social security, professional safety, protection of young workers, or weekly rest seemed insufficient to sway all clients.* But he conceived of Conventions—irrespective of their subject matter—as a means for saving the working population of newly industrializing nations from the anguish

---

* Henceforth the capital letters "C" and "R" will be used with reference to ILO conventions and recommendations, as distinguished from the conventions and recommendations of other international organizations.

and suffering of the epoch of the industrial revolution. Hence he held that such nations were obligated to ratify Conventions even if the Treaty was silent on the matter. Further, he argued that since social needs always take priority over purely economic considerations, underdevelopment and early industrialization could not be cited as excuses for not ratifying Conventions. He supported the cooperative movement, sought to include agricultural workers in ILO Conventions, and held that professional employees were entitled to benefit from them as well. In short, he sought to fashion the kind of program, by way of research leading to labor Conventions, that would include every conceivable kind of employee and economic pursuit, and thus transform an environment dominated by free-enterprise thinking.[11]

If we bear in mind the composition of the international environment at the beginning of the first phase of the ILO's history, this emphasis becomes entirely reasonable. In 1920, 67 per cent of the membership was European, 70 per cent possessed democratic political institutions, 48 per cent were either mature industrial nations or on the road to rapid industrial development, and 81 per cent possessed economic institutions stressing free enterprises; the 19 per cent that were beginning to introduce government regulation and welfare legislation were also the ones that already possessed mature industrial institutions. By 1930, however, a sharp change had set in. The European component had declined to 54 per cent, and the Latin American had risen to 27 per cent. Democracies accounted for only 46 per cent of the membership, totalitarian regimes for 8 per cent, and oligarchies for the remainder. The industrial and industrializing nations comprised only 34 per cent of the membership, and the underdeveloped countries now amounted to 49 per cent. Eighty-one per cent still professed free-enterprise institutions, 6 per cent had adopted corporatist ways, and the number of welfare-oriented regimes had shrunk to 13 per cent.[12] With the sharp decline in the type of environment that could reasonably be expected to be amenable to the Functional penetration Thomas had in mind, both ideology and program were rapidly becoming irrelevant after 1930.

To what extent did the clients permit Thomas and the Office to put such a program into actual operation? First, let it be said again, the bulk of ILO activity was confined to the drafting of labor Conventions and Recommendations, based on continuing research by the Office. By 1933, 40 Conventions had been completed. Only two of them (Nos. 11 and 29) dealt with the advancement of the position of labor in a pluralist society; five (Nos. 1, 5, 10, 14, and 33) dealt with maximum hours and protection of young workers in a sufficiently general manner to approach the aims of the ideology.[13] All the others were confined to very specific measures for selected segments of the labor force and thus clearly peripheral to the Thomas thesis. Since the record of unconditional ratification and implementation for the most important Conventions did not result in uniformity, the leadership saw itself compelled to follow the path of least resistance, i.e., to draft Conventions on very specialized topics appealing to a well-defined portion of the clientele in the major industrial nations. In short, subgoals soon became dominant over the general program. One ILO official explained this development by the need to cater to the governments and workers most active in and demanding of the ILO—in fact, the Western Europeans representing industrialized economies and polities already committed to increasing social justice—and by the desire to score immediate practical successes in an easily defined field. In so doing, the program came to stress higher standards on purely humanitarian grounds, and to separate social progress from economic development and stability. But the complexity of the topics selected for Conventions and the heterogeneity of the clientele nevertheless combined to reaffirm the leading role of the Director and the Office.[14]

The very eagerness of the leadership to transform the environment produced the unexpected consequence of reducing the ILO to a modest program. Yet the first phase of the ILO's history was also a period of consistent constitutional expansion into new fields, a trend that ran counter to the shrinking of a program likely to influence international integration. This expansion was least successful with respect to migrant workers and civil servants. Although the Office claimed competence to deal with civil servants and drafted some Conventions to allow for this interpretation, actually little use was made of such provisions by prospective clients. Ingenious arguments were advanced holding that any person seeking work in another country qualified as a "worker," and hence was entitled to the protection of ILO Conventions when seeking work, aboard ship, and upon arriving in his new domicile. But even if this notion could be justified doctrinally, governments feared an extension of ILO competence into the delicate area of immigration policy, and even certain worker delegates showed similar fears. Consequently, apart from one unimportant Convention, no new powers accrued to ILO in these fields.[15]

If Britain and France, in 1918, thought that they were merely satisfying the demands of *industrial* workers, the 1920's soon demonstrated the naïveté of that assumption. First, several of the social security Conventions simply extended the benefits provided to the widows and orphaned children of workers. No challenge arose. Four other cases, however, required prolonged discussion in ILO organs and advisory opinions from the Permanent Court of International Justice before the extension of competence was confirmed.[16] In 1921 the Conference wished to inquire into the "condition of *agricultural* labor," a desire challenged by a number of European governments and agricultural associations as going beyond the intent of Part XIII of the Treaty. The Court upheld the Office interpretation, declaring that the Treaty was "comprehensive" and had to be read

in its entirety—including the generously drawn Preamble![17] Further, the
Office was free to determine the political opportuneness of intervention,
since this was irrelevant for interpreting the text. At the same time, Venezuela demanded that the Office launch an inquiry into "the organization
and development of agricultural production," i.e., concern itself with an
economic rather than a social welfare issue. France challenged this demand
as implying ILO penetration into "production." Thomas granted that the
ILO had no such powers, but ingeniously pointed to the continuity between matters of economic and social concern and the impossibility of
drawing artificial lines. Again, the Court agreed with him in general terms
and affirmed the ILO's power to make studies and inquiries spilling over
into production if they resulted from genuine matters of social reform,
even though it denied the competence of the Office in the specific case.[18]
British master bakers, claiming that they were *self-employed*, objected to
having to adjust their working hours to the ILO Hours Convention; but
the Court once more ruled that the Treaty applied comprehensively to all
types of work, and that no particular social philosophy, not even individualism, could be taken into account in interpreting the Treaty. The ILO was
not the prisoner of any doctrine, either with respect to defining principles
or with regard to implementing them.[19] Finally, the same ruling was handed
down once more when Britain sought to remove *supervisory employees*
from the purview of the Convention regulating women's night work.[20]

When Thomas died, then, the constitutional basis for a wide program
was indeed established, over the protests of employers and several important governments. But the industrial-democratic environment in which
the first phase of programming had evolved, and to which it was geared,
underwent a drastic change at that very time as the Great Depression and
fascism appeared in Europe.

ENVIRONMENT AND IDEOLOGY, 1933–43

Even before the death of Albert Thomas, significant changes had taken
place in the international environment, spurring a series of new demands
and leaving their mark on ILO ideology and program. In 1929 the Great
Depression struck the United States, soon to spread to Europe and eventually to most of the world; free enterprise capitalism was put on the defensive as the economics of Lord Keynes achieved the respectability of public
policy; politics was radicalized in formerly democratic member states with
the advent of fascist regimes, as it was infused with the first breath of anti-
colonial Marxism and Asian resentment. Statistically, the membership of
International Labor Conferences reflected these changes in the environment. European membership slipped from 55 per cent in 1935 to 46 per
cent in 1939; African-Asian membership had risen to 18 per cent by 1939
and Latin American to 28 per cent. By 1935, the democratic polities had

shrunk to 39 per cent, and the oligarchical to 43 per cent; the totalitarian had risen to 18 per cent.[21] Mature industrial systems, in 1935, accounted for 16 per cent of the membership, and rapidly industrializing countries for 29 per cent; mature agricultural systems declined to 12 per cent, and underdeveloped economies to 43 per cent. The most dramatic change is revealed in the economic institutions now becoming prevalent; free enterprise economies shrank to 63 per cent; social welfare economies accounted for 27 per cent of the membership in 1935, and 35 per cent in 1939.[22] Finally, the world political alignments now made themselves felt in that the membership reflected the rival alliances taking shape.

Now, according to a functional theory of organization, a changed environment can produce the very opportunity for programmatic revaluation that may lead to further international integration. On the other hand, if the opportunity is misunderstood by the leadership, or if the leadership neglects the appropriate alliances and coalitions, a changed environment can impose new restraints and lead to routinization. The principles on which the ILO was based postulate a separation between "social" and "economic" objectives, a distinction somewhat ambiguously reaffirmed by the 1922 advisory opinion of the International Court. Integration, in theory, could be advanced by minimizing the distinction in terms of practical programs, a course that would lead the Organization inconspicuously into the realm of economic intervention; a humanitarian social policy would lead—under the benevolent aegis of the Depression and its miseries—to welfare economics. Further, the simultaneous advent of regimes challenging the doctrine of pluralistic politics and trade union freedom might be conceived as opening up numerous interstices for international intervention, especially if linked with economic programs. Finally, the African and Asian demand for industrialization and rejection of imperial influence could be considered as reinforcing both of the other new opportunities. Combined with specific client demands for industrialization and democracy, general interest in alleviating the hardships of the Depression could cause, willy-nilly, a spilling over of ILO programs into socio-economic revolution.[23]

The ideology of Thomas, further, was a distinct spur to such a development. True to his conception that the role of the ILO was to strengthen the labor "thesis" in the direction of the global transformation of capitalism, he indeed attempted a sweeping revaluation of ILO ideology by casting the Organization in the part of initiating international structural reforms. In terms of program, he preached the new gospel by advocating the creation of a European employment service to encourage the migration of the unemployed to labor-deficit areas—especially when augmented unemployment insurance (which he also advocated) would prove inadequate to create new demand and thus spur production. Viewing the beggar-my-neighbor policies of the major industrial states after 1930, he sought to remedy the wrong by initiating large-scale projects for international public works, and thus apply the Keynesian medicine under ILO auspices. He singled out European railway, telegraph, and road construction as particularly appropriate here. Increased participation of voluntary groups would strengthen the democratic character of such ventures, and stepped-up research by the ILO would infuse them with the proper planning emphasis. Not unreasonably, Thomas invoked the sections of the Constitution stressing the comprehensive character of "social justice," as well as the decisions of the Permanent Court of International Justice, in seeking to catapult the ILO into the position of a global economic planning agency.[24]

This daring attempt at ideological revaluation had the firm support of the workers affiliated with the International Federation of Trade Unions, as far as the economic planning component was concerned. But these workers also stood for the reaffirmation of democracy against the suppression of trade union rights by the fascist states, and on this point the ILO gave them little solace. Thomas was unwilling to risk the wrath of the major governments by urging a clear political issue, and therefore recurrent majorities of government and employer delegates continued to seat "worker delegates" from fascist countries in ILO organs over the protests of the Workers' Group. The program, further, was clearly consonant with the domestic policies adopted in the thirties by the major Western member nations, and thus could be regarded as meeting domestic demands for welfare state measures. If Keynes was now the prophet enshrined at the national level, why could he not be used to strengthen the prescription internationally? In point of fact, however, employers never did see matters in this light and could not be relied upon as a client group supporting Thomas. More important, governments were quite content to continue beggar-my-neighbor policies in their international conduct (thus, incidentally, meeting certain employer and trade union demands at the national level) while practicing a species of planned welfare economy domestically.

The United States joined the ILO in 1934. Its demands and expectations are, in many respects, typical of the reaction of industrialized member states now rapidly developing a social consciousness. Domestically, the New Deal was committed to overcoming the Depression by the creation of new purchasing power and the enactment of social legislation.[25] But it was also committed, under the National Industrial Recovery Act, to avoiding competition and, in particular, to standardizing wages and hours throughout the nation in order to eliminate differentials in labor costs as an item in competition. Prior to the depression, labor and government had been indifferent to the ILO doctrine of standardization because it seemed to bear little relationship to the nature of American industrial capitalism and the political and economic ideology of the American Federation of Labor. The situation now, however, was sharply different: as Thomas moved away from the standardization doctrine toward an ideology of international countercyclical policies, the United States—for domestic economic reasons—embraced standardization! It did so with energy and consistency, pressing for the adoption of two general Conventions on working hours, and, when these failed to be widely ratified, for industry-by-industry technical conferences designed to impose the 40-hour week on selected industries. In addition, spirited American participation was responsible for the institutionalization by the ILO of regional conferences and technical tripartite meetings, a tactic that indicated the shift to piecemeal approaches to standardization when the method of frontal assault had failed.[26]

Moreover, American influence was manifested in other ways: upon the retirement of Director Harold Butler, the United States succeeded in getting the American John Winant elected as his successor.[27] Further, the introduction of new consultative techniques and the demand for more standard-setting did not produce any actual expansion of the program. To be sure, the American delegates lent their full support to the *study* of public works and of countercyclical investments; they were anxious to see studies and reports explaining the policies of other member states; and they contributed generously, through ILO publications, with information about the American experience. But they did not clamor for the initiation of international public works any more than the European governmental and employer delegates.

By 1938, therefore, the efforts of Thomas and Butler to revalue and expand ideology and program had not profited from the conversion of the United States to an earlier phase of the ILO approach; in fact American enthusiasm was matched less and less by the support of the older member nations. As war came closer and the uncertainty of the Western European governments with respect to the totalitarian regimes grew apparent, the worker members, in concert with the United States government, sought to convert the ILO into a dynamic successor to the obviously moribund League of Nations. Because of its commitment to social welfare and reform and because of its tripartite structure, this coalition of interests lauded the ILO as the only "democratic" international institution worthy of being saved and expanded, in contrast with the power-politics-tainted League. In terms of program, the United States and the workers now demanded ILO research on arms reduction, and discussion linking peace through arms reduction with social progress. In 1940 Roosevelt spoke of saving the ILO with United States and Latin American protection in order to retain a progressive liaison agency for all "democratic" nations.[28] On the basis of this kind of encouragement and unique support, Acting Director Edward Phelan, at the unofficial International Labor Conference of 1941, boldly claimed a new mandate, a "social mandate," for the Organization by demanding for it the task of coordinating all post-war plans for national reconstruction and social democracy.[29] If the Office and its Washington supporters had prevailed at that time, the original, partly concealed, Thomas ideology would have carried the day.

As it was, the Depression and reconstruction doctrine of Albert Thomas met more than one environmental challenge. It was not only that European governments and employers were indifferent to the ILO doctrine, which had belatedly received some support from the United States. The first stirrings of quite a different set of demands from non-Western underdeveloped sources were also noticeable, though hardly influential yet. During this period, the Indian workers progressively demanded the inclusion of agricultural labor in ILO standards and a larger ILO task with respect to agriculture generally. They called attention to the existence of forced labor in India and demanded international measures against it, including ILO investigations on the spot. They stressed the common lot of all workers in colonies as suffering from capitalist imperialism, and wanted the ILO to undertake special new tasks to undo colonialism. Housing and unemployment were suggested as specific topics for new international standards, and the first demands for rules against racial discrimination in employment were heard. More significant still, on certain issues the Indian worker and employer delegates spoke with one voice: they called attention to the neglect of Asia by the ILO; to the now familiar theme of unequal economic development and the special problems, with respect to labor standards, created by conditions of underdevelopment; and to the connection between the struggle for independence and the struggle for development.[30]

Organizational ideology, though exposed to the possibility of growth owing to the new environmental challenges and demands, did not succeed in infusing the Organization's program with a dramatic new task. The heterogeneity of the body of clients produced a program only slightly different from that of the preceding period. Yet it is also true that the very challenge of a drastically changed international environment did result in a revitalized Office which, more and more, assumed the role of the leader and executive, the initiator and promoter of policy. This was certainly true of Thomas and his utilization of the directorship; and he was not slow to seek to profit from the new environmental demands to expand the ILO program. Upon his death, Harold Butler attempted to follow in his footsteps, as did Edward Phelan after Winant's return to the United States government. In other words, successive executive leaders of the ILO took identical positions on the major ideological and constitutional questions, all in conformity with the functional postulates of integration.[31] In doing so, they sought to rely on the one client group that most nearly met the ideology of "Official Functionalism," with its depression-hardened demands for international unemployment relief and reform: the workers.

The problem of world unemployment was first taken up by the Governing

Body in 1930, which upon the demand of the workers created an Unemployment Committee. Subsequently it decided to have the Office study the problem and communicate its recommendations to other international conferences and meetings seeking to deal with the Depression. At the same time, Thomas kept up his pressure for the initiation of international public works, and had the Office do a series of independent studies on that topic. By 1934, the Governing Body had cautiously endorsed the idea, but in essence had confined itself to recommending to member governments the introduction of the 40-hour week and the abolition of overtime in order to mitigate unemployment.[32]

By 1932 the International Labor Conference had endorsed the idea of international public works; but the Governing Body confined itself to "examining" the plans submitted by the Office, and nothing was done about implementing the Conference resolution to encourage economic democracy by associating workers and employers with planning to spur mass consumption.[33] Various European and world economic conferences failed to halt the trend toward increasing national autarky, despite Governing Body and Office efforts to sell the gospel of international Keynesian planning to them. In 1936 the Governing Body agreed to let the Conference grapple seriously with the possibility of international public works, though at first merely stressing desirable identity of national policies and the exchange of information.[34] In its 1937 session, the Conference adopted two Recommendations that carried Keynes as far as he could be carried in the international arena, given the continued lack of enthusiasm on the part of most governments and employers. Recommendation 50 urged member governments to exchange information on public works, to cooperate with a new Governing Body Committee on Public Works in "studying" the information exchanged, and to plan new national public works on the basis of the studies and reports of the Office. Recommendation 51 sought to persuade all member governments to adopt, at the national level, the fiscal, administrative, monetary, and investment policies associated with vigorous pump-priming.[35] The scene seemed set for ILO task expansion—on paper—but the Governing Body Committee on Public Works found it impossible to meet until 1938, and thereafter it decided to confine its mission to collecting information submitted by member governments. By 1939 it had decided that its "reports should deal more particularly with the effect exercised by armament policy on public works of a non-military character."[36] This formulation might well serve as the epitaph forced by a hostile environment on Official Functionalism.

The Functional logic relies heavily on the use of dispassionate inquiries, based on value-free modes of research, to expose problems and lay the groundwork for eventual policy compromises. Experts, not politicians, are singled out as the agents for defining the limits for accommodation, preferably along lines of pure computation and problem-solving. In launching its ambitious series of studies and reports in the fields of unemployment and international public works, the ILO bureaucracy was acting wholly within the confines of this logic. It clearly succeeded in establishing its competence to invade the field of economics and to recommend policy going far beyond the social welfare considerations spelled out in the Constitution. Had it also succeeded in confirming the independence of its experts and the absolute reliability of their studies, it might have created a standard of substantive expertise that troubled governments might have found difficult to rebut and ignore.

The Office, however, was once more forced to stop short of this summit of autonomy by the nature of its clients. As Thomas and Butler staked out greater and greater claims for Office competence during the Depression, the Governing Body increasingly demanded a share in approving questionnaires before they were mailed out, in sampling the replies before they were used, and in considering the final reports before they were published. Several inquiries were stopped; others were deprived of their most telling points. Further, the major groups of clients were not at all convinced that truly independent experts were desirable, and they successfully exerted themselves in determining who would serve on expert commissions. Governments were agreed in obtaining persons unlikely to expose or embarrass them; employers—often hostile to the ILO program—insisted on having their spokesmen included; and the dominant worker faction, the IFTU, was most anxious to exclude smaller and hostile trade union movements from having a voice in research. Hence the experts chosen to conduct research, and thereby propose policy, were selected on the basis of political compromises that tended to obscure the independence of research.[37] The possible integrative role of "pure" research was contaminated by the tensions in the international environment, and the autonomy of the Office was thus restricted.

And so the great effort at ideological and programmatic revaluation failed. During the period under review, 27 new Conventions were adopted. Six of them merely revised older instruments, and fifteen dealt with very specific conditions in narrowly defined industries; three took a first step in the direction of protecting the human rights of colonial workers,[38] and three more sought to create fundamental new industrial conditions meeting the ideological challenge of the Depression.[39] The bulk of the legislative program, therefore, did not reflect the effort at revaluation, though the colonial aspect was to receive greater attention at a later time. Further, the rate of ratification slowed down considerably during this period, since member states cited the Depression as a reason for delaying the progress of standardization!

It is an interesting and functionally instructive paradox that it was the war—the very condition, according to its ideology, the ILO was to have averted—which furnished the occasion for the next and even more dramatic effort at revaluation. After 1939 the ILO increasingly came under the protection of the United States. As political participation by most governments and all European voluntary groups sharply declined, the Office—under the leadership of Phelan, now ensconced in exile in Montreal—found a clear field for the doctrine of a global social reconstruction mandate, a doctrine first openly argued in 1941. As long as the governments were fighting a war for survival and the League of Nations had gone into eclipse, the ILO had no competing interests and no rival bureaucracy to worry about. It was in this context that the bold new claim for functional expansion was made.

THE BID TO REVALUE THE PROGRAM:
THE PHILADELPHIA DECLARATION

Exile and war, combined with the sponsorship of the American New Deal, led to the most comprehensive effort at ideological and programmatic revaluation attempted by the ILO. The formal culmination of this effort is the Declaration of Philadelphia, adopted by the 26th International Labor Conference in 1944 and subsequently incorporated as the central article of faith in the amended ILO Constitution. What does this document proclaim?

It affirms that labor is not a commodity, that freedom of expression and of association are essential to sustained progress, that poverty anywhere constitutes a danger to prosperity everywhere, and that an unceasing war against want must be carried out through concerted international and national efforts based on free and democratic discussion among representatives of governments, employers, and workers. This much of the declaration reaffirms in stronger terms what had already been established in 1919. But the ILO was to strike out in two new and clearly marked directions in drawing on its original ideology: the primacy of human rights in the context of social policy, and the need for international economic planning.

The emphasis on human rights took the form of asserting that "all human beings, irrespective of race, creed or sex, have the right to pursue both their material well-being and their spiritual development in conditions of freedom and dignity, of economic security and equal opportunity"; moreover, "the attainment of the conditions in which this shall be possible must constitute the central aim of national and international policy."[40] Elaborating this principle, the Philadelphia Declaration lays down ten specific programmatic points aimed at realizing, in the field of social policy considered very broadly, the conditions held relevant. In so doing, the ILO membership reinserted or strengthened the very points that had been slighted in 1919, adding a sweeping assertion in favor of policies of full employment. It is of the greatest ideological significance that *economic* need, unequal conditions of international competition, and the prevention of war are no longer cited as justification for this program: elementary human rights provide the only justification.

More significant from the viewpoint of organizational analysis is the emphasis on economic planning. The Philadelphia Declaration asserts that "all national and international policies and measures, in particular those of an economic and financial character," should be judged in the light of their contribution to the attainment of the above conditions and should be accepted *only* if they contribute to that attainment. To cap the bid for leadership in post-war international economic planning, we read:

It is the responsibility of the International Labor Organization to examine and consider all international economic and financial policies and measures in the light of this fundamental objective; in discharging the tasks entrusted to it the International Labor Organization, having considered all relevant economic and financial factors, may include in its decisions and recommendations any provisions which it considers appropriate.[41]

These responsibilities the ILO would be willing to share with other international organizations; but they should extend to measures to expand production and consumption, to deal with economic fluctuations, to contribute to economic development, and to establish commodity price stabilization.

If the Philadelphia Declaration had been taken literally by those who voted for it, the ILO would have developed into the master agency among the emerging family of functional international bodies; it would have taken the place intended for the United Nations Economic and Social Council—though not in fact attained—by some of the drafters of the Charter. What pressures and demands were responsible for this remarkable document? The backbone of the demands was furnished by the now familiar alliance of Western trade unions with the exiled Office. As in 1918, trade unions in the Allied nations argued that the victory over Nazism was hollow unless it included new international measures in favor of social justice. Many of the Allied governments had committed themselves during the war to follow policies of full employment and planned expansion or development once peace was restored. The government of Australia, for example, consistently argued that, in post-war planning, policies of full employment should set the tone for everything else. One consequence of the Labor Party's participation in the wartime British coalition government was a similar sweeping commitment to trade unions in the United Kingdom. The United States government contributed to the cause. President Roosevelt, in addressing delegates to the 1944 Conference, stressed the role of the ILO as the supreme world body dealing with labor standards, and added: "But more than that, it [the ILO] must be the agency for *decision* and for *action* on those economic and social matters related to the welfare of working people which are practical for industry and designed to enhance the opportunities for a good life for peoples the world over."[42]

Labor and certain governments thus came to the aid of the beleaguered Office, which was then battling the major fear of any organization: that important new tasks would be entrusted to new organizations. The projected UN was viewed as a dangerous rival in 1943 and 1944. The Office desperately sought to develop a sweeping program that would preempt the entire field of social and economic policy. This stance was encouraged by Western trade unions, who felt that the ILO had been the only successful portion of the League of Nations, and by many governments who were convinced that the Office was the world's foremost collection of technical experts on social policy questions. Both opinions, therefore, strongly favored an ILO that would be independent of an unproved general international organization, and supreme in its own rather sweeping field.

In the cruel light of history, this vision seems ill-designed to accord with the environment in which Official Functionalism put forth its claims. It is important, therefore, to keep in mind a variety of features which, in 1944, made the sweep of the Philadelphia Declaration quite defensible. The Office, we have reason to surmise, did not expect to attain everything it claimed. It did not expect the membership to endorse each of the sweeping assertions, and it did not anticipate the full implementation of everything the member governments did endorse. In short, making the widest possible claims was, in one sense, a bargaining gambit to assure some considerable slice of the post-war pie for the ILO. Further, in the spring of 1944, there was as yet no Dumbarton Oaks draft of the UN Charter and no Economic and Social Council; moreover, the Soviet Union—which was invited to attend the Philadelphia Conference but refused—was known to be unenthusiastic about the idea of providing the future UN with an economic and social organ. On the other hand, the Office was not alone in advocating and preparing ambitious post-war schemes based on a commitment to welfare: similar pressures were underway with respect to food production and commodity trade, international lending activity, and currency stabilization. In the absence of an overall plan for the organization of the post-war world, the Office could take courage from the prevalence of ambitious economic thinking and seek to profit from the competition among existing and nascent international agencies. The fact that the Philadelphia vision was not entirely crowned with success does not release us from the obligation to analyze the convergences that produced it.

Typical of the convergence of bureaucratic, trade union, and certain governmental aims was the British proposal for the creation of Industrial Committees within the ILO framework in 1945. These bodies were set up as international tripartite research and negotiating agents for specific industries. They were to be composed of the nations most concerned with the industry in question, in their capacity as *producers*; there was no provision for the representation of consuming nations. They were to do painstaking and continuous research on every aspect of labor and social policy in their respective sectors. But, more important, they were to make proposals for the regulation of wages, conditions of employment, and welfare arrangements for all the producer countries involved. They were to make "agreements of an international character not less effective than national collective agreements."[43] And, finally, they were to be allowed to participate in "the international organization of social and economic measures designed to secure stable prosperity and reasonable social standards in the industry concerned," and thus to be geared to world-wide economic planning.[44] If successful, these committees would combine the tasks of international collective bargaining with cartel-like production rules as far as the labor costs of normally competing nations were concerned.

The nature of convergences of inputs here illustrates the kinds of phenomena illuminated by a functional theory of organization. The nature of the national environment provided the motives for two groups of clients: trade unions and governments in industrialized, welfare-oriented countries. International collective bargaining and standardization of labor costs among competing producer nations would effectively factor out labor from competition, thus facilitating national policies of full employment and welfare services without endangering the loss of foreign markets. Britain, Australia, and the United States were able to subscribe to such a program without simultaneously having to favor an active economic planning function for the ILO: national planning could be made effective if the planners did not have to worry about foreign competition. But the major organizational need of the ILO leadership—survival in a new and potentially hostile environment—was also met by this program because it assured the ILO of a major and vital new role while opening up new channels, in the Committees, for acquiring more loyal clients in the environment. The generous social welfare doctrine of the Philadelphia Declaration, moreover, appeared to rest on a fairly wide consensual base if measured against the distribution of relevant attributes in the environment.[45]

If these were the environmental and organizational impulses favorable to task expansion, the doctrinal arguments adduced by the Office remain to be summarized. Little is left of the earlier insistence that social justice requires uniform international labor standards, and that the progress of labor eliminates a major cause of war. Economic policy, on the other hand, is treated as an indissoluble part of social policy; the relationship of both to war is a theme treated cursorily and almost incidentally.[46] Instead, certain fundamental human rights are adduced as justifying a much broader attack on poverty than the mandate granted the ILO in 1919. It is no longer sufficient merely to combat discrimination on the basis of sex or race, or to fight for better working conditions on the grounds of humanitarianism: economic insecurity and inequality of opportunity are the basic conditions that must be eliminated now. Put positively, economic security and equality of opportunity *are* the basic human rights that beget and define an international program.[47] Once the nations are committed to this principle by a solemn declaration, they have to grant the corollary principle that all national and international financial and economic policies must be scrutinized in order to assure their conformity with the objectives of economic security and equal opportunity—and the ILO would be best equipped of all international agencies to do the scrutinizing.

The document then goes on to enumerate specific economic policy fields to be so scrutinized: namely, policies of full employment, placing new industries so as to benefit the population, fitting jobs to human needs, regulating and aiding migration, assuring worker participation in economic planning, and stimulating collective bargaining. In addition, the document urges the continuation of the more specific policies of dealing with well-defined welfare issues that formed the bulk of the ILO program before the war. But, again, the justification for dealing with the health of mothers and children, or with safety in mines, is no longer mere humanitarianism or the need to assure equitable competitive conditions; it is a matter of elementary human rights. Hence all aspects of economics—such as resource allocation, monetary stabilization, commodity controls, investment planning, and productivity programs—must be dealt with by the ILO in order to make the attainment of the more elementary rights a possibility. Jurisdiction over all economics is legitimated, in effect, by putting forth a sweeping human rights doctrine. Commitment to these principles, the Office argued, would not require the drafting of a convention to be specially ratified, as long as a "solemn declaration" were adopted and incorporated into the peace settlement.[48] Experience, relations with other international bodies, and, above all, the Organization's unique tripartite structure that assures democracy, combine to make the ILO the logical agency for achieving the millennium.[49]

This reformulation of what was originally a rather simplistic social reformist creed is extraordinarily ingenious. The fact that it largely failed to be implemented, despite its unanimous endorsement in the terms of the Philadelphia Declaration, is due to a misjudgment of the nature and performance of the environmental forces on the part of the leadership, especially a misjudgment of the depth of the United States attachment to the ideas of comprehensive international planning.[50]

What is more immediately relevant, however, is the role that Official Functionalism played in the elaboration of the expanded program. We are dealing here with the explicit Functionalist assumptions made by the Office, with ascertaining how the Thomas ideology had evolved by 1944 to serve as an inspiration for new demands. This ideology is given to us in explicit form in an "unofficial" book by an ILO official.[51] The earlier emphasis on need and spontaneity, the reliance on natural forces, and the commitment to a piecemeal approach remain intact. "We explore a world task and a world opportunity, in which for the most part the coordination of national economic policies will be a happy maximum attainable at this stage of international relations."[52] Specialized agencies already created or inherited from the League of Nations, because they arose historically and in response to spontaneously experienced needs, are the proper channels for carrying out the world task: they understand their functions and should meet them. "What the General Assembly and the [Economic and Social] Council have to try to inject into international economic and social collaboration is the *simultaneous collaboration of the parts as a whole,* and the collaboration at the very inception of policy: simultaneity and incipiency of action are the twin factors of success in administrative coordination."[53]

Although the UN task remains confined to coordination, the nature of the need is nevertheless poignantly defined. Minimizing any direct relationship between welfare standards and the preservation of peace (a point on which Functionalists have always had difficulty making up their minds), Finer stresses that poverty anywhere threatens prosperity everywhere because of the essential unity of domestic and foreign trade. The network of economic interdependence has become an irrevocable commitment under prevailing welfare expectations.[54] The Functional task thus becomes one of affirming and maximizing the network in order to assure everybody's physical welfare. Specifically, Finer called for tariff reduction, exchange stability, freer migration, economic development, equal access to raw materials, the improvement of labor standards, the protection of the general interest in commodity agreements and cartels, the regulation of international communication facilities, the improvement of dietary standards, food distribution, and world health, and the creation of "better understanding among peoples of each other's way of life and special problems, so as to provide a sound basis for international cooperation."[55]

Not unexpectedly, the ILO's program is a large beneficiary of this creed. The establishment of labor standards remains in the forefront; but, interestingly, it is now argued that standards depend less on legislation than on industrial prosperity. Therefore a new task for the ILO must be to penetrate the whole area of industrial expansion by means of a cooperative program with the International Bank. Further, similar cooperation with other specialized agencies must give the ensemble the power to assure full employment everywhere, and thus to partake in the international coordination of national public works to provide countercyclical stimuli! A parallel expanded role for the ILO is suggested in the encouragement of migration and the protection of both the migrant and the working force in the new country. A larger ILO role in protecting the working population in dependent territories is suggested on the ground that this is implied by the Charter principles on trusteeship; but the need for such action is justified merely in terms of stimulating world trade by eliminating pockets of poverty.[56] In short, a Functional ideology still focused primarily on welfare considerations and tied to a presumed global consensus on the primacy of welfare, is the basis for putting forth a greatly expanded organizational program. This program was given legitimacy by the stress on the prior need for prosperity and democracy, all justified by the popular post-war emphasis on human rights.

THE BID TO REVALUE THE STRUCTURE:
CONSTITUTIONAL REVISION, 1945–46

But a Functionally legitimated new program still requires some kind of constitutional basis. Was the 1919 Constitution of the ILO adequate for the new task the Office put forward? The curiously muted answer provided by the ILO legal adviser is another faithful reflection of Official Functionalism. In a closely reasoned opinion submitted to the 26th Conference, the legal adviser, in effect, minimized the need for constitutional revision. The Constitution, he argued, "has acquired as the result of history and usage an existence distinct from that of the treaties in virtue of which it was originally brought into force."[57] Functions and competences have expanded naturally over the years, in response to needs and demands, a trend supported by the permissive decisions of the Permanent Court of International Justice. Because "the practice of the ILO has in general been based on a dynamic or functional approach to problems of constitutional interpretation," he hoped that, if this tradition continues, "the need for constitutional amendment as a method of constitutional development will be greatly reduced."[58] The great bulk of the new program, and its extension to new categories of clients, is implied in the evolving tradition of the Organization and requires no new overt legal sanction; because the Constitution "is not a strait waistcoat but the *skeleton of a living body*, the scope for further development without constitutional amendment is even greater."[59]

Yet there is one exception to this projection, so clearly based on the assumption of the immanent world community evolving from a consensus on practical tasks. Existing constitutional provisions *not* clearly favoring this continued evolution must be eliminated, on the assumption that a future world environment might impose a strict constructionist view on the living Constitution. Thus the leadership sought to institutionalize the tendency toward automatic expansion of the Organization.[60] To the Office this implied amendment of the 1919 text so as to buttress the autonomy of the

Organization and of the Office, and ease the amendment process itself.[61]

From the viewpoint of organization theory, the most important of these constitutional changes is the increase in ILO autonomy. This trend reflects, if read in conjunction with the organizational ideology advanced by the Office to justify it, an evolution in the action-oriented Functionalism of Mitrany, Thomas, and Jenks toward an appreciation of the sociological functionalism here advanced as a basis for a theory of international integration. The chief ideological innovation over the earlier period in the history of the ILO is not merely the substitution of a basic human rights concept for an earlier social reformism. It is the insistence on the importance of *structure* in organizational growth, the point so largely neglected by the Functionalist school of the Mitrany parentage. Constitutional revision advocating structural independence from, but regular access to, other international organizations indicates an appreciation of the importance of an institutionalized leadership that combines the advantage of legally sanctioned "office" with functionally determined "roles." A wholly autonomous Secretariat, with control over its own budget, with power to participate in the choice of new members and clients, with enhanced prestige flowing from legally recognized international civil service status, and with the authority to aid governments, represents such a step in institutionalization, in structure, instead of relying purely on the inherent logic of task-oriented action.

This conclusion is based on the actual constitutional changes considered important by the Office, which were subsequently accepted by governments, workers, and employers and incorporated into the 1946 text. They comprise the absolute divorce of the ILO from the League of Nations, with the consequent autonomy of the Organization as regards budget and membership. They also include the ability of the Governing Body itself to determine the states of "chief industrial importance," and the reaffirmation of the absolute independence of the international civil service. It should be added that these provisions were accepted by the membership almost without discussion as self-evidently desirable.[62]

The Office also urged that the amendment procedure itself be liberalized; but its adoption of the Functionalist doctrine was flexible enough to allow it to insist that even under the new procedure the amendment process would be so weighted as to give three of the major industrial powers a *de facto* veto. Phelan was even willing to extend this recognition so as to exempt powerful federal states from accepting *any* new obligations under the liberalized procedure. Although the Office had no difficulty in persuading governments and voluntary groups to accept the new procedure, it succeeded in doing so only after it withdrew its proposal to exempt the United States and after the major governments combined to defeat efforts by smaller states and some workers to eliminate the big-power veto.[63]

To this extent, then, the leadership succeeded in equipping itself with the freedom it felt it required in order to realize the Philadelphia program. But viewed from another perspective the victory is quite hollow. In the first place, while the Office succeeded, without encountering opposition, in having the Philadelphia program inserted verbatim as an Annex into the new Constitution, the leadership at the same time tended to weaken its new autonomy by itself suggesting the revision of the old constitutional provisions dealing with investigations and sanctions.[64] More important, however, the leadership essentially failed in persuading the emergent United Nations to cast the ILO in the central role envisaged in the Philadelphia program. The San Francisco Conference was in session as the Governing Body began to grapple with the issue of constitutional revision, a task hardly facilitated by the fact that the ILO had no notion of the extent of its future recognition by the United Nations. The Office doctrine had cast the ILO on a plane of equality with the United Nations, as the economic counterpart to a world political directorate, with other economic and social agencies subordinate to the ILO by virtue of the scrutiny function. The San Francisco Conference produced a scheme in which all economic agencies were equal, and all were to be subordinate to the Economic and Social Council. An ILO delegation that had been present in San Francisco reported back with fear and disappointment, which resulted in a decision of the Governing Body to seek an agreement with the United Nations confirming the autonomy of the ILO rather than its apotheosis.[65]

It is time we turned to the reverse side of the coin: quite apart from what the Office wished done in terms of program and constitution, what kinds of demands were put forth by the membership during this crucial period in the Organization's life? One major proposal was the demand championed by France, Belgium, and the Latin American workers to change the formula of tripartite representation, a demand defeated by the Office in alliance with most governments and employers.[66] Other claims not endorsed by the Office and not incorporated into the new Constitution, despite demands that this should be done, actually reflected deeply held convictions on the part of certain client groups and had direct repercussions with respect to the implementation of the Philadelphia program.

Thus most of the Latin American delegations, India, Australia, and Egypt inveighed against the continued overrepresentation of industrial Western states in major ILO organs, and wanted reforms introduced. They also argued for more ILO regional offices and conferences, and many advocated regional Conventions in addition. Further, the same nations, as well as Poland, pressed for the recognition of agriculture as a vital field for ILO activity, but cautioned against treating it in terms of codes and Conventions. Even though neither the Philadelphia discussions nor the deliberations of the various constitutional committees paid much attention to the future role of the ILO in rendering technical assistance, such demands began to be heard in 1945 from the spokesmen of underdeveloped countries. In contrast, representatives of employers, as well as the British and American workers and governments, began to voice the opinion that increased productivity was more important than higher legislative standards in raising worker welfare. Belgium stressed that the future program should encourage freedom of association, most Latin American workers called for direct and drastic ILO help to national unions in organizing and modernizing, Poland demanded ILO aid for national economic planning, and Mexico wanted the Philadelphia principles incorporated in national constitutions![67] Finally, many of the smaller underdeveloped countries sought to convince the Office of the utility of preparing a minimum code of labor standards of universal applicability, a suggestion bitterly opposed by workers from industrialized countries.

On all these issues the Office preference for implied powers and gradualism won the day over the advocates of "action." But on two additional points it lost: the constitutional provisions regarding the handling of Conventions and Recommendations were tightened, and new specific obligations were assumed by the colonial powers for their dependencies. Neither point had been recommended by the Office; in fact, the general tenor of those of the Office staff who participated in the discussions suggests that a crossing of legal *t*'s was not considered desirable. Both changes illustrate the way strongly held subgoals tended to penetrate into a normative and programmatic structure that the leadership sought to preempt; as such they deserve our attention.

By virtue of a greatly expanded Article 35 of the Constitution, the colonial member states assumed the obligation to apply Conventions to their possessions, to explain where and why a given Convention was not applicable, and to submit special reports on the progress of application. Further, in the event that a given possession was legally competent to deal with labor legislation itself, the colonial power assumed the obligation to communicate new texts to it and to submit declarations of acceptance on its behalf. Britain took the leading part in advocating this new body of norms; and it was also specifically requested by the Conference's Committee on Social Policy in Dependent Territories. It fitted in well with the general trend of British colonial welfare policy at the end of the war, and with the decisions of the conference that drafted the UN Charter. It should be added that the Indian worker and government delegations favored even stronger action, including the automatic appointment of a commission of inquiry to ascertain, on behalf of the ILO, whether a given territory should be exempted from the application of the Conventions.[68] With this support, the new obligations were accepted with little discussion and no dissent.

A variety of demands for changing the system of Conventions and Recommendations was heard during the two-year debate on constitutional amendments; but they all came from governments, workers, and employers, with the Office maintaining a discreet silence throughout.[69] Thus all American delegates tended to minimize the importance of Conventions and to suggest their de-emphasis. Greece, Mexico, Uruguay, Poland, and the New Zealand and Indian workers, by contrast, demanded fuller ILO powers for supervising the implementation of ratified Conventions.[70] A curious intermediate position was taken by the French and British employers, often supported by others. On the one hand, Messrs. Waline and Forbes Watson tended to argue that the Convention system did not work because states that vote lightly for the adoption of texts then neither ratify nor apply them, thus suggesting that Conventions *should* be ratified and that Recommendations *must* be applied.[71] But, on the other hand, the same gentlemen suggested various ways of watering down the content and universality of the Conventions while compelling governments who voted in the affirmative to ratify them. It is thus not entirely clear whether, by demanding tighter obligations with respect to ratifying texts, submitting them to the competent national authorities, and reporting on implementation or the reasons for non-ratification, the employers wished to strengthen or discredit the system.[72] In any event, enough workers and governments, almost certainly for reasons quite opposed to those of the employers, supported enough of these suggestions to result in the new obligations of Articles 19 and 23. They were submitted to the Conference Delegation, not as a result of an Office initiative, but as a consequence of a report of the Committee on the Application of Conventions of the 29th Conference.[73]

An especially delicate point was involved with respect to the obligations of federal states. Under the 1919 Constitution, federations were obligated to nothing: they were free to treat Conventions as if they were Recommendations. This happy state of affairs, of course, was due to the reluctance of the American delegation at Paris to commit itself to any binding norms. However, it aroused the impatience of most worker delegations, and it particularly annoyed Forbes Watson. More important, the Canadian government suggested that federal states re-examine their constitutional abilities to handle labor matters, and the Canadian workers proposed that provincial officials be henceforth included in delegations going to ILO meetings.[74] In 1945, Phelan very cautiously endorsed these suggestions, and proposed the three-point amendment eventually adopted by the Conference Committee on the Application of Conventions.[75] Federal states were to treat Conventions as must all member states in fields in which they have the proper competence; but they were to refer other texts to the authorities of the constituent units, as well as to worker and employer organizations, with the obligation to report on their progress. The United States agreed to this formula as harmless and consistent with actual federal practice. It became the basis for the suggestions of the Conference Delegation, eventually finding its way into the new Constitution.

Thus, except for the world economic planning role claimed in 1944, the leadership succeeded in all its major undertakings. It espoused and carried to victory an ambitious new program, and it succeeded in obtaining a permissive new Constitution confirming its autonomy. It fought off a series of very specific demands that might already then have punctuated subgoal dominance and the subordination of general standards to specific aims. While it had not sought an extension of organizational competence with respect to the system of Conventions, the fact that it had to accommodate itself to such demands from its clients can hardly be considered a defeat. Moreover, it frustrated both the attempts of some governments to subordinate the Office to the Governing Body and the efforts of employers to force a tripartite pattern on its staff. The leadership was able to profit from the very deep sense of commitment experienced by civil servants, trade unionists, and employers associated with ILO meetings since the twenties to weather the various challenges to its existence. A unique organizational style of negotiation and bargaining that had evolved since 1919 survived, largely because the officials who had been engaged in it felt wedded to its survival. All this, however, did not prevent the ILO from following a course very different from the one that had been charted in Philadelphia.

THE BID THAT FAILED: ENVIRONMENT AND PROGRAM, 1946–48

The actual work of the ILO during the immediate post-war years was concentrated on an intensified continuation of the drafting of labor Conventions. Between 1946 and 1948, no less than twenty-three new Conventions were completed; some of them had long been in preparation, completion having been interrupted by the war years. Did these Conventions reflect the spirit of the Philadelphia Declaration? A brief survey will show that the bulk did not.

Thus nine of the new Conventions dealt with maritime matters exclusively, the results of the 28th Session of the Conference (Seattle); four of these had not entered into force by 1963, and the remaining five were poorly ratified.[76] Five new Conventions dealt with labor conditions in dependent territories, and some of them sought to establish a sweeping set of new rights for indigenous populations.[77] Five additional instruments continued the pre-war work of seeking to establish higher welfare standards for specific segments of the working population, but they also contained rules applicable everywhere.[78] One Convention amended the ILO Constitution, and another sought to standardize national employment service administration.[79] Only two post-war Conventions clearly reflected the pioneering spirit of the Philadelphia Declaration, the instruments dealing with labor inspectorates and with freedom of association; only in these is the new emphasis on the primacy of human rights over piecemeal social reform clearly expressed.[80]

The great bulk of the output reflects not so much a general dedication to universal rights as the continuation of a programmatic emphasis that corresponds to the wishes of specific groups of clients, i.e. marked subgoal dominance. The new emphasis on labor standards in colonial territories, to be sure, is a response to Latin American, Indian, Egyptian, and European socialist demands. As such it does correspond to the marked non-European breeze that swept through the Philadelphia discussions; but the content of the texts remains subgoal-oriented just the same, even if a new group of clients happened to be the beneficiary. These same clients, almost all delegates from underdeveloped countries, continued to ask for certain programmatic points that were *not* yet reflected in the output: demands for technical assistance were heard more and more; the agricultural sector was to receive more attention; productivity increases rather than legislative changes in welfare standards were now advanced as arguments by some Asian employers. With respect to the issue of human rights, the Indian workers after 1947 were not slow to attack their own government's Preventive Detention Act as a violation of the ILO Constitution.[81]

Of global planning there was hardly a trace. The future of a harmoniously coordinated world economy was held in limbo as the negotiations for an International Trade Organization dragged on, only to end in failure. In the councils of the International Bank and the International Monetary Fund—the agencies with power to shape a world economic policy—the emphasis was simply on the speedy restoration of a pre-Depression pattern of a maximum of free trade. Discussion of global economic trends and policies in the UN Economic and Social Council soon proved to be as sterile as the negotiations for an ITO. The ILO's scrutiny function was the victim of this trend, as was the FAO's attempt to deal dramatically with the twin issues of commodity surpluses and famine. Instead, the ILO in these years followed the general world pattern of lending its support to an intensified discussion of social and economic issues at the regional level, thus again meeting the special demands of several groups of clients.*

The protection of human rights, then, can be considered the only point

---

* There is a certain chilling contemporary parallel to this story. In 1944, Functionalists felt certain that the presumed internationally shared goal of post-war reconstruction, full employment, and orderly international trade *compelled* an international program of economic planning, even if the national officials in the chief decision-making positions were not ideologically committed to such a stance. A "situation" was held sufficient to bring about a certain pattern of conduct even in the absence of clearly articulated, identical national ideologies or commitment to a specific constitutional structure. The preoccupation of the European industrial states with *nationally* planned reconstruction, linked with the reassertion of anti-planning views in the United States, combined to defeat this grand design. In other words, this species of Functionalist logic was insufficient to encompass the total scope of demands and aspirations emanating from the international environment.

We may be running the same danger now, with the focus having been shifted to globally planned disarmament. In 1962 a report was issued by a group of United Nations experts advocating cutbacks in arms production adjusted and geared so as to avoid hardship and unemployment. This is presented as a technical problem in international economic plan-of the Philadelphia program that meaningfully reshaped the doctrine and ideology of the Organization in these years. Yet official ILO statements stoutly maintain that everything which happened since 1944 is consonant with the Philadelphia program, which is said to inspire and guide all action. The continuation of subgoal-dominated standard-setting is justified because it now extends over a broader scope of concerns, and embraces new categories of workers and of welfare issues. But the yardstick of the achievement is still provided, according to the Office argument, by the texts of Conventions and Recommendations, and by the intensified supervision and follow-up procedures incorporated in the new Constitution. The Office, in short, sought to have its cake and eat it, too: it followed essentially the same policy as before the war, but it justified its dependence on the goals of disparate clients by invoking the hallowed words of Philadelphia, by continuing to pretend that there was an essential connection between the continuation of social reform policies and dedication to human rights on the one hand, and the cementing of world peace on the other.[82]

It is therefore ironic that the success of the ILO in the field of human rights can be attributed less to the adequacy of the Philadelphia Doctrine than to the very condition the program was to have averted: the Cold War. Jenks, in line with Official Functionalism, rightly argued that the standardized advancement of human rights constitutes one of the most promising of functional tasks—if only a modicum of international political and military security can be assured first! But he wants the best of all worlds. He stresses that "there is nothing in the diversity of the legal traditions out of which a universal law of nations must be built which makes the concept of a universal law of civil liberties unreasonable"; yet he also feels that progress can be made on the basis of continuing confrontations of specific occupations and groups in the kind of forum provided by the ILO.[83] As we shall show later, the ILO's success in this field is due less to the legal substructures and political aspirations common to all nations and groups than to specifically channeled hostilities in which the aspirations of certain governments happened to converge with those of voluntary groups. Consequences unintended by both Functionalists and governments somehow appear as more significant causative agents than the claims of Official Functionalism.

---

ning. A new "situation," a very specific "need" on which all can agree presumably, can give rise to the planning structure required. In view of the experience of the ILO, can we expect subgoal dominance here to be excluded in favor of a truly grand design? The mechanism of unintended consequences did not suceed in ushering in a greatly magnified task in 1944; it is unlikely that the same mechanism could now be expected to go unnoticed by hawk-eyed officials in communist, neutralist, and unrepentant capitalist capitals.

7. *Organizational Ideology, 1948–63*

Since 1948 the Director-General of the ILO has been David A. Morse. An American labor and industrial relations specialist, and Assistant Secretary of Labor in the Truman Administration, Morse had not been identified with the Functional mode of thought. Nor was he known as an advocate of international integration by way of standardization. Instead, his name has become linked with an approach to international labor problems that stresses technical assistance, education, and promotional activities in preference to legislative action.

The environmental forces that fathered the new emphasis will be sketched in a moment. First, however, it must be stressed that Morse's approach is as firmly anchored in a conception of "situation" and of "need" as the earlier Functionalism. The source of the need is the impact of technology on society, and the desirability of securing human adaptation with a minimum of social strain. Thus we find emphasis on the emerging relationship between an unchecked population explosion on the one hand, and the need for planning employment opportunities for burgeoning nations on the other. We find stress on productivity programs designed to minimize the impact of alien ways of life, to increase production by adapting and shaping indigenous ways, and to obviate the introduction of possibly unnecessary machinery. Labor-management relations can be regarded as a forum to modernize underdeveloped societies by means of special modes of discussion and conciliation, instead of being viewed merely as an institutionalized confrontation of interest groups. Automation and the growth of synthetics create trade and employment problems that could be met by new forms of industrial and agricultural retraining. Industrialization may generate the need for rearranging the trade patterns of the older and wealthier nations.

And all this, adds Morse, is what constitutes the real challenge to the future program of the ILO.

We have sketched the leadership's programmatic thinking in order to stress the difference in emphasis over the earlier periods. Although the new Director-General was undoubtedly motivated to move into novel directions by his own convictions and those of the United States government, the programmatic revaluation did correspond to vigorous new environmental pressures that confronted the ILO after 1948. The membership was distributed as follows during these years, expressed in per cent (rounding error of ±1 per cent):

Characteristic	1950	1962	Characteristic	1950	1962
Location			Economic Development		
Europe	39	32	Mature industrial	20	17
North America	5	2	Rapidly industrial-		
Latin America	20	14	izing	25	23
Australasia	5	2	Mature agricultural	11	5
Asia	27	20	Underdeveloped	44	55
Africa	4	30	Economic Institutions		
Political System			Free enterprise	41	48*
Democratic	64	39	Social welfare	50	32
Oligarchic	27	39	Communist	0	12
Totalitarian	10	22	Corporatist	10	8

The great influx of non-Western, underdeveloped nations seeking rapid modernization provided an enormous pressure for the initiation of massive ILO technical assistance programs. Further, owing to the ambivalence of most of the new members with respect to the categories of social welfare and political democracy long accepted by the older European members, there was a marked de-emphasis on the drafting of additional Conventions: the new countries were more interested in productivity and manpower-training programs than in the rights of the working man. Still further, the continuing reservation of most employers with respect to Conventions also made itself felt, especially since many elements in the older trade union movements now began to evince a strong interest in long-range social and technological problems. The influx of non-European states now provided the environmental stimulus for putting into practice demands heard for years, such as the institutionalization by the ILO of regional meetings, committees, and offices, as well as consistent attention to the problems of agricultural modernization, thus further derogating from the earlier central role of the International Labor Code.

* This category includes a number of former French African territories that are not in principle committed to free enterprise, but whose actual economic institutions and policies cannot be characterized as anything very definite. The same is true of some Latin American and North African countries.

Moreover, the most recent period of the ILO is the period of the Cold War. This implied, before 1954, an attempt on the part of Western trade unionists and governments to exploit the ILO machinery in order to embarrass the Communist bloc over the lack of freedom for labor. The stress on Conventions and Recommendations dealing with larger human rights dates from this concern. After the return of the Soviet bloc nations to the ILO in 1954, this debate took an even sharper turn as the communist delegations retaliated in kind by seeking to exploit the ILO machinery as part of their ideological campaign against the West. With the admission of scores of non-Western and non-aligned states since 1955, both Cold War contestants increasingly turned to these new elements for support, and in turn had to support their new demands in areas of industrial concern not previously part of the ILO ideology. The setting was one of proliferation of program demands, begetting an intensified bargaining process for translation into organizational outputs.

This was the context in which Morse sought to "sell" his new emphasis; it was sufficiently unstructured and heterogeneous to give him a good deal of room for maneuver, especially since the possibilities for special pay-offs to client groups remained part of the picture: technical assistance funds were now augmented through ILO participation in the United Nations Technical Assistance Board, occasional Conventions could still be drafted, and the Industrial Committees provided a forum for very specific confrontations among the representatives of certain industries dealing with very specialized concerns.

No simple ideology of "peace through social reform" or "our commitment to universal human rights demands a comprehensive economic program" could do justice to these complex and contradictory environmental pressures. Moreover, the articulation of an ideology had to take place within the constraining vise of recurrent crisis. It was more than a matter of pleasing new member nations that shared the earlier Functional consensus only within sharp limits. Morse found it necessary to base his program on the support of an indispensable hard core of friendly nations, notably the United States. When American policy showed the effect of the negative sentiments of the business community, American employers acted as a precipitant of crises and a source of restraint. After the communist nations returned to Geneva, he faced the task of assuring the continuity of universal membership without seriously damaging the liberal and pluralistic values of Official Functionalism. He had to interest the Soviet Union in remaining a member without appearing unfaithful to the values of the trade union movement and the Western democracies. The preference for promotional programs over legislation and direct action is the natural formula for bridging these environmental chasms.

MIGRATION POLICY: THE LAST EFFORT AT PLANNING

Before the new Director-General could turn to programmatic revaluation, he had to deal with one inherited program. This was the coordination of world migration policy, one of the chief fields in which the Office sought to approximate the global task implied by the Philadelphia Declaration. The effort was a daring stab at acquiring for the ILO an "operational" program, going beyond standard-setting and research, to supplement the operations then being conducted by the United Nations Relief and Rehabilitation Administration and the International Refugee Organization. The failure of this final effort is instructive in itself as well as setting the scene for the subsequent programmatic revaluation of which Morse became the architect.

The program was launched by two meetings of the ILO's Permanent Migration Committee, an intergovernmental body with the task of discussing ways and means of encouraging the orderly overseas migration of persons anxious to resettle.[1] At these meetings it was decided to revise several older ILO Conventions dealing with migrant workers, and to aid other international agencies with research and advice in questions of resettlement. But, in addition, the hope was expressed "that the ILO would . . . receive exclusive jurisdiction in migration questions which concern workers in any permanent arrangement regarding divisions of work among the several agencies."[2] Discussions between the ILO and the UN then produced a consensus that no new organization should be established to deal with migration, but that the ILO should step up its general assistance to governments with respect to fitting migrant workers for easy resettlement.

Apparently not content with these modest developments, the government of Peru asked the Governing Body to take the initiative in a more ambitious operational program of encouraging European emigration. At its third (and final) meeting, the Permanent Migrations Committee empowered the Director-General to assume leadership in migration and to call a major conference designed to give the ILO new and active powers in this field. A preliminary conference was convened in May 1950, attended by most of the governments that had previously participated in the meetings of the Committee. They encouraged the ILO to draw up a comprehensive plan for organizing orderly migration, and gave the Office what appeared to be a free hand in defining this new opportunity for task expansion. The United States and Britain overtly supported this gesture, and the Organization for European Economic Cooperation offered the ILO almost a million dollars for carrying out an active operational policy.

The Office was not slow in seizing the opportunity. It prepared a plan calling for the establishment within the ILO of a Migration Administration that would "encompass the total European migration situation and reduce it to a short-term problem," and also "assist overseas countries to obtain the manpower and technical know-how desired for current economic and social development."[3] The Administration, while acting only upon governmental request, was to draw up migration plans, negotiate agreements between sending and receiving countries, select, train, inform, and transport migrants, raise and disburse funds for transportation, and give loans to migrants in order to enable them to establish themselves in the receiving country. It was estimated that the first year of operations would call for $25,000,000. The policies of the Migration Administration were to be supervised by a Council of interested governments. This ambitious proposal was then discussed by the 1951 Naples Conference on International Migration, which was attended by most of the countries that had so far participated in the ILO discussions, predominantly European senders of migrants and Latin American receivers.

Apparently as a result of a sudden *volte face* by the United States, the Conference proceeded to kill the proposal. The American rejection of the scheme resulted in decisions to study the matter further and to encourage the ILO to concentrate on technical assistance for migrants. A Consultative Council on European Migration was also to be created. When the governments were subsequently asked by the Director-General to define the functions of the Council and to participate in its work, the response was so lukewarm that it never came into existence. Instead, the same governments that had first encouraged the ILO venture into migration, almost immediately proceeded to establish the totally autonomous Intergovernmental Committee for European Migration, which, while never joining the United Nations system, acquired many of the powers and functions originally claimed for the ILO by the Office.

Yet the ILO was not the complete loser. The work of the period resulted in improved technical assistance techniques for aiding migrants and in a more extended definition of their rights in the International Labor Code. In terms of expanded tasks and powers, however, the ILO plan became a victim of the Cold War. The United States, as well as a number of other Western governments, refused to give the ILO jurisdiction over substantial additional funds and tasks involving direct access to individuals, because communist countries—Poland and Czechoslovakia—might have been among the beneficiaries and participants.[4] The enthusiasm of Australia, Britain, and the United States for a true international program remained intact from the earlier period; but they were unwilling to have it delegated to an organization in which the enemy might participate. Thus, although major ideological confrontations may lead to an upgrading of organizational powers in some tasks, the migration episode illustrates the limits of this thesis when the program involved calls for field operations and large funds.

OFFICIAL FUNCTIONALISM REVISED

The Morse revaluation has become known as the "promotional program." Far from evolving in a simple and consistent line in reaction to the limits and failures of earlier efforts at revaluation, the program grew by bits and pieces and continues to retain much of the earlier approach. It is our task now to summarize the thought pattern of the Director-General, the points he has come to consider important in his effort to make organizational leadership triumph over environmental heterogeneity, competing Functionalisms, and international crisis. The ensemble is less a finished ideology than single points of emphasis that remain to be tied together. Its acceptance into actual ILO policy will concern us later in this chapter.

The primordial needs of underdeveloped countries provide the first new point of emphasis, a point that Morse stressed immediately upon assuming office.[5] It was precisely at the same time that the United Nations inaugurated its Expanded Program for Technical Assistance, from which most of the ILO technical aid funds were derived. Economic development, in addition to the obvious dependence on capital and technical personnel, was also held to depend heavily on sound planning by national governments and on enthusiastic popular participation and understanding. Only thus can the necessary programs for manpower recruitment and training be made to succeed. To this extent Morse remains true to the earlier ILO doctrine in insisting on the necessity for establishing and strengthening voluntary groups.[6]

Further, this change of emphasis still sought refuge in a shadowy claim of helping to preserve peace:

No longer can the poverty, disease, ignorance and miserable conditions of life of the vast majority of the people of the world be hidden from view or from the spotlight of world political opinion. . . . It is discernible even to the most unenlightened that these are the ugly facts of life and that the rapid improvement of these conditions is essential to the elimination of internal national strain, to the easing of international tension, and to the promotion of world peace.[7]

Morse insists on continuous improvements in the standards of living of the people in process of industrialization. He emphasizes that it is essential that every step in industrialization be accompanied by a perceptible improvement in the workers' condition. However, he recognizes the basic conflict between this view and the principle of accelerated economic development. If gains of increased production were to be passed on to workers in the form of improvements in their standard of living, this would seriously diminish the savings or capital acquired for accelerated development. Hence Morse holds that large-scale capital investment is not the only route

to economic development. It can also be promoted by introducing new
methods of production that require little capital outlay. Efficient utilization
and better organization of existing capital resources can generate the surplus necessary for industrialization. Similarly, he believes that it is possible
to use surplus labor in underdeveloped countries for capital-building activities.[8]

His approach stresses the social aspects of reducing the frustration
present in economic development processes. He is greatly concerned with
the various economic and other forces that push the rural populations of
industrializing countries to seek employment in urban surroundings. He
advocates measures that provide fuller employment in rural communities,
and that give the rural populations a greater degree of security and an
improvement in their living standards, such as agrarian reform, cooperative societies, handicraft industries, and community development. However, social stability will not be established unless rural migrants to the
cities secure adequate housing, working conditions that maximize decent
human relations, and wholesome ways to pass their leisure time. If
labor Conventions are not adequate for dealing with such problems, ILO-
administered technical assistance might be.[9] And, among the various kinds
of technical assistance emphasized, none is more important in Morse's
thought than the encouragement of the productivity of labor, with the consequent stress on manpower-training programs. While Morse remains faithful enough to the old ideology by mentioning the importance of increasing
the workers' share of the national product in the form of more highly
developed social security systems, he still puts the main emphasis on raising living standards by increasing the overall size of the national product.[10]

It follows from the emphasis on underdeveloped regions that Morse
must devote much greater attention to the problems of agriculture. The
present concern for agriculture is manifest in the various forms of technical assistance that the Organization offers in order to raise the level of
village life.[11] Agricultural development rests on a convergence of the interests of Asian governments with the "promotional" component of Morse's
ideology; it is quite outside the traditional concerns of worker and employer delegates. The tripartite principle of organization does not apply
to organs charged with the agricultural program, and some workers even
oppose the program because it does not lead to legislative texts that can be
used for bargaining purposes at the national level.

An appeal to the social aspects of economic development as the basis for
a revalued ideology cannot very well rest on a notion of dialectical confrontation among clients. Under Morse, the employers are no longer the
"enemy." Management, because of its integral role in modern industry, is
now a legitimate part of the ILO approach. Industrial progress demands
collaboration among the chief social partners—not conflict. Hence stress

is now put on management development and better labor-management relations. In Morse's words:

Management and labor have a vital role to play in laying the basis for economic growth and social change. Moreover, as I have emphasized before, the relations between management and labor are a significant factor in transition towards industrialization and in the maintenance of social stability during the transition. These relations measure a country's capacity to absorb change. . . . If labor-management relations are poor, relationship throughout the social structure will be poor. If labor-management relations are good, this provides a solid practical foundation on which to build the new attitudes and institutions needed to keep pace with the dynamics of modern industry.[12]

And again:

If I were to express this new program emphasis in one word, that word would be "promotional." It differs from most other aspects of the ILO's work in this respect: it is dependent upon the force of education, persuasion and *promotion*. Its basic aim is to spread the idea of labor-management cooperation in ever-widening circles within each country through nationals of the country.[13]

This emphasis on labor-management relations is an integral part of Morse's broader concern for increasing productivity and the social product. It applies to the industrialized as well as to the underdeveloped member nation. But whereas in underdeveloped countries the ILO should be concerned with the various social, labor, and economic problems connected with economic development, in the industrialized countries its main emphasis is on social and labor problems arising from the impact of automation and other modern technological advances. Morse regards the fast pace of technical change and the difficulties arising from it as the major problems of the developed countries. These forces do not create overall unemployment. On the contrary, they may create new employment opportunities and new skill requirements. But since they also cause labor dislocation locally and nationally, they may in some instances create specific transitional problems of re-employment—whether in certain localities, or for certain groups of workers, or for certain individual workers. Hence these forces do pose the need for specific measures of social protection: for unemployment insurance and other forms of social security, and for all social assistance and services designed to protect the ordinary worker from hardship and to promote general community welfare.[14]

The challenge of world-wide technological change provides Morse with the major justification for legitimating and expanding the task of the ILO. Here and there, when he speaks of the challenge of employment problems, of management techniques, of labor-management relations that are as true to the principles of Vinoba Bhave as to Walter Reuther's or Léon Jouhaux's, or to the need for motivating modern youth, the Philadelphia principles come to the fore again. Morse claimed for the ILO the duty to alert governments to the dangers of technological unemployment and to prepare measures for mitigating it; this is an especially apt task for a United Nations agency, he says, because these technological issues occur in all types of economies and in all social and political systems. The stabilization of commodity prices and the regularized flow of investment of surplus capital from developed nations to Africa, Asia, and Latin America again show up as special tasks of the ILO, now in the context of conditioning the world to the challenge of technological upheavals.[15]

If it were not for the ILO's heritage of the liberal-pluralistic ideology, these points of emphasis would not require an interest in human rights. But, still true to the Philadelphia Doctrine, the ILO in recent years has shown increasing concern for the problem of fundamental human rights and freedoms. The Organization has sought to promote the extension of such rights and freedoms in all countries. It has concentrated its efforts on trade union rights, and on the elimination of forced labor and discrimination in employment and occupation.[16] Morse conceives of this broader problem of human rights in relation to the functions of the ILO as follows:

Freedom of association, equality of opportunity and respect for human personality are fundamental to the achievement of the ILO's other objectives of material welfare; and broader material welfare without these is a negation of all that ILO stands and works for. The promotion of human rights is therefore of the greatest concern to the ILO; and it is accordingly a matter of extreme importance for the ILO to consider in each instance how best it can exert its influence for the achievement in practice of wider respect for human rights.[17]

But he no longer claims this task as legitimating the total ILO program: "Action to promote respect for human rights is a *corollary* to the ILO's activities directed toward the improvement of the material circumstances of life and is of fundamental importance to the achievement of the organization's objectives as laid down in its Constitution."[18] It is predominantly in this area that Morse continues to rely on Conventions and Recommendations, which are so drastically downgraded in other aspects of his approach.

Clearly, the ILO under the leadership of Morse gave up any notion of transforming the world environment on the basis of a hierarchically arranged body of principles following the pattern of reformist Functionalism. The method of direct confrontation between the progressive challenger (labor) and the reluctant enemy (management) is minimized; the medium of legislative labor standards as the issue on which the confrontation can be brought about is reduced to a lower level of action. And thus instead of developing a universal network of new ties and loyalties by means of a functionally very specific *law*, the more elusive technique of discussion, education, and demonstration is advocated. As Morse himself said:

To put it bluntly, an implicit purpose of the early ILO was to prevent any country, and particularly the less industrialized countries, from entering into international trade competition on the basis of cheap labor standards . . . Now by contrast a very great part of our effort is directed towards enabling countries to develop their industries and particularly towards promoting economic expansion and social growth in the less developed countries. Nowadays we know that the importance of differences in labor costs as factors affecting international competition has been greatly exaggerated, that by and large the high labor cost countries have not encountered any special difficulties in selling their goods abroad.[19]

Therefore, the ILO has become "a means to promote the realization of *the practical social aims* of the different countries which now make up our membership."[20] In Morse's mind, the heterogeneity of the new environment begets, by necessity, a more diffuse task in which past sacrosanct principles of Official Functionalism are in effect questioned. Tripartism is no longer an organizational fetish; the Director-General declines to worry unduly over the issue of "voluntary" associations that result from political systems in which ILO standards of freedom of association are not fully implemented.

To the suggestion that the ILO is likely to lose its purpose and soul in the process of diffusing its ideology and program, Morse has this answer:

The ILO, as I see it, is an organization of people, a human organization working through and amongst people for the attainment of certain human goals. It is neither the embodiment of an absolute moral law revealed forty years ago and enshrined in the Constitution, nor is it a supra-national judicial authority empowered to enforce certain defined standards. The ILO works in the world as it finds it and it works in the world for the attainment of its purpose. This purpose . . . is the improvement of conditions of men and women throughout the world. The fact that this purpose has not been attained is the greatest argument for the continued existence of the ILO. To work effectively for its attainment the Organization must have the confidence and sympathy of all people in all countries and of none more than those who are the furthest from its goals. Principles, it seems to me, for the ILO should thus be a guide, an inspiration for action, and not a test of respectability.[21]

Let us note that these "principles" do not call for any very specific rules governing personal freedom; they are broad guides for securing greater freedom for all those who are trying to eliminate the causes of war. Thus, with the introduction of the "peace" theme, we can close the Functionalist circuit.

Morse's conception of peace and the role of the ILO in relation to peace is a watered-down version of the Thomas doctrine. The ILO is related to peace only in the sense that economic and social dissatisfaction is one cause of tension: "The conditions of poverty, disease, ignorance and injustice stunting the lives of millions today, the enslavement of other millions, the injustices which can result from too rapid industrialization and impersonal bureaucracy, the effects of war, petty nationalism . . . these are among the real threats to peace."[22] He therefore called for an attack on poverty, exploitation, and injustice wherever they exist. But in so doing he provided no more than a very fragile bridge between the Old Functionalism and the New. Organizational leadership must not only satisfy clients but inspire the staff as well. In order to grasp the impact of Morse's revised Functionalism, we must now turn to the degree to which the ILO program reflects it, and to the measure of unity that it lends to the Office.

Has Morse succeeded in drawing all clients into his wide web of aims? Has he succeeded in infusing his staff with the spirit of the new ideology and thereby reduced special understandings between select clients and divisions of the Office? We shall approach an answer by first sketching the role of the Director-General in program-making, and then outlining the program itself.

IDEOLOGICAL REVALUATION AND THE NEW PROGRAM

Neither all clients nor all segments of the staff have been firmly tied into the new web of non-hierarchical aims. Matters of freedom of association, trade union rights, and specific benefits to labor that can accrue by way of legal obligations remain in the forefront of the workers' demands. While they find their natural counterpart in the aims and arguments of the Labor Standards Division of the Office, these aims are *not* shared consistently by the technical divisions or by the new units created to advance Morse's "promotional" ideal. Nor are they shared by a consistent majority among the governments; and the employers continue to oppose standard-setting. New Conventions and Recommendations, therefore, almost invariably originate in the Office itself, and rely for support on a portion of its staff as well as on the workers. As for routine technical assistance operations within the purview of the United Nations Expanded Program or the Special Fund, these are the primary interest of the Office technical divisions and their specialists and of the governments of underdeveloped countries. However, they are not of central importance to Morse, the workers, or the older staff members of the Office. By contrast the promotional approach, with its aim of gearing the future ILO task to the challenge of technology and social issues, is of direct interest only to a segment of the Office close to Morse and to some governments, including the United States. Workers and employers are interested only in limited aspects of this work, and the technical specialists and labor standards staff remain to be convinced of the full legitimacy of the approach.

This being the situation, the Director-General arrives at his programmatic synthesis by a variety of routes, sometimes sidestepping the ideas of his staff and of the national trade unions on which earlier leaders tended to rely. Morse develops his proposals for a program largely on the basis of his continuous contacts with national governments and elite groups who are not necessarily consistently active participants in the work of the ILO. As these clients put their demands to him, he picks and chooses among them in terms of what he feels will be acceptable to majorities on the Governing Body and in the Conference. This process determines which topics the Office will propose for the agendas of the policy-making organs, which expert consultations will be held, and which preliminary reports will be prepared and circulated. Naturally, he exercises what influence he can in the selection of experts to draft preliminary proposals, and he attempts to co-opt influential national figures for such commissions in order to be assured of their support. In short, to the extent that his ability to maneuver among disparate clients permits this, the Director-General holds the initiative in program preparation and task expansion. In doing so, however, he consistently has to conciliate dissenting clients *and* staff members, and thus continues to include aspects of the earlier ILO doctrine in his program. But the bulk of the inspiration comes from governments and no longer from the workers.

The opportunities for an imaginative leadership would be immense if it were solely a question of maneuvering for support among disparate governments, and of appealing to them on the basis of an ideology that combines stress on economic development, social policy, technological adaptation, and certain basic human rights. If the leader could be assured of a staff solidly united on these programmatic points and inspired to feed them back into a representative decision-making structure that increasingly depends on the initiatives of the leader, his task would be much simpler. Such, however, is not the situation in the ILO. While it is true that the representative organs exercise less and less initiative in ideology and program-formulation, Morse has not yet succeeded in making his revision of Official Functionalism the dominating creed of his staff. What beliefs, then, do prevail among the various segments of the staff?

One segment of the Office retains strong links with the Functionalism of Thomas and Phelan. It remains faithful to the underlying Western values of pluralism, popular participation, and workers' rights that inspired the drafting of the International Labor Code. Far from denying the overwhelming importance of economic and social development and the necessity for technical assistance and cognate operational responsibilities, this segment of the Office feels that such activities should be geared to—if not subordinated to—the continuation of standard-setting. Among the specific programmatic points singled out by the older Functionalists, we find the insistence on broad human rights (especially freedom of association), absence of forced labor, non-discrimination, and equal rights for men and women. Stress is placed, too, on the encouragement of group participation in national economic planning or in policies for working out income guaranties. Labor-management relations, negotiation, conciliation, and collective bargaining are also emphasized. Finally, the older Functionalists insist on the need for maintaining close ties with the political-representative organs of the ILO. They want to advance on the liberal and pluralistic front by means of attracting and persuading the major client groups through the medium of the Conference and the Governing Body. They deplore the reverse technocratic emphasis that is sometimes associated with the technical and economic divisions of the Office.

This technocratic theme is the property of the segments of the Office that are preoccupied with rapid, dramatic, and unflinching economic development and modernization in Africa, Asia, and Latin America. They see the economic development doctrine of Morse's Functionalism as the key determinant of the whole program. Governed by a feeling of immense crisis and challenge, they would come close to scrapping most of Official Functionalism. They do not believe in the human rights program because it tends to interfere with national efforts at dramatic labor recruitment and human investment. Impressed with the need for rapid capital formation, they willingly subordinate social advancement to industrialization. Advocates of economic development are eager to cooperate with any national regime that is able to plan and administer effectively, and they therefore refrain from asking questions about democracy and pluralism. In terms of program, of course, these segments of the staff stress technical education, productivity measures, manpower recruitment and allocation, and such measures of encouraging popular support as appear necessary to sustain the drive for industrialization. Naturally, they are not particularly perturbed by the lack of intimate liaison with the ILO representative organs.

The program that has prevailed since the defeat of the last major measure to realize the Philadelphia Declaration is neither clear nor consistent. Morse's formula is obviously an attempt to straddle the two positions described. The program not only retains the concern with human rights, but continues to cater to the economic and social interests of the industrialized members, a commitment that the advocates of economic development would like to eliminate. In discussing the program, we shall follow the distinctions used by the Office with respect to available *means*: (1) the continuation of the preparation of an International Labor Code, (2) massive technical assistance and the research connected with it, and (3) the "promotional" program with respect to labor-management relations, management development, worker education, and labor studies.[23] As for fundamental *aims*, it was only in 1963 that a formal attempt at synthesis was made. For the bulk of the Morse period, the Office contented itself with noting that "the main objective will remain social progress, pursued in a climate of freedom, founded on increased productivity and directed toward higher standards of living."[24]

Conventions and Human Rights

The lack of emphasis placed upon new legislative texts under the Morse regime is evident from a brief look at the twenty-six new Conventions adopted since 1948. Of these, seven are merely revised versions of earlier specific subject-matter texts; eight are new texts establishing norms for specific industries and specific categories of workers, i.e. they are subgoal-oriented; one makes minor procedural changes; and the remaining ten deal with human rights generally, or at least with a substantial segment of the working force in many countries.[25] The ratification figures for this last category, the least subgoal-oriented texts, are the most impressive of the total record. Legal texts and institutionalized supervision dealing with human rights are particularly vital for the benefit of the working populations of dependent territories and for newly independent nations anxious to foster social development. But a word of caution is voiced by the Office even here. It is laudable that new nations should be concerned about freedom of association, "but their primary concern in this field is not so much to enact legislation as to set up the institutional framework which they lack, and without which it is not possible to give a practical content and effect to legislation."[26] Hence, in the long run, Conventions and their supervision by the ILO may be the most effective means of supplying information on actual conditions, which in turn can then be improved through the ILO educational program rather than through standard-setting itself.

The areas really singled out for effective treatment through legal standardization are fields that bear a minimal relationship to international integration. They include the establishment of a variety of health and safety codes for occupations that at present do not possess them. They also include a group of measures for improving rural welfare that correspond to the policy demands of certain Asian governments concerned over agricultural stagnation and unrest. In addition, and justified again by virtue of the appeal to human rights, many of the colonial and former colonial powers take great satisfaction in special texts seeking to protect indigenous and tribal groups from the inroads of forced industrialization, though it cannot be said that the new nations themselves are so concerned with this aim.[27]

It is equally important to review other fields that in the past have featured ILO standard-setting activities, but that are now downgraded. The Office feels that standardization measures in specific industries, as discussed in the Industrial Committees, have about exhausted their potential. There seems to be little that can be done to standardize hours, wages, and social security benefits by way of universal texts. Instead, regional meetings and texts, as well as intensified technical assistance operations, are now advocated as the proper technique for influencing these fields. Nor does the Office go out of its way to stress the complaint procedure available to aggrieved workers for safeguarding their rights to freedom of association and collective bargaining.[28] Instead, the Office seems to be associating itself with those governments and employer groups that cite underdevelopment as a reason for resisting the standard-setting procedure:

The fundamental balance between what economic development can afford and what social progress demands will largely depend on [employers' and workers'] sense of responsibility; shorter hours of work, equal remuneration, family allowances or old-age pensions are all elements of social progress, but only on the condition that the economic infrastructure is strong enough to carry them. Striking this balance is a difficult art, and it may well be that the Organization will increasingly be called upon to assist governments, employers and workers in assessing what advances can reasonably be achieved.[29]

Technical Assistance

What standard-setting loses technical assistance gains in the new program. Underdeveloped countries have first call on the services of the ILO; meeting their manpower, productivity, housing, and employment problems constitutes the Organization's primary task, particularly with respect to agricultural workers and the problems attendant on their moving to urban centers. Here the research and publication activities of the Office are of capital importance, as is the functioning of a variety of specialized information centers in Geneva. Help in creating cooperatives, rural handicrafts, and small-scale industries is part of the program. Manpower organization and vocational training will continue to receive the most attention, since 50 per cent of UN-financed technical assistance operations under ILO control have been devoted to this end. The organization of employment services, recreation centers, and services to migrant rural workers goes hand in hand with this concern. Administrative means and motivational incentives for increasing productivity will continue to preempt important ILO energies. Technical assistance and research will be geared increasingly to deal with the social consequences of technological change, particularly automation, the effective use of youth in the labor force, and the growth of the portion of the labor force employed in service occupations. Greater emphasis, too, will be given to the training of labor inspectors and administrators of other labor services.[30]

Yet the Office realizes that the emphasis on technical assistance, temporary though it presumably is, not only implies a drastic shift away from the earlier program in terms of techniques, but has important implications for the institutional and ideological character of the ILO. For it implies even more pronounced dependence on specific subgoals of certain clients, and minimizes the role of worker and employer organizations. Hence, "to a very large extent the operational activities of the ILO are not under the direct control of its constitutional governing organs, though the latter keep those activities under constant supervision."[31] Since the technical assistance specialists on permanent or temporary service with the Office are usually not deeply interested in the larger tradition and program of the Organization, a serious problem of staff cohesion is created, impeding the revaluation of ideology and program that an effective international organization requires.

When technical assistance acquires the relative permanence of a centralized approach and an institutionalized administrative framework aimed at a clientele that may be expected to associate with the program for a long time, it may become more relevant to international integration than the present ad hoc approach has allowed it to be. Such a refocusing of technical assistance comes very close to the "promotional" approach and sometimes begins to overlap with it. When this does occur, we must take it seriously as a possible item in task expansion advancing integration. An example of such a development may be furnished by the ILO's Center for Advanced Technical and Vocational Training, which commenced operations in 1963.[32] The Center caters to an elite in the economic development process: highly skilled workers, foremen, technical instructors, technicians, and senior management personnel. Trainees are not eligible unless they have already mastered the basic skills of their professions. Their attendance at the Center is intended to increase their technical skills in the design, use, and maintenance of machinery; to deepen their understanding of human and group relations, in the context of the development problems of their native countries as well as in management techniques; and to enable those of them who are instructors to improve their teaching techniques. With proper selection and indoctrination of trainees, it may be possible to avoid the extremes of subgoal dominance that normally characterize technical assistance operations.

The Promotional Program

"The educational approach," says the Office, "is a means of reaching ever widening circles of the population in the various countries, learning from them of their problems and needs and giving to them the services most appropriate for meeting them."[33] It is a permanent approach, more effective—it is hoped—than Conventions and Recommendations because it relies exclusively on persuasion, and less disruptive to the unity of the Organization than a large number of otherwise poorly coordinated technical assistance measures. Furthermore, it approximates the Functionalist creed because of its insistence on dealing directly with representatives of voluntary groups at the national level, "to facilitate the working out of solutions rather than to advocate particular policies or methods."[34] If successful, therefore, it could reknit the contacts and ties that might transform the international environment, contacts that were not measurably increased by the standard-setting program unsuccessfully revalued at Philadelphia and the technical assistance program bestowed on the ILO by the United Nations.

The promotional or educational approach advocates the creation of a climate of labor-management relations in which problems will be solved cooperatively, particularly the problems raised by rapid social and economic change and the social consequences of developing technology singled out by Morse. Although the Office insists on the need for a number of new institutions and programs it also emphasizes that the new approach can be advanced by utilizing such existing mechanisms as the Industrial Committees, the International Labor Conference, and a variety of regional committees and conferences. Whereas Conventions do not constitute an appropriate means of action, Recommendations sometimes do.[35] We shall deal with the promotional program by singling out the aspects stressed by Morse himself: the Management Development Program, Labor-Management Relations, Worker Education, and the Institute of Labor Studies.

The Management Development Program is a relatively modest affair initiated in 1958, adding only very slightly to what had been done for the preceding decade in the productivity field by way of technical assistance. Substantively, it covers productivity, supervisory training, and improvement in job performance. It relies primarily on the skills of management specialists in industrialized countries to teach their art in developing nations. The methods include technical assistance on the spot, as well as visits by management trainees of new countries to Management Centers in developed nations. One major procedural innovation is proposed that may hide an important substantive step: the ILO headquarters is to initiate research on the relationship between local economic and social structures and training needs for management specialists; this training would include the study of general economic planning and of welfare measures. Since this emphasis is to be coordinated with advice to governments on the setting up of management centers, it is at least conceivable that the new ILO ideology on social harmony and cooperative problem-solving will trickle into the minds of the trainees, and thus contribute to the changing of the national and international environments. Such is certainly the formal intent of the program.[36] Let it be added that Morse proposed this aspect of his educational approach partly in order to satisfy segments of the Employer Group, to demonstrate that it no longer constitutes the institutionalized "enemy" and that it is of interest to the governments of underdeveloped countries rather than to the workers. The American employers accepted the program only after they realized that it was not being used to teach "socialism" to managers from underdeveloped countries.

The ILO task might grow more dramatically if various initiatives for a new approach to labor-management relations bear fruit. Morse's thought on his preferred type of social harmony—peculiarly a product of the recent American collective bargaining and mediation experience—has already been exposed. In an effort to infuse the ILO with this attitude, the Office in 1956 commissioned David L. Cole, an American industrial relations specialist, to make appropriate proposals for international action. The Cole Report stresses the need for minimizing the loss of productivity through strikes and lockouts, and therefore advocates a general system of collective bargaining in which parties show self-restraint and an overwhelming appreciation for the interests of the community.[37] The Report professes the belief that adequate training in human relations will infuse the negotiating parties with reason and patience; if only they are given enough cold economic facts of a statistical nature, they will resolve their differences peacefully. Cole proposed that the ILO assume the task of furnishing these statistics, as well as circulating model collective agreements and the texts of important contracts previously negotiated. Thus he hopes to spare industrializing countries the strife and bitterness that accompanied the Industrial Revolution in the West.

The Office then convened a meeting of experts on industrial and human relations to consider the Cole Report further. After duly noting a wide range of differences between nations and industries with respect to collective bargaining, arbitration, and administrative regulation of wages, the experts more or less agreed to endorse the principles of the Cole Report and to urge the Office to expand its activities in line with Cole's recommendations.[38] Two years later the Conference adopted a resolution endorsing the same principles. It called on the Office to expand its research program so that it would include the kind of material Cole considered useful, to become a global center for information on collective bargaining, and to foster the creation of national and international institutes for training in labor-management relations. In addition, the normal technical assistance activities were to include training in improved industrial relations. The resolution was approved by the Governing Body, and the Office thereafter began to undertake the research requested, and to convene a series of bipartite technical meetings to consider the application of these principles. It also decided to refer the issue to a number of Industrial Committees.[39]

The present program of labor-management relations is the result of these consultations. In terms of relations with an important group of clients—the American business community—the procedure for launching the program was an example of successful penetration of the environment by means of co-optation. A doctrine acceptable to American employers was enshrined as a result of technical consultations with American specialists. In terms of substance, the program aims at making industrial managers conscious of their obligation to the community; it hopes to temper their interest in productivity with concern for satisfactory human relations in plants and offices.

Worker education constitutes the third formal promotional and educational program. In principle, it is designed for the workers of countries in which trade unions either do not exist or are still rudimentary, and it aims to teach them the basic skills of organizing, negotiating, and participating in economic planning. It hopes to make the workers effective partners in the process of administering economic development and running a developed industrial system. The Office produces a certain amount of instructional material for this purpose, but the actual implementation of the program has thus far been in the hands of the International Confederation of Free Trade Unions and the International Confederation of Christian Trade Unions. These anti-communist groupings have, not unnaturally, used the funds given them by the ILO to organize, in the underdeveloped countries, trade-union training programs that reflect their ideologies. They have also come to consider the operation as a private fief that can be reintegrated into the formal ILO program only with some difficulty.

To a very considerable degree, the success of these three educational programs depends heavily on the interest shown by member governments and the various ongoing ILO committees. Hence the capstone of Morse's promotional approach is a new institution associated with the ILO but free from government control: the International Institute for Labor Studies. The Institute offers courses on a variety of topics in the field of industrial and labor relations; these courses are designed to link the study of major social issues with the research and experience of academic social scientists and national research centers. But who are the students? Morse's approach is exemplified by his insistence that the students be members of the national elites active in the field of industrial relations, personnel managers, trade union leaders, social workers, and middle-level civil servants specializing in labor matters. Social science is to influence established power-holders, not young trainees or the operational specialists to whom normal technical assistance activities are addressed.

In a sense, the Institute represents a hard-headed effort to penetrate indirectly the international environment, to achieve indirectly the ends Thomas sought to impose directly on the world through the medium of the International Labor Code.[40] The material consists of the topics commonly found in "crash" courses designed to familiarize persons of widely differing backgrounds with the chief aspects of economic development, and it puts special emphasis on the labor and employment facets. Thus the lectures include general discussions of economic development, wage policy and wage determination, employment policy, manpower statistics and characteristics, productivity and manpower planning, social security, cooperation, and labor-management relations. Care is taken to have a variety of experiences with modernization represented in both the material and the lecturers, the latter including representatives of planning approaches of differing scope and intensity.[41] However, in view of the relatively short training period and the mixture of topics, it is far from clear whether the original objectives of the Institute will be realized.

The creation of this Institute represents an instructive case study in ILO decision-making. In part, it is the culmination of a generation of trade union demands for a "workers' university" under ILO auspices, a demand that had always been opposed by the employers and many governments. It comes close to meeting a series of worker demands for an expanded program of worker education in collective bargaining, freedom of association, social security, occupational health and safety, etc. At least the curriculum of the Institute corresponds to this aim, if not its government and trainees. The similarity sufficed to assure Morse of worker support when, in an effort to remove all possible objections beforehand, he took up the matter privately with governments before presenting it to the Governing Body. Only the Soviet and United States governments voiced objections. The Soviets were successfully reassured that the purpose of the Institute was not to disseminate capitalist propaganda and cement capitalist institutions. The United States at first objected to the mode of financing by way of private endowments, and wished to subordinate the Institute to the Governing Body in order to minimize the teaching of socialist principles. These doubts were met by the heavy share of Governing Body control over finances and curriculum that was finally adopted, even though the Institute and its Director were made autonomous. Some employers were initially hostile because they feared communist control, but eventually acquiesced in the decision; now the Institute enjoys wide support from the employers. Morse had succeeded in walking a very narrow ideological tightrope; while it is impossible to say anything on the success of the venture, it remains an interesting example of the unique approach of programmatic revaluation attempted in the years since 1948.

IDEOLOGY, PROGRAM, FUNCTIONALISM, AND INTEGRATION

According to the thesis developed in Chapter 4, we would expect global integration to proceed most smoothly through the instrumentality of an international organization with a functionally specific program geared to the major welfare expectations of crucially placed client groups in member nations. We would expect the process to be facilitated by the prevalence of maximal autonomy on the part of the organization, and the ability of its leadership to sound out a hostile environment and to adjust the program so as to revalue and upgrade common welfare expectations. Finally, the greater the freedom to participate enjoyed by voluntary organizations and experts, the more rapid the process of integration would be, with the understanding that the concern of these client groups would work toward a constant broadening of the functionally specific task. The progress of integration could then be observed by watching for signs of increasing organizational authority and legitimacy. What can we learn from the forty-five years of the ILO's experience, an organization whose program and ideology superficially resemble our analytical model?

A detailed answer is obviously impossible in the absence of empirical evidence of the increase—if any—in authority and legitimacy. Such empirical material will be presented in the next chapters. Here we must confine ourselves to conclusions culled from the ideological and programmatic development pattern. Obviously, the ideology of the ILO has evolved markedly since 1919; but it is not self-evident that the evolution has been both adaptive *and* designed to maximize integration. By 1932, the social reformism of Thomas, based on specific items of labor legislation designed to appeal to a group of allied clients and to convert a group of skeptical enemies, gave way to an effort to profit from the world depression by obtaining for the ILO a major world planning task. In the process, the content of "social" reform became coterminous with "economic" planning. Phelan's attempt to convert depression planning to global economic reconstruction based on a doctrine of universal human rights, far from marking a new ideological departure, merely continued the emphasis and thinking of the thirties. In a sense, the Philadelphia Declaration is merely the apotheosis of the Thomas ideology. Both efforts at dramatic revaluation failed because they were based on a mistaken assessment of the environment: the leadership mistook governmental words and phrases for real and lasting intentions, and it failed to convert governments to the ILO viewpoint when the shallowness of the post-war "consensus" became apparent. Revaluation was achieved at the level of fundamental declarations, of ritual, but not in the minds of the chief environmental forces. An unintended consequence of this era was the eventual evolution of the human rights doctrine as a lasting inspiration for a new programmatic emphasis, unintended because it required for its realization the stimulus of the Cold War rather than commitment to reconstruction.

Official Functionalism, at best, had succeeded in creating additional loyalties on the part of the workers for specific benefits, and, after 1948, for the general protection of freedom of association. With Morse's revaluation of the ideology, a totally new and functionally less defensible dimension was introduced. As the program grew ever more comprehensive in terms of the topics included, its appeal to specific client groups was reduced. As Morse deliberately sought to satisfy the central decision-makers—the governments—the program became less closely focused on the demands of the functionally specific clients that had provided the earlier links with national communities. This transition required no ideological legitimation in terms of a doctrine unique to the ILO and calculated to appeal to its particular clients: the global consensus with reference to economic development and social modernization was quite sufficient; only the stress on freedom of association and related human rights retained a link to the unique organizational ideology.

It is doubtful whether the Morse program, because of its universal aspects and its functional diffuseness, contributed much to integration. Technical assistance expended on improving productivity and vocational training has little to do with transforming the international environment. By its very nature, technical assistance corresponds only to what governments think they require for their own purposes; even if the activities are officially legitimated by appealing to the Philadelphia slogans, their effects are unlikely to bear any relationship to global loyalty patterns, and instead remain firmly anchored in the programmatic subgoals dear to the hearts of limited groups ·of clients. The same is true of Conventions and Recommendations geared to fishermen, marine cooks, office workers, and bricklayers, so long as the rights conferred upon them concern only certain fringe benefits. Subgoal dominance within a comprehensive program is manifest here, too. On the other hand, this danger is avoided in ILO work dealing with the cementing of basic human rights, and with the slow infiltration into the minds of client groups of the content of Morse's promotional program. Improved labor-management relations and creative approaches to the social challenges of technology, if inculcated through the medium of a carefully selected elite, possess both general significance and functional specificity. Within the interstices of Morse's very general approach, we may still discover evidence of the functional model of integration as far as *program* is concerned; while the earlier ideology is muted, it is neither forgotten nor clearly redefined.

In Morse's revaluation of Official Functionalism, we have, in essence, an ideology subordinated to a very pragmatic selection of program items with varying degrees of relevance to integration. By putting the program ahead of a viable organizational ideology that unites the staff, and the staff with the clients, Morse's Official Functionalism has sought to have the best of the Old and the New without fully satisfying either. The supreme challenge of organizational leadership, therefore, consists of so reformulating ideology *and* program, so welding the two into a cohesive whole, as to overcome the schisms among staff members and clients. This Morse sought to do in the agonizing reappraisal he submitted to the 1963 session of the International Labor Conference.

The Director-General's Report for 1963 contains the germ of a creative compromise designed to "rescue" Official Functionalism by submerging it in a development doctrine. The situation which, in the mind of the leadership, makes possible such a new departure is seen in these terms: (1) ILO programs are thought to be capable of growth and impact only when international tensions are relatively quiescent. In times of major crisis, the Organization must concentrate on sheer survival and cannot think about integrative measures. However, with the advent of almost full universality of membership and the *détente* in the Cold War following the Cuban missile crisis, bolder plans are possible. The survival of the Organization is no longer the major issue. (2) The mere fact of the increasing complexity of technology and science begets patterns of interdependence that transcend political and ideological differences. These patterns can be used to build bridges among social systems and to interrelate constructive international programs. (3) UN agencies are the only available instruments that can aid economic development and be entirely free from the charge of fostering "neo-colonialism." They offer possibilities that are closed to bilateral programs, and to efforts made by regional bodies such as the European Economic Community and Comecon. (4) The possibility of disarmament under conditions of avoiding mass unemployment sets a new challenge for global economic planning to which the ILO is uniquely able to respond.[42] (Shades of 1932, 1944, and 1951!)

Morse now proposes to gear the ILO program centrally to rapid economic development in such a way as to strengthen the normative thrust of the Organization's tradition. The generally accepted objectives of developing countries are taken for granted. The unique purpose of the ILO is to keep the *social* component of economic development in the forefront, to make sure that drastic labor mobilization, planned wages and investment, and the stress on industrialization at all cost remain compatible with the welfare and dignity of workers. This implies insistence on non-discriminatory employment policies, freedom of association, and an enlightened social policy. An enlightened social policy, in turn, implies the advancement of human rights, the protection of the agricultural and otherwise disadvantaged population, fiscal and land reform, and the promotion of governmental stability.[43]

The specific content of this program is most ambitious. Technical assistance would continue to be given for the planning, recruitment, and training of manpower. Employment planning would be added to the general emphasis on economic development planning, thus perhaps finding alternatives to the common African habit of quasi-compulsory manpower drafts.[44] Income policies would be geared to overall economic development planning, but with the main emphasis on maximizing labor participation and the protection of marginal groups in the population through social security. Since the relationships between such special protective measures and overall economic planning are not always clear, a special research program should be launched to work them out.[45] The participation of labor in planning is of foremost concern to Morse. All means available to the ILO, through worker education, should be marshaled to make the emerging trade unionists of Africa, Asia, and Latin America active partners in a pluralistic society. This demands the speedy ratification of the key ILO Conventions on Freedom of Association, and follow-up procedures for determining whether governments accused of violating this freedom have mended their ways. For the advocate of promotional programs, Morse proposes technical assistance to trade unionists in skills required for meaningful participation in national planning, and the use of existing programs relating to management development, labor-management relations, and worker education.[46]

What about legal standards? To be sure, Morse proposes the extended use of the ILO Human Rights Conventions, but only as a promotional and educational device. In the place of firm wage, hour, and employment rules, he proposes studies and conferences designed to assure flexible employment stability in the face of automation. Instead of legal norms he advocates further promotional programs in human relations, and technical assistance for a progressive personnel policy, the extension of works councils and plant committees, and the encouragement of worker welfare. New Conventions are flatly opposed except in the field of occupational health and safety.[47]

The expert must share power with the delegate in the future, the *Report* concludes. A general political consensus must be at the basis of the upgraded program as worked out in the annual sessions of the Conference. That body would debate broad policy choices involving the human values implicit in economic development, instead of considering a further elaboration of the International Labor Code. Hence, in the future, little use should be made of the Convention-drafting process; instead, Recommendations should be used to an ever-increasing extent to realize the social policy objectives urged by Morse. Finally, the ILO would participate ever more actively in regional economic planning, together with other specialized agencies and the regional UN commissions.[48] In short, social policy would temper the rigors of economic development policy. But educational activity, rather than legal standards, would be the central means. And, in the process, the representational organs would be re-attracted to the center of power as the authorizing agent for policies worked out by the experts and the leadership. Yet the leadership would undertake the actual upgrading of common interests through programmatic task expansion.

However, is even revised Official Functionalism an essential ideology for legitimating such an approach? It proved undoubtedly useful in persuading some of the Office staff and the workers. For many of them the sociological properties of Functionalism had served as a practical political ideology as well. The congruence of the two features certainly eased Morse's job of retaining the loyalty of his own staff and of one central group of clients. Yet as far as the employers and most of the governments are concerned, Functionalism—in either its sociological or its ideological guise—is not a requisite for supporting the Morse program. While Official Functionalism could be used to justify an expansion of organizational competence, and was so used by Morse's predecessors, it was neither necessary nor sufficient for obtaining a wider task and mandate during the era of the Cold War. Integration following the functional model may be attainable *without* a doctrine of Official Functionalism in the minds of the central actors.

Hence it is the pattern of organization prevailing among these actors, the way in which they attain consensus, and the success they enjoy in influencing and molding the leadership to which we must now turn.

8. *The Organizational Clients*

If the crosscurrents of political demands exposed in the preceding chapters permit of no flat and sweeping generalization about who "runs" the ILO and whose wishes prevail, this much at least can be said: the leadership, by itself, can do almost nothing. The ILO's permanent bureaucracy depends at all times upon converging patterns of demands flowing from groups of associated clients who have exhibited no consistent commitment to the doctrine of Official Functionalism. Clearly, the Office is not merely sensitive, but hypersensitive, to the demands of groups of clients and powerful governments. The consequences of this dependence are revealed in the ILO program; whether this program is still capable of bringing about integrative transformations in the international environment depends on whether its unintended consequences can be safely resisted by member states.

Obviously, the Office has committed serious mistakes in the past in its assessment of what the environment would encourage or even permit. In the language of organization theory, the Office has greatly overestimated the feedback force of its policies. The question, then, is this: have the client groups shown *any* proclivity toward facilitating feedback? Have they, through a process of long interaction in the councils and meetings of the ILO, developed *any* corporate spirit and agreement on substance that might make possible an eventual transformation of the national scene?

This chapter will attempt an answer. It will therefore have to extract, from the material presented in the preceding chapters as well as from the additional facts presented here, an idea of whether client demands emanating from a variety of national settings are mutually complementary. What do workers, among themselves, agree on? Do employers from the United States, Germany, Ceylon, and Mali have common interests? On what issues do governments speak with one voice? The facts of unequal economic development, competing social doctrines, and hostile political institutions may make it difficult to conceive of complementary demands. But, clearly, unless some complementarity existed, no program at all would have taken shape.

Further, we must investigate how the various groups of organizational clients respond to each other's demands. Is there any mutual responsiveness? If so, on what issues and with what regularity? Do workers and employers agree merely on subgoal-dominated technical issues, or on the major questions of human rights? Most important, is there a temporal trend toward greater or lesser responsiveness among workers, employers, and governments? The answer may well determine whether such programs as the ILO's new approach to labor-management relations are consonant with global trends stressing conciliation by experts, or whether they fly in the face of local patterns. If it can be demonstrated that voluntary groups achieve such mutual responsiveness more readily than governments, the Functional ideology will receive considerable objective support.

Our discussion will begin an examination of the crucial test of functional theory, the degree of legitimacy and authority enjoyed by the ILO, as observed by the implementation of its central consensus on the part of possibly reluctant member governments. Is there a relationship between central consensus, organizational pressure, and local implementation on the one hand, and the degree of economic development, attitudes toward social progress, and yearning toward international respectability on the other? Do cold wars, depressions, and local revolutionary situations bear a relationship to such organizational authority? A self-confident totalitarian regime may be less responsive to such pressures than a military dictatorship in a stagnant underdeveloped country. Only a series of case studies of the reaction to the ILO consensus on the part of regimes that are deviant in some important respects can provide meaningful answers. Such cases will be presented in this chapter as a sequel to our discussion of consensus, complementarity of demands, and mutual responsiveness among groups of clients. Other evidences of authority and legitimacy will appear later.

VOLUNTARY GROUPS AND THE ILO CONSENSUS

As the exponents of Official Functionalism never cease to emphasize, the ILO is unique among United Nations agencies because of the institutionalized participation of worker and employer representatives in almost all of the Organization's work. This participation rests on the celebrated tripartite formula of representation, under which each national delegation is made up of two government delegates and one delegate each from the most representative national organization of employers and trade unions. The rationale underlying this unique arrangement is, of course, closely tied to the Functional ideology: experts representing vital social interests are more likely to reach agreement on substantive policy than spokesmen for governments preoccupied with questions of power, prestige, and national sovereignty. But the originally unspoken premise in this rationale held that in each member state conditions of freedom of association must prevail. Only then was it possible to speak meaningfully of voluntary industrial groupings representing, spontaneously and without governmental interference, the vital social interests of their adherents. The rationale, in short, was tied to presumptions of pluralistic democracy in the environment.

What happens when this presumption is violated by the facts? The history of the ILO is long in examples of arguments over the proper tripartite formula; the recurrent disagreements over the credentials of worker and employer delegates to the International Labor Conference demonstrate the continuing importance of the issue. A crucial index to the study of consensus and mutual responsiveness among voluntary groups, therefore, is provided by the attitudes of workers and employers toward the tripartite formula and the credentials question.

One preliminary explanation is necessary. It is a commonplace that parliaments cannot function without parties; international conferences permitting the full and equal participation of voluntary groups require an institutional structure for organizing the great clusters of interests represented in them. In the ILO, the tripartite formula is given institutional expression by the existence of two permanently organized groups, the Worker Group and the Employer Group. Each has its own secretariat, and each is tied to global trade-union and employer associations functioning outside and apart from the ILO.

Both Groups came into existence in 1919; the framers of the ILO Constitution had "probably not foreseen that the employers and worker delegates, being necessarily bound by strong ties of common sympathy and interest, would inevitably tend to form distinct blocs with a view to united action."[1] Worker unity of action was assured, even before the opening of the first Conference in Washington, by the International Federation of Trade Unions, to which all the labor members of the national delegations in Paris belonged. The IFTU was informally accepted by the diplomats as labor's mouthpiece. Its demand that Austria and Germany be admitted to the negotiations was accepted; its request that the IFTU, rather than national governments, choose the labor representatives to the ILO was turned down. In any event, the IFTU constituted the ILO Worker Group two days after the opening of the Washington International Labor Conference, obtained recognition for it, and for itself as the Group's secretariat, and immediately proceeded to put forth amendments to the Washington Hours Convention then being debated. Its major initial procedural success was to persuade the Governing Body to modify the 2:1:1 formula of representation for all committees of the Conference (except for the Selection Committee) into a 1:1:1 system.

The employers also organized immediately. As early as 1911, a certain Mr. Olivetti had organized an International Congress of Industrial and Agricultural Employers Organizations, which in turn set up an International Employers Information Center under the leadership of the Belgian employers federation. The war interrupted these efforts, but they were resumed by the same Belgian industrialists in 1919. These men, in their capacity as members of the Belgian delegation to the Washington Conference, convened a meeting of employer delegates and constituted the Employer Group that has functioned ever since.[2]

The Trade Union Consensus in the ILO

Since labor regarded the creation of the ILO as a major step in assuring the respectability of free trade unions in industrial societies, it is hardly surprising that the workers took the presumptions implicit in the tripartite formula very seriously indeed. Between 1923 and 1938, the Worker Group challenged the credentials of no less than twenty-seven "worker delegates" belonging to corporatist unions in fascist member states. The indifference of employers and governments to the issue of freedom of association as an essential constituent in the tripartite formula doomed to failure each of the challenges. The issue was confused further by the disintegration of the IFTU during World War II, and the emergence of rival communist, socialist, and Christian unions in many member states, resulting in 1945 in the creation of the World Federation of Trade Unions, an attempt to unify all workers under Soviet leadership. How would the "most representative" national trade-union federation be selected? Who would speak for labor in the international arena?

This question was to preoccupy the ILO during the discussions of constitutional revision, and it began to overlap the question of whether the Soviet Union would rejoin the ILO.[3] Molotov was trying to obtain official United Nations recognition for the WFTU's predecessor, the World Trade Union Conference, as a specialized agency, and he would neither join nor officially recognize the ILO. The impasse was broken by assuring the representation of major trade unions in the new UN Economic and Social Council, whereupon the Soviet Union ceased to oppose the recognition of the ILO as a UN specialized agency, without, though, reducing its overt hostility to it or offering to join.[4] The future of the tripartite formula, however, was thrown into doubt by this issue because the French and Belgian ILO delegations urged its modification to allow for *two* delegates each from national trade-union and employer organizations. The change was justified because it would allow more than one national organization to be represented at one time, and because it would facilitate the admission of "employer" delegates from nationalized enterprises, thus presumably making it easier for communist states to join the ILO.[5] The proposal failed to receive the support of any other government.

The Worker Group was sharply divided on the issue. Jouhaux argued, in effect, that the original ILO doctrine had been so successful as to have rendered capitalism largely obsolete. New socialized forms of production, which "are simply the development of what has gone before," are emerging as the dominant ones, and they demand recognition through the medium of a different tripartite formula. Lombardo Toledano, on behalf of all Latin American workers represented in the ILO, repeatedly demanded a 2:1:2 formula, doubling worker representation while keeping the employers in a minority. According to his argument,

The world is divided into two large sectors from the point of view of the economic and social structure of nations. Most countries are still under a capitalist regime based on private property. But one-sixth of the inhabited world is living under a socialist regime. To ignore that fact, or to keep silent about it, to make no reference to it in this Conference . . . would be a most serious error . . . We must not give the impression that there is only one social system in the world.[6]

Both speakers lauded the principle of *universality* in representation as being necessary to complete the victory of socialism. They made no reference to freedom of association of the prevalence of comparable political institutions.

Despite their vigorous attack, the bulk of the Worker Group, especially the American Federation of Labor, adhered to the established formula. But the principle of universality managed to emerge as the operative consensual feature in the Worker Group just the same. Universal membership, as a principle, has triumphed over freedom of association as a precondition for participation. Since 1945, the Worker Group has sought to challenge the credentials of "fascist" and communist worker delegates on over a dozen occasions; only three of the challenges were upheld by the Conference. By 1960, the Worker Group had tacitly accepted the principle urged by Jouhaux and Toledano in 1945.[7] The consensus in no longer seeking to exclude workers representing unions that do not profit from freedom of association is matched by that of the ILO Credentials Committee. The operative rule seems to be to seat any worker delegate who genuinely represents whatever union organization happens to exist nationally.[8]

However, the Worker Group's shift from an earlier consensus in favor of free trade unionism toward universality of participation was not a painless one. Upon failing to exclude the communist worker delegations in 1954, the Worker Group in the Governing Body sponsored discussion of an amendment to the ILO Constitution to "ensure that Workers' and Employers' representatives could only be appointed after nomination by organizations of workers and employers which are free and independent of their governments."[9] Whereas the Employer Group supported this move, the governments sidetracked it by appointing the famous McNair Committee to make a study of freedom of association. The Committee reported in 1956 that freedom of association was seriously impaired in roughly one-third of the ILO member states. Realizing that its proposed amendment would exclude these countries, the Worker Group dropped the issue. A last unsuccessful effort to exclude communist workers was made in the 1958 Maritime Conference. After that experience, those who had previously urged the importance of universality within the Workers' Group had won the day.

Material introduced in the preceding chapter made it amply clear that nothing approaching a deep consensus obtained among the workers on the other constitutional and procedural issues. Many, but by no means all, favored a strengthening of the obligations assumed by member governments with respect to Conventions and Recommendations. Some isolated worker delegates urged the adoption of more stringent sanction powers—such as the disruption of shipping services or the withholding of international loans—to put pressure on states reneging on their obligations. But the Worker Group did not endorse these ideas, and apparently felt satisfied with the possibilities offered by the established ILO mechanism.

Before we can deal with the complementarity of demands and the mutual responsiveness of the workers on substantive issues of social and economic policy, the anatomy of the Worker Group must be examined. Before 1945 the IFTU spoke for labor in the ILO; although it was unsuccessful in excluding worker delegates of different affiliations and views from the Organization, it was wholly successful in keeping them from exercising any influence. Since 1945 the situation has been more complex. Consonant with the Soviet Union's hostility toward the ILO, the World Federation of Trade Unions (WFTU) boycotted the ILO until 1947. However, the American Federation of Labor, which, unlike the CIO, had not joined the WFTU, threw its influence behind the ILO while concurrently starting an active union-organizing and educational program of its own in Latin America in order to weaken WFTU influence there. Thus in 1947, the WFTU, apparently recognizing a tactical error in having thrown its entire weight into the ECOSOC, solicited and obtained consultative status with the ILO, along with the International Confederation of Christian Trade Unions (ICCTU) and the Inter-American Confederation of Workers. To complete the round robin, the AFL now obtained consultative status in the ECOSOC, and immediately used this forum to initiate its anti-Soviet forced labor campaign, to which we shall return later. In 1948, the WFTU fell apart as a result of the defection of all the non-communist affiliates, who in 1949 united to form the International Confederation of Free Trade Unions (ICFTU).

Since that time, the ICFTU has been the voice of labor in the ILO, a status formally recognized by virtue of its serving as the secretariat for the Worker Group. While all the Soviet bloc and some African worker delegates are affiliated with the rump WFTU, the influence of that grouping has been minimal. In the Governing Body, the Worker Group does not even bother to consult WFTU members, whose names are never put forward for election in any case. While they do attend worker caucus sessions in other ILO meetings, they do not assert themselves and make no effort to influence worker policy. WFTU members served Soviet policy prior to 1954 by echoing general communist denunciations of the capitalist-imperialist nature of the ILO, a behavior that further undermined WFTU influence.* Since 1954, not even the Soviet government has bothered to avail itself of the faction's presence.[10]

Although relations between the ICFTU and the ICCTU are free from the ideological strain introduced by the Cold War split in world labor ranks, the ICCTU is hardly better off than the WFTU in terms of formal influence in the Worker Group. Before 1945, the ICCTU was assured of access because one of its most prominent leaders was a long-time member of the Governing Body. With the advent of the ICFTU after the war, this changed, leading to some years of neglect and uncertain access to the ILO leadership. In 1953, an agreement was struck with the ICFTU reserving two seats on the Governing Body for the Christian unions, but formal relations with the Worker Group continued to be strained. ICCTU members complain that ICFTU functionaries do not consult them regularly, that their views are ignored in meetings of the Worker Group, and that coordination of policy is both sporadic and ineffective. Further, the Christians tend to feel that they are a more progressive and realistic trade union organization than their socialist and American colleagues in the ICFTU; they complain that anti-communism seems to provide the only reliable common denominator for free labor.[11]

In terms of informal access and influence, however, the ICCTU is in a much better position because Morse consults its leaders regularly. The sub-

---

* Interviews in Geneva indicated that the Soviet government does not directly instruct WFTU delegates, does not consult them, and frequently embarrasses them by taking public positions contrary to earlier "party line" WFTU statements, which the Soviet delegation then chooses to ignore without informing the WFTU workers. Even though excluded from the Governing Body, the WFTU keeps open its access lines to the leadership of the ILO. The Director-General confers once a year with the WFTU Executive Board and sends representatives to WFTU congresses and meetings. Policy matters of interest to the WFTU are thus presented to the ILO, which acts on them whenever feasible in terms of relations with the other clients.

stantive demands of the ICCTU often demonstrate a very different emphasis from those of the ICFTU. Rather than being interested in the International Labor Code, the Christian unions prefer to invest their limited funds and considerable energies in African, Asian, and Latin American trade-union educational efforts. They operate schools and training programs for young labor leaders in underdeveloped countries, particularly in the fields of social and economic planning. Hence they support ILO policies of that nature, and they urged Morse to undertake his promotional program. At the same time, they take an interest only in Conventions dealing with human rights, freedom of association, and the equality of women. They no longer have much interest in refighting the issues of representation in Geneva, and they expect no great benefits from ILO activities for workers in industrialized countries.[12]

Thus, the oligopolistic position of the ICFTU puts the world leadership of the workers into the hands of trade union functionaries who head old, entrenched organizations representing, overwhelmingly, democratic and industrialized national settings. Moreover, the nature of the Worker Group makes this leadership markedly oligarchical. ICFTU initiatives for ILO action almost invariably originate in the central secretariat in Brussels. They very rarely come up in the deliberations of the top decision-making organs of the ICFTU. Moreover, there is a considerable overlap in membership between the ICFTU Executive Board and the worker representation on the Governing Body. At best, an ICFTU initiative on a major new demand will not be put forth until after the major national affiliates have been consulted. This amount of coordination suffices to result in a considerable degree of harmony among the workers in the deliberations of the Governing Body.

On the other hand, it is equally important to note the possibility of a marked personal style of commitment *to the ILO* rather than to the ICFTU, as far as the leadership of the Worker Group is concerned. Such, for instance, was the sentiment of Sir Alfred Roberts, who headed the Group for the bulk of the post-war period. Under his direction, the Worker Group functioned as an autonomous corporate agent; on such issues as the accommodation to the Soviet bloc, it was dedicated to the survival of the ILO rather than to serving merely as the mouthpiece of the ICFTU. At the Maritime Conferences, however, where the leadership of the Worker Group lay with the ICFTU-affiliated International Transport Workers Federation and its president, Omar Bécu, the reverse was the case. In short, there is no consistent and reliable separation of leadership roles in the Group as between loyalty to the Organization or to a subgroup of clients.

The oligarchical character of the ICFTU is even more evident in the conduct of the Worker Group in the International Labor Conference and its permanent committees. The national worker delegates are almost invariably unprepared for the meetings; there is no contact among them prior to the sessions; and the ICFTU provides no intersession briefings. Ideas and decisions, therefore, are prepared ahead of time by the ICFTU central secretariat, and cautiously fed into the various committees of the Conference by way of selected briefings to certain members of the Worker Group. Although the Group caucuses regularly during the Conference, the ICFTU in fact attempts to present the caucus with a minimum of choices. Decisions in the caucus are reached on the basis of majority voting, and since the ICFTU-affiliated delegates outnumber all the others, the ICFTU position always wins out. WFTU members readily accept the leadership of the ICFTU, reserving their right to dissent only on obvious major Cold War issues. A vote once taken binds the delegates not to speak or vote against the worker position in sessions of the Conference or its committees, *unless* a minority makes clear in the caucus that it cannot be bound. Departures from this rule are very rare.

The impression of great and consistent mutual responsiveness here created should not be overestimated. The worker leadership is careful not to go beyond what a minimum common denominator of agreement permits. National union positions are regularly expressed and argued in the caucus. The preceding chapter made it quite clear that, on major substantive points, the expectations of national delegates representing industrialized countries are quite different from those entertained by their colleagues from underdeveloped countries. The compromises that ensue are adjustments not so much of varying positions among labor internationals, as of different national viewpoints among ICFTU affiliates.

Hence it is possible to speak of a substantive worker consensus only in the broadest terms. In principle, all the ICFTU delegates defend the virtue and importance of Conventions and Recommendations; in fact, they take a sustained interest only in the major human rights instruments, leaving the technicalities of the ILO's major work in the social security field, for example, to experts and government delegates. Although the ICFTU has not opposed the promotional program of the ILO, it continues to maintain a reserved attitude toward it. The free unions claim no credit for launching a program that runs counter to their tradition of directly attacking labor standards through the medium of legal texts or collective bargaining. Although they were consulted by Morse in the preparation of the new approach, they claim direct responsibility and interest only in the worker education program. As a major client group, they quite clearly remain to be assimilated into the promotional program so long as they continue to profess a doctrinal attachment to an earlier aspect of ILO work which, itself, is far from commanding detailed and sustained support from the Group as a whole.

The Employer Consensus in the ILO

Before we can consider the complementarity of demands among employers from a variety of national settings and their degree of mutual responsiveness, the central institutional vehicle of employer cooperation must be described. This vehicle is provided by the International Organization of Employers (IOE), created just before the Washington Conference of 1919 and the creator, in turn, of the Employer Group in the ILO. It is, if anything, even more of an oligarchy than the worker organizations. The IOE is composed of the leading national employer federations in all West European and North American nations, with a sprinkling of participants from underdeveloped nations.[13]

The General Assembly of IOE merely ratifies the decisions made in private negotiations among the representatives of the leading national affiliates. In fact, the same persons represent the employers on the Governing Body and compose the IOE Executive Committee. The IOE was headed until 1930 by the Belgian industrialist who founded it; he was succeeded by a Dane, who held the office until 1939. Sir John Forbes Watson, the strongest leader the employers ever had, headed the organization and the Employer Group during the crucial war years; Pierre Waline has headed both groupings ever since. Votes are rarely taken; a *de facto* unanimity rule tends to prevail. If unanimity is unobtainable, the Employer Group in the Governing Body tends to abstain *en bloc*.

The IOE does little advance planning and undertakes no coordination of national viewpoints before ILO meetings. Its efforts are concentrated on such procedural questions as are likely to embarrass the Communists, and on immediate tactical matters, primarily the election of employers to ILO committees. Nor is it possible to speak of anything like an IOE ideology—except for a bitter anti-communism and a general commitment to using the ILO as a vehicle for containing communist influence. At best, the IOE acts as a downward communications channel, informing national affiliates of centrally made decisions.

Employer attitudes on the procedural questions of the extent of ILO powers have undergone a curious development. During the Thomas and Butler periods, the employer attitude on the major constitutional issues was one of keeping ILO powers from expanding. Yet a lingering attachment to the proposition that international competition can be moderated by the equalization of labor costs—an aim especially strong among West European industrialists but hardly shared by their American colleagues—was responsible for the employer position with regard to Conventions and Recommendations voiced during the debates on constitutional revision. Forbes Watson and Waline then seemed to be saying that if there had to be ILO standards, they should be applied faithfully and uniformly. Their arguments for a wider and more compulsory ratification and reporting procedure, especially at the expense of federal states, must be explained on this basis. Yet the fact remains that the employers, in principle, were opposed to almost all the Conventions that were offered for ratification. But when confronted with the *fait accompli* of unequally and imperfectly ratified and applied Conventions, they adapted to the institutional logic by advocating that the system should be perfected, rather than scuttled—even if their motives were mixed. Moreover, employer interest in the application of Conventions increased with the general shift toward basic human rights.

Employer reaction to the issue of tripartism was very different from the workers'. Before World War II, the employers had generously sacrificed freedom of association to universality by joining governments in voting for the seating of corporatist trade union delegates. During the constitutional debates, they had resisted a change in the existing tripartite formula, and in the early post-1945 arguments over the seating of fascist unions they remained disinterested.[14] With the return of the East European communist nations in 1954, their attitude suddenly changed. When the workers wished to drop the issue of freedom of association in the wake of the McNair Committee's findings, the Employer Group insisted that the issue be faced, only to be defeated by a solid coalition of government and worker votes in the Governing Body. Failing to have their demand for the exclusion of communist "employer" delegates accepted by the Credentials Committee, the employers shifted the focus of their attack to the Selection Committee, the organ that makes committee assignments for the International Labor Conference. Here they succeeded until 1958 in keeping the communist employers from being given the right to vote because they were seated merely in the formal capacity of "deputy members." Efforts by communist and neutralist governments to override these decisions were voted down by the Conference. In 1958 the communist governments demanded full voting rights for their employer delegates, and threatened withdrawal from the ILO if they did not receive satisfaction. The result was the so-called Ago formula, adopted over the opposition of non-communist employers but with the concurring votes of the Worker Group and most governments.[15] In 1959 the free employers decided to boycott committee meetings; but by 1960 the bulk of them had reconsidered, and decided to rejoin major Conference organs in order to be able to counter communist charges—with the exception of three of their number, including the American delegate, who continued their walkout.

There is equally suggestive evidence, when we turn to the substantive positions of the employers, that their attitudes have undergone change in the direction of reassociation with organizational objectives. Prior to

World War II, the apparent schizophrenia of the employers had meant that they opposed—as Thomas meant them to—the ILO legislative program. They considered themselves the international spokesmen for capitalism in a world given over to the "creeping socialism" of the thirties. But it meant, too, that the anti-competitive instincts of Western employers unexpectedly compelled them to seek an occasional strengthening of ILO procedure in order to get the most out of the initially unwanted Conventions. The schizophrenia quite clearly resulted in an institutional and emotional commitment to the ILO at the very time when Forbes Watson and others were trying to demonstrate that the ILO "does not work."

As in the case of some of the workers' leaders, this commitment also contained a personal dimension. For many of the West European employer delegates, the work of the ILO commands commitment because it constitutes one of their major reasons for claiming leadership over their home organizations. Being a member of the Governing Body is a symbol of status and importance at home. Long periods of such service enhance the delegate's position in his national organization; but they do, of course, tie him more closely to the ILO as well. Hence he must make some effort to "sell" the ILO program to his national affiliates, and thereby to legitimate an approach that had not previously commanded national respect. The chief exception to this trend has been the delegate of the U.S. National Association of Manufacturers; but American employers affiliated with the Chamber of Commerce and the Committee for Economic Development have tended to be more receptive to ILO programs and policies.

Employers by and large still oppose the ILO legislative program; but now they have allies among governments and in the Office. They still stress anti-communism as their major plank; but the manner in which they combat communism has implied an unplanned reaffirmation and support for the ILO program. The mechanism of this transformation must now be described.

In the first place, it must be understood that during the post-war years neither the Employer Group nor the various voluntary employer organizations with access to the ILO have defended anything like a profound common position on substantive issues. More frequently, national delegates merely sought to defend demands emanating from their national environments and perceptions. Their collective demands meant little to the ILO or to them; their primary reason for participating lay in the opportunities for meeting and discussion.[16] No wonder that until the physical return of the communist delegations, the sole theme in employer demands was the defense of capitalism against communism.

But it was not merely the physical confrontation with very articulate communist spokesmen in the sessions of the ILO that produced the change. Until the mid-fifties the Employer Group was run by an oligarchic coalition of American, British, French, Belgian, and Swedish federations of industrial employers; the Latin American and Asian delegates present during that period exercised no independent initiative and followed the leadership. With the mass admission of new states from Asia and Africa, this picture changed dramatically. Employer delegates from these countries were already committed to considerable state intervention in economic planning and development; they had no interest in legislative texts, but demanded instead technical assistance and educational programs in management science and industrial relations; the Cold War themes held no overpowering interest for them in view of the neutralist commitments of their governments. Thus the IOE, after initially opposing the Morse promotional program, soon chose to embrace it because that is what the employers from underdeveloped countries wanted most.[17]

Even though not all employers, and most particularly not the American employer, embrace the new consensus of accommodation, Waline seems to be speaking for the bulk of the Group when he claims that the era of Convention-drafting is over. The ILO, he argues, is now the leading world forum in which self-confident and progressive employers can explain and defend progressive capitalism to the young and confused Asian and African trade unionists and employers who must choose between East and West. Hence employer participation in ILO activities is essential. Employers must make clear that the system of industrial relations perfected in the Netherlands and the Scandinavian countries contains the key to the future, and that ILO promotional and technical assistance programs can spread this gospel; in alliance with unflinching support for the principle of freedom of association, this approach can defeat the appeal of totalitarianism. Indeed, the communist challenge impels the ILO to strengthen its procedure for supervising the application of Conventions in order to promote this and other human rights principles. Waline said: "Faced with the proponents of Communism, let us not underestimate the value and power of attraction of these principles. Rather should we take every opportunity not only to defend them, but to emphasize their merits. At the same time, we must not forget that they may seem a luxury to certain less-favored nations, which we must help not to fall victim to the material temptations of totalitarian discipline."[18] In short, the new employer consensus converges markedly with the program and ideology of the Office.

Non-Governmental Organizations

In the labor and management field there are literally hundreds of specialized non-governmental organizations, each anxious to gain access to intergovernmental policy-making institutions. The attitude of the Office has been one of reserve toward such groups, and it has grown more reserved over the years as the number of groups has multiplied. The Office deliberately makes it difficult for such bodies to establish consultative status with the ILO, both because of its organizational commitment to certain preferred voluntary associations, and out of a desire to protect itself from demands and ideas considered peripheral to ILO objectives.[19] Hence, in an effort to appear hospitable without being unduly so, the Office has established a "Special List" of non-governmental organizations with some restricted rights of access to certain ILO meetings. To qualify for inclusion such organizations must accept the aims of the ILO as their own, have a large membership, and carry on successful and respectable international professional activities. In this way, the Office at least leaves open a certain channel of communication with new voluntary groups which, at some later time, might well acquire sufficient standing to become an important client.[20]

Whereas the activities of the "preferred" organizations are closely meshed with the regular ILO program, the same is by no means uniformly true of the other voluntary groups with consultative status. With most of the social service organizations, cooperation is smooth and frictionless because their programs parallel the ILO's. In the field of vocational training, for instance, the ILO solicits and accepts the advice of the World Veterans Federation. Hence such organizations exchange documents with the Office, and make use of their access to the technical divisions to make suggestions and share experiences. The same applies to the Red Cross, though that organization has encountered some difficulty in persuading the ILO to exclude volunteer disaster-relief workers from the scope of ILO Conventions. The World Medical Association (WMA), on the other hand, actively lobbies at the ILO to protect the position of the private physician in Conventions dealing with medical coverage and health insurance. The Office, further, went out of its way to accommodate the heavily American-influenced WMA by using its staff to undertake some ILO expert studies. Women's organizations, especially the Federation of Business and Professional Women, are quite indefatigable in approaching the Office in their efforts to write the legal equality of women workers into every relevant international document. Occasionally they complain of neglect and indifference on the part of the ILO. Most of the marginal employer groups, while demanding the right of access, rarely make use of it and take no sustained interest in the ILO program. The activities of the groups interested in the protection of human rights consist of submitting petitions and memoranda to the standing and ad hoc expert bodies that investigate the implementation of the major ILO human rights Conventions. Much of the information alleging violations of the texts comes from these sources, though such charges are not taken as seriously by ILO organs as their initiators wish. Hence none of these groups has in fact become an important ILO client organization. The ILO is merely one international forum in which they voice their demands, and the Office has hardly strained to absorb these groups into its network of friends and supporters.

This, of course, is not true of the specialized and regional trade union federations. The Office takes them much more seriously, and they do participate regularly in the work of Industrial Committees. In view of the possibility that some of the currently dominant trade union internationals will decline in influence, notably in Africa and Latin America, it is the better part of organizational wisdom on the part of the Office to cultivate client relationships with younger forces, whose objectives may complement those of the leadership more closely than those of the ICFTU and WFTU.

An altogether different position is occupied by the International Cooperative Alliance (ICA). This non-governmental organization has been closely associated with the ILO for forty years, and shares the interest of the Office in the development of cooperatives of all kinds. Moreover, it has more experience in this field than the ILO, a feature the Organization was quick to recognize when governments of major underdeveloped countries, notably India, demanded ILO technical assistance in the development of cooperatives. Such help has increasingly been provided by the ILO's Division on Cooperatives, with emphasis on setting up national training institutes for future administrators of rural cooperatives. In carrying out this work, officials of the ICA constantly advise the ILO staff and, further, undertake their own technical assistance activities on the basis of an agreed division of labor between the two organizations.

Much the same is true of the International Federation of Agricultural Producers. Unlike the ICA, the overwhelming bulk of its membership is drawn from Western-developed countries. Like the ICA, it has a very strong interest in fostering rural democracy and local self-confidence, and hence encourages the formation of all kinds of agricultural cooperatives. Since its primary interest, however, lies in protecting farm incomes, most of the Federation's ties and lines of access are with the Food and Agriculture Organization rather than with the ILO. Agricultural Producers do have direct access to the ILO as well, where they participate in all ILO meetings dealing with rural labor problems. They are frequently consulted by the Office with respect to technical assistance and research work relating to agricultural cooperation, complementary occupations and sources of income for underemployed rural populations, and vocational training for farmers.[21]

GOVERNMENTS AND THE ILO CONSENSUS

Even when an interpretation favorable to the importance of tripartism is adopted, the special position of governments in the ILO decision-making process is generally recognized. It is not only a question of voting power, though the superior position of the governments is obvious here. In the preparation of Conventions and Recommendations, only governments are consulted by the Office; nor do all the governments consult national worker and employer groups as they are supposed to do. Governments alone receive certified copies of these texts. Only governments, obviously, incur international legal obligations. This fact is recognized in the differing procedures listed in the ILO Constitution for dealing with "complaints" (i.e. charges of non-implementation of ILO norms brought by governments) and with "representations" (i.e. identical charges advanced by voluntary groups).[22] Enough has been said about the preparation of the ILO program during the Morse period to make it plain that here, too, governments exercise the effective final vote. After all, it is on the basis of their contributions that the ILO budget is made up, not the demands of workers and employers.

It is true that the dominance of governments is mitigated in fact by three conditions. Ideally, when all worker and employer delegates are united, they can block the united vote of governments. Actually, of course, the alignments are never as unambiguous as this, since some governments are likely to favor the Worker Group. Hence governments are not, in practice, able to "run" the Organization. More important, on most routine issues, including the discussion of future program and agenda items, the Office actually takes the initiative. Since it is the repository of most expert knowledge and enjoys considerable prestige among all the client groups, the Governing Body tends to defer to its suggestions. When the Office acts in tacit alliance with the Worker Group, its authority is all the greater. This feature is especially pronounced in the realm of operational ILO programs, in which the Office receives a minimum of detailed instructions from the political policy-making organs. Finally, since the limited constitutional powers of the ILO make it safe to vote for measures that need not be implemented, there is no consistent force compelling governments publicly to oppose policies to which they are privately hostile.

The special position of governments was made evident to the ILO in its early years. Albert Thomas in 1920 suggested to the Governing Body a system of "national correspondents." These persons were to be national agents of the ILO, appointed by the Office from among national trade unionists, with the task of communicating trade union aspirations directly to Geneva by means of regular reports, and conveying ILO policy to the worker clients. The system actually approved by the Governing Body provided for the appointment of the correspondents *by governments*. The persons chosen are usually officials in the Ministry of Labor; their appointment is not regularly based on consultations with trade unions. The monthly reports on national labor conditions sent to Geneva, therefore, are written by persons who simultaneously serve a national and an international authority.[23] The need for co-opting national officials into the ILO process, if the environment were to be transformed at all, thus became clear early. Such cooptation has been successful in the instance of collaboration between Geneva and the national capitals in the field of social security legislation; it has been far less spectacular in efforts to organize and attract national labor inspectors into a special client group.[24]

In formal parliamentary terms, the ILO processes feature a Government Group whose composition, rules, and procedure are similar to those of the Worker and Employer Groups. However, the Government Group possesses even less corporate life than its counterparts: it engages in no inter-session activities of any kind; its deliberations do not bind the participants, and no particular moral importance attaches to statements of its spokesmen. The Group concentrates on the discussion of procedural issues. Its major purpose is to put forward candidates for election to ILO organs and Conference committees. On these questions, matters are decided by majority vote, and the participating diplomats have learned to reach agreement by sidestepping otherwise divisive major political issues. Matters of substance are broached very rarely. If they do come up, they refer to immediate issues before the Governing Body or the Conference, not to long-range ideology, planning, or program. Such discussions are for information only; they are not ended by a vote and lead to no Group position. The Government Group is not used as a forum in which the conduct of one regime is reviewed by others. In addition, there are regional clusters of governments who carry on more intimate consultations. Standing caucuses exist for the Soviet bloc, the Arab League states, and the Latin American governments. The West Europeans, Africans, and Asians consult regularly among themselves without the benefit of an organized caucus. The United States tends to remain aloof from these groupings. Such working out of common positions ahead of time as does take place among governments, then, occurs in the regional meetings.

Hence consensus among governments is minimal. Collectively, they do not constitute an identifiable client group for the ILO leadership, though regional clusters of certain governments can be so considered for some programmatic points. On the issue of tripartism, the governments—with the exception of France and Belgium in 1944–46—took their stand on the original ILO formula. They consistently stressed the principle of universality over any freedom of association issue, and took no sustained interest in either the Worker or the Employer Group preoccupation. When the Soviet Union and its clients rejoined the ILO, most governments favored any formula that would satisfy the Soviet bloc, a position made all the more palatable for many non-Western governments by the Soviet Union's espousal of "progressive" causes and its identity on most substantive issues with the Worker Group's position. Their eagerness to satisfy the Soviets was matched by the Soviet delegation's oft-professed willingness to abide y majority decisions and to play the ILO game by the constitutional rules. Hence most governments supported the formula developed by Roberto Ago in 1958 for overcoming the problem of how to seat the communist employers over the veto that the Employer Group had exercised in the Selection Committee. The formula provides (1) that all delegates have the right to be assigned as voting members to committees; (2) that normally the Groups have the power to nominate the voting members. But in order to avoid the continuation of discrimination against communist employers, the Ago formula also provides (3) that in the event of a dispute within a Group, the dissatisfied delegates can appeal to an outside Appeals Board, which has the power to assign a maximum of *two* additional voting members to each committee.[25]

It appears that the present settlement of the dispute over the tripartite formula gives everyone satisfaction, except those who are wedded to the principle of freedom of association. This goal of the ILO has, in fact, been balanced with the ideal of universal membership, an ideal in which the aims of the Office, the Director-General, the bulk of the governments, the Worker Group, and an increasing portion of the employers actually converge.* As compared with the earlier appeal to the Functional principle of autonomous voluntary groups, the Morse era has wrought important changes. Although much ritual homage is still paid to the principle of tripartism, the numerical majority of ILO members not exhibiting the characteristics of the democratic-pluralistic society has undermined its dominance in fact.

On the major procedural issue of tripartism, we can speak, at least, of a consensus of indifference. What can be said of degrees of agreement among governments with respect to substantive policy? No collective move away from or toward a common position can be discerned. We shall have occasion to examine the extreme positions typical of the United States and the Soviet Union later in this chapter. Generally it can be said that all governments representing underdeveloped and impatient economic environments are interested in technical assistance and promotional programs geared to their national social philosophies. Industrial countries were not initially vitally concerned with this issue, but went along. Western European governments tend to be interested in specific Conventions dealing with industrial conditions of concern to them; they were in the vanguard of this program before World War II, and they constitute the core of countries that maintain this interest. Most underdeveloped countries are not interested in advanced labor standards; their concern is with promoting the kind of

---

* The Office had argued all along that representatives of socialized enterprises should attend meetings in their capacity as employers, since the ILO is open to all types of economic systems. The Conference adopted a resolution in 1954 which declared that freedom of association is an *aim* of the ILO but not a precondition for participation in its work.

labor conditions that will foster economic development. Several of them have evinced an interest in accepting ILO norms originally worked out for industrial countries in the 1920's. At the verbal level, at least, all governments pay homage to the universal protection of trade union and human rights; but the bulk of neutralist governments tends to prefer the patchwork of relatively innocuous compromise resolutions on issues flowing from the concern over human rights to rigid ideological confrontation and condemnation.* Western industrialized regimes and the Soviet bloc showed eagerness to subordinate substantive policy to annual exchanges of propaganda broadsides; but the advent of the underdeveloped and neutralist government as the "average" regime in the ILO has tended to dampen these attempts, turning them into an inconsistent and spineless mixture of sentiments consonant with an uneasy coexistence of clashing ideologies.

PATTERNS OF ACCOMMODATION

Our survey of consensual patterns has so far encountered two types of bodies of men gathered together to make decisions: groups of delegates united by a common occupation and position in society, informed by the interests perceived on the basis of their occupation, and assemblies of delegates uniting the three occupational divisions into one aggregate. Each of these units loosely corresponds to the type of decision-making structure in which organized interests are represented.[26] Earlier we identified this structure with a decision-making process labeled "compromise," based on bargaining among the representatives of interests. "Compromise" was conceived as the kind of decision made whenever the participating actors are able to agree in their beliefs about causation, about anterior events and facts, but disagree about the outcome they prefer. Such decisions depend on voting, and may result in agreement at the level of the minimum common denominator, in splitting the difference, or in upgrading common interests. Our job now will be to determine which of the three results has in fact dominated in the ILO. We shall also need to discover whether the pattern bears a close enough resemblance to the decision-making scheme to establish its relevance to functional studies of international organizations.

It has become obvious that representative assemblies and groups are not the only decision-making units in the ILO. The International Labor Conference, the Governing Body, the committees established by them and composed of their members, as well as the three "parliamentary" Groups, are only constitutionally the major decision-makers. The ILO also convenes technical conferences, usually called to discuss the feasibility of or need for a new program proposed by some client group or the Office. Such con-

---

* One major exception to this trend is the Afro-Asian concern with racial discrimination, which posed a major survival crisis for the ILO in 1963 (see Chapter 11).

ferences are, of course, merely advisory to the chief decision-making units.[27] Yet their participants are carefully chosen to include members of major client groups in the various nations or among international associations. Are their decisions "compromises," too? Does the advisory character change the pattern? The same questions can be raised with respect to the Industrial Committees that were made a fixed feature of ILO standard-setting in 1945.*

Matters become more complicated when we consider units that are not primarily representative of fixed client interests. The Governing Body frequently appoints commissions of outside experts to review situations and make recommendations for policy. Other commissions are given quasi-judicial functions to evaluate the performance of member states in carrying out their obligations or to receive complaints.† Some of these commissions carry out permanent advisory functions and include persons who are also prominent in national labor relations circles; others are created ad hoc and are given a membership not necessarily representative even in an indirect sense. In addition, the Governing Body creates mixed commissions, composed of delegates and of outside experts. In principle, such units might be expected to render "judgmental" decisions, based on a collegial structure, seeking and often attaining unanimity but resorting to a vote when matters have to be brought to a head. In this pattern our earlier discussion assumed that the actors could agree on outcomes even though they might differ in their beliefs about causation. One might expect here that decisions would upgrade common interests or split the difference because the non-representational character of the collegium permits a maximum of mediation. If actual conduct matches the ideal pattern sketched, we would expect international integration to be advanced most consistently through such agencies because of the stimulus they would give to organizational growth and the transformation of the environment.

The Deterioration of Consensus within the Groups

First we shall examine patterns of accommodation within each parliamentary Group. Table 1 recapitulates the voting cohesion of the Groups. Quite obviously there was less consensus in each group after thirty-nine years of confrontation and interaction than in the earlier period of the

---

* The Industrial Committees will be analyzed in detail in Chapter 10.
† Commissions to make dispassionate surveys are exemplified by the Ad Hoc Committee on Forced Labor. Quasi-judicial commissions include the Committee of Experts on the Application of Conventions, discussed in Chapter 9. The Committee on Freedom of Association, discussed in Chapter 12, is a standing organ of the Governing Body; it is tripartite and composed of members of the Governing Body, and is therefore a representational organ. Commissions of Inquiry appointed to investigate charges of non-compliance with obligations are composed of outside experts and are therefore of a collegial nature. See Chapter 11 for a discussion of the mixture of investigation and conciliation typical of the work of such bodies.

TABLE 1

Voting Cohesion of Groups in the International
Labor Conference, 1919–58

(*Deviation from unanimity in per cent, as based on all recorded roll-call votes*)

Subject of vote	1919–29	1930–44	1945–58
Government Group			
All votes	12.6	9.9	15.5
Conventions	12.4	17.3	14.5
Agenda	15.0	4.5	22.7
Credentials	3.3	1.0	28.0
Worker Group			
All votes	2.6	0.8	10.6
Conventions	1.3	0.5	4.1
Agenda	0.5	0.0	15.2
Credentials	2.5	7.8	31.7
Employer Group			
All votes	10.6	10.7	16.7
Conventions	8.7	10.5	22.3
Agenda	12.5	8.5	15.8
Credentials	2.0	0.4	20.8

Source: Ernst B. Haas, "System and Process in the International Labor Organization," *World Politics*, XIV (1962), 342–44, 347–50. The number of roll-calls was as follows: all votes, 416; Conventions, 177; agenda, 49; and credentials, 48.

ILO's history. In the case of the Government Group, the growing dissensus is not very significant, since the Group was not spectacularly cohesive at any time, though the deterioration of earlier indifference to the procedural issues of credentials and agenda is marked. Differences of opinion within the major regional caucuses, except for the Soviets, are even greater than the aggregate figures.[28] The Cold War and the anti-colonial revolt have destroyed whatever pattern of accommodation might have existed before 1945.

Deterioration of consensus as the composition of the world trade union movement has grown more complex is also evident in the case of the Worker Group, especially on the major procedural points. On the other hand, the bedrock of agreement among all the workers has remained the attachment to sweeping texts designed to raise labor standards and to the protection of trade union rights. There has been evolution in the sense that whereas before World War II this consensus was easily achieved because of the homogeneity of the trade union movement, it is still intact now even though the Worker Group is quite obviously divided into communist, western-industrial-anti-communist, and underdeveloped-neutralist clusters of interests.

Considered regionally, worker delegations from NATO, Asian neutralist, and communist countries are more cohesive than the Group's average, whereas Latin America, European neutral nations, and Asian allies of the West are consistently more divided among themselves. However, the bargaining that does dominate the pattern of accommodation in the Worker Group rarely progresses beyond the level of the minimum common denominator. Further, our decision-making scheme is peripheral to the situation, since the participating delegates tend to agree on the outcomes they prefer though disagreeing in their beliefs about causation. The bargaining that prevails seems to be correlated with the characteristics associated with judgmental decisions even though the structures involved are representational. The pattern of accommodation, therefore, is such as to contribute significantly to integration. However, the ideal functional preconditions are not clearly the cause.

The employers, perhaps because they have been cast as the villains of the ILO drama, really display an amazing pattern of mutual responsiveness. The deterioration of their consensus, though marked, is less pronounced than in the case of the workers, especially when it comes to credentials and agenda items. Their disagreement over Conventions reflects a long-standing difference of opinion between American and European employers to the whole issue. Sharp regional differences are also apparent. Employers from the Soviet and NATO blocs constitute very cohesive—though opposing—groups; those from European neutral countries, Asia, and Latin America reflect deep divisions and instability, which are gradually being reconciled in the emergent employer consensus on seeking mutual accommodation despite major ideological cleavages. Interestingly enough, this is being achieved even though the actors agree *neither* on their preferences *nor* on their beliefs about causation. Where only charisma, in principle, should be able to save the situation, actually the institutionalized game of interest politics is compelling the parties to scale down their initial positions and to make a common front that will enable them to live in the same structure. No early substantive consensus can be expected from this trend, but the procedural life of the Group is being saved, when—according to our functionalist decision-making matrix—it should wither of anomie. While the minimum common denominator rules at the level of substantive discussion, something akin to splitting the difference is appearing at the procedural level.

But, typically, the three Groups show mutual responsiveness only in order to be able to confront their opponents in the decision-making process in the Governing Body and in the Conference, as well as in their committees and in technical meetings of a representational nature. Is there a general ILO consensus that emerges from the encounter among nations and Groups? Is it based on "compromise"? Does it upgrade common interests?

Does it result in a growing pattern of mutual responsiveness *among* the Groups rather than *within* them? Again, we must distinguish between consensus on the procedural issues of tripartism and constitutional powers and the substantive questions of ILO policy.

Procedural Consensus Among the Groups

There can be little doubt that the meaning of cumulative ILO decisions has been to confirm the pattern of tripartism written into the Constitution in 1919, with the understanding that its nature has been progressively watered down by minimizing the question of freedom of association. There is and has been an intergroup operational consensus in which one outcome has been preferred—the survival of the ILO—over all obvious differences in anterior reasoning. Even employers as hostile to much of the substantive work and the doctrine of the ILO as Forbes Watson devoted much of their energies to preserving the Organization and espousing its causes vis-à-vis their own constituents at home. Even workers as cynical of major results or as satisfied with their powerful national organizations as American and British trade unionists devoted much effort to strengthening the tripartite structure and justifying it at home.

But what kind of interaction among Groups, governments, associations, and bureaucratic leadership is possible in such a context? The story of the revision of those sections of the Constitution dealing with sanctions and inquiries is exceedingly instructive because it confirms a trend toward a procedural consensus aimed at "satisfying" demands at the center of the spectrum. The emasculation of the original competence with respect to inquiries and sanctions was actuated by the severe difference of opinion among the participants. The need for reform was further demonstrated by the years of disuse into which these provisions had fallen. The full procedure under the 1919 and 1946 Constitutions for the receipt of complaints and representations, the appointment of commissions of inquiry, the referral to the Permanent Court of International Justice, and the authorization of economic sanctions against a defaulting state are described in Chapter 11. Here we are concerned merely with the forces responsible for the different attitude prevailing since World War II.

Under the old Constitution, a complicated procedure for launching inquiries into alleged non-observance of ratified Conventions linked the Governing Body with the Secretary-General of the League of Nations and the Permanent Court as the authorizing agents. The same combination of organs could also recommend sanctions against a defaulting government. At the Philadelphia Conference these issues were barely mentioned. In the discussions of the Governing Body and the Conference committees concerned with constitutional revision that followed, the New Zealand and Netherlands workers, as well as the Polish government, argued for stronger and internationally coordinated sanctions, whereas the Mexican employer demanded ILO inspection locally of whether Conventions had been faithfully implemented. On the other hand, the French government and employer argued for less emphasis on sanctions; these delegates joined the British worker in advocating more reliance on adverse publicity. Let it be said immediately that the whole issue was a very subordinate one, barely ever considered worthy of major emphasis by any speaker and ignored by most.[29] Further, opinion was quite divided within the Worker and Employer Groups.

When this confrontation accomplished nothing, the Office proposed to the 27th Session of the International Labor Conference a compromise deduced from the discussion, implying a diminution of the competence of the ILO. While the Governing Body was to receive full powers in *independently* appointing commissions of inquiry, the automaticity of the process was to be reduced by eliminating the standing panels of experts from which the members of such commissions might be speedily drawn.[30] References to possible sanctions against defaulting states were to be deleted altogether from Articles 28, 32, and 33. On the other hand, whenever the old text made a reference to the PJIC, the Office proposals merely substituted the name of the new International Court of Justice.[31] The net impact of the Office ideas would have been to leave ILO competent to launch investigations, subject to the right of appeal of the alleged defaulting state to the new Court.

Following this deduction of the leadership, the Conference Delegation on Constitutional Questions in the spring of 1946 completed the process of downgrading ILO powers. Noting curtly that complaints and investigations "should whenever possible be dealt with through the machinery of the ILO rather than through international legal proceedings," the Delegation proceeded to diminish further the references to the ICJ by eliminating its power to review sanctions and the non-submission of Conventions to competent authorities.[32] Commissions of Inquiry, while considered potentially useful, would prove so only if their functions were "confined to finding the facts and making recommendations concerning the measures which it would be appropriate for members to take to discharge the obligations which they have assumed."[33] More generally, the Delegation held that it would not be opportune to strengthen the enforcement powers of the ILO in any way other than to encourage the growth of more efficient national labor inspectorates:

The conclusion which it has reached is that the problem is primarily one of *national standards of law enforcement* and that international action must therefore be directed towards promoting progressive development of more effective *national* administrative machinery, a more vigorous insistence on the part of trade unions . . . and a whole-hearted willingness on the part of employers to cooperate fully . . . rather than towards measures which would inevitably be regarded as unwarranted international interference.[34]

Substantive Consensus Among the Groups

The trend in the realm of constitutional revision is to reaffirm the behavior pattern that had prevailed in fact—irrespective of changes in the international environment. The same cannot be said when we turn to the evolution of substantive consensus. In fact, given the premises of the Functionalist in analyzing the growth of an international task, we are here in the presence of a number of disquieting paradoxes. Thus, if we recall the content of the Morse program, there is an evident consensus on concrete policy even though the client groups in the ILO have been far less united internally during the current stage of international relations than in the post-1919 period. Confrontations within increasingly heterogeneous clusters of occupationally similar clients have split them, thus making it possible for the same delegates to support colleagues from rival occupational groups in the plenary policy-making meetings. Further, this overall consensus on policy has emerged even though the number and force of environmental pressures since 1945 has been much more diffuse and beset with more contradictions than during the earlier environmental phases. The first consensus, though narrower in scope, was more passionately held because it rested on homogeneous environmental factors and relatively cohesive client groups; the contemporary consensus is diffuse in scope and negligently held; but it exists despite the diffuseness and lack of passion. Does it, perhaps, exist *because* of these conditions? If so, Official Functionalism would suffer a reverse, and sociological functionalism score a minor point.

As our discussion of the Morse leadership has shown, consensus has been attained since 1955 as a result of a pattern of accommodation in which something is accepted from each group of clients without great concern for overall organizational and programmatic unity. The program is made by the leadership, which functions in a permissive context of increasingly heterogeneous client demands in which the notion of a recognizable "group interest" is more and more irrelevant. Support is bought by catering to subgoals; substantive consensus emerges as a result of the manipulations of the leadership, which is able to profit from the very heterogeneity of the environment and its clients. As long as no final and millennial support for (or attack on) the ultimate values of any government or group is implied, the game of swapping concessions and support on questions involving secondary interests can go on for a long time.

But this pattern tends to result in "compromises" at the level of the minimum common denominator of all-around acceptability. When this occurs, the diagrammatically neat resemblance of the ILO decision-making process to the modal pattern of collective bargaining in industrialized societies breaks down, a victim of the diffuseness of the post-1945 international environment.[35] But let us note the exceptions. Even within this pattern of accommodation, issues arise in which the client groups retain some of their earlier cohesiveness, thus begetting a pattern of accommodation that results in the splitting of the difference between initial bargaining positions.[36] This is confined, however, to efforts at setting very specific labor standards that may never see the actual implementation on which their validity to Functionalists rests.

The paradox is made greater by the fact that this consensus cannot be attributed in any thoroughgoing sense to the decision-making matrix sketched earlier. In the pre-1945 environment, collegial and representative committees and assemblies could exercise an integrative effect because of the commitment of the chief actors to the survival of the ILO as an institution. Even when Jouhaux and Mahaim, Delevingne and Guérin, Barnes and Fontaine, and Hallsworth and Forbes Watson could agree neither on outcomes nor on the social philosophies that conditioned their beliefs about causation, they could and did agree on the preservation of a tripartite ILO with some kind of social-economic program. This is no longer true. It cannot be established that the representatives of communist states attach any overwhelming importance to a given international institution; the attitude prevailing among the Asians and Africans who had no role in shaping these institutions is one of manipulative detachment. The survival of the ILO is no longer an aim that is valued for its own sake by the chief clients, or even by many of the trade unionists.

The diffuse and heterogeneous environment, of course, implies that agreement on causation is next to impossible; to assume it, one must imagine the capitalist converting the communist, the racist persuading the African nationalist. Agreement is possible only insofar as assessments of past economic and social conditions, and their relationship to future higher living standards, are grossly similar—an area tolerating a great variety of perceptions. Further, agreement on outcomes is even less likely to eventuate; the victory of one set of client aims is more likely to be regarded as a defeat by a rival group. *Yet there is a consensus in Geneva.* If we can attribute its growth neither to ideological convergences nor to constitutional pressures, nor yet to the mutually persuasive effects of continuous interaction among members of conferences and committees, to what can we ascribe it?

Environment and System as Makers of Consensus

The explanation can be found in the effects of the new environment itself. Continued deadlock among clients and bureaucrats leads to the reciprocal scaling down of demands among actors anxious to get something out of the Organization. Accommodation is sought *de facto* when the actors tacitly agree no longer to engage in the same fruitless controversy year after year, when propaganda is silenced in favor of less spectacular efforts to meet interests of subordinate priority. Credentials and Cold War issues are brought up less frequently *even though* they symbolize the chief ideological components in the international environment, and even though the doctrine of Official Functionalism suggests that they be discussed. After all, the actors in Geneva perceive issues and interests besides those contained in the program of the ILO. They are aware of the arms race, the pacification of the Congo, the malaria campaigns, and Cuban missiles, which may form the subject of simultaneous discussion among their governmental colleagues in another building in Geneva, not far from the ILO's. A total systemic context conditions actor responses in any one international organization. If the pressures of that context conduce toward accommodation, toward a downgrading of issues, and toward compromise on matters of real but secondary interest, then conduct is conditioned by the systemic pressures of the total context, rather than by the behavioral attributes of committee meetings and expert reports.

This explanation runs the grave risk of committing the same error that I earlier attributed to certain types of systems theory.[37] I there warned of reification and of attributing behavioral consequences to abstract formulations of process; I insisted that systemic forces, to be relevant to functional analysis, must be recognized and identified in the conduct of actors. And I suggested the test of consistency as the applicable yardstick: accommodative behavior deduced from systems analysis must be consistently discovered in the behavior of the key actors whose responses are supposed to "make" the system, and it must be consonant with their explicit motives.

In our functional model, the "system" is the Organization, and its "rules" would be the pattern of accommodation that the actors consistently display, even if they derive from perceptions flowing from the environment, the total world context within which the UN family functions. One kind of systemic impact could be alleged, in line with the test of consistency, if the ideological tenets of actors had demonstrably changed, or if the setting of the committee meetings had resulted in one side persuading the other. Neither of these events in fact transpired, as indicated in our discussion of the adequacy of the functional decision-making matrix. But something else occurred: the actors devote less time to discussing ideological issues that divide them, and concentrate more on exchanging concessions with respect to technical assistance, labor-management relations programs, worker education, and trade union rights. In short, the inability to resolve anything by means of the immediate post-1948 style of confrontation led the actors to recognize that the sheer game of interest politics *without* shared preferences or beliefs could still pay off in terms of benefits for specific clients; in this sense the system itself brought about the low-level consensus that concentrates on partially shared interests of secondary priority. The Organization was saved as its clients proliferated; *but the program can acquire sharper immediate integrative potential only if the consensus comes to include the revalued ideological content urged by Morse in 1963.*

Yet if our concern with unintended integrative consequences of earlier consensual patterns has any validity, we should not dismiss the matter at this point. Even minimal accommodations can yield new rules and commitments. Even compromise at the level of the lowest common denominator can result in new committees, new reports of experts that cannot be easily rebuffed, new ideological appeals. Actors may still be the prisoners of their earlier commitments and willy-nilly be drawn into unforeseen consequences of earlier lighthearted cooperation. It is in this situation that the manipulative role of the leadership becomes crucial. And one of the most effective ways available to heads of international secretariats is the recourse to respected outside experts. Experts can help trigger the growth of a new and wider task based on claims the clients themselves cannot reject because of their own earlier commitments. The case of forced labor in the ILO will illustrate my argument.

FORCED LABOR: A CASE STUDY IN INTEGRATIVE ACCOMMODATION

The story began when, in 1947, the American Federation of Labor raised in the ECOSOC the question of forced labor in communist countries. The AFL called for a survey of forced labor in all UN member states, and for the preparation of a new Convention covering types of forced labor not included in the 1930 ILO instrument. The ECOSOC took the matter up in 1949 by asking member governments whether and to what extent they were prepared to cooperate in such a survey. The response was mixed: governments anxious to use the AFL charge as part of the Cold War propaganda offensive supported the inquiry; governments anxious to minimize this offensive opposed it, notably the Soviet Union and several Latin American nations who were unenthusiastic about having their labor practices scrutinized.

After initially postponing further discussion of the charges, combined pressure from the International Labor Office and the American and British governments induced the ECOSOC in March 1951 to set up the joint United Nations-ILO Ad Hoc Committee on Forced Labor. Its task was "to study the nature and extent of the problem raised by the existence in the world of systems of forced or 'corrective' labor, which are employed as a means of political coercion or punishment for holding or expressing political views, and which are on such a scale as to constitute an important element in the economy of a given country."[38] The Committee was to do its job by studying national legal texts to ascertain their compatibility with the UN Charter, and "by taking additional evidence into consideration."[39] It concluded its inquiry in May 1953, and nobody was surprised that its report confirmed the widespread existence of forced labor. By the time the ECOSOC got around to considering the Report, however, a certain relaxation in Cold War tensions had set in, which induced the British government to suggest a postponement of debate. On April 27, 1954, the ECOSOC adopted a mild resolution condemning forced labor for purposes of political correction and massive economic undertakings; but it neglected to single out any specific delinquent governments, and urged *all* UN members to examine their legal codes so as to eliminate such practices. The ECOSOC then virtually voted to wash its hands of the issue, and called on the ILO to keep the matter under review.[40]

The ILO had already anticipated an inconclusive end to the UN inquiry. The Governing Body in June 1955 had voted to set up its own Ad Hoc Committee on Forced Labor; and in 1954 it had put before the International Labor Conference suggestions for a new and more comprehensive convention on the subject, aimed at the complete abolition of all forms of forced labor. The Governing Body's decision to establish an ILO Committee on Forced Labor was made unanimously, with the exception of a Soviet dissent. However, this result was obtained only after a solid alliance of the Worker and Employer Groups had succeeded in persuading an initially divided Government Group to go along. The workers urged a definition of forced labor to encompass not only the categories already investigated, but also mass deportations and concentration camps. Initially, the British, French, and Canadian governments had tried to delay a decision, arguing that the establishment of a committee was not necessary and not conducive to better international relations. The chairman of the Government Group (Sir Guildhaume Myrddin-Evans, U.K.) had even suggested that this view represented the majority position among the governments. A. A. Arutiunian, for the Soviet Union, protested against the "holy alliance of capitalist employers and some trade union leaders, who were more interested in propaganda than in an impartial scrutiny of the problem," and justified his negative vote as being "in the interest of international relations and cooperation." While the workers insisted successfully on the right of non-governmental organizations to submit evidence to the Committee, they acquiesced in the compromise restricting the life of the new organ to two years.[41]

The ILO Committee thus had a very wide mandate. In addition to the more traditional reliance on laws and decrees, it was encouraged to use, if found to be consistent and mutually corroborative, allegations and reports on forced labor contained in individual affidavits submitted by voluntary groups, and press reports. The conclusions derived by the Committee from this factual analysis were then tested against norms contained in the UN Charter and ILO texts. In all cases the confirmation or rejection of allegations was obtained by a unanimous vote of the Committee.[42] The results of the Committee's inquiries are summarized in Table 2.

The Committee also called attention to the existence of a form of forced labor, namely as a punishment for infringement of labor discipline, that prevailed in addition to the varieties dealing with political correction and massive economic development; it roundly condemned all three types, while meting out specific blame and praise for continuing violations and evidences of improvement. The ILO Committee, in contrast to its predecessor, the Joint UN-ILO Committee, assimiliated mass deportation into the category of forced labor for economic development purposes, and suggested that it be reviewed by the ILO. In general, the Committee pinned its hopes to the power of public opinion; it suggested that in the future the matter of forced labor be dealt with through the medium of more sweeping ILO Conventions, enforced through the play of public opinion in the expert and political organs of the Organization. It stressed, further, the potential use of commissions of inquiry and appeals to the International Court of Justice to give meaning to the findings of ILO organs.[43] Shortly after the submission of the report, the sweeping Abolition of Forced Labor Convention (No. 105, 1957) was adopted by the Conference.

When in 1957 the Governing Body reviewed the report of the Committee, it was clearly impressed with the work of three independent experts, who came from very different legal and political backgrounds and yet had arrived at unanimous and strong conclusions. Over the continued opposition of the Soviet Union, now vigorously supported by India, the Governing Body voted to continue the mandate of the Committee until 1960, with instructions to evaluate new allegations of forced labor practices expected from voluntary groups and governments.[44] In fact, few such allegations were received. Instead, the Committee merely noted with satisfaction that India, Belgium (with respect to the Congo), Australia (with respect to Papua), Nigeria, and Zanzibar had eliminated legislation that was in conflict with ILO standards. Whereas the situation in Bulgaria and the Soviet Union was improving, conditions in Communist China were not.[45]

Clearly, the improvements in conditions were not *caused* by the ILO spotlight or by the authority of independent experts following up on a political consensus. But they did coincide with these efforts. It is therefore reasonable to suppose that the autonomous internal forces in the communist world that strive toward some relaxation in totalitarian controls were reinforced by the pressure of the global consensus and the sensitivity to charges formulated by labor and humanitarian voluntary groups. It should also be stressed that the charges taken most seriously by the experts always

TABLE 2
Work of the ILO Committee on Forced Labor

Accused state	Accuser	Government replied	Charges confirmed	Degree of improvement noted
Albania	United States ILRM	no	yes	some
*Bulgaria	United States ILRM	no	yes	some
China (Peking)	China (Taiwan) United States ICFTU ICCCP	no	yes	none
*Czechoslovakia	United States ILRM	yes	yes	substantial
*East Germany	ICFTU	no	yes	none
Great Britain (Kenya) ..	ILRM	no	no	–
*Hungary	United States ILRM	yes	yes	some
*Poland	United States ILRM	yes	yes	substantial
Portuguese colonies	ILRM ASS	yes	no	–
*Rumania	United States ILRM	yes	yes	some
*South Africa	ASS	yes	yes	none
*Soviet Union	United States ILRM ICFTU Ukrainian refugee organizations	yes	yes	substantial
Yugoslavia	ILRM	yes	no	–

Asterisk denotes allegations previously investigated and confirmed by the Joint UN-ILO Committee. On two additional allegations, involving the charge by Egyptian trade unions that Britain, France, and Israel had engaged in forced labor practices in Cyprus and Port Said during the 1956 Suez invasion, the Committee ruled that it had no jurisdiction. The following abbreviations have been used: ILRM, International League for the Rights of Man; ICFTU, International Confederation of Free Trade Unions; ICCCP, International Commission Against Concentration Camp Practices; and ASS, Anti-Slavery Society.

involved *joint* accusations by such groups *and* a single powerful government. This suggests that a convergence of key governmental pressures with voluntary group aspirations is the crucial trigger for eliciting consensus among independent experts who have no access to the actual situation other than the close reading of legislative texts and the internal consistency of affidavits and press reports. Some governments, acting alone, dropped their interest when the immediate political situation suggested caution, as evidenced in the work of the ECOSOC. But voluntary organizations, with their concern for the merits of the issue, continued their pressure in the ILO despite the post-Stalinist thaw. There is therefore ample objective justification for the recommendations of the Committee that the ILO, rather than the UN, be the forum for future action in this field:

The Committee noted that action bearing directly or indirectly on forced labor had been or was being taken by various international or regional bodies . . . It noted that certain other instruments which were intended to be general statements of aims or principles nevertheless attempted to define forced labor practices. It found that, as a result of this, different international texts contained a variety of definitions. This, in the view of the Committee, could only lead to difficulties of interpretation and application. It therefore suggested that any declarations of principle which might be adopted in fields which fall within the purview of some specialized agency should be restricted to very general statements, leaving it to that agency to work out detailed rules for the implementation. *This, the Committee felt, was particularly important in the case of forced labor since this was a matter for the International Labor Organization, which had a long-established machinery for supervising the application of the standards it set up.*[46]

The Organization may attempt to translate a moderately successful global intergroup consensus into policy that receives some implementation from its members; it can hardly be blamed if it then seeks to use its success as a justification for further functional autonomy. Here, at any rate, the external functional analysis completes and supplements the claims of the Official Functionalist ideology.

THE LIMITS OF CONSENSUS AND THE EXTREME CLIENTS

During the Thomas period in the ILO's history, the major "deviant" states in the international environment were marginal to the system: the United States and the Soviet Union were latecomers to Geneva, and the Soviets never took much interest in the ILO at that time. But both were deviants in the sense that the United States represented the polar anchor of the extreme employer opposition, and the Soviets the dialectical opposite in worker impatience, to the Functionalist formula of social reconciliation. ILO consensus developed on the continuum between these opposites. During the Morse period, with the programmatic emphasis less consistently on social reconciliation, the older continuum has become subordinate to broader and asymmetrical concerns. But, in many respects, deviancy persists. American and Soviet acquiescence in the broad consensus hides active opposition and malaise with respect to many policies. If they nevertheless submit to systemic pressures, the test of consistency compels us to spell out the mechanics. In addition, there is another type of marginal client: the underdeveloped country whose oligarchic government is impelled by rhetoric and insecurity to seek participation in the ILO, but is neither able nor always willing to pay the price of membership in terms of fidelity to the program. Perhaps this type of client is the most susceptible to systemic pressures. Panama and Venezuela will illustrate the argument.

The Insecure Client

Panama, as is generally known, is an economically very underdeveloped country whose oligarchic government sought to earn some revenue by permitting its flag to be flown by ships owned elsewhere, notably in the United States. By, technically, transferring to another nationality, the shipowners were released of responsibility of applying United States labor legislation. As a result the bulk of the crews on ships thus transferred was composed of non-Americans who were willing to accept lower wages and work under conditions illegal under American regulations. In 1948 the International Transport Workers Federation (ITF), a trade secretariat of national transport unions, called an international boycott of Panamanian-flag vessels, after failing to extract a condemnation of Panama from the ILO's bipartite Joint Maritime Commission.[47] Panama, in an effort to head off the boycott, convened a special conference of interested parties to consider the situation, while also calling upon the Governing Body to appoint a special tripartite committee to investigate. Pending the work of these bodies the ITF postponed its boycott.

The committee took six months to complete its investigation; it interviewed officials of the Panamanian government, the shipowners, and the unions; in addition it inspected thirty Panamanian ships picked at random in many ports. The report filed by the committee confirmed the charges of the ITF that the Panamanian-flag ships tended to be old, that they were able to evade health and safety regulations, and that Panamanian legislation protecting seafarers was inadequate. This report was turned over to the Governing Body, which submitted it to the government of Panama for its comments before making it public. The government of Panama took strong exception to the committee's findings, claiming that they were based on an inadequate sample of the merchant fleet. Furthermore, it threatened to bring suit against the ILO in the International Court of Justice. Thereupon the Governing Body toned down the charges and published the report with the note that the findings applied only to the ships inspected; but it also took "formal note that the Government of Panama has made an earnest endeavor to improve conditions in its merchant marine."[48] Simultaneously, the ILO encouraged the continuation of direct negotiations between the Panamanian authorities and the interested parties, in the hope of giving effect to the pious wish expressed in publishing the condemnatory report. At the same time the ITF continued its threat to launch a world-wide boycott.

This combination of private and public pressures upon a government possessing few sources of revenue, highly dependent upon the support and good will of other nations, and having no developed public opinion standing behind its ruling clique brought some results. Collective agreements between the ITF and the shipowners met some of the workers' demands; some obsolete ships were withdrawn; and the government of Panama offered to enact a health and safety code for seafarers. In 1950, Panama had ratified no ILO conventions; by 1962 it was a party to eleven texts, even though none referred specifically to maritime questions, and only four related indirectly to the matter under dispute earlier. Yet Panama was constantly being censured for non-implementation and non-reporting, which suggests that the compliance with world pressure was still largely manifest at the rhetorical level.[49]

Venezuela is somewhat more developed economically than Panama, and by 1949 its greater rate of social mobilization was demonstrated by the growth—with Western assistance—of an articulate trade union movement. In that year the military junta of Perez Jiménez assumed power; and since autonomous voluntary groups seemed to have no place in his oligarchy, he proceeded to suppress trade unions. Léon Jouhaux called this situation to the attention of the Governing Body, demanding also that the ILO launch an investigation. The Director-General was then authorized to gather all pertinent facts. Following this very mild gesture, the Venezuelan government invited the Director-General to send a mission to Caracas to investigate economic problems, including the development of trade unions. The mission went to Venezuela and minced no words in condemning the government's trade union practices. The government, for its part, restored certain trade union rights even before the mission's report was officially published.[50] Again there was rapid verbal compliance, accompanied with protestations of fidelity to international standards and solidarity with an international consensus—a type of conduct not usually found on the part of totalitarian or democratic regimes with diversified and developing economies. But once the verbal gestures had been made, implementation remained questionable. On the occasion of a meeting of the ILO Petroleum Committee, in 1955, the worker delegates took advantage of their session in Caracas to denounce the government of Perez Jiménez, an act followed by their expulsion from Venezuela. Thereupon the entire Committee left

Caracas and reconvened in Curaçao, while Venezuela retaliated by withdrawing from the ILO. The rupture, incidentally, terminated a previously successful manpower training program that had been conducted by the ILO in Venezuela. Normal relations between Geneva and Caracas were not re-established until the overthrow of the Perez Jiménez regime.

The experience indicates that the aggressive use of publicity may goad the insecure regime into an act of defiance. The reverse occurred in yet another instance. In Pakistan, the regime of Ayub Khan, upon taking power in 1958, changed the status of trade unions in such a way as to infringe on certain obligations previous governments had assumed by virtue of ratifying ILO Conventions. The new regulations, apparently, were not deliberately intended by the government to violate international obligations. Quiet and unofficial representations by the Office persuaded this insecure client to amend the regulations.

The Totalitarian Client

In terms of continuity of Communist Party control and success in dramatic industrialization, it would seem that the Soviet Union is the secure totalitarian state *par excellence*. Wherein then lies its deviancy with respect to the ILO consensus? During the Morse period, the ILO is dedicated to the indefinite coexistence of rival economic forms and doctrines; but the Soviet Union is at best temporarily reconciled to this situation. The ILO process is based on freedom of association for voluntary groups that are presumed to defend permanently opposing social and economic interests; in the Soviet Union, class conflict has been abolished by definition, and trade unions, therefore, are performing functions of a social service nature and are helping to maintain labor discipline. The ILO is dedicated to the improvement of labor conditions through standard-setting, technical assistance, and education; Soviet doctrine maintains that such improvement is an automatic consequence of the revolutionary displacement of capitalism and feudalism. Why, then, did the Soviet Union and other communist states rejoin the ILO?

The answer will be suggested in what follows. It seems to hinge on a Soviet sense of self-confidence considerably less strong than that suggested by the Stalinist stance of total boycott of the ILO. Khrushchev was clearly more concerned over his country's world image than was Stalin; but there is also a stronger sense of self-confidence than Stalin's in the new expectation of meeting the West on its own grounds and successfully defending the Soviet pattern to the world.[51] In any event, the exposure to the meetings, experts, committees, and commissions of Geneva seemed to have produced some systemic impact, even though there is no shred of evidence that the Soviet Union has somehow been "converted" to the ILO consensus.[52] We shall support this thesis by reviewing the Soviets' demands and the ILO pressures with respect to representation, substantive ILO policy, and the Cold War.

As a result of the adoption of the Ago formula in 1959, the Soviets won the essence of their fight for equality of representation irrespective of the issue of freedom of association. The decisions of the Appeals Board, by which communist employer delegates with voting rights were added to Conference committees in 1959 and 1960, confirm this victory, as does the return of Hungary to Geneva. The same conclusion must be derived from the new practice of the Governing Body of including Soviet workers and employers in the composition of the Industrial Committees, of increasing Soviet-bloc governmental membership on the Governing Body, and of adding Soviet government delegates as well as "independent" experts to various Governing Body commissions. The Soviet industrial manager has been accepted as a fully qualified representative of "management" in terms of his industrial and administrative skills, even though he is not an "employer." In terms of global consensus, the Soviet Union has yielded nothing, and has instead succeeded in bending the organizational doctrine in its direction; hence it is here no longer deviant.

The Soviets did not reap these benefits, however, without first having to join the ILO on terms considerably less favorable than they had initially demanded. In 1953 they attempted to obtain a species of conditional membership that would give them access to the debates at Geneva without incurring all the obligations of membership. They demanded that they be exempted from the sweep of Article 37 of the Constitution, the provision that gives compulsory jurisdiction to the International Court of Justice in any question or dispute dealing with the interpretation of the Constitution or a Convention. Further, they stipulated that past ILO decisions would not be automatically binding on the Soviet Union. Finally, they demanded that the Constitution be changed so as to provide greater representation for the workers. When Morse flatly refused to negotiate a Soviet return to Geneva on these or any other special terms, the Soviets withdrew their demands.[53] Clearly, the desire for substantive benefits made Moscow swallow a slightly unpalatable procedural pill.

The list of substantive issues and demands submitted by the Soviet Union is impressive. Communist delegates, in general, have pressed for new international standards as Western and Afro-Asian governments have grown less interested. On several occasions, communist-bloc votes in the Conference were responsible for turning sentiment initially favoring a Recommendation into a move for a Convention. While the West has argued for de-emphasizing standard-setting in favor of increased technical assistance activities, the Soviet bloc has advocated both aims simultaneously. But even this field yields evidence of a systemic impact on Soviet attitudes. At first the Soviet Union condemned all technical assistance as imperialist exploitation in disguise, and attacked many specific assistance projects. Since nobody paid any attention, the Soviets muted these charges and came to accept ILO technical assistance as given, confining themselves to an occasional complaint that their offers of participation were not accepted by the Office—to which the Office rejoined that the offers were unacceptable because strings regarding personnel and finance were attached to them. Even though the Soviets apparently realize that technical assistance may divert rather than foment revolutionary change, they now pose as champions of the program. The record of the Soviet bloc in carrying out ratified Conventions has often been censured by ILO organs; but the Soviet Union's counterargument—that actual conditions in the USSR are such that ILO texts do not really apply to them—is almost identical with the United States argument. Actually, the Soviets had ratified twenty-two Conventions as of 1962: six of the major texts dealing with basic human rights, three maritime instruments, and thirteen very specific Conventions calling for standards in the fields of wages, hours, and protection of women and the young that corresponded to already existing national practice. This record in no way compares unfavorably with that of most ILO member states.

It is likely that the Soviet Union returned to the ILO, in part, to defend itself against Western charges of communist violations of trade union rights—and to level similar charges against the West. In any event, the communist delegations have consistently demanded that WFTU-endorsed trade union rights be used as the supreme world standard. They have also demanded that more rigid provisions for the protection of trade unions in colonial territories be voted. Though defeated on the first issue, they were quite successful on the second. It is hardly surprising that the communist delegations have flatly declined to cooperate with the work of the Governing Body's Committee on Freedom of Association, which they—correctly—charge with being under Western dominance; but the majority of the membership has refused to alter the methods and composition of that Committee in line with Soviet suggestions. Repeated ICFTU charges in the ECOSOC and in the Governing Body that no trade union rights existed in communist countries were answered by the Soviet Union's thesis that, in a socialist economy, trade unions fulfill different functions from those applying under capitalism, and that therefore the weaknesses alleged by Western workers were actually points of strength. After repeatedly refusing to submit the charges to ILO investigation, the Soviet Union in 1958 decided to admit a party of ILO experts, appointed by the Director-General, to undertake a factual, on-the-spot survey of freedom of association.

Some degree of responsiveness was equally apparent in the Soviet reaction to the forced labor charges leveled by Western workers and governments. Moscow was unsuccessful in seeking to block the Governing Body's decision in 1955 to appoint an ILO expert committee on forced labor. But the Soviets had a considerable degree of success, in 1956–57, in inserting their ideas on forced labor into the Abolition of Forced Labor Convention then being drafted. Initially, the Western sponsors of that text merely wished to stigmatize the three major types of forced labor that the expert committee had unearthed, i.e. use the Convention primarily as an anti-communist device. The Soviets, with help from many underdeveloped countries, counterattacked by successfully inserting provisions against forced labor as a punishment for strikes and as a means of racial persecution. Whereas the Soviets announced that they had ratified the 1930 Forced Labor Convention, several other governments (including India, Japan, and the United States) admitted that the breadth of the new Convention made ratification impossible for them. When, in 1957, the Worker Group in the Governing Body moved to make the expert committee on forced labor a permanent organ (whose task would be to supervise the degree of national implementation of the new Convention on the part of states *not* likely to ratify it), the Soviet position received sufficient support to result in the compromise that made the life of the new committee subject to Governing Body review in 1960. Yet in 1959 the Committee of Experts on Forced Labor reported that very substantial improvements in Soviet law and practice had taken place. Whether the subsequent inaction of that Committee can be attributed to Soviet recalcitrance remains a moot point.

Determined, clearly, to improve the negative world image conjured up by the work on freedom of association and forced labor, and to counterattack in a field in which the West was very vulnerable, the Soviet Union in 1957 made itself the champion of a very far-reaching Convention against discrimination in employment, putting the stress on racial discrimination. Although the Soviet proposals were rejected, including a demand that a permanent committee to investigate discrimination be set up, the attack probably compelled the United States to vote for the Convention, even though American opinion remained ambivalent on the merits of the text.

With regard to substantive ILO program demands, then, the Soviets on many occasions were compelled by the pressures built into the system at Geneva to moderate earlier demands and to cooperate when they would have preferred to remain aloof. When we deal with matters directly relating to the Cold War, however, the Soviet demands failed to penetrate the ILO consensus on substantive work relating to labor standards and human rights. The effort to use Geneva as a general propaganda platform was made frequently: general resolutions were proposed calling for the reduction of international tensions, for complete and immediate disarmament, and for the immediate dissolution of all empires. While these efforts always received some support, none was actually adopted. In 1959 the International Labor Conference amended its Standing Orders to make general

resolutions of this kind irreceivable in the future.[54] The Soviets appeared
to be unperturbed at having to accommodate themselves to what the general substantive consensus proved willing to tolerate.

The extremes in deviant demands slough off as the regime concerned
discovers secondary areas of interests in which its demands and expectations overlap with those of other member states. And thus the deviant regime joins in the consensus along the middle ranges of the continuum, even
if this step occurs as a result of consequences not initially perceived or
intended. Later perceptions, driven home by the system itself, made it
clear to the communist delegates that many of their concerns were quite
reconcilable with the diffuse consensus at Geneva. But unlike the insecure
client state, the totalitarian client extracts his pound of flesh in *penetrating*
the consensus rather than simply *joining* it. He is a force to be reckoned
with. The Organization, even though willing to censure specific practices,
is unlikely to stigmatize him. The Report of the ILO Mission to investigate
the trade union picture in the Soviet Union will illustrate my point.

That Mission was composed of four members of the Office, which devoted two months in 1959 and two more weeks in 1960 to the survey. It
began its work following an invitation of the Soviet government, but under
the shadow of charges of interference with trade union freedom then *sub
judice* in the Governing Body. The Mission interviewed government economic officials, as well as functionaries of the All-Union Central Council of
Trade Unions, both in Moscow and in various other industrial centers. It
inspected some factories, talked with officials of plant and regional unions,
attended some union meetings, and visited various social service facilities
administered by the unions. It apparently did not watch elections or engage
in free discussion with individual workers. The itinerary of the Mission
was negotiated between the Director-General and the Soviet government,
rather than being left entirely to the ILO. Finally, the Report notes that "the
Mission was accompanied throughout by a representative of the State
Labour and Wages Committee and a representative of the AUCCTU, who
gave every assistance in overcoming the problems which inevitably arise
on a long journey."[55]

The Mission, of course, found and noted that the doctrinal and legal
situation of trade unions in the Soviet Union differs completely from the
accepted Western model. But it concluded that even though Soviet trade
unions lack certain functions and rights associated with organized labor
in Western countries, they participate continuously and importantly in
their country's total industrial effort. In short, the Mission accepted the
Soviet contention that in a socialist economy trade unions fulfill the new
and different functions associated with the building of a classless society,
rather than "representing" the interests of workers. The Mission was especially impressed with the post-1957 trend toward increasing the role of the

AUCCTU in overall economic planning and in the determination of the general "wage fund."[56] Participation in plant management, the enforcement of labor discipline, social insurance, and educational and recreational activities are all described with sympathy. Cautious support is expressed for the thesis that autonomous trade unions, closely geared to State and Party but with their own corporate identity, are arising. With respect to the central question of freedom of association, the only evaluative statement the Mission permitted itself is this:

Much has been said in this report about the extent of trade union power in the USSR. It is interesting to consider how far this power is a measure of trade union freedom. Many people feel that the Soviet trade unions, instead of becoming more independent, are being more closely integrated with the system of government. They doubt whether the unions can continue to develop on the lines followed in recent years and still remain trade unions. These are problems on which the reader must form his own judgment. It has been said that the Soviet trade unions, with other social organizations, will eventually replace the State. Be this as it may, while carrying out their functions in regard to the planning and organizing of production, and while continuing their efforts for the protection and welfare of the workers, the unions remain one of the pillars of the Soviet system.[57]

It appears, therefore, that the Organization respects "deviant" practices as the Soviet Union accepts and joins in parts of the ILO's substantive consensus, even at the occasional expense of national Soviet law. As a result, fears expressed in 1954 that the Soviets would destroy the ILO system proved as unfounded as the hope that the ILO could merely rebut, expose, and embarrass the deviant state and continue unscathed along the grooves of the earlier consensus. Embarrassment has been mixed with acceptance, Western-inspired rebuff with the legitimation of new forms. In the process, the program of the ILO has undoubtedly become much more "political" than it was. But since the deviant state has been partly the beneficiary while exposing itself to more "political" countercharges, neither the autonomy nor the task of the Organization has suffered by this broadening of the consensus.[58]

The Free-Enterprise Client

What makes the United States, unmarred by underdevelopment, oligarchy, or totalitarianism, a deviant client with respect to the ILO consensus? The issues are many and they interlock. American industrial opinion generally is hostile to the idea of improving living standards by way of legislation, preferring the mode of increasing productivity linked with free collective bargaining. Hence the very principle of a code that establishes otherwise desirable standards by legal action is not readily accepted by either the workers or the employers. Further, the dedication to the principle of free enterprise capitalism is generally shared by both groups. Though labor has certainly favored much social legislation tending toward a welfare-oriented economy, its principles remain doctrinally hostile to "socialism." In general the employers have opposed all ILO texts as evidence of "creeping socialism" or worse, and have sought to insulate the United States from their jurisdiction. Workers, because of the fact that, in most sectors, actual standards prevailing in the United States were in excess of what the ILO texts demanded, were indifferent to the International Labor Code; the facts of industrial prosperity made the Code irrelevant for the most part. Since 1947, at any rate, the United States has considered itself the leader of a global anti-communist campaign that officially scorns notions of coexistence, a feeling again shared by industry and labor. It is true that the existence of a federal constitution is usually invoked by American spokesmen from all camps as good and sufficient reason for aloofness toward the ILO consensus. But one suspects that this claim is usually made in order to disguise a more basic hostility, a hostility less easily explained to the world at large. Finally, it should be noted that of the various American groups, employers affiliated with the National Association of Manufacturers provide the backbone of the opposition.

Until 1948 these evidences of deviancy were hidden for a variety of reasons. Under the New Deal, the U.S. government did expect—however mistakenly—to reap benefits from the Code, and the trade unions took the same position. Employer opposition was then sidestepped because the government followed the practice of appointing only "progressive" employers to the American delegations. The uncertainty among various government departments concerning the nature and shape of the world to be created in 1945 was reflected in the hiatus between glowing declarations and unwillingness to make specific commitments at the Philadelphia Conference. Again, however, workers and employers associated themselves with the government's position of cautious global welfare-statism. Employers previously hostile to the ILO then supported a program of extended social security coverage, and of wholesome and cooperative labor-management relations through constant joint participation, the practice made familiar in American industrial relations during the war.[59] The "progressive industrialism" associated with the Committee for Economic Development was the point of view represented in American employer dealings with the ILO through the person of James D. Zellerbach; and this attitude was predicated on the legitimacy of strong trade unions cooperating with a management that identified its own security with an expanding capitalism based on greater mass purchasing power and social reform.

But even this attitude was hostile to standard-setting and extensive legislative work. Hence progressive American employers took the initiative in

1948 in persuading David Morse, a labor specialist considered to share their views, to accept the post of Director-General. The price for this support was the expectation that Morse would de-emphasize standard-setting, and concentrate instead on technical assistance operations that would create the world conditions under which progressive capital could coexist cooperatively with progressive labor. This position again converged with the attitudes of government and American unions, resulting in solid United States support and lobbying for the election of Morse. As far as the unions and the Democratic Administration were concerned, then, the United States fully identified with the successfully restructured ILO consensus; the United States. also, had penetrated rather than merely joined that consensus.

The bulk of American employers, however, now struck out in the opposite direction. Encouraged by the passage of the Taft-Hartley Act, they were determined to prevent the infringement of different ILO standards on the American labor scene. The ILO program was now openly identified with "creeping socialism" and communism; the ILO was represented as being dominated by a coalition of socialist governments and workers, thus threatening American values; the return of the Soviet Union was cited as evidence of the imminent victory of communism. Its threat to the rights of the American states was singled out, thus marking a convergence between employer economic doctrine and the general anti-United Nations sentiment symbolized by the Bricker Amendment movement. Furthermore, after 1948, United States employer delegates were all chosen from this group and the Republican Administration increasingly deferred to its pressure.[60]

The government never went so far as to admit that participation in ILO programs meant commitment to a policy of bankrupting the United States in order to create world socialism—as W. L. McGrath repeatedly charged on behalf of the American employers. But it did identify itself with the employers' view to a great extent. The United States successfully insisted in Geneva that the number of new Conventions be held to a minimum, that the representation of employers on ILO committees be increased, that the seating of communist "employers" be opposed, and that massive surveys into freedom of association be launched. The United States, in short, made itself the mouthpiece of active anti-communism and deliberately sought to use the ILO for Cold War purposes. Instead of being interested in pushing the human rights issue to the point of drafting comprehensive new international agreements, it was concerned merely with their propaganda value. But it continued to advocate technical assistance programs complementing bilateral activities in the fields of productivity and vocational training. As far as American workers were concerned, they shared the commitment to using the ILO as an active anti-communist propaganda forum, even if they did not accept the more extreme employer charges. Employer unrest reached a high point in 1955, with demands for a congressional investigation of the ILO and with Senator Bricker's successful blocking of increased American contributions to the ILO budget.[61]

The Administration met this attack by appointing the Johnson Committee, a group of eminent specialists called upon to make recommendations on future relations with Geneva.[62] In general, the Johnson Report defended the work of the ILO, and advocated full and continued United States participation. It also minimized the legislative powers of the Organization, and reaffirmed that it was in no way able to commit the United States legally. It recommended that Conventions and Recommendations be de-emphasized, but that American delegations should not oppose them merely because of skepticism regarding the principle of the Code; however, it made no recommendations regarding the actual ratification of any texts. On the other hand, increased support for the technical assistance program was recommended. The Committee stressed continued recognition of the principle of tripartism as buttressing freedom and democracy, *including* the admission of communist employers, if properly voted on; but it also reserved the right and duty of American delegates to challenge the credentials of communist employers. In general, the ILO was pictured as a representative and democratic organization, fully capable of furthering American long-range interests in the Cold War, even though short-range frustrations might occur. Not only did the government act on many of the detailed and administrative recommendations advanced by the Committee, but a less defensive tone was adopted by American government delegates at Geneva after 1956. In addition, a slightly less conservative employer delegate was then nominated by the National Association of Manufacturers, following a government threat that otherwise a more responsive candidate would be found elsewhere. After 1960 the task of appointing a U.S. employer delegate was given to the Chamber of Commerce. The result was to confirm American adhesion to the general consensus.

One of the most significant steps taken by the United States in its efforts to use the ILO as a forum for attacking communism, while at the same time defending its national way of life, was the offer to welcome a purely factual survey of freedom of association on its soil. The suggestion was made by the American worker delegate in the Governing Body, and was speedily tendered officially by Secretary of Labor James P. Mitchell. It was this offer which, apparently, triggered the Soviet Union's identical response soon after. The survey was carried out by four members of the Office during the spring of 1959. It included interviews with government, union, and management spokesmen in Washington and the major industrial centers, meetings with local labor councils, and visits to plants. The Mission's Report stresses that "the Mission was not accompanied on its journeys by any representative of the Government, the trade unions or of the employers," and that the authorities "left the Mission entirely free to go wherever it wanted and to talk to anyone it pleased."[63]

One is entitled to wonder, however, whether a great deal of propaganda mileage was gained by the United States. The Mission duly noted the power of American trade unions, and accurately summarized major labor legislation and court decisions creating freedom of association. However, it also noted quite correctly the difficulties faced by unions in various regions and branches of industry to make the law prevail at all times. Further, it suggested a slight deterioration of the legal right to freedom of association as a result of restrictions on certain trade union practices introduced by the Taft-Hartley and Landrum-Griffin Acts. It described the instrumental attachment of American employers to trade unionism, and expressed the opinion that corrupt as well as undemocratic practices in union government were exaggerated out of their true proportions. It mentioned the ambiguous status of civil servants with respect to freedom of association, collective bargaining, and the right to strike, but it also felt that the actual status of these workers is more favorable than the legal situation suggests.

On balance, the Mission took an unflinching pro-trade-union position, which insisted on the justice and legitimacy of freedom of association, not only in terms of actual prevailing conditions of freedom, but also in the sense that this freedom be accepted in good faith by the society in which it is being practiced. And on this score the United States was reported to be remiss. The Mission felt that the Taft-Hartley Act is, on occasion, so interpreted by employers and local authorities as to restrict the ability of unions to organize and be recognized. It stressed that labor legislation is not applied and interpreted uniformly throughout the United States, and that therefore unions are becoming more "legalistic" and less militant. "Right to work" legislation is cited to support the allegation that, with respect to organizing and recognition, the unions are now on the defensive. This was found to be the case because acceptance of the unions was still not total:

There is an increasing acceptance of the labor movement in the United States as an integral part of the national society, and there does not appear to be a climate of opinion in which any fundamental attack on the principle of freedom of association is to be expected; in addition the trade union movement now plays a very important part in the national life. In the minds of many people, however, *the acceptance of trade unionism is more in the nature of resignation to the fact that the unions exist than of positive approval. Such persons are willing to accept the unions and to deal with them because they have succeeded in establishing themselves; but they would not go so far as to say that trade unions are desirable or necessary.*[64]

Undoubtedly this observation of the Mission is quite accurate. But the ILO experts also drew the inference that "a person who is prepared to recognize a trade union only if it corresponds to his own idea of what a trade union should be or do can hardly claim to be a believer in freedom of association."[65] In the mind of the Office, the principle of freedom of association is not firmly established unless a society accepts it on intrinsic rather than purely instrumental or interest-determined grounds. It is not enough merely to tolerate your partner and to negotiate with him in a context of interest confrontation; you must actually love him too!

The continuing reservation in the American attitude to ILO doctrine and program is manifest in the hesitancy with which government delegates approach discussion of basic issues in Geneva. It is equally apparent in the qualifications present in the Johnson Report, and it stands revealed in the somewhat reticent conclusions published in the survey on freedom of association. Yet the United States has not cut down irrevocably on its financial contributions to the ILO and continues its full participation. It has stepped up its demands for multilateral technical assistance operations and has continued its support for the ILO social security program. More important still, even though the opposition to Conventions and Recommendations is as strong as ever, and even though many of the human rights texts adopted since 1947 by the ILO imply American shortcomings with respect to these standards, government and worker delegates have supported these efforts at Geneva.[66] The United States, in its formal demands, rarely called for more than resolutions condemning communist practices in the field of human rights; on more than one occasion, sweeping legal standards were enacted in place of resolutions, standards sometimes effectively amended as a result of Soviet demands. Further, standing institutions were created for enforcing some of these rights—if only by way of adverse publicity. Instead of sulkily withdrawing into its tent, the United States has availed itself of these institutional pressures; it has come to play the game implied by the imposition of a system that American policy-makers initially opposed and continue to oppose in formal terms. In short, by adapting itself to unintended consequences of earlier measures, the United States has reinforced the consensus among clients. The adaptation itself is no more than a recognition that secondary objectives can still be gained by submission to the system, even though certain primary aims were deflected.

THE FUTURE OF TRIPARTISM

The demonstration that consensus may prevail and grow at the level of overlapping but secondary national objectives is not likely to support the thesis that tripartism is essential for international integration. According to Functional teaching, tripartism seeks to subject the international environment to integration along the lines of a specific economic and social doctrine by proceeding on the basis of the institutionalized confrontation of occupational interests. The present tripartite formula is considered a necessary condition for this approach. But is it really? We shall now argue that Functional tripartism has failed to contribute significantly to international integration. But we shall also argue that an alternative principle of tripartism has been tacitly introduced, which, though consistent with the nature of the international environment, will not necessarily transform the environment in an integrative manner.

The classic Official Functionalism assumed class conflict to be "natural" in an industrial society. Implicit in this assumption were a number of institutional and behavioral premises that require spelling out. Although industrial class conflict was natural, it could be transcended through organization, confrontation, and bargaining. Eventually a new national and international environment would emerge, based on a synthesis of progressive worker and employer ideologies. The process of conflict resolution, at the national as at the international level, then called for the participation of organized workers able to persuade and cajole reluctant employers into the synthesis, habituating the employer to the thought of his own eventual abdication. Further, freedom of association for both types of clients was clearly a requisite. If all these premises had been met in the real international environment, the Functional ideology would have come close to providing the explanation for, and the guide to, massive systemic transformations: experts, representing organized voluntary interests, in tackling directly experienced practical tasks, would have automatically found solutions and formed new habits of an integrative nature.

The institutional tripartism that was the corollary of this doctrine has simply failed to reflect the realities of the international environment since 1945. The clients who represent this environment in the Geneva system had neither the presumed requisites nor the typical perceptions associated with the formula. Major ideological issues have caused the fissures and alignments of the day, not occupationally derived interests. The membership has faithfully reflected the major fissures by introducing the anti-communist and anti-imperialist themes into the discussions. The presence of the colonial issue hardly requires special stress. The clients, instead of clustering consensually around their occupational and administrative concerns, tend to reflect their country's position in the East-West-Unaligned spectrum. Workers and employers no longer readily and predictably support their comrades; whenever the issue before the meeting reflects considerations of race, social equality, colonial evolution, investment, freedom of association, collective bargaining, or the image of any of the blocs, national-ideological allegiance triumphs over economic group interest. In short, the major premise of a division of opinion among three groups to facilitate confrontation and synthesis along Functional lines is simply not found in the real international world.

Yet a different kind of tripartism has quietly crept into the interstices of ILO operations. It manifests itself not in formal representation on standing organs, but in the way in which the technical assistance operations are carried out; it has moved from the confrontations in the Conference to the discussions and seminars of the promotional program. These ILO activities are carried out by the Office and special boards almost without any continuing supervision on the part of the standing tripartite organs. Technical assistance projects are discussed and approved in New York because they are largely financed by the United Nations Special Fund, or by the Expanded Technical Assistance Program, which is administered by the UN Technical Assistance Board. ILO influence in these bodies is entirely handled by the Office. Formal relations take place between requesting governments and international civil servants, entirely sidestepping the tripartite formula.

These programs are hardly ever controversial. They involve no formal confrontation of interests, and they require no institutionalized means of resolving conflict. Hence the Office, in conformity with the Morse program, seeks to influence the transformation of the environment by other means. It aims at transcending industrial conflict on the local scene by reconciling workers and employers, by socializing them into modes of cooperation and mutual understanding under which neither side will work for the elimination of the other. Further, the formal confrontation of interests is avoided. Technical assistance experts "lead" the parties in training them; Office personnel takes the initiative in demonstrating and praising conciliatory and cooperative techniques. With education, with awareness of each other's perceptions, the workers and employers of developing countries are to be weaned away from the historical confrontation of class-based interests. In more formal language, the Office reverted to the computational model of decision-making. Experts who agree on the outcomes they prefer, and who share each other's technically based sense of causation, dispense "truth" to trainees, fellowship holders, and other beneficiaries of technical assistance programs. Tripartism remains in the picture because the trainees include workers, employers, and government administrators; it is still central because these occupations furnish many of the experts who administer technical assistance and educational programs.

This attenuated tripartite formula is far from guaranteeing continued international integration. Some members of the Office hold that the mere fact that identical experts dispense their truth in country after country has a standardizing and integrating effect. Others, more realistically, admit that the conditions of such aid are largely defined by the recipient government, and that ILO staff members are not well placed to bring about standardized integrating results. Experts must be *personae gratae*; many have been rejected and a few expelled by governments because they were not. The Soviets seek to attach various strings with respect to equipment and personnel o their aid. Although the UN Resident Representative, in principle, enjoys great powers in influencing the recipient government and could therefore exercise a standardizing and integrating effect, such powers in fact prevail only as long as the government is weak and unable to plan its own development.[67] Further, the preponderant portion of technical assistance, being financed from United Nations sources, effectively escapes such special conditions as ILO might wish to impose in line with its own doctrine, even though ILO experts provide the actual services. In short, while the post-1945 international environment offers new opportunities for the Office leadership to capitalize on the computational mode of decision-making, the dominant voice of the governments still acts as a very major restraint on any rapid integrating consequences.

The impact of the new tripartite formula may be explored further in connection with the ILO's productivity program, a major item in technical assistance. These programs, as a matter of principle, are so administered as to maximize the participation of trade unions and trade associations. Since they are designed to win over both reluctant workers and skeptical employers, they insist on avoiding any increase in unemployment attributable to productivity growth. Such programs, instead of stressing pure physical increases in per capita productivity, as some employers might wish, emphasize human relations, morale incentives, worker participation in decisions affecting production, and the professionalization of attitudes and skills among managerial personnel. In short, they are designed to transcend industrial conflict by creating an aura of creative participation for all parties, a climate in which knowledge, facts, and understanding are substituted for confrontation based on hostile perceptions of interest. In view of the strangeness of this doctrine in many local settings, it is hardly surprising that very different degrees of success have marked the many productivity projects.[68]

Tripartite participation in some educational programs aims at similar results. The very principles underlying the ILO Labor-Management Relations program bespeak the same attitude of reconciliation and transcendence of clashing industrial interests. The Office seeks to achieve these results by appointing experts and consultants who have no ideological commitment, or by making up panels of experts so as to accommodate several ideologies forced to coexist in the process of tendering assistance. The hope is always that missions so composed will then persuade their trainees in underdeveloped countries to adopt similar attitudes of accommodation and understanding.[69]

The sweep of Office-based tripartism is, however, severely limited by the current era in the international environment. Although the tripartite approach is wholly consistent with the industrial relations practices in the developed democracies of the West, practices that increasingly eschew any

simple confrontations of interest, activities implementing this approach are
confined to the rare instances when a Western country requests ILO help
with reference to adjustment to automation or the launching of a productivity program. The approach is also applicable to developing nations
whether neutralist or not, who are anxious to combine industrialization
with a minimum of social friction. Nations whose traditional cultures legitimate compromise and conciliation, whose values stress accommodation
over confrontation, provide particularly fruitful soil for the new tripartism
India is the outstanding example. The attraction that the formal tripartite
structure exercised in India is partly due to its family resemblance to gradual social transformation based on mutual understanding among social
antagonists. There is an obvious similarity betwen *satyagraha* as a doctrine
of conflict resolution based on persuasion and the pattern of tripartite participation in policy-making that aims at frictionless industrialization. Small
wonder, then, that the Indian Congress Party proved hospitable to the ILO
ideology as early as 1930.[70] Whether hospitality to these ideas can outlast
the growth of strong and self-confident trade unions and employer associations is another question.

What is clear, however, is the non-applicability of the tripartism of technical experts to communist countries. Communist countries in the ILO
have made themselves the exponent of the original ILO tripartite doctrine;
they favor confrontation and antagonism at the very time the bulk of the
membership has come to care less and less about the principle. This is true
even though the communist countries meet few of the structural and behavioral requisites associated with Official Functionalism. Their insistence
is verbal, and their argument remains unrelated to the reality of the international environment in which occupational-interest clusters do not determine the disposition of issues. In fact their conduct in insisting on the
full representation of all delegates—even those whose existence is the result of external repression as in the case of the Hungarian delegation after
1956—belies the advocacy of the principle and reinforces the trend away
from the Functionalism of Albert Thomas and the founders of the ILO.

Nor is the new formula easily applied to traditional oligarchies, regimes
not yet consistently motivated to introduce industrialism or a larger measure of egalitarian social relations. Where there is no will to raise productivity, appropriate technical services will not be requested. Where the will
is part of a continuing malaise concerning social change, and where the
prestige of a family enterprise cannot accommodate managerial ideologies,
tripartite technical advice will fall on deaf ears. Such conditions continue
to prevail among many of the member states. They limit the appeal of the
new tripartism, while positively excluding the exercise of the old.

The only kind of tripartism that has a chance of survival in the contemporary international environment is the type that corresponds to the actual needs and perceptions of clients *in their interaction*. It is a tripartism that is representational only in a formal sense, and that no longer seeks to remain true to the original premises of Official Functionalism. It would accept in the future, without challenge, the designation and self-identification of workers' and employers' associations at the national level.

Such a principle of tripartism would dispense with decision-making based on representation and bargaining, a style that no longer faithfully describes the actual process in any event. It would rest instead on computational techniques in which the expert—whether a member of the Office or a specialist recruited from the environment—manages and manipulates agreement on the basis of relatively non-controversial subordinate social objectives. While this approach would undoubtedly slow down the pace of environmental transformation, it would also succeed in coopting the largest possible number of clients into an ongoing consensus, and thereby enmesh them in a decision-making process from which they may no longer wish to extricate themselves. The relaxed tripartism here described is regarded by some members of the Office as the best mode of weaning the bulk of the employers away from their rigid anti-communism, of persuading these clients that *all* employers have some common interests in some form of industrial coexistence. But if a doctrinaire and purely representational form of tripartism is left to its own devices, this result is unlikely to be achieved. Tripartism can be an educational device for habituating antagonistic clients to live with one another only if it is manipulated by the Office. This the leadership hopes to do by means of the promotional program. Thomas was groping toward the same results when he refused to make an issue over the *bona fides* of corporatist worker delegates, and accepted them into ILO policy-making as the only national workers' organization available.[71] The expert associated with interest groups will prove a more willing instrument in this process than the bureaucratic representative of interest groups.

The ideological Functionalism reflected in the ILO's constitutional tripartite formula has failed to bring about a consensus on program and task; that consensus has been demonstrated as resulting from quite a different process. Nevertheless, this way of putting the matter overstates the case. C. Wilfred Jenks himself argues that the autonomy of the Office, rather than the constitutional tripartite formula, accounts for the success of the ILO; the expert in the organizational leadership emerges as the hero of systemic transformation, not the interest group spokesman. But he also suggests that the governments would never have permitted the requisite autonomy to evolve, as it did during the Thomas era, if the interest group spokesmen had not backed the Office.[72] Thus we must also conclude that the tripartite formula was probably a requisite, during the environmental phase of the 1920's, in permitting the Office to develop. But this is no longer the case in the environment of the 1960's.

Ideological Functionalism has been superseded. We must then rely on analytical functionalism to suggest the limits of the integration that can be expected to result from a relaxation of the tripartite formula. By pinpointing areas of secondary interests among clients in which convergences could take place, analytical functionalism has shown us the way in which new organizational tasks can develop, producing consequences unintended by the clients but successfully enmeshing them in a larger consensus. The danger remains that indiscriminate organizational adaptation to new environmental forces will undermine the Organization's uniqueness and its political relevance. It makes sense to adapt to new client groups by admitting communist delegates without making a fetish of freedom of association; but it makes no sense to adapt so completely as to jettison the whole principle of freedom of association, thus abandoning what, politically, is a very relevant concept. By simply dropping the issue, as the International Labor Conference did in readmitting Hungary (even though that government had flouted every request and wish addressed to it by the Governing Body), the Organization runs the risk of overadapting. If it loses the role of political gadfly completely, it ceases to be a force for international integration and becomes merely a technical body.

9. *International Labor Standards*

LABOR STANDARDS: A FUNCTIONALIST NIRVANA

It is hard to conceive of a field of international practical action more appropriate to the functional perspective in projecting international integration than the setting of labor standards. The preoccupation is both highly specific and of immediate interest to large numbers of people, groups and governments of all types. Though not concerned directly with power, it is a type of welfare activity that influences national prosperity and morale. Though born in the Western-pluralistic social milieu, it is the subject of generous verbal tribute by Buddhist and Christian, Muslim and Hindu, oligarch and democrat, capitalist and proletarian, yogi and commissar. It allows us to discern not only the outlines of a universal and constantly expanding consensus—at least at the level of words—but also a fixed and routinized mode of international deliberation for determining these standards, for specifying their legal scope, and for supervising, criticizing, and investigating their implementation. National environments could thus be transformed by routinized central action; expert and lay spokesmen for voluntary groups are given an international forum; converging national aims could either produce direct consequences, or work themselves out in an integrative direction through unintended results apparent only much later.

The fact that the rules governing ILO methods for setting labor standards are subject to considerable ambiguity and debate hardly changes the relevance of the field for a functionally informed inquiry. The very ambiguity could create a constitutional and attitudinal hiatus in which skillful organizational leadership could accelerate the production of unintended consequences. In order to assess the ILO record in transforming the international environment, then, the basic legal structure governing the setting of labor standards must be sketched.

Conventions

As of 1963, the ILO has adopted 119 legal texts, 116 of which seek to set minimum labor standards, technically called "international labor Conventions." The process of drafting the texts is optimistically identified by the ILO officials as "international legislation," a description that creates the misleading impression that these instruments constitute "law." At best, they constitute treaties that become part of the law of member states only *if and when* they are ratified. There is agreement only on the principle that such instruments pose an obligation for governments to *consider* ratification. But even if they do ratify, the scope of the obligation assumed is subject to dispute.

Certain member states and the Office take the position that a ratified Convention constitutes a full legal obligation that must be carried out within twelve months by means of the necessary municipal legislation or administrative machinery. But a number of governments argue that ratification is determined by the convenience of the national legislative calendar, and that acceptance of a Convention need not be followed in short order with appropriate translation into municipal law. Finally, a certain number of states maintain that ratification constitutes merely an endorsement of the standards *in principle,* without creating any immediate obligation to revise national law or enact new law. In that case, the Convention is no more than a moral stimulus that the ratifying state creates for itself for an eventual adoption of the standards envisaged.[1]

This, however, is not the only ambiguity involved in the task of setting labor standards. It was not always clear whether the task of the Organization extended to all workers, to industrial workers only, to the families of workers, to agricultural workers, or to salaried employees. Practice resulted in a gradual expansion of the scope, undoubtedly aided by the ambiguity of constitutional provisions. On the other hand, the constitutional desideratum for *uniform* international standards was subjected to the Organization's tendency toward regionalism. The ILO was also challenged by uncertainty concerning the level of standards to be fixed: if they were made too low, many of the industrialized states would not benefit from them because their national standards already exceeded the ILO norms; if made too high, the underdeveloped states would decline to ratify. In fact, as early as 1919, the ILO permitted certain underdeveloped countries lower standards than required of the industrial members, and in 1952 it completed a Convention explicitly permitting two standards and authorizing ratification by sections. Conventions found to be too demanding are often revised downward by later conferences; upward revision occurs less often. Furthermore, states have been permitted to ratify conditionally, the condition specifying that their major competitors in world trade also ratify before acceptance enters into force.[2] The net result of this ambiguity over the level and geographical scope of norms has been to seek an average level that can accommodate the demands of most members.

A final ambiguity of the legal effect of Conventions concerns federal states. Under the 1919 Constitution, and owing to the American delegation's objection to binding international standards, federal states were permitted to treat Conventions as if they were merely Recommendations. As a result of the post-1946 revision of the Constitution, federal states can decide whether the subject matter of the Convention falls under central or local jurisdiction. If it falls under federal law, the formal obligation is the same as for the unitary state; if not, the central government is bound to communicate the text to local authorities within eighteen months of adoption, undertake consultations for federal-state coordination on common measures to carry out the Convention, and inform the Director-General of what measures have been taken. Further, federal states remain subject to the basic reporting obligation concerning unratified Conventions and Recommendations.[3] Article 19, paragraph 5, of the Constitution requires that any instrument adopted by the International Labor Conference by a two-thirds majority, labeled either a "Convention" or a "Recommendation," must, within eighteen months of adoption, be brought "before the authority or authorities within whose competence the matter lies, for the enactment of legislation or other action."*

A distinction is often made between "general" and "specific" Conventions. General Conventions are presumed to apply to all countries and all types of occupations. They are exemplified by the ILO instruments governing the abolition of forced labor, labor inspectorates, freedom of association, the right to organize and to bargain collectively, equal remuneration, non-discrimination in employment, and general social security coverage.[4] The great bulk of the Conventions, however, deal with workers in specific occupations (plantation labor, seafarers, miners, glass workers, etc.), or are aimed at eliminating specific practices (long working hours for young workers and women, excessively heavy weights for dockers, fee-charging employment services, unsafe machinery, etc.). A third type of specific Conventions creates special social security coverage for certain types of workers.

For the Functionalist, the general type of Convention is the more signifi-

* An ambiguity regarding scope, akin to that of the federal state, is introduced by the provisions of Article 35 of the Constitution, which deals with non-metropolitan territories. In principle, Conventions are declared applicable to such territories if the metropolitan power is responsible for legislation within the scope of the Convention. If the colony is self-governing, the metropolitan power has the same obligation as a federal government with respect to state authorities. If it is not, the metropolitan government must deposit a declaration with the ILO, stating whether a ratified Convention is to be applied to a given colony, and if so, whether with or without such "modifications as may be necessary to adapt the Convention to local conditions." Colonial powers therefore enjoy wide discretion with regard to applying ratified Conventions to their colonies, either in part or integrally.

cant one. Being less technical, it is likely to elicit the interest of a broader range of groups during the drafting process; for the same reason it is likely to be invoked on behalf of broader sections of the public after completion. In terms of implications, Conventions of general application are much more likely to transform the international environment than specific Conventions. This point is illustrated by examining the role of the International Confederation of Free Trade Unions in the progress of some of the major Conventions.

Convention 81 had its origin directly in the Office, though it was supported by the free workers; nevertheless the workers are disappointed by its lack of scope, and claim that there is inadequate ILO control over governmental practices. The Freedom of Association and Equal Remuneration Conventions were initiated by the free workers; but even though they persuaded the ILO to enact the provisions assuring the equality of the sexes, the ICFTU prefers to supplement the Office's work in supervising implementation by conducting its own national surveys. Convention 102 was the brainchild of a number of European social security administrators who had formerly been trade unionists. These men sought a Convention with advanced standards, but their efforts were rejected by the majority in the International Labor Conference, and a minimum standards instrument was the result. The ICFTU is itself divided on the issue, with many unions in underdeveloped countries echoing their governments' claim that they cannot afford ambitious systems of social insurance. Convention 105 resulted from previous United Nations discussion and a series of Governing Body investigations. This instrument was adopted unanimously by the Conference; it has since been so easily and widely ratified that the ICFTU promises itself very little from it, even though it provides an excellent legal basis for mobilizing political pressure against the use of forced labor for political suppression or forced economic development.

Recommendations

Instruments adopted by a two-thirds majority in the International Labor Conference and embodying desirable labor standards not intended to become binding obligations are labeled "Recommendations." The only duty incumbent on the member governments is to submit the instrument to the competent authorities for their consideration within a period of eighteen months, and to keep the ILO informed of future action. There is no other obligation. The use of this technique is justified by the ILO because it offers the possibility of creating an international social conscience without posing the immediate necessity of changing national law. Recommendations can precede Conventions by calling attention to desirable benefits for workers before governments are ready to act. But Recommendations can also be used to complete and amplify Conventions by spelling out technical and administrative details that may be found useful in implementing the Convention. The technique can thus add flexibility to the process of generating new universal norms—though the ambiguities in the system of Conventions would hardly seem to call for greater flexibility.

Even though 117 Recommendations had been adopted by 1962, the political reality is somewhat different from ILO doctrine. The very origin of the system of Recommendations bespeaks this fact, since the system found its way into the Constitution as a compromise to enable federal states in general, and the United States in particular, to remain interested in the new Organization.[5] In subsequent years, Recommendations have sometimes been adopted in lieu of Conventions, when it proved impossible to mobilize the necessary two-thirds majority. It is common for employers to press for Recommendations in order to prevent the adoption of new standards; and it is equally common for the workers to hold out for Conventions when employers and governments oppose the creation of higher norms.[6] The Office may propose a Recommendation in instances in which the actual diversity of national practices would make a Convention too cumbersome, but the workers are likely to oppose such a move.[7] Occasionally, governments that are in sympathy with a given draft Convention (and perhaps already committed in their domestic policies to carry out its substance) may argue for a Recommendation when they are certain that wide ratification and conscientious implementation are unlikely.[8] In short, the technique of Recommendations tends to be used as a political compromise, or delaying tactic, when the adoption of more rigorous standards runs into opposition.

ILO Conventions and Recommendations, supplemented by important resolutions adopted by the Conference and the Governing Body as well as by decisions of international tribunals interpreting these instruments, together constitute the International Labor Code. The term is misleading because it overstates the actual extent of international authority and legitimacy. A legal code is a systematically arranged body of binding norms; it is not a collection of separate agreements and resolutions, no single one of which is binding for all the members of the community, all of which can be denounced, and none of which can be submitted to adjudication that automatically binds the member governments.[9] For the sake of convenience, we will speak of the ensemble of Conventions and Recommendations as the International Labor Code; but it should be understood that the term contains a certain amount of inflated legitimacy.

Drafting the Instruments

A word should be said about the routine invariably followed by the ILO in arriving at a Convention or Recommendation. The formal decision to consider a given subject as appropriate for a new Convention is made by the Governing Body. This organ may arrive at its decision on the basis of suggestions received from the United Nations Economic and Social Council, the Office, the Worker or Employer Groups, or individual governments. The Office and the workers, through the ICFTU, are the most common sources of demands. Once the decision is made, the Office is instructed to make a complete survey of law and practice in member nations with respect to the subject chosen. Next, the Office prepares and circulates a questionnaire to member governments, soliciting their views on the desirability of a new instrument. If the response is sufficiently favorable, the Governing Body places the subject of a new instrument on the agenda of the International Labor Conference. The topic is then discussed in two successive sessions of the Conference, the first taking up the general principles, the second passing on the draft of a text. The actual text is drafted by the Office and discussed subsequently with a technical committee of the Conference, a procedure obviously necessary if the Office is to have an idea of what is politically feasible. On occasion, it may also be considered necessary to appoint an outside committee of experts to consider the need for and wording of a text before the matter is submitted to the Conference. Adoption of a text takes place in a plenary session of the Conference. Sometimes, the submission of a new topic to the Conference is preceded by regional tripartite conferences, or by a separate tripartite conference for a specific industry. In general, the more controversial a topic is, the more preliminary consultations and negotiations will be undertaken.

The Reporting Obligations

As a result of the constitutional amendments voted in 1946, member states are obligated to submit four kinds of reports every year, irrespective of whether they have ratified any Conventions. The first and most sweeping of these obligations is that laid down by Article 22, a duty already incorporated in the 1919 Constitution as Article 408: "Each of the members agrees to make an annual report to the International Labour Office on the measures which it has taken to give effect to the provisions of Conventions to which it is a party. These reports shall be made in such form and shall contain such particulars as the Governing Body may request." Annual reports on ratified Conventions are returned on the basis of a very exhaustive questionnaire, for each Convention, prepared by the Office and approved by the Governing Body. The questionnaire demands information on national law, administrative regulations, and court decisions with respect to *each* provision of *each* Convention. A survey of the fidelity of reporting since 1931 shows obvious oscillations; performance is least satisfactory at times of post-war adjustment and during periods when large numbers of new states enter the world arena.[10]

Second, members possessing colonial territories have a special reporting obligation. In addition to reports due under Article 22 with respect to Conventions accepted with or without modification on behalf of a non-metropolitan territory, the colonial powers are obligated to submit reports with respect to the degree to which unratified Conventions are actually applied in the law and practice of *each* colony.[11]

Third, member states assume the obligation of reporting on whether they have submitted new ILO Conventions and Recommendations to the competent national authorities for action, whether they intend to ratify or not, and what the results of such submission have been. It should be repeated that the obligation to submit does not imply the duty to ratify or implement the instrument. The constitutional provision for reports on submission is intended merely to prod member nations to consider ratifying texts previously adopted.[12]

Fourth and last, since 1949, member states have been under the obligation to submit reports on the degree to which they, in fact, apply unratified Conventions and Recommendations in their national law and practice.[13] The Governing Body selects each year a group of Conventions and Recommendations for this purpose, so that member states are not burdened with submitting such reports for all ILO instruments annually.

What is done with these voluminous reports after they reach Geneva? According to the Constitution, the Director-General of the Office and the Governing Body are responsible for administering the reporting procedure; in practice, however, matters are handled somewhat differently. The reports are received, read, and analyzed by the International Labor Standards Division of the Office, i.e., by international civil servants. They are concurrently referred to a special committee of independent experts, appointed by the Governing Body upon nomination by the Director-General, which scrutinizes them and decides on what remarks should be addressed to the reporting governments. This Committee, which is known under the imposing title of Committee of Experts on the Application of Conventions and Recommendations, is the true supervising agent; its authority is accepted by all other organs of the ILO *sine die*. After completing its annual evaluation, the Committee of Experts forwards its report to the International Labor Conference, whose Committee on the Application of Conventions and Recommendations (known familiarly as the Conference Committee) is composed of delegates to the Conference, following the tripartite formula. Its task is to debate the report of the Committee of Experts; it invariably approves the report, endorsing—and often strengthening—the remarks addressed to specific governments. The evolution, powers, and autonomy of these organs constitute important evidence of organizational development and, as such, deserve our attention.

INSTITUTIONAL AUTONOMY AND STANDARD SETTING

The Functionalist theory of international integration relies heavily on the old adage "Big oaks from little acorns grow." Neither the constitutional provisions implying supervision of national policies nor the organs designed to provide it arose full-grown and pure. In a very real way, they gradually insinuated themselves into the fabric of international discussion until they became autonomous agents of integration, asserting opinions and demands different from the initial preferences of governments. How did this come about?

Until 1925, the annual reports on ratified Conventions—until 1946 the only type of report that members were obligated to submit—were examined directly by the Conference, a practice soon made impossible by the sheer bulk of the reports. In 1925, the Conference—on a motion by the Irish government delegate, supported by the United Kingdom—decided to create a standing committee to consider the reports. After operating for one year, the committee found itself unable to cope with the volume of material, and suggested to the Governing Body the creation of a standing committee of experts to digest the reports before the Conference acted on them. There was ample opposition to this step: many governments seemed to fear that the experts would act as a commission of inquiry investigating violations of Conventions. These fears were overcome by assurances that the committee would be "technical," without power to evaluate performance or interpret Conventions; its task would be confined to comparing the texts of national legislation and ratified Conventions, and to pointing out discrepancies.[14] Further, to assure impartiality, it was to be composed of nationals of small countries. Nevertheless, the creation of both committees was vigorously fought by the Italian and Spanish government delegates.

The Committee of Experts thus began to function in 1927 with a very restrictive mandate. However, with the almost constant support of the Worker Group in the Conference, it soon enlarged its cocoon. Its members included nationals of the major powers from the beginning. In 1929, it demanded that it should have the power to raise questions regarding the *effectiveness* of application of ratified Conventions. The Governing Body consented, provided that no actual investigations and evaluations were undertaken! Soon the Governing Body admitted the Committee's demand that states be asked to make observations on difficulties encountered in applying Conventions, and that voluntary associations be invited to add their observations to the reports. Further, federal states were invited to indicate to what extent they actually applied Conventions that were, in law, only Recommendations for them. The Committee suggested, too, that governments be invited to appear before it to explain special difficulties, and again the Governing Body agreed.[15]

However, the Governing Body also refused a number of Committee initiatives to expand its mandate. When the Committee introduced the word "criticism" into its reports, the Governing Body edited it to read "observation." When, in 1932, the Committee proposed a blacklist for perennial violators of Conventions, it found no support. Similarly, the Governing Body refused to sanction a workers' suggestion that non-ratifying states be compelled to explain their inaction. A demand by the Committee that colonial powers be induced to explain why they did not apply Conventions in non-metropolitan territories was blocked by the French and British governments. Attempts by the workers to duplicate the machinery of the Committee by asking for the creation of specialized bodies to investigate conditions in coal mines, colonies, and forced labor situations failed to receive the necessary support. And when the workers demanded that they, too, be given the right to appear before the Committee, the Governing Body turned a deaf ear.[16] Yet a careful observer writing in 1937 could affirm that the Committee "no longer limits itself in giving the Governing Body a simple report on the cases of non-application it finds. It goes much further. It presents critical observations, acknowledges responses of governments, discusses them, refutes them, formulates commentaries on the interpretations presented, and advances suggestions. We see that the Committee begins to strip itself of its original purely consultative capacity. It begins to take the form of a semi-autonomous organ with its own authority."[17]

The dramatic increase in powers occurred in connection with the constitutional revisions of 1946, which we treated in Chapters 6 and 8. All the earlier accretions in institutional autonomy and responsibility were reaffirmed and expanded. Many of the indirect suggestions and insinuations that had crept into the supervisory procedure were now formalized. Specifically, the increased reporting obligations of member states under Article 19 were referred to the Committee for supervision, almost as a matter of course, by the Governing Body. Thus, the indirect practice of studying the impact of unratified Conventions, and the informal pressure for submission of instruments to competent authorities evidenced earlier, were now translated into formal powers for the Committee of Experts, as was the new mandate to investigate, occasionally, the impact of Recommendations. It is hardly surprising, then, that in the most recent period of the Committee's history, its reports have been ever more detailed, its "observations" ever more pointed, and its suggestions for remedial action more specific. Finally, let it be noted that the proposal for a blacklist of delinquents, turned down in 1932, has, in the hands of the Conference, become a standard technique of moral pressure in the post-war period.

We must now take a closer look at the Committee of Experts itself. Certain features concerning its composition stand out.[18] In terms of membership the Committee has enjoyed remarkable stability. During the pre-war period its membership was usually ten; after the war it was expanded to eighteen, but five of the pre-war members carried over into the later period. Again, several of the members served also on the League's Permanent Mandates Commission; others had served as governmental delegates to the Governing Body and the International Labor Conference, such as Sir Atul Chatterjee; almost all of them had had experience as national specialists on labor law or the administration of labor legislation, or as professors of law. Many of them had served as consultants to national ministries and administrative services; four members before the war, and eight after, were high government officials. Distinguished international figures, with experience in the League of Nations, United Nations, and international tribunals, include William Rappard, Paul Ruegger, Lord McNair, Sir Ramaswami Mudaliar, Georges Scelle, Baron Van Asbeck, Max Sørensen, and the Begum Liaquat Ali Khan. Paul Tschoffen, a prominent Belgian lawyer, served as chairman of the Committee for over thirty years; H. S. Kirkaldy, a British professor of industrial relations and frequent delegate to the Conference, has functioned as its *rapporteur* for most of the post-war period. Before the war all but three of the members were Europeans, but after the war there were fifteen non-Europeans, twelve from underdeveloped countries and eight from countries that attained their independence since 1945.

A special word should be said about the legal and political systems represented by the membership. Clearly, there is overrepresentation of democratic polities and legal systems stressing individual rights. Before the war, all members represented systems at least formally in this category. Since the war, the only persons appointed from totalitarian settings have been the Portuguese, Polish, and Soviet members.

How does the Director-General select names of candidates for appointment? In an effort to achieve a membership that will be acceptable at once to governments, workers, and employers, names are chosen through consultation with trade unions and national specialists with whom the Office confers routinely. The presence of jealous governments in the picture is dramatically reaffirmed by the fact that the name of each nominee is submitted to his home government to make sure that he is *persona grata*.

The material provided by the reports is not the only source of information available to the Committee. Since it works in close cooperation with the Office, which provides its secretariat, it has access to additional sources of information, such as national official documentation, press reports, com-

plaints from trade unions, information furnished by national ILO correspondents, conversations with visiting national officials, reports from re-
turning technical assistance experts, and—last but by no means least—
information picked up informally by secretariat members on home leave.
Hence, though the bulk of the supervisory effort still hinges on the examination of legal texts, more and more time is being devoted to the indirect
investigation of actual practice and implementation, and informal contacts
can sometimes be used to persuade delinquent governments to mend their
ways.*

How does the Committee make its decisions? In Chapter 4 we contrasted decision-making based on "judgment" with that based on "compromise." Judgmental decisions are most easily made by an uninstructed,
collegial group of specialists, who agree on the preferred outcomes of
deliberations while disagreeing on notions of background and causation;
the principle of strict majority voting suffices to make decisions that are
recognized as legitimate. Compromise decisions are made by instructed
representatives of constituent interests on the basis of negotiations, if
possible avoiding a vote; in such situations the decision-makers tend to
disagree on preferred outcomes, though they may agree on background
and causation. Now, structurally, the Committee of Experts resembles the
collegial body. The members are mostly specialists committed to the advancement of labor standards, though their individual economic and social
philosophies may and do differ. Specialization is recognized to the extent
that certain Committee members habitually assume responsibility for reading and evaluating reports on certain Conventions, a practice that results
in an internal standing division of labor. The members have habitually
deferred to each other's special competence.

In another vital respect, though, the Committee's habits do not meet
the requirement of our model. Until 1960, the Committee had never voted
on its report; all decisions had been made unanimously and as a result of
the pattern of mutual deference linked to informed discussion. Further,

---

* Yet the assessment of practical application, as distinguished from legal and parliamentary action, continues to present a great many difficulties. In 1963 the Committee listed the
data available to it for such assessments and cautiously evaluated them. See *RCE, 1963,*
pp. 12–16.

One major source of information is the evidence afforded by national judicial decisions;
but this is obviously limited by the extent to which litigation is known and accepted nationally as a routine way of resolving labor conflicts. Another source is provided by the observations that worker and employer groups are supposed to append to the annual reports of
their governments. Yet the Committee admits that the number of such observations has
"always been small"; member states lacking strong voluntary groups are unlikely to forward evidence of this kind. Further, the Committee relies on the reports of national labor
inspectors; but these vary in quality and quantity, and depend on the extent to which
nations have accepted the ILO standards regarding labor inspectorates. A final source is
provided by statistical information requested of member states; but the Committee has had
occasion to complain of the inadequacy of national response to many such requests.

the Committee has never found it necessary to draw up any rules of procedure. Finally, members of the Office have always been intimately associated with the deliberations. All this strengthens the impression that the decision-making procedures represent a hybrid between the judgmental and the computational-bureaucratic modes, a position that strongly supports the movement toward autonomy.[19]

Since 1960, a different trend seems to have been under way, something like a mixture of the judgmental with the compromise mode of making decisions. Prior to 1960 the ideological tone in the Committee had been set by the overwhelming majority of members representing democratic-pluralistic social settings; and the presence of the Portuguese member ever since the war had produced no noticeable effect on the reports and the computational-judgmental pattern. With the appearance of a Polish member the picture began to change. Values challenging the pluralist doctrine underlying ILO-endorsed standards were, for the first time, openly expressed; and the member involved, Arnold Gubinski, declined to associate himself with the Committee's critical observations concerning the limitations on freedom of association in Soviet-bloc nations.[20] In the following year the same problem arose in connection with the abolition of forced labor. Since the Committee concluded that there was evidence of the use of forced labor for political and economic development purposes in communist countries, the Polish member requested that the whole matter be dropped from the Committee's agenda.[21] Thus far, the Committee has simply noted the dissenter's view and hewed to its customary procedure. But since the appointment to the Committee, in 1962, of a distinguished Soviet jurist, E. A. Korovin, such a course may not prove feasible in the future. Far from destroying the supervisory machinery, however, the introduction of a less compliant attitude is merely likely to make majority voting the customary means for resolving conflict, thus perhaps even strengthening the Committee's institutional autonomy with regard to the surrounding international environment.

Firm evidence of the recognized independence of the Committee is provided by the fact that since World War II it has been almost free from direction by the Governing Body. Decisions of the Governing Body concerning the supervisory machinery have been made exclusively on the basis of notes and recommendations prepared by the Office. Even the questionnaires guiding the preparation of reports, which are periodically revised, are in reality drafted by the Office, though sometimes considerably modified by the Governing Body before being sent out. But the Governing Body no longer comments on the reports of the Committee of Experts; it merely notes them and sends them on to the Conference. The Committee, for its part, no longer approaches the Body for an enlarged mandate, but proceeds on its own in making ever more searching inquiries and addressing ever more critical comments to governments. However, while noting this growing autonomy, the limits on Committee action should be kept in view: unlike the Ad Hoc Committee on Forced Labor, the Experts do not carry out pinpointed investigations of specific complaints, or suggest basic new norms; unlike the Committee on Freedom of Association, the Experts do not persuade specific governments to respect the rights of specific trade unions; and, unlike the Governing Body's committees of inquiry, the Experts do not make on-the-spot investigations of allegations of delinquency. Their growing autonomy, therefore, depends on the fact that they deal mostly with documentary evidence tied to overall constitutional obligations assumed by members.

The Committee's persistence in demanding full implementation of ratified Conventions is extraordinary. Year after year, in the case of certain recurring delinquencies, pressure continues to be exerted, with the wording of the "observations" developing more and more pungency. This is accomplished while maintaining a public quasi-judicial stance. The conclusions of the Committee are considered by it as proposals based on law, to be submitted to the Conference and to be acted upon by that body. Nevertheless the pungency of the "observations" is unmistakable as the scale of terms is raised from surprise to amazement, incredulity, disapproval, reprobation, and finally condemnation.

Director-General Butler, in the mid-thirties, appraised the effectiveness of the persistence thus: "The work of the Committee of Experts permits us to achieve incontestable results, even though the relationship between cause and effect is not always apparent. In fact, many of the measures that one might regard as spontaneous at first sight have been taken by governments following observations made by the Committee."[22] Instances of national compliance with previous remarks of the Committee are revealed in each annual report and at each session of the International Labor Conference.[23] It is a standing feature of the Committee's skillful persistence that ordinarily no evidence regarding a non-implementation of a ratified Convention is published for two years after discovery, thus giving the Office and the Committee time to persuade the delinquent government to make the appropriate changes in law or practice before word of the situation reaches the Organization and the public. The information is made public only when the Committee is convinced that the infraction will continue, or when a serious infraction comes to light.

How effective is this supervisory procedure? How can effectiveness be measured? A painstaking study of *all* cases examined by the Committee of Experts, involving the conformity of national *law* with the norms of ratified Conventions, disclosed that, between 1927 and 1963, 3,248 ratifications and declarations of acceptance with respect to non-metropolitan territories came up for scrutiny. Of these, 73.1 per cent (or 2,374 cases) required no critical observations. The remaining 26.9 per cent involved infractions, which led to these results:

	No. of cases	Per cent
State undertakes full remedial action	293	31.9
State undertakes partial remedial action	258	28.1
State so far fails to remove infraction	346	37.7
State denounces Convention	21	2.3
Total	918	100.0

If we add the instances involving denunciations and refusal to comply, we arrive at a total "defiance score" of 11.3 per cent of obligations scrutinized by the Committee. This, it should be stressed, is a record of which any international agency can be intensely proud.[24]

The Committee's success may thus be attributed to the mixture of judgmental deliberations with bureaucratic-computational methods, the former being undertaken by uninstructed and wholly independent experts dealing with a set of constitutional rules capable of expansion. It is doubtful, however, if this would have sufficed to explain the evolution of the supervisory machinery if these organizational elements had not, in fact, profited from the support of the major client of the ILO—the trade unions. In order to complete this analysis, then, we must examine the relations of the Committee of Experts with the International Labor Conference, and especially with the Conference Committee on the Application of Conventions.

Governments, unless the setting be that of a sharp ideological battle, do not go out of their way in international organizations to criticize and embarrass one another. Trade union delegates suffer from no such inhibitions. Hence it is natural that the worker delegates have used the Conference and its Committee as the main forum for calling attention to the inadequate implementation of Conventions. Further, they have done so ever since the creation of the Committee in 1926. The Conference has followed the practice, while respecting the principles of tripartism and equality of delegates, of reappointing the same delegates to the Committee over long periods, thus creating a cadre of employer and worker members intimately familiar with the Conventions and recurrent cases of non-compliance.[25] Worker delegates habitually seek to compel their own governments to explain why certain Conventions are not applied completely, and they supported all efforts of the Committee of Experts to widen its mandate. This trend was particularly marked during the earlier stages of ILO history; since 1946, the autonomy of the Committee of Experts has been so well entrenched that each year the Conference Committee merely goes through the same motions of congratulating and thanking the Experts for their valuable work.[26]

Why, though, have the trade unions been so successful in using the Conference to back up the supervisory machinery? Paradoxically, the employer delegates have usually supported the workers in their efforts to extract explanations and compliance from delinquent governments, since this gave them the opportunity to portray the system of Conventions as useless. Employers delighted in uncovering evidence of non-compliance, especially instances of member states' refusal to ratify Conventions they had supported in Geneva, in order to paint the Code as a failure.[27] Governments, for their part, present no common front. Their positions have varied with the party in power at home. They have usually been exceedingly sensitive to criticism and have missed few opportunities to use the forum of the Conference to explain and justify their policies, and even to promise reforms.[28] Since the discussions of the Conference Committee can be used as a forum by the opposition, and the accusations can find their way into the domestic press, these confrontations can be very effective.

But the advent of very self-confident non-pluralistic and non-democratic member states may change the picture. Soviet-bloc "employers" and workers do not automatically side with their colleagues from democratic countries. In recent years the breakdown of perfect consensus in the Committee of Experts has been mirrored in much sharper controversy in the Conference Committee, with communist delegations opposing *en bloc* Committee texts that criticize national practices in the human rights field. A corollary of this trend has been the tendency of trade unionists from Western countries to come to the defense of their governments on Cold War issues. In the field of human rights, at least, Functionalism can be expected to transform the international environment by indirection only if the major ideological political cleavages do not always happen to coincide with the voluntary group positions in the ILO. Crosscutting rather than coinciding cleavages favor functional expansion. The Committee of Experts can hope to overcome this trend by turning more and more to compromise solutions, but the Conference Committee, which is already a negotiating body, may be pushed further into the direction of *immobilisme* if crosscutting cleavages are not maximized.

AUTHORITY AND PEACEFUL CHANGE IN STANDARD SETTING

We now turn to an examination of the success attending the ILO reporting procedure on the progress and implementation of the International Labor Code. The purpose, at the moment, is not to evaluate the Code itself; it is to analyze the ILO's reporting record in order to assess the *authority* possessed by the Organization, its capacity to oblige member states to implement their obligations despite their apparent unwillingness to do so. To the extent that this authority prevails in practice, the procedures of the ILO are helping to bring about a peaceful transformation of the international environment.

Four indicators of authority are available. All cover obligations derived from the ILO Constitution that are experienced as onerous by the member states. Filing reports on ratified and unratified Conventions, giving details on submission of new instruments to national agencies, and cooperating with studies on the extent to which the Code is applied even with respect to non-binding injunctions are burdensome tasks administratively and may well be embarrassing politically. Our indicators, then, are provided by (1) the fidelity with which annual reports on ratified Conventions are submitted, (2) the regularity with which new ILO instruments are submitted to the competent national authorities, (3) the degree of cooperation with ILO studies of the reasons for non-ratification, and (4) the responsiveness shown by persistently delinquent states after they are placed on the blacklist.

The actual record of member states in ratifying Conventions is deliberately omitted from our catalogue of indicators of organizational authority. This choice calls for an explanation. Certain aspects of the assumption of new obligations by way of ratifying Conventions will be treated when we consider the *legitimacy* enjoyed by the ILO in the standard-setting field. Enough is known of the reasons for ratifying or refusing to ratify a Convention to cast doubt on the usefulness of this criterion as an indicator of authority. Many ratifications are deposited for trivial reasons, totally unconnected with a reasoned decision to submit local labor conditions to the upward dynamism of the International Labor Code. During the tenure of Albert Thomas, it was customary to extract ratifications at the end of intimate conversations with national officials and in the course of banquets in which social conviviality prevailed over social consciousness. Conventions ratified under such circumstances during the twenties are frequently not applied very diligently today. In more recent years, the minister of labor of a Latin American country, for instance, was anxious to ratify a certain Convention, not because he was interested in implementing it, but to impress his colleagues in the cabinet with his progressive ideas; ratification was undertaken for reasons of immediate prestige of a particularly short-term nature, given the nature of the minister's regime. Hence ratifications as such should not be considered indicators of authority, a choice on my part matched by the recent policy of the International Labor Office in *not* seeking premature ratification, even to dissuade member states from ratifying Conventions when there is some ground for believing that the Convention would not be implemented soon.

The recurrent reasons advanced for non-ratification are a matter of public knowledge. They are taken sufficiently seriously by the Office to have yielded the policy of restraint. These reasons may be spurious or sincere, but they are real. At the same time, they tend to undermine the ILO ideology with respect to the equalization of labor standards among developed and underdeveloped countries; and to the extent that the Office respects these reasons, it fails to live up to its own values. Thus governments will frequently argue that they cannot accept a given Convention because local social and climatic conditions make it inapplicable; in point of fact, the purpose of the Convention may well be to overcome those very social conditions. Other nations suggest that the Convention refers to economic circumstances not yet encountered in their country, even though the point of the Convention may be to foster the development of those very circumstances. Frequently member states complain that the scope of a Convention exceeds existing national legislation, even though the purpose of the instrument was to extend that very scope. At the same time, such nations often make it clear that they are unwilling to change national law to cover additional categories of workers or to make available additional benefits to all workers. States with federal constitutions regularly claim that specific Conventions cannot be ratified because they constitute part of the competences of the local units.[29] Officials of the ILO will suggest to national voluntary groups that they put pressure on their governments for ratification only when they feel that conditions have developed so as to make ratification relatively painless, i.e., when these objections no longer apply. In other words, ratification tends to take place only when it is no longer considered onerous, thus not constituting a valid indicator of authority.

Reporting on Ratified Conventions

The simplest way to get an idea of the degree of the ILO's authority in extracting annual reports is to establish the identity of members who, during the period since World War II, have regularly, intermittently, or only sporadically submitted reports. The situation for the period 1946–62 is shown in Table 3.

TABLE 3

Member States Reporting on Ratified Conventions, 1946–62

Reporting regularly: Australia, Austria, Belgium, Burma, Byelorussia, Canada, Ceylon, Chile, Denmark, Dominican Republic, Finland, France, Ghana, Greece, Guinea, Honduras, Iceland, India, Ireland, Italy, Japan, Malaya, Morocco, Netherlands, New Zealand, Norway, Pakistan, Philippines, South Africa, Soviet Union, Spain, Sudan, Sweden, Switzerland, Tunisia, Turkey, United Kingdom, United States, Viet Nam, West Germany.

Reporting intermittently: Afghanistan, Argentina, Brazil, Bulgaria, Cuba, Czechoslovakia, Ecuador, El Salvador, Guatemala, Haiti, Hungary, Indonesia, Iraq, Israel, Liberia, Luxembourg, Mexico, Poland, Portugal, Romania, Ukraine, United Arab Republic, Yugoslavia.

Reporting sporadically: Albania, Bolivia, China, Colombia, Iran, Nicaragua, Panama, Peru, Uruguay, Venezuela.

Source: This table was compiled on the basis of information presented in *RCE, 1946–62.* The following rules were observed: (1) States that have ratified one or no Conventions were omitted. (2) States admitted to the ILO since 1960 were omitted. (3) Since many states failed to submit reports in the years immediately following World War II, performance until 1947 was treated generously in the scoring. (4) A state's performance was assessed not only with respect to its actual submission of annual reports, but also with respect to its fidelity in responding to the requests of the Committee of Experts for "supplementary information," a request regularly addressed to many states whose annual reports were ambiguous or incomplete. Thus, some states that performed quite well in regularly submitting reports were nevertheless delinquent in supplying supplementary information, which placed them in the "reporting intermittently" column. States that for many years did not report and then began to submit reports regularly were similarly classified.

We see, therefore, that the industrialized democracies as well as the economically developed totalitarian systems report faithfully. Underdeveloped countries, irrespective of political system, that possess a well-organized administrative service also perform well. Furthermore, a number of underdeveloped countries with rather authoritarian regimes and vigorous nationalisms nevertheless defer readily to ILO authority with respect to submitting reports. Even though they may resent the exercise of that authority, their eagerness to project a progressive image in world affairs seems to spur them to full cooperation. On the other hand, the list of occasional delinquents includes some Latin American countries anxious to project a progressive image but not blessed with the most efficient of civil services or the most stable of governments. Others, such as Haiti and Guatemala, are not progressive, efficient, or stable, but they are sufficiently insecure and sensitive to respond to external authority. However, it is the record of the communist states in this category that is most interesting. They uniformly show a trend of moving from complete noncompliance to increasing efforts to send reports in on time and to respond to requests for supplementary information; they thus show some sensitivity to ILO authority. Those who report only sporadically fall mostly into the category of underdeveloped countries that possess an inefficient, crisis-ridden, insurrection-prone oligarchical regime, unable to carry out any kind of continuing public functions. Albania's case is *sui generis*; Uruguay's is puzzling because it cannot be explained on any of the above grounds.

There is a good deal in this record of interest to a functional theory of integration. The faithful performance of the bulk of industrialized and democratic states is of minor significance. Their record merely confirms an exposure to functionally specific international criticism and thus maintains voluntary groups in positions of political importance relative to labor standards; but since they were already in this position before 1945, no net gain for integration can be scored. The case is otherwise with respect to the totalitarian countries that report regularly. In reporting they expose themselves to criticism, if criticism is warranted under the terms of any applicable Convention. External and internal centers of opposition are thus given a forum for undermining the monolithic quality of the state through functionally specific charges. To the extent that such charges are met by greater compliance to ILO authority, the international system grows at the expense of some of the most recalcitrant national actors. The case can be stated more strongly in the instance of totalitarian systems lacking the self-confidence and internal security of the Soviet Union, the very states that reported intermittently. In their case, international criticism was undoubtedly one factor that prompted them to comply with ILO requests. It should be noted that, for them, this was an unintended consequence of participation in the ILO to which they submitted, not always in the best of grace, because they felt they could not risk continued exposure as violators when they also sought to convey a picture of dogged work toward a new society. We may conclude that the unplanned growth of organizational authority can evolve even from actor motives that were initially purely propagandistic. More important still, even if a net increase in welfare standards cannot be demonstrated on the basis of the ILO approach, the increase in authority resulting from the reporting procedure remains of immediate relevance to the evolution of the international system because of the bureaucratic habits of compliance it may engender.

Fidelity in Submitting Instruments to Competent Authorities

In general the record of member states in abiding by the ILO Constitution in submitting unratified Conventions and Recommendations to the proper agency of the national government for examination within the prescribed time limit—or at any time—is poor. The situation for the period 1948 through 1962, as of March 15, 1962, is shown in Table 4.

Each year the Committee of Experts draws up a long list of states failing to carry out this obligation. Often this results in improved conduct the following year.[30] But in many cases the appeals fall on very deaf ears.[31] Sometimes the reason is to be found in the nature of the national legislative calendar, but more often it lies simply in the indifference of the national government, or its certainty that the instruments will be received with hostility by segments of the national public. At other times, a government

TABLE 4

FIDELITY OF SUBMISSION OF ILO INSTRUMENTS TO COMPETENT AUTHORITIES

Session[a]	Number of decisions submitted			Total members of Organization
	All	Some	None[b]	
31st Session, 1948	46	9	5	60
32nd Session, 1949	44	12	5	61
33rd Session, 1950	44	—[c]	19	63
34th Session, 1951	46	12	6	64
35th Session, 1952	45	9	12	66
36th Session, 1953	48	—	18	66
37th Session, 1954	45	—[c]	24	69
38th Session, 1955	49	5	15	69
39th Session, 1956	56	1	19	76
40th Session, 1957	55	10	12	77
41st Session, 1958	51	2	26	79
42nd Session, 1958	51	8	20	79
43rd Session, 1959	43	7	30	80
44th Session, 1960	39	1	43	83

SOURCE: *RCE, 1962*, p. 187 (slightly altered). A similar table, summarizing the situation as of March 15, is published annually in the Report.

[a] Except for the 41st Session (April-May), all sessions of the Conference were held in June.
[b] Includes cases in which no information has been supplied by the government.
[c] At this session the Conference adopted one Recommendation only.

hostile to a given text will postpone submission to parliament in order to deprive the opposition of the opportunity to call for ratification.[32] Again, the largest number of the hopeless delinquents are underdeveloped countries with oligarchic governments. But, clearly, this particular obligation is not taken very seriously by a large number of states of all types.

This indicator thus shows no growth whatever in ILO authority. Further, what is of even greater import to the Functional approach, there is a good deal of evidence that member states neglect to show the ILO instruments to representative organizations of workers and employers, as they are bound to under the Constitution.[33] The purpose of this rule, once more, is to expose the progress of international labor standards to the logic of pluralist politics. With respect to the rule to permit the regular participation of voluntary groups in examining the instruments, member nations of all types are delinquent and thus shield themselves from the integrating potential of the ILO.

Fidelity in Reporting on the Scope of the International Labor Code

In order to encourage the widest application of the International Labor Code, the ILO Constitution requires member states to submit reports, when requested to do so, on the extent to which their national legislation and practice makes use of ILO instruments even when these are *not* ratified, and therefore constitute no binding commitment in any sense. The Governing Body singles out certain Conventions and Recommendations each year for purposes of eliciting these reports. The fidelity shown in replying constitutes a particularly sensitive indicator of organizational authority because of the onerous nature of the burden and the possibly embarrassing character of the member state's response. To be sure, if the response shows the member state to be ignoring the International Labor Code, no legal delinquency exists, and the Committee of Experts is not entitled to address admonitions to the state involved. Yet an ideological embarrassment is created, and the reporting state is put on the defensive in terms of ILO doctrine if it is shown to be unconcerned with international labor standards. The failure of a state to reply to a questionnaire constitutes no evidence, by itself, that substandard labor conditions exist; but it creates presumptive evidence in the minds of the complying states that such is the case. Hence non-compliance involves a risk of tacit exposure; but compliance in the absence of general application of the Code creates an even less favorable image. By submitting reports and thus braving various risks, a member state would display great deference to the ILO's authority, particularly if it is generally known that high labor standards do not prevail.

As Table 5 makes plain, less than half of the ILO membership defers to such authority. In some instances, again, this is clearly due less to a

TABLE 5

Reporting regularly: Australia, Austria, Belgium, Bulgaria, Byelorussia, Canada, Chile, Cuba, Denmark, Finland, France, Greece, India, Ireland, Israel, Italy, Japan, Malaya, Morocco, Netherlands, New Zealand, Norway, Pakistan, South Africa, Soviet Union, Spain, Sweden, Switzerland, Tunisia, Turkey, Ukraine, United Kingdom, United States, Viet Nam, West Germany.

Reporting intermittently: Argentina, Burma, Ceylon, Czechoslovakia, Dominican Republic, Ghana, Guatemala, Guinea, Honduras, Hungary, Iceland, Iran, Luxembourg, Mexico, Nicaragua, Philippines, Poland, Romania, Sudan, Thailand, Uruguay, Yugoslavia.

Reporting poorly: Afghanistan, Albania, Bolivia, Brazil, China, Colombia, Costa Rica, Ecuador, El Salvador, Ethiopia, Haiti, Indonesia, Iraq, Jordan, Lebanon, Liberia, Panama, Paraguay, Peru, Portugal, United Arab Republic, Venezuela.

SOURCE: This table was compiled on the basis of information presented in *RCE, 1950–62*. The following rules were observed: (1) States admitted to the ILO since 1960 were omitted. (2) Performance during the years 1950–52 was treated generously, since apparently the new constitutional rules were not yet well understood by all members. (3) A state was scored as "reporting intermittently" if years of faithful reporting alternated with the non-submission of information, or if a prolonged period of non-reporting was followed by a prolonged period of compliance. (4) A state was scored as "reporting poorly" if it never reported, or if occasional years of compliance far outweighed years of non-reporting.

desire to "cover up" than to a shortage of administrative personnel able to complete and return the questionnaires. This is probably the case with respect to Iceland, Luxembourg, and Uruguay. The table shows that states known, because of economic development and prevailing social doctrine, to possess standards meeting or exceeding the demands of the Code are also faithful respondents. Furthermore, many underdeveloped nations committed to planning and anxious to increase welfare, though in many cases not yet meeting the standards of the Code, also reply faithfully—thus acknowledging ILO authority. But a larger number of underdeveloped states, as well as the bulk of the newer communist members, apparently prefer defiance of the rules to the risks of exposure. It takes little empirical work to demonstrate that Bolivia, Ethiopia, Panama, and Venezuela, to single out names in the last column at random, are far from meeting the standards of the Code.

The Blacklist

Perhaps the most telling way of observing the ILO's authority over its member states is to investigate the "special list" to which the annual International Labor Conference condemns certain perennial violators. The criteria used by the Conference for drawing up the list are in themselves highly significant. Far from including all, or even the major number, of violations brought to the attention of the ILO by the reporting procedure every year, the list includes only "certain cases where special and persist-

TABLE 6

ANALYSIS OF MEMBER STATES ON SPECIAL LIST, 1948–62

| Member state | Total | Violations | | | Improvement as a result of blacklisting[a] |
		Non-submission of annual reports	Non-implementation of observations	Non-submission to competent authorities	
Albania	14	6	5	3	None
Liberia	12	4	5	3	None
Nicaragua	10	4	3	3	None
Panama	9	3	–	6	None
Uruguay	8	3	4	1	None
Bolivia	7	3	–	4	None
Chile	6	–	6	–	None
Mexico	6	–	6	–	None
Ethiopia	6	–	–	6	None
Lebanon	5	–	–	5	None
Libya	5	–	–	5	None
Colombia	5	3	2	–	Some
Hungary	5	4	1	–	Some
China	4	2	–	2	Some
Peru	4	2	1	1	Some
Venezuela	4	2	–	2	Good
Cuba	4	3	1	–	None
Czechoslovakia ...	3	1	2	–	Some
Guatemala	3	–	2	1	Some
Ecuador	3	1	–	2	Some
Indonesia	3	2	–	1	Some
El Salvador	3	1	–	2	Some
Jordan	3	1	–	2	None
Paraguay	3	–	–	3	None
Belgium	2	–	2	–	No word
Argentina	2	1	–	1	Good
Bulgaria	2	1	1	–	Good
Costa Rica	2	–	–	2	Good
Iraq	2	1	–	1	Some
Italy	2	–	2	–	Good
Yugoslavia	2	2	–	–	Good
Haiti	2	–	1	1	No word
Egypt	2	2	–	–	No word
Afghanistan	1	1	–	–	Good
Brazil	1	–	1	–	Good
Burma	1	1	–	–	Good
France	1	–	1	–	Good
Greece	1	–	1	–	Good
Iran	1	–	–	1	No word
Iceland	1	1	–	–	No word
Austria	1	–	1	–	No word
Somali Republic .	1	1	–	–	No word
Philippines	1	–	1	–	Good
Romania	1	–	–	1	Good
Thailand	1	–	–	1	Good
Turkey	1	1	–	–	Good
Sudan	1	1	–	–	No word
United Kingdom .	1	–	1	–	No word

ent problems seem to have prevented the discharge of obligations." To qualify for blacklisting, a state must have (1) "persistently disregarded" its obligations, (2) been given the opportunity to explain itself before the Conference, and (3) been judged on *all* the evidence available in reports and discussions.[34] Let it be noted, then, that even with this wide margin of latitude in favor of the delinquent state, about half of the ILO member states have appeared on the list at some time since 1948.

The varieties of violations possible are not of equal seriousness with respect to assessing the authority of the ILO. As made clear in Table 6, the most persistent violators are delinquent with respect to all types of obligations. It should be realized, though, that non-submission of Conventions and Recommendations to the national legislature is not so serious an infraction as failure to submit reports on the application of ratified Conventions, since unsettled political conditions in the member state may make such submission impossible (as in Ethiopia, China, Venezuela, and Ecuador). Further, failure to submit reports may be due less to ill will than to administrative incompetence or domestic political upheaval (as in Colombia, Venezuela, and Indonesia). However, failure to submit reports or advance ratification cannot be blamed on unsettled conditions in the cases of Lebanon, Paraguay, Uruguay, Libya, or Mexico. Hence, lack of interest or ill will may well be present. Administrative failings in these countries are certainly no greater than in many other underdeveloped states that have responded to blacklisting by improving their performance. The most serious infraction, from our viewpoint, is the failure to heed observations, in all cases *repeated* observations, of the Committee of Experts to make national labor practices conform with the content of ratified Conventions. Failure to respond to blacklisting here constitutes the most telling evidence of lack of authority.[35]

Who, then, are the perennial bad boys? They are the members with a total score of five or more violations, unmatched by any kind of improvement. With the possible exception of Uruguay, all are underdeveloped or rapidly industrializing. They consist of only one totalitarian state, two or

---

NOTES TO TABLE 6

SOURCE: International Labor Conference, *Proceedings*, 31st Session through 46th Session, *Report of the Committee on the Application of Conventions and Recommendations*. Normally, the information on which this table is based is presented under heading III, "Special Problems," in the report for each session.

The following method of scoring the violations was employed. Each member state, theoretically, may be delinquent on three counts each year: non-submission of annual reports, non-implementation of previous observations made by the Committee of Experts with respect to ratified Conventions, and non-submission of unratified Conventions and Recommendations to the competent national authorities. The total number of violations scored against each state represents the number of occasions on which that state was blacklisted *on all counts* during the period under review, as broken down more specifically in the remaining columns. A given state, therefore, may have three violations scored against it in any one year, while in the following year it may have only one or none at all.

[a] In this column, *No word* means that violation was noted for the first time in 1961 or 1962, thus not permitting observation on rectification. *Some* means that violations were noted irregularly, and blacklisting in any one year was followed by several years of full compliance. *Good* means that violations were noted rarely, and blacklisting resulted in many years of full compliance or in complete absence of recurrence. *None* means that violations were noted without interruption since 1959, or longer.

three democracies, a number of traditional oligarchies, and Bolivia, a modernizing oligarchy. There seems to be no common denominator. Among communist countries, Czechoslovakia, Hungary, Bulgaria, and Romania have all appeared on the list, but all have shown themselves responsive to pressure; they are accepting ILO authority despite ideological disagreement. It remains to be seen whether Cuba, regularly delinquent only since the advent of Castro, will join Albania in the most prominent spot. Other traditional oligarchies, as underdeveloped as the most serious violators, have similarly displayed responsiveness to ILO authority, though many of them backslide. Nor has the fact that Cuba, Bolivia, Mexico, and Uruguay are self-consciously welfare-oriented induced them to heed the pressure of the Conference.

The reasons for non-compliance must therefore be sought in the specific infractions and in specific national conditions. For example, Chile has consistently refused to grant freedom of association to agricultural workers; Albania declines to outlaw night work for women; Mexico has long refused to enact legislation to protect dockers against accidents; both Nicaragua and Uruguay seem to have made no efforts to enact a long list of specific obligations. Yet in all these cases the states in question had ratified the Conventions, only to refuse their implementation later. The only conclusion that suggests itself is that ratification was undertaken lightly, without seriously considering the implications for the economy. Once the implications were clear, the delinquents preferred to defy the authority of the Organization rather than take the trouble to adjust national practices. Yet, interestingly enough, the International Labor Code continues to enjoy a certain amount of authority even in these instances, as evidenced by the fact that the delinquent states have not simply denounced the undesired Conventions. One thing is clear: blacklisting does not necessarily produce compliance, irrespective of the form of government or economic ideology of the violating state.

In the majority of cases, however, the blacklist does work: ILO discussion is authoritative even when it is not legitimate. States that are delinquent in submitting reports and advancing ratification do make efforts to mend their ways. This is as true of industrialized democracies as of underdeveloped oligarchies and rapidly industrializing totalitarian states. In many instances there is a sensitivity to criticism that leads to partial or complete compliance; sensitivity of this kind is perhaps not surprising in the case of Guatemala, Costa Rica, or Afghanistan. But it does suggest the reality of the authority of international criticism even in the instance of self-reliant and ideologically self-conscious totalitarian regimes anxious to project a "progressive image" of themselves. And this remains true when the infraction concerns a deliberate disregard of observations. Those who continue to defy the authority of the ILO are confined to the category of countries which, apparently, regret having ratified a given Convention. Many of these countries are, in fact, insecure and sensitive to external pressure. If pressure were carried beyond blacklisting, it is likely that Panama, Nicaragua, and Liberia could be made to defer to international authority.[36] Whether this is also true of the more self-reliant type of regime characteristic of Albania, Mexico, Uruguay, and Chile is subject to doubt.

LEGITIMACY AND VALUE CHANGE

If decisions and directives are obeyed without approval or commitment by the member state, ILO authority may be established, but the organization does not necessarily acquire the reputation that its acts are good, just, and desirable. To be regarded with approval, to be the repository for demands which, when cast in the form of new international obligations, are then implemented by those who made the demand, to be respected as a source of new norms—this constitutes legitimacy. A functional preoccupation does not require us to assume that when member states show evidence of considering the ILO "legitimate," they are acting from motives other than perceived self-interest. They may even demand performance and action from the ILO without really intending the action to take practical shape—as in initiatives introduced for propaganda reasons. But if such action results in the implementation of new obligations anyway, as an unintended consequence as far as the sponsoring state was concerned, then that state recognizes the legitimacy of international action. To the extent that such compliance creates habits and expectations for similar future action, value change in the direction of more international power is under way. How, in the case of the ILO, can we judge the presence of legitimacy?

The voluntary acceptance of new obligations, in the form of ratifying Conventions, constitutes an act of subordination to international power. To be sure, no state consciously ratifies a Convention that it considers to be detrimental to its policies. But even the convergence of a certain national interest with the content of a Convention constitutes evidence of legitimacy, since after ratification the state becomes subject to ILO criticism and review. Further, since, in the future, the state will have to enact legislation to give substance to a Convention accepted at an earlier time, in many cases a real burden is created. In short, our criterion of legitimacy is national adherence to the International Labor Code.

Four specific indicators can be used here. (1) We shall analyze the fidelity with which present and former colonial powers extend the provisions of the Code to their non-metropolitan territories—a step to which they are in no way legally obligated. (2) Upon reaching independence, these territories have the choice of retaining or denouncing Conventions accepted on their behalf by their former rulers; their degree of fidelity to these obligations constitutes a fascinating indicator of legitimacy. (3) States may be willing but unable to implement the Code; in that case they may request the International Labor Office to give them technical assistance in improving labor standards. Such requests constitute a further indicator of legitimacy. (4) Finally, a certain number of monographic studies have been prepared in order to ascertain the full scope of influence exercised by ILO action in specific states. These will be briefly reviewed.

ILO Conventions in Non-metropolitan Territories

During the first decade of ILO's history, the conduct of the colonial powers furnished little positive indication of the kind we seek. Conventions applying to colonial territories were confined to certain cautious social security measures, such as workmen's compensation and maternity benefits, minimal industrial safety and health regulations, measures for the protection of the young, minimum wage-fixing machinery and rudimentary trade union rights, and, somewhat later, the first serious measures to abolish forced labor.[37] World War II both hindered and accelerated this trend. At first, the demands for manpower and increased production resulted in large-scale retrogression in labor standards, the suspension of many ILO Conventions, and a marked decrease in ILO authority. At the same time, however, the social forces unleashed by the inclusion of many colonial populations in the war effort resulted in a new awareness on their part, which led to local demands for higher standards and more consistent welfare policies. This pressure, in turn, was met by the resurgence of welfare doctrines in the home policies of most colonial powers, and by 1945 a number of colonial welfare and development schemes had been enacted. At that point, the International Labor Code once more became relevant, and the legitimacy of ILO rose as national policies began to converge with international standards. The Conference, in the immediate post-war years, adopted a series of very sweeping Conventions designed especially for colonial territories, which furnished the bulk of the new obligations assumed by the metropolitan governments during the 1950's.[38]

Since 1955, Geneva has been deluged with declarations of acceptance.[39] Table 7 contrasts the situation at the end of World War II with the state of affairs obtaining when the bulk of colonial territories attained independence. What is especially striking with respect to the legitimacy of the Code is the startling contrast between the number of Conventions applied selectively in 1960, and the number of the Conventions formally accepted in that or previous years. The record of Belgium, France, Italy, the Netherlands, New Zealand, the United Kingdom, and the United States merits recognition. On the other hand, it should come as no great surprise that

TABLE 7

APPLICATION OF INTERNATIONAL LABOR CONVENTIONS IN NON-METROPOLITAN TERRITORIES, 1947 AND 1960

State	No. of ratified Conventions		No. of Conventions accepted on behalf of nmt territories				No. of Conventions applied in nmt territories			
			Almost all[a]		Selectively[b]		Almost all[c]		Selectively[d]	
	1947	1960	1947	1960	1947	1960	1947	1960	1947	1960
Australia	11	18	2	6	0	4	1	5	0	10
Belgium	30	53	3	17	0	8	2[g]	8	0	24
Denmark[e]	18	26	?	7	?	2	?	4	?	5
France	29	62	4	13	20	29	2	16	8	48
Italy	20	57	1	10	3[f]	7	0	16	2	39
Netherlands	23	41	7	3	11	28	2	3	7	39
New Zealand	22	37	2	5	0	4	0	5	0	19
Portugal	9	15	3	1	0	0	3	1	0	11
So. Africa	5	7	?	3	?	0	?	3	?	3
Spain	—	38	—	1	—	0	—	0	—	0
United Kingdom[h]	27	49	9	7	12	20	6	6	12	35
United States[i]	3	4	3	5	0	0	?	1	?	17

SOURCE: *Report of the Committee of Experts on the Application of Conventions and Recommendations,* 1948, pp. 32–46. *RCE, 1961,* Pt. IV, Appendix II. A query means that no information was available; a dash means "not applicable."

[a] A Convention is considered "accepted" on behalf of "almost all" colonial territories under the jurisdiction of a specific member state if that state submitted a declaration of acceptance *without* modification for the overwhelming majority of such territories.

[b] A Convention is considered "accepted selectively" on behalf of the colonial territories under the jurisdiction of a specific member state if that state submitted a declaration of acceptance *with* modification and/or has accepted the Convention only on behalf of a portion of its colonies.

[c] A Convention is considered "applied in almost all" territories if the member state is reported by the ILO as "fully applying" the Convention, or if the state enacted legislation to give effect to the Convention in the overwhelming number of the colonies under its jurisdiction.

[d] A Convention is considered "applied selectively" if the member state is reported by the ILO as applying the "substantive provisions" of the Convention, or where "there appear to be beginnings of application" in all or some of the colonies under the member state's jurisdiction.

[e] With the changed status of Greenland, Denmark ceased to be considered a state administering non-metropolitan territories. The 1947 figures exclude the Faroe Islands. The figures listed under 1960 actually refer to the situation in 1956.

[f] The figure reported in 1948 is unclear. A maximum of three Conventions appeared to have been accepted selectively.

[g] Applied to non-indigenous population only.

[h] Excluding the Channel Islands and the Isle of Man.

[i] Excluding the Panama Canal Zone.

little evidence of value change is apparent in the case of South Africa, Portugal, or Spain.

Further, since 1948 the Organization has adopted a number of additional instruments, which, even though not designed exclusively for colonial territories, are especially applicable to them by virtue of the conditions dealt with.[40] Many of these came too late to be relevant to the colonial powers; but the extent to which the newly independent territories accepted them is a further indicator of the legitimacy of the Code.

As an internationally sanctioned means of improving social policy in colonies, the Code became increasingly legitimate, and in this context the

ILO's authority increased because the Organization triumphed over several challenges. Several of the colonial powers have argued that certain territories did not have a "non-metropolitan" status under municipal law and therefore were not subject to the reporting obligation, an interpretation regularly rejected by the majority in the Conference. Britain had denied any obligation to report with respect to Conventions ratified before April 20, 1948. Yet, in 1962, "in deference to the views expressed by the Committee [of Experts] on this matter over a number of years," she removed her objections and undertook to submit all reports requested in the future.[41]

Another challenge to both the authority and the legitimacy of the procedure came from the communist bloc with respect to Article 35. Beginning in 1960, spokesmen for the bloc contended that colonialism was being perpetuated by virtue of the special provisions contained in Article 35, whereby colonial powers were empowered to accept Conventions selectively and with modifications for their remaining holdings. The universalization of labor standards should go hand in hand with the elimination of colonialism; hence Article 35 should be repealed altogether. As of 1964, the Soviet bloc had found sufficient support for this position to change the established rules.*

---

* Actually, this whole effort could also be interpreted as an incipient attempt to legitimate a new and controversial work program for the ILO. The scheme grew out of the communist bloc's attempt to bolster its global anti-colonial policy by invoking ILO doctrines, but had implications going beyond the consequences intended by Soviet propaganda. The sequence of events was as follows:

In 1961, the Soviet Union introduced a resolution into the International Labor Conference, invoking the ILO Constitution, the Philadelphia Declaration, and the UN General Assembly resolution on the immediate termination of colonialism. The operative portions called for a complete plan of action, to be prepared by the Director-General, not only for eradicating the effects of colonialism, but for intensifying the application of the International Labor Code and giving technical assistance. In addition, the resolution called for the deletion of Article 35 from the Constitution.

In that year, the resolution was not adopted because the necessary quorum was not present at the time of the final vote, even though a majority supported it. During the discussion, it became evident that the major colonial powers wished to retain Article 35, since they felt that its obligations were responsible for the progressive content of their colonial policies, a position also defended by the American Worker delegate. Whereas the governments of Australia, Belgium, Denmark, France, Germany, Japan, the Netherlands, Portugal, Spain, Switzerland, and the United Kingdom demonstrated their reservations by abstaining on the vote, Egypt, Iraq, Guinea, and Dahomey supported the communist bloc in urging the ILO to take this opportunity to expand its program into a field of vital concern. They seemed ready to legitimate new operational authority, for obvious political reasons, even though this would have meant submission to stronger international rules! Most of the Workers supported the resolution, and most of the Western Employers opposed it. International Labor Conference, 45th Session (1961), *Record of Proceedings*, pp. 682–83, 629–32, 706–10.

Essentially the same resolution, however, passed at the 1962 session. The Director-General was urged to prepare a program to overcome the "adverse consequences" of colonial rule. But as for the controversial Article 35, the Governing Body was merely requested to "consider placing on the agenda of an early session of the International Labor Confer-

The supreme test of legitimacy, however, lies in an impartial assessment of the influence of the Conventions on colonial policy. In its most recent study, the Committee of Experts concluded cautiously that it had found a favorable situation on the whole. In general, forced labor was found to be a dead issue. Freedom of association seemed permitted almost everywhere; minimum wages, protection of wages, and labor clauses in public contracts were all adequately dealt with. But equal remuneration for men and women workers was far from general practice! Health and safety measures introduced for specific industries and occupations are generally observed, as are the rules regarding medical examinations and night work for young persons. With respect to hours of work, weekly rest, and annual vacations, practice was too divergent to permit the Committee a flatly favoring finding. As regards social security, coverage is restricted to compensation for accident and illness connected with the job. Though legislation concerning labor inspectorates is generally in accord with Convention 81, the Committee expressed some doubt whether the quality and size of the public service makes possible adequate supervision and satisfactory staffing of inspection services.[42] Finally, in the general field of social policy, the Committee found it impossible to make a wholly favorable judgment because of the wide variety and great unevenness of actual practices.[43] Thus, as far as the former colonial powers are concerned, their implementation of obligations with respect to minimal safety and welfare regulations (minimal as compared with comparable norms in the metropolitan countries), and certain fundamental human rights, gives a very positive picture of the legitimacy enjoyed by the ILO.

The Assumption of the International Labor Code by New Countries

It is a commonplace to argue that the rules of international law are of Western origin and were in large part designed to protect private property. New nations in Asia and Africa, as well as many older ones in Latin America, have often objected to these two facts. While few have gone as far as did Soviet international lawyers in casting doubt on the interpretations of customary and treaty law advanced by Western governments and jurists, many of the new nations contend that the traditional rules tend to perpetuate institutions and policies unacceptable to them; such rules are unacceptable not only because they were imposed by imperialism, but because they conflict with dominant policy demands in the field of eco-

---

ence the question of revision." In committee sessions, the Employers had unsuccessfully attempted to delete this request. The resolution was passed unanimously, with 24 abstentions, apparently mostly from the Employer side. Then, at the 1964 session of the Conference, the repeal of Article 35 was made a reality in the form of a draft constitutional amendment certain to receive the necessary ratifications. International Labor Conference, *Record of Proceedings*, 46th Session (1962), pp. 508–23, 630–31, 638–41.

nomic and social development. Hence, it is hard to conceive of a more telling indicator of the legitimacy of ILO policy than the degree to which the new nations, despite the prevalence of this attitude, have voluntarily perpetuated norms imposed on them by their former rulers. Another indicator, of course, is their record in taking the initiative in accepting new obligations and exposing themselves to the hazards of the reporting and supervisory procedure.

Table 8 presents some startling trends. With few exceptions the nations listed have retained almost all the Conventions previously accepted by the European powers. Many have begun to ratify ILO Conventions on a massive scale. Some of the states most critical of "bourgeois" international law, such as Algeria, Ghana, Mali, and Guinea, nevertheless show amazing fidelity to that law. The denunciations, in short, are of minor importance, whereas the accessions and new ratifications show impressive evidence of legitimacy.

The pattern of denunciations that developed was largely shaped by the authority of the ILO itself. Former colonial territories, in their letter of application for admission to the Organization, are asked to make a "declaration of loyalty" to the Code. That is, they are asked to declare that they will continue to be bound by Conventions accepted on their behalf *without modification* by the former metropolitan nation. While they are permitted to denounce those Conventions referring specifically to non-metropolitan territories (Nos. 82, 84, and 85), they also pledge themselves to apply their content pending ratification of the corresponding generally applicable texts.[44] If practice has lived up to this formula, the evidence of legitimacy is impressive. What is the trend?

The texts intended for non-metropolitan territories have been uniformly denounced, and these comprise the bulk of the reduction in ratified Conventions scored against new nations. Conventions 87 and 98 have been overwhelmingly ratified, as have the texts dealing with discrimination and forced labor. Of the former French subsaharan territories, only Guinea and Senegal ratified Convention 81. On the other hand, all former British colonies except Burma and Malaya accepted 81 in getting rid of the obligations of 85. There is a general commitment to freedom of association, even though there appears to be no uniform enthusiasm about creating labor inspectorates.

Convention 82, the comprehensive text dealing with social policy, posed a special problem. There was no correspondingly sweeping text for metropolitan nations, and hence a new nation could not be expected to exchange its denunciation for the ratification of a parallel instrument. At the request of the First African Regional ILO Conference (1960), a new Convention was drafted and approved by the 46th Session of the International Labor Conference in 1962, making possible the continuation of measures

TABLE 8

ACCEPTANCE OF ILO CONVENTIONS BY SELECTED NEW STATES, AS OF JUNE 1963

State and date of entry	Conventions accepted by former metrop. state for colony[a]	Conventions accepted at independence	Conventions ratified since independence[b]	Net increase or decrease in Conventions accepted
Algeria (1962)	9	7	35	+33
Burma (1948)	14	14	7	+ 7
Burundi (1963)	17	15	2	0
Cameroun (1960)	15	8	1	− 6
Central African Rep. (1960)	16	12	0	− 4
Ceylon (1948)	5	4	15	+14
Chad (1960)	15	12	4	+ 1
Congo, B (1960)	16	12	0	− 4
Congo, L (1960)	18	16	0	− 2
Cyprus (1960)	17	11	0	− 6
Dahomey (1960)	16	13	2	− 1
Gabon (1960)	15	13	12	+10
Ghana (1957)	5	3	20	+18
Guinea (1959)	17	13	7	+ 3
India (1919)[c]	16	16	12	+12
Indonesia (1950)	9	3	3	− 3
Ivory Coast (1960)	17	14	11	+ 8
Jamaica (1962)	19	15	0	− 4
Malagasy Rep. (1960)	16	12	6	+ 2
Malaya (1957)	15	7	5	− 3
Mali (1960)	17	13	1	− 3
Mauritania (1961)	17	13	0	− 4
Niger (1961)	17	13	6	+ 2
Nigeria (1960)	24	18	6	0
Pakistan (1947)	16	16	12	+12
Rwanda (1962)	17	13	2	− 2
Senegal (1960)	17	13	13	+ 9
Sierra Leone (1961)	23	20	7	+ 4
Somali Rep. (1960)[d]	22	13	1	− 8
Tanganyika (1960)	23	18	6	+ 1
Togo (1960)	16	12	0	− 4
Trinidad and Tobago (1963)	20	10	0	−10
Uganda (1963)	21	12	5	− 4
Upper Volta (1960)	17	13	4	0

[a] The number of Conventions accepted on behalf of the colony by the metropolitan power was determined by adding the Conventions accepted "without modification" to those accepted "with modification." With the exception of the states mentioned below, this information was derived from *Chart of the Application of Conventions in Present and Former Non-Metropolitian Territories, RCE, 1961*, Pt. IV, App. II. For Malaya, the same information was derived from a similar chart published in *RCE, 1957*, App. II. For Ghana, Indonesia, and Ceylon approximately the same information was derived from *RCE, 1948*, pp. 38–41. Since, however, this information is not as complete as in the case of the other reports, the figures should be treated with some caution. For Burma, India, and Pakistan, the same information was taken from International Labor Office, *Chart of Ratifications*, March 1, 1950.

[b] This information was taken from International Labor Office, *Chart of Ratifications*, June 5, 1963.

[c] Even though India has legally been a member of the ILO since 1919, for purposes of this tabulation, independent decisions with respect to ratifying ILO Conventions were assumed to have begun with the 31st Session (1948).

[d] The figures for the Somali Republic represent the sum of declarations of acceptance previously deposited by Great Britain and Italy, respectively, for their former Somaliland possessions. As of 1963, the Conventions still in force were not necessarily applicable to all of the territory of the Somali Republic, with the former British and Italian sections enjoying different rights under the Conventions.

previously covered by Convention 82.[45] This effort, incidentally, to preserve international norms after independence was due largely to the demands of the worker delegates.

In the overwhelming number of instances, the denunciation of other instruments has been confined to those that had been accepted with modifications. In other words, the new states have in general abided by the rules imposed by the ILO in preserving the essence of the network of obligations assumed by the colonial powers.[46] The sharp reduction in the number of accepted instruments in the case of Malaya, Cyprus, Trinidad, and Uganda is chiefly due to the fact that Britain had accepted many texts with modifications on their behalf. The same is true of the Netherlands with respect to Indonesia. On the other hand, Burma, Ceylon, India, Nigeria, Sierra Leone, Malaya, and Ghana have begun to ratify on their own initiative many of the pre-World-War-II Conventions on hours, minimum age, workmen's compensation, and minimum wage-fixing machinery, which created standards long surpassed by the older nations. The same tendency is manifesting itself with respect to Gabon, the Ivory Coast, Malagasy, Niger, Algeria, and Senegal (especially the last two). In the case of the Somali Republic, the situation is particularly complex even though no untoward denunciations took place. The net reduction indicated in Table 8 is due to the fact that very few of the fourteen Conventions are applied in the entire territory of the country; whereas all Conventions fully applicable to the former Trust Territory and former British Somaliland, respectively, were accepted, the relevant obligations apply only to those parts of the Republic that were formerly subject to them.

Yet the returns are not all in. Earlier, we suggested that an international organization can enjoy authority without the concurrent prevalence of legitimacy. The colonial record indicates that the reverse of this proposition is equally true. I suggest that the contribution of international organization to the transformation of the international environment can take place only when authoritative actions are also legitimate actions, and vice versa. At least, the initial exercise of authority must produce legitimate reactions and value change eventually, if it is to contribute to integration; conversely, the demand for new international competences and programs must eventually bring with it a growth in authority. There is much to suggest that this is not about to occur with respect to the acceptance of the International Labor Code by revolutionary-reformist new nations.

Despite the acceptance of international labor legislation by many new states, the Committee of Experts noted in 1961 that "attempts have already been made in many countries . . . to achieve economic development through the establishment of systems of compulsory labor to carry out certain major projects. This question has been discussed in detail by the Conference, which in 1957 adopted the Abolition of Forced Labor Convention. This instrument prohibits the use of forced labor, *inter alia*, 'as a method of mobilizing and using labor for purposes of economic development.' "[47] The Committee goes on to condemn such practices, and to warn that they threaten to become general in Africa unless they are modified into a voluntary community-development approach. Further, the right to organize and to bargain collectively seems to exist on paper rather than in reality in many new states. The Committee expressed its apprehension that, in the drive for social mobilization, freedom of association would disappear. It tried to persuade new nations that the assumption of social security charges and measures for the protection of the workers need not retard economic development, since the portion of the population about to profit from such measures was relatively small. In arguing doggedly for the continued application of the Code to advance human rights and to gear economic development to the immediate enjoyment of higher welfare standards, the Committee seemed to be expressing a deep fear that revolutionary nationalism was about to sap two decades of growing ILO legitimacy.[48]

Technical Assistance to Implement the Code

Technical assistance operations of all kinds provide only the most intangible indicator of legitimacy or of authority. Their authoritative character can be assessed only when the advice of the foreign expert or the Resident Representative conflicts with the desires of the receiving government; if the relevant information were available, one could then seek to trace patterns of who prevails over whom. It may be suggested, however, that a test of legitimacy is provided if a member state requests technical assistance of the ILO in order to be able to apply a portion of the International Labor Code, whether by way of ratification or not.

Such requests are addressed to the ILO, but they occur primarily in areas of little relevance to the transformation of the international environment. They concern highly technical matters in the fields of social security, hours, working conditions and manning rules on ships, and the protection of women and children. Little such work is carried on in the field of human rights, comprehensive social policy, or the improvement of labor inspectorates, fields in which a standardization of conditions would contribute directly to the functional penetration and integration of national polities.

In the maritime field, for example, underdeveloped nations now in the process of acquiring merchant marines sometimes ask the Office for advice about which of the older maritime Conventions they should ratify in order to bring their standards into line with practice in older developed countries. But they also seek ILO action to help them write new Conventions setting *lower* standards.[49] Further, through the discussions of the

Joint Maritime Commission, the Office succeeds in making unratified maritime Conventions the basis for collective bargaining negotiations and collective agreements. This procedure is made possible by the fact that employers and unions often look for some kind of fixed framework in which negotiations can go forward, particularly in Western Europe.

Technical assistance seems to be requested most commonly for social security measures, since the extreme administrative and financial complexity of the field makes underdeveloped countries reluctant to accept the relevant Conventions.[50] Technical assistance has taken the form of regional seminars for national officials in Central and South America as well as in the Middle East, efforts designed to acquaint these officials with techniques and possibilities for applying the Code. In addition, various individual Latin American countries have requested and obtained ILO expert advice in the preparation of national social security legislation, as have India, Ceylon, Greece, Egypt, and the Philippines. Both Britain and the United States have acknowledged that they learned lessons from ILO instruments in the development of their national social security legislation during the 1930's. The Deputy Director-General of the ILO makes the following claim:

> By far the most important part of Latin American labor legislation has been enacted since the foundation of the ILO, under the direct inspiration of the standards laid down by the ILO Conference. . . . The Organization can claim to have provided a powerful stimulus, to have supplied essential technical advice and information and to have kept attention fixed upon the importance of strict enforcement and the means by which this can be secured. . . . [There is] hardly any Latin American social security . . . [that] . . . has not at one time or another been influenced by the Organization's research or other work.[51]

The importance of this type of activity can also be demonstrated in the context of regional problems arising among industrialized states. In the years immediately following World War II, international navigation on the Rhine was hindered by sharp discrepancies in the six relevant national labor codes with respect to the social security benefits and contributions, as well as the hours and working conditions, of barge and tug crews. In 1952, two regional Conventions, negotiated with the assistance of tripartite conferences convened by the ILO, overcame these obstacles by creating a common Western European body of norms applicable to all river crews, irrespective of nationality or the flag of their vessel. The rules can be enforced in any riparian state, with differences subject to compulsory arbitration; a tripartite international commission was created to examine the application of the treaties.[52]

Additional examples of the linking of technical assistance with the progress of the Code are provided in connection with the application of the Conventions dealing with fee-charging employment agencies and public employment services (Nos. 34 and 88). Mexico and Guatemala requested help from the ILO in making these already ratified Conventions a reality as far as domestic administrative arrangements were concerned.[53] However, it was the Committee of Experts that suggested to the governments of Argentina and Cuba that they ask for technical assistance in order to implement Convention 88.[54] On other occasions, the Committee politely suggested to Chile, Uruguay, and Pakistan that they request ILO technical assistance to enable them to carry out ratified Conventions.[55] With respect to the Convention on Indigenous and Tribal Populations (No. 107, 1957), the Committee delivered this general admonition:

The Committee would wish . . . to refer to . . . [a] method whereby the various Organizations [i.e., FAO, WHO, UN, UNESCO] can help governments in advancing their implementation of the Convention: they can provide technical assistance to deal with the special problems encountered in giving effect to the Convention. The Committee is aware that such assistance is already being provided in certain cases. It trusts that the governments of all states bound by the Convention will keep this possibility in mind.[56]

Frequently the context in which these suggestions occur involves the plea by a ratifying, and usually underdeveloped, country that "administrative" or "personnel" problems prohibit the application of the Convention. When the government requests technical assistance, the legitimacy of the Code seems reaffirmed; but when such assistance must be "sold" to the government, this inference can hardly be drawn.

National Case Studies

Ideally, a detailed case analysis of each ILO member state should be available to enable us to study the aura of legitimacy attending the acceptance of labor Conventions; unfortunately, I know of only six such studies, covering pre-1939 Czechoslovakia, Switzerland, Italy, Greece, Nigeria, and India. Despite the smallness of the sample, however, much interesting information is presented on the possible convergence of self-interest with international legitimacy.

The first pair, Czechoslovakia and Switzerland, represents industrialized members.[57] In Czechoslovakia the bulk of labor legislation antedates the establishment of the ILO, but the coverage provided by various laws depended on which portion of the old Austro-Hungarian Empire bequeathed territory to the new nation in 1919. Hence, the Czech government ratified some of the social security Conventions in order to have a basis for introducing uniformity into its own code. In general, Czechoslovakia declined to ratify Conventions until after national legislation met or exceeded the ILO standards. Whenever a government sought ratification in order to compel parliamentary action in improving national legislation, it withdrew its request when opposition developed in any sector of the interested public. With the onset of the Great Depression, Czechoslovakia all but ceased ratifying Conventions, though the Czech trade union movement stood in the forefront of those who constantly lobbied in Geneva and Prague for higher labor standards. This loss of interest on the government's part has been attributed to preoccupation with budgets overburdened by relief measures and to the conditions of international trade. Czechoslovakia repeatedly refused to ratify Conventions unless its major international competitor—Germany—did likewise.[58]

The Swiss example does not dramatically differ from the Czech one. In general, Switzerland's federal authorities ratified Conventions when they sought to unify, undo, or evade existing constitutional restraints in the labor field, in which case they would invoke the superior normative character of international obligations. This occurred with respect to the Conventions governing unemployment, minimum wage-fixing machinery, and night work for young persons and women, which in some instances raised and in others actually lowered previous national standards. A number of ratifications had no results because they merely confirmed existing standards in the fields of the right of association (agriculture), forced labor, statistics, and labor inspection. Some of the safety, age, and hours Conventions were ratified in order to raise and unify previous standards. But, on the whole, the impact of the International Labor Code was no more decisive in Switzerland than in Czechoslovakia. Mention should, however, be made of the possibility of using unratified Conventions to obtain a base for desirable national standards when such a base is suddenly needed. Thus, Switzerland, upon deciding to acquire a merchant marine in 1941, immediately applied six maritime Conventions without ratifying them, in order to have a yardstick for collective bargaining. The same thing happened when she decided in 1938 to enact legislation governing a minimum age for employment; then the 1932 ILO Convention on that subject became a useful model.

The second pair of cases, Italy and Greece, represents member nations making rapid strides toward industrialization and development, but until recently still underdeveloped.[59] There is no doubt that the Code did influence the progress of Italian labor legislation quite considerably. Italy is among the few states that have ratified over half of the Conventions; though frequently a given Convention was not translated into domestic legislation until some time after ratification: in short, the Conventions have tended to provide a model and a standard toward which national legislation has aimed. Whenever the Committee of Experts had occasion to point to inconsistencies between ratified Conventions and legislation, the government has usually undertaken to eliminate the discrepancy. With respect to the human rights Conventions, the rights involved already existed by virtue of the Italian Constitution, while pre-existing national laws in such fields as equal remuneration and social security permitted ratification without involving net improvement.[60]

Greece has ratified far fewer Conventions. In the instance of night work for women, ratification merely reaffirmed previous national law, thus enabling the government to resist demands for lowering the standards. In the case of some instruments regulating hours and age limits, ratification resulted in trivial adjustments slightly widening the scope of coverage. Some ratifications, moreover, took place as much as thirty years after the standards were first established by the ILO. Only in eight cases did the ratification of a Convention result in the creation of an entirely new body of rights and standards: namely, some of the older maritime Conventions, and the 48-Hour Week and Unemployment Conventions of 1919. According to our source, "analysis reveals occasional delays or restrictions in the effective application of international standards; but it has almost always been possible in the end to overcome these difficulties, so that . . . the result can be described as definitely favorable."[61] Considering the modest scope of the obligations assumed, this is a fair statement, though it suggests that the Greek conception of ILO legitimacy is hardly impressive. With the ratification of Conventions 87 and 98 in 1962, however, this picture may be changing.

Our last pair of cases, Nigeria and India, represents underdeveloped and post-colonial nations. It is evident in the Nigerian case that Britain made systematic use of the International Labor Code to legitimate progressive measures that she wished to introduce on her own volition.[62] For instance, the forced labor Convention of 1930 was applied in Nigeria in conjunction with efforts to eliminate forced labor practices rooted in tribal tradition; the Convention governing the recruitment of native labor was ratified in the context of preventing the impressing of native labor for work in Fernando Po. When Britain wished to introduce minimal rules protecting women and young workers and regulating hours and age, she turned to the applicable ILO Conventions for appropriate models. The Nigerian labor code reflects the International Code still. The Colonial Office ordered the Nigerian authorities to use the Conventions dealing with minimum wage-fixing, labor clauses (public contracts), and dockers' safety as a basis for establishing local rules, long before actually ratifying the Conventions. However, this step sufficed to induce the Nigerian Railway Workers Union to stand on these instruments when it negotiated with the government in 1946. Finally, it is claimed that the abolition of penal sanctions for breach of contract, public employment services, and freedom of association were introduced by Britain without any stimulus from the ILO. This case study, as well as the Indian, confirms that imperial nations anxious to improve working conditions for reasons of their own have generously used the ILO machinery as a means of publicly legitimating their decisions.

The Indian case is unusual because it represents a recognition of ILO legitimacy to an extent unmatched by any other member nation.[63] During the 1920's, the government of British India ratified a number of Conventions protecting workers against industrial abuses and the hardships encountered during the first steps in industrialization. According to one source, the government's aim was, in part, to increase Indian textile production costs and thus to protect competing British industry.[64] Since that time the pace of ratification has slowed down, a fact perhaps attributable to the general increase in international knowledge and literature regarding industrial conditions, as compared with the period after World War I, when the ILO was the prime forum for such lore. Still, independent India ratified some of the human rights Conventions and amended her national legislation in some twenty instances in order to bring it into line with ratified international standards. Three maritime and three social security Conventions, though unratified, largely shaped the substance of existing national legislation. Although these instruments were not very important, India solicited and received ILO technical assistance in preparing the necessary legislation. British and independent India followed the practice of *not* ratifying a Convention until national legislation met the standards involved, but of using the Convention in the interim as the guide in preparing that legislation.

ILO doctrines are most apparent, however, in the procedure used by the Indian government in preparing labor legislation. As early as 1929, a Royal Commission on labor legislation urged that administrative measures be taken to achieve a maximum of consistency and uniformity among the central government and the then provinces, a desire intensified by the system of diarchy created under the 1935 Constitution and the federal system introduced in 1947. The Commission proposed the creation of a tripartite advisory body, which was, in fact, set up in 1942 and has been functioning ever since. The structure follows the ILO representation formula, with the government members consisting of delegates from local, state, *and* central governments—thus overcoming the common argument of federal states that they lack jurisdiction with respect to the ratification of many ILO instruments. The tripartite organization examines all Indian labor legislation, and pays special attention to old and new ILO Conventions, with a view to a possible recommendation to the central government for ratification. Interest group participation and pressure is thus built into the ratification process, thereby meeting the fondest hopes of the ILO's founders that their Organization would act as a spur to pluralism at the national level. It appears that the tripartite organization, through its equally tripartite sectoral subcommittees, is actually at work applying the International Labor Code to new Indian legislation.[65]

India's case, however, is hardly typical for all of independent Asia. In an effort to spur ratification among countries reluctant to plunge into the Code, the ILO Constitution permits a great deal of "flexibility": member states may ratify Conventions with various exceptions and exclusions if underdevelopment or climate make industrial conditions differ from the Western norm.[66] No matter how such "flexibility" may be justified, it results in watering down obligations and obstructing true standardization. Such a permissive attitude toward standards was urged at the 1947 Asian Regional Conference of the ILO, resulting in a decision by the Asian members to draw up a list of "priority instruments" from among all ILO Conventions, instruments considered especially applicable and urgent for Asian countries. By 1961 the ratio of priority Conventions actually ratified, as compared with what could have been accepted, was only 23 per cent.[67]

This record with respect to ILO legitimacy in Asia is hardly reassuring, and it is scarcely improved by spotty evidence that some standards, as usual, are applied in the absence of ratification, and that many are not applied despite ratification.[68] "Flexibility" in the acceptance of standards has produced disappointing results. Only India, Pakistan, and Nationalist China seem to have been induced to accept new Conventions on the basis of the permissive "special country" clauses. The bulk of the Asian countries remains far behind in records of ratification, and continues to cite the well-known socio-economic conditions associated with underdevelopment as good and sufficient reason for not accelerating the pace. Legitimacy, then, is linked with a pre-existing national commitment to provide higher welfare standards or to unify scattered existing standards; it is not generated and produced liberally by exposure to international criticism or authority.[69]

THE INTERNATIONAL ENVIRONMENT AND
THE INTERNATIONAL LABOR CODE

A final test for assessing the role of the ILO in transforming the international environment remains. Even if neither legitimacy nor authority *regularly and predictably* flows from organizational decisions and actions, it is still possible that the program of the Organization may gradually transform the environment: it may create, at the national level, new institutions, habits, attitudes, and relations among groups that will constitute —in the aggregate—a new and different source of demands. This could occur even in the absence of new organizational powers; it might, however, be prevented from occurring by the lack of consistent legitimacy associated with ILO instruments. Hence, the acceptance of the International Labor Code, the major organizational program, must be assessed in very general terms on the supposition that this most indirect of all integrative impulses might be operative.

Particular cogency is given to this assessment by the argument that the wide acceptance of the Code proves that a global humanitarian concern dominates over rival aims, even though these rival aims made possible— in the short run—the embedding into the international order of the basic humanitarian concern. If this argument can be sustained, much comfort can be derived by the Functionalist devotee of indirection and of the legitimation of ultimate global values through the intermediary agency of expediential motives.

The argument, as developed by Francis G. Wilson in a perceptive early monograph on the ILO, runs as follows. The ILO's original goal was the achievement of world peace by the creation of social and industrial peace, a goal based on the assumption that social discontent and revolution were one of the causes of war. This, however, was to be accomplished through international labor legislation that represented formal cooperation among classes; the new order was designed to make capitalism bearable rather than to replace it by means of the class struggle. In short, it was the enthronement at the international level of the socio-political doctrines of the revisionist Socialists and their trade unions. These unions and their leaders, however, were motivated essentially by pure humanitarianism, the desire to increase welfare for its own sake—not because of any specific economic doctrine or political ideology—an approach inherited from Owen and Fourier.

To this, governments remained indifferent, if not opposed, until the year 1918. Even then the pure humanitarian argument did not move them much. Instead, they were induced to embrace the trade union position because of a prevalent conviction that they needed a strong influence to restore "the confidence of the workers in a temporarily bankrupt social order"; i.e., to co-opt the European masses with their revolutionary mood into the existing order.[70] But it was widely believed that since unequal economic and social conditions were responsible for differential production costs, the introduction of progressive legislation could not raise living standards unless labor costs ceased to be a portion of the competitive world trade picture. In short, international standardization was required to eliminate the competitive component introduced by certain low labor standards. With this immediate tangible interest in mind, governments were willing to accept the socialist trade union position without committing themselves to the underlying humanitarianism.[71]

Now, however, comes the triumph of ultimate values over immediate ones, though immediate aims ushered in that victory: since demonstrably the major competitive nations have *not* widely ratified the Conventions that would equalize labor costs, the anti-competition argument has not

TABLE 9

INFLUENCE OF ILO RECOMMENDATIONS ON NATIONAL LEGISLATION

Recommendation	Date of survey	Total member countries	Countries reporting	Conclusion re uniform application[a]
Forced Labor (Indirect Compulsion) No. 35 (1930)	1950	63	26	Yes
Forced Labor (Regulation) No. 36 (1930)	1950	63	26	Yes
Income Security No. 67 (1944)	1950	63	30	No
Social Security Armed Forces No. 68 (1944)	1950	63	27	No
Medical Care No. 69 (1944)	1950	63	23	No
Vocational Training Seafarers No. 77 (1946)	1950	63	28	No
Protection against Accidents, Dockers, Reciprocity No. 40 (1932)	1951	64	26	No
Vocational Training No. 57 (1939)	1951	64	24	No
Apprenticeship No. 60 (1939)	1951	64	25	Yes
Labor Inspection No. 81 (1947)	1951	64	27	Yes
Labor Inspection Mining & Transport No. 82 (1947)	1951	64	28	Yes
Unemployment Provision No. 44 (1934)	1952	66	27	Yes
Unemployment Young Persons No. 45 (1935)	1952	66	27	No
Public Works National Planning No. 51 (1937) ..	1952	66	27	No
Public Works National Planning No. 73 (1944) ..	1952	66	26	No
Employment, Transition from War to Peace No. 71 (1944)	1952	66	27	Yes
Employment Service No. 83 (1948)	1952	66	27	Uncertain
Migration for Employment No. 86 (1949)	1953	66	33	No
Labor Clauses Public Contracts No. 84 (1949) ...	1954	69	38	Yes
Protection of Wages No. 85 (1949)	1954	69	37	Yes
Medical Examinations Young Persons No. 79 (1946)	1955	69	38	No
Night Work Young Persons Non-Ind. Occupations No. 80 (1946)	1955	69	37	No
Collective Agreements No. 91 (1951)	1956	76	47	Yes
Equal Remuneration No. 90 (1951)	1956	76	44	Yes
Labor Inspection (Mining & Transport) No. 82 (1947)	1957	77	52	No
Labor Inspection No. 81 (1947)	1957	77	52	No
Minimum Wage Fixing Machinery No. 30 (1928)	1958	79	58	No
Minimum Wage Fixing Machinery (Agriculture) No. 89 (1951)	1958	79	58	No
Collective Agreements No. 91 (1951)	1959	80	74	Uncertain
Cooperation at the Level of the Undertaking No. 94 (1952)	1959	80	60	Uncertain
Forced Labor (Indirect Compulsion) No. 35 (1930)	1962	83	50	Uncertain
Forced Labor (Regulation) No. 36 (1930)	1962	83	50	Uncertain

[a] In scoring the descriptive evaluations of the Committee of Experts, as presented usually in Part III of the annual report since 1950, I had to use personal judgment. Usually the Committee enumerates the countries that seem to be giving effect to a Recommendation. I have therefore described application as "uniform" when a numerical majority was reported as applying the Recommendation, and as "uncertain when the Committee expressed its inability to make a clear evaluation on the basis of information received.

been vindicated in fact.[72] Instead, the ILO has happily pursued the drafting of labor legislation that it could then justify only on humanitarian grounds, and that member nations have accepted on the basis of whether they were, or were not, interested in higher labor standards, again on humanitarian grounds. The chief element underlying acceptance of the standards, Wilson argues, has not been international competitiveness but the gains in labor productivity justifying higher standards. The test we must now make, however, is whether—even on humanitarian grounds—there is a general adherence to the standards established by the Code. Is humanitarianism widely accepted as a legitimate goal?

One test is provided by the degree of observance bestowed on the Recommendations adopted by the International Labor Conference. The results that can be deduced from the Committee of Experts' annual review of selected groups of Recommendations are given in Table 9. The picture, clearly, is mixed, and the surveys are made less than satisfactory by the low percentage of countries replying to the questionnaires. It appears, moreover, that Recommendations that were uniformly applied when first surveyed no longer showed this trend when revaluated later. Whereas the general uniformity demonstrated in the case of certain procedural safeguards regarding collective agreements and equal remuneration is reassuring, the same is not true in the fields of labor inspection and minimum wage-fixing machinery. Thus, the effect of Recommendations on uniform standards remains spotty. But this overall picture should be contrasted with the usefulness of Recommendations in specific instances. It is reported that Recommendations are sometimes used as models for national legislation and for contracts in collective bargaining, simply because they frequently contain more authoritative detail than can be included in a Convention, detail based on the accumulated experience of the specialists working in the Office. One commentator concludes his survey of Recommendations by arguing that a "gamut of possibilities, a richness of formulas, enable us to understand all the implications of the system. If Robinson, Barnes and A. Fontaine could judge the results thirty years after, we would wager that they would be very astonished and that they would compare all these types of Recommendations with the rabbits and flowers which the magician pulls from his hat."[73]

Roughly the same criteria were used in evaluating the Committee of Experts' annual survey regarding the effect given to unratified Conventions, as presented in Table 10. ILO officials often cite examples of governmental use of unratified Conventions to perfect legislation; they also point out that unions frequently seek to include ILO-endorsed provisions in collective agreements.[74] The Committee's studies, however, seem to indicate that such practices remain confined to less than half of the Conventions surveyed. Uniformity seems to be achievable in the fields of social security

TABLE 10
APPLICATION OF UNRATIFIED ILO CONVENTIONS

Convention	Date of survey	Total member countries who had not ratified	Countries reporting	Conclusion re uniform application[a]
Forced Labor No. 29 (1930)	1950	41	17	Yes
Food and Catering Ship's Crews No. 68 (1946)	1950	61	29	No
Certification of Ship's Cooks No. 69 (1946)	1950	60	31	No
Seafarers' Pensions No. 71 (1946)	1950	61	29	No
Medical Examination Seafarers No. 73 (1946)	1950	61	30	Yes
Certification of Able Seamen No. 74 (1946)	1950	62	31	No
Protection against Accidents, Dockers No. 32 (1932)	1951	49	18	No
Labor Inspection No. 81 (1947)	1951	53	20	Yes
Labor Inspection Non-Met. Territories No. 85 (1947)	1951	10	7	Uncertain
Unemployment Provision No. 44 (1934)	1952	59	23	No
Employment Service No. 88 (1948)	1952	53	20	Yes
Right of Association Non-Met. Territories No. 84 (1947)	1953	8	5	No
Freedom of Association & Right to Organize No. 87 (1948)	1953	52	23	Uncertain
Migration for Employment No. 97 (1949)	1953	60	31	Yes
Labor Clauses Public Contracts No. 94 (1949)	1954	57	28	Yes
Protection of Wages No. 95 (1949)	1954	59	30	Yes
Minimum Age Non-Ind. Occupations No. 60 (1937)	1955	64	36	No
Medical Examination of Young Persons No. 78 (1946)	1955	60	34	No
Night Work Young Persons Non-Ind. Occupations No. 79 (1946)	1955	60	33	No
Right to Organize & Collective Bargaining No. 98 (1949)	1956	56	31	No
Equal Remuneration No. 100 (1951)	1956	60	38	Yes
Labor Inspection No. 81 (1947)	1957	49	29	Yes
Freedom of Association & Protection of Right to Organize No. 87 (1948)	1957	51	37	No
Minimum Wage Fixing Machinery No. 26 (1928)	1958	42	33	Yes
Minimum Wage Fixing Machinery (Agriculture) No. 99 (1951)	1958	67	49	Uncertain
Freedom of Association Protection of the Right to Organize No. 87 (1948)	1959	44	38	No
Right to Organize & Coll. Bargaining No. 98 (1949)	1959	40	34	No
Right of Association Non-Met. Territories No. 84 (1947)	1959	8	6	No
Minimum Age (Industry) No. 5 (1919)	1960	48	25	Yes
Minimum Age (Industry) Rev. No. 59 (1937)	1960	70	49	Yes
Night Work Young Persons (Industry) No. 6 (1919)	1960	49	25	Yes
Night Work Young Persons (Industry) Rev. No. 90 (1948)	1960	62	42	No
Medical Examinations Young Persons (Industry) No. 77 (1946)	1960	66	47	No
Social Security (Min. Stan.) No. 102 (1952)	1961	73	47	Yes
Forced Labor No. 29 (1930)	1962	22	11	No
Abolition of Forced Labor No. 105 (1957)	1962	48	28	No

[a] The methodological note at the foot of Table 9 applies here too.

dealing with specific categories of workers and specific contingencies, such as compensation for shipwrecked sailors. The Office argues that the effort to standardize labor legislation establishing maximum hours for women and young workers is unusually successful, if considerable time for ratification is allowed. The early Conventions in this field were first ratified only by industrialized states; others accepted them as their own industrialization gathered momentum.[75] The same seems to be true of the establishment of minimum standards regarding the operation of employment services.[76]

In the less technical fields, however, the picture is quite the reverse. The attempt to unify the various social security standards into one comprehensive document (Convention 102, 1952) failed to result in a striking flood of ratifications, even though acceptance in sections is encouraged. More striking still is the actual diversity prevailing with respect to freedom of association, despite the corpus of Conventions, Recommendations, resolutions, and exhortations regularly produced by the ILO. In 1956, the famous McNair Report established that the following restrictions on the freedom of trade unions and employer associations prevailed: [77]

Restriction	No. of countries
Registration of associations by government required	35
Restrictions for public employees imposed	25
Membership in associations limited by occupation	22
Officers of association must have specific occupation	11
Prohibition on political activities for associations	18
No use of union funds for political purposes	8
No right to form federations	20
Government controls association meetings	12
Government controls union elections	18
Government subsidizes associations	25
Government controls association finances	20
Power to dissolve association without court order	20

Lord McNair concluded that "in many of the less advanced countries restrictions and limitations exist which would afford opportunities of domination and control to a government desirous of using them."[78] Yet the diversity was so great that one simply cannot generalize about which restrictions tend to prevail in what type of political and economic system.

We possess a great deal of detailed information about the situation in Latin America.[79] While Latin American legal codes, in very general terms, permit freedom of association, wide variations in details persist just the same. Bans on political parties often extend to trade unions; trade union aims must often be subordinated to very specific legislative aims, as in Bolivia, Mexico, and Brazil; unions are prevented from participating in politics in Brazil, Chile, and Peru; in El Salvador, Chile, Honduras, and Brazil restrictions are placed on a union's affiliation with national or international federations; in seven countries, the state claims the right to prohibit, or participate in, trade union meetings; in ten countries, trade unions must be registered by the state and may be penalized in various ways for not doing so. On the other hand, union leaders are widely protected by law against dismissal or discrimination by employers. It is not uncommon, however, to find flat prohibitions against association for agricultural workers. With respect to collective bargaining, the situation is equally confused. Since voluntary associations in general are recent arrivals on the Latin American social scene, one commonly finds a great deal of dependence by trade unions on the patronizing protection of the state; collective bargaining is inhibited not so much by legal obstacles as by the weakness of organizations and the diffuse character of the economic setting. Naturally, the obstacles to freedom of association that do prevail cannot be expected to facilitate rapid change in these conditions. Significantly, compulsory arbitration and/or conciliation machinery, limiting the right to strike, exists for all, or certain, branches of the economy in most Latin American countries.

This evident and pervasive lack of uniformity in standards has given rise to two kinds of reaction among delegates to the International Labor Conference. One school, predominantly among the worker delegates, feels that the situation calls for more intensive efforts to prescribe new norms and supervise their implementation—in sort, they find that the unsatisfactory situation calls for an *expansion* of the ILO task. Otherwise, as one Swiss worker said, "the workers would gradually become estranged from the Organization."[80] Interestingly enough, this position was also defended by the Soviet Union and Brazil: both claim to consider the standard-setting work of the ILO as the Organization's greatest task.

The other school, and by far the larger, consists of delegates who seem to favor a further diffusion of standards and relaxation of efforts to devise new universal norms (although they couch their comments in phrases advocating "greater flexibility"); in short, they want a *reduction* of the organizational task. Spokesmen for underdeveloped countries complain regularly that the Conventions are too demanding for them and would impede rapid economic growth if applied now. Some delegates recommend that no new Conventions be drafted at all; others propose that the ILO concentrate for a while on obtaining more ratifications and implementation of existing Conventions before drafting new instruments. And a French worker delegate admitted frankly that "differences in economic and social conditions between different regions of the world made it virtually impossible to draft Conventions applicable to all countries."[81] In 1960, the Director-General answered these doubts as follows: "To those of you who, in this debate, have stressed the need for a reappraisal of our standard-setting work, I would only say that I am very much alive to this matter and will continue to study and come forward with new practical possibilities."[82]

As the failure of the effort to introduce uniform international labor standards becomes increasingly evident, we find a specific remedy being suggested time and again, by underdeveloped as well as industrialized member nations: namely, the formalization of regional labor Conventions. The African, Asian, and American Regional Conferences of the ILO have all endorsed this demand—but have done nothing about it. If they were to take action, such measures would merely underline the failure of a universal humanitarian impulse to overcome differentials in labor conditions. On the other hand, an approximation to such a development has occurred in Western Europe. Although only two regional Conventions have been formally prepared under ILO auspices, four additional European instruments were drafted in close consultation with the ILO and almost wholly within standards previously established as desirable by the ILO.[83]

The most comprehensive general regional Convention concluded under these auspices is the European Social Charter, drafted by the Council of Europe in close consultation with a tripartite European conference called for this purpose by the ILO. The Charter is vague and hortatory in its general provisions regarding the rights of the family and the need for social services and full employment; but in these respects it exceeds the standards laid down by the International Labor Code. However, with respect to detailed rules regarding hours, medical examinations, labor inspection, and the right to organize, the Charter does *not* meet the standards of ILO instruments, even though the actual labor conditions prevailing in most European countries are far in excess of the standards laid down in the Charter. Finally, despite the efforts of the ILO, the Charter does not provide for as consistent a pattern of worker and employer participation in securing implementation and providing supervision as is to be found in ILO instruments. But it is also true that on a variety of other detailed provisions the recommendations of the tripartite conference and of the ILO were accepted by the Council of Europe.[84] Again, then, the record regarding ILO influence is too inconclusive to justify an exuberant evaluation of the impact of labor standards on the international environment.

One highly indirect means of approaching the universalization of labor standards remains: the creation of a cohesive and united body of labor inspectors, committed to enforce a common set of rules in their daily work. Ever since 1933 the Committee of Experts and the Conference Committee have called attention to this possibility. Regional and universal conferences and seminars of labor inspectors have been convened by the ILO; repeated suggestions have been heard for the creation of an international inspectorate, for the exchange of national inspectors, and for direct technical assistance by the ILO to national inspection services. Thirty years later, we have an indifferently applied Convention on the minimum standards to be met by national inspection services and some sporadic technical assistance; but we are no closer to effective supervision that goes beyond the textual analysis of legal documents and the airing of an occasional complaint.[85] It appears, then, that neither the direct stimulus of worker dissatisfaction and international competition nor the indirect pressure of humanitarianism has given us a marked and uniform transformation of the international environment.

10. *International Collective Bargaining*

The title of this chapter is a deliberate misnomer. Strictly speaking, there is no such thing as international collective bargaining. If, however, the international setting could demonstrate developing habits, organizations, and processes that would approximate the species of interest politics we usually identify as collective bargaining, such a trend would be of enormous significance to a functional theory of integration. It could be expected to exhibit many of the traits familiar from the national political context, and to presage their replication at the international level. Task expansion and integration might be expected to follow the steps outlined in Part I of this study.

The habits, organizations, and processes most closely approximating a species of collective bargaining at the international level are represented by the ILO's ten Industrial Committees and by its Joint Maritime Commission. Whereas the former came into existence only at the end of World War II, the latter had its origin in the earliest period of the ILO. Their activities and the degree to which they penetrated the national industrial and labor fields provide the evidence for judging the thrust of international collective bargaining with respect to transforming the world environment.

INTEGRATION AND
THE ORIGIN OF THE INDUSTRIAL COMMITTEES

The Industrial Committees of the ILO originated in the economic expectations that industrialized countries developed during World War II. Nations with socialist governments were anxious to provide the proper international setting for national policies of planning and full employment, and this concern was expressed at the Philadelphia Conference and fully reflected in the draft program presented to that meeting by the Office.[1] Machinery had to be devised, in the judgment of these governments and the Office, to permit industries that were especially dependent upon international trade and competition to work out joint labor standards. The aim was to assure order and stability for the labor cost structures of such industries, thus permitting national planning to go forward without fear of interruption or interference from international competition. This machinery would consist of studies, discussions, negotiations, and the possible drawing up of industry-wide agreements that would differ from collective bargaining contracts in name only.

The official father of this idea appears to have been Britain's Ernest Bevin. But even before he made the proposal on behalf of the British government, the ILO had been receiving requests from trade unions representing the mining, steel, metal, textile, and transport industries that special international arrangements for common standards be made for them.[2] Such requests had been coming in since 1938. Bevin, in 1943, based his suggestions on Article 5 of the Atlantic Charter, which spoke of post-war economic cooperation for purposes of improved labor standards for all; he singled out the ILO as the proper forum, arguing that in the past it had not been able to deal in sufficient depth with working conditions in specific industries. He proposed that those engaged in the main industries consult together.[3] The new machinery, apparently, was to be a club of producing countries. We know that the suggestion was received with favor by the Office and the 26th International Labor Conference.

Britain and those who joined her in 1944 were especially interested in industries heavily involved in international trade. That the analogy to collective bargaining was not far from the minds of the sponsors is made evident by the following suggestions. Bevin proposed first that the conclusions of the Committees take the form of international collective agreements; alternatively, he mentioned the possibility of their taking the form of model clauses to be inserted into collective agreements concluded at the national level. The effect on economic planning and international competition would have been about the same. In 1949, the Belgian government went even further by proposing that conclusions of Industrial Committees be converted into simplified Conventions, while the International Transportworkers' Federation suggested the use of ILO Recommendations.[4]

These views did not prevail in the Governing Body, and the system of Industrial Committees at no time approximated the plan initially put forth by Bevin. International collective bargaining within, or cartel-like arrangements among, competing industries could have evolved. In either case, only the interests of industrialized ILO member states would have been protected, and the principle of universal standards would have suffered another blow. In fact, the Governing Body proceeded with extreme caution once it officially launched the Committees in 1945. It prescribed an identical initial agenda for all Committees, so that each could work out its own program and priorities only within the confines of general ILO policy. First, each Committee was to examine the social problems facing its industry during the period of transition from war to peace; and, second, each was to study "future international cooperation concerning social policy and its economic foundations in the industry."[5] So large and vague was this mandate that most of the Committees ranged broadly and unevenly over the entire socioeconomic horizon, their discussions culminating after the first few sessions in massive requests that the Office should undertake further technical studies of specific industrial conditions. Even if the complexity of the task facing the Committees had been mastered sooner, by the time more studies were available the initial *élan* toward collective bargaining had dissipated considerably.

The success or failure of the initial British scheme, however, is not our primary concern. The creation of a massive structure of representative organs, assembling the spokesmen for major voluntary groups in a quasi-bargaining setting at the international level, poses the tempting possibility of systematically analyzing behavior aiding or blocking international integration. These civil servants and interest group spokesmen represent important national elites. They meet periodically, caucus, study, negotiate, and draft instruments that may—if implemented—seriously modify national habits and conditions, thus leading through intended or unintended consequences to a more integrated international order.

The Industrial Committees constitute representative structures, whose members may be expected to agree in their assessments of background factors but to differ in the outcomes desired. Their negotiations may result in compromises at the level of the minimum common denominator, or they may upgrade common interests. Conflict may be resolved creatively or minimally. In any event, they make possible almost continuous participation by public and private leaders in the elaboration of norms vitally related to industrial peace and prosperity. *If* their participation leads to joint decisions that are perceived as good and just by the members, *and if* they are implemented with fair regularity, we could trace positive behavioral and structural integration. However, even if perceptions of justness are uneven and implementation is spotty, the decision-making structure and process created in 1945 afford a striking body of data for gauging the legitimacy of the ILO program. Functionalism can be put to the test by observing the legitimacy that its associated processes enjoy in the minds and practices of the participants. Nationally, collective bargaining constitutes a legitimate pattern of resolving industrial conflict; the participants feel engaged and committed to the resulting contract because they mixed their minds, voices, and pens in its elaboration. Clearly, we must examine the processes and internal political patterns of the Industrial Committees in order to determine whether a similar international feeling prevails in them. If so, does it follow the functional presuppositions of confrontation among experts, or the functional requisites of rational interest adjustment?

A political structure, however, may possess authority even without enjoying legitimacy. Participants may implement decisions or resolutions without, at first, considering them good, just, or binding. A demonstration of authority attending these quasi-collective bargaining sessions in the ILO, even in the absence of legitimacy, would constitute an even more powerful measure of international integration. Centrally determined norms would be fed back into the national environments despite initial opposition or indifference. Hence, in addition to observing patterns of legitimacy in the Committees, we must investigate their authority by examining the degree to which member states carry into policy what they may *not* have favored at the negotiating table. The supreme test of both legitimacy and authority, then, is the degree to which the Industrial Committees are effective in introducing new national industrial practices.

Before we can undertake either of these investigations, however, the evolution of the powers of the Committees must be sketched.

THE STRUCTURE AND POWERS
OF THE INDUSTRIAL COMMITTEES

Established by the Governing Body in 1945, and soon thereafter called into session, the Committees immediately departed from the usual tripartite formula of representation. Instead of doubling the number of government delegates in relation to those of voluntary groups, they adopted the principle of absolute parity of representation, or the very 2:2:2 formula rejected by the Governing Body when France and Belgium urged it during the debate on constitutional revision. Travel expenses of non-governmental delegates are borne by the ILO in order to assure the presence of full delegations from smaller countries. Non-governmental delegates are appointed by their respective governments; although the ILO "suggested" that such appointments be made in consultation with representative national organizations of employers and workers, this rule is apparently optional and need not be used "in cases where that method was not considered practicable."[6]

So constituted, the first sessions of the Committees were characterized by lack of uniformity and free-wheeling discussion, despite the agenda directives established for them. Further, no special rule was used by the Governing Body in selecting member states for each Committee. States were initially chosen if they possessed an obvious stake in the industry concerned; but countries who expressed an interest in being added to the membership, even if they were not among the world's leading producers of coal, chemicals, oil, or textiles, were readily accommodated for a number of years. In short, there was, at first, no consistent criterion for selecting Committee members.

Governing Body concern over this state of affairs soon led to the creation of a standing Committee on Industrial Committees as a device for assuring continued and close Governing Body control over the new, sprawling structure. In 1948, this Committee adopted a series of principles designed to guide the future debates and conclusions of Industrial Committees. The purpose of the new structure was redefined, and little trace of Bevin's scheme remained:

The International Labour Conference effectively covers the field of general policy. These Committees are to provide machinery through which the special circumstances of the principal international industries can receive special and detailed consideration. By bringing together representatives of those engaged in the industries, the Committees afford an opportunity for the discussion of common problems on the international plane in the same way as within the individual countries.[7]

The Governing Body then went on to make clear that the Committees were not to encroach on the general policy competence of the Conference, but to confine themselves to "particular and practical" industrial problems. General issues settled by the Conference could be discussed to the extent that they applied to specific industries. Only "exceptionally" were Committees to take up general issues not yet disposed of by the Conference.[8] The power to determine the agenda was again firmly lodged in the Governing Body. Agenda items not previously approved should be brought up for discussion only if approved by a majority in *each* of the three groups that make up every Committee. The technical preparation of the meetings was to be undertaken by the Office. Office members, in participating in Committee sessions, were cautioned not to lay draft conclusions or resolutions before the delegates for their approval, though they were able to point out which agenda items should be singled out for summary in a formal conclusion. "The duties of the Secretariat should be to assist the Committees in their work, but not to direct that work."[9]

In practice, this admonition is somewhat wide of the mark. Each Committee discusses the agenda for its next session—normally two to three years later—before adjourning. Invariably, the Office then refines, reorganizes, and reduces the scope of agenda items before submitting it to the Governing Body. That organ, true to its guidelines, discusses the draft agenda in detail and usually trims the Office suggestions; but it must of necessity rely heavily on Office advice in terms of technical documentation when it seeks to determine agenda items. In the early years, the Governing Body also stressed that thoughtful discussion was more important than sweeping resolutions. It emphasized the need for sound technical inquiries to precede discussion, specified that sessions should last at least two weeks, and insisted that meetings be interspersed with visits to factories and with field trips.

The most important directives, however, were laid down with respect to the effect to be given to Industrial Committee deliberations. The innocuous terms "conclusions," "reports," "memoranda," and "resolutions" were chosen rather than the more authoritative "recommendations." If a Committee adopts conclusions, these are to be addressed *to the Governing Body*, though they may call for action by employers' and workers' organizations, governments, the Office, the Conference, or other international organizations. The Governing Body then reserves the right to communicate the conclusions to governments or to bury them. The guiding directives of 1948 were vague on the precise extent to which governments and voluntary organizations were to implement conclusions; further, they referred to the duty to submit reports to the ILO in most circumspect tones.[10] In the Standing Orders given to all Committees in 1948, the normal tripartite operating procedures of the Conference were in essence repeated. However, the Governing Body assured standing representation for itself on all Steering Committees of Industrial Committees. Simple majority voting was ordained, and the Government, Employer, and Worker Groups were given the same parliamentary roles that they have in the Conference.[11]

Apparently in subsequent years the Governing Body felt that these rules were still too permissive. In 1949 it was decided that henceforth the conclusions of Committees would be sent to all governments with the observations of the Governing Body. In fact, the practice was then adopted of merely "noting" the conclusions and sending them on with the official observation that the Governing Body was not technically competent to assess their merits. Governments were then to (1) examine the conclusions, (2) communicate them to employers' and workers' associations, (3) solicit the comments of these associations, and (4) send to the ILO, nine months before the next session of the Committee, a report "setting out the position in their respective countries on the matters dealt with in the resolutions, including details of any action taken or which it is proposed to take."[12] This decision was taken in response to the Office's disappointment with respect to the adequacy of the follow-up procedure and the role of national voluntary organizations.

The procedure governing the Industrial Committees has been periodically revised right up to the present time. In 1955 and 1962, the Governing Body, apparently still concerned about proliferation and duplication of Industrial Committee activity with the work of other agencies, amended the Standing Orders so as to tighten the powers of Steering Committees in examining the receivability and expediency of resolutions adopted by the plenary Committees.[13] Further changes were also made with respect to the reporting and follow-up procedure. In 1954 the Governing Body enjoined the Committees to observe restraint in the number and scope of reports requested from governments, and it authorized the governments to confine themselves to general descriptions in specifying effect given to resolutions or in furnishing information on existing industrial conditions.

Nevertheless, in 1961 the procedure was again tightened. Each Industrial Committee was to appoint a three-man Working Party whose task it would be to examine and classify reports received, specify areas in which additional information seemed required, and determine which resolutions should be singled out for renewed follow-up steps in subsequent Committee sessions.[14] In the 1962 version of the Standing Orders, the Governing Body decreed a new procedure for assuring internal consensus in each Committee. In order to reduce prolonged wrangling among the three Groups, an automatic mechanism for determining the composition of subcommittees was established. A procedure was laid down, too, for arriving at "positive conclusions based on the widest possible measure of agreement": meetings were to combine a fixed order of study, debate, and confrontation with an opportunity for every viewpoint to find expression.[15] The same rules were to apply to the meetings of the Working Parties on effect given to conclusions. The Office felt that the inauguration of the Working Party system had contributed to the more effective consideration of Industrial Committee action at the national level.

However, by far the most extensive changes initiated by the Governing Body concerned the membership of the Committees. Two pressures forced reconsideration of the original formula. Countries that are not important producers of the international commodities covered by the Committees increasingly clamored for admission to membership, especially underdeveloped countries, since membership was becoming a mark of respectability and recognition. This threatened to extend the size of the Committees beyond manageable bounds and was therefore resisted by the Governing Body. But perhaps more important, the return of the Soviet Union in 1954 pushed to the forefront the issue of admitting a major deviant state. Obviously the Soviets were qualified, on grounds of production and employment, for admission to each of the ten Committees; but repeated secret ballots in the Governing Body defeated positive action on the Soviet application until 1959. In that year the Governing Body undertook a basic review of the membership rules, a job it had postponed since 1954. The Director-General was authorized to make a statistical study of production and employment magnitudes in all countries that had applied for Committee memberships, so that the most prominent might be selected fairly. But he was also authorized to submit a survey of past interest shown by applicants in the work of Committees of which they had been members, particularly with respect to regularity of attendance at sessions. Countries with insufficient interest were in the future to be penalized by exclusion. Finally, recognition was to be given to equitable geographical distribution, thus reducing the earlier monopoly of the major producing nations.[16] Eventually the Governing Body adopted a formula, proposed by Britain, whereby one third of the membership of each Committee would be chosen automatically on the basis of production and employment figures, a second third might be voted on if the figures were ambiguous, and the final third would be selected on the basis of geographical distribution. The Soviet Union thus became an automatic member of all Committees. Here, as elsewhere, the principle of universality had triumphed over rival principles of representation.

Before we examine in detail those aspects of the Industrial Committee structure that relate immediately to the questions of functional analysis of organizational development, a word must be said about the impact of the work as seen by the Office.[17] Conclusions adopted by certain Committees, for instance, stimulated other international organizations to adopt new international norms. The ECE Road Transport Agreement contained employment clauses drafted by the ILO Inland Transport Committee; the same Committee also produced the Conventions protecting the rights of Rhine River Boatmen. The European Coal and Steel Community code for assuring safety in coal mines issued from the ILO Coal Mines Committee. More general resolutions dealing with the stability of employment found their way into the inconclusive debates of the UN Economic and Social Council. Many conclusions on the subject of wage levels were stated, endorsing all the accepted means of fixing wages in free economies; but agreement on specific wage levels or guaranteed wages proved quite impossible. All the Committees endorsed the 40-hour week, but left the attainment of this aim up to national collective bargaining; only in the case of road transport did it prove possible to negotiate a detailed schedule of hours providing for maximum driving time and rest periods. More concrete agreement was reached in the field of job welfare services. All the Committees have adopted conclusions laying down detailed recommendations on recreation facilities, lockers, rest rooms, and drinking fountains. In the case of the Petroleum and Building Trades Committees, agreement was also reached on minimal standards of housing and worker health services. The same is true of industrial health and safety, which proved to be an area in which agreement could be reached relatively easily. The Committees here endorsed measures for training supervisory personnel, and recommended the creation of joint committees at the plant level for carrying out safety rules. Productivity is another field in which many detailed resolutions were adopted. The Committees stressed that workers must be provided with the proper incentives, that worker representatives should always be consulted in the introduction of new production techniques, and that vocational training should be undertaken by the employers in order to fit workers for more advanced production methods.

In terms of the original purposes of the Industrial Committee structure, activities with respect to industrial relations and employment are of special interest. Several Committees have endorsed the creation of machinery for associating workers with management decisions, though the full panoply of powers associated with co-determination was not adopted. They have also recommended the institution of elaborate conciliation and mediation procedures. Generally, the usual invocation of the hallowed principles of freedom of association and free collective bargaining has gone hand in hand with the description of the standard methods for third-party intercession in industrial disputes. It would appear, therefore, that the Industrial Committees have gone some way in furthering the "human relations" approach to industrial conflict, rather than the mere confrontation of hostile parties. With respect to a stable employment policy, however, the results of ten years of action have been confined to well-known platitudes. The Building Trades and Iron and Steel Committees advocated the planning of public works to serve as a countercyclical reserve force. The standard Keynesian prescription was frequently expressed in Committee conclusions. But of actual international action there was no trace.

In general, then, what can we say about the impact of this elaborate effort? On occasion, the discussion has launched a detailed investigation into prevailing conditions in a national industry, such as the ILO inquiry into the condition of Iranian oil workers in 1950. At other times, it has led to the calling of a subsequent meeting of experts, which drafted more detailed regulations, such as the unification of symbols for labeling dangerous chemicals. But these cases are rare. Very few items broached by the Committees have found their way into the agenda of the Conference or into the International Labor Code. The main impact, as seen by the Office, has been educational. Workers, employers, and administrators with experience in advanced industrial techniques are able to share their knowledge with those less experienced. The conclusions and resolutions are designed to find their way into local plant planning, local collective bargaining, the programming of public works, and the activities of labor inspectors. Far from devising new principles, the Committees serve as a vehicle for diffusing ideas long accepted by economists and industrial relations specialists in industrialized countries.

The accuracy of the Office view will be assessed when we turn to the discussion of legitimacy and authority. It is already clear, however, that the reluctance of most non-socialist governments to adopt the British view expressed itself, first, in the stringent control the Governing Body seeks to exercise over the life of the Committees. Next, it resulted in a watering down of the Committees' mandate, so that increasingly they came to concern themselves with very specialized welfare issues confined to specific industries, rather than with general international economic policy. As the Committees became larger, more diffuse in membership, and more hemmed in by procedural regulation, their work became increasingly non-political and subgoal-dominated. An imperfect consensus at the top of the power pyramid resulted in such a diffusion of function that the central international task intended in 1945 was all but lost from view. Small wonder, then, that the Office suggested in 1959 "that certain of the major Committees have now accomplished most of the useful technical work that they can immediately perform."[18] This opinion is shared by the governments of several countries, notably that of the United States.

LEGITIMACY: THE POLITICAL PROCESS IN THE INDUSTRIAL COMMITTEES

We began this chapter with a disquisition on the relationship between international collective bargaining and the integrative potential of the ILO. Yet we have all but concluded that the Industrial Committees engage in little that resembles collective bargaining. The Office seems to regard them as a forum for the dissemination of technical information by way of tripartite parliamentary procedure. The fact remains, however, that the procedure *does* approximate a collective bargaining structure, even if the results are of a different character. Further, the structure may yield results of an integrative nature, even if they do fall short of international collective agreements binding private groups and governments. It may provide evidence of the extent to which the participants attach specific notions of legitimacy to the ritual. We will now survey the internal politics of the Committees with this possibility in mind, turning our attention to the tripartite, bipartite, and multipartite representative bodies.

Tripartite Bodies: Industrial Committees

One indicator of the extent of legitimacy enjoyed by an institution in the minds of its members is the degree of interest they display in joining and utilizing the institution for their individual ends. It is therefore of great significance that *no* country has ever voluntarily withdrawn from an ILO Industrial Committee; all who have enjoyed membership have wished to continue to exercise this apparent claim to international respectability, even if their past interest in the work and the standards of the Committees had been minimal.

When the Governing Body, in 1959, undertook its review of the Committee membership, fifty countries applied for admission to the Committees, at a time when the overall membership of the ILO was approaching eighty. All the applicants submitted material and arguments stressing the importance of the respective industries in their economic life. Several of them advanced additional arguments that shed some light on their perception of legitimacy. Twelve past members applying for reappointment to membership claimed that they had faithfully sent delegations to meet-

ings, had taken the resolutions seriously, and had tried their best to implement them locally in cooperation with workers' and employers' groups.[19]
These countries, then, supported their claim to membership by citing conduct closely connected with the transformation of national environments.
With three exceptions, they are old industrialized or rapidly industrializing
nations. Three applicants, however, advanced a different argument concerning legitimacy. They contended that underdevelopment, the desire to
modernize, and the principle of equitable geographical distribution justified their admission.[20] Finally, three communist applicants argued that
their admission was necessary because a variety of economic systems should
be represented in the ILO; the overall size of the Committees should be
extended to thirty countries in order to allow the world's workers maximum
opportunity to participate in discussions involving the advancement of
their living standards.[21]

Clearly, governments consider membership important and desirable.
But this by no means implies that they take the work of the Committees
equally seriously. On the contrary, most government delegations are very
passive in the actual discussions of the ten Committees. Individual governments, on occasion, make strong presentations on specific points. But the
Government Group in the Committees initiates nothing. Governments tend
to prefer to permit workers and employers to argue out matters; their
Group has no position to defend and takes no sustained interest in guiding
the work of the Committees. With respect to participation, therefore, a
feeling of legitimacy comprises the fact of belonging, but *not* the functional
correlative of active interest in the consequences of belonging. This, at
least, is true of the majority of governments. As we shall see later, certain
welfare-oriented industrial states display legitimacy feelings comprising
both elements of the concept.

The Employer Group functions well in the Committees. Its members
come well-prepared and thoroughly briefed on the implications of agenda
items. Their positions are the result of previous caucusing and information
received from subject-matter specialists of the International Organization
of Employers. These specialists, as well as representatives of other international employer associations, attend Committee sessions and confer with
the regular employer delegates. Yet the long-standing dispute within the
ranks of the employers on the question of communist employer delegates
also arose in the Industrial Committees. When credentials were challenged,
as they invariably were between 1954 and 1960, a compromise was adopted
by which the communist members were seated as "deputy delegates,"
normally without the right to vote. This, however, did not prevent these
delegates from intervening consistently and effectively in the deliberations.

As for the worker delegates, their cohesion varies. If their activities have
previously benefited from briefing and coordination on the part of the

central organizations of ICFTU and ICCTU, the workers will present a solid common front; and even in the absence of adequate preparation, they will attempt to maintain a cohesive voting bloc. The communist delegates from Eastern Europe have minimized propaganda and have associated themselves constructively with the general position in the Worker Group; but the communist workers from France and Italy have followed the opposite line, thus countering the policy defended by the Group. Unlike the employers, it appears that the workers have no consistent program or continuity of policy aims that can be advanced in successive sessions. Workers, to be sure, consider the Committees and participation in them as indicators of respectability and influence; but, as in the case of governments, they do not consistently link the legitimacy of belonging to sustained interest in producing and implementing concrete policy. As a rule, workers go to the sessions and then attempt to make up their minds on outstanding policy questions after they arrive in Geneva. If their respective International Trade Secretariats (ITS's) have done a good job of guidance, they will be cohesive; more often, this is not the case.

The ITS, therefore, is the central focus of effective worker participation. In general, the ITS's that are affiliated with the ICFTU—because of their size and complexity—fail their affiliated workers. But their counterparts in the Christian Federation do a much more thorough job in preparing positions and advancing initiatives within the Industrial Committees. Yet for all the ITS's, whatever their affiliation, the very existence of the Committees is a welcome channel of expression. They leave no doubt that the mere opportunity of participation is considered highly desirable, thus giving proof that the institution holds legitimacy for them. The ITS's consistently approach the Governing Body Committee on Industrial Committees with requests to include on the agenda matters close to their hearts. The Industrial Committees are the chief international lobbying channel open to these trade unions, and they make full use of it.[22]

Industrial Committees are representative of fixed interests which, in advanced economies, bargain with one another at the national level. Do they bargain similarly at the ILO even though the results of their confrontation have not been sweeping international labor contracts? The evidence is that workers and employers do, but that governments do not; and—what is more—that governments assume no clear responsibility for aiding the implementation of the bargain that has been struck. Representative structures tend to make decisions on the basis of majority voting. Industrial Committees are empowered to do so, and they do, in fact, adopt many of their resolutions on this basis. Are such decisions considered legitimate by all? Apparently they are not. On several occasions when the Governing Body reviewed the work of specific Committees, the employers disputed the legitimacy of conclusions adopted by narrow margins. This review, in fact, serves as an opportunity for reopening issues that had not been settled to the satisfaction of all participants at the Committee level. The operative principle of legitimate decision-making, therefore, is not simple majority voting but quasi-unanimity. As Price remarks:

What has in fact happened is that there has been a large measure of accommodation on all sides and that general agreement has usually been reached on the maximum that was possible at the moment. If that maximum has sometimes seemed too little to some of the delegates, they have nevertheless appreciated the difficulty of making spectacular progress when the interests of three groups and a great variety of countries have to be reconciled.[23]

This cautious summary by a member of the Office suggests that the actual pattern of accommodation takes place at the level of the minimum common denominator. Decisions made on other grounds lack legitimacy in the eyes of some participants, even though these same elements cherish belonging to the structure.

Bipartite Bodies: The Joint Maritime Commission

The contrast to the Industrial Committees is provided by the purely bipartite Joint Maritime Commission (JMC) of the ILO, which acts as a unique and successful international forum for "pre-collective bargaining." Its success is closely related to the nature of the industry it covers. Maritime transport is probably the most keenly competitive international industry. Minute cost differentials among national shipping lines may spell large differences in earnings. The world commercial setting is characterized by sharp cyclical fluctuations in the volume of trade available for shipping and the amount of tonnage competing. Seamen's unions in all maritime countries, therefore, have a common interest in preventing this competition from taking place at the expense of their welfare. Shipowners in countries with strong unions have an interest in imposing standards relating to catering, certification, manning, crew quarters, and wages on their competitors. While the same principle should apply in all industries, the narrow margin of profit in shipping makes the issue particularly acute in the case of seamen. Not surprisingly, therefore, the International Transportworkers Federation (an ITS affiliated with the ICFTU) and the International Federation of Shipowners are among the most cohesive and disciplined international interest groups.*

The seamen's unions agreed to support the establishment of the ILO in

---

* In the case of the ITF, cohesion is also partly the result of the long and strong leadership of Omar Bécu, who exercised immense influence on the leaders of national maritime unions. Seamen's unions tend to defer to the decisions worked out at the level of the ITF; international positions become national positions. Consultation between the two levels is continuous, so that the national union leaders feel the ITF position to be their own once negotiations take place in the ILO setting.

1919 only on condition that special arrangements be made for the accommodation of their interests. The arrangement, which headed off the creation of a special international organization dealing with maritime labor matters, was twofold: (1) periodically the annual International Labor Conference would be devoted exclusively to maritime matters and to the drafting of maritime Conventions; (2) a standing bipartite commission for the industry would be set up within the ILO to prepare for the Conference. And thus the JMC came into being, the institutionalized meeting-ground of organized seamen and shipowners.

The JMC has the task of working out the items that the parties wish the Governing Body to place on the agenda of the maritime sessions of the Conference. In addition, the JMC is the forum in which any number of other contentious issues are negotiated that never find their way formally into the International Labor Code. Normally, the ITF takes the initiative on both grounds. It presses the Office for action on issues of concern to seamen. The Office then communicates these demands to the Shipowners' Federation and mediates toward an agreed list and definition of issues. Thereupon, the Governing Body is given a statement of demands, which is then referred to the JMC for further refinement, leading to discussion by the Conference, or alternatively to direct negotiation in the JMC. In either case, the deliberations of the JMC itself—though formally bipartite—obviously rely consistently on the mediatory services of the Office. The decision-making structure is no longer purely representative, but includes a bureaucratic component that is able, on occasion, to upgrade common interests through its mediatory services.

The JMC, acting alone or with the cooperation of the Office or Governing Body, has headed off any number of international seamen's strikes. When informed that the JMC was getting ready to consider a specific grievance, the ITF has postponed strikes; it has used the need to negotiate in Geneva as an argument to persuade its more militant national affiliates to stay their pickets.[24] At other times, negotiations in the JMC have fixed the outlines within which national collective bargaining took place; such confrontations have successfully standardized international practices with respect to crew welfare in ports and the air-conditioning of crew quarters, even in the absence of ILO Conventions.

Preparation of new Conventions relies even more heavily on the Office. Whereas the parties define the area they wish covered by new standards and the Governing Body formally authorizes submission to the Conference, the Office does the technical work of preparation and actually drafts the standards and the final Conventions. In the JMC no effort is made to elaborate a final text. "Pre-collective bargaining" sums up a process under which outstanding issues are narrowed down, especially as the items being negotiated become more technical all the time. The JMC provides the forum in which the preliminary sweeping demands are voiced, countered, refuted, rejected, and eventually compromised into a narrower range of negotiable issues. By the time such a compromise is reached, all talking for effect has been completed, and the list of issues that remains constitutes the preliminary agreement between the two parties. This agreement represents, not a new contract, but an agenda of agreed items calling for new international norms to be elaborated by the next maritime session of the International Labor Conference.

The maritime Conventions adopted by the ILO tend to be very specific. If generally ratified, they would constitute the equivalent of a universal seamen's code and would almost obviate the need for additional collective agreements at the national level for the matters covered. Negotiating them would constitute effective international collective bargaining. However, many of the Conventions are not widely and generally ratified. In fact, their entry into force is usually conditional upon ratification by the major shipping nations, who are both inconsistent and slow in ratifying.[25] The faithful ratifying states include the West European ones; but most of the underdeveloped countries that operate large merchant marines fail to ratify. The most comprehensive set of standards ever written, the Seattle Conventions of 1946, by and large never entered into force.

Hence the major value of the Conventions lies in the spur to national collective bargaining that many of them provide. Some countries, notably the United States, apply the standards contained in Conventions in the absence of formal ratification. Many underdeveloped countries make an effort at implementing early maritime texts because they wish to have some minimum standards, but feel unable to introduce the levels that now obtain on European and American ships.[26] Agreements worked out in the JMC are important even in this context because the chief actors in Geneva are the same persons who later negotiate collective agreements at the national level. Hence, even in the absence of ratified Conventions, principles arrived at in the JMC can find their way back into collective agreements simply because the same parties negotiate both.

Pre-collective bargaining still falls short of the ultimate confrontation desirable for the success of integration along functional lines. But it comes a great deal closer to it than the diffuse activities of the tripartite Industrial Committees. If bipartite negotiations aided by the central bureaucracy seem fruitful for continued integration, what can we say about the multipartite approach?

Multipartite Bodies: The Permanent Agricultural Committee

For the sake of contrast, one variant representative body will be described here even though its work is not such as to become relevant to the study of environmental transformations due to functional impulses. The

ILO Agricultural Committee, after limited experience before 1944, was reconstituted after the Philadelphia Conference at the special request of Asian underdeveloped countries and of Poland. Its work is not of direct concern to industrial trade unions or employers, and tends to overlap with that of the Food and Agricultural Organization. In short, the Committee was to provide services for certain governments preoccupied with agricultural modernization and thus stood outside the normal pattern of interest confrontation in the ILO. Although its work has proved largely irrelevant to our analytical concern, the principle governing its composition remains germane.

The Governing Body intended the Committee to be broadly representative of all types of agricultural interests, but wished the members to be appointed by it rather than by governments or voluntary organizations. Actually the members are formally appointed by the Governing Body, upon nomination of the Director-General. They comprise (1) six representatives of the Governing Body, two from each Group; (2) one representative each of eight major national organizations of agricultural employers and workers; (3) sixteen agricultural experts, connected with smallholders' organizations, governmental administration, universities, and research institutions; (4) one representative each for the International Federation of Agricultural Producers and the European Confederation of Agriculture; and (5) one representative each for three International Trade Secretariats of agricultural workers. Although all these people are broadly "representative" of interests, they nevertheless serve in their personal capacities at the pleasure of the Governing Body.[27] Their initial agenda consisted of studies and discussions of vocational training in agriculture, child labor, the effects of technological improvement on agricultural employment, and the highly charged issues of tenancy and sharecropping.

Obviously, an organ so diffuse and so dependent on central direction as the Agricultural Committee is unlikely to trigger an interaction process similar to that of the JMC, or even to that of the Industrial Committees. It is merely able to serve the Governing Body and the Director-General as a guide to the international consensus existing in the agricultural field. A multipartite committee, therefore, is ill-adapted to the maximization of the integration process.

AUTHORITY AND LEGITIMACY: MEMBER STATE PERFORMANCE

The elaborate follow-up procedure built into the operations of the Industrial Committees suggested the possibility of a rigorous quantitative evaluation of organizational authority. Each Committee reviews from time to time the resolutions, memoranda, conclusions, and statements it has adopted, and selects at each session certain of these for specific attention. Questionnaires are then drawn up by the Office and sent to *all* ILO member states in the hope that member governments will reply and thereby indicate the extent to which the Committees' standards have found their way into national policy and practice. Further, each ILO member state receives a copy of the Committee texts at the end of each session, irrespective of whether or not it is a Committee member. In short, all members are able to implement the standards laid down, even when they do not participate in the discussion and elaboration of norms. By using the replies returned to Geneva in response to the Office inquiry—replies that are systematically summarized and assembled—I have attempted a quantitative assessment of organizational authority.[28]

My survey of performance has omitted resolutions addressed to organs and audiences other than national governments or voluntary groups. Each text may contain several specific recommendations; if so, each was counted separately. On occasion, a Committee adopted, at a later session, a text substantially similar to an earlier set of recommendations; if so, I have combined the two texts and counted responses only once.

Replies were coded as follows:

No reply—Government furnishes no response to a specific recommendation singled out for follow-up information by an Industrial Committee.

Evasive—Governmental response is vague and general.

Does not apply—Governmental response contends that local conditions render the recommendation inapplicable.

Complies fully—Government indicates that recommendation was used in introducing new national labor standards.

Complies in part—Government indicates that a portion of the recommendation was used in introducing new national labor standards.

No intent—Government makes clear that it has no interest in the recommendation and no intention of applying it.

Describes existing conditions as good—Government merely describes existing conditions in the industry that seem to conform essentially with the content of the recommendation.

Describes existing conditions as fair—Government merely describes existing conditions in the industry that seem to conform to some extent with the content of the recommendation.

Describes existing conditions as poor—Government merely describes existing conditions in the industry that seem not to conform with content of the recommendation.

But only states participating in the work of the Committees are clearly under an obligation to furnish the ILO with periodic reports on the use they make of these texts.[29] Others may or may not report; some do, some do not, and others do intermittently. Since there is no clear obligation for *all* member states to report *all* the time, there appears to be no equitable and meaningful measure of total possible positive performance. Given the enormous unevenness in the actual reporting pattern of all ILO member states, our first gross measure, then, will be a statement of *individual performance of all reporting countries* (Table 11, p. 311) and a summary of *total performance in each Committee of all reporting countries* (Table 12, pp. 314–16). The analysis will be confined here to ascertaining which countries most frequently comply with all or parts of resolutions, and to stating which countries report existing industrial conditions to be roughly consonant with the texts of resolutions.

A second measure restricts quantitative analysis to those states that at one time or another had actively participated in one or more Industrial Committees. Such an analysis enables us to judge whether fidelity of implementation continues after active participation ceases, whether a member state once exposed to the negotiating process of a Committee continues to feel committed to it and carries the commitment over into its national policy. A full quantitative analysis was once more impossible because of the tremendous variations in national reporting. Some former Committee members continue to report, others stop completely, and still others report selectively. Again, there appears to be no consensus in the ILO about whether former members remain under an obligation to continue their reports. In the absence of such an agreement, it would seem unfair to penalize states that do not report or to credit governments that do. Since there is no unambiguous norm of possible perfect performance, a wholly comparative picture of fidelity resulting from earlier participation has not been attempted. Instead, the episodic information derivable from the ILO reports on Industrial Committee activity concerning this type of performance has been summarized as *special performance* beyond the clear call of duty. Rather than constituting a measure of organizational authority, this analysis tends to pinpoint countries and activities with which a special sense of legitimacy is evidently associated (Table 13, pp. 320–21).

A third measure, however, proved both feasible and meaningful in comparative terms. It seeks to measure the *degree of fidelity in implementing recommendations that accompanies active participation in the work of the Committees.* My criterion for fixing active participation was the legal position of a country on a Committee; a country was considered an "active member" for the term for which it was elected to full membership by the Governing Body. This criterion therefore excludes states that attended as observers, or whose full membership was ambiguous; and it includes states that enjoyed full membership, but chose not to exercise it by absenting themselves from certain sessions. This procedure enables us to exclude responses received from countries not enjoying membership at any time, or at a time when they were not legally required to respond. Two exceptions to this rule were introduced. Some governments enjoying membership at a certain point so interpret their obligations as to assume that they still owe the ILO a response for the session following their retirement from a Committee. Hence, responses received in the session immediately following the last session during which a country enjoyed membership were included in the analysis. Similarly, countries newly elected to a Committee often feel obligated to submit reports immediately upon election, but before having actually participated in the elaboration of norms. Such diligence was rewarded by including the responses in our tallies.

Hence, the basic measure of ideal fidelity of a full participant is the category "Total replies possible." It represents the sum of separately coded items (for each country and each Committee), taken from texts selected by the Committees for follow-up of action carried out at the national level. Percentage values for each category were then computed by using "Total replies possible" as the base figure. The number of "Total replies possible" therefore represents the responses a given government *could* have given to all specific recommendations for action addressed to it. If a government had faithfully carried out all these recommendations, the category "Complies fully" would read "100 per cent," i.e., 100 per cent of all replies possible (Tables 15 and 16, pp. 324 and 326). As such it is the most rigorous test of organizational authority.

Total Performance

Our gross measure of organizational authority is the degree to which all member states—irrespective of membership on the Committees—comply fully or in part with resolutions of the Committees. The results of sixteen years of experience with the system are summarized in Table 11. The top category of countries comprises those reporting more than fifty instances of full and/or partial compliance; the second category comprises those reporting between twenty-five and fifty instances; and the last—and largest—category consists of those reporting fewer than twenty-five instances.

The range extends from those confessing to no compliance at all to India's high score of one hundred instances of compliance.* What do these clusters suggest about the relationship between member state characteristics and organizational authority? The countries in the top category of fidelity are all democracies. They possess old industrial economies, or are in the process of rapid and energetic industrialization. With the exception of Japan and Turkey, they profess the doctrines of the welfare state. Moreover, the same countries report that existing industrial conditions approximate the standards recommended in the ILO resolutions. In short, ILO authority is strongest in democratic countries whose social and economic

---

* The United Kingdom's score of 127 instances is slightly misleading, since it includes the performance of colonial governments that may not have been acting under instructions from London.

TABLE 11

INDUSTRIAL COMMITTEES: INDIVIDUAL PERFORMANCE OF ALL
REPORTING COUNTRIES

(*Number of instances as reported by countries*)

Country	Complies fully	Complies in part	Conditions good or fair	Country	Complies fully	Complies in part	Conditions good or fair
Belgium	23	63	145	Dominican Rep.	0	3	46
Canada	13	48	248	Greece	0	0	2
France	29	75	293	Guatemala	1	1	6
Germany	26	38	210	Haiti	0	0	4
India	20	80	158	Indonesia	0	1	30
Japan	10	58	153	Iran	0	0	10
Netherlands	14	39	224	Iraq	0	0	6
Turkey	18	36	55	Ireland	0	0	1
U.K.	22	105	666	Israel	2	3	22
				Liberia	0	0	0
Australia	10	19	96	Luxembourg	2	2	3
Austria	6	24	188	Malaya	0	6	43
Denmark	7	34	87	Mali	0	0	1
Finland	2	28	83	Mexico	2	5	43
Italy	17	30	141	Morocco	1	0	0
Norway	5	40	131	New Zealand	0	15	128
Poland	7	21	43	Nigeria	0	4	49
Sweden	6	23	162	Pakistan	2	3	40
Switzerland	5	23	87	Peru	0	0	1
U.S.	2	25	146	Philippines	0	5	59
				Portugal	0	0	6
Argentina	0	13	49	Saudi Arabia	0	0	1
Brazil	2	4	12	Spain	0	2	19
Burma	4	8	37	Syria	0	0	0
Cameroun	0	0	0	Thailand	0	0	1
Ceylon	5	14	92	Tunisia	1	0	7
Chile	1	6	57	U.A.R.	12	4	36
China	0	1	2	So. Africa	2	5	33
Colombia	0	1	1	Uruguay	3	3	13
Costa Rica	0	0	8	U.S.S.R.	0	1	13
Cuba	0	2	19	Venezuela	0	1	7
Cyprus	1	0	0	Vietnam	0	1	36
Czechoslovakia	0	4	12	Yugoslavia	0	0	27

Total number of countries reporting: 64.

conditions are in harmony with the organizational ideology. This finding
suggests that the countries requiring *least* persuasion and encouragement
to make their national economic life conform with international standards
are *most* disposed to obey; conversely, those most in need of persuasion
are the least amenable, as shown by the large number of underdeveloped
free-enterprise nations possessing oligarchical regimes that appear in the
third category.

The bulk of the countries appearing in the second category are also
democracies. Further, all of them are welfare-oriented with respect to

social policies pursued at home. Their economies are fully industrialized, rapidly industrializing, or maturely agricultural. By and large they report their existing industrial conditions to be essentially in conformity with ILO standards. So why do they not submit to the authority of the ILO more frequently? There is no uniform answer. Australia, Austria, Switzerland, and the United States are federations and therefore precluded constitutionally—according to their own claims—from applying some of the ILO standards by way of central action. Poland, the only totalitarian country here to show some responsiveness to ILO authority, can hardly be expected to be a top performer. And it may well be that the four Scandinavian countries that appear in this category have relatively little to gain from submission to ILO authority, since standards already exceed the recommendations of the Industrial Committees.

Is there, then, little hope for increasing organizational authority with respect to the bulk of the underdeveloped countries? The examples of India and Turkey would seem to suggest that whenever political democracy is combined with a determined drive to industrialize *and* to attain a modicum of planned social-welfare benefits, ILO authority is likely to increase as such countries turn to Geneva for examples and advice. Clearly, the present task of the ILO—or any other United Nations agency—is insufficient to make much of an impact nationally with respect to the intensification of these characteristics. But if autonomous national forces tend in the appropriate direction, the authority of the Organization will probably increase as an incidental consequence.

Table 12 summarizes data on the instances of compliance with the recommendations of Industrial Committees so as to permit us to assess the authority of specific Committees with reference to individual countries. I have tried to answer two questions in compiling these statistics: (1) which Committees display the highest degree of authority in terms of the number of instances of compliance reported; and (2) which Committees have sufficient influence over their members to produce a generalized compliance pattern among *all* members, irrespective of the national political and economic characteristics that have been shown to be favorable to ILO authority.*

The committees, in terms of the sum of full and partial compliances, rank as follows from the most to the least authoritative:

---

* In order to answer the second question, a statistical measure of general distribution of compliance had to be devised. I chose the cut-off point of 5 per cent of the total compliance score for each Committee. In other words, if all member states, on the average, had complied to the same extent with all recommendations, each would account for approximately 5 per cent of the total compliance score. If the 1959 membership figure of the Committees (average 22) had been used, the cut-off point actually should have been fixed at 4.55 per cent. But since average membership before 1959 was somewhat lower, I felt justified in rounding the figure to 5 per cent.

1. Coal Mines	More than 200 compliances
2. Building Trades 3. Chemicals 4. Metal Trades	More than 100 compliances
5. Plantations 6. Iron and Steel 7. Textiles 8. Salaried Employees 9. Inland Transport	More than 50 compliances
10. Petroleum	Fewer than 50 compliances

Apparently, the work of the Committee on Coal Mines struck a very distinct chord of responsiveness among the membership, whereas the Petroleum Committee worked in a complete vacuum. To some extent, of course, this record is to be explained in terms of the particular resolutions that engendered the compliances, a point to be explored later. But the crucial task at the moment is the pinpointing of specific countries which responded most to organizational authority.

The least successful Committee—Petroleum—also shows a very lopsided distribution in the reporting of satisfactory existing conditions. Only one of the many underdeveloped countries with an oil industry reported conditions comparable to the four industrialized countries that scored high. Neither industrial nor underdeveloped countries were interested in complying. A similar relative lack of authority can be imputed to the Committee on Plantations. Three of its twenty-one member states accounted for *all* the full compliances, while a further six were responsible for 70 of the 78 instances of partial compliance. Of the many underdeveloped countries concerned with work on plantations, only four were among those who considered the work of the Committee authoritative. On the other hand, the reporting of satisfactory conditions seems relatively well distributed over the membership. Finally, the organ dealing with Salaried Employees must be included among the unsuccessful Committees. There were no instances of full compliance, while partial compliances were dominated by eight of the twenty-one members. But, again, since only five countries accounted for the 94 reports of concentrated satisfactory conditions, the incidence of such conditions must be fairly general in the member states. Once more, only one underdeveloped country is on the list of prominent states—Ceylon.

At the opposite end of the continuum, we find two Committees with an approximately even spread of compliances: Coal Mines and Iron and Steel. Both organs feature many countries who comply with resolutions and who report satisfactory existing conditions. Whereas the Committee on Coal Mines included no underdeveloped and few industrializing countries among its faithful, the Iron and Steel Committee can boast Brazil and Chile among newly industrializing countries who consider its work authoritative.

TABLE 12

Industrial Committees: Total Performance of All Reporting Countries

(Number of instances as reported by countries)

Committee and number of members in 1959	Full compliance		Partial compliance		Good & fair conditions	
	Chief countries[a]	No.	Chief countries[a]	No.	Chief countries[a]	No.
Coal Mines (18) ...	Australia	5	Belgium	37	Belgium	26
	Canada	9	France	32	Canada	22
	France	9	India	33	France	33
	Germany	13	Japan	27	Germany	22
	India	5	Poland	17	Japan	21
	Netherlands	8	Turkey	16	Netherlands	47
	Poland	6	U.K.	40	New Zealand	14
	U.K.	7	Total	202	U.K.	27
	Total	62	*Total partial compliance*	271	U.S.	17
	Total full compliance	70			Total	229
					Total good & fair conditions	278
Petroleum (20)	None		None		Austria	20
	Total full compliance	0	*Total partial compliance*	2	Burma	22
					France	25
					Germany	20
					U.K.	18
					Total	105
					Total good & fair conditions	278
Textiles (25)	None		Argentina	5	Canada	28
	Total full compliance	6	Belgium	3	France	19
			Brazil	3	Germany	16
			Canada	3	India	17
			Denmark	4	Norway	19
			India	3	Sweden	21
			Japan	3	U.K.	21
			Turkey	3	U.S.	18
			U.K.	4	Total	159
			Total	31	*Total good & fair conditions*	322
			Total partial compliance	54		
Metal Trades (24) ..	Belgium	8	Finland	16	Austria	26
	Germany	4	France	7	Canada	34
	Denmark	2	India	8	Finland	30
	India	2	Japan	8	France	37
	Japan	2	Netherlands	9	Germany	29
	Switzerland	2	Norway	13	Italy	25
	Total	20	Switzerland	7	Netherlands	27
	Total full compliance	27	U.K.	6	Norway	25
			U.S.	6	Sweden	43
			Total	80	U.K.	33
			Total partial compliance	115	Total	309
					Total good & fair conditions	498

TABLE 12 (*continued*)

Committee and number of members in 1959	Full compliance Chief countries*a*	No.	Partial compliance Chief countries*a*	No.	Good & fair conditions Chief countries*a*	No.
Building Trades (25)	Denmark	3	Canada	12	Austria	31
	France	7	Denmark	10	Canada	56
	Turkey	9	France	11	France	44
	U.A.R.	12	Germany	10	Germany	41
	Total	31	India	11	Japan	44
	Total full		Netherlands ...	9	Netherlands ...	34
	compliance	49	New Zealand ...	7	Norway	44
			U.K.	12	Sweden	36
			Total	82	U.K.	34
			Total partial		Total	364
			compliance	135	*Total good & fair conditions*	621
Salaried Employees (21) ..	None		Belgium	3	Austria	19
	Total full		Ceylon	3	Canada	22
	compliance	9	Denmark	3	France	18
			Germany	7	Germany	17
			Netherlands ...	5	Norway	18
			Norway	4	Total	94
			Sweden	4	*Total good & fair conditions*	307
			Switzerland ...	3		
			Total	32		
			Total partial compliance	51		
Inland Transport (27) ...	Belgium	2	Finland	3	Austria	23
	Ceylon	1	France	5	Canada	27
	India	2	Germany	4	Germany	27
	Italy	4	Netherlands ...	3	Italy	35
	Total	9	New Zealand ...	3	Netherlands ...	37
	Total full		Turkey	3	New Zealand ...	27
	compliance	14	U.K.	6	U.K.	22
			Total	27	Total	198
			Total partial compliance	45	*Total good & fair conditions*	383
Chemicals (21)	Australia	3	Denmark	15	Austria	26
	Belgium	8	Italy	11	France	23
	France	3	Japan	9	Germany	22
	Germany	6	Norway	16	India	17
	India	3	Sweden	8	Italy	19
	Italy	5	Switzerland	7	Japan	23
	Sweden	3	Turkey	7	Sweden	16
	Turkey	3	U.K.	9	U.K.	24
	Total	34	Total	82	U.S.	23
	Total full compliance	49	*Total partial compliance*	122	Total	193
					Total good & fair conditions	312

(*continued on following page*)

TABLE 12 (*concluded*)

Committee and number of members in 1959	Full compliance		Partial compliance		Good & fair conditions	
	Chief countries*a*	No.	Chief countries*a*	No.	Chief countries*a*	No.
Plantations (21) ...	Burma	4	Australia	4	Ceylon	54
	India	5	Burma	7	France	59
	U.K.	9	Ceylon	6	U.K.	443
	Total	18	France	9	Total	556
	Total full compliance	18	India	10	*Total good & fair conditions*	995
			Malaya	6		
			Nigeria	4		
			U.K.	24		
			Total	70		
			Total partial compliance	78		
Iron & Steel (21) ...	Australia	2	Belgium	8	Austria	24
	Belgium	2	Canada	8	Belgium	21
	Brazil	2	Chile	4	Canada	20
	Canada	2	France	5	France	21
	France	7	India	6	Germany	16
	India	2	Italy	3	India	17
	Italy	3	Japan	4	Japan	15
	Japan	3	U.K.	3	Netherlands	27
	Luxembourg	2	Total	41	South Africa	15
	Mexico	2	*Total partial compliance*	53	Sweden	20
	Netherlands	2			U.K.	30
	South Africa	2			Total	226
	Sweden	2			*Total good & fair conditions*	292
	U.K.	2				
	U.S.	2				
	Total	37				
	Total full compliance	39				
	Grand total full compliance	281	*Grand total partial compliance*	926	*Grand total good & fair conditions*	4286

a Countries accounting for 5% or more of the total number of reported instances. Reporting countries never scoring 5%: Cameroun, China, Colombia, Costa Rica, Cuba, Cyprus, Czechoslovakia, Dominican Republic, Greece, Guatemala, Haiti, Honduras, Indonesia, Iran, Iraq, Ireland, Israel, Liberia, Mali, Morocco, Pakistan, Peru, the Philippines, Portugal, Spain, Syria, Thailand, Tunisia, Uruguay, U.S.S.R., Venezuela, Vietnam, and Yugoslavia.

The remainder of the Committees falls between the two extremes described. Building Trades, Inland Transport, and Textiles perform poorly, i.e., compliances tend to be concentrated; but the incidence of satisfactory conditions is relatively widespread. Further, even though these industries are particularly widely distributed among underdeveloped *and* industrial countries, very few underdeveloped economies actually figure among the consumers of ILO resolutions. Egypt is prominent in recognizing the authority of the Building Trades Committee, and Ceylon that of the Inland Transport Committee, but that exhausts the roster. Predictably, Brazil and Argentina, as rapidly industrializing nations, find the authority of the Textile Committee quite palatable. The Metal Trades and Chemicals Committees performed somewhat better in terms of a generalized spread of compliances, though less well than Coal Mines or Steel. However, the work of neither proved authoritative for countries other than the core of Western industrial nations who, together with Turkey and India, make up the bulk of the faithful. Other newly industrializing countries took less interest in their work, and underdeveloped countries can hardly be expected to report on industries that they do not possess and are not installing.

Thus, in general, the Committees with the best record in securing compliances are also the most successful in securing a wide incidence of their norms. However, evidences of authority remain heavily and disproportionately concentrated in democratic-industrial-welfare-oriented states in *all* Committees, even in those dealing with industries widely encountered in underdeveloped and newly industrializing countries. Typically, the Committees most successful on all counts are the ones responsible for the industries symptomatic of a high degree of industrialization. Authority, then, is far from evenly recognized. Countries least in need of help in securing higher standards are the most faithful. Only those among the presumed consumers of aid in securing social justice who have made a democratic or revolutionary commitment to dramatic modernization recognize the authority of the Committees.

This conclusion suggests the way in which the ILO's international authority will develop in the future. Underdeveloped countries being guided toward modernity under the aegis of relatively stable democratic governments will continue to identify with ILO norms. They can do so without violence to their nationalism or the dominant values of their leaders. However, nations in Africa, Asia, and Latin America that are being weaned away from traditionalism under the forced draft of quasi-totalitarian single parties, revolutionary oligarchies, or charismatic leaders are also potential consumers of the same norms and thereby become, indirectly, subject to ILO authority. These leaders—and the same is true of the post-Stalinist communist parties of Eastern Europe—can identify with international values and rules only if the symbols of world authority are minimized, if the service of world organizations to national demands is stressed instead. Hence the Official Functionalism of David Morse is wholly compatible with the extension of ILO authority in a heterogeneous world environment; in fact, it is the only organizational ideology that could hope to accomplish this feat. Environmental heterogeneity makes the cementing of ILO authority difficult but not impossible; the uneven distribution of national values and demands preserves that field of maneuver which a task-conscious inter-

national organization requires for increasing its own authority while satisfying its clients.

Special Performance

So far we have concerned ourselves with the total performance of all
ILO members in paying heed to the work of the Industrial Committees.
Now we turn to an examination of a sense of special interest, special commitment, and continuing attachment to the work of the Committees, in an
effort to single out countries and tasks peculiarly sensitive to organizational
authority. Here we select for attention the record of those countries who
continue to take seriously the work of specific Committees after they cease
to be members.

Before we turn to the special performers, however, a word must be said
about a few countries who submit reports without ever having been a
member of any Committee. The countries are Spain, Ireland, Haiti, Cameroun, Mali, Syria, Saudi Arabia, Cyprus, and Guatemala. Spain constitutes
a special case. She reported for resolutions of three of the Committees,
recording no full and only two partial compliances, but 17 instances of
satisfactory existing conditions. One suspects that Spain, always under
some ideological pressure in ILO councils, seeks to profit from the Industrial Committee system to boast of relatively progressive industrial conditions. The other states on this list are all underdeveloped and—Ireland
excepted—oligarchical. While there are practically no instances of compliance among them, each reports, for one Committee of interest to it, a
certain number of satisfactory existing conditions. For Saudi Arabia it
was petroleum, for Guatemala building trades, and for Syria textiles. I
am uncertain what, if any, significance to attribute to this pattern, other
than the evident desire of these countries to demonstrate their interest and
eagerness to be considered loyal members.

The identity of the special performers reveals few surprises (Table 13).
The countries scoring high on reported compliances in the absence of continued membership on the Committees are among those whose total performance indicated considerable interest in the work of the Committees:
Australia, Ceylon, New Zealand, and Turkey. Australia and Turkey are
interested and successfully engaged in rapid industrialization; New Zealand is a successful welfare state with a mature agricultural export economy; and Ceylon is an underdeveloped country with a strong commitment
to welfare planning. These clients are typical of member states who should,
ideally, profit most from the type of work done by the Industrial Committees. However, it is hardly a compliment to the legitimacy enjoyed by the
ILO that only four member states display such a record.

A special word must be said about Turkey, since she has shown an unusual degree of interest. Of Turkey's total of 55 compliances, 33 occurred

in the absence of membership on the Committees, with the bulk occurring in the context of Committee work of special concern to developing economies: namely, the construction industry, salaried employees, and the chemical industry. This is indeed model performance from the point of view of a maximal integrating effect; but it is not matched by any other country in a similar economic and social situation. In fact, it should be noted that Turkey accounts for almost one-third of all the "special" compliances discovered.

Overall, the number of countries reporting in excess of a strict construction of their obligations is impressive. Forty member states submitted replies after leaving the Committees, out of a cumulative total membership of fifty-five since the inception of the system. However, it is quite evident from the figures given in Table 13 that the bulk of these governments merely made use of the reporting procedure to give evidence of satisfactory existing conditions in certain industries. Many of the reporting countries submitted no evidence of any compliance whatever, but gave a good deal of information on the factual situation in industries of concern to them. It is especially noteworthy that Chile, New Zealand, the Philippines, Poland, Turkey, Uruguay, and Viet Nam submitted a great deal of information on industries that do not yet occupy a crucial role in their economies. Others seemed to be anxious to profit from the publicity attending the Committee sessions to display their progressive social spirit. Australia appeared to do this with reference to her plantations in New Guinea; Chile and New Zealand did so in all industrial categories; Egypt and Iraq with reference to the oil industry; Norway in textiles and the building trades; and Viet Nam with reference to plantations. Most of these countries, however, have a very poor record of implementing the concrete recommendations of the Committees.

The distribution of special performance with respect to the individual Committees is summarized in Table 14. The order in which the Committees are listed follows their relative degree of success as determined from total member state performance. The distribution of frequency among reporting countries has no special significance by itself, since it is a function of the rapidity of turnover in the membership of the Committee. Thus the very small number of "special" reports submitted for Coal Mines and Steel is due to the fact that the membership of these two Committees has been relatively stable. What is of greater significance is the ratio of compliances to the number of reports. Coal Mines and Steel continue to display a great degree of success according to this indicator; so do the Chemicals and Building Trades Committees. On the other hand, Metal Trades, Plantations, Textiles, and Salaried Employees scored far fewer "special" compliances than one might expect as a result of the relatively high number of "special" reports submitted; and the catastrophic total record of the Petro-

TABLE 13

Industrial Committees: Identity of Special Performers
(*Number of incidents reported*)

Country and committee	Complies fully	Complies in part	Conditions fair or good	Country and committee	Complies fully	Complies in part	Conditions fair or good
Argentina	0	3	13	**Germany**	0	0	13
Coal Mines	–	2	3	Petroleum	–	–	13
Metal Trades	–	–	7	**Honduras**	0	0	2
Salaried Employees	–	1	3	Inland Transport ..	–	–	2
Australia	3	4	46	**Iraq**	0	0	6
Petroleum	–	–	5	Petroleum	–	–	6
Chemicals	3	–	8	**Israel**	0	0	3
Salaried Employees	–	–	4	Inland Transport ..	–	–	3
Plantations	–	4	29	**Italy**	0	0	3
Belgium	0	2	6	Salaried Employees	–	–	3
Petroleum	–	–	1	**Japan**	2	1	9
Building Trades ...	–	2	5	Inland Transport ..	–	1	1
Brazil	0	1	8	Salaried Employees	–	–	8
Petroleum	–	1	8	Iron and Steel	2	–	–
Burma	0	1	5	**Luxembourg**	0	0	2
Inland Transport ..	–	–	1	Metal Trades	–	–	1
Building Trades ...	–	1	–	Building Trades ...	–	–	1
Salaried Employees	–	–	4	**Mexico**	0	2	0
Canada	0	2	22	Textiles	–	2	–
Salaried Employees	–	2	22	**Morocco**	1	0	0
Ceylon	5	5	25	Chemicals	1	–	–
Metal Trades	–	–	2	**Netherlands**	2	1	2
Inland Transport ..	1	2	6	Salaried Employees	–	1	2
Building Trades ...	2	3	17	Iron and Steel	2	–	–
Salaried Employees	2	–	–	**New Zealand**	0	15	129
Chile	0	0	28	Coal Mines	–	2	14
Petroleum	–	–	6	Textiles	–	–	9
Textiles	–	–	6	Metal Trades	–	2	23
Metal Trades	–	–	3	Inland Transport ..	–	3	27
Inland Transport ..	–	–	5	Chemicals	–	–	6
Chemicals	–	–	1	Building Trades ...	–	7	27
Salaried Employees	–	–	7	Salaried Employees	–	1	7
Colombia	0	0	1	Plantations	–	–	16
Plantations	–	–	1	**Norway**	0	4	36
Cuba	0	0	1	Textiles	–	–	10
Petroleum	–	–	3	Building Trades ...	–	1	21
Salaried Employees	–	1	3	Salaried Employees	–	3	5
Denmark	0	2	16	**Pakistan**	1	1	10
Inland Transport ..	–	–	4	Building Trades ...	–	–	1
Chemicals	–	–	4	Salaried Employees	1	1	9
Salaried Employees	–	2	8	**Philippines**	0	3	17
Dominican Republic	0	2	10	Petroleum	–	–	1
Textiles	–	1	2	Textiles	–	–	1
Building Trades ...	–	1	–	Metal Trades	–	2	3
Salaried Employees	–	–	8	Chemicals	–	1	–
Finland	0	1	9	Building Trades ...	–	–	2
Building Trades ...	–	1	7	Salaried Employees	–	–	8
Salaried Employees	–	–	2	Iron and Steel	–	–	2

TABLE 13 (continued)

Country and committee	Com-plies fully	Com-plies in part	Condi-tions fair or good	Country and committee	Com-plies fully	Com-plies in part	Condi-tions fair or good
Poland	0	2	16	Chemicals	3	7	4
Textiles	–	1	5	Building Trades ...	9	1	7
Inland Transport ..	–	–	3	Salaried Employees	3	2	4
Building Trades ...	–	–	4	Iron and Steel	–	2	11
Salaried Employees	–	1	4	**United Arab Republic**	0	0	13
Portugal	0	0	1	Petroleum	–	–	13
Plantations	–	–	1	**Uruguay**	2	2	10
South Africa	0	1	13	Petroleum	–	–	3
Inland Transport ..	–	–	4	Metal Trades	1	–	5
Salaried Employees	–	1	9	Inland Transport ..	1	–	–
Sweden	0	0	11	Chemicals	–	1	–
Textiles	–	–	11	Building Trades ...	–	1	2
Switzerland	0	1	0	**Venezuela**	0	1	6
Salaried Employees	–	1	–	Plantations	–	1	6
Thailand	0	0	1	**Viet Nam**	0	1	36
Plantations	–	–	1	Metal Trades	–	–	2
Tunisia	1	0	5	Chemicals	–	–	1
Salaried Employees	1	–	5	Building Trades ...	–	1	5
Turkey	16	17	37	Plantations	–	–	28
Petroleum	–	–	1	**Yugoslavia**	0	0	6
Textiles	1	3	5	Inland Transport ..	–	–	6
Metal Trades	–	2	5	**GRAND TOTAL**	33	76	582

leum Committee is in no way improved when we consider special performance. According to the number of reports submitted, Plantations, Inland Transport, Petroleum, and the Building Trades are of strong interest to member countries. Since these industries are of concern even to underdeveloped countries, this is what one would expect. However, success in terms of significant numbers of compliances is evident only in the case of the construction industry, where job safety and vocational training accounted for much of the Committee's work. In other words, ILO legitimacy is not significantly demonstrable as a result of this analysis. The submis-

TABLE 14

INDUSTRIAL COMMITTEES: DISTRIBUTION OF SPECIAL PERFORMANCE BY COMMITTEES

Committee	No. of countries reporting	No. of incidents[a]	Committee	No. of countries reporting	No. of incidents[a]
Coal Mines	3	16	Iron and Steel	4	8
Building Trades	14	30	Textiles	9	8
Chemicals	9	15	Salaried Employees	22	24
Metal Trades	10	12	Inland Transport	12	8
Plantations	7	5	Petroleum	11	1

[a] This figure is the sum of full and partial compliances.

sion of special reports for these industries by underdeveloped countries was not often enough accompanied by evidence of compliance with resolutions.

Participant Performance

The analogies to political behavior frequently urged by social psychologists would lead us to expect the behavior of consistent participants in the work of the Industrial Committees to show more deference to organizational authority than that of the total ILO membership. Participation supposedly engenders sentiments of legitimacy. It is alleged to give rise to a commitment to the work of the group with which the delegate is involved, irrespective of the subject matter of that work. Participant performance, according to this argument, would combine the highest ratings of both legitimacy and authority with reference to quasi-collective bargaining. It may be recalled that the argument is not altogether fanciful. The behavior of long-time members of the Governing Body and of the Committee of Experts on the Application of Conventions shows traces of this type of commitment. Could not this apply to the behavior of government delegates to sessions of the Industrial Committees? The only empirical proof adequate to substantiating this argument—of tremendous importance to a theory of international integration if true—consists in analyzing once more the pattern of fidelity to Committee resolutions displayed by the participating governments.

Table 15 summarizes their conduct since the inception of the system. Let us note first the remarkably narrow range of variation with respect to the possibility open to member governments to furnish evasive replies. A maximal score of 3 per cent was discovered, contributed—not altogether unexpectedly—by South Africa and the Soviet Union. Further, relatively few governments reported that resolutions did not apply to their economies. Only Yugoslavia, South Africa, and Burma so reported in excess of 5 per cent. Finally, a heavy reliance on reporting no intention of applying a resolution, with its implication of national truculence, is encountered rarely. Burma's 6 per cent is the extreme; Turkey's 5 per cent is equally unusual, and the European countries that scored 4 per cent have excellent records on other grounds.[30]

Participants who lack sustained interests in the work and feel no overwhelming sense of commitment obviously do not demonstrate these traits by being evasive or truculent; they show their indifference by not reporting at all. The "no reply" column contains the first damning indictment of the social psychologist's hypothesis. Of the forty-nine participants appearing in our table, only twenty-one reported 30 per cent of the time or better; thirteen passed the 40 per cent mark; only six reported as much as half of the time.[31] The participants who rarely bother to report, those scoring between 90 and 100 per cent in the "no reply" column, are overwhelmingly underdeveloped economically, as well as frequently being oligarchical or authoritarian politically. In short, fidelity of reporting is positively correlated among participants with democracy, industrialization, and an interest in welfare planning. Those who participate but do not share this syndrome of traits seem unaffected by the benign change of attitude dear to the social psychologist.

Relatively little of interest emerges from an examination of behavior with respect to reporting on existing industrial conditions. Not unnaturally, very few participating governments admit to poor conditions. The honesty of Pakistan and the Philippines is as refreshing as their consistent zeal in reporting. Also not unnaturally, it is the economically developed participants who contribute most of the reports attesting to good or fair conditions.[32] Since the existence of such conditions is not apparently related to fidelity in implementing resolutions or reporting regularly, no general conclusions with respect to legitimacy and authority can be culled from this type of conduct.

What, then, is the picture regarding compliance with Committee resolutions? Does it differ for the regular participants as opposed to the total membership? Only seven countries can boast a combined score of full and partial compliances of 10 per cent or better: Belgium, Finland, France, Germany, India, Japan, and Norway. Another eleven score 5 per cent or better: Burma, Canada, Ceylon, Denmark, Italy, Luxembourg, the Netherlands, Poland, Sweden, Switzerland, and Turkey. Again, those already developed or planning for full industrialization are the chief participants consistently interested both in reporting and in implementing the results of the Committee deliberations. Burma's and Ceylon's fidelity is a reflection of the serious interest of these countries in improving working conditions among plantation workers; but the odd dozen of other underdeveloped countries also possessing plantation economies show no similar enthusiasm. In this roster we find one communist state and two states that might be classified as oligarchies; all the others are democracies.[33]

Authority and legitimacy, then, go hand in hand with a commitment to planned social welfare measures, whether in the context of the already developed (who require no persuasion from Geneva), or in the aims of democratic and autocratic elites committed to the speedy and drastic modernization of their nations.

This finding does not differ significantly from our conclusions regarding total or special performance. The same names and the same syndromes of characteristics recur throughout. Participation does *not* clearly improve performance; some of the more marginal participants conscientiously implemented resolutions after leaving a Committee or without ever having been members. The intrinsic importance of the subject matter of a Com-

TABLE 15

Industrial Committees: Participation and Fidelity of Member States[a]

Country and no. of committees participated in	No. of replies possible	PERCENTAGE OF REPLIES								
		No reply	Evasive reply	Does not apply	Complies fully	Complies in part	No intent	Desc. existing conditions		
								Good	Fair	Poor
Argentina (6)	284	84	0	0	0	2	0	1	12	0
Australia (6)	621	85	1	2	1	2	0	2	6	0
Austria (7)	383	48	1	4	1	2	3	17	22	1
Belgium (9)	910	68	1	2	3	7	3	6	9	1
Brazil (10)[b]	462	97	0	0	0	1	0	0	1	0
Burma (2)	166	57	1	10	2	4	6	3	16	1
Canada (8)	745	52	1	4	2	6	2	12	18	3
Ceylon (2)	158	42	1	4	0	6	3	8	34	2
Chile (7)	340	82	1	4	0	1	3	2	5	2
China (7)	278	98	0	0	0	0	0	0	0	0
Colombia (2)	48	98	0	0	0	2	0	0	0	0
Costa Rica (1)	64	86	0	0	0	0	0	0	13	2
Cuba (2)[b]	124	88	0	0	0	1	0	0	10	1
Czechoslovakia (7) .	346	94	0	1	0	1	0	2	2	0
Denmark (6)	448	68	1	3	2	7	4	4	11	1
Dominican Rep. (1) .	73	45	0	4	0	1	0	7	38	4
Finland (6)	270	58	0	3	1	9	2	9	17	1
France (10)[c]	1039	52	2	3	3	8	2	11	18	1
Germany (9)	537	45	0	3	5	7	3	15	21	0
Greece (3)	91	97	1	0	0	0	0	0	2	0
India (10)	876	57	1	5	2	9	3	4	15	4
Indonesia (2)	152	72	1	0	0	1	1	3	17	5
Iran (1)	48	79	0	0	0	0	0	4	17	0
Israel (4)	139	80	1	1	1	2	0	5	9	1
Italy (9)	642	65	1	2	2	5	1	5	16	2
Japan (9)	466	48	0	2	2	12	2	9	22	2
Liberia (1)	32	100	0	0	0	0	0	0	0	0
Luxembourg (2)	79	92	0	1	3	3	0	0	1	0
Mexico (10)	699	90	0	1	0	0	0	1	5	2
Netherlands (10) ...	826	60	1	3	1	4	2	10	17	2
Norway (6)	363	58	1	2	1	10	3	7	16	1
Pakistan (3)	207	67	2	1	0	1	2	1	13	12
Peru (5)	321	100	0	0	0	0	0	0	0	0
Philippines (2)	130	48	2	2	0	2	2	5	27	13
Poland (7)	355	83	1	1	2	5	1	1	6	0
Portugal (2)	137	96	0	0	0	0	1	1	3	0
South Africa (5) ...	333	76	3	10	1	1	2	2	4	2
Sweden (7)	557	62	1	4	1	4	1	12	15	1
Switzerland (6)	515	71	2	3	1	4	1	5	12	1
Thailand (1)	32	100	0	0	0	0	0	0	0	0
Tunisia (1)	5	60	0	0	0	0	0	20	20	0
Turkey (3)	247	75	0	2	1	8	5	0	7	1
U.A.R. (5)	353	83	1	3	3	1	0	1	6	3
U.K. (10)[c]	3517	65	1	3	1	3	2	5	16	3
Uruguay (3)[b]	58	84	0	2	2	2	0	0	5	5
U.S. (10)	837	72	1	3	0	3	2	5	12	2
U.S.S.R. (10)[d]	37	65	3	3	0	3	0	8	19	0
Venezuela (2)	104	99	0	0	0	0	0	0	1	0
Yugoslavia (3)	64	59	2	8	0	0	2	25	5	0

mittee's work, seen in the context of a government's policy commitments, is the crucial variable underlying interest and compliance.

We finally turn to an examination of the authority enjoyed by the various Committees themselves among the participating states, as distinguished from their role among the total ILO membership. Table 16 provides the necessary data. As in the case of the total membership, the Committee on Coal Mines is clearly the most successful in terms of the amount of compliance its resolutions receive; and again, the Petroleum Committee is the least authoritative, even (perhaps especially) for its constant members. With the exception of the oil industry, the Committees having the best compliance score also enjoy the most faithful reporting pattern from the member governments. The steel and chemical industries even approximate a rate of reporting that is half of the possible performance. But there are several significant shifts bearing on our hypothesis. Why do certain Committees improve and others decline when participant performance is contrasted with total performance?

The explanation would seem to lie in the unequal industrial development of the participating countries, reflected in different ways in the composition of the various Committees, as opposed to the total compliance pattern. The hypothesis of improved performance as a result of participation does not receive consistent support from this finding. Thus, the construction industry and plantations suffered from *poorer* compliance in terms of participant performance as compared with the total membership. Both are Committees whose work is of general interest to all types of economies; both enjoyed the participation of many underdeveloped countries. The better total performance for Plantations seems due to the interest taken by Australia and New Zealand; in the case of the construction industry, the non-participant performers responsible for the higher degree of success were Belgium, Ceylon, New Zealand, and Turkey. In both cases, then, the better total performance was contributed by the developed and industrializing nations that do not require the psychological stimulus of participation in order to perform well.

Steel and Salaried Employees improved their standing in terms of participant performance. Both are of interest primarily to developed and industrializing countries, and the Iron and Steel Committee, at least, has been dominated by them. Here it is normal that the participants would take greater interest in the work, an argument that applies equally to coal mines, chemicals, and the metal trades. Hence, we are left with the case of Sal-

---

NOTES TO TABLE 15

a Countries participating on a Committee for one session only were excluded.

b Scores do not include the work of Committees that have held no sessions since the member began to participate. Therefore the following countries were not scored at all, even though elected to membership since 1960: Ecuador, New Zealand, Honduras, Morocco.

c Includes reports submitted on behalf of colonies.

d Even though the U.S.S.R. is now a member of all ten Committees, only reports due with respect to sessions held since her admission have been analyzed.

TABLE 16

PARTICIPATION AND FIDELITY OF INDUSTRIAL COMMITTEES

Committee and no. of resolutions adopted	No. of replies possible	PERCENTAGE OF REPLIES								
		No reply	Evasive reply	Does not apply	Complies fully	Complies in part	No intent	Desc. existing conditions		
								Good	Fair	Poor
Coal Mines (21)	2187	64	0	3	3	12	4	2	10	2
Petroleum (13)	665	65	1	1	0	0	0	8	25	0
Textiles (18)	1288	70	2	2	0	4	1	2	19	1
Metal Trades (16) ..	1955	66	1	2	1	5	1	10	11	1
Inland Transport (11) ...	1859	77	1	1	1	2	1	7	9	2
Chemicals (11)	1156	54	0	1	4	10	4	6	19	1
Building Trades (14)	3964	77	1	3	1	3	1	5	9	2
Salaried Employees (8) ...	621	63	1	3	0	5	1	5	21	1
Plantations (19)	4822	70	1	2	0	2	2	3	16	4
Iron & Steel (15) ...	999	51	1	10	4	5	2	22	5	0

aried Employees, a Committee that enjoyed a diffuse membership in terms of degrees of economic development. It is conceivable that in this case the act of participation was the crucial variable that accounted for the improvement in performance.

THE QUALITY OF AUTHORITY AND LEGITIMACY

It is high time we turned from the numerical incidence of authority to its quality. What is the *content* of the most authoritative resolutions? Do they deal with trivia, or with the core of collective bargaining? Is authority, even for the few industrialized and industrializing members who submit to it, confined to minor items that are unlikely to affect the national environment? Clearly, the real test of organizational authority is the subject matter of the successful resolutions. Subgoal dominance of a particularly trivial character might well obtain here as elsewhere in the generation of international norms, thereby minimizing the integration process. The fact, however, that the resolutions deal with conditions peculiar to specific industries should not be mistaken for subgoal dominance; in the context of collective bargaining, this is natural and inevitable. What would constitute a departure from the core of concerns vital to integration is exclusive concern with the non-controversial type of activity associated with routine technical assistance.

First, we must single out the resolutions most successful from the point of view of their incidence of *full* compliance. Table 17 summarizes resolutions that had obtained fifteen or more such evidences of deference.

TABLE 17

RESOLUTIONS OF INDUSTRIAL COMMITTEES OBTAINING FIFTEEN
OR MORE FULL COMPLIANCES

Subject of resolution (Committee and date in parentheses)	No. of compliances	
	Full	Partial
Statistical reporting (Iron & Steel, 1947)	30	0
Mineworkers' charter (Coal Mines, 1947)	24	12
Vocational training (Building Trades, 1949)	20	22
Manpower recruitment (Coal Mines, 1947)	16	15
Dangerous substances (Chemicals, 1955)	15	6

Three of these successful resolutions deal with issues that are far from vital. The Iron and Steel Committee's top scorer merely sought to standardize the reporting of steel production statistics; the Chemical Industries Committee sought to persuade governments to adopt standardized labels for five categories of dangerous substances;[34] and the Building, Civil Engineering, and Public Works committees adopted an omnibus resolution laying down the customary suggestions for improved vocational training for various categories of workers.[35]

By contrast, the two resolutions adopted by the Coal Mines Committee are of general importance. In 1947, the European countries, in an effort to rehabilitate their war-devastated collieries and work forces, were extremely interested in making mining as attractive an occupation as possible. There was much discussion about drawing up general principles to single out mining as an occupation to be favored, and it was suggested that a Mineworkers Charter be drafted. The principles to be incorporated into such a statement were laid down by the ILO in sweeping terms, including provisions for special pensions, health and safety measures, shorter working hours than in comparable industries, and stable employment.[36] Many of these principles were indeed translated into public policy in Western Europe. In a kindred resolution, the Coal Mines Committee laid down detailed suggestions for inducting new miners into the working force by way of special pensions, for encouraging migration through improved multilateral social security coverage, and for recruiting displaced persons.[37] Again, in Western Europe many of these suggestions were translated into national policy.

We now turn to thirty-six resolutions that fared less well in terms of compliance, but still ranked considerably above the bulk of the output of the Industrial Committees. Table 18 summarizes all resolutions whose *combined score for full and partial compliances* stood at 10 or above. It is obvious that we have adopted a very permissive criterion of success here; but the vast majority of resolutions cannot even meet this modest test.

TABLE 18

RESOLUTIONS OF INDUSTRIAL COMMITTEES OBTAINING TEN OR MORE
FULL OR PARTIAL COMPLIANCES

Subject of resolution (Committee and date in parentheses)	Number of compliances
Productivity/consultation (Coal Mines, 1953)	59
Vocational training (Chemicals, 1955)	56
Productivity/consultation (Chemicals, 1955)	56
Social welfare services (Coal Mines, 1953)	31
Productivity/consultation (Metal Trades, 1952)	29
Vocational training (Coal Mines, 1947)	28
Minimum income (Metal Trades, 1948)	26
Miners' housing (Coal Mines, 1947)	26
Vocational training of handicapped (Coal Mines, 1949)	24
Productivity and health measures (Coal Mines, 1951)	22
Mine safety (Coal Mines, 1956)	22
Productivity and vocational training (Building Trades, 1953)	20
Safety in construction industry (Building Trades, 1956)	17
Seasonal unemployment (Building Trades, 1951)	17
Technological unemployment (Iron & Steel, 1949)	16
Vocational training and general education (Plantations, 1950)	16
Industrial relations (Building Trades, 1946)	16
Productivity (Building Trades, 1953)	15
Recruitment of manpower (Coal Mines, 1956)	15
Job welfare facilities (Building Trades, 1951)	14
Regularization of employment (Metal Trades, 1954)	14
Regularization of employment (Iron & Steel, 1947)	13
National housing programs planning (Building Trades, 1951)	13
Hygiene in shops and offices (Salaried Employees, 1952)	12
Regularization of employment (Building Trades, 1946)	12
Industrial consultation (Chemicals, 1958)	12
Conditions of work (Inland Transport, 1957)	12
Conditions of employment/vocational training (Salaried Employees, 1958)	12
Food and clothing for workers (Plantations, 1950)	11
Labor recruitment standards (Plantations, 1950)	11
Job classification (Plantations, 1953)	10
Unemployment (Salaried Employees, 1954)	10
Industrial relations (Inland Transport, 1948)	10
Industrial relations (Metal Trades, 1952)	10
Plant safety (Textiles, 1950)	10
Vocational training (Textiles, 1949)	10

How shall we separate those resolutions crucial to an assessment of authority and the process of integration from those that are too specific to be relevant? Our criterion is the controversiality of the policy advocated in the resolution. Measures already considered routine, technical, and self-evidently desirable in all industrial settings are the following: suggestions dealing with vocational training, industrial safety, job welfare, hygiene arrangements, and job classification. Vocational training took up much of the time of the Industrial Committees, but the suggestions that resulted rarely went beyond the obvious advocacy of more and better schools, apprenticeship programs, managerial indoctrination, and adult education centers.[38] Industrial safety resolutions stressed the responsibility of employers in indoctrinating workers on the importance of safety rules, procuring machinery likely to minimize accidents, and introducing proper labeling. Further, the importance of organizing plant safety committees was singled out.[39] Job welfare resolutions dealt with the number and quality of drinking fountains, lockers, and washrooms.[40] It can hardly be argued that these concerns vitally affect the progress of international integration, or that even perfect compliance would so transform the national scene as to mark the advent of a major new type of environment.

It is therefore striking that the routine and subgoal-dominated resolutions are far from monopolizing the total score of compliances. At least as successful are resolutions dealing with employment generally, the encouragement of productivity without loss of employment, minimum income, industrial relations, and the encouragement of general social welfare services. All these involve major and often controversial—if not costly—public and private measures. Some of them strike at the root of modern industrialism and the degree of public intervention in the private sector. Stabilization of employment was dealt with relatively successfully for miners, steelworkers, metalworkers, construction workers, and even salaried employees. Stress was placed on manpower forecasts, the planning of construction so as to overcome seasonal lags, housing construction coordinated with business cycle policy, and manpower recruitment in an organized employment market.[41] The encouragement of productivity programs is closely related to this interest. Afraid of automation and the unplanned displacement of workers made redundant by successful productivity measures, almost all the Committees adopted resolutions stressing the creation of consultative labor-management machinery to plan new productivity measures and to cushion displacement with retraining programs.[42] Advocacy of increased productivity was almost always accompanied by the demand that workers share in its benefits, and that it be linked with social justice. Income security measures were successfully recommended only in the Metal Trades Committee; standardized systems for calculating minimum wages and bonuses were advocated here.[43] The defense of freedom of association was linked with the demand that wholesome industrial relations be fostered through standing labor-management committees. The recommendation that employers be indoctrinated in the importance of human relations in industry was tied to these suggestions; but conciliation and arbitration machinery was also recommended in some instances.[44] At least some of the principles of the ILO Labor-Management Relations Program are reflected in these resolutions. Their general implementation would clearly transform the national scene in many countries. Finally, recommendations for generally improved social services range from the advocacy of special medical centers for miners to the responsibility of employers to furnish plantation workers with food and clothing.[45]

Our analysis of the particularly successful resolutions would be incomplete without an effort to characterize the content of those that failed to obtain a sum of ten full or partial compliances. Do these resolutions differ from the relatively successful ones in being more, or less, controversial? Is there a differential pattern among the Committees to explain relative lack of success? Table 19 summarizes the distribution of the resolutions and arranges them according to the subjects covered.

Obviously, more of the controversial resolutions failed to attain the minimum of compliances considered essential for "success," though the ratio to the technical resolutions is not dramatically unfavorable. Moreover, the Textile, Metal Trades, Building Trades, and Salaried Workers Committees were particularly unsuccessful in making their more demanding resolutions succeed, though, admittedly, the texts they tried to draft were much more ambitious than those of some of the other Committees. At the opposite extreme we find the Chemical Industries Committee, which attempted very

TABLE 19

INDUSTRIAL COMMITTEES: DISTRIBUTION OF RESOLUTIONS
OBTAINING FEWER THAN TEN COMPLIANCES

(Number of resolutions)

Subject	Total	Coal	Petro-leum	Tex-tiles	Metal Trades	Inl. Trans-port	Chem-icals	Build-ing Trades	Sala-ried Emps.	Plan-tations	Iron and Steel
Technical	**44**	6	5	5	4	5	5	1	1	6	6
Safety 5		–	1	–	1	–	2	–	–	–	1
Vocational training 7		1	1	–	2	1	1	–	–	–	1
Job welfare 13		1	2	3	–	1	1	–	–	4	1
Job classification 2		–	1	–	1	–	–	–	–	–	–
Min. age/prot. of women..... 7		4	–	1	–	–	–	1	–	1	–
Labor inspection 4		–	–	–	–	2	–	–	1	1	–
Miscellaneous .. 6		–	–	1	–	1	1	–	–	–	3
Controversial	**59**	5	8	11	8	4	2	4	4	8	5
Productivity 8		–	–	3	3	1	–	–	–	1	–
Employment ...12		2	–	2	2	2	–	2	2	–	–
Income/wages .. 9		1	2	1	–	–	–	1	–	3	1
Industrial relations 13		–	2	2	2	–	1	–	2	1	3
Social welfare .. 8		–	3	–	1	–	–	1	–	2	1
Hours/vacations 5		1	1	1	–	–	1	–	–	1	–
World trade.... 3		1	–	2	–	–	–	–	–	–	–
Miscellaneous .. 1		–	–	–	–	1	–	–	–	–	–
Grand Total	**103**	**11**	**13**	**16**	**12**	**9**	**7**	**5**	**5**	**14**	**11**

few of the more controversial issues and limited itself to highly specific matters.

Are the subjects covered by the unsuccessful resolutions identical with the forty-one that scored high in compliances? By and large they are. However, among the more technical texts, the unsuccessful ones also include efforts to improve labor inspection services and to protect women and younger workers, efforts that were not authoritative or legitimate enough to appear on our scale of success. Among the more ambitious and controversial resolutions, we find several attempts to guarantee minimum wages and to standardize working hours and paid vacations at the national level; none of these achieved sufficient compliance to be represented in the earlier tabulation. As far as the great bulk of the Industrial Committee effort is concerned, though, it is less the subject matter that is correlated with compliance than the industry involved. Essentially similar resolutions adopted by various Committees differ widely in the legitimacy and authority they enjoy.

The most interesting among the unsuccessful, but controversial, resolutions are a few attempts to regulate the international conditions of competition that motivated Britain to propose the Industrial Committee principle in the first place. These resolutions, had they been successful, would have constituted a true approximation to international collective bargaining, even though they merely attempted to set standards at the national level. Identical procedures and principles of action at the national level would have produced indirectly a measure of homogeneity in the international environment. In the field of regularized employment, the concern was with complex and interconnected economic trends calling for coordinated national planning to assure stable employment within the sector covered by a single Committee. It is here that we find reference to countercyclical planning in the steel and construction industries, interest in a general fuel policy to aid threatened miners, a coordinated transport policy to save the jobs of railroad workers.[46] The Iron and Steel, Building Trades, and Textiles Committees unsuccessfully sought to introduce guaranteed weekly wage scales.[47] The Plantations and Petroleum Committees, responsible in general for unorganized workers in underdeveloped countries, had to content themselves with recommending the creation of minimum wage-fixing machinery.[48] The effect on world petroleum and commodity prices could have been considerable. The efforts of the Textiles and Plantations Committees to set up international regulations for hours of work and vacations might well have had the same effect.[49] It is significant that most of these efforts occurred during the first few years of the life of the Industrial Committees. With few exceptions, the more recent period saw the abandonment of these ambitious attempts at general regulation and the withdrawal to the routine realm of vocational training, job welfare rules, and industrial safety.

The slow descent into the realm of the more technical is epitomized by four resolutions that sought directly to stabilize the international economy by treating world trade as a subject for Committee resolutions, brave attempts that have not been repeated recently. In 1950 the Textile Committee called attention to the effects of international disparities in the wages of textile workers and sought to diminish them. It drew attention to the relationship between international commodity trade and full employment in the textile industry, calling for adequate supplies at equitable world prices. In 1953 it went further and called upon governments to prevent international competition in textiles in order to protect employment.[50] Similarly, the Coal Mines Committee in 1947 concluded that "an international economic agreement between the coal producing countries, which would remove unfair competition, would facilitate greatly the solution of the social problems mentioned in the suggested principles for incorporation in a coal mineworkers Charter."[51] These conclusions were of interest to the developed Western countries that originated the system of Industrial Committees. That the heterogeneity of the international environment did not favor their emergence as meaningful United Nations policy is a matter of record. That the entire approach to international collective bargaining gave way to more modest efforts at advice to specific industries has been made clear here. What authority and legitimacy there is, therefore, is increasingly concentrated on the routine and the technical. And thus the promise of dramatic transformations of the international social and industrial environment by way of quasi-collective bargaining went the way of the ILO's overall post-war reform program.

THE FUTURE OF COLLECTIVE BARGAINING

A pall of uncertainty overshadows any notion of collective bargaining, on the national as well as on the international scale. In the West the discussion has centered on the rival principles of negotiating national, regional, and plant-level agreements, on the role of bargaining in the context of overall national wage and income policies, and on the virtues of third-party intercession as opposed to bipartite confrontation. The two central concepts in the problem are the *unit* that does the negotiating and the *level* at which the negotiation is to be effective. As Arthur Ross puts it, "we should think not of a single bargaining unit, but of a *structure* of decision-making levels. The real problem is to identify the types of decisions which should ideally be made at each level."[52] But if collective bargaining results from the interaction of a multiplicity of bargaining units connected in an intricate network of legal and economic relationships, why should not the ILO Industrial Committees become the apex of a negotiating pyramid, with each subordinate level exercising its proper role?

Such a future for the ILO is exceedingly unlikely because of the pervasive asymmetries that attend the role of collective bargaining in determining the pattern of industrial relations throughout the world. Furthermore, the evolution of national bargaining practices seems to be tied to the socio-economic experiences of workers and employers, to stages of development and future expectations. These, as we shall now demonstrate, represent the extremes in asymmetry.

In the capitalist economic history of the West, collective bargaining developed from the plant to the regional and national levels. It originated at the local level as a simple device to give the individual workers additional bargaining strength vis-à-vis the local employer. Subsequently, a general protective ideology sought an overall organization of the larger labor market, mainly with a view to shielding workers against displacements due to depressions. National collective bargaining arose, either at the level of the total economy (as in Sweden, the Netherlands, and—in a different sense—Italy), or with respect to industrial sectors (as elsewhere in Western Europe and in certain American industries). Although the tendency toward centralized bargaining has gone further in Europe than in the United States, the trend is manifest there as well. This was the "traditional" system that prevailed at the end of World War II, and that inspired the work of the ILO Industrial Committees.

Now, however, "prosperity, full employment, modern technology, and rising living standards have undermined traditional systems of industrial relations in Western Europe. Established institutions and routines have been outdated while new tendencies have begun to appear."[53] Fear of recession no longer dominates people's thinking. Production has grown rapidly. Labor shortages have prevailed, and real earnings have increased markedly. The large-scale impersonal and bureaucratized corporation has displaced the small family-run enterprise; and professional managers, concerned with productivity and human relations, have displaced indifferent or paternalistic *patrons*. "Wage drift" has caused wage and fringe benefits at the plant level to exceed the norms laid down in national or regional agreements. Political unionism and the authority of national federations have declined, and the rate of expansion in union membership has slowed down. More and more *de facto* negotiation goes on at the plant and company levels, negotiation in which local works councils, plant committees, and shop stewards are perhaps as important as trade unions. Issues of job security, fringe benefits, job evaluation, and relations with management have become more important as the issue of basic wages has slipped out of the hands of the parties directly involved.

This combination of circumstances may have set the scene for a certain division of labor among interlocking negotiating units. Basic wage policy is increasingly determined by the government through the work of central planning bodies in which trade unions are represented. A wage and income policy is sought through these means, designed to gear wage levels to growth targets and investment objectives. To the extent that labor and management participate and acquiesce in this approach, they surrender the earlier capacity to negotiate autonomous collective agreements. At the same time, local and company-level organs of worker representation re-enter the scene by acquiring the power to negotiate local benefits of a non-wage character. The central negotiating function of national trade union federations declines as a result of both pressures.

Western Europe represents the acme of this development. In the United States and Japan the trend is still toward industry-wide national bargaining, mixed with steps toward compulsory arbitration and a decline of union militancy, especially with respect to wages. Hence, relations are asymmetrical even within the industrialized-democratic world. In the Soviet bloc, of course, there is no collective bargaining at all and no recognized role for trade unions in "confronting" other units in industrial planning. Yet there is evidence of increasing trade union influence in the drafting of national development plans. There is no point in predicting a role of equality for the unions in the planning process; yet the Soviet pattern parallels the Western trend insofar as traditional collective bargaining is becoming obsolete. Collective bargaining was left behind in Western Europe; it is competing with administrative pressure on wages and with arbitration in the United States; it was never the practice in communist systems and is unlikely to become accepted there.

While collective bargaining is being left behind in industrialized nations, it has not yet made its appearance in most of the underdeveloped and industrializing world. In the totally agricultural and socially unmobilized nations, of course, the process is irrelevant. In such countries as Brazil, Argentina, Chile, Indonesia, and India, there are the beginnings of collective bargaining at the local and regional levels—though usually within the framework of political and ideological unionism. However, in Pakistan, Burma, Malaya, Turkey, and large parts of Latin America, unions are too weak or too timid to claim such a role. They have not yet reached the stage attained by Western Europe in 1900. In almost all of the underdeveloped world, wage policy and labor welfare issues are treated—with the consent of trade union leaders—as an aspect of overall development planning rather than as issues to be negotiated by private groups. The prospects for free collective bargaining along "traditional" Western lines appear dim.

It follows that the global pattern is straining toward more asymmetry, at least for the time being. There can be no international pinnacle for collective bargaining, no logical central unit, as long as the subordinate units show more and more diversity. A reintegration at the global level seems conceivable only in the context of a universal income and commodity policy, in the context of some kind of global planning. The piecemeal approaches currently typical of the United Nations system are unlikely to usher in a planning process capable of giving the ILO a true role at the apex of a collective bargaining pyramid.

11. *Human Rights*

"A NEW BIRTH OF FREEDOM"

With this ringing phrase C. Wilfred Jenks opens the argument for the central and most challenging task confronting the ILO: the protection of the rights of individuals against infringement on the part of governments. We have encountered this theme before in our exploration of the ILO task and program. Here it is our aim to examine it systematically in terms of the transformation of the world environment it implies. Normally we would reserve the analysis of organizational ideology for a later phase of the discussion, concentrating first on the significance of the human rights field to a functional dissection of the organizational dynamic. Jenks, however, who has done more than any other international official to determine the doctrinal and programmatic role of human rights in the work of the United Nations system, makes this separation of themes partly redundant. Jenks is a Functionalist. His approach, today as in 1944, bears a very close resemblance to the themes we introduced in our first chapters. What is more important, his Functionalism is already tempered with a good many of the manipulatory insights we associated earlier with sociological functionalism. Hence his statement of the case, in part, is quite germane to our first duty: to explore the possible significance of the task of protecting human rights in the functional expansion of international organizations.

The contemporary world, Jenks argues, is characterized by two self-contradictory trends that can be resolved only by global action. On the one hand, the populations of almost all countries increasingly demand "rights" for themselves that correspond to the heritage of nineteenth-century liberalism: the political freedoms of political participation and the economic freedoms of a better material life. In the West this trend has culminated in

e democratic welfare state; in the rest of the world the revolutions of the
mid-twentieth century are belatedly bringing forth similar mass demands.
On the other hand, the modern state is less and less able to satisfy these
aspirations because of the changes wrought by technology. Self-sufficient
economies and polities, able to satisfy the aspirations of their citizens for a
free political life and a wholesome standard of living, are a thing of the past.
Technology has created a military and economic interdependence that deprives the state of the ability to carry out its functions satisfactorily. Hence,
the network of international organizations inherits—if only by default—
the task of meeting the demands belatedly born of nineteenth-century
liberalism.[1]

But there is no automatic dialectic at work here, according to Jenks. The
heavy hand of *fortuna* must be stayed, must be overcome through the artifice of the *virtú* of law. Governments tend to be recalcitrant and not to recognize the dual forces sketched. Reactionary minorities in the nations will
seek to halt the advance of freedom and to stunt majority public opinion.
Law must come to the rescue of freedom. The law in question, however, is
not traditional international law, which governs only states and is based
on a territorial principle of jurisdiction. It is what Jenks calls the "Common
Law of Mankind," a law which recognizes *ab initio* the rights of individuals and whose jurisdiction is functional rather than territorial, thus becoming global in scope by sleight of hand.[2] The present international
system is the proper one for ushering in this law.

Freedom through law is also thought to rest on the direct perception of
interests that Functionalists single out for attention. Major industrial countries are likely to entertain the interests that make them ready consumers
of new "common law" norms protecting human rights. But let us note,
before proceeding, that the argument here begins to slip into wishful thinking and covert advocacy rather than resting on functional givens. First,
among such interests, Jenks finds that

the Constitution of the International Labour Organisation . . . declares "the
failure of any nation to adopt humane conditions of labour is an obstacle in the
way of other nations which desire to improve the conditions in their own countries." While the precise inter-relationships of labour standards, labour efficiency and competitive capacity in the international market may be complex
and subject to debate, no one who is familiar with the political history of international commercial policy, including such chapters as the reciprocal trade
agreements programme in the United States, the economic integration movement in Europe, and the problem of competition with established industries
from new industries in underdeveloped countries, can doubt that this proposition reflects a widespread view of governments, management and labour alike,
which is a substantial factor in contemporary international economic relations.[3]

Second, such states have an interest in inducing foreign countries to which they export goods and capital to adopt labor standards that meet the best judgment of the international community, standards resting on informed and reasonable compromise rather than local improvisation based on distrust of foreigners. Finally, such countries are thought to have a continuing interest in using the international protection of human rights as a means for establishing stable democratic conditions in new and underdeveloped countries. These interests cannot be met by recommendations and resolutions; they require the binding force and authority of law, i.e., ILO Conventions.[4] Converging interests (at least among Western industrialized states) combine with the logic of the international system to set the scene for the new task.

The final Functional argument that we rediscover here relates to the theme of world peace. Reciprocal guarantees of freedom are sought by governments in order to protect freedom at home, to secure their citizens civil liberties that would be jeopardized if unrest elsewhere were to make the garrison state inevitable. "Civil liberties have become a leading and legitimate object of foreign and international policy because historical experience shows that without a wider acceptance of civil liberties we are unlikely to be able 'to save succeeding generations from the scourge of war.' "[5]

Obviously, a functional theory of integration cannot accept this argument in its entirety, even though much of it is based on massive trends whose existence cannot be denied. The ringing phrases on which Jenks relies occur in such documents as the Universal Declaration of Human Rights, the European Convention for the Protection of Human Rights and Fundamental Freedoms, and in innumerable resolutions of international conferences. Governments pay at least lip service to them, as do conclaves of trade unionists, industrialists, veterans, and displaced persons, while lawyers passionately invoke them. The United Nations Commission on Human Rights, in the absence of a legal mandate, has received tens of thousands of individual petitions asking the UN to protect individual rights; the Trusteeship Council, with a full legal mandate, has received as many. From the streets of Birmingham to the slums of Johannesburg the same demand is heard. Freedom of association, non-discrimination, equality of opportunity, abolition of forced labor, and national self-determination (whoever the "self" may be) are universal demands from La Paz to Havana, Elisabethville to Algiers, Saigon to Warsaw. For certain purposes, mutual economic and technological interdependence is recognized even bilaterally between Moscow and Washington, to say nothing of London, Paris, and Bonn. Differential labor standards are of concern to governments, workers, and industrialists throughout the world, though the greatest incidence of this trend is in areas undergoing active common-market formation. Minimum standards for world trade and political rights are matters of moment to the West, even if the industrialized giant of the East attaches less importance to them. But whether the alleged tie between peace and the universal protection of human rights is consistently perceived today may well be doubted. In short, the Functional case for an expansion of the ILO task into the field of human rights rests on a real substructure of perceptions and pressures. The central weakness of the case, in the 1960's as in the 1940's, lies in the uneven incidence of the perceptions.

Jenks's Functionalism recognizes this fact. He admits that "the effectiveness of these international guarantees of freedom of association depends to a substantial extent on the degree of protection accorded to civil liberties in general and in particular on 'the protection of human rights by the rule of law on the basis of fundamental liberties such as freedom of opinion and expression, freedom of peaceful assembly and association, and freedom from arbitrary arrest, detention or exile.' "[6] The very groups and countries now clamoring for certain human rights in the social and economic fields seem less concerned with the traditional civil liberties. Communist countries, with the possible exception of Poland, minimize these civil rights unless they are put into a class context. Developing nations whose trade unions function as an adjunct of single political parties do not fit the picture of ideal requisites.

Of what use, then, can ILO law be? What happens to the common law of mankind when the Functional pressures for its extension are unevenly distributed among clients and consumers? The crucial criterion for judging functional success is the extent to which countries *not* previously part of the human rights consensus come to accept centrally made norms as a result of whatever systemic pressures are brought to bear, pressures that run *contrary* to pre-existing perceptions and aims. Jenks can do no better than argue the merits of continual invocation of international norms in the hope that rhetoric will itself somehow transform the system: "What legal vitality the Declaration [of Human Rights] has depends on the effect of invoking it in a wide range of national and international proceedings and here the future may show that we are at present only at the beginning of the story. In retrospect the Universal Declaration may yet come to be regarded as the Magna Carta of mankind."[7]

Despite these cavils, the Functionalism of the advocate and the functional stance of the analyst remain essentially united in positing human rights as an issue most likely, at this time, to result in task expansion of the international system, a conclusion based on a series of converging expectations on the part of governments. At this point, however, several analytical features inherent in the international protection of human rights must be thrown into relief, features that Official Functionalism has not considered.

Unlike the bulk of efforts invested in the preparation of international labor standards, the protection of human rights, especially freedom of association, concerns everybody. Subgoal domination, almost by definition, cannot occur in this realm. Hence if the program of an international organization expands to include this new area, the task thus taken on becomes the epitome of vitality. It becomes a task that pits citizens of a state against their own government, workers against employers, and employers against monolithic governing groups. It is a task that may involve formal appeal for a redress of individual grievances to an international forum. And this forum becomes the visible and direct agent for giving aid and comfort to the individual in a field of human endeavor that involves the most fundamental of values. In analytical terms, the expansion of an organization's task into the field of human rights is a powerful indicator of capacity to bring about a transformation of the international system.

Further, the field can serve as a vital indicator of organizational legitimacy. If states consistently demand the protection of human rights, participate in the preparation of appropriate texts, ratify these, invoke them, *and then implement them* when called upon to do so, considerable legitimacy attaches to the Organization in the perceptions of its members and clients. If members differ in their perceptions of organizational legitimacy, an analytical treatment of their reaction to the human rights issue will clarify the systemic impact of the international agency under review. In addition, the same field can be used as an indicator of authority. Human rights, because they deal with universal, non-technical, highly political, and controversial matters, provide a sensitive litmus paper for determining which governments will defer to central pressure even when they do *not* consistently demand international norms, participate in their preparation, or ratify the resulting texts. Of course, failure to participate in preparing internationally protected rights is evidence of an absence of that very converging of expectations singled out by Jenks. When, after complaints have been voiced and an international hearing instituted, such states comply anyway, the national scene *is* changed. Any international step that reduces the internal monolithism of a member state, that creates self-conscious autonomous groups within it, is a step toward a non-territorial, non-national pluralistic international environment. Any step that divorces national trade unions or employer associations from an exclusive concern with national legitimacy and authority is a step toward a different international system, especially if the national disaffiliation results in an international realignment of concrete social interests. Human rights protection may provide merely a procedural and instrumental link here; but it is surely a vital link if it facilitates the confrontation of economic interests on a scale larger than the national one.[8]

We can now summarize which requisites implicit in the field of human rights are of central importance to task expansion and system transformation. The rights to be protected must be such as to minimize the common organizational tendency toward subgoal-dominated programs. They must comprise the most general list of freedoms, cutting across occupational and national-cultural lines. Freedom for migrant workers to have access to the social security legislation of the host state is not enough, because there simply are not that many migrant workers and because their demands are too insignificant to change any environment.

Further, the rights to be protected by international action must comprise those in the forefront of national and international agitation if they are to rest on a measure of convergence of interests. The traditional Western preoccupation with political and civil rights is insufficient to meet this requisite. The bulk of the politically articulate population in non-Western countries does not seem particularly concerned with freedom of speech, religion, assembly, or the right to oppose the government—unless of course the claimant happens to be in opposition. The rights to hold free and secret elections, to form and maintain parties, and to publish newspapers critical of the regime are not the ones most ardently sought in Asia and Africa or in parts of Latin America. To argue that these procedural political rights are of vital value in securing substantive economic and social benefits is to underestimate the passion for immediate improvement, for radical self-assertion. It misses the passion for the kind of collective dignity that is associated with the vague espousal of the unqualified right to national self-determination, the "right" highlighted in the opening articles of the United Nations draft covenants on human rights.

In short, the functional requisites of a vital human rights program must focus on economic and social rights, an emphasis increasingly recognized also in Western countries. Freedom of association, the central right of concern to the ILO, is here both instrumental and substantive. Instrumental significance derives from its importance in so changing a national setting that the government involved is forced to direct its attention to the demands of new groups; substantive significance attaches to the results—through collective bargaining or otherwise—of the aroused attention. As Jenks puts it:

Freedom from forced labour, freedom of association for trade union purposes, and freedom from discrimination in respect of employment also constitute a group of closely related rights in another sense. They all have a close bearing on personal freedom, not only in the enlarged sense of freedom from fear and from want . . . but in the primary sense of freedom from arbitrary restraint upon the action and opportunities of the individual. They provide, of course, particularly in the case of freedom of association, for freedoms which may introduce new elements of constraint, but they do so primarily to enlarge the area of personal freedom rather than primarily to promote a particular economic or social policy.[9]

In long-range terms Jenks is undoubtedly right. However, in the shorter run of the convergence of national expectations in the current international system, it is doubtful that the actors of importance to our requisites will embrace freedom of association *except* in terms of a particular economic or social policy. Advocacy of freedom of association and other political rights is likely to manifest itself dialectically. It will occur as a result of the West against the communists. On the other hand, it may be possible for the ILO to capitalize on an interest in human rights that derives from a specific economic program in such a way as to turn it into a protection of political rights more generally. If so—and whether this is the case remains to be demonstrated here—the protection of primordial political and civil rights would be an unintended consequence of a slightly different policy input, and as such of immense importance to the analysis of international integration.

In any event, our functional requisites also demand that actor conduct go beyond the invocation of desirable norms. Meaningful new standards do not arise merely as a result of rhetorical broadsides. Nor do they automatically follow from the ritual ratification of Conventions. A feedback into the national scene must be demonstrated in concrete behavioral terms. The actual implementation, through national legislation and practice, is the crucial indicator of organizational success.[10]

The tension between the expectations of the chief actors, especially the conflict between the espousal of political rights and the espousal of economic rights, suggests that the systemic impact of the protection of human rights is likely to manifest itself dialectically. It will occur as a result of heated charges and demands intimately tied to the Cold War and the anticolonial revolution. Judicial restraint and the careful sorting of facts—though such virtues could enhance the legitimacy of the system—are not the central factors; the impact on the environment can only come from the actual passions that provide the fuel for organizational outputs. Orderly transformation of the national—and hence the international—scene can thus come about as an unintended consequence of disorderly claims and confrontations.

Jenks, on the contrary, argues that since human rights involve mass attitudes and deep-seated social habits, legal techniques and discipline must be used for their protection. "Moral judgment has a vital role to play in world affairs, but when moral censure is over-frequently or indiscriminately employed or intemperately expressed, its edge is blunted."[11] Hence detach-

ment is of the essence in dealing with specific allegations; judicial restraint
is imperative unless the fire of passionate controversy is to be fed. "Moral
judgment ceases to be moral when it ceases to be judgment and becomes
special pleading or invective."[12]

No systemic transformation will come about unless the organization
deals with the mass of special pleading of which international politics is
made up. Invective is inseparable from confrontation. Indeed, the confrontation itself is just the type of crisis situation which, if properly exploited, can result in dramatic task expansion and eventual feedback. It is
useful for the ILO to maintain a façade of detachment and restraint. But
unless the Organization glories in the interideological strife of its members
and seeks to surmount these tensions with a consensual synthesis of central
action, the field of human rights will afford no more dynamic opportunities
than the elaboration of specific labor standards.

ILO PROCEDURE AND HUMAN RIGHTS

These considerations pinpoint the importance of human rights in the potential transformation of the international system. Moreover, they provide
evidence of the extent to which they have been absorbed into Official Functionalism. Yet they do not exhaust the theme. Official Functionalism also
contains a number of theses concerning the *unique* role of the ILO in this
process, theses that retain and reaffirm the claim made originally at Philadelphia in 1944.

Why does the Office argue that the ILO has been specially chosen to
act as midwife at the "new birth of freedom"? One justification advanced
is the relative continuity of the ILO's concern with the questions of freedom of association and forced labor. The early history of ILO efforts is
invoked, but the main argument derives from the claim that the Philadelphia program implied a new global consensus on the primary importance
of human rights as ends in themselves, a consensus translated into an action
mandate with the ILO as the beneficiary.

In addition, the Office invokes a specific mandate given by the United
Nations. Recalling the Economic and Social Council's discussions with
regard to violations of freedom of association in communist and capitalist
countries, the Office proudly stresses that the subsequent work of supervising the application of the 1948 Convention was bequeathed to the ILO by
the ECOSOC's resolutions. We shall return to this theme later. Let it be
pointed out, though, that the parentage here established rested precisely
on a brutal confrontation of opposed ideologies, not on restraint, and that
the evolution of the Governing Body's machinery for quasi-judicial supervision was an unintended consequence of that confrontation. Because of

the authority of the UN, however, Jenks feels able to argue that the principle of freedom of association must be viewed as having "taken its place among 'the general principles of law recognized by civilized nations' which . . . are indicated in Article 38 of the Statute of the International Court among the sources of law to be applied by the Court."[13]

In addition, and more directly, Official Functionalism invokes the mystique of tripartite deliberation as its special justification. If a new functional law of individual rights is to be become meaningful, the argument runs, representative spokesmen of important groups other than delegates of governments must participate in the drafting process. Only thus can a transterritorial identity of interests be fashioned. The true interest of mankind is an eventual universal and genuine consensus among workers and employers, universal because it rests on occupational experience, and genuine because it flows from confrontations of that experience. Thus, the most generally recognized standard of individual human rights can be written into international law. Consensus flows from group ideas on progress, and the incorporation of that progress in ILO documents spells freedom. Since pluralism is thus elevated into one of the causative agents of consensus formation, it follows easily that the ILO—the most pluralist of international organizations—is the natural agent.[14] Again, however, we are entitled to ask whether this assumed tendency toward universal reason and justice is not the result of an earlier confrontation of clashing ideas that are far from uniformly committed to progress; or whether, somehow, the commitment to progress is considered immanent in the major interest groups whose consensus eventually results in new human rights. The weight of the "official" argument rests on the second alternative.

The tripartite ILO is particularly well equipped to advance human rights, the argument concludes, because of long organizational experience in conducting restrained, careful, and intensely practical negotiations. ILO efforts are by definition very functionally specific; they are flexible in that they do not seek to impose identical rules and procedures for all types of human rights; they aim at generality even though the context is specifically in the field of labor law; and they profit from the unique ILO procedure of discussion, review by experts, and continuous supervision over the implementation of obligations.[15]

Unfortunately, the argument is not quite convincing. Apart from the untenable proposition that consensus for the progress of freedom is inherent in the structure of autonomous social groupings and need merely be triggered by the tripartite international process, the functional limits on the mechanism are not spelled out. Is the impact of the confrontation uniform with respect to the global clientele? We suspect, on the basis of our previous inquiry, that it is not. Does unevenness destroy the neatness of the demonstration? It should. Forces that merely transform a part of the environment are unlikely to engender the new system so eagerly sought. And the stronger the stress on very functionally specific, step-by-step methods is, the greater the distortion of the potentially universal impact of the new rules becomes. We must therefore turn to the instruments and procedures available to the ILO for creating and enforcing new human rights standards in order to discover to what extent these limits are operative.

How, then, does the ILO define new internationally protected human rights? It does so by relying on the Conventions and Recommendations that we encountered before. In fact, the human rights of interest to us are simply one aspect of the International Labor Code. Therefore, the rules and procedures governing the drafting, ratifying, and implementing of Conventions discussed above apply fully to our present concern. Conventions and Recommendations are subject to the annual reporting procedure and to the supervision of implementation made possible by the work of the Committee of Experts on the Application of Conventions. Finally, the very limited value of Recommendations already noted applies fully to the field of human rights.[16] Hence, our attention will be focused on Conventions.

As far as some ILO spokesmen are concerned, almost all the texts adopted by the Organization deal with human rights. In the largest sense, one might include such matters as social security, protection of women and young workers, minimum wage-fixing machinery, maximum hour rules, manpower recruitment, protection of labor contracts, employment services, paid vacations, protection of tribal populations, and special measures in favor of indigenous workers in colonies. The difficulty here is that most of such efforts, all of which are represented in one or several ILO Conventions, fail to meet our requirement of generality. They establish basic rights of an economic or social character for specific groups in the population, but they lack general applicability. Further, the many specific texts adopted on behalf of non-metropolitan territories have lapsed with the independence of the countries concerned. In general, the very specific texts have not enjoyed wide ratification either. If we wish to avoid subgoal domination, by definition we cannot include every text that indirectly creates human rights; we must confine ourselves to the general instruments which, by making possible a spilling over into new and wider social contexts, are likely to transform the international system. To be sure, texts must be functionally specific. But they cannot be so specific as to preclude a spill-over.[17] Hence, we shall single out for detailed analysis the Conventions dealing with (1) labor inspection, (2) freedom of association, (3) the right to organize and collective bargaining, (4) equal remuneration, (5) forced labor, and (6) discrimination.[18]

With the exception of the labor inspection Convention, each of these crucial texts originated as a result of, or at least in conjunction with, discussion and pressure in the ECOSOC. The text dealing with equal remuneration resulted from interest expressed by women's organizations, and the ILO's efforts followed previous discussion and study in the UN Commission on the Status of Women. The four remaining texts, however, sprang directly from Cold War and colonial confrontations. The two Conventions covering trade union rights followed a bitter debate in the 1947 session of the ECOSOC, which pitted the Soviet and American governments against each other, the former representing charges by the WFTU directed against "imperialist" practices, and the latter acting on behalf of the AFL, which attacked Soviet practices. The story behind the issue of forced labor at the UN has already been told.[19] ILO action followed as a direct consequence of the ECOSOC's uncertainty about how to handle the anti-communist findings of its Special Committee. And the Anti-Discrimination Convention, as might be expected, had its origin in Soviet, Asian, and African demands that racial discrimination be barred on a global scale.

In short, the very texts on which Official Functionalism relies for staking out a new organizational task had their origin in controversy, acrimony, and deep political conflict. There was little restraint and moderation in evidence. Autonomous social groupings were only intermittently and inconsistently involved. Governments were the crucial actors, and they may be suspected of having entered the fray for propagandistic reasons rather than from a desire to impose new international legislation. Once the forum shifted to the ILO, of course, the functional logic of interest group participation did enter as an independent force, resulting in formal norms that may indeed have been unexpected in their eventual role as far as the original aims of governments were concerned.[20]

We now turn to the content of these six texts, reserving a discussion of supervisory machinery, success, and fidelity of implementation to a subsequent section.

(1) Convention Concerning Labor Inspection in Industry and Commerce (No. 81), 1947. Convention 81 requires ratifying states to "maintain a system of labour inspection in industrial workplaces" (Art. 1); the system is to be operated by trained personnel who are independent of pressure from employer or political sources. Inspectors must have the right to enter workplaces at will and without previous notice, question personnel, inspect books and facilities, post notices, and remove materials for analysis (Art. 12). Further, they are to have the power to order alterations in plant conditions to make them conform with the law (Art. 13). The central labor inspection administration must publish an annual report on its work, giv-

ing information on the number of visits made, and the incidence of violations, penalties, industrial accidents, and cases of occupational disease; this report is to be submitted to the ILO (Arts. 20, 21). But the Convention also contains loopholes. In many instances its injunctions are qualified by the phrase "in such manner as may be prescribed by national law or regulations." Mining and transport undertakings may be exempted. Application to commercial offices is optional, as is extension to "territory which includes large areas where, by reason of the sparseness of the population or the stage of development of the area, the competent authority considers it impracticable to enforce the provisions" (Art. 29). Finally, the substance of the law to be enforced by the inspectors rests entirely within national discretion.

(2) Convention Concerning Freedom of Association and Protection of the Right to Organise (No. 87), 1948. The crucial provision of this text is that "workers and employers, without distinction whatsoever, shall have the right to establish and, subject only to the rules of the organisation concerned, to join organisations of their own choosing without previous authorisation" (Art. 2). Public interference of any kind with the formation and life of associations is forbidden, and this applies to units at the local, municipal, regional, national, and international levels. "Organisation" is defined broadly to include any interest group other than the military and police (Arts. 9, 10). Member states must "take all necessary and appropriate measures to ensure that workers and employers may exercise freely the right to organise" (Art. 11). The only possible remaining loophole is the provision that the rights here guaranteed must be practiced with respect for the law of the land, though this law "shall not be such as to impair . . . the guarantees" (Art. 8).

(3) Right to Organise and Collective Bargaining Convention (No. 98), 1949. This text is a supplement to Convention 87, protecting workers against acts of anti-union discrimination in respect to their employment. Workers cannot be punished or penalized for organizing or participating in unions, or engaging in collective bargaining. The text does not formally recognize the closed or union shops, but it is so drawn as to be acceptable to countries in which these institutions exist.

(4) Convention Concerning Equal Remuneration for Men and Women Workers for Work of Equal Value (No. 100), 1951. Because of widely differing national methods governing the determination of wages, it proved impossible to lay down a flat prohibition against unequal pay scales. The text is therefore "promotional" in tone. "Each member shall, by means appropriate to the methods in operation for determining rates of remuneration, promote and, in so far as is consistent with such methods, ensure the application to all workers of the principle of equal remuneration for men

and women workers for work of equal value" (Art. 2, para. 1). The "methods" include national law, collective bargaining, other recognized machinery for wage determination, or a combination of all these. Convention 100, however, does not tackle a standardization of the methods themselves, or deal with the difficult matter of job classification that may impair the purity of the "equal pay for equal work" rule (Art. 3).

(5) Convention Concerning the Abolition of Forced Labour (No. 105), 1957. Convention 105 goes far beyond not only the earlier ILO Convention on this subject, which was adopted as a result of discussion in the League of Nations, but also the League's Anti-Slavery Convention (1926). Forced labor with respect to "political coercion or education or as a punishment" is prohibited, as is using labor as a means of economic development, as a device for enforcing labor discipline, or as punishment for having participated in a strike. Finally, it eliminates forced labor as a means of racial, social, national, or religious discrimination (Art. 1). There are no visible loopholes here.

(6) Convention Concerning Discrimination in Respect of Employment and Occupation (No. 111), 1958. Like Convention 100 this text is "promotional." Members undertake "to declare and pursue a national policy designed to promote, by methods appropriate to national conditions and practice, equality of opportunity and treatment in respect of employment and occupation, with a view to eliminating any discrimination in respect thereof" (Art. 2). This is to be done by any or all of the following methods, depending on local conditions: discussion with voluntary organizations, enactment of legislation, educational programs, repeal of legislation inconsistent with the text, adoption of a rigorous non-discriminatory national employment policy, and the application of this policy to vocational guidance and training and to placement (Art. 3). Persons "justifiably suspected of, or engaged in, activities prejudicial to the security of the State" do not profit from these provisions (Art. 4). Equality of opportunity is considered to be impaired if distinctions and preferences are made on the basis of race, color, sex, religion, political opinion, national extraction, or social origin (Art. 1).[21]

Such are the central texts. What are the provisions for supervision and enforcement? We may distinguish, first of all, between procedures written into the ILO Constitution and as such deliberately devised, and methods that have evolved ad hoc and that have gained acceptance without, or in spite of, the declared intentions of the member states. Obviously, the second category holds a greater interest for our thesis.

Among the constitutionally sanctioned procedures, the most important is the annual review of member state reports concerning ratified and unratified Conventions that is undertaken by the Committee of Experts. Although the field of human rights is treated no differently by the Committee than the rest of the International Labor Code, it is worth recalling that, in its origins, this organ evolved ad hoc and assumed constitutionally sanctioned status as a result of custom and political pressure.

Another procedure of continuing importance here is the investigating power of the Governing Body. That organ has often launched inquiries into practices relating to human rights. Some were of an ad hoc nature, resulting from specific complaints received by the ILO and ending in the dispatch of a mission to the country concerned in order to ascertain the facts and—less often—assist the government in correcting the situation if a violation was uncovered.[22] Such ad hoc investigations are launched only if the allegedly delinquent government consents to the sending of the mission and is willing to negotiate with it. Other investigations deal with generalized problems and do not involve the dispatch of a special mission. Although a committee of distinguished specialists is set up to undertake special inquiries, most of the work is done by the Office on the basis of national legislation, available newspaper and monograph sources, and the replies to questionnaires submitted to governments. This was the procedure used in two massive inquiries on freedom of association undertaken on behalf of the Governing Body, the investigation of 1926 and the McNair studies of 1955–56.[23] In both cases the purpose of the inquiry was to lay the factual basis for a subsequent systematic program on the part of the ILO. To a considerable extent these inquiries must also rely on the cooperation and consent of governments, at least as far as the use of questionnaires is concerned.

In addition, the Constitution makes provision for a formal complaint and representations procedure that we have so far considered only in the context of constitutional revision.[24] It is therefore important to spell out the provisions and the formal interpretations to which they were subjected, before we turn to the use that has been made of them. The drafters of Part XIII of the Treaty of Versailles were overwhelmingly in favor of putting strong measures of control and enforcement into the labor legislation machinery they were fashioning. They were convinced that economic pressure would be an important way of achieving uniform international labor standards when used in conjunction with adverse publicity, machinery for judicial settlement, and impartial fact-finding. Only the United States delegates at all times made plain their strong opposition to such an approach. The resulting machinery was to function as follows.[25]

Any group of workers or employers may address a "representation" to the Governing Body alleging that a member state is violating a Convention that it has ratified. The Governing Body may invite the comment of that government and, if an adequate response is not obtained, publish a report giving both the text of the allegation and the government's reply, if any. This ends the power of voluntary associations directly to seek enforcement of the Code.

Any government, however, may address a "complaint" to the Governing Body containing the same kind of allegation. If the reply of the defendant government is deemed insufficient, or if the Governing Body does not wish to consult with it, the ILO may apply to the League of Nations for the appointment of a Commission of Inquiry. Further, the Governing Body may request the appointment of such a commission on its own initiative or on the request of any delegate to the International Labor Conference. Member states, further, are under obligation to set up panels of three specialists in industrial matters, one representing labor, one the employers, and an independent expert; from among these the Secretary-General of the League was to select a Commission to deal with the allegation at hand. The Commission would then investigate (governments having pledged to cooperate with it by virtue of having become members of the ILO), ascertain the facts, and if necessary recommend a settlement. It might also recommend "measures of an economic character against a defaulting Government which it considers to be appropriate, and which it considers other Governments would be justified in adopting."[26] This was the extent to which "sanctions" were provided. It must be stressed that Commissions were mobilizable *not* by the ILO, but by the League of Nations, and that the procedure applies exclusively to governmental grievances or matters brought up by a Conference delegate.

After the Commission had completed its work, the Secretary-General of the League was to publish a full report. The defaulting government might accept the report and its recommendations, in which case the procedure would be terminated. If it declined, it had the right to appeal to the Permanent Court of International Justice, whose decision was final. The PCIJ could affirm, reject, or change the Commission's recommendations, and confirm also the "economic measures" that may have been suggested. If the defaulting government chose to ignore either the report of the League or a PCIJ decision, the other member states were free to take the "economic measures" recommended, but they were under no obligation to do so. The defaulting government could at any time inform the Governing Body that it had accepted the Commission's report and invite a new visit to verify the claim, whereupon all sanctions would stop.

Before we consider the emasculation of this procedure in the 1946 Constitution, let us note that neither the Office nor the Governing Body ever took the enforcement procedure very seriously. The Office never claimed to possess any power to recommend "sanctions," and preferred to use the term "a measure of control" in connection with the annual report procedure.

The Governing Body, for its part, failed to mention in its Standing Orders of 1932 the possibility of sanctions. And many member states declined to set up the tripartite panels of persons eligible for appointment to commissions of inquiry, claiming either that such commissions had no right to act on their soil or that qualified persons could not be found.[27]

As already mentioned, the new Constitution sought to avoid all reference to agencies other than the ILO. It eliminated the United Nations as a possible successor to the powers previously vested in the League, and it considerably reduced the role assigned to the International Court of Justice. Further, it eliminated all references to "economic measures" and abandoned the standing tripartite panels. Otherwise the original procedure was left intact; but the only "sanction" remaining provides that "the Governing Body may recommend to the Conference such action as it may deem wise and expedient to secure compliance" with the report of a Commission of Inquiry or a judgment of the ICJ.[28]

What extraconstitutional practices can we detect in the history of the ILO that might influence the enforcement of human rights? The onset of the Cold War and the anti-colonial campaign of the Afro-Asian bloc have resulted in the creation of one ad hoc organ which, unlike the ones discussed above, does *not* rest on the consent and cooperation of governments. This is the Committee on Forced Labor, discussed previously. So far no additional or similarly imposed investigatory bodies have been created. But the continuation of the type of interest confrontation that the anti-colonial struggle implies makes the creation of such bodies almost a certainty. In the United Nations General Assembly several imposed commissions have been set up to deal with colonialism, *apartheid,* and national self-determination in Portuguese colonies. There is no reason to suppose that the task of ILO makes it immune from the same pressures. Again, however, an initial propagandistic impulse may well lead to unintended consequences as far as international supervision over human rights is concerned. What evolved at South Africa's expense in 1964 may by 1966 be used against Indonesia or Iraq. Other types of central supervision may be evolving. The Office has prepared a study of the conditions necessary to assure the independence of trade union funds. Once it receives official endorsement in the form of a resolution by an authoritative ILO organ, it may proceed to protect threatened union treasuries on that basis. In a politically sensitive field in which international concessions are considered necessary by governments, unplanned and unforeseen control powers may emerge from superficially very "technical" studies.

Office-conducted surveys of trade union freedom on the soil of member states may constitute another evolving supervisory technique. Naturally such visits take place only with the consent and cooperation—if not under the supervision—of governments. But if they are conducted systematically as part of a long-range program of protecting trade union rights, they may well acquire the character of a feared and respected outside "audit" to whose authority member states will respond. So far, such surveys have been conducted in the United States, the Soviet Union, Britain, Sweden, Burma, and Malaya.[29] The observations of the mission were always understanding and mild. But they may not always be so if the field of human rights remains in the forefront of international political demands.

This judgment must stand even though these surveys of freedom of association went into—possibly temporary—eclipse in 1963. And the circumstances of their decline illustrate some of the limits inherent in the functional logic. It will be recalled that the surveys originated in a Cold War confrontation between the United States and the Soviet Union: eager to embarrass and expose the Soviet system, American trade unionists offered the formula of the surveys and immediately obtained a declaration from the United States government that it would welcome an ILO visit. The Soviets, of course, very soon followed suit. However, the results of these two missions so displeased the American workers that they later insisted on the abolition of the Office section devoted to the surveys and on the discontinuance of the whole technique. What appeared to be developing into a new type of international activity was left to wither as the initial expectations of the chief clients were disappointed.

However, by far the most interesting and powerful supervisory device that has evolved in an extra-constitutional fashion is the Governing Body's Committee on Freedom of Association, which has become the quasi-judicial global guardian of trade union rights. Let us recapitulate the story of the ILO's efforts to enforce freedom of association. The 1919 Constitution affirmed this freedom as fundamental and requisite for membership in the ILO. But when in 1921 the Governing Body was seized of instances of alleged interference with unions in Spain and Hungary, it proved unwilling and unable to do more than discuss the issue: no condemnation was directed to the governments concerned, who were under no specific contractual obligation to respect trade union freedom. Efforts were therefore launched to draft a Convention specifically guaranteeing freedom of association, inspired in part by the desire of the IFTU to ban fascist "union" representatives from full participation in the Conference. This effort failed because a sufficient majority could not be mobilized, in the 1927 session of the Conference, to adopt the questionnaire to be sent to governments prior to the drafting of a text. Whereas the Worker Group wanted a sweeping Convention, the Employer Group insisted on so formulating the questionnaire as to highlight the issue of public order and the general interest. The resulting text was a compromise that so dissatisfied the Workers that they combined with some Employers to defeat it.[30] There followed the period of passive ILO accommodation to totalitarian regimes, with the muting of the credentials issue and neglect of freedom of association, a policy that was not reversed until after World War II.

When, after the adoption of Conventions 87 and 98, charges of the violation of trade union freedom became part of the Cold War debate in the United Nations, the Economic and Social Council proposed the establishment of a standing Fact-Finding and Conciliation Commission, whose procedures were made to sound very much like those of the Commissions of Inquiry described in the ILO Constitution. Like them, of course, the new Commission could function only with the consent of the alleged delinquent government. Unlike them, the new Commission, though appointed by the Governing Body, was automatically to receive complaints and petitions addressed to ECOSOC's Commission on Human Rights, and it was to deal, too, with situations *not* confined to the alleged violation of ratified Conventions. In other words, a significant step in expanding the international task appeared to have been taken.[31]

The first complaints arrived in 1950. They involved a series of allegations formulated by the ICFTU and the AFL against Peru, implicating the Peruvian government in the murder of a high Peruvian trade union official; but the Peruvian government refused to admit the competence of the Commission, thus stopping the new procedure at the outset. This, in turn, gave rise to the procedure in use ever since, the "preliminary" sifting of allegations by a Special Committee of the Governing Body to determine their receivability. The Special Committee became *the* organ for protecting trade union rights, having dealt since 1951 with almost four hundred complaints. An unplanned and unexpected "provisional" organ took the place of the intended one, and built up a body of international trade union judgments that "may prove to be of pioneer importance as an experiment in the development of quasi-judicial processes of a growing body of accepted international doctrine on crucial social and industrial issues which will profoundly influence legal development in many countries and may at some stage harden into customary international law."[32]

We shall deal with the details of the Commission's transfiguration in Chapter 12. The essential point is to note the birth of an unplanned supervisory organ with a spill-over potential in the human rights area, a birth aided by an international ideological crisis. Thus far this has happened only in the context of protecting freedom of association. But efforts are already being made to perfect new "special machinery" to consider complaints concerning violations of the Anti-Discrimination Convention; these efforts are being strongly endorsed by the very Soviet Union that on other occasions sharply challenges the constitutional propriety of creating new international organs with supervisory competences. No doubt the motives of Moscow are as expediential here as were Washington's in 1948, when the United States strongly supported the creation of machinery to protect trade union rights. But the functional logic has a tendency to ignore and transcend the initial aims of governments.*

"Special machinery" for combating discrimination in member states was first proposed by the International Labor Conference in 1960. The Conference asked the Director-General to make proposals to that effect to the Governing Body, a unanimous request backed on the floor by the government delegates of Ghana, the U.A.R., and Poland, who made it very clear that the target in their minds was the Republic of South Africa.[33] Three years elapsed before agreement could be reached. Whatever proposals the Director-General might have made were submerged in the Governing Body's own pursuit of the matter. It decided in 1963 that it was not advisable "at this stage" to create "a special procedure for the examination of any allegations of acts of discrimination," but rather to continue the mandate of the Governing Body's Committee on Discrimination to watch the effectiveness of more modest measures proposed.[34] These measures were identical with the position long defended by the United States on the UN Commission on Human Rights: promotional and educational programs to spread knowledge concerning steps for combating discrimination in employment, technical assistance for teaching appropriate steps, ILO research on the extent to which discrimination exists in national law and practice. Even the Soviet government delegate rallied to this position, unanimously accepted by the Governing Body, even though he was disappointed with its modesty.

The treatment accorded the Republic of South Africa in the 1963 session of the Conference illustrates the extent to which, in response to converging but temporary global political pressures, the protection of human rights may result in an expanded but unanticipated task for the ILO. But at the same time this situation illustrates once more the functional limits on task expansion when there is no reliable and profound consensus. This is particularly true when the demand for an expanded task coincides with a constitutional issue, the gravity of which poses a survival crisis for the Organization. All these features were present in the South African case.

In 1961 the Conference had adopted a resolution urging South Africa to withdraw "voluntarily" from the ILO until it abandoned *apartheid*, the discrimination issue *par excellence*. Upon South Africa's failure to heed the resolution, the African nations in 1963 announced that South Africa was no longer a member of the ILO, a declaration rejected by the Conference's legal advisor.[35] Thereupon a major constitutional crisis developed,

---

* In 1959, the ECOSOC adopted a resolution urging UN member states to ratify the Anti-Discrimination Convention. Similar supervisory machinery may be evolving ad hoc in the Organization of American States' Commission on Human Rights, and has evolved, with full legal sanction, under the European Convention on Human Rights.

involving challenges to the rights of South Africans to address the Conference, the validity of their credentials, and ending in a boycott of the Conference on the part of all African and Soviet bloc delegations, joined by many Asians.[36] At this stage, Director-General Morse took the initiative in proposing a plan to the Governing Body that would not only preserve legality and satisfy the Africans, but upgrade common interests by further extending the task of the ILO in the field of anti-discrimination measures. The plan envisaged the temporary exclusion of South Africa from all ILO meetings other than the Conference; the full cooperation of the ILO with all United Nations activities aimed at South Africa, including expulsion from the UN system and the encouragement of resistance movements in Southwest Africa; and the appointment of a special commission to investigate—with or without South African consent—practices regarding forced labor, freedom of association, and discrimination.*

The Governing Body, after a bitter and substantively inconclusive debate, accepted the first two of Morse's suggestions and authorized the sending of a tripartite delegation to New York to aid the Security Council in proceeding against South Africa. But it turned down the idea of creating a new commission with new powers; and it avoided the expulsion issue by postponing any discussion of revising the Constitution to facilitate such a step.[37] No task expansion has taken place yet; but the Office took the initiative for such a development in pushing for new investigatory powers. The next crisis over discrimination may well confirm the evolution of that power.

REPRESENTATIONS AND COMPLAINTS IN PRACTICE

Before the enforcement procedure can be evaluated in terms of functional analysis, it is, of course, necessary to survey the use that has been made of the constitutional and extra-constitutional provisions we have just described. During the pre-1945 period, efforts were made by national trade unions to apply the representation procedure against their own governments; but almost no use was made of the more formal complaint procedure under which governments were able to challenge each other's fidelity

---

* "Papers Before the Governing Body Concerning the . . . Question of South Africa," Geneva, June 28–29, 1963, Doc. GB 156-1400, Annex II. There is some irony in this proposal if we bear in mind that the Office, in 1944 and 1945, went to considerable lengths in seeking to eliminate political ties of this kind between the ILO, the League of Nations, and the incipient United Nations. The new environment repoliticized the Organization. In the Governing Body debate, the Worker and Employer Groups, as well as the government of Australia, demanded that the Constitution be revised to provide for the expulsion of a member. Even sanctions are becoming popular again, as evidenced in India's demand that diplomatic, economic, and transport ties with South Africa be broken by ILO members, a move that would align the ILO with previous resolutions adopted by the General Assembly. In fact, South Africa withdrew from the ILO in 1964, while the Conference adopted a draft constitutional amendment permitting expulsion in similar future cases.

to the Code. During the post-1945 period, however, the representation procedure has all but lapsed, whereas the complaint procedure has gained a new lease on life even though the possibility of sanctions no longer exists.

Let us consider representations first. The twelve allegations received and processed in Geneva before the revision of program and Constitution are summarized in Table 20. The fate of six of them immediately suggests the inherent limitations of the International Labor Code itself. No effective supervision was possible if the legal rigor of the system of Conventions was subjected to doubt. Thus, three representations dealing with the suppression of trade unions by fascist governments were rejected because no specific Convention on the subject then existed.[38] The complaints of the Mauritius Labor Party and the French Indian workers could not be heard because neither of these associations was considered a bona fide trade union. And since France was legally quite competent to decline the application of the Code to its overseas territories, the aggrieved unions in Pondicherry had no legal basis for advancing their claims. In two additional cases, however, the procedure took a course quite consonant with the aim of using publicity and pacific settlement techniques to give reality to the Code. In Chile and Mauritius, the complainants eventually withdrew their representations because the governments concerned began to take an interest in the non-application of ratified Conventions. Presumably, the workers' objectives were attained without resorting to a full international confrontation.

The four remaining cases, however, illustrate the extreme caution with which the Governing Body approached enforcement of the Code. The representations of the Japanese and Latvian seamen were found to be well-substantiated. Neither government had conscientiously applied the Convention it had ratified. Yet the Governing Body accepted the explanations informally offered by the two governments and declined to pursue the matter further: the Japanese authorities claimed that they were attempting gradually to abolish fee-charging employment agencies, and the Latvian government protested its inability to proceed because of the intransigeant attitude of radical seamen's unions and obdurate employers.[39]

The Governing Body hardly showed outstanding courage here. It proved even more self-effacing in the case involving the suppression of trade unions in Estonia. In prolonged discussions between a special Governing Body committee and the Estonian authorities, the latter claimed that they were justified in ignoring Convention 11 because they were suppressing not only agricultural trade unions, but industrial agricultural ones as well. Thereupon the committee recommended to the plenary Body that the matter be dropped, a proposal adopted by a vote of 14 to 9. The Governing Body then asked the Estonian government to agree to the publication of a

TABLE 20

Representations Submitted to the Governing Body, 1919–40

No.	Date	Complaining organization	Government indicted	Subject	Disposition by ILO
1	1920	Spanish Trade Union Congress	Spain	Freedom of association	Not receivable because no Convention involved
2	1924	Japanese Seamen's Union	Japan	Suppression of fee-charging employment agents (Conv. 9)	Explanation of government accepted
3	1930	Latvian Seamen's Union	Latvia	Same as 2	Same as 2
4	1935	Madras Railway Workers	France	Non-application of Conventions 2, 4, 6, 11, 12, 13, 14, 18, 26, because of "local conditions"	Not well-founded because France has right to determine applicable "local conditions"
5	1936	Textile and Dock Workers of French India	France	Same as 4	Not receivable because complainants are not a "professional organization"
6	1936	Salaried Workers International (ITS)	Austria	Freedom of association	Not receivable because no Convention involved
7	1936	Madras Textile Workers	India	Non-application of Unemployment Convention (No. 2)	Substance upheld by GB, but India denounces Convention and gives jurisdiction over employment to provinces under new Constitution
8	1936	Mauritius Labour Party	Britain	Non-application of Conventions 2, 5, 6, 7, 8, 11, 24, 25, 26	Not receivable because complainants are not a "professional organization"
9	1937	Estonian Agricultural Workers Union	Estonia	Freedom of association in agriculture (Conv. 11)	Not well-founded because government was suppressing industrial trade unions as well, hence not discriminating
10	1937	Mauritius Workers Society	Britain	Same as 8	Withdrawn because government undertook review of conditions
11	1938	Chilean Bakers' Union	Chile	Hours of work at night (Conv. 20)	Same as 10
12	1938	Yugoslav Metalworkers' Union	Yugoslavia	Freedom of association	Not receivable because no Convention involved

Source: Adaptation of material in Troclet, pp. 659–67.

report summarizing the procedures, a request that the government opposed. Consequently no report was published.[40]

However, the case showing the greatest lack of ILO legitimacy or authority with respect to enforcing the Code concerned the British Indian reaction to the Governing Body's finding that violations of the Convention on Unemployment had occurred. The Governing Body unilaterally published a report on the situation, an act followed by the Indian denunciation of Convention 2, justified by the entry into force of the new Indian Constitution that gave jurisdiction over employment questions to the provinces. Clearly, these experiences were not calculated to reinforce the tendency toward an enlarged task involving active supervision.

Since 1945 there has been no formal recourse to the representation procedure. Such allegations as have been received in Geneva concerning violations of the Code have been dealt with by the Director-General and Office Missions of Inquiry, sometimes in consultation with the Governing Body.[41] The complaint procedure, by contrast, has finally come into its own. Let us review the cases that have come up.

Before World War II there was not a single case in which the full panoply of constitutional possibilities was even attempted, a state of affairs that may have been instrumental in persuading the 1945 Conference Delegation on Constitutional Questions to take the whole matter very lightly. In 1920, the British government complained before the Governing Body that the rugmakers of Kerman worked under subhuman conditions. In response, the Governing Body merely instructed the Director, Albert Thomas, to initiate "friendly representations" with the Persian government.[42] In 1934, the Indian worker delegate to the Conference charged the British Indian authorities with not applying Convention 1 to railway workers. The Governing Body accepted the charge and appointed a committee of its own members to investigate; but this group accepted the explanation of the government that it was doing its best to apply the Hours Convention as rapidly as possible. Instead of appointing the Commission of Inquiry foreseen in the Constitution, the Governing Body in effect used the representation procedure in order to exonerate the British authorities.[43]

After the war a distinct political aura began to suffuse the complaint procedure. In 1951, the Egyptian government complained that Britain had violated the forced labor Convention and had infringed on freedom of association in the Suez Canal Zone. The Governing Body, while denying the right of Egypt to lodge a complaint because Egypt was not a party to the relevant Conventions, agreed to the British suggestion to have the Director-General dispatch a fact-finding mission to the area. The mission undertook this task and reported to the Office. Thereupon the parties agreed to withdraw the matter from the agenda.[44] Again, a quiet and unpublished settlement was arranged before the procedure could be tested. But the full procedure came into its own after forty-three years of disuse with the revival of the forced labor issue in 1962. Ghana proceeded to complain against Portugal, whereupon Portugal struck back by depositing a similar complaint against Liberia. Friendly settlements and legal formulas permitting a sidestepping of the issue were no longer possible. International conditions in 1962 were very different from those in 1935, and the alignment of interests in the ILO now presages an affirmation of the enforcement procedure as a direct—if unintended—result of the Cold War and the anti-colonial revolt.

Before exploring these possibilities, we must return to the oscillations in the ILO procedure governing representations and complaints before 1962, for they tell a story of environmental restraints upon constitutional possibilities. The Worker Group, during the interwar period, was clearly anxious to make the most of the enforcement provisions, but it received no support from governments, employers, or the Office. At the time of the Latvian representation, the Worker Group argued that a Commission of Inquiry should be requested by the Governing Body by virtue of that organ's right to undertake an investigation on its own initiative. The implication of such a step would have been the automatic conversion of a representation into a complaint by the ILO itself. The Office reacted first by reiterating the legal distinction between the two procedures; however, in the 1932 Standing Orders of the Governing Body, the right to make the conversion was recognized. On the other hand, the same Standing Orders do not touch the procedure for handling complaints, thus implying that representations were preferred, and that nothing should be done to facilitate recourse to the complaint procedure by governments or delegates to the conference.[45]

Further, the actual procedure used in processing representations was considerably diffused in the practice of the ILO. Instead of proceeding immediately to a formal consideration of a representation, the Governing Body permitted a number of preliminary steps to evolve in connection with the first cases. First, the legal receivability of a communication had to be ascertained. Second, the allegedly delinquent government was given an informal opportunity to exchange views and offer explanations. If the Governing Body's committee charged with looking into the representation felt satisfied, the union communication was never even formally submitted to the national authorities. This is what happened in the Japanese seamen's case, for instance. As that and other cases showed, the Governing Body's committees were also quite ready to accept all sorts of excuses which, on a rigorous reading of ILO obligations, might not have been considered germane. Further, the time limit set for informal exchanges of views and replies to communications was repeatedly extended, thus allowing more opportunity for remedial action to occur, or tempers to cool, before formal steps were initiated. Perhaps most important, the Office's role constantly expanded in these situations because the preliminary negotiations and exchanges of views were delegated to the Director. This practice, having evolved ad hoc after the war, developed into a full investigatory power on the part of the Office when the parties felt desirous of fact-finding and mediation. It is also true, of course, that the Office did not translate this expansion of its powers into an extension of its authority.

The Standing Orders formally recognize these reductions of authority. Proceedings are confidential until they are completed. The Director is to amass all the facts before the Governing Body is formally informed of the situation. The Governing Body must set up a tripartite committee of three of its own members to consider the receivability of the representation. If it is considered receivable, it may then be decided (1) to refer it to the government concerned without inviting a reply (which is a method of terminating the procedure), (2) to request further information (which is a method of delay), or (3) to communicate the representation to the government *with* a request for a reply. Only the final step can be said to meet the enforcement rules defined in the Constitution.[46] If a formal reply is indeed invited, a "reasonable" time limit is fixed. Further, a representative of the government concerned is invited to appear before the Governing Body's committee. As a result of these steps, the Governing Body is still free (1) to find that the explanations are satisfactory and close the procedure; (2) to adjourn a decision by requesting further information; or (3) to consider the representation well-founded in substance and publish it in a report together with the replies of the government. Again only the final step is a full application of the constitutional rules. At this point, too, the Governing Body is free to convert the representation procedure into the mode of action that has been devised for complaints. These rules remain in effect today.

Both in the case of representations and in that of complaints, the report of the Governing Body is the crucial item. It constitutes the chief act of publicity available to the international organization if friendly inquiries and quiet conciliation fail to work. The Constitution gives the Governing Body leeway to publish or not to publish a report. If there are hopes of obtaining a friendly settlement, a report will normally not be published. But in fact—as opposed to law and standard legal commentary—two kinds of reports have evolved: unilaterally published reports and what we might call "negotiated" reports. A unilateral report contains an overt or implicit condemnation of a government, as in the unsuccessful criticism of India. A negotiated report contains recommendations for a settlement previously cleared with the delinquent government and accepted by it. In other words, when the Organization publishes such a report with specific recommendations, it has previously assured itself that this will not be considered an unfriendly act and will be implemented. It serves to save face for the government, while simultaneously disguising the authority of the Organization. The Estonian case (1937) and the Venezuelan Inquiry (1950) provide examples of attempts at obtaining a negotiated report; both attempts were rebuffed by the government. The subsequent evolution of this unplanned technique, however, saw its acceptance in certain kinds of situations.[47]

The procedure in use during the interwar period was the victim of an essentially hostile environment. As charges became more general and political, they also stood a smaller chance of being accepted by the ILO, which was constrained to seek refuge in a narrow legalism that effectively undercut its authority. It is striking, of course, that the representation procedure was utilized predominantly by weak trade unions in developing or colonial countries. Possibly, older and stronger unions were content to use purely national procedures to gain redress for grievances, since recourse to the ILO procedure might have jeopardized the ratification of new Conventions by embarrassing their governments over old ones.[48] Further, if the rules spelled out formally and informally are taken seriously, there did exist a real difficulty in ascertaining the "facts"; and if the time limits set for governments were to be respected, there was no point in insisting on immediate and full application of a ratified Convention—especially if such an insistence was suspected of hindering new ratifications or even giving rise to denunciations. Given this reasoning, it may well be true that the main value of the enforcement procedure lay in the informal pressure exerted on governments either to heed ratifications so as to head off a representation, or to take action quietly, once one was submitted, as in the Chilean Bakers' case.[49] In any event, Western trade unions saw little value in the procedure for their own ends, and workers from underdeveloped countries could not have been encouraged by the success of their efforts to use the ILO machinery. Consequently, the procedure has lain dormant as far as the enforcement of specific labor standards is concerned. Since 1940, no national union has sought national enforcement of any of the specific texts through international representations. As regards the subgoal-dominant aspect of the Code, therefore, the evidence suggests a flat deterioration of organizational legitimacy and authority in practical enforcement.

THE REVIVAL OF THE COMPLAINT PROCEDURE

One cannot escape the conclusion, then, that the reinvigoration of the complaint procedure, in the formal sense and in the special machinery for protecting freedom of association, is linked to the transcendence of subgoal domination and the brutal introduction of extralegal political issues. The post-war agitation has concerned itself with the more general human rights, whether protected by a ratified Convention or not. Forced labor, discrimination, and persecution of trade unions—often in a colonial context—have provided the substance of the charges. In 1950 and 1951, these could still be sidetracked into "friendly inquiries" on the part of the Office, and could result in a negotiated report that did not have to emerge from the full-blown panoply of international powers. But the apotheosis of the colonial revolt that is being played out within the ground rules of the Cold War may have made obsolete even this effort at restraint.

The formal complaint procedure was tested for the first time in 1961–62. On February 25, 1961, the Office received a communication from Ghana containing the following formal charge: "The Republic of Ghana is not satisfied that Portugal is securing effective observance in . . . Mozambique, Angola, and Guinea of Convention 105. . . . Accordingly, the Republic of Ghana requests that the Governing Body of the ILO take appropriate steps, for example, by setting up a Commission of Inquiry to consider this complaint and to report thereon."[50] Morse consulted with the officers of the Governing Body (the chairman, the employers' vice-chairman, and the workers' vice-chairman),[51] who unanimously recommended to the full Governing Body that since Ghana had a full right to lodge a complaint, and since the Governing Body had never drawn up any Standing Orders for the complaint procedure, a Commission of Inquiry might well be appointed. Until a report from this Commission had been received, it would be inappropriate for the Governing Body to discuss the merits of the complaint. Ghana was to furnish further particulars concerning her allegation, and Portugal was to have an opportunity to comment in writing and send a representative to Geneva. Upon receipt of these materials, the Governing Body would be in a position to decide whether to appoint a Commission. If it did so decide, the Commission members would "serve as individuals in their personal capacities . . . chosen for their impartiality, integrity, and standing" and, upon assuming their duties, would be asked to make the same solemn declaration that was requested from judges of the ICJ.[52] The Governing Body approved these recommendations of its officers.

There followed a sharp written exchange between Ghana and Portugal. Ghana furnished "particulars," which consisted mostly of vituperative statements impugning Portuguese economic policy in Africa in very general terms, including some claims concerning forced labor, but nothing resembling evidence. Portugal was quick to point this out and to deny the complaint in its entirety, a task made simple by the Ghanaian decision not to divulge the names of "witnesses" and merely to cite newspaper reports and monograph accounts. Yet Portugal declared that she "is sure that Governing Body . . . will not allow itself to be swayed by the completely unfounded statements of the Government of Ghana and will instead seek to discover the truth and nothing but the truth. We count firmly on this and await with equanimity the decisions that the Governing Body may take to this end."[53] Ghana, when pressed for her lack of detailed documentation, replied that "it is for the members of the Commission to find out whether Ghana's complaint is true or not. All the facts stated in Ghana's letter of complaint stand and members of the Committee are invited to investigate either from witnesses or from a first-hand fact-finding mission to Angola and Mozambique."[54]

Despite this somewhat unsatisfactory state of affairs concerning the facts, Portugal had inferentially committed herself to submit to ILO jurisdiction. Consequently the three officers recommended to the June 1961 session of the Body that a Commission of Inquiry be appointed. The Commission was to fix its own rules of procedure, collect such information as it needed, and negotiate with Ghana and Portugal—"without being bound by the views of either of them"—for access to additional information, including investigations on the spot. The Governing Body approved this recommendation on June 3, and on June 19 appointed the Commission of Inquiry; the members, proposed by the Director-General, were Paul Ruegger (chairman), Enrique Armand-Ugon, and Isaac Forster.[55]

The Commission proceeded to hold two sessions in Geneva, which were devoted to reading background information furnished by the parties and to interrogating numerous witnesses. Both parties were represented by agents during the interrogations and intervened actively in examination and cross-examination. The Commission addressed requests for additional information to the governments of the Congo (Brazzaville), the Congo (Léopoldville), South Africa, Britain, and the United Arab Republic. The two Congos did not reply; Britain answered that she could furnish no new information; the U.A.R., without giving any new information, associated herself fully with the complaint; and South Africa merely provided texts of agreements with Portugal. A number of non-governmental organizations were invited to submit evidence, and most of them did so. Those invited consisted of all the organizations with full consultative status in the ILO and those on the "special list" with an interest in the protection of human rights. A good deal of evidence was heard from missionaries and missionary societies. In fact the bulk of the Ghanaian witnesses were missionaries, since the Portuguese African exiles and nationalists alluded to by Ghana as its principal witnesses did not make an appearance at the hearings. Portugal produced witnesses drawn from the colonial administration and from the managers of various enterprises in Africa.[56]

Thereupon the Commission visited Angola and Mozambique. It inspected mines, railways, ports, road works, various plantations, factories, and the major areas of labor recruitment. "It questioned a large number of African workers *selected by it* in the various places of work and recruitment, as well as directors of undertakings, personnel managers, recruiters, doctors and nursing staff of companies, and engineers. It also spoke to divisional administrators, chiefs of posts, native chiefs and trade union representatives."[57] The Commission devoted thirteen days to the trip, and three weeks in February 1962 to formulating its conclusions and drafting its report for the Governing Body.

What did it find? Although forced labor was reported to have been commonly used in Africa, "far-reaching changes had occurred in Portuguese policy, legislation, and practice in connection with the ratification" of the forced labor Conventions. "The Commission is fully satisfied of the *bona fides* of these changes of policy, legislation, and practice and rejects as entirely without foundation the suggestion made in support of the complaint that 'Portugal only ratified the Convention as a cover to continue her ruthless labour policies.' "[58] The Report then makes its main point:

The Commission is not satisfied that all of the obligations of the Abolition of Forced Labour Convention, 1957, were implemented in full as from the date of the coming into force of the Convention for Portugal, namely 23 November 1960. It has noted a number of cases in which important changes for the purpose of bringing the law and practice into full conformity with the requirements of the Convention have been made since the complaint was lodged, but in which the provisions of the Convention were not fully applied immediately after its coming into force for Portugal. It has also noted certain respects in which further steps are necessary to give full effect to the . . . Convention.[59]

In general, therefore, the Ghanaian complaint failed to achieve what was probably the immediate objective of Accra, to embarrass Portugal internationally and thus support the struggles of the Angolan independence movement. But it did result in a hurried Portuguese effort to improve labor conditions in areas in which practices approaching forced labor had prevailed previously; the most striking reform adopted while the complaint was being processed was the initiation of a labor inspection service and the ratification of Convention 81.[60]

The Commission's Report then proceeded to describe in detail reforms initiated in various places, and to call attention to certain labor practices still prevalent in specified estates and installations in violation of the Convention. But the dominance of reform over abuse was stressed consistently. In addition, the Commission produced a long list of laws, decrees, and administrative orders which—though apparently no longer being applied—are still inconsistent with the Convention and should be repealed. As for the general condemnation of colonial policy, the Commission noted that it "regards the general allegations concerning labour standards formulated in the communications submitted to it by the Government of Ghana as inappropriate for consideration in detail because they raise matters going beyond the obligations of the Abolition of Forced Labour Convention, 1957, which is the subject of the complaint."[61] Portugal received its pat on the back for having bowed to the authority of the ILO; Ghana could feel some satisfaction in having indirectly brought about new reforms in labor practices even though the main allegation was rejected by the Commission; and a fundamental new procedure for asserting central power was added to the ILO armory. To grasp this procedure we must now throw into relief the novelty both of the measures taken and of the Commission's *obiter dicta*.

Perhaps the most important innovation was introduced by the Governing Body itself. The officers, in cooperation with the Office, made all the important initial decisions without appointing a special committee. Further, they all but committed themselves to the appointment of a Commission of Inquiry *before* the full Governing Body had considered the matter, and *before* Ghana had made even the shoddy case that she finally produced. In other words, the new international setting confirmed the Ghanaian claim that it was the duty of the ILO to prove or disprove whatever unsubstantiated charges were made by a government. Although this tendency may be legally objectionable, its effect on the growth of organizational legitimacy could be considerable. The Governing Body, in short, opened the door to a centralized approach totally at variance with the restrictive attitude it had taken during the interwar period.*

Scarcely less important is the role that accrued to the Office. The Office staff made the initial decision of whether to go ahead with the complaint, resolving to do so despite the vagueness of the charges. It was the Office that initially persuaded the Portuguese authorities to participate in the procedure, and that prevailed on the Ghanaians to give a modicum of formal status to their *démarche*. In other words, the Office legitimated the steps in the new procedure and the necessary governmental consent. Finally, the members of the Commission were picked by the Office, two of them

---

* The Commission itself did not take a consistent attitude on this crucial point, thus confirming the tendency toward task expansion. The Commission was troubled by the absence of substantiation in Ghana's complaint, and remained dissatisfied when Ghana failed to supply details after being given additional opportunities to do so. "Unless the complainant government makes a *prima facie* case it would appear to be entirely within the discretion of the Organisation whether to pursue the matter further," the Report says. Although, at various points in the procedure, the Commission was aware that a *prima facie* case had not been made, it decided to visit Angola and Mozambique "without prejudging the question of whether or not it had any satisfactory evidence." In other words, the absence of satisfactory evidence to make a case *against* Portugal seems to have been taken as the excuse for going ahead with the investigation. Somewhat lamely, the Commission concludes its soul-searching by remarking that although it "considers that the extent of its inquiry in this case has been fully justified by the importance of the issues at stake, it does not consider that it should be assumed that so full an inquiry is called for as a matter of course in the absence of the submission by the complainant of substantial evidence." International Labor Office, "Report," *Official Bulletin*, XLV (1962), 228–29.

from among the small family of international experts long familiar with the machinery for supervising the International Labor Code.[62]

The Commission itself not only confirmed all these procedural developments, but contributed several of its own. It proved extremely permissive in the number and types of witnesses admitted. It universalized the procedure by inviting other governments to comment. The hearings gave opportunities for non-governmental organizations to make themselves heard in the United Nations forum. And the interrogation of witnesses took the form of a quasi-judicial procedure because of the generous participation permitted to the agents of the parties. The visits, though short, confirmed the freedom of movement of international inspectors, since it was the Commission that insisted on an itinerary, rejected military escorts, and selected the respondents with whom it would talk. Further, the agents for the parties were not permitted to accompany the Commission to Africa.

However, it may be the Commission's *obiter dicta*, rather than its specific allegations and conclusions, that turn out to be the crucial feature in an expansion of the ILO task regarding investigations of this type. Undeterred by its own repeated admission that political matters and general economic policy were outside its mandate, the Commission affirmed that member states were under a positive obligation to encourage freedom of association even though forced labor was the immediate issue.[63] Portugal was under obligation to undertake general economic development measures, with full and equal African participation, because only such steps would decisively deal with questionable methods of labor recruitment.[64] Trade unions must be permitted to function without danger of reprisals or persecution. "Freedom is not a purely negative concept; it does not consist only of, and does not necessarily exist by reason of, the absence of compulsion and constraint; it includes an element of choice which represents its positive aspect."[65]

Finally, the Office could take delight in a suggestion of the Commission that henceforth states subjected to a complaint must report annually on measures taken to carry out recommendations of the Commission of Inquiry.[66] The Governing Body, for its part, terminated the inquiry on March 7, 1962, by noting that both parties had formally accepted the recommendations of the report. Many speakers expressed satisfaction with the new assertion of ILO authority, and voiced the hope that the Commission's procedure would constitute a firm precedent. Dissatisfaction was expressed only by the Soviet bloc countries. They complained that the Commission had failed to specify a time limit within which the remaining reforms were to be made, had been too generous in exonerating Portugal, and did not provide adequate follow-up procedures. Further, forced labor could be expected to disappear only with the complete demise of colonialism.[67]

The functional logic suggests that an international procedure that has acquired authority in the pursuit of one party's national interest will be applied sooner or later by the opposing party for its private purposes. In the process, the procedure will become generally authoritative as various blocs, nations, and ideologies all seek to rely on it in order to score off their opponents. To put it another way, what is sauce for the goose may be expected to become sauce for the gander. And so it happened with respect to the use of complaints in the ILO. Let us turn to our second example.

On August 31, 1961, the government of Portugal submitted a complaint to Geneva alleging that Liberia had been remiss in giving effect to the Forced Labor Convention of 1930. The Liberian government replied by demanding the immediate dismissal of the complaint on the grounds that it was politically motivated! Liberia was suggesting that the complaint had been lodged in reprisal for her siding with the African bloc in advancing United Nations measures against Portugal in Angola. True to the procedure in the first case, however, the Governing Body decided not to prejudge the question of motives and to permit the Commission of Inquiry to deal with it. It then appointed a new Commission of Inquiry, composed of Enrique Armand-Ugon (chairman), T. P. D. Goonetilleke, and E. J. S. Castrén.[68] Furthermore, Portugal had assimilated the new technique fast, for she had carefully included some documentation in her complaint, drawn for the most part from the many critical statements of the Committee of Experts concerning Liberia.

Liberia was accused of (1) failing to remove from her legal code measures permitting the use of forced labor, such as porterage, compulsory participation in public works, and compulsory cultivation; (2) failing to furnish the ILO with annual reports on ratified Conventions (including Convention 29); and (3) tolerating the use of forced recruitment practices by the Firestone Plantations Company. The Commission ruled that until 1962 Liberia had indeed failed to amend her labor laws in line with Convention 29, even though changes introduced in that year remedied the worst malpractices. Further, the Commission rejected the Liberian contention that ratification of the Convention automatically repealed earlier legislation, since the text was held to be non-self-executing. While noting that it had no power to enforce Article 22 of the Constitution, the Commission sharply reprimanded the Liberian government for failing to submit annual reports and insisted that the reporting procedure be used in the future; only in this way could it be determined whether Liberia was living up to the admonition to remove additional "anomalies" from its legal code. For this purpose, the Commission prescribed that henceforth two high Liberian officials be personally informed whether the necessary reports had been dispatched! As for the charges against Firestone, the Commission held that they were "not proved," though suggesting that they had probably had some foundation in the past.[69]

Not content with this almost unqualified acceptance of the Portuguese charges, the Commission saw fit to add some *obiter dicta*. Noting the rapid rate of Liberian economic development and the social tensions usually associated with it, especially in connection with the pressures upon tribal society, the Commission strongly advised the government to link its suppression of forced labor with a more progressive social policy generally. It called on the government to accelerate the application of all the human rights Conventions already ratified, as well as to ratify the texts covering Indigenous and Tribal Populations (No. 107, 1957) and Labor Inspection (No. 81, 1947).[70] Congratulating the government both on its policy for developing the hinterland and on the growth of trade unions, the Commission concluded its Report by saying: "A people whose proudest boast is that 'the love of liberty brought us here' will in taking such action perpetuate and honour the oldest and dearest of its national traditions."[71]

Except for making certain procedural reservations, Liberia reacted submissively enough. Between August 31, 1961, and May 30, 1962, she "eliminated all the major discrepancies between the laws of Liberia and the requirements of the Convention."[72] In accepting the Commission's Report, the government, in effect, bound itself to remove the remaining legal "anomalies" as well. It suddenly submitted reports on ratified Conventions that had been outstanding for years, and agreed to the rather humiliating procedure governing their submission in the future. Finally, it ratified Conventions 87 and 98 after Portugal pressed its charges, but before the Commission had completed its inquiry. This sequence of events can hardly be considered coincidental. However, as regards the central question of application in practice, the situation remains ambiguous. The Commission, in not pressing the charges against Firestone, had ruled that "the purpose of the inquiry is neither inquisitorial nor historical but remedial; in these circumstances it becomes a question of judgment how far it is profitable to explore further the facts relating to the application of legislation which has now been repealed."[73] Its judgment was that "no useful purpose would be served by examining further the factual allegations."[74] True, the Commission adopted the precedent set by the Ghana-Portugal Commission in using the Committee of Experts as a formal device for following up on its rulings; but since the factual allegations were never fully investigated, this provides a poor basis for follow-up measures.

The Commission's reticence may be explained by certain aspects of the procedure adopted in the second ILO Inquiry under Article 26. In general, the Portugal-Liberia Commission followed exactly the same procedure as its predecessor, which comprised the hearing of initial statements by the parties, the admission of agents for each, the full communication of information, the request for additional information, the request for information from interested governments and non-governmental organizations, the calling of witnesses, and the conducting of negotiations with each party for full cooperation with the inquiry. It is this last point that calls for comment. Unlike Portugal in the first case that arose, Liberia did not "throw itself on the mercy of the Court." The Liberian agent, on the contrary, requested that the proceedings be stopped as soon as his government notified Geneva of its amendment of the labor code and its readiness to submit missing annual reports. Further, he hinted broadly that his government would not cooperate in any searching investigation; nor did he, at any time, invite the Commission to visit Liberia:

Obviously, the Commission is entitled to assurance that the amendatory Acts are in effect and to that end the Chairman of the Liberian Delegation has formally certified the laws to the Commission. *It would be neither necessary nor appropriate for the Commission to question the authenticity of this certification. It would be even less appropriate for the Commission to undertake, on its own initiative, to search through the legal code or system of a Member for the existence of laws which have not been made the subject of complaint.*[75]

Although the proceedings were not stopped at this point, the Commission did find that it had sufficient information for its report to make a visit to Liberia unnecessary.[76] Liberia, for its part, accepted the Commission's recommendations on March 6, 1963.

This decision raises the whole question of the sufficiency of evidence in international proceedings of this type. In the Portugal-Liberia case, the Commission reaffirmed the inherently expansive conclusion of its predecessor in using the absence of detailed information as a justification for continuing the inquiry, if convinced that a *prima facie* case existed.[77] But it received no information from other governments or non-governmental organizations. The witnesses available for interrogation were confined to officials of the Liberian government and of foreign corporations active in Liberia. No spokesman for the workers appeared.[78] Yet the Commission treated as "not proven" the factual allegations against Firestone because they were based merely on scholarly reports and not on official government documents![79] If an on-the-spot investigation is judged not to be "appropriate at the present time," and if no worker witnesses are available, it would seem that, despite the declared willingness of the Commission to be its own judge of the need for further information, the precedure favors the defendant government.

Clearly the authority of investigations of this type remains precarious. The precariousness is plainly illustrated by the role of "negotiation" in the proceedings. To be sure, the ritual adopted stresses detachment and insists on a purely judicial posture. The members of the two Commissions not only presented a "politically balanced ticket" to the extent possible, but possessed outstanding judicial qualifications and wide experience in international labor law. Their reports were not in any sense "negotiated" with the parties. In contrast with the reports of ad hoc missions or the surveys of freedom of association, which remain true to an even more precarious pattern of international authority, the findings and recommendations of the Commissions of Inquiry were not "cleared" with the parties before publication. Yet an element of "negotiation" remains just the same. It enters at the preliminary stage when the Office and Governing Body must obtain the consent of the "defendant" to cooperate with the ILO; it enters even more stringently when the Commission must assure itself of the willingness of the parties to furnish information and permit on-the-spot activities. The experience of the Portugal-Liberia Commission shows how precarious the ILO position remains in this respect.

I suggest that at the present stage of international development no other procedure can be expected. An international environment favoring anti-colonialism is unlikely to accept as authoritative investigative procedures favoring the colonialist. Indeed, the Director-General encountered considerable difficulty in proceeding against Liberia. The New African nations were far from eager to cooperate; employers from the older African countries were especially leery of opening the door to international inspection. The carefully "balanced ticket" that was drawn up in the Ghanaian case could not be duplicated. Yet a Commission *was* constituted, and the Liberian countercharge was *not* used as an excuse for dropping the case. The road seems open for a mushrooming of the procedure once the immediate colonial context becomes obsolete.

HUMAN RIGHTS CONVENTIONS: LEGITIMACY AND AUTHORITY

These two instances of the invocation of the ILO's complaint procedure illustrate the application of our analytical concept of authority. Both cases involved the imposition of international norms on two states—Portugal and Liberia—that previously had been hostile or indifferent to the standards of conduct implied. Neither had actively participated in the preparation of the forced labor Conventions; both had either not ratified one of the texts or ratified very recently; neither had evinced any great consistency in its past policy in actually implementing the provisions against forced labor; neither has an outstanding international reputation regarding a progressive social policy or the domestic encouragement of such human rights as are associated with democracy. Yet both bowed to the international forum in undertaking measures of improvement consistent with standards not previously supported or invoked. In larger terms, then, international authority will be demonstrated to exist if and when a government "improves" its domestic conduct to conform with ILO human rights standards, even though it was hostile or indifferent to the original enunciation of these standards. It will now be our task to survey the entire field of human rights as defined by the ILO, for similar instances of compliance.

The legitimacy of human rights legislation in the perceptions of member states, however, must be measured differently. Here the degree of interest shown in the preparation of new Conventions is a crucial indicator. But the mere expression of approval for a new text, and an affirmative vote cast, do not suffice to establish a perception of legitimacy. Nor does the invocation of the texts at the expense of another government, usually an enemy state in terms of the world political context. In addition to favorable expression and invocation, legitimacy is established only if the state in question also ratifies and/or applies the texts on its own territory. If invocation alone were accepted as a sufficient criterion, a content analysis of speeches made in Geneva would prove almost all member states to be faithful and loyal servants of international norms. Integration might be expected to proceed automatically and directly, without the functional detours into dialectical confrontations. But invocation alone proves nothing. Only by using it in conjunction with the more meaningful indicators of performance can we arrive at a "human rights observation score."

The method used in deriving a "human rights observation score" for each member state was as follows. First, it should be remembered that the score seeks to pinpoint state behavior with respect to two variables: sustained interest in the preparation of new human rights norms, *and* faithful implementation of the norms after they acquire the form of a Convention. Hence it was possible to use only states that were members of the ILO at the time the six Conventions singled out for analysis were prepared; thus most of the new African members were disqualified from consideration. For the same reason it was not possible to include the communist-bloc states in scoring the Conventions prepared before 1954. Finally, it proved impossible to include Convention 111 (Discrimination) in the scoring, since the first report of the Committee of Experts dealing with its implementation was not sufficiently explicit.[80]

The coding and scoring of interest in and implementation of Conventions 81, 87, 98, 100, and 105 was handled as follows. The items of conduct that interest us are (1) the response of the government to the Office's questionnaire inquiring about interest in preparing a Convention; (2) the vote of the government on the final text of the Convention; (3) ratification or non-ratification; and (4) the degree of implementation, irrespective of ratification. Thus:

Behaviorial alternative coded	Score assigned	Behavioral alternative coded	Score assigned
Response to questionnaire[81]		Ratification[83]	
No response submitted	0	Ratified	2
Negative response	−1	Not ratified	0
Positive response	1	Implementation[84]	
Vote[82]		No report received	0
Absent at time of vote	0	Report insufficient	0
No delegation present	0	Convention is applied	
Abstention	0	in part	1
No	−1	Convention is fully	
Yes	1	applied	3

A word of amplification is required with respect to the item concerning implementation. I relied in all cases on the judgment expressed by the Committee of Experts and used its criteria as my own. These criteria are admittedly very stringent: No state is certified as applying a Convention fully unless it and *all* its constituent units (especially in the case of federations) seem to apply *all* provisions of the text in question. Legal anomalies, unused constitutional provisions, unenforced decrees, if possibly inconsistent with the Convention, will invariably be censured by the Committee. For this reason, very few states qualify as fully applying a Convention, but many states emerge as implementing portions of the text; cases of complete non-implementation cannot be scored, since the obdurate non-applying state will not submit reports to the ILO. The total number of various types of responses analyzed is summarized in Table 21.

It was judged that replying to a questionnaire and voting in the Conference are not actions as critical, suggestive, or binding as ratification and application. Failure to reply may be due to lack of administrative personnel rather than lack of interest; failure to attend the Conference is explicable on many grounds and need not argue lack of interest. Ratification is a serious act implying possibly onerous legal and propagandistic consequences; hence it was scored more heavily than the behavioral items relating solely to interest. But non-ratification does not necessarily imply lack of interest or commitment. Implementation, however, is the real proof of the pudding, and hence it was scored more heavily still. Some credit was given for partial application. A maximal score of sustained interest and perfect application is 7; a minimal score of complete disinterest and non-application is −2. A score between 7 and 5 suggests sustained interest and full or at least partial application. The range between 4 and 2 indicates uneven interest in preparation and imperfect implementation; this range includes the possibility of uneven interest in preparation, later followed by full application. The lowest range covers those with little or no interest in preparation and partial or no application. Thus the final score assigned

TABLE 21

NUMBER AND TYPE OF RESPONSE OF ILO MEMBER STATES TO
HUMAN RIGHTS LEGISLATION, 1947–62

Type of response	Convention					
	No. 81	No. 87	No. 98	No. 100	No. 105	No. 111
Office Inquiry						
Not a member at time	48	43	41	37	28	22
No reply	26	27	38	27	16	33
No comment	0	0	9	9	13	25
Affirmative	27	27	11	15	36	20
Negative	1	5	3	14	9	2
Vote[a]						
Yes[a]	134	127	115	105	240	189
No	0	0	10	33	0	24
Abstain or absent	0	25	30	55	1[b]	13
Ratification (1962) [c]						
Ratified	47	60	57	38	57	36
Not ratified	55	42	45	64	45	66
Implementation[d]						
Not a member at time	26	21	32	32	0	–
No report	27	5	23	25	11	–
Insufficient information	2	9	12	5	16	–
Not fully applied	33	49	19	27	57	–
Fully applied	14	18	19	13	18	–

[a] The vote here recorded is the total vote cast, not merely the governmental vote. If the total for each Convention does not tally with the ILO membership during the session of the Conference in question, the difference is accounted for by the failure of states to be represented (as distinguished from temporary absence at a given meeting).

[b] Actually there appeared to have been more absences and abstentions than the formal record indicated.

[c] The ratification figures for 1963 are as follows: Conv. 81, R 53, NR 55; Conv. 87, R 65, NR 43; Conv. 98, R 66, NR 42; Conv. 100, R 44, NR 64; Conv. 105, R 64, NR 44; Conv. 111, R 39, NR 69.

[d] When several follow-up reports were requested by the Committee of Experts, the volume and kind of response to the latest available report was used. On June 1, 1962, ILO membership was 102 states.

to each country represents the average of the five separate scores assigned it, as derived from its conduct with respect to each Convention.

The member states' performance scores for the five Conventions are given in Table 22. The national average scores as presented in Table 22 were used in compiling Table 23, which shows the perceptions of legitimacy concerning human rights texts by classes of states, the classification being by political, social, and economic characteristics as explained in note *a* of Table 22.

High legitimacy perceptions (5.0 and over) are confined to countries possessing democratic-pluralistic political institutions; further, these are overwhelmingly industrialized nations committed to welfare planning. Norway, Sweden, Germany, and Britain would have scored even higher if they had not staunchly opposed Convention 100; France, which gave full sup-

TABLE 22

HUMAN RIGHTS: RANKING OF MEMBER STATES WITH RESPECT TO PARTICIPATION
IN PREPARATION AND IMPLEMENTATION OF ILO CONVENTIONS, 1947–62

Country	Average score	Convention					Code[a]
		No. 81	No. 87	No. 98	No. 100	No. 105	
Philippines	6.0	–	4	6	7	7	D-U-FE
Libya	n.s.[b]	–	–	–*	–*	6	O-U-FE
Austria	5.8	6	7	7	5	4	D-OI-S
France	5.6	7	5	7	7	2	D-OI-S
U.K.	5.6	7	7	7	0	7	D-OI-S
Germany	5.5	–	–	–	4	7	D-OI-S
Belgium	5.4	5	5	6	5	6	D-OI-S
Norway	5.2	7	7	4	3	5	D-NI-S
Sweden	5.2	7	7	7	0*	5	D-OI-S
Honduras	n.s.	–	–	–	–	5	O-U-FE
Jordan	n.s.	–	–	–	–	5	O-U-FE
Denmark	4.8	5	5	6	3	5	D-MA-S
Finland	4.8	7	5	6	1*	5	D-MA-S
Netherlands	4.8	7	5	5	0	7	D-NI-S
Costa Rica	4.6	3	4	5	6	5	D-U-FE
Dominican Rep.	4.6	4	4	5	6	4	O-U-FE
Iceland	4.6	2	7	6	4	4	D-MA-S
Italy	4.6	6	5	4	3	5	D-NI-S
Cuba	4.4	4	5	5	4	4	O-U-FE
Switzerland	4.4	7	5	5	0	5	D-OI-S
Greece	4.4	4	7	6	1	4	D-U-FE
Israel	4.25	–	5	4	3	5	D-NI-S
Argentina	4.0	3	4	3	4	6	D-NI-FE
Luxembourg	4.0	3	4	6	3	4	D-OI-S
Mexico	4.0	3	5	0	7	5	D-NI-S
Turkey	4.0	7	2	5	3	3	D-NI-FE
Ghana	n.s.	–	–	–	–	4	T-U-S
Ireland	3.8	7	5	3	0	4	D-U-FE
Poland	3.8	3	4	3	4	5	T-NI-CM
India	3.6	7	3	3	2	3	D-NI-S
Peru	3.6	3	4	1	3	7	O-U-FE
Yugoslavia	3.6	2	2	5	6	3	T-NI-CM
Bulgaria	3.4	5	3	2	5	2	T-NI-CM
Chile	3.4	2	1	5	5	4	D-NI-S
Pakistan	3.25	–	5	4	0	4	O-U-FE
Australia	3.2	3	3	3	0	7	D-NI-S
Uruguay	3.0	3	7	3	2	0	D-MA-S
Guatemala	2.8	3	3	2	2	4	O-U-FE
Haiti	2.6	4	1	2	3	3	O-U-FE
U.A.R.	2.6	4	2	1	1	5	T-U-CP
U.S.	2.6	3	3	2	3	2	D-OI-S
New Zealand	2.6	5	3	3	0	2	D-MA-S
Hungary	2.6	2	3	2	5	1	T-NI-CM
Ecuador	2.6	1	3	2	3	4	O-U-FE
China	2.4	4	1	1*	2	4	T-U-CP

TABLE 22 *(continued)*

Country	Average score	Convention					Code[a]
		No. 81	No. 87	No. 98	No. 100	No. 105	
Iraq	2.4	5	2	0*	0	5	O-U-FE
Ceylon	2.33	–	–	1	1	5	D-U-S
Syria	2.25	–	3	2	1	3	O-U-FE
Brazil	2.2	3	2	1	3	2	D-NI-FE
Iran	2.2	2	2	1	1	5	O-U-FE
Portugal	2.2	4	1	1	0	5	T-U-CP
Panama	2.2	3	6	0	2	0	O-U-FE
Canada	2.2	3	3	2	0	3	D-NI-FE
Burma	2.0	1	6	1	1	3	D-U-S
Tunisia	n.s.	–	–	–	–	2	O-U-FE
Romania	n.s.	–	–	–	–	2	T-NI-CM
Spain	n.s.	–	–	–	–	2	T-NI-CP
Ukraine	n.s.	–	–	–	–	2	T-OI-CM
Indonesia	2.0	–	–	–	3	1	T-U-FE
Liberia	1.8	0	2	2	1	4	O-U-FE
Thailand	1.6	0	3	1	0	4	O-U-FE
Colombia	1.6	2	2	1	1	2	O-U-FE
El Salvador	1.25	–	1	0	0	4	O-U-FE
Albania	1.2	0	2	2	2	0	T-U-CM
Japan	1.0	–	–	–	1	1	D-OI-FE
Vietnam	1.0	–	–	–	1	1	O-U-CP
Byelorussia	n.s.	–	–	–	–	1	T-OI-CM
U.S.S.R.	n.s.	–	–	–	–	1	T-OI-CM
So. Africa	0.8	3	0	0	1	0	T-NI-FE
Afghanistan	0.8	1	0	1	0	2*	O-U-FE
Venezuela	0.75	1	1	0	1	–	D-U-FE
Lebanon	0.67	–*	–	0	0	2	O-U-FE
Czechoslovakia	0.5	–	0	0	1	1	T-OI-CM
Bolivia	0.2	0	0	0	0	1	O-U-S
Ethiopia	0	0	0*	0*	0	1	O-U-FE

NOTE: Asterisks indicate ratification in 1963. In addition, the following new member states ratified the following Conventions: Algeria, 81, 87, 98, 100; Burundi and Rwanda, 105; Tanganyika and Uganda, 81, 98, 105; Jamaica, 81, 87, 98, 105; Trinidad and Tobago, 87, 98, 105; Paraguay, 87; Senegal, 81, 100; Malagasy Rep., 100; Cameroun, 81.

[a] *First unit (political)*: D Democracy; O Oligarchy; T Totalitarian State. *Second unit (economic)*: OI Old Industrialized; NI Newly Industrializing; MA Mature Agricultural; U Underdeveloped. *Third unit (social)*: FE Free Enterprise; S Social Welfare; CM Communist; CP Corporatist.
[b] Not scored.

port to the Equal Remuneration text, spoiled its high score by opposing the Forced Labor Convention. The only high scorer not yet committed to the welfare state is the Philippines. Her case illustrates that underdevelopment and the absence of the modal pluralistic society do not prevent internationally determined human rights from being observed, so long as the national elites are committed to a form of government that respects the rule of law.

Low legitimacy perceptions (under 2.0) are overwhelmingly character-

TABLE 23

Human Rights: Performance Scores of Member States Classified by
Political, Economic, and Social Characteristics

Type of country[a]	Number of countries in type	Number of countries with performance scores				
		Under 2	2–3	3–4	4–5	Over 5
Democracies						
D-OI-S	9	–	1	–	2	6
D-NI-S	8	–	–	3	4	1
D-U-FE	5	1	–	1	2	1
D-MA-S	5	–	1	1	3	–
D-NI-FE	4	–	2[b]	–	2	–
D-U-S	2	–	2	–	–	–
D-OI-FE	1	1[c]	–	–	–	–
Oligarchies						
O-U-FE	18	7	7	2	2[d]	–
O-U-S	1	1	–	–	–	–
O-U-CP	1	1	–	–	–	–
Totalitarian states						
T-NI-CM	4	–	1	3	–	–
T-U-CP	3	–	3	–	–	–
T-OI-CM	1	1	–	–	–	–
T-NI-FE	1	1	–	–	–	–
T-U-CM	1	1	–	–	–	–
T-U-FE	1	–	1	–	–	–
Total	65	14	18	10	15	8

Note: The following countries were not included in the table because complete information for only one Convention was available: Libya, Honduras, Jordan, Ghana, Tunisia, Romania, Spain, Ukraine, Byelorussia, U.S.S.R.

[a] For explanation of code symbols, see Table 22, note a.

[b] Includes Canada, which might perhaps more reasonably be classified as social-welfare-oriented, i.e., as D-NI-S.

[c] Japan. Data are limited to Conventions 100 and 105, and it seems likely that the classification is wrong.

[d] Cuba and the Dominican Republic. The classification is correct only if the ILO reports on implementation are considered credible.

istic of oligarchies saddled with underdeveloped economies. These regimes will support human rights legislation in Geneva by voting for whatever draft is before the Conference; but they usually do not reply to the preliminary Office inquiry, they generally fail to ratify, and they are almost always remiss in implementation. Support for international measures is a rhetorical gesture. It is, however, worthy of note that only three totalitarian regimes rank at the bottom of our legitimacy scale. Two of them (Albania and the Republic of South Africa) are deviant states with respect to a wide variety of international norms and expectations. Their indifference to the ILO is merely part of their general preoccupation with unique national doctrines. The only "regular" communist state in the lowest range is Czechoslovakia; unlike several of its Warsaw Pact partners, it has remained indifferent to the norm-generating trend in Geneva, a fact perhaps attributable to the relative persistence of the Stalinist leadership in the Czech

Communist Party. But two democracies are also found in this range of our legitimacy scale. The data for one—Japan—is incomplete, and the classification is possibly wrong. The other is Venezuela; its low score is largely due to the poor performance of the non-democratic Perez Jiménez regime; the subsequent democratic leadership has been preoccupied by considerations more urgent than cooperating with an international organization.

This much could have been predicted without statistical verification. The remainder of our findings, however, is less self-evident and therefore more suggestive with respect to the evolution of the ILO human rights task. The eighteen lowest scorers in the intermediate range of legitimacy include seven more of the underdeveloped, free-enterprise-committed oligarchical regimes; such totalitarians as Hungary and Nationalist China, and authoritarian regimes committed to some form of corporatist organization of society and economy (Portugal, U.A.R.); and, finally, certain democracies that invoke federalism, institutional uniqueness, special economic problems, or the possession of high human rights standards in the absence of formal ratification as justifications for not bestowing much legitimacy on the ILO proceedings. The United States, Canada, New Zealand, Ceylon, Brazil, and Burma are in this last group.

The very mixture of institutions, beliefs, and stages of economic development represented by the twenty-five states scoring between 3 and 5 on our scale would seem to suggest that whereas democracy does not necessarily imply a high legitimacy perception, oligarchy and totalitarianism do not necessarily preclude a growing sense of legitimacy. In other words, between the predictable extremes of lively interest *cum* loyalty and indifference *cum* non-application, there is a large gray area of permeability in which the role of existing national institutions with respect to the future world environment cannot be predicted. Relatively few of the underdeveloped oligarchies are found here, and two of them are probably so classified because of inaccurate data. But the presence of Pakistan and Peru suggests that this syndrome of traits, because it is obviously changing, may create a receptivity among the elites seeking to adapt themselves to new standards of conduct legitimated by international action. The bulk of the democracies not scoring above 5 is found in this range. For the most part, these are countries in which exemplary standards of human rights already prevail, with the possible exception of Greece and Argentina. The departures in conduct known to exist in the case of these two members are faithfully reflected in their score. Denmark, the Netherlands, Australia, and others did not score more highly because interest and implementation with respect to one or two of the five Conventions was poor, even though performance with respect to the remainder was high. Typically, some European democracies opposed Convention 100, which was not acceptable to either their trade unions or their employer associations, and no aura of legitimacy bestowed by the ILO could change their minds. In other cases the low score is attributable to a failure to cooperate with the Office in the preparation of new Conventions. Obviously many of the democracies found here are actually very close to the highest range.

As we have seen, communism and the desire to industrialize rapidly are not necessarily a bar to some receptivity to the international process. Thus Bulgaria, Yugoslavia, and Poland are found in the intermediate range. If complete participation had been forthcoming from the Soviet Union, the Ukraine, and Byelorussia during the whole period under review, their scores (in terms of implementation of texts other than the Forced Labor Convention) might have been similar. Obviously, communist states do not fully apply any of these Conventions, with the exception of the instruments on equal remuneration and labor inspection; they cannot fully apply them and remain totalitarian in nature. But when internal pressures associated with a greater social division of labor and higher levels of industrial production combine with international propaganda exchanges, domestic transformations consonant with international demands become conceivable.

This finding suggests that the phenomenon sometimes described as the *embourgeoisement* of communist societies is a factor favorable to international integration in the human rights field. The support given to civil liberties by the international society would stimulate social transformation in communist societies that had already attained industrialization and an articulate and fully mobilized population segmented into functionally specific groupings. International integration would follow from continuing domestic transformation meeting world standards. If this hypothesis derives some support from the human rights score of Poland and Yugoslavia, can it be expected to apply to non-European countries engaged in massive planned development under totalitarian (or at least highly authoritarian) auspices?

We are here dealing with an aspect of organizational authority rather than legitimacy. Underdeveloped countries ruled by single parties or revolutionary oligarchical elites tend to concentrate on problems of internal stability and modernization. Their participation in the preparation of new international texts is at best sporadic. Yet they invariably vote in favor of new Conventions, and their record of ratification is no worse than that of many developed countries. The real difficulty arises in the field of implementation. Non-communist totalitarianisms and revolutionary oligarchies are not by temperament likely to encourage freedom of association, equal remuneration, non-discrimination, and the prohibition of forced labor for economic purposes or "political education." Their self-image precludes adherence to the institutions of autonomous and competing social groupings; all social organizations should fit into the national development plan and be subject to the national purpose as articulated by the leader, the party, or the ruling junta. But if, despite these forces, the leadership is prevailed upon to apply human rights Conventions and to take seriously its earlier ratification of these instruments, it is in effect submitting to the authority of the organization in the absence of an earlier consistent interest. Would the pressures we isolated in the case of the European communist nations operate here too?

So far we have little evidence that they do. Bolivia is a consistent low scorer. Egypt, Burma, and Indonesia cluster at the lower end of the intermediate range. The data for Ghana, Mali, Guinea, Tanganyika, Iraq, Sudan, Algeria, and Tunisia are too fragmentary to permit any statement. What would we say of Colombia, Ecuador, Peru, and Venezuela if they were taken over by modernizing nationalist elites much more radical and authoritarian than the present ruling groups, though not necessarily communist? What of Central America and the many African nations not yet fully in the throes of this development? The superficial answer is that developments of this kind would destroy both the legitimacy and the authority of the ILO task by diffusing standards and expectations still further.

But this may turn out to be a short-range view that ignores the functional logic. Revolutionary regimes are troubled by a pervasive ambivalence on which the functional logic may rely. On the one hand, they are intolerant of internal dissent and therefore cannot in practice favor civil liberties; but, on the other, they are the chief international exponents of the kind of human rights represented by Conventions 100, 105, and 111. And the evolution of Yugoslavia, Poland, and the U.S.S.R. has shown that at a certain point even the provisions of Conventions 87 and 98 can become at least partially acceptable. In other words, to pursue relentless policies of anti-imperialist, progressive modernization and to shout these policies from the rooftops of Geneva and New York is to invite the unkind commentary that Ghana or Indonesia, for example, do not practice at home what they preach abroad. If revolutionary elites seek international respectability *and* support for their declared policies favoring certain kinds of human rights, submission to ILO authority may well be the tribute that vice will pay to virtue.[85]

Perhaps this is why the Committee of Experts continues to stress the lack of validity of various justifications for non-ratification advanced by governments. With reference to Convention 98, the Experts explained that special legislation need not be passed in order to live up to the terms, and that the Convention neither encourages nor prohibits compulsory trade unionism.[86] Differing socio-economic systems, whether communist, corporatist, or pluralistic in nature, offer few insurmountable obstacles to the ratification of Convention 87, the Committee somewhat surprisingly declared. It arrived at this optimistic evaluation by comparing the texts of laws and constitutions with the terms of the Convention, and it concluded by hoping that the progress of economic development would result in the formation of autonomous professional organizations.[87]

"Upward mobility" in perceiving the legitimacy of international norms regarding human rights is clearly possible. National demands for change, when supported by international interest groups and political confrontations, may result in a country's moving from the intermediate range of performance into the high range. The older democracies, both in the highest and in the upper intermediate ranges, did not require any international stimulus because autonomous economic and constitutional developments account for the establishment of human rights here. The oligarchies and totalitarianisms in the lowest range will almost certainly remain immune to any international stimulus as long as underdevelopment goes hand in hand with stagnant and unmobilized masses ruled over by traditional elites. But the bulk of the world's nations is found in neither camp; it is engaged in massive social transformations involving the removal of stagnancy and the mobilization of hitherto inert masses, both under totalitarian and under democratic auspices; in short, the crucial variable that characterizes the "mobile" state on our scale is the commitment to welfare planning, to systematic economic development under some vague "socialist" label. These are the clients—especially if their domestic struggles are exposed to international criticism and ideological blackmail—that provide likely, if involuntary, consumers of ILO efforts. They offer some empirical justification for the analytical projection of the human rights task as the chief ILO contribution to international integration.

12. *Freedom of Association*

Freedom of association as an aspect of individual liberty stands out clearly among the various freedoms that have become subject to ILO activity. The pre-eminence of this freedom is manifest in the special machinery that has evolved for hearing allegations of infringement. Whereas the international control afforded by the Committee of Experts and the complaint clauses of the Constitution is confined to instances in which governments have ratified a human rights text, the authority vested in the Committee on Freedom of Association applies to the right to form industrial interest groups in *all* countries, irrespective of "sovereign consent." Moreover, freedom of association occupies a special position in that it can activate subsidiary freedoms of enormous significance to the evolution of an international environment dominated by autonomous interest-dominated groups. In that sense, it is a prerequisite liberty for the evolution of a pluralistic society. We shall devote a special chapter to this aspect of the human rights program because of its unique role in a functional theory of integration, and because of its special position in the work of the ILO.

THE ORIGIN OF THE COMMITTEE ON FREEDOM OF ASSOCIATION

In 1948 and 1949, in the context of the Cold War, the Governing Body and the ECOSOC were confronted with a mounting wave of complaints about suppression of trade union rights. They therefore jointly decided to set up a standing Fact-Finding and Conciliation Commission on Freedom of Association. ILO circles felt that wholly impartial investigations of the facts "may be of great assistance to the governments concerned in clarifying situations which have become the subject of international controversy."[1] The guarded phrasing suggests that neutral conciliation, under the guise of ascertaining the facts, might induce beleaguered governments to mend their ways in order to head off world criticism. In any event, a Commission of nine persons appointed by the Governing Body was jointly decided upon. These persons should have judicial or similar experience, and enjoy general confidence in terms of impartiality. They would hear complaints forwarded by the UN to the ILO, as well as complaints directly addressed to the ILO emanating from organizations of workers or employers, or from governments.[2] The Commission was prohibited from entertaining complaints without the consent of the defendant government. But if such consent was refused, the Governing Body could consider the refusal as grounds for publishing a report on the alleged violations of trade union freedom, thus invoking international publicity as a sanction. Before an allegation had been considered by the Commission, neither the ECOSOC nor the Governing Body was to discuss the case in order not to prejudge it. It was the requirement of national consent that aroused opposition. Most of the Worker Group, led by Léon Jouhaux, denied the need for the requirement and predicted that insistence on it would condemn the procedure to impotence. This prediction was made despite the fact that the Governing Body assured the ECOSOC that its guiding principle would be "to provide facilities for the impartial examination of the facts in an atmosphere free from political prejudice of any kind or of propaganda in any interest whatsoever."[3]

The predictions of the Workers were almost immediately proven correct with the refusal of the Peruvian government that we discussed previously. Since 1950, only one government has given its consent to launching the procedure entrusted to the Fact-Finding and Conciliation Commission. Worker indifference about the official exclusion of "political prejudice" and "propaganda" was equally manifest in the unions' activities. The WFTU was obviously interested in using the machinery for discrediting "imperialist" and "feudal" regimes. The ICFTU was similarly concerned with politically inspired attacks. The free trade unions were not even fully satisfied with the content of Conventions 87 and 98, which provided the legal standards for the new machinery. They had opposed the clause providing for respect for national law and had unsuccessfully insisted on the unambiguous inclusion of coverage for public service workers. On the other hand, they had succeeded in fighting down the desire of some governments to include a sweeping "public order" clause. Because the ICFTU was primarily motivated by the political objective of attacking communist and traditional regimes, even when it did not expect any concrete improvement to result from issuing charges, it objected to the rigid national consent requirement and preferred a machinery more closely linked to the tripartite traditions of the ILO; thus ICFTU participation in contentious proceedings could be assured.[4]

In November 1951 the workers got their way. The Governing Body had previously entrusted the preliminary examination of complaints to its own officers. Now it decided to appoint a standing tripartite Committee of nine of its own members, who would conduct a preliminary examination of each allegation to determine whether the case was worth submitting to the full Governing Body; if so, and if the Governing Body decided to take up the case, the Committee would ask the consent of the defendant government before giving the allegation to the Conciliation Commission.* If consent were withheld, the new Committee would recommend "appropriate alternative action" to the Governing Body.[5]

It is doubtful whether the Governing Body majority that voted for this step foresaw its consequences. In effect, the Committee has become the Conciliation Commission.[6] The Committee, being a creature of the Governing Body alone, is not bound by ECOSOC rules and is therefore free from the consent requirement. Practice since 1951 has confirmed that the "preliminary examination" of the worthiness of a complaint is in reality a full investigation of the facts and, where warranted, an effort at ILO conciliation and pressure. A supposedly harmless procedural device has become a mechanism for investigating the merits of a case, a transformation subsequently upheld by a long series of ILO resolutions and declarations. As an unintended consequence of propagandistic motives, the ILO clients came to acquiesce in a totally unplanned growth in institutional competence.

This species of institutional growth as a result of the permutation of original aims is, of course, familiar to the adept in functional analysis. Since there is no evidence of any governmental or employer initiative to explain the growth of an almost supranational organ for the protection of trade union rights, we must conclude that the Office, in alliance with the workers, provided the legal and institutional idea for bypassing the Conciliation Commission; the Governing Body, of course, approved this development. Secretariat members work on the complaints in cooperation with the Committee members; they draw up the texts of the Committee recommendations to the Governing Body, recommendations that are invariably approved by the plenary parent organ. Governing Body approval became *pro forma*. The Office, as the font of legal doctrine and the repository of factual information (which, in turn, was obtained partly from the trade union Internationals), was in a position to influence the substantive Committee decisions.

It is true that all decisions of the Committee have been unanimous; yet

* In this chapter, reference to "the Committee" always means the Governing Body's standing Committee on Freedom of Association.

it is also true that the Committee is a "representative" body in the sense of equal tripartite representation of the major occupational groupings. According to our decision-making matrix, unanimity is the last thing to be expected here if each member were to act in terms of his group interest; bargaining capped by a contentious vote would have to be the rule of conduct. How do we explain the paradox?

The simple truth of the matter is that the Committee is only "representative" in a very limited sense. A look at its composition during the period 1951–63 will illustrate this:[7]

Governments: France (1951–61, P. Ramadier);[8] India (1951–63, V. K. R. Menon and S. T. Merani); Mexico (1951–54 and 1957–63, P. de Alba, C. Puig, and Bravo Caro); Colombia (1954–57, L. G. Barros); Italy (1961–63, R. Ago).[9]

Employers: J. Forbes Watson (1951, U. K.); M. Ghayour (1952–54 and 1957–63, Iran); P. Waline (1951–63, France); J. B. Pons (1951–57, Uruguay); G. A. Allana (1954–57, Pakistan); J. O'Brien (1957–63, Ireland).

Workers: J. Möri (1951–63, Switzerland); A. Roberts (1951–52, U.K.); L. Jouhaux (1951–54, France); A. Vermeulen (1952–54, Netherlands); A. Cofino García (1954–57, Cuba); R. Bothereau (1957–60, France); A. Sánchez Madariaga (1957–63, Mexico); J. J. Hernandez (1960–63, Philippines).

Western European trade unionists, and the politicians associated with them, have been represented far in excess of their proportional strength in the ILO. Many of these men have close ties also with the ICFTU. As far as the governments are concerned, the supremacy of reformist-socialist ideas and anti-communist convictions was assured by the almost permanent membership of France and India, and especially by the chairmanship of former Socialist French Premier Paul Ramadier, whose party maintains ties with the ICFTU. Despite the apparent intention to have one representative each for Europe, Latin America, and Asia, it is the socialist European trade unionists who have provided continuity on the Worker side; moreover Möri, Jouhaux, Bothereau, Vermeulen, and Roberts are all associated with the leadership of the ICFTU. As for the employers, the Western European influence has manifested itself in the continuous membership of Pierre Waline, the long-time leader of the ILO Employer Group.[10] Small wonder that in 1957 the Soviet government's representative on the Governing Body protested that the composition of the Committee was "one-sided, since the Eastern European countries were not represented in any of the groups."[11] In 1960 he amplified his protest by announcing that henceforth the Societ-bloc countries would take "no part in the decisions" of the Governing Body regarding the reports of the Committee.*

While homogeneity thus undermines the Committee's authority, there is still sufficient heterogeneity to make the achievement of consensus a difficult matter. Unanimity was actually a device adopted for assuring consensus along the lines of a minimum common denominator, and for establishing the legitimacy of the procedure in the eyes of the clients. It was in fact tied to an early policy of dismissing complaints alleging generalized repression of trade union freedom, if the events cited occurred in a setting of civil unrest. The Committee then put the burden of proof on the complainant, by asking him to demonstrate that suppression of human rights involved specific discrimination against trade unions. Only by factoring out the "political" issues inherent in oligarchical politics could unanimity actually be achieved at the level of the minimum common denominator. Unanimity thus served the dual function of legitimating the Committee's work and of constraining the scope of its earlier rulings. However, it remains to be seen whether this has continued to be the case.

ISSUES BEFORE THE COMMITTEE

The accepted method of categorizing the multitude of issues with which the Committee has dealt since 1951 is that of the lawyer. He is concerned with the subject matter of each allegation in terms of the rights defined in Conventions 87 and 98. Further, he is interested in relating the evolution of a rule of law to each subject. The point of departure for the legal categorization of the Committee's work, then, is the text of the basic Conventions and the subject matter of the facts alleged.

Functional reasoning compels me to adopt a different mode of categorizing issues. I am concerned with the trend—if any—evident in the decisions made by the Committee with reference to the evolution of rules, habits, and institutions not necessarily willed or foreseen by the actors. Such a trend, though perhaps not recognized in the actors' explicit aims, must be consistent with them. Further, the context of my functional analy-

---

* 146th Session, June 24, 1960, *Official Bulletin*, p. 13. It should be added that a variety of other devices also militate against the perfectly representative nature of the Committee. If possible, the officers of the Governing Body are to serve concurrently as members of the Committee; Waline and Möri have served in both capacities. Further, the non-representation of communist workers and employers in the two Groups on the Governing Body distorts the picture. Apparently an effort was once made—and then quickly denied—to depart from the tripartite formula by adding a fourth government member to the Committee. This stratagem might have changed the voting alignments. See 143rd Session, November 17–20, 1959, *Official Bulletin*, p. 118. Finally, the practice of appointing nine regular members assures continuity of non-representational composition because the alternates almost automatically move on to full membership when a member retires.

sis is the overall integration of the society of nations, a consideration perhaps not inconsistent with actor motives but certainly not central to them. Hence the categories of issues here chosen reflect primarily the analytical context and only secondarily the legal subject matter. Yet the two overlap and occasionally converge completely. The content of a case considered by the Committee will illustrate the distinction.

In 1953, the ICFTU alleged that the government of Poland had suppressed free trade unions and compelled all associations of workers to follow the lead of the Communist Party: the aspirations of the workers were being subordinated to the realization of the economic plan. Because trade unions had been, in effect, converted into appendages of state and party, freedom of association was not possible. Strikes and collective bargaining were not permitted. Further, dissident trade union leaders had been imprisoned.[12] In 1956, the ICCTU joined the free unions in lodging a further complaint alleging the imprisonment of workers and the breaking of a strike in connection with the events in Poznan.[13]

In the legal terms, these charges involve the following issues: (1) the right of workers to join organizations of their own choosing, (2) the free functioning of unions, (3) the right to organize unions freely, (4) the capacity to bargain collectively, (5) the right to strike, (6) freedom to hold meetings, and (7) freedom from arrest and imprisonment. Considered somewhat differently, but still in legal terms, these charges could also be divided into allegations referring exclusively to the unrestricted functioning of trade unions, and allegations referring to the exercise of civil liberties more generally. To this distinction we shall return later. Now we must juxtapose these legal-issue categories to the issues that are functionally relevant to the process of integration.

For our purposes, it is not important to differentiate, for example, between the right to strike and the free functioning of unions. We are interested in the growth of a task, of legitimacy, and of authority; our concern is the depth of the feedback into national practice. Hence we are preoccupied with the *context* in which charges are made, rather than with the charges themselves. Our argument has been that the vitality of the integration process depends to a large extent on the degree of generally relevant controversy implicit in international action. We have also contended that one major yardstick of systemic transformation is provided by the degree to which the monolithic nation-state ceases to be a monolith, i.e., the extent to which autonomous social groups with articulate interests to defend make their appearance as actors. Hence our chief criteria for categorizing human rights issues are (1) controversiality and (2) the trend toward pluralism.

The least "controversial" type of claim relating to the flourishing of pluralism involves specific charges of specific violations of the rights of a given union or a discrete set of persons. In our Polish example, the charges made with reference to the Poznan riots would fall into this category of issues. The rights of specific individuals are at stake here, but not the capacity of a trade union movement as a national whole. We shall label this type of issue "trade union rights." It will include labor controversies— irrespective of violence or brutality and notwithstanding the incidence of murder and false arrest—that are confined to the life of individual unions and their conflicts with specific national law or policy. Instances of the violation of trade union rights can occur in any political system. The contextual setting is confined to the aims, claims, and interests of a relatively small number of workers and a government agency or a single employer.

Next on the scale of "controversiality," and more germane to the flowering of pluralism, is the category of issues we label "human rights." They may involve the same legal and subject-matter categories that appeared in the Polish example, though the first three would normally be classified here. What matters is the different context: here we are concerned with a challenge to the trade union movement as a whole, with efforts to destroy or weaken it. Typically, this issue category applies to authoritarian political systems, whether fully totalitarian or merely repressively oligarchical.

In both categories the issues are not related to the general currents of world politics: they are of interest primarily to workers in the countries where the events are alleged to have occurred. Our third category—"colonial issues"—takes cognizance of one of the major international currents of our period. Charges referring to any subject matter leveled in a context in which a national movement is seeking to weaken or discredit a colonial administration provide issues of this type. So do complaints lodged by governments of newly independent countries, or by trade union internationals that are trying to strengthen an indigenous workers' movement and hasten the process of decolonization. Trade union violations put forth in the context of the Afro-Asian revolt against colonialism, then, provide our third type of issue. The substantive charges may be the same as in the first two issues; what matters is the different context and the higher pitch of controversy.

Finally, the Cold War setting provides a rather typical context for charges of repressing trade unions. Again, the substantive charges may be the same as in the trade union and human rights categories. But the context is the discrediting of either West or East. This type of issue is applicable to most of the charges leveled by the democratic systems against communist regimes and vice versa. Hence the two Polish cases are classified as "Cold War" issues in our scheme, even though, in terms of subject matter alone, they would figure as trade union and human rights issues.

Are "political" issues, then, our real focus of interest? To answer this question is to differentiate once more between ILO practice and analytical procedure. In the jurisprudence of the Committee, "political" complaints are not receivable; ILO jurisdiction is confined to "trade union" issues. But the Committee considers "political" such acts as the imprisonment of rebels, the shooting of political opponents, the repression of all voluntary groups, the censoring of mail or the press, etc. Naturally these acts involve freedom of association and general civil liberties as well. But unless it can be proven that these acts, too—though perhaps only incidentally—affect the exercise of trade union rights, the Committee will not deal with them.[14] However, the very distinction made by the Committee is irrelevant to our purposes. We are vitally concerned with the politicization of the quasi-judicial process of protecting union freedom of association and with its expansion into the field of civil liberties. Hence the degree of *political content and controversy* is of the essence in our scheme of classification.

How does the ILO membership rank on our scale of issues? Table 24 summarizes the situation. In all, 64 countries were the victims of complaints, and they represent every kind of regional bloc and set of characteristics. Although the colonial charges leveled against Britain and France contribute much to the total of 272 cases analyzed,[15] the Cold War charges leveled against the United States and Greece bulk almost as impressively. As far as violations of trade union rights in the narrow sense are concerned, no category of member state has enjoyed immunity. Further, the high

TABLE 24

FREEDOM OF ASSOCIATION: INCIDENCE OF ISSUES

Country	Total cases	Issue (number of cases)					Relevant political context
		Trade union	Human rights	Colonial	Cold War	Other	
Argentina	17	12	4	–	–	1	Before 1955 suppression of anti-Peronista unions; after 1955 suppression of Peronista unions
Austria	2	–	–	–	2	–	
Belgium	4	2	–	1	1	–	
Bolivia	2	–	2	–	–	–	
Brazil	5	2	2	–	–	1	Attempts of communist unions at recognition
Burma	7	6	1	–	–	–	
Cameroun	2	1	–	–	1	–	
Canada	2	2	–	–	–	–	Newfoundland union freedom issue
Ceylon	1	–	1	–	–	–	
Chile	7	2	3	–	–	2	Law for Defense of Democracy issue
Colombia	4	–	3	–	1	–	
Congo (B) ...	1	1	–	–	–	–	
Congo (L) ...	2	–	1	–	–	1	
Costa Rica	4	2	2	–	–	–	

TABLE 24 (*continued*)

Country	Total cases	Trade union	Human rights	Colonial	Cold War	Other	Relevant political context
Cuba	6	–	5	–	–	1	Before 1959 suppression of anti-Bastista unions; after 1959 suppression of anti-Castro unions
Czecho-slovakia	1	–	–	–	1	–	Right of non-communist unions to exist
Denmark	1	1	–	–	–	–	
Dominican Rep.	2	–	2	–	–	–	Anti-Trujillo movement
Ecuador	1	1	–	–	–	–	
El Salvador	1	1	–	–	–	–	
France	20	3	1	13	3	–	Chiefly colonial-national movement
Germany	3	1	–	–	2	–	
Greece	29	13	4	–	7	5	Earlier complaints deal with aftermath of civil war, recent ones with government efforts to control union movement
Guatemala	4	–	2	–	1	1	Post-Arbenz situation
Guinea	1	1	–	–	–	–	
Haiti	2	–	2	–	–	–	
Honduras	3	2	1	–	–	–	
Hungary	4	–	–	–	4	–	Right of non-communist unions to exist; revolt of 1956, Soviet intervention
India	6	3	3	–	–	–	Preventive Detention Act issue
Iran	6	–	2	–	4	–	Mossadegh period disturbances
Iraq	2	–	2	–	–	–	Opposition to Kassem regime
Israel	1	1	–	–	–	–	
Italy	3	–	–	–	3	–	CGIL conflicts with government
Ivory Coast	1	–	–	1	–	–	
Japan	4	1	–	–	2	1	Trade union movement's resistance to increasing government controls
Jordan	2	–	1	–	–	1	
Lebanon	2	1	1	–	–	–	
Liberia	1	–	–	–	–	1	
Libya	1	–	1	–	–	–	Government efforts to curb a Nasserite trade union movement

(*continued on following page*)

TABLE 24 (*concluded*)

Country	Total cases	Trade union	Human rights	Colonial	Cold War	Other	Relevant political context
		Issue (number of cases)					
Mexico	2	1	–	–	–	1	
Morocco	4	3	–	–	–	1	Government efforts to control dissident trade unions
Netherlands ..	4	2	1	1	–	–	
New Zealand ..	1	1	–	–	–	–	
Pakistan	3	–	2	–	–	1	
Paraguay	3	1	1	–	–	1	
Peru	3	1	2	–	–	–	
Philippines ...	1	–	–	–	1	–	
Poland	2	–	–	–	2	–	Right of non-communist unions to exist; Poznan riots
Portugal	2	–	1	–	–	1	Legality of corporatist unions
Saar	1	1	–	–	–	–	
Senegal	2	1	–	–	1	–	
So. Africa	10	1	7	–	–	2	Suppression of Communism, Industrial Conciliation, and Native Labour Acts
Spain	3	–	3	–	–	–	Legality of trade union system
Sudan	2	–	1	1	–	–	Military control of unions
Switzerland ...	2	2	–	–	–	–	
Syria	1	–	–	–	–	1	
Thailand	1	–	1	–	–	–	Military control of unions
Turkey	2	–	1	–	1	–	Protest against Menderes regime
U.A.R.	3	1	1	–	–	1	
U.K.	33	2	–	29	–	2	Colonial-national movements
Uruguay	2	1	–	–	–	1	
U.S.	12	2	–	1	9	–	Application of National Security Program to seamen
U.S.S.R.	3	–	–	–	3	–	Right of non-communist unions to exist; intervention in Hungary
Venezuela	2	–	2	–	–	–	Military control of unions under Perez Jiménez regime
Yugoslavia ...	1	–	–	–	1	–	Right of non-communist unions to exist
Total	272	79	69	47	50	27	

totals tallied against Argentina, South Africa, Chile, Cuba, and India give
testimony to the fact that trade unions have not been slow to make use of
the procedure to press home generalized attacks on the enjoyment of civil
rights.

Table 25 summarizes temporal trends in the incidence of our four issues.
Cold War issues, which had represented almost 30 per cent of the total
during the first years of the Committee's work, declined to a mere 7.4 per
cent in the most recent period. The decline of the colonial issue has been
almost equally precipitous. Concurrently, the incidence of pure trade union
issues has doubled, while allegations of general human rights violations
have declined slightly. Quite obviously, as functionally specific matters
gain in scope and attention, general world issues are becoming less and less
important in the process. Thus far, at any rate, this trend has not re-
dounded to the benefit of civil liberties as a recognized subject for international quasi-judicial action, at least not quantitatively. Controversiality has
declined with the waning of colonial empire and periodic lulls in the East-
West confrontation; but so long as human rights issues do not take the
place of the colonial and Cold War charges, no great ILO contribution to
the international growth of pluralism can be demonstrated.[16]

TABLE 25

FREEDOM OF ASSOCIATION: INCIDENCE OF ISSUES OVER TIME
(*Per cent*)

Period	Issues				
	Trade union rights	Human rights	Colonial	Cold War	Indeter- minate
1950–53 (92 cases)	17.4	27.2	26.0	29.4	0
1954–59 (111 cases)	34.8	25.9	13.4	19.7	6.2
1960–63 (69 cases)	35.0	20.3	9.0	7.4	28.3
Average 1950–63 (272 cases)	28.9	24.9	16.5	19.8	9.9

PARTIES BEFORE THE COMMITTEE

The ILO procedure for protecting freedom of association is open to any
"industrial organization." Moreover, the Committee has made it amply
clear that it is for the ILO rather than for municipal law to define this term.
Thus, complaints against a government may be deposited by any national
association of workers or employers with a demonstrable interest in the
allegations. A union that has been dissolved by national action may still be
recognized as a complainant. A union official dismissed by administrative
action can still have a *locus standi* before the Committee. An exiled trade
union or employer association is considered a bona fide industrial organization, as is an individual lodging his complaint from abroad. The exis-

tence of a political animus on the part of the complainant is considered irrelevant, and the presumption of innocence—if this term is appropriate at all in a situation in which governments are not supposed to be on trial—lies with him.[17]

This, then, means that charges can be brought by national organizations complaining against *their own* governments, and by international confederations of such organizations acting on behalf of their national affiliates. In fact, about 85 per cent of all cases have originated with such groups. Furthermore, the Committee takes the view that national organizations complaining against the practices of a foreign government normally do *not* have a genuine interest in the matter.[18] As is apparent from Table 26, about 10 per cent of the cases have come from such groups, and the incidence appears to be rising. Yet the Committee has dismissed summarily all but four of these complaints on grounds of vagueness or irreceivability. Finally, the Committee categorically refused to deal with complaints addressed to it by such groups as political parties, student associations, groups of political exiles who are not trade unionists, and individuals whose institutional affiliations cannot be ascertained. Four per cent of the cases have originated with such groups, and their incidence seems to be growing too. Although employers' associations may bring charges, only one has in fact done so.[19] All other cases have come from trade unions or indeterminate political bodies.

In compiling these statistics about the nature of the complainants, I have followed certain rules. In all, well over five hundred complaints have been received by the Office, even though only 310 numbered cases had appeared in the records as of the spring of 1963. The explanation lies in the fact that, in many instances, several national unions will bring substantially identical

TABLE 26

FREEDOM OF ASSOCIATION: SHIFTS IN THE IDENTITY OF COMPLAINANTS
(*Per cent*)

Period	WFTU	ICFTU	ICCTU	WFTU, ICFTU	ICCTU, WFTU, ICFTU	Nat. union vs. own govt.	Nat. union vs. foreign govt.	Non-occup. group
1950–53 (92 cases)[a]	60.8	9.7	0	3.5[d]	1.1[g]	13.0	9.7	1.1
1954–59 (111 cases)[b]	31.4	9.0	9.0	5.4[e]	1.9[h]	31.5	6.3	4.5
1960–63 (69 cases)[a]	21.6	3.0	6.0	4.4[f]	0	37.7	18.7	7.2
Average 1950–63 (272 cases)[c]	38.8	7.7	5.1	4.2	1.2	27.1	10.6	4.1

[a] Two complaints involving only independent international confederations were not tabulated.
[b] One joint complaint of WFTU and ICCTU was not tabulated.
[c] Shortage of 1.2% due to the exclusion of the three cases from tabulation.
[d] Cases 12, 16, 40.   [e] Cases 102, 134, 136, 152, 156, 178.   [f] Cases 220, 221, 266.
[g] Cases 72/122.   [h] Cases 143, 153.

charges against the same government with respect to the same situation. Further, the international confederations do not follow identical policies in this field. Thus the WFTU, responsible for almost 40 per cent of all cases, prefers to handle complaints through the central machinery, rather than delegating them to national affiliates. Hence I charged all cases to the communist federation when they were presented by the Prague office, by an international trade secretariat affiliated with the WFTU, or by the Latin American Confederation of Workers, to which the WFTU likes to delegate its Latin American cases. The ICFTU, by contrast, prefers to let national affiliates present their own cases, though help, information, and instruction are generously furnished by Brussels just the same.[20] I have charged to the ICFTU all cases argued by free trade secretariats, by national unions working with the ICFTU, and by the ICFTU acting alone. The same rule has been used in dealing with the complaints presented by the Christian federation. Only when there was no evidence that a national union was acting in conjunction with an international confederation was a case charged under the heading of a national union attacking its own or a foreign government. Two cases involving charges by independent regional confederations were excluded from Tables 26 and 27. So was a single case argued jointly by the WFTU and the ICCTU.

Tables 26 and 27 make it plain that the WFTU is exercising more and more restraint. In the early years, the communists specialized in using the procedure for bringing Cold War and colonial disputes to Geneva, at the expense largely of the Western industrialized democracies. As their "litigation" declined, emphasis shifted to genuine human rights issues advanced against South Africa, India, and especially Latin American oligarchies. In this they were often joined by the free trade unions and occasionally even by the Christians. Spain and Portugal, not unnaturally, have provided a favorite target for the WFTU.

ICFTU complaints have never been many, and over the years they have become fewer still. The ICFTU specializes in Cold War indictments of Soviet-bloc countries and human rights complaints against Latin American oligarchies, Thailand, Spain, Portugal, and South Africa. It also launched a certain number of very effective colonial charges against France and Britain. The general performance of the ICCTU follows roughly the same pattern as that of its socialist colleague in Brussels. To the ICFTU should go the credit for first alerting strong and articulate national unions to the possibility of turning to Geneva and to the world forum for protection against conservative governments. The most telling case is that of Japan, whose unions, together with the ICFTU, have fought a continuing battle since 1958 in seeking to force the Japanese government to undo a variety of anti-union measures.[21] An intensification of this pattern, in the case of

TABLE 27

Freedom of Association: Complainants, Defendants, and Issues
(Number of complaints)

Defendant (type and no. in type)	WFTU				ICFTU				ICCTU				Nat. union vs. own govt.				Nat. union vs. foreign govt.				Total Complaints
	TU	HR	Col.	CW	TU	HR	Col.	CW	TU	HR	Col.	CW	TU	HR	Col.	CW	TU	HR	Col.	CW	
D-OI-S (9)	3	2	29	11	1	–	8	–	2	–	2	–	9	–	7	5	1	–	5	2	87
D-OI-FE (2)	–	–	–	2	2	–	–	–	1	–	–	–	–	–	–	–	–	–	–	–	5
D-NI-S (5)	2	5	–	3	1	1	–	–	–	–	–	–	4	1	–	–	1	–	–	–	18
D-NI-FE (1)	1	2	–	–	–	–	–	–	–	–	–	–	1	–	–	–	–	–	–	–	4
D-MA-S (3)	1	–	–	–	–	–	–	–	–	–	–	–	1	–	–	–	–	–	–	–	2
D-U-S (1)	–	–	–	–	–	–	–	–	–	–	–	–	–	1	–	–	–	–	–	–	1
D-U-FE (4)	5	1	–	5	–	4	–	–	–	–	–	–	10	6	–	–	–	–	–	–	31
O-NI-FE (3)[a]	5	4	–	1	1	4	–	–	–	–	–	–	4	2	–	–	–	2	–	–	23
O-U-FE (25)[b]	4	14	1	6	–	3	–	–	4	3	–	–	5	2	–	1	2	–	–	1	46
O-U-S (2)	–	–	–	–	–	–	–	–	–	–	–	–	6	–	–	3	–	–	–	–	9
T-OI-CM (2)	–	–	–	–	–	–	–	3	–	–	–	1	–	–	–	–	–	–	–	–	4
T-NI-CM (4)[c]	–	–	–	–	–	–	–	4	–	2	–	1	–	1[c]	–	–	–	–	–	–	8
T-NI-FE (1)[d]	1	5	–	–	–	2	–	–	–	–	–	–	–	1	–	–	–	–	–	–	9
T-U-S (1)[e]	–	–	–	–	1	–	–	–	–	–	–	–	–	–	–	–	–	–	–	–	1
T-U-FE (1)[f]	–	2	–	–	–	1	–	–	–	1	–	–	–	1[f]	–	–	–	–	–	–	5
T-U-CP (2)	1	1	–	–	–	–	–	–	–	–	–	–	–	–	–	–	–	1	–	1	4
Total	23	36	30	28	6	15	8	7	7	6	2	2	40	15	7	9	4	3	5	4	257[g]

note: Symbols in first column are explained in Table 22, note a. Abbreviations in the column heads are as follows: TU, trade union issues; HR, human rights issues; Col., colonial issues; CW, Cold War issues; WFTU, World Federation of Trade Unions; ICFTU, International Confederation of Free Trade Unions; ICCTU, International Confederation of Christian Trade Unions.

Two types of complaints were excluded from the tabulation: complaints submitted by non-occupational groups and independent regional international confederations, and complaints alleging an indeterminate violation of trade union rights.

[a] Includes Argentina. The bulk of the complaints deals with the post-1955 situation. Further, the Perón regime was not clearly totalitarian.

[b] Includes pre-1959 Cuba.

[c] Includes post-1959 Cuba. The single national complaint in this row involved a case submitted by an exiled Cuban union.

[d] Republic of South Africa only.

[e] Guinea only.

[f] Spain only. The single national complaint in this row involved a case submitted by an exiled Spanish union.

[g] The total number of cases used for the table was 238. Joint complaints were credited to each complaining international confederation.

industrializing and democratizing nations, would be of enormous significance to the growth of a pluralistic international environment.

National unions attacking their own governments have made steadily increasing use of the ILO machinery. Their efforts are directed against all non-totalitarian governments. These complainants concentrate on genuine trade union issues, though human rights issues do arise in complaints against Greece, Burma, and Bolivia. Colonial and Cold War issues have furnished the theme only for some early complaints by communist European unions against the governments of France and Italy. Although national unions attacking foreign governments have resorted to the ILO machinery more and more, their charges do not seem to fall into any meaningful pattern, apart from their tendency toward vagueness and tendentiousness.

While no type of economy or regime was immune from attack, the charges were by no means evenly distributed. Nine industrialized countries of the West were the victims of a third of the complaints. But of that third almost 80 per cent consisted of colonial and Cold War attacks. The twenty-five underdeveloped oligarchies singled out for attack accumulated one-sixth of the total complaints; over half of these charges, however, were concerned with infringements of basic human rights not readily connected with the colonial or Cold War contexts. Democracies in the early stages of industrialization or still underdeveloped economically also emerge as favorite victims, with Greece scoring quite disproportionately in this category. Cold War charges vie with human rights as the main contexts here. Communist regimes have been indicted rarely in terms of the number of complaints; however, the quality of the complaints was such as to give rise to the most severe condemnations ever enunciated by the Committee. Among other totalitarian regimes, Spain and South Africa, of course, continue to be most frequently under trade union attack.

For the advance of pluralism as a pervasive feature of the international environment, it is undoubtedly good that the WFTU should no longer pre-empt the field. Yet if the communists had not profited from the controversiality of the colonial issue, it is unlikely that the ICFTU would have embraced that issue. Intemperate and propagandistic though the early WFTU charges were, they served the purpose of sensitizing the system to the possibilities of the machinery; the other actors "learned" from the communists. The result is a slight decline in the activity of the international confederations and a wave of interest on the part of newly articulate national unions, who are advancing trade union issues close to their hearts. So long as they continue to pose general human rights issues along with trade union questions, the general functional transformation may still be served, especially if the Internationals continue to interest themselves actively in the larger questions.

DECISIONS OF THE COMMITTEE

We must now look more closely at the Committee's disposition of the three hundred cases submitted to it if we want to grasp the impact of this quasi-judicial procedure at the international level. The evolution of this aspect of the Committee's procedure is one of the most significant indicators of development.

There can be no doubt that the initial justification advanced by the ILO for instituting its own organ to protect trade union rights was based exclusively on the notion of *conciliation*; at first there was no public suggestion of a *judicial* dimension. As Jenks disarmingly put it:

This development in the procedure corresponds to a real and generally recognized need; there is a widespread recognition that it is to the general advantage that allegations of infringements of trade union rights should be impartially and dispassionately examined internationally as a contribution to the relaxation of both international and social tension, and a procedure which provides facilities for such examination informally by a body so composed as to ensure a reasonable equilibrium between divergent views and interests, without a formal investigation analogous to legal proceedings against the State concerned, presents great advantages over a procedure which, while doubtless affording more formal guarantees of judicial independence, tends, by reason of its formality, to assume the character of an intervention in domestic affairs which gives recourse to the procedure a political aspect which it is preferable to avoid.[22]

Even if the conduct of those who were party to these proceedings hardly supports the explanations given by Official Functionalism, the argument is significant as representing the cautious official façade designed to reassure skittish governments. The purpose of the procedure was not to punish guilty governments, but "to promote respect for trade union rights in law and in fact."[23] If governments are protected against unreasonable charges, the Committee continued, they will then voluntarily cooperate with the ILO in avoiding the infringement of trade union rights merely to ensure their good name. Hence the Committee does not seek to pursue a case when it receives information that the initial grievance has been redressed; but it reserves its right unilaterally to reopen the case if new evidence of malpractice is received. The Committee determines when a case ought to be referred to the Fact-Finding and Conciliation Commission; moreover, a government's initial refusal to admit the Commission will not prevent the Committee from recommending to the Governing Body that the case be submitted to the Commission.[24]

So why do we persist in calling the procedure "quasi-judicial," especially when the Committee members are far from being judges or jurisconsults? Conciliation did not remain the exclusive aim for long. The Committee, cautious at first, insisted on very full documentation and was exceedingly reluctant to entertain complaints of a general nature. Initially, its procedure admitted that complaining trade union organizations and governments were not on an equal footing; hence the replies of governments to a complaint were not directly communicated to the complaining organization. In recent years, however, the Committee has moved toward a notion of the judicial equality of the parties. Witnesses for the complainants are not formally heard by the Committee, in order to avoid the impression of judicial proceedings; but government spokesmen have on occasion been permitted to appear. In one sense, of course, the special position of governments is counterbalanced by the special position of representatives of international trade union confederations, who, incidentally, sit as members of the Committee in their capacity as worker members of the Governing Body. Since often it is their organizations in Brussels (Prague not enjoying representation) that initiate the proceedings in the first place, it might appear that the procedure permits the plaintiff to function as judge and jury. In order to eliminate this impression (by no means inconsistent with international conciliation),* the Committee strengthened its rules regarding the disqualification of members. Whereas at first only nationals and colleagues of the parties had to disqualify themselves from participating in the deliberations, in 1958 it was decided that an international trade union official "may not take part in the consideration of a case by the Committee if he has taken any personal part in the decision to refer the case or in the formulation or submission to the Committee of the allegations under consideration."[25]

Perhaps equally important in the trend toward a quasi-judicial forum is the evolution of the Committee's procedure with respect to its autonomy in relation both to the Governing Body as a whole and to the parties. Let it be noted first that the Committee, with the eventual approval of the plenary Governing Body, is the author of its own rules of procedure; it has always taken the initiative in reviewing and revising the rules. These have in fact changed constantly—and autonomously. The cumulative effect of the self-administered change has been the growth of the Committee's discretionary power, its capacity to dispose of issues without referring them to the plenary Governing Body except in the most *pro forma* of ways. Yet it remains true that this evolution was possible only within the limits set by the dominant opinion in the Governing Body.

Thus the Committee alone determined the criteria governing the receivability of a complaint, the circumstances under which further information should be requested, and whether the complaint was sufficiently well-

---

* The conciliation practiced in the UN under the auspices of most General Assembly commissions almost always includes the parties or their allies. Conciliation in the Security Council by definition includes the parties or their allies if the dispute is of any major scope.

formulated to call for communication to the allegedly delinquent government. In addition, the relative degree of urgency implicit in various allegations is determined by the Committee, which thus fixes its own priorities in
terms of the nature of the allegations before it. Although its initial mandate was merely to determining the worthiness of an allegation on behalf
of the Governing Body, the Committee soon claimed and exercised the
power to request additional information from governments while the decision on receivability was still pending. In this way, the dispute was kept on
the Committee's active docket while the national authorities were given a
chance to mend their ways. The Committee instructed the Director-General
to follow up on the extent to which governments had implemented its
recommendations, and to keep the Governing Body informed. It soon successfully asserted the right not to drop a case from its docket, even though
the complainant withdrew it, if it suspected that the withdrawal was due
to pressure from the government accused.

It remains entirely within the discretion of the Committee whether to
refer a case to the plenary Governing Body for full and public debate, to
recommend the publication of a report, or to suggest the interposition of
the Fact-Finding and Conciliation Commission. It has the capacity to determine when and under what circumstances weightier measures are to be
adopted, and this is a powerful weapon for dealing with uncooperative
governments. Even the capacity to dismiss ill-founded or vague allegations
has been turned into a weapon, since the decision to dismiss is often accompanied by recommendations to the government to review its law or practice, thus implicitly threatening a reopening of the case.

Only in the matter of visits to trouble spots has the initial tenuousness
of the international conciliation procedure remained unchanged. Having
been refused admission in two of the earliest cases (Venezuela and the
Dominican Republic), the Committee requested the Director-General, in
any future case calling for visits, to negotiate as a precondition the full and
free access of the visiting Committee to all sources of information, and the
right of the Governing Body to publish the Committee's report without
governmental permission. Even though the Conference in 1955 overwhelmingly adopted a resolution inviting governments to permit visits by
the Fact-Finding and Conciliation Commission and revising the Committee's procedures to facilitate this development, few invitations and only one
request for visits have been forthcoming.[26]

We are now ready to examine the patterns of severity into which the
decisions of the Committee fall. They are summarized in their application
to each "defendant" government in Table 28. The categories advanced,
once more, depart from the rubrics customary in the procedure of the
Committee, although they were inspired by it and can in all instances be
related to it. Our interest lies in pinpointing which governments have been

treated with leniency and which with severity, which cases the Committee has regarded lightly and which with great misgivings. In all instances, each case has been listed under only one heading. This means that each case has been considered *as a whole*, even though it may have been composed of a series of separate allegations disposed of in varying ways by the Committee. If a given case consisted of three allegations, one of which was dismissed *sine die*, one held over for continued discussion with the government, and one singled out for a pointed suggestion that certain laws were inconsistent with freedom of association, the case as a whole was assigned to the rubric "Recommends change in law and practice." In other words, the most drastic action taken by the Committee in a given case was my criterion.

Dismissal of a case, in our context of controversiality and pluralism, may occur as a result of two very different approaches. "Dismissal without inquiry" can mean one of three things: first, that the Committee did not find it necessary to communicate an allegation to the defendant because it was too vague, came from a complainant whose *locus standi* was not recognized, or referred to matters not considered in the jurisdiction of the ILO (i.e., political persecution unrelated to trade unionism); second, that the Committee dismissed the complaint after convincing itself that the facts alleged either were incorrect, or, if correct, did not constitute a violation of freedom of association; or, third, that the Committee received information that the situation described had been rectified. "Dismissal after inquiry" implies a stronger approach. It covers cases in which the Committee did not finally decide to dismiss the charges until after it had communicated with the defendant government, and had elicited an explanation which satisfied the nine members that no violation of union rights was involved. It may well be that cases in this category cover situations in which the mere act of communication amounted to covert conciliation resulting in a change in national practice.

"Dismissal with request to review" covers cases in which the matter as a whole was dismissed on the basis that no evidence of violation had been uncovered; *but* the dismissal was accompanied by a request that, because future violations might be implicit in the practices alleged, the government should re-examine its law and policy to make sure they did not violate Conventions 87 and 98. In other words, this form of dismissal incorporates another of the indirect modes of conciliation-*cum*-pressure that rests on the Committee's self-asserted power to elicit information and keep cases under review. This form of dismissal may occur either "without inquiry" or "after inquiry" (i.e., after prolonged negotiations and numerous requests for further information). It may occur after the exhaustion of local remedies or the completion of an inquiry into the alleged abuses launched by the defendant government on its own initiative. It may occur after

TABLE 28

FREEDOM OF ASSOCIATION: DEFENDANTS AND THE DISPOSITION OF COMPLAINTS
(*Number of cases*)

Defendant	Total cases	Dismissal		Dismissal with request to review		Inquiry still in progress	Recommendation to change law or practice	"Sanctions"
		Without inquiry	After inquiry	Without inquiry	After inquiry			
Argentina	17	8	–	1	–	–	8	–
Austria	2	2	–	–	–	–	–	–
Belgium	4	3	1	–	–	–	–	–
Bolivia	2	1	–	1	–	–	–	–
Brazil	5	3	–	1	–	–	1	–
Burma	7	5	1	–	–	–	1	–
Cameroun	2	–	1	–	–	1	–	–
Canada	2	1	–	–	–	–	1	–
Ceylon	1	–	1	–	–	–	–	–
Chile	7	3	–	–	–	2	2	–
Colombia	4	2	–	1	–	–	1	–
Congo (B)	1	–	–	1	–	–	–	–
Congo (L)	2	1	–	1	–	–	–	–
Costa Rica	4	2	–	1	–	–	1	–
Cuba	6	3	–	–	–	1	2	–
Czechoslovakia	1	–	–	–	–	–	–	1
Denmark	1	1	–	–	–	–	–	–
Dominican Rep.	2	–	–	–	–	–	1	1
Ecuador	1	1	–	–	–	–	–	–
El Salvador	1	1	–	–	–	–	–	–
France	20	12	3	2	–	–	3	–
Germany	3	2	1	–	–	–	–	–
Greece	29	18	1	2	–	1	7	–
Guatemala	4	1	–	–	–	–	3	–
Guinea	1	–	–	–	–	1	–	–
Haiti	2	1	–	1	–	–	–	–
Honduras	3	2	–	–	1	–	–	–
Hungary	4	1	–	–	–	–	1	2
India	6	2	–	3	1	–	–	–
Iran	6	4	1	–	1	–	–	–
Iraq	2	1	–	–	–	1	–	–
Israel	1	1	–	–	–	–	–	–
Italy	3	3	–	–	–	–	–	–
Ivory Coast	1	–	–	–	1	–	–	–
Japan	4	2	–	1	–	–	1	–
Jordan	2	1	–	–	–	–	1	–
Lebanon	2	2	–	–	–	–	–	–
Liberia	1	1	–	–	–	–	–	–
Libya	1	–	–	–	–	–	1	–
Mexico	2	2	–	–	–	–	–	–
Morocco	4	3	–	–	–	–	1	–
Netherlands	4	3	–	1	–	–	–	–
New Zealand	1	1	–	–	–	–	–	–
Pakistan	3	1	–	2	–	–	–	–
Paraguay	3	2	–	–	–	–	1	–
Peru	3	3	–	–	–	–	–	–

TABLE 28 *(continued)*

Defendant	Total cases	Dismissal		Dismissal with request to review		Inquiry still in progress	Recommendation to change law or practice	"Sanctions"
		Without inquiry	After inquiry	Without inquiry	After inquiry			
Philippines	1	1	–	–	–	–	–	–
Poland	2	–	–	–	–	–	2	–
Portugal	2	1	–	–	–	–	1	–
Saar	1	–	–	1	–	–	–	–
Senegal	2	–	–	–	–	1	1	–
So. Africa	10	3	–	1	1	–	5	–
Spain	3	2	–	–	–	–	1	–
Sudan	2	1	–	–	–	–	1	–
Switzerland	2	2	–	–	–	–	–	–
Syria	1	1	–	–	–	–	–	–
Thailand	1	–	–	–	–	–	1	–
Turkey	2	1	–	–	–	–	1	–
U.A.R.	3	3	–	–	–	–	–	–
U.K.	33	23	1	2	1	–	6	–
Uruguay	2	2	–	–	–	–	–	–
U.S.	12	11	–	1	–	–	–	–
U.S.S.R.	3	1	–	–	–	–	–	2
Venezuela	2	–	–	–	–	–	1	1
Yugoslavia	1	1	–	–	–	–	–	–
Total	272	159	11	24	6	8	57	7

either defendant or complainant has been given time and opportunity to furnish additional details. In other words, it is a device for keeping the issue alive as long as the inquiry could have any possible merit.

The heading "Inquiry still in progress" represents an even severer approach. It covers charges considered serious enough by the Committee to warrant extensive communication with the parties and many requests for further information; it may involve waiting for the exhaustion of local remedies or the consummation of confidentially communicated indications that the government is ready to change its practices. Since the Committee had made no final decision either to dismiss or to recommend specific remedial action at the time of our survey, the eight cases in this column could not be incorporated in most of our later tabulations.

The two final columns represent the strongest measures available to the Committee. A "recommendation to change law or practice" is the ILO's diplomatic formula for finding a government "guilty" of specific violations of Convention 87 and/or 98, and for indicating precisely what measures ought to be taken to eliminate the violation. It is not customary to make such a recommendation until all the modes of conciliation implicit in the various gradations of review and dismissal have been exhausted. And even after such a recommendation is made, the Committee usually keeps the case on its docket and continues its efforts to obtain a change in national policy. Usually this is done by way of quiet negotiations and unpublicized consultations between the Office and the government concerned, either in Geneva or locally. In certain cases, though, more public steps are taken, steps we have summarized in the column headed "Sanctions." What do these comprise? They may include some or all of the following measures: referral to the plenary Governing Body for full and public debate, request that the Fact-Finding and Conciliation Commission be dispatched to the scene, referral of the matter to full debate in the ECOSOC or General Assembly, and the publication by the Governing Body of a full report describing the guilty government's misdeeds.

Who has been singled out for the "full treatment"? A report has been published only in the cases of Czechoslovakia, Hungary, and the Soviet Union. The Fact-Finding Commission procedure was recommended in the cases of the Dominican Republic, Venezuela, Japan, Hungary, and the Soviet Union. Referral to the United Nations was decided upon with reference to Hungary and the Soviet Union. But the lesser pressure of recommendations for changes in law and practice has been brought to bear on a wide variety of governments, notably Argentina, Guatemala, Greece, Poland, South Africa, and the United Kingdom.

Table 29 tells us something about the incidence of these types of decisions over time. The decline in the number of dismissals suggests that the Committee's criteria are becoming more severe. While the average rate of dismissals without inquiry remains around 60 per cent, the decline from the 67 per cent of the earliest period indicates both improvement in the care and detail with which complaints are drafted and a growth in the Committee's severity. Dismissals with request to review are sharply declining, a development correlated, however, with a sharp decrease in the number of reported cases in which charges were dismissed after the situation had been rectified. In short, it appears as if there is less occasion to resort to this mode of action. On the other hand, such dismissals following lengthy communication with the defendant are growing, once more suggesting a stricter

TABLE 29

Freedom of Association: Shifts in the Type of Decision
(*Per cent*)

Period	Dismissal		Dismissal with request to review		Inquiry still in progress	Recommendation to change law or practice	"Sanctions"
	Without inquiry	After inquiry	Without inquiry	After inquiry			
1950–53 (92 cases) ..	67.4	4.3	15.2	0	1.2	6.5	5.4
1954–59 (111 cases) ..	53.0	3.0	5.8	3.0	1.6	32.0	1.6
1960–63 (69 cases) ..	58.2	6.5	4.6	3.5	6.5	20.7	0
Average 1950–63 (272 cases)	58.7	4.5	9.0	2.2	3.3	19.8	2.5

attitude on the part of the Committee. The same is suggested by the sharp rise from 6 to almost 21 per cent in recommendations for change of national policy. Finally, the futility of the sanctions procedure is driven home by the disappearance of this weapon from the Committee's armory during the most recent period, a conclusion supported by the obvious fact that there has been no discernible decrease in the violations of trade union rights.

It may be true, as Jenks argues, that even the large number of dismissals has a positive effect on international integration, since only by rigorous insistence on full documentation can the legitimacy of the Committee be established in the minds of skeptical governments. Its reputation for impartiality, judiciousness, and detachment is considered a prerequisite to full legitimacy. If this is so, however, the weight of judiciousness should have been felt evenly by all complainants, and the rigor of the judgments should have been dispensed in equal measure to all defendant governments. While this seems to have been the trend in recent years, it was not the case earlier. A certain "double standard" was then perceptible, related to the Cold War and the *de facto* predominance of the ICFTU and its governmental allies on the Committee. In the earlier periods the Committee found ample reason to dismiss without inquiry numerous complaints having their origin in civil unrest, in efforts to overthrow traditional oligarchical regimes, and in the repression of political trade unionism by military dictatorships.[27] Other dismissals or milder censure occurred in the colonial context, resulting in the immunity of colonial administrations if they were engaged in suppressing trade union movements that were allied with political nationalism.[28] In still other instances, the "immaturity" of the trade union movement was cited as a reason for allowing administrative interference with union affairs.[29] Only in two instances did such conditions give rise to efforts at the strongest measures on the scale of pressure. Yet the same measures were invoked against three communist countries on five occasions, although their departure from the modal democratic-pluralistic trade union pattern could be as easily justified as Peru's or Argentina's in terms of the escape hatches left open by the Committee. Admittedly the work of protecting freedom of association began to unfold in the highly political context of the anti-colonial revolt and the Cold War, and admittedly the major trade union Internationals were often merely jockeying for propaganda vantage points, but the legitimacy of judiciousness does not gain if one side more or less consistently "wins."

Whose complaints, then, were most often unheld in relatively strong terms against which defendants? The answer appears in Tables 30 and 31. But before we try to interpret the tables, one point should be made clear. No claim is being made that the Committee automatically favors some complainants, in terms of the frequency and severity of types of decisions.

TABLE 30

FREEDOM OF ASSOCIATION: DISPOSITIONS, DEFENDANTS, AND COMPLAINANTS
(Number of cases)

Defendant (type and no. in type)[a]	Dismissed					Dismissed with request to "review"					Government requested to change conduct					"Sanctions" recommended[b]			Total complaints[c]
	WF TU	ICF TU	ICC TU	NTU vs. own	NTU vs. foreign	WF TU	ICF TU	ICC TU	NTU vs. own	NTU vs. foreign	WF TU	ICF TU	ICC TU	NTU vs. own	NTU vs. foreign	WF TU	ICF TU	ICC TU	
D-OI-S (9)	30	1	2	21	8	6	4	1	1	1	8	4	—	—	—	—	—	—	87
D-OI-FE (2)	1	—	1	—	1	1	—	—	—	—	2	—	—	—	—	—	—	—	6
D-NI-S (5)	7	—	—	3	1	2	—	—	2	—	2	1	—	—	—	—	—	—	18
D-NI-FE (1)	1	—	—	2	—	1	—	—	—	—	1	—	—	—	—	—	—	—	5
D-MA-S (3)	1	—	—	—	1	—	—	—	—	—	—	—	—	—	—	—	—	—	2
D-U-S (1)	—	—	—	1	—	—	—	—	—	—	—	—	—	—	—	—	—	—	1
D-U-FE (4)	10	—	—	11	1	1	—	—	3	—	4	—	—	—	3	—	—	—	33
O-NI-FE (3)	5	1	—	2	1	—	—	1	1	—	1	3	2	6	—	—	1	—	24
O-U-FE (25)	12	2	2	7	5	6	1	1	1	—	5	3	—	1	—	1	2	—	49
O-U-S (2)	—	—	—	7	—	—	—	—	1	—	—	—	—	1	—	—	—	—	9
T-OI-CM (2)	—	1	—	—	—	—	—	—	—	—	—	2	—	—	—	—	1	—	4
T-NI-CM (4)	—	—	—	1	2	—	—	—	—	—	—	2	2	1	—	—	1	—	9
T-NI-FE (1)	—	—	—	—	2	2	—	—	—	—	4	2	—	—	—	—	1	—	11
T-U-S (1)	—	—	—	—	—	—	—	—	—	—	—	—	—	—	—	—	—	—	0
T-U-FE (1)	1	—	—	1	—	—	—	—	—	—	—	1	1	—	—	—	—	1	5
T-U-CP (2)	2	—	—	—	2	—	—	—	—	—	—	1	—	—	—	—	—	1	6
Total	70	5	5	56	24	19	5	3	9	1	27	19	5	9	3	1	6	2	269[c]

NOTE: Three types of cases were excluded from the tabulation: pending decisions; complaints by non-occupational groups and groups with ambiguous identity; and complaints by independent international confederations.

The heading "NTU vs. own" refers to cases brought by national trade unions against their own government; "NTU vs. foreign" analogously.

[a] The letter symbols are explained in Table 22 (p. 375), note a. The classifications are qualified by notes a through f of Table 27 (p. 394).

[b] No cases in "NTU vs. own" and "NTU vs. foreign."

[c] The total number of cases used for the table was 251. Joint complaints were tabulated separately for each international confederation.

ILO circles insist that the political identity of the complainant is wholly irrelevant, as is the political context in which the complaint is lodged. The fact that the ICFTU is successful far more often than the WFTU is attributed, by the ILO, to the care with which the free unions prepare their cases and to the merits of the allegations. Nothing in Table 30 contradicts this argument. The table merely shows the sharp statistical differences between the nature of the complainant and the degree of success the complaint has achieved; it does not offer data on the reasons for the differences. With this word of caution, let us examine the figures.

The Western democracies, the target of the single largest bloc of complaints, got off relatively lightly. Not only were no sanctions ever imposed against them, but the request to change conduct was used on only a dozen occasions. Four involved ICFTU charges in the colonial context, and eight involved WFTU charges predominantly in the colonial and human rights realms. The great bulk of the complaints presented by the WFTU and national unions was dismissed. But note that the ICFTU fared much better in the charges brought against democracies with a free enterprise orientation, namely Japan and Canada. On the other hand, national unions complaining against their own governments in the democracy/underdeveloped/free enterprise syndrome did quite well, whereas the WFTU did not. The countries involved were primarily Greece and Costa Rica. All complainants were quite successful in castigating violations of trade union rights in rapidly industrializing oligarchies with a free enterprise orientation, namely Argentina, Venezuela, and Turkey. Against underdeveloped oligarchies with free enterprise doctrines, the WFTU did relatively well; so did the ICFTU when the free unions made the effort to intervene. It is only here, incidentally, that national unions acting against a foreign government were ever successful in obtaining the Committee's indictment of a government.[30] Whenever the ICFTU and ICCTU complained against a communist regime, their efforts were crowned with success. But success also attended the WFTU and ICFTU complaints against South Africa, Spain, and Portugal. One cannot escape the conclusion, then, that WFTU complaints, whatever their merits, tended to be effective against regimes not actively engaged in a domestic or international struggle relating to the Cold War, as well as in certain colonial situations also championed by other unions. The WFTU was equally successful in pushing genuine human rights issues against regimes which, for all their anti-communism, were also anathema to the free unions.

As Table 31 shows, however, the ICFTU was almost always successful, no matter who provided the target, since the number of plain dismissals stands at a mere 20 per cent. And charges brought jointly by the WFTU and ICFTU scored some measure of success in all but 8 per cent of the cases. These figures suggest that the chances are almost overwhelming that

TABLE 31

FREEDOM OF ASSOCIATION: COMPLAINANTS, DISPOSITIONS, AND ISSUES
(Per cent)

Complainant and no. of complaints	Disposition of case																	"Sanctions" recommended		
	Dismissed						Dismissed with request to "review"					Govt. requested to change conduct							
	TU	HR	Col.	CW	Not clear	Total	TU	HR	Col.	CW	Total	TU	HR	Col.	CW	Total	HR	CW	Total
WFTU (103)	14	11	16	22	5	68	2	8	2	2[d]	14	5[e]	7[e]	5[k]	1[m]	18	–	–	0
ICFTU (21)	5	5	5	5	–	20	5	5	–	–	10	9[f]	27	–	9[n]	45	5	20	25
ICCTU (12)	24	8	8	–	–	42	–	8	8	–	16	16	8	–	8	32	–	8	8
WFTU, ICFTU (12)	8	–	–	–	–	8	–	–	17[b]	–	16	–	34[h]	42[l]	–	76	–	–	0
WFTU, ICFTU, ICCTU (2)[a]	–	–	–	–	–	0	–	–	–	–	0	–	50	–	–	50	50	–	50
National union vs. own govt. (74)	38	11	11	10	6	76	3	3	–	3	9	8[g]	7[i]	–	–	15	–	–	0
National union vs. foreign govt. (28)	15	3	11	11	46	86	–	–	3[c]	–	3	–	8[j]	–	3[o]	11	–	–	0

NOTE: Percentages are rounded to nearest full number upward. Three types of cases were excluded from the tabulation: pending decisions; complaints by non-occupational groups and groups with uncertain identity; and complaints by independent regional confederations. The single joint ICFTU-ICCTU complaint was credited to ICFTU; the single joint WFTU-ICCTU complaint was credited to ICCTU. Total number of cases used: 252.

[a] Cases Nos. 72 (Venezuela), 143 (Spain).
[b] Cases Nos. 40 (France-Tunisia), 178 (U.K.-Aden).
[c] Case No. 59 (U.K.-Cyprus).
[d] Cases Nos. 48 (Japan), 104 (Iran).
[e] Primarily Latin American cases and South Africa.
[f] Cases Nos. 179 (Japan), 211 (Canada).
[g] Almost exclusively Greek cases.
[h] Cases Nos. 12 (Argentina), 102 (South Africa), 134/111 (Chile), 266 (Portugal).
[i] Cases Nos. 185 (Greece), 193 (Burma), 224 (Greece), 239 (Costa Rica), 253 (Cuba).
[j] Cases Nos. 109 (Guatemala), 167 (Jordan).
[k] Cases Nos. 75 (France-Madagascar), 103 (U.K.-Southern Rhodesia), 194 (U.K.-Singapore), 200 (South Africa), 251 (U.K.-Southern Rhodesia).
[l] Cases Nos. 16 (France-Morocco), 136 (U.K.-Cyprus), 152 (U.K.-Northern Rhodesia), 156 (France-Algeria), 221 (U.K.-Aden).
[m] Case No. 146 (Colombia).
[n] Cases Nos. 58 and 148 (Poland).
[o] Case No. 131 (Guatemala).

national unions, unaided by the large Internationals, will not prevail in
Geneva, often because their complaints are poorly drafted, ill-substantiated,
and considered by the Committee to raise points not essential to trade
unionism. Although the WFTU's total record of success is only slightly
better, it is clear that the communists' best chances of finding a sympathetic
hearing lie in the field of human rights. As far as the Cold War context is
concerned, only 3 per cent of the WFTU's total charges were in some measure successful, whereas their opponents' score stands at 29 per cent for
the ICFTU and 16 per cent for the ICCTU. Even though, in terms of successful hearings accorded by the Committee, pure trade union issues have
been gaining ground at the expense of all other types of issues, they continue to occupy a poor third after human rights and colonial issues. And
if subgoal dominance is to be avoided in the quasi-judicial protection of
trade union freedom, it is just as well that this should remain the case.

SPILL-OVER: FROM TRADE UNION RIGHTS
TO CIVIL LIBERTIES

This conclusion suggests that measures for the protection of trade union
freedom will not automatically enlarge an authoritative and legitimate
international task. Cumulative blows in the cause of international integration, to be successful in terms of transformations of the environment, must
"spill over" from the specific into a more diffuse context. Trade union
issues must increasingly appear in the guise of general human rights issues
in order to demonstrate a spill-over capacity. The Committee must progressively facilitate the application of its dispositions to an ever-widening
circle of contexts, and thus rule on a larger and larger variety of cases in
which the circumstances may not be of a purely trade union character. To
what extent, then, has the twelve-year record of the Committee demonstrated a spill-over capacity?

Two answers are possible. One indicator of spill-over capacity is provided by Official Functionalism itself, the self-conscious concern of ILO
personnel to extend the influence of the Committee's work; the other, however, must be superimposed by the analyst on his subjects and cannot therefore be isolated simply by recapitulating ILO doctrine. We must proceed
to place that doctrine into the context of functional analysis. First, let us
examine the argument of Official Functionalism.

The dispositions of the Committee, notwithstanding their origin in a context of conciliation rather than adjudication, are held to be "law." Further,
the purpose of this law is to jog member governments into the maximum
degree of compliance with the norms of freedom of association defined in
Conventions 87 and 98. This doctrine gives us the first implicit tenet of a
spill-over capacity: *Conventions 87 and 98 are used as the relevant yard-
sticks for blaming or exonerating governments, irrespective of whether*

they have ratified these texts. The McNair Committee had already proceeded on this assumption in making its factual survey. Being explicitly bound by these Conventions is held to be unnecessary because of the more general terms of the ILO Constitution and its capacity to generate binding norms. The rigor of the argument is moderated only by the admission that certain procedural niceties must be observed in presenting allegations of violations, and that the application of the Conventions may vary with the degree of political and economic development.[31]

But this admission contains a major drawback. Is freedom of association for trade unions an autonomous right that can be presumed to demand recognition regardless of the general respect for civil liberties? Obviously, an admission of unequal conditions of political development would suggest a negative answer. Sociologically, freedom of association must be regarded as only one aspect of a general respect for individual and group liberty anchored in public law. It can be administered only if public law also recognizes a whole series of cognate immunities, such as freedom from arbitrary arrest, exile, and detention, freedom of speech and assembly, and the right to the due process of law. Logically, it would follow that unless the ILO procedure is used to advance the progress of civil liberties on a broad front, there can be no meaningful anchoring of trade union freedom.

Official Functionalism can hardly be blamed for shunning this blatant inference. "The extent to which freedom of association for trade union purposes is to be regarded as a particular application of freedom of association in general," says Jenks, "or as a distinct right governed in certain respects by special rules remains open to debate, and there continue to be considerable divergences of view as to what the concept of freedom of association implies and the relationship of freedom of association to varying forms of political and economic organization."[32] And it turns out that the Functionalists in Geneva hope to be able to protect trade union rights as an independent entity, even though these liberties are admitted to be part of a larger whole. But to make such an admission, and to grant at the same time that unequal development makes application difficult, is to condemn a program to inertia, if not to failure. Hence a judicious effort at separating annoyingly interconnected contexts is a reasonable way to attempt to escape the dilemma.

There is, of course, an inevitable footnote to this argument, contributed by Official Functionalism itself. If contexts have to be separated, the Committee cannot be expected to deal fully and formally with complaints originating in a context of political instability and nationalist fervor. While the ILO points proudly to the Committee's consistent refusal to accept a *government's* claim that a given complaint is purely political, it also stresses that when the *Committee* discovers such to be the case, it will dismiss the complaint. And, claims Jenks, "the rejection of complaints on account of their political nature has not been a source of weakness in the procedure but an element in its strength."[33] Gratifying though it must be to transform, by the magic of words, a functional drawback into a source of strength, a continuation of this policy would surely destroy any spill-over capacity inherent in the protection of trade union freedom.

This conclusion, however, is the result of a different type of functional analysis, the type that provides our other indicator of spill-over. The successful transformation of the international environment by way of an expanded central task does rest on the separability of contexts. If every aspect of policy funneled into a United Nations agency were imbued with Cold War controversy, there would be very little spill-over and less task expansion. The growth of legitimate and authoritative international tasks, furthermore, depends on a high degree of functional specificity: the task must relate to directly experienced needs and demands of important national elites. Why then insist that there is a connection betwen trade union freedom and a free society in a larger sense? Why not rest the argument on the specific needs of trade unions? An excess of functional specificity condemns a task to triviality in terms of larger social concerns. An overconcentration on trade union issues would seriously delay the growth of a genuine functional law of human rights because, once trade union demands have been established and gratified, there is little left to spill over from mundane contract negotiation to civil liberties. Integration in the field of human rights requires an enlargement of the functionally specific realm to comprehend more and more varied aspects of freedom, though it is quite desirable— given the nature of the international environment—that the process begin with trade union rights in the narrower sense. And the enlargement of functional specificity, in turn, demands that the initial field of action be imbued with a high analytical spill-over capacity. Viewed in this way, the tendency toward more and more trade union issues in the flow of complaints is undesirable; but the efforts of the WFTU to push into the limelight—for whatever propagandistic and malicious reasons—genuine human rights matters in Latin America provide a "eufunctional" impetus. Yet the Cold War issues introduced by the ICFTU, ICCTU, and WFTU, irrespective of the fact that the anti-communist variety has been endorsed and the anti-Western rejected by the ILO, are "dysfunctional" because in the nature of things they cannot lead to a constructive spill-over.

Official Functionalism rests its argument in large measure on the law-creating propensity of the machinery that has been set up for protecting trade union freedom. The "law" involved consists of procedural and substantive decisions on the part of the Committee, couched in the language and form of conciliation. The ILO seems content to consider as "law" anything officially pronounced and publicly invested in the ceremonial aura of law; it seems less concerned with insisting on a regular measure of observation and implementation on the part of the defendants. If "law" is the equivalent of formal invocation, this would do very well. But functional law rests, not on invocation, but on the experiencing of converging needs on the part of elite actors, needs that give rise to norms accepted in subsequent conduct because they facilitate order, are predictable, and satisfy demands. If the trick of the functional dialectic results in the acceptance of norms that had their origin in mutually antagonistic claims and the desire for disorder, the argument would still remain intact. Subsequent "learning" by the chief actors persuaded them to accept the new norms despite the hostile context from which their opposing claims first arose. Their very hostilities, via political learning, lead to convergences. But these in turn must lead to a spill-over into tasks of roughly equal interest to all, not into the excessively specific context of trade union issues nor into the excessively general realm of gross ideological confrontation. The escape formula of Official Functionalism, because it seeks to sidestep this need, commits itself to a notion of law far too vague and hortatory to be of utility in the process of international integration.

In fairness, however, it must be admitted that this formula dates from the experience accumulated by the ILO Committee during its first six years of operation. It has not been reformulated since. Yet I suggest that the trend of the decisions made since 1958 is such as to suggest a definite spill-over into the human rights field and a much greater readiness to deal with civil liberties in general terms, whether these arise in a colonial or trade union context. It may be undesirable to admit this trend from the viewpoint of the Official Functionalist. Our functional preoccupation, however, gives us no right to ignore it; and if we wish to substantiate our claim that the specific trade union context is growing ever wider, we must examine the substantive legal rulings of the Committee.

We shall divide the Committee's pronouncements into (a) rulings defining areas of permissible governmental regulation of trade unions, (b) ambivalent rulings seeking to steer a middle course between full trade union freedom and residual governmental powers, and (c) rulings unambiguously defining areas of trade union autonomy. We shall contrast the trend that prevailed during the period 1950–57 with what developed thereafter. For the first period, I shall rely exclusively on the magisterial presentation of Jenks, without citing specific cases; for the subsequent period, however, reference to the Committee's cases will illustrate the evolution of its jurisprudence.

(a) *Permissible governmental regulation.* One line of decisions ruled that national law remains supreme and governs a variety of situations that relate to trade union activities. Thus, no state is under obligation to permit the headquarters of international unions to be established on its territory, or to issue passports to union officials. Union security arrangements are wholly a matter of national law, provided due process is used in administering them. The state may supervise union treasuries to guard against misuse, though it may not control union finance or selectively subsidize unions. The Committee approves of tripartite arrangements that institutionalize trade union representation on administrative boards and recommends their use; but no state is obligated to adhere to this procedure. Although the right of assembly is insisted on as absolute for trade union purposes, the Committee also holds that no violation of freedom of association occurs when political meetings, riots, or demonstrations of unions are prohibited or broken up. Normal criminal conviction of trade unionists cannot be considered suppression of freedom of association. Such conviction may properly disqualify a worker from union membership, or may result in his expulsion from the country. The arrest of trade union officials is not anti-union discrimination if the government can show that the arrest was unrelated to trade union duties.

Two doctrines operated particularly strikingly in favor of the state before 1958: the distinction between "political" concerns and "proper trade union" activity, and the Committee's rulings that certain countries "in their present state of development" may properly regulate key trade union activities. We find that the conviction of trade unionists for political offenses is considered a normal criminal conviction; hence a variety of national measures taken for the purging of Communists from the trade union movement have been upheld as legal.[34] National regulation of union funds, the official registration of unions, and governmental insistence on separation between political and trade union activities on the part of organized workers are all acceptable in "the early stages" of economic development. Finally, the Committee does not consider general racial discrimination—as distinguished from discrimination for purposes of preventing a worker from joining the union of his choice—a violation of freedom of association.

The sweep of both doctrines was considerably attenuated after 1958. It is true that in several new African states the "early stages of development" doctrine was seemingly reaffirmed. In any event, no severe condemnations were pronounced against governments suppressing unions accused of "anti-national" activity, political manifestations, or attendance at proscribed trade union meetings.[35] In a good many other cases, however, the reverse trend appeared. Dahomey was reprimanded for suppressing unions, and Britain was admonished to be less restrictive with respect to a wide sweep of trade union activities in colonial areas.[36] Several military dictatorships under which rudimentary trade unions were struggling for survival were admonished to cease regulating trade union meetings, elections, and organization.[37] No allowance for pre-democratic and pre-industrial conditions was made in favor of the Libyan government when it sought to suppress pro-Nasser unions.[38]

The distinction between "political" and "trade union" activities is also giving way. In a number of recent Middle Eastern cases, the Committee took jurisdiction over complaints and remonstrated with governments, even though the allegations referred to union activities bordering on sedition and involved government suppression of communist sympathizers.[39] But the most striking *volte-face* has come about in the case of Greece. Before 1957 the Committee had found it expedient not to interfere consistently with the Greek government's efforts to isolate and remove trade unionists suspected of communist ties, citing the civil war and political unrest as reasons for non-intervention. In more recent rulings, however, the Committee has shown increasing impatience with this argument, justifying its change of attitude on the grounds that the Greek situation had become more stable. Greece was sharply reprimanded for interfering with trade union elections, dismissing, arresting, and deporting workers without due process for trade union activities, suspending trade union newspapers, and intimidating workers.[40] In short, with the ebbing of Cold War charges, the Committee has permitted this type of complaint to spill over into the realm of general human rights, thus cutting away at the earlier immunity of governments.

(*b*) *Governmental regulation subject to some control.* The Committee dislikes the custom followed in some countries of bestowing favors on certain unions through a special registration procedure, and has recommended "reconsideration" of such measures to assure their non-discriminatory nature. Civil servants must have the right to organize and protect themselves against anti-union actions; but the state may properly prohibit them from striking, and may insist that they do not affiliate with the general trade union movement, provided other measures for independence and equality are allowed. Governmental certification of unions is an interference with freedom of association only if genuine union activities are thereby controlled; registration to control political activities, especially in time of acute civil unrest, is permissible. In "the early stages of development," it may be legal for governments to establish model union constitutions and by-laws, and to exercise some supervision over union elections. But no union official may be removed because of the loss of his regular employment. Yet the Committee often calls on governments "to review" this kind of legislation to ascertain whether it does not limit freedom of association. Loyalty and security programs are legal if the worker is protected by due process; but they constitute an infringement of freedom of association if a worker is prevented from joining a union of his choice. The Committee affirmed that there is no generally accepted definition of the right to strike.

Therefore it upheld national measures limiting strikes, while affirming the general right, by noting the superiority of national law with respect to civil servants, essential services (though their scope was hedged with limitations), existing collective agreements, and the observance of conciliation and arbitration terms. Governmental suppression of strikes affecting national security or bordering on political demonstrations was deemed not to interfere with trade union rights.

The difficulty, clearly, lies in determining what is "political." As far as the ILO is concerned, the purpose of trade unions is to protect the economic and social interests of workers. Hence the Committee often recommended that unions minimize their involvement in politics, especially in revolutionary contexts. It has been unwilling to examine complaints of governmental favors to allied trade union movements. General martial law and the suppression of civil rights are not regarded as interference with trade unions, unless the unions are singled out for punishment. Unions dissolved as a result of the conviction of their leaders for subversion or sedition are not deemed victims of anti-union activities. In the "early stages of development," governments may restrict the right to join federations and internationals, though they are asked to "review" such decisions.[41] Similarly, governments may restrict attendance at international union meetings and the international exchange of union publications if political activity suggesting subversion is implied. When there is no political involvement, no restrictions on national or international meetings and publications for genuine trade union purposes are to be tolerated. The distinction may make sense in a society in which the habits of functionally specific pluralism are already established; its application to the developing and underdeveloped world, in which actors are not always conscious of these distinctions, may defeat the very purpose of the ILO program.[42]

Since 1958 this recognition has been reflected increasingly in ILO decisions. The exonerating circumstances implicit in the "early development" doctrine have been minimized. Several governments have been admonished, notwithstanding the youth of the trade union movement, to permit affiliation with Internationals, to cease discriminating in registration formalities against anti-government unions, and to permit the right to strike.[43] More significant, the distinction between political and trade union activities has been weakened in fact, though not in the *obiter dicta*. Repeated blows have been imparted to induce governments to extend the right to strike and to organize to such civil servants as teachers, municipal employees, and railway workers. Trade unionists imprisoned for participating in "freedom movements" are still entitled to prompt and fair trials. Governments are no longer able simply to arrest trade unionists for threatening "the security of the state." In several cases, colonial authorities were admonished that they should not deregister unions, search union premises, arrest union leaders, merely because the men involved were suspected of sedition.[44] The recourse to "emergency legislation" in order to prohibit strikes, and to the military mobilization of workers about to go on strike, came in for sharp denunciation in Argentina, in conjunction with intensified efforts on the part of the Committee to abolish the discrimination practiced in favor of "registered" unions.[45] Again, the area left to governmental discretion seems somewhat reduced as compared with the earlier period.

(c) *Trade union autonomy.* Under no circumstances may workers be forced to join a union or be prevented from joining on the basis of racial distinctions. Under no circumstances may workers in colonial territories be forced to join unions or affiliate with federations under the control of the metropole; instead they must be free to establish and maintain their own organizations.[46] Administrative regulation of unions, including registration, certification, or supervision of union business, is not permissible under the "without previous authorization" rule of Convention 87, *if* the administrator has sole discretion, not subject to judicial review.[47] The "due process" requirement here applies to the situations encountered earlier in which some administrative regulation is nevertheless tolerated. Governments are absolutely prohibited from engaging in unilateral administrative dissolution of unions. Federations have the full right to draw up and follow their own programs, even if these do not conform with government policy. Union officials, with the exception of the cases noted above, cannot be removed in order to weaken the movement. Federations and locals must have untrammeled opportunity to bargain collectively, though the government is not obligated to enforce the terms of an agreement. Further, governments may properly insist that parties to collective bargaining play a "constructive" role in general consultations regarding national policy.

Nothing in the more recent decisions of the Committee has weakened these tenets. On the contrary, in two very sweeping, protracted, and exhaustive cases these principles have been extended and anchored in such a way as to deny openly the international legitimacy of totalitarian trade union systems enshrined in national constitutions.[48] With this development, the "double standard" whereby communist countries were previously denied the escape hatch afforded by the doctrines of "early development" and "political activity" has been eliminated. The communist countries might have profited from these doctrines if the Committee had been willing to consider the special conditions of a socialist economy as warranting exemption. As it was, they were singled out for special rebuke.[49] Now, at least, other political systems, claiming equally unique and nationally anchored doctrines and institutions, are also denied immunity. And human rights norms have spilled over as a result.

THE AUTHORITY OF THE COMMITTEE: GOVERNMENTS
AND IMPLEMENTATION

Such, then, is the "law" of trade union freedom as developed and pronounced by the ILO Committee on Freedom of Association. But unless we place this jurisprudence into the crucible of actual implementation, we shall be unable to carry the law beyond the level of invocation. Hence we must ask: Which governments tend to carry out the recommendations of the Committee? In what situations do these governments cooperate with the Committee, and when do they seek to block it?

An initial test of the Committee's authority is given us by national acceptance of ILO jurisdiction over complaints alleging violations of trade union freedom. Characteristically, the South African government objected as early as 1950 to the establishment of the Fact-Finding and Conciliation Commission, on the grounds that it had not been based on a mandate from the Conference and the member states. Although the Governing Body was competent to create investigatory bodies, South Africa argued, it had no right to create agents possessing powers of sanction without the express consent of the government concerned. Australia agreed with this general indictment of a slow drift toward supranationality. The criticism was sufficiently telling to induce the Office to make clear that the requirement of national consent remained intact, and that the Commission therefore enjoyed no supranational judicial powers. France, Lebanon, and the Soviet Union sought to block the creation of the Commission on somewhat different grounds. They argued in the ECOSOC that because trade union freedom was an important and central aspect of human rights in general, the United Nations should not delegate any powers connected with it to a specialized agency.[50] Once these initial charges had been made, the jurisdiction of the Governing Body's Committee was formally challenged only by South Africa and Argentina, whose invocation of the non-intervention clause of the U.N. Charter had no effect. No significant challenge to central authority, then, was heard throughout the Committee's life.

This, of course, does not mean that governments have been uniformly enthusiastic and cooperative. The major democracies never liked the Committee, but they learned to live with it as the best way to counter communist charges with full publicity. France, Britain, and the United States respond to ILO requests for information, and have a good record of implementing Committee decisions.* Although they do not seek an expansion

---

* The major exception to France's cooperative attitude was the Algerian situation. Here France refused to furnish full information or to change its repressive policies in response to Committee admonitions. The eventual dismissal of the charges stems from the change of regime.

of the Committee's mandate or revel in supranationality, they appreciate the importance of the publicity in defending their policies. Communist countries, too, have had an excellent record of cooperation since 1954, meeting all requests to supply full information about their trade union practices. The Soviets, between 1954 and 1958, took special delight in exploiting the procedure for anti-colonial and Cold War purposes, and thus could not very well denounce the machinery when it was turned against them. However, with regard to changes of conduct (as opposed to supplying information), no communist government ever acted consistently on any Committee request. Latin American oligarchical regimes cooperate fitfully; they tend not to answer requests for information, and when they do, the replies are often inadequate. But their record in introducing improvements in response to Committee requests is far from bad.* Japan is exceedingly responsive to requests for explanations and information, and moderately responsive to requests for changes in policy. In short, there is no ready correlation between cooperativeness in furnishing information and accepting the jurisdiction of the Committee, on the one hand, and implementing its decisions on the other. Even South Africa and Argentina find it useful to reply to requests for explanations and information. Iran, Greece, and Egypt supplied information in answer to "political" allegations after initially resisting the requests. Libya and Costa Rica invited ILO visits.

How, then, can we evaluate the record of national implementation? There is no unequivocal test. ICFTU officials, for example, are far from certain in many instances about whether there has been compliance with ILO decisions.[51] They agree with Office personnel in believing that in many situations improvements are introduced in response to the mere submission of a complaint, the placing of a complaint on the docket, and the receipt of requests for explanation from Geneva. In the huge majority of cases in which the complaint merely alleges the illegal arrest of a trade union leader in a non-totalitarian country, the person concerned is released upon the threat of action from Geneva.[52] Obviously, there is no way of summarizing the success of the procedure in quantitative terms. But we know that requests to "review" legislation or policy, appended to a dismissal, may be effective. We also know that a mere request for information can have the same result. In short, the actual procedure of the Committee is not very different from that of the Committee of Experts on the Application of Conventions, and the manner in which it slowly obtains compliance falls into the same category of international pressure.

A quantitative evaluation is possible only with respect to the complaints that reached the stage of specific recommendations to governments to

---

* The Committee feels that Paraguay and the Dominican Republic improved law and practice as a result of the complaints against them.

change their conduct or the suggesting of sanctions. There were 64 such cases in our sample of 272. How can we tell whether improvements have taken place, since neither the government concerned nor the ILO makes any public announcement on this point? The conclusion must be inferred from the context. Whenever the Committee's report acknowledges a change in policy or congratulates the government for having made improvements, our problem is solved. But often the Committee does not express itself in such clear terms. I have assumed that a violation of human rights continued to prevail whenever, in the later phases of a case, the original allegations are made once more, whenever the Committee proclaims itself unable to dismiss the case because the government does not submit adequate replies, and whenever new cases are submitted alleging the same infractions already ruled on by earlier Committee decisions. Prolonged correspondence with a government over a given situation, not accompanied by remarks about the removal of the violation, is also assumed to imply non-improvement. In many cases, a part of the alleged violation was eventually rectified, although some other part might continue to give rise to correspondence. Such situations have been scored as implying "some improvement."

In all, 30 member governments were requested to change their conduct; eight of them were democracies, eight were totalitarians and fourteen were oligarchies. As Table 32 shows, the attainment of "great improvement" is confined to democracies. Three of the five instances involved also the withdrawal of colonial rule and the reforms associated therewith; two involved a violent change of regime in Venezuela. But we should note that neither France nor Britain proved responsive to the Committee's authority in colonial cases in which the issue of sedition figured largely, or in which the governments were seeking to implement a far-reaching and ambitious policy of "integration" into another nation. Barring this complication, the democracies were responsive to international criticism and introduced reforms in line with Committee requests. Some improvement was also registered by Brazil and Canada.

The same cannot be said of the totalitarians. The communist nations have proved quite impervious to sanctions and requests for changes in conduct. Changes in the position of trade unions did occur in Poland and Hungary, but this cannot be attributed to the ILO, even if pressure from Geneva acted as a supplementary stimulus, and acceptance of ILO requests served as a mode of gaining international respectability for Gomulka and Kadar. Neither Portugal nor South Africa has reacted in any way. Spain, however, has liberalized some of the restrictions under which trade unions had lived for so long, though she is still far from applying in full the principles of freedom of association that the Committee preaches to Madrid in the continuing confrontation. In this case, as in the cases of Poland and Hungary, it is likely that gradual domestic reform is increasingly desired by the

TABLE 32

Freedom of Association: National Implementation of ILO Decisions

TOTAL NUMBER OF CASES: 64

> *Great improvement: 5.* United Kingdom, 2; France; Venezuela, 2.
>
> *Some improvement: 27.* Argentina, 3; Greece, 2; United Kingdom, 2; Chile; Hungary, 3; Cuba; Dominican Republic, 2; Poland, 2; Brazil; Canada; Japan; Jordan; Libya; Morocco; Paraguay; Senegal; Spain; Sudan; Turkey.
>
> *No improvement: 32.* Argentina, 5; Greece, 5; United Kingdom; South Africa, 5; Chile, 2; France, 2; Guatemala, 3; Cuba; U.S.S.R., 2; Burma; Colombia; Costa Rica; Czechoslovakia; Portugal; Thailand.

Argentina (8 cases)

> *Some improvement:* Case No. 140: Suppression of union activities during civil war. Cases Nos. 172, 231: Right to strike of civil servants; deregistration of public employees and bankers' unions.
>
> *No improvement:* Cases Nos. 12, 190, 258: Discrimination in favor of registered unions. Cases Nos. 192, 216: Suppression of strikes.

Greece[a,c] (7 cases)

> *Some improvement:* Case No. 105: Suppression of bankers' union. Case No. 157: Control over local elections; loyalty screening.
>
> *No improvement:* Case No. 256: Control over union administration. Case No. 234: Dismissal of trade union leaders. Cases Nos. 185, 224: Arrest and deportation of union leaders. Case No. 240: Interference in union elections.

United Kingdom (6 cases)

> *Great improvement:* Case No. 136: Suppression of union activity and strikes during civil war in Cyprus. Case No. 152: Restrictions on activities of African unions in No. Rhodesia.
>
> *Some improvement:* Cases Nos. 103, 251: Prohibition of African unions in So. Rhodesia. Case No. 221: Restrictions on civil servants' union activity in Aden.
>
> *No improvement:* Case No. 194: Control of unions suspected of sedition in Singapore.

South Africa (5 cases)

> *No improvement:* Cases Nos. 102, 145, 183, 200, 261: Suppression of all African unions and prohibitions of right to strike.

Chile[d] (3 cases)

> *Some improvement:* Case No. 271: Discrimination against certain union leaders.
>
> *No improvement:* Cases Nos. 10, 134: Control of union elections, meetings and administration to control sedition.

France (3 cases)

> *Great improvement:* Case No. 16: Right of workers to organize without restriction in Morocco.
>
> *No improvement:* Case No. 75: Restrictions on union publication (Madagascar). Case No. 156: Restrictions on all union activities, arrests, and repressions for sedition (Algeria).

Guatemala (3 cases)

> *No improvement:* Cases Nos. 109, 131, 144: Restrictions on all union activities; arrest of leaders for sedition.

TABLE 32 (*continued*)

Hungary[a,b] (3 cases)
Some improvement: Cases Nos. 19, 158: Position of unions in communist system. Case No. 160: Suppression of 1956 revolt.

Cuba (2 cases)
Some improvement: Case No. 159: Interference in union meetings; intimidation.
No improvement: Case No. 253: Shooting of workers.

Dominican Republic[a] (2 cases)
Some improvement: Case No. 3: Repression of independent unions. Case No. 151: Prohibition of right to strike; prior approval for collective agreements.

Poland[a,b] (2 cases)
Some improvement: Case No. 58: Position of unions in communist system. Case No. 148: Suppression of strikes.

U.S.S.R. (2 cases)
No improvement: Case No. 111: Position of unions in communist system. Case No. 155: Suppression of Hungarian revolt.

Venezuela[b] (2 cases)
Great improvement: Cases Nos. 2, 72: Suppression of trade unions.

Brazil (1 case)
Some improvement: Case No. 125: Discrimination against civil servants.

Burma (1 case)
No improvement: Case No. 193: Restrictions on union activities of civil servants.

Canada (1 case)
Some improvement: Case No. 211: Anti-union legislation in Newfoundland.

Colombia (1 case)
No improvement: Case No. 146: Massacres of workers; prohibition of right to strike for civil servants.

Costa Rica (1 case)
No improvement: Case No. 239: Restrictions on right of plantation workers to organize.

Czechoslovakia (1 case)
No improvement: Case No. 14: Position of unions in communist system.

Japan (1 case)
Some improvement: Case No. 179: Right of civil servants to strike, organize, and bargain.

Jordan (1 case)
Some improvement: Case No. 167: Dissolution of union during civil war.

Libya (1 case)
Some improvement: Case No. 274: Interference with right to organize; persecution of union leaders.

Morocco (1 case)
Some improvement: Case No. 232: Restrictions on right to organize.

(*continued on next page*)

TABLE 32 (*concluded*)

Paraguay[a] (1 case)
   Some improvement: Case No. 168: Suppression of union activities, right to organize anti-govt. unions; prohibition of strikes.

Portugal (1 case)
   No improvement: Case No. 266: Position of unions in Corporatist system.

Senegal (1 case)
   Some improvement: Case No. 248: Persecution of dissident union leaders.

Spain (1 case)
   Some improvement: Case No. 143: Prohibition of right to organize and strike.

Sudan (1 case)
   Some improvement: Case No. 191: Suppression of all trade unions.

Thailand (1 case)
   No improvement: Case No. 202: Suppression of all trade unions.

Turkey (1 case)
   Some improvement: Case No. 169: Prohibition of right to affiliate.

---

[a] Ratified Convention 87 and/or 98 as a result of pressure by Committee.

[b] Improvement in the situation cannot be credited directly to work of the Committee but is connected with change in government. The same is true in Case No. 13 (Bolivia) and Cases Nos. 1 and 92 (Peru), even though these never resulted in formal requests to change conduct.

[c] In Case No. 18, clemency was asked for trade union leaders condemned to death for sedition. The appeal was successful.

[d] Case No. 271 is still pending despite the seriousness of the charges.

---

government itself. Hence compliance with ILO requests can be used as a means for gaining international respectability and legitimacy without major cost to desired national policy. The net impact of the ILO machinery in these countries may be dismissed as negligible.

There remain fourteen oligarchies and two democracies with underdeveloped economies (Greece and Costa Rica) that cannot be treated in such direct terms. The case of Greece is especially instructive. After playing a minor role in the Cold War drama staged by the WFTU, the early indictments of the government's repressive practices were all dismissed on "political" and "civil war" grounds. However, as Greek national unions learned to use the ILO machinery, proceeding to embarrass their government unmercifully, the character of the Committee's decisions began to change too. The fact remains that violations continue, and that the responsiveness of Athens has at best been sporadic. But it has been better than Argentina's, where the Cold War issue could not be cited as an excuse for repression. The ponderous nature of international diplomacy and the ILO machinery is evident when we find the same issue—discrimination against unregistered unions—still alive in 1963, even though it was dealt with as early as 1951.

Greece, Argentina, Guatemala, Chile, and Colombia all seem to point to the same lesson: trade union repression connected with civil unrest and general modernizing-revolutionary activity will not be checked by international criticism so long as the national scene remains in turmoil. Such criticism may be effective after the turmoil subsides with the victory of the ruling oligarchy. The cases of Jordan, the Dominican Republic, Libya, Morocco, Paraguay, and Turkey suggest that some reforms will be made once the oligarchy feels secure and experiences the need to satisfy world critics. Obviously such reforms tend to be short-lived; the very next attempt to overthrow the regime and supplant it with a modernizing group will bring into play new repressions that cannot be rapidly stopped by complaints from Geneva. And we should bear in mind that the new repressions will be practiced by whichever group wins: the traditional oligarchy will reimpose the earlier restrictions; its challenger will almost certainly proceed to repress trade unionists not allied with the revolutionary group.

In a final pair of countries—Thailand and Burma—international criticism is of no great avail because the policy of repression forms part and parcel of the efforts of a reformist-military oligarchy to stifle criticism and modernize the country in line with the junta's plans. Though reformist in intent, the politics of reform in these contexts are too authoritarian to permit toleration of possible rival centers of organized influence. In short, the record suggests no permanent structural changes of the national scene in favor of increased freedom. The feedback of the Committee's work on modernizing oligarchies has been minimal.

I suspect that the authority of the machinery will be greatest in countries that have already achieved the "take-off" stage in the evolution of a democratic-pluralistic society, irrespective of their degree of industrialization. They already possess the structural requisites of pluralistic democracy, though the ideological underpinnings of that elusive faith may still be weak. They have a syndrome of domestic political demands pushing toward the welfare state, even though these voices have not yet prevailed. The case of Japan may well be of symptomatic significance here.

The conservative government of Japan, since 1958, has been attacked by its General Council of Trade Unions, the All-Japan Postal Workers' Union, the Japan Teachers' Union, the Japanese Congress of Government Employees' Unions, the National Railway Workers' Union, and the All-Japan Prefectural and Municipal Workers' Union.[53] The allegations all hinged upon the apparent efforts of the government to "roll back" the very liberal rules regarding trade union rights introduced under the Occupation. The government was accused of placing legal restrictions on the right of these civil service unions to organize autonomously and to strike, and of refusing to bargain collectively with them.[54] In 1960 the allegations were expanded to include charges of police search of trade union premises, interference with union meetings, and the dismissal from their jobs of active unionists. The Committee has been negotiating with the government for five years over these charges. At first it requested merely additional information, including details of how judicial remedies had been exhausted by the complaining unions (who lost their case). It then strongly recommended that Japan ratify Convention 87, while holding that violations of Convention 98 had indeed taken place. It also requested that she amend or repeal the legislation involved in the charges, and make arbitration available as a compensatory guarantee for civil servants deprived of the right to strike. Finally, it suggested that these unions be registered in such a manner as not to expose them to the unilateral administrative control of the National Persónnel Authority. At the same time the government was exonerated from various charges alleging local procedural violations.

The response of the Japanese government has been equivocal. It agreed to ratify Convention 87 and to amend the disputed legislation. It introduced the necessary bills in the Diet—but as of 1964 they had not been passed. Negotiations with the unions involved were resumed, and some bargaining has apparently taken place. Yet the issue as a whole remains unresolved. It represents the international manifestation of a domestic struggle among Socialist unions eager to weaken the power of a conservatively controlled government apparatus and to accelerate the modernization of Japanese society in a pluralistic direction. Many of these unions represent the "new" middle class in Japan. They and their allies in the Socialist Party are able and willing to use domestic parliamentary means, among others, to attain their end. After the Ikeda government had already acceded to the ILO request to cooperate with the Fact-Finding and Conciliation Commission, the Socialists in June of 1964 sought to topple the government. This constitutes the first instance ever in which a parliamentary motion of no-confidence was used in the attempt to realize the implementation of a major ILO norm. The Socialists rejected attempts of the Liberal-Democratic Party to settle the ILO Committee's requests by means of a compromise and made the issue of ratifying Convention 87 a matter of confidence. Even though they lost, the effort is symptomatic of future possibilities.

Irrespective of the precise success of the ILO suggestions, it is of the greatest significance to the transformation of the international environment that ILO machinery should be utilized by national and world trade union federations. The proliferation of instances of this kind would deepen the feedback into national habits and structures, and speed up systemic transformation as a whole. But an intensification of this process is wholly dependent upon its taking place in a national setting in which pluralism is sufficiently established structurally not to slip back into patterns of repression once power is transferred to rising groups.* Hence the variegated

---

* Other countries in which analogous developments are conceivable are Turkey, Costa Rica, and the Dominican Republic since the demise of Trujillo. Perhaps Argentina and Greece, after a period of relative tranquillity, would also qualify.

oligarchies in which the Committee has brought about "some" improvement will not substantially feed the trend.

The fact remains that in at least half the cases that involved a request to change national conduct, no improvement was scored. The authority of the procedure is not yet fully established in the rules of the system. The most we can say is that governments hostile or reserved toward the machinery have muted their opposition. No major state welcomes being the target of charges by trade unionists challenging an aspect of national policy. Yet no government, since the famous flat refusal of Czechoslovakia, has declined to furnish information or engage in negotiation, even if these led to no improvement. All governments seem to realize that the tide of labor complaints is publicly irresistible, no matter how much they dislike the procedure privately. Governments are the prisoners of the functional dialectic: committed publicly to the human rights of workers and the progress of labor, they cannot consistently block the consideration of human rights issues even if these do flow from the hostile confrontations implicit in the Cold War and colonial contexts. Although substantive improvements are not easily squeezed from this vise, the procedural autonomy of the central machinery is confirmed nevertheless; and, in the appropriate national context, substantive reform may come about eventually. How else can we explain the fact that a number of states have ratified Convention 87 *after* that text had been used to embarrass and coerce them?

HOW MUCH INTEGRATION?

It is this dialectical quality of the process that is slighted by the Official Functionalist satisfaction with the system. ILO officials see the evolution of the "law" as taking an essentially unilinear causative path: there has allegedly emerged a genuine world consensus on the primacy of human rights; this consensus has been translated by the ILO into an authoritative mechanism for assuring the enjoyment of these rights, giving rise to a uniform world "law" concerning trade union freedom; the repercussions of this "law," as cemented by the ILO, will eventually produce a pluralistic international environment which, because it can deal with social tensions by cooperative means, will shore up world peace.

Let us follow Jenks's development of this theme. He argues that "this cooperation has been forthcoming because this development in the procedure corresponds to a real and generally recognized need; there is a widespread recognition that it is to the general advantage that allegations of infringements of trade union rights should be impartially and dispassionately examined internationally as a contribution to the relaxation of both international and social tension."[55] The Functional theme could hardly be developed in a more pristine manner. Jenks also argues that the authority of the ILO has fomented attitudes of cooperation among associations of workers and employers, and that governments have come to accept such associations as "necessary partners in the formulation and administration of public policy in regard to industrial and labor questions."[56] He continues disarmingly that "these influences are nonetheless real because they cannot be precisely measured in a survey" of ILO methods.[57] But they developed as a result of the cogency of the Philadelphia Doctrine, of the validity of a vision that correctly analyzed the "needs" of the world environment.[58] And they gain in strength because the various approaches and techniques of the ILO organs are all mutually complementary. The Organization grows in proportion to the success of its mystique and its acceptance in the consensus among its clients.[59]

As for the success of the machinery, Jenks claims that it stopped infringements by early international attention and publicity, cleared the air and clarified standards by dismissing large numbers of unwarranted charges, established a measure of international accountability even in the absence of ratified Conventions, promoted negotiations between governments and unions, and persuaded certain governments to change their law.[60] In short, the thrust of the system has been toward international pluralism and harmony. Not that Jenks sees the way as completely smooth. He concludes: "While, therefore, the ILO guarantees and standards are unequivocal, and substantial progress has already been made in their implementation, the task of securing their general application under infinitely varied national conditions remains one of herculean proportions."[61] Indeed it does. Perhaps, even, the vast heterogeneity of the international environment invalidates the very notion of a consensus that lies at the base of the argument.

Our survey of demands in the international system has given us no firm evidence of a programmatic consensus among the clients of the Organization. The same can be said of the quasi-judicial machinery for protecting trade union rights. To be sure, the ICFTU is quite satisfied, since it succeeded in bending the system to its ends. It has reason to congratulate itself for its successes in inducing governments to cooperate, sometimes very much against their initial inclinations. It can take comfort from the fact that improvements in national conditions have been made in a variety of socio-economic and political systems. And it knows that its best chances of long-run success lie neither in the Cold War nor in the colonial context, but in the field of basic human rights. The employers, however, have given little evidence of sharing this attitude. As for the governments, their uneven and inconsistent record in actually implementing Committee decisions speaks for itself.

In short, the Official Functionalist thesis seems to err in imputing a substantive consensus on human rights from the confrontation of demands. It errs further in mistaking the invocation of legal rules for the substance of law. And its projection of a unilinear pluralist path is untenable, despite the fact that many of the observations concerning the success of the machinery are both accurate and telling. There is as yet no autonomous intergroup consensus on the legitimacy of the function to protect human rights. At best there is a procedural consensus on the inevitability of the machinery's survival in the present international environment. But let us note again that this consensus stems from a dialectic of its own; it did not spring, in full beauty, from some universal commitment to the sanctity of human rights. It developed from hostile confrontations having their roots in basic ideological incompatibilities; such confrontations, far from being based on "need" or "convenience" or any other Functional magic, were brutally political. It may well be doubted that this phase of the international environment has yet been transcended. The final test of success, in terms of integrative impact, lies not so much in the jurisprudence of the Committee as in the use made of the procedure by national unions groping toward a pluralistic order. These, in turn, are much more likely to respond to the logic of hostile confrontation than to the will-o'-the-wisp of orderly and lawful cooperation.

It is the merit of functional analysis to point to indirect and circuitous paths of integration, rather than to rely on straight and narrow approaches that involve sonorous but empty phrases. The field of human rights is impregnated with indirect functional consequences closely related to the transformation of the international system. Its growth and constantly expanding legitimacy in the minds of groups in many nations surely reinforces the authority already accumulated by the ILO machinery. The relevance of this pursuit by the Organization, therefore, is in no way impaired by the imperfections of the ideology chosen to justify it. Tasks grow from needs even if these oppose one another. And authority increases in proportion to the involuntary commitment of elites to forces they had ill assessed and mistakenly nurtured.

PART III

The Utility of Functionalism

13. *World Integration and International Organization*

We began this study at the lofty level of general inquiry into the total network of strategic relationships at the international level. Much of the loftiness was lost as we began to consider certain very specific relationships in the realm of human welfare. I suspect that the initial exaltation reached vanishing point when we examined the functional relationships among welfare demands and policies in the specific structural context of the International Labor Organization. Our purpose, in concluding our survey, is to try to recapture that initial loftiness.

Such an effort must concern itself with linking the realm of welfare demands and policies in the ILO with the broader field of international welfare policies. More important, it must re-establish an analytical link, at least, between the network of international politics in general and its welfare component. This, then, brings us back to the world of systems and systemic relationships, and to the functional mode of analysis in understanding the transformation of international systems.

SYSTEM AND SUBSYSTEM

The ILO—contrary to its own earlier wishes—is but one of many institutions set up to deal with the advancement of man's welfare. For the actors whose inputs provide some of the policies eventually produced, the ILO represents only one of many channels for advancing their interests. Most of these actors concern themselves with welfare demands in the context of larger preoccupations involving the advancement of national and regional ways of life. In short, the ILO is a small component of a much larger network of relationships, a network established by the same units that articulate the life of the ILO. The specific structures covered by the label "ILO" operate as a part of other structures; the functions carried out by them flourish alongside and usually in subordination to other functions; the advancement of labor welfare engenders relationships that are merely a subsystem within the larger international system. It follows that the possible transformation of that system—the process we call "integration"—cannot be understood if we concentrate exclusively on the structural and functional properties of one subsystem.

Of what utility, then, is a study of the ILO? Since the ILO is not even a "typical" international agency, how can we justify the elaboration of a "case study"? The justification hinges on the conviction that the kinds of inputs and outputs evident in the ILO subsystem are symptomatic of the international environment. It derives hope from the fact that the units articulating inputs are the very actors who remain central to any transformation of the international system. I am persuaded that the ILO offers the opportunity for insights with respect to voluntary organizations at the international level not available in the context of other United Nations agencies. The attributes of the ILO subsystem are the same as those of the overall system, since the participating actors are identical. Although the structures are unique and the functions do not necessarily lend themselves to generalization, they still illustrate one strategic range of relationships. In short, the propositions derived from a study of the ILO may be viewed as hypotheses concerning integration in the context of the overall system.

The range of this utility remains subject to a number of strictures that must be set forth at the outset. We had best deal with them by distinguishing (a) the impact of the structures on the environment, (b) the impact of the evolving environment on the structures, and (c) the adequacy of our functional paradigm with respect to describing both sets of relationships.*

With respect to organizational impact on the international environment, our study of the ILO cannot "prove" anything about the transformation of the system; it can only suggest trends. ILO outputs remain comprehensible only as a part of the total UN output; actor inputs into ILO remain an integral part of the total world policies of these actors. Although the international environment undoubtedly underwent very dramatic changes since 1919—moving *simultaneously* toward and away from integration (depending on which set of functions is examined)—not even the most committed Functionalist would attribute these changes overwhelmingly to the work of the ILO. In many respects, the environment has changed so as to make national units converge in terms of policies and values; and in many respects this reflects convictions dealing with welfare. But to claim that this has been "caused" by the outputs of the ILO would be ludicrous. Nevertheless, the evolution of the ILO's organizational task remains im-

---

* At this point the reader may find it profitable to scan the definitions and formulations presented in the last two sections of Chapter 3, and the Paradigm presented in Chapter 5.

mediately relevant to our problem. New tasks have resulted from new inputs, which in turn resulted from interaction with earlier organizational outputs. The environmental forces, which earlier had evinced little interest in such tasks, acquiesced in them as a consequence of lessons learned and incorporated into their demands and expectations. The reverse, of course, has also occurred, thus giving rise to disintegration. To repeat: it is essential for the study of integration to highlight such structural impacts on the environment; but because they are confined to one subsystem, they remain illustrative, heuristic, and suggestive with respect to the larger system.

The impact of evolving environments on the structure of the subsystem, however, can be treated in more definitive terms. In other words, it is difficult to relate the performance of a given organization to a change in values, habits, and institutions in the environment of the system; it is hazardous to argue a direct integrative impact attributable to organizational performance. But it is quite safe to generalize about the effect of environmental inputs on the evolution of the organization. The movement toward greater institutional autonomy and authority can easily be correlated with the evolution of an organizational task that corresponds to patterns of environmental inputs. Here functional analysis is able to say something definite. Whereas its contribution based on the indicators of legitimacy and value change must remain suggestive, its conclusions based on the indicators of authority, autonomy, and peaceful change may be treated with less modesty.

Does our paradigm accurately predict the evolution of the organization toward greater autonomy and authority? Does it suggest patterns with respect to growing legitimacy and value change among the nations? Does it come to grips with such limited impact on systemic transformation as can reasonably be associated with a functionally specific subsystem carrying out strategic tasks? The cautious distinction here introduced between the evolution of the organization and the transformation of the environment suggests a scaling down of the claims advanced in Chapter 5. Only a review of the history of the ILO in systemic terms can answer these questions.

INTERNATIONAL SYSTEMS AND THE ILO

Any given international system of the concrete, actor-oriented variety, must be able to specify these constituents: the relationships being abstracted, or the pattern of inputs and outputs; the units formulating inputs and expecting to benefit from outputs; the environment from which the inputs flow and toward which the outputs are directed; the attributes that the system is presumed to possess as a result of the interaction among these constituents, e.g., stability, adaptiveness, self-maintenance; the structures through which inputs are translated into outputs; and the functions (either as purposive action or unintended consequences) that result from the activity of the structures. Systems are differentiated from each other on the basis of the *type* of functions resulting from *different possible combinations* of input-output relationships, actors, and environmental conditions. Obviously, if we bear in mind the variety of environments in which the ILO has functioned, the Organization (i.e., a specific structure) has experienced participation in several systems.

Let us now try to describe these systems. I shall profit here from a kindred attempt undertaken by Richard N. Rosecrance, who sought to circumscribe nine historical systems that have prevailed since the eighteenth century. Rosecrance was concerned not merely with power and ideological relationships, but with the totality of major environmental forces, with system transformation as opposed to maintenance, with instability as opposed to the eternal search for equilibrium. Hence his intent closely parallels my own, despite certain differences in definition and emphasis.* Two of his systems will provide the organizing framework for "placing" the ILO as a subsystem.

How can we tell one system from another in empirical and historical terms? "System-change occurs when the constituents of disruption and regulation undergo major change. . . . The different categories composing actor disturbance have been transformed. There have been changes in the patterns of direction, control and resources. In addition, the activity and power of regulative and environmental forces has also been altered."[1] But the question of whether a new kind of outcome is stable or unstable is not directly related to the change in systems in Rosecrance's analysis. Stability is determined by whether or not the *acting units* consider the change acceptable; hence it follows that "system-change, stability and instability are not interdependent."[2]

On the basis of this apparatus, Rosecrance divides history since World War I into two systems. "System VIII" prevailed between 1918 and 1945, and the balance of disturbing and regulative forces is summed up as bipolarity, or diametric opposition. "System IX" has prevailed since 1945; its outcome is described as tripolarity, or dissension. System VIII was characterized by great instability, whereas the dominant attribute of System IX is moderate stability (in the sense established above).

However, System IX might well be subdivided into four further phases.

---

* Richard N. Rosecrance, *Action and Reaction in World Politics* (Boston: Little, Brown, 1963). These differences in definition may be noted: (1) The systemic attribute of most interest to Rosecrance is stability vs. instability, rather than transformational and adaptive quality as in my case. (2) Whereas for me the relevant structures are necessarily international organizations, Rosecrance prefers the notion of a "regulator" or "regulatory device," under which he subsumes international organizations as well as any other technique for dealing with disturbing inputs. (3) Instead of functions, Rosecrance prefers to speak of "outcomes," viewed as the resultant of disturbing and regulative forces interacting on the international stage; a given outcome of input-output relations flowing from environmental forces is the balance of disturbing and regulative forces, which may either confirm the old system or usher in a new one possessing different attributes (pp. 11–14, 219–30).

These would comprise (1) an attempt at a Great Power concert, 1944–47; (2) bipolarity with the regulative mechanism under the control of the United States, 1947–51; (3) an interregnum of tripolarity and unstable bargaining patterns between the blocs, 1952–55; and (4) the confirmation of a bipolar military balance functioning within an institutionalized multipolar bargaining pattern, in which the initiative lies with the non-aligned blocs preoccupied by post-colonial and economic issues.[3] In both structural and functional terms, the first and second pairs of phases, respectively, show more similarity than diversity. We may subsume each pair under its own major rubric, one implying the non-acceptance of a new regulative balance by one major actor (i.e., the United States before 1952), and the other the tripolar and multipolar interfunctional bargaining pattern that has prevailed since the Korean War. In short, I shall use three international systems: the interwar pattern, the immediate post-war pattern, and the network of relationships confirmed since the mass admission of new states to the UN.

(*a*) *System 1, 1919–44.* The environment was dominated by a basic bifurcation among national elites: on the one hand, groups anxious to preserve the territorial, economic, and ideological status quo of the peace settlement of 1919, and, on the other, a constantly growing body of groups anxious to overthrow the status quo in all its aspects. Further, this division was correlated with sharp ideological differences regarding the merits of the presumed modal pattern of capitalism-democracy-pluralism. Those who challenged this syndrome as a desirable pattern of national and international organization—the communists, fascists, and proto-fascist authoritarians—followed correspondingly bellicose international policies. They courted large-scale war, met the disintegration of the capitalist world economy with heroic (but disturbing) autarkic policies, and profited from rapid technological change to mobilize their populations into manipulable mass societies. As the acting units were increasingly bifurcated into democratic and totalitarian governments, the possibility of meeting diametrically clashing inputs with an output pattern of compromise became impossible, since the compromise would have involved dismantling one of the modal positions. The structures—the League of Nations and the alliance system—after some initial successes against states not directly involved in this confrontation, assumed a vacuous position outside the real conflict. Dysfunctions triumphed over functions in diplomacy, economics, social relations, and armaments, whether seen as purposive action or unintended consequences. The central attribute of this system was transformation in a disintegrative direction.

So much for the general situation. What did it imply for the ILO? Was it rescued by Functionalism from the general maelstrom? In a very real sense it was. The ILO grew up in the lee of the global storm. Global dysfunction produced some very real functional results in the realm of labor welfare. Because the ILO originated as a sop that the dominant status-quo actors sought to give to portions of their own populations, it was able to rely on the relative constancy of these motives to build up its program. The withdrawal or inactivity of the revisionist powers factored the subsystem out of the global system. As a result, it survived the bipolar confrontation as the tacit ally of the democratic bloc. We must now specify the consequences of this condition, with respect both to the environment and to organizational growth.

One test is provided by the effectiveness of ILO legislation as regards labor standards. As predicted, within the confines of the restrictive ideology of Official Functionalism, the Organization was able to agree only to a minimal, special-client-oriented legislative program. Efforts to break out of this mold, by means of general anti-depression and anti-armaments policies, ended in complete failure. The labor standards so elaborated were implemented primarily in industrial countries possessing functionally specific interest groups. Few modernizing oligarchies in the system took an interest in the program; of the modernizing totalitarianisms, only Italy showed sporadic evidence of interest. Recommendations, though less controversial, were not widely implemented either. However, again as predicted, the discussion of the legislative program *did* give rise to closer, face-to-face relations among representatives of industry, labor, and governments, who were more willing than before to regard as legitimate the continued examination of industrial issues at the international level. Nevertheless, this readiness was confined to the democratic states of Western Europe, North America, and Australasia.

Certain unintended consequences followed from this purposive setting characteristic of the major actors. As a result of judicial decisions, programmatic scope was increased with reference to agriculture and additional categories of "workers." The dissatisfaction of key client groups with the implementation of ratified Conventions gave rise to the annual review and discussion procedure. Several member states objected to this development, but proved unwilling to deny their overt ideological commitment to Functionalism and block the procedure. However, these were invariably unstable regimes lacking self-confidence. The review and investigation procedure was generally useless against strong and self-confident states determined not to implement terms of Conventions. Although such members did not openly challenge the legitimacy of the "law without force" procedures that grew up, they found ample scope in the written law of the system to do so effectively. States never resorted to the officially sanctioned complaint procedure, and no effort to invoke the "law with force"—the provision for sanctions—was ever made. On the other hand, the functional logic was correct in predicting that voluntary groups striving for a pluralistic-industrial order would seek to avail themselves of the intended and unintended procedures at hand. Admittedly, the authority of these procedures did not improve discernibly during the interwar years; but since they were not openly challenged, and since they were utilized by some voluntary groups, it may be said that at least their legitimacy improved. The ready acceptance of the unintended new procedures in 1944 certainly gives substance to this claim.

The interwar system, however, conspicuously failed to bear out the hypotheses advanced under the general heading of international pressure in favor of worker welfare. Technical assistance was not used as a stratagem to advance standardization. The leadership did not prove receptive to entertaining complaints that were not clearly subject to ILO jurisdiction. The strain of subgoal specificity was not successfully resolved in terms of a more comprehensive program. Indifference to the Organization's aims, and division among various client groups, did not enable the leadership to expand into new fields of endeavor. On the contrary, its *de facto* dependence on the goodwill and interest of one bloc in the global confrontation imposed as mandatory restrictions the aims and motives entertained by that bloc.

It cannot be said that Thomas and Butler did not seek to escape this dilemma. But since they could appeal to very few reliable clients, their room for maneuver was sharply limited. Hence the development of organizational autonomy—as distinguished from impact on the environment—was barely sufficient to assure survival. As for impact on the environment, the basic objective of the ILO, as enshrined in Official Functionalism, was clearly not achieved, and no net increase in integration can be asserted. However, an organizational ideology was elaborated just the same, and the leadership did succeed, in 1944, in legitimating it as a generally expansive doctrine of welfare under international auspices. Moreover, this doctrine could cite the lack of success of the first two decades as justification for a new and larger program. The enlarged scope of the Philadelphia Declaration was, itself, an unintended consequence of the foundering of the program written in Paris, even if it did not result from the earlier dialectic that presented the trade unions as friendly clients and the employers as hostile ones. Employers, in general, also supported the new program. In the work of the leadership, disparate subgoals among trade unions and governments *did*, in 1944, force an expansion and dilution of the older program. It *did* provide a programmatic redefinition at a more comprehensive level. The field of standard-setting came to include technical assistance for labor efficiency, the protection of human rights, and the modernization of pre-industrial societies. But it is also true that the successful redefinition strained Official Functionalism, sacrificed specificity and coherence, and opened the door to new crises and disputes over program among the clients.

Thus, even though the environment was hardly changed, the Organization made sufficient alteration to its program and appeal to survive. Would it have survived without the victory of the industrial-democratic bloc in 1945? Few would be audacious enough to make such a claim. The ILO managed to survive because it vegetated in the shelter of one power bloc, and eventually upgraded its program by maximizing the environmental features and national inputs which happened to flourish at the end of World War II among the members of that bloc. The story of post-war international planning and the construction of the United Nations agencies surely does not support any contention that the ILO, as an autonomous subsystem, significantly contributed to the greater integration of the international system that took place after 1945.

(b) *System 2, 1945–51.* The actors in the immediate post-war environment were both more numerous and more variegated than those of the preceding system. The fascist bloc disappeared. Its role as the disturbing force —with respect to the values and inputs represented by the industrial-democratic bloc—was taken by a strengthened and expanded communist bloc. In addition, the environment contained a relatively small number of newly independent underdeveloped states (India, Indonesia, Egypt, Burma, the Arab countries) that followed a self-conscious policy of non-alignment. The inputs furnished by these actors varied with their national perceptions of value and interest, and are far too familiar to require recapitulation. The outputs of the system, overwhelmingly, represented the aims of the Western bloc, led by the United States, united in NATO after 1949, and allied for the most part with the Latin American states, themselves united in the OAS. Military strength was polarized between the two superpowers, both equipped with nuclear weapons by the end of the period. In the remainder of the world, the buildup of military capacity had to compete with welfare demands and the allocation of resources for satisfying them; in general, the demands for welfare triumphed over military considerations everywhere except in the United States and the Soviet Union, and sometimes there too.

Among the acting units, voluntary groups assumed a more important role than before in the field of labor and business contacts (though still less important than governments), as the Cold War became linked to policies of massive foreign aid and ideological intervention. Technical assistance became an accepted tool in international politics in the effort to prevent the spread of communism to the underdeveloped countries. The central structure was the United Nations and the specialized agencies, through which Western-sponsored policies of collective security, economic aid, and technical assistance were funneled to some extent. Regional organizations arose at the same time, but were not yet of central importance. The functions of the system, as produced by the United Nations structure, were at first confined to the purposive mobilization of the symbols of law and collective security on behalf of the Western bloc, a mobilization that reached its high point in the Korean War and the enlistment of all specialized agencies on behalf of the West. Unintended consequences, with respect to these Western inputs, did not appear until 1951. The attributes of this system were loose bipolarity, sharp ideological confrontation, and a very precarious stability.

Given this overall setting, what was the ILO's impact on the international environment? In line with the ideological revaluation of 1944, emphasis in the field of international legislation shifted from subgoal-dominant Conventions to the drafting of basic human rights texts. These standards were adopted as part of the Cold War climate and corresponded to the inputs of Western-oriented governments and voluntary groups. They were implemented, by and large, only by the European and Commonwealth governments. Subgoal-dominant Conventions became of some interest to certain underdeveloped countries, which now, for the first time, were appearing as full-fledged actors in the system; conversely, these Conventions lost appeal in the industrialized West, whose standards already exceeded the ILO norms. At the same time, the polarization of world ideologies tended to reduce the integrative impact of continued consultations and confrontations in Geneva.

The bifurcation of industrial interests between the West and the newly emerging countries manifested itself strongly in the attempt to regulate international conditions of industrial competition by means of global collective bargaining in the Industrial Committees. Programmatic diversification took the form of providing the producing countries with a special forum in which they could negotiate agreements for standardizing labor conditions and costs. The flexibility of the procedure resulted in permissive rules and very uneven implementation. Personal contacts among interest group representatives, contrary to our prediction, did *not* produce a meaningful consensus along functionally specific lines.

But the revaluation did produce the initially unintended consequence of new institutional machinery claiming some degree of supervisory power. Human rights Conventions called for a strengthened annual reporting procedure and additional scope for the experts examining the reports. They called, too, for a special complaint procedure, true to the functional jurisprudence of "law without force," by means of which specific infractions of the Conventions could be handled through a quasi-judicial conciliation process. Again, it proved difficult for regimes objecting to this development to dispute its legitimacy, while at the same time protesting their loyalty to ILO principles. Voluntary groups availed themselves of the procedure to the extent that they were striving for a pluralistic order. Totalitarian groups also resorted to it in order to punish and expose their class enemies! Implementation of decisions remained uneven, and in some measure correlated with the self-perceived insecurity of a regime. Secure autocracies paid little attention to the rules or the procedure. The legitimacy of the approach seemed to grow without concurrent improvement in authority.

Technical assistance became the programmatic mainstay of the ILO after 1949. However, it assumed an autonomous position and resisted inclusion either in the UN-sponsored collective security program or in the older ILO doctrines of Official Functionalism. Technical assistance with regard to manpower training, social security, and productivity was given without making any consistent effort to use it for inculcating general respect for the International Labor Code. Relations with and among clients became more diffuse. The workers increasingly reflected the tensions of the Cold War, some of the employers (notably those of the United States) developed a generalized hostility to the whole program, and governments increasingly attempted to use the ILO as an appendage of their overall policies. Hence demands for new programs posed a disruptive threat that could not be met by the leadership's appeal to a non-existent general consensus. Clients were divided—a favorable condition—but the nature of their division was such that the leadership could devise no easy and ready formula to take advantage of the division. Subgoal specificity increased to the extent that new programmatic departures were made difficult; the older standard-setting activities joined the new technical assistance operations in catering to very specific groups of clients.

The ILO was the victim of the inability of the major actors to fashion a coherent global economic and social machinery. The Organization was too technical to lose all relevance; but it was not technical enough to be immune from the effects of the political winds that swept the world. Moreover, because it had so few supranational powers of its own, it could not assert itself against the onslaught of ideology and the lashes of national policy, as was clearly demonstrated in the failure to acquire the central role in world migration policy.*

This brings us to the evolution of the ILO's autonomy during this period. The leadership, basing itself on a poorly assessed convergence of client inputs in 1944–45, made a supreme bid for increased organizational autonomy in conjunction with a global economic and social task that was to go far beyond the mere standardization of labor norms. It certainly attempted to make the establishment of higher labor standards a dynamic

---

* The ILO was not the only victim of the breakdown of the illusory world consensus that fashioned the UN system between 1944 and 1946. The FAO was prevented from making a meaningful entry into the world commodity problem; the IMF was unable to assume international exchange stability; UNESCO failed to elaborate a coherent educational doctrine or program; the ICAO soon gave up trying to deal with the commercial and economic aspects of aviation; and the comprehensive International Trade Organization failed to come into existence during this period. All these agencies were too "political" to remain unaffected by the attributes of the global system, but not autonomous enough to transcend it. All, though, were sufficiently "technical" to survive. WHO, the most technical among them, actually flourished.

doctrine of world economic and political progress through planning. It assuredly laid the basis for claiming new powers and tasks as the original task foundered on spotty implementation by member governments and uneven interest by voluntary client groups. The choice of program was indeed dictated by the search for allies among trade unions; but at the same time the leadership sought to conciliate employers, now no longer the "enemy," by watering down labor's demands.

The fact remains that these efforts were in vain. The topics advanced for inclusion in an expanded ILO task were sometimes given to regional organizations or handled bilaterally, as in the case of the migration plan. More often, they were not made part of any international agenda for action. Although during this period the ILO functioned in the shadow of the Western bloc and its allies, these actors took no great interest in the Philadelphia program, except when it suited their general policy aims—as in the case of the texts and machinery dealing with freedom of association. Autonomy and expansion of jurisdiction, therefore, could be achieved only in the context of international ideological confrontations, not on the basis of a Functionalism that extolled welfare for its own sake. Paradoxically, it was probably subgoal domination that saved the ILO during this period from suffering the fate of the International Trade Organization.

(c) *System 3, 1952 to the present.* The characteristics of the world environment since the Korean War are common knowledge. As the superpowers assumed a mutual, increasingly impregnable, thermonuclear deterrent stance, the system was "opened up" to diplomacy, conventional war, guerrilla war, conciliation, and international supervision. Relations within each bloc loosened up, though the blocs remain. But bipolarity was finally laid to rest, in all fields except the thermonuclear weapons balance, by the admission to the system of fifty new Asian and African nations, almost all of them underdeveloped, overwhelmingly preoccupied with economic modernization and the elimination of colonialism, and only peripherally interested either in the Cold War or in collective security. The new nations quickly formed (or joined) several blocs of their own. These blocs are for the most part devoted to the principle of non-alignment, a doctrine of increasing appeal in certain Latin American countries that had been faithful allies of the West in the earlier system. The pattern of inputs changed accordingly, with decolonization and economic development acquiring thematic supremacy.

The two major powers have responded to these events by downgrading total war as an instrument of policy (they had additional systemic reasons for doing so, apart from the Afro-Asian challenge) and by setting out to woo the non-aligned world with economic and technical aid as well as promises of support in the anti-colonial struggle. The Cold War was not buried; but its strains were increasingly interwoven with these new inputs.

The resulting output pattern is a mixture of international policies in which some security arrangements are bartered for steps in aid and decolonization. The system is far more stable than its predecessor, owing to the fact that the range of punishment considered acceptable by the actors has increased. They no longer consider a bloody guerrilla war the occasion for major hostility, even if they are losing. The system's structures are, as before, the United Nations and its growing multitude of specialized and regional agencies, as well as the proliferating regional organizations that assert themselves as bloc actors in the UN. As the task of these structures has become more and more economic, and as supervisory powers in some political and military settings have been acquired, functions have developed rapidly along lines obscured and blocked during the earlier period. The chief instances of functional and initially unintended expansion are the growth of autonomous UN financial agencies, the Special Fund, the Congo Operation, plebiscites and inquiries in post-colonial crises, and the growing independence in military and political affairs of the UN Secretariat. Space, drugs, population control, and the resources of the ocean bed may provide the tasks for future functional expansion as decolonization becomes a thing of the past.

How did the direction of the system affect the subsystem? Multipolarity provided the environmental setting in which a dramatic revaluation of ideology and program was initiated. Multipolarity also implies heterogeneity in client demands and expectations. A legislative program can therefore be successful only if the standards invoked are of roughly equal appeal to the bulk of the membership. Since subgoal-dominant specific standards are no longer of much interest to Western workers and cannot be easily fitted into heroic development programs in Africa and Asia, the legislative program has been sacrificed in two ways. Emphasis has been placed on general human rights texts that could not be effectively opposed even by regimes likely to be embarrassed by them; and the standardization program has tended to give way to the ad hoc special educational measures advanced as part of the "promotional" approach. The environment was to be penetrated by way of persuading key elites in the direction of progressive social policies, rather than by way of legal uniformity.

This development took place at a time of dramatic changes in membership: the Soviet-bloc countries returned to the ILO as the new African and Asian states were admitted. Latin America lost its earlier peripheral relations with the international system, and Western voluntary groups—who had initially been the important clients—lost some of their earlier commitment. Diffusion in membership meant diffusion in legal uniformity. Hence such integrative trends as could be associated with labor standards in the first two periods of the ILO's history declined, in fact as well as in the ideology, during the current phase.

One victim is the machinery of quasi-collective bargaining. Attitude integration did not take place during the current period of the Industrial Committees' work. The procedure was too flexible to make any uniform impact on the environment except in the maritime field. On the other hand, the shift in emphasis to human rights protection, and the promotion of attitudes favoring a progressive social policy, *did* imply an unintended growth of the ILO machinery. The constitutional complaint procedure finally seems to have come into its own; the machinery for protecting freedom of association is swamped with cases, the perennial violators of the Code are publicly blacklisted each year, and the sweep of the annual reporting machinery seems to expand year by year. It remains true, as predicted in our paradigm, that national loyalty to these techniques improves as governments come to believe that their security and "image" somehow depend on the views of the non-aligned. At long last, the authority of these procedures seems to be growing along with legitimacy, and sometimes in its absence.

The promotional approach means that technical assistance operations, in the widest sense, *are* being used as a covert technique for introducing ILO-sanctioned norms. The emphasis on human rights and on the superiority of social objectives over brute economic development *is* fed into the environment by way of educational, training, and promotional activities. One result is an ever-increasing flow of new demands for new programs and more drastic measures, provided for the most part by the African and communist member states. The leadership is increasingly receptive to these demands insofar as they can be justified in terms of the promotional approach, thus implying an unintended politicization of the ILO's work. With the demise of standards and the stressing of universal values calculated to appeal to the new members, subgoal specificity may eventually be sharply reduced, though it is too soon to announce such a state of affairs. The heterogeneity of the membership, somehow held in line and in mutual interdependence by the interfunctional and interregional network of ties, has been used by the leadership to announce new programs upgrading common interests and to persuade the more critical older clients of their efficacy in terms of their own national aims.

It is obvious that this has not yet produced a discernible change in the international environment. It is equally obvious that the appeal is addressed primarily to a consensus among the new members, made politically possible by the enmeshment of Western and Soviet objectives in the underdeveloped and non-aligned world. Even though the major powers do not share or show any great enthusiasm for the new program, they have acquiesced in it and legitimated it in their national demands and general compliance with ILO measures. And this has meant an increase in the authority and autonomy of the Organization itself. The new environment has resulted in a higher task, wider action, and somewhat stronger structures than ever before. However, this development has taken place in the face of growing heterogeneity in the environment, rather than greater integration in the sense in which we have defined it thus far. Whether the stronger structures will now lead to an invigorated integration of the environment is something only the analyst of the next international system can establish.

We shall return to this point later. First we must summarize the trend toward structural autonomy. With the failure of the Paris and Philadelphia programs, the ILO now addresses itself to the positive consensus of the underdeveloped and non-aligned to stress an ideology of social progress that takes place alongside economic development and within the confines of the norms of the Code. The leadership is able to stress this consensus because the communist and Western blocs find its implications to converge with their own revised and moderated national objectives in the current system. By a circuitous route, therefore, the protection of labor standards in industrializing nations has become paramount as the interests of workers in the older countries are no longer susceptible to ILO support. The leadership thus did evolve an ideology that joins the protection of labor's demands with the new global development consensus. The new powers claimed by inference involve a follow-up procedure for Governing Body decisions on infringements of freedom of association. They comprise formal powers to abolish forced labor and promotional powers to advance freedom from discrimination. What the leadership sacrifices with respect to formal legal powers is amply compensated by the more intangible capacity to intervene with institutionalized conciliation and education, with structured persuasion in labor-management relations, industrial peace, trade union organization and administration, and humane management science. Formal legal bonds are relaxed as the substructure for the informal legal ties of functional obligations is built up.[4]

Our paradigm erred in ascribing the shift in program and the upgrading of common interests to the search for allies among voluntary groups, especially among the workers. The support for the new program comes overwhelmingly from governments which are unwilling to tolerate pluralism at home. The support of workers and employers is becoming secondary, though the insistence on the observance of standards in supporting economic development is a gesture in their direction. The leadership, after a phase of mutually antagonistic and simultaneous policies of advancing standards *and* rendering ad hoc technical assistance, has found a formula for programmatic reintegration. Disparate subgoals among clients forced the re-examination, after the survival crises posed in the mid-fifties by the return of the Soviets, American hostility, and the advent of the Afro-Asians had been weathered. As long as the forces of the overall system continue to work themselves out in their current manner, further organizational authority and autonomy are likely to follow.

The overall conclusion is inescapable: organizational autonomy has increased despite the fact that organizational outputs had little to do with the transformation of the environment. The Organization grew and the structures developed *even though* structures in the previous system had not discernibly changed the environment of that system. In other words, organizational autonomy grew as a result of later environmental inputs that owed little or nothing to what the Organization had previously done. The ILO was the unwitting beneficiary of changes in the system that had occurred autonomously. It may well be that this will not be true in the future. The legitimacy of the International Labor Code with respect to many new nations was demonstrated earlier. The authority of various enforcement procedures seems to be growing. If the new members and the communists continue to feel the ILO's pressure (along with that of other agencies) for mitigating authoritarian controls, there *will* be environmental transformations associated with the upgraded program. This has not yet occurred on a significant scale. But its advent within the interstices of the technical assistance and promotional program is consistent with the general systemic forces isolated in our analysis.

Our conclusion is wholly consonant with a certain principle of systems theory, the principle of Requisite Variety. This principle holds that only variety in the regulating forces can overcome the variety due to disturbing inputs; "only variety can destroy variety."* Systems 1 and 2 were characterized by bipolarity, i.e., a scarcity of regulating forces. The ILO managed to survive, but not to grow. It "adapted" to the systems by seeking shelter under the wings of one bloc; but that bloc was not consistently interested in the Organization's program; survival crises occurred in each period. Another kind of adaptation, a creative adaptation advanced by a leadership taking advantage of the multipolar and diffuse environment, could take place only after the system itself had appreciably changed. The change itself increased the number of actors and their demands, but permitted the interplay of demands to be reduced to a bargaining pattern of which the entire UN system partakes. Programmatic and organizational growth were the result, within a focus of more limited but more generally appreciated outputs. The price exacted by heterogeneity was legal uniformity and ideological purity; the prize gained was a tentative program based on a dynamic consensus that permitted growth and avoided the more Puritan forms of Official Functionalism.

* The term is Ashby's, and my rendering is a paraphrasing of his more abstract definition. W. Ross Ashby, *An Introduction to Cybernetics* (New York: Wiley, 1956), p. 206. Rosecrance adduces the same principle in his System IX to explain its relative stability as compared with System VIII. Increasing the number of actors, and multiplying their often disturbing inputs, actually *reduces* the number and kind of outcomes produced by the system. Rosecrance, p. 264.

THE ORGANIZATIONAL MODEL RE-EXAMINED

The hypotheses advanced in our paradigm were verified with respect to the internal growth of the Organization, with respect to the impact of the environment on the Organization. They were proved false, by and large, by the experience of forty-five years of attempted international standard-setting in the labor-welfare field; the environment was not markedly influenced by the program. Whether the same conclusion will ultimately apply to the reformulated program, as constructed by the leadership from the attributes of the current international system, remains to be seen. In the meantime, intellectual honesty compels us to admit that the predictive accuracy of our paradigm, deduced as it was from experience in a variety of diverse international organizations, is limited. In part, these limits stem from the inability of the ILO's leadership, in certain periods, to separate Official Functionalism from the functional dynamic. Official Functionalism often made possible the survival of the Organization, but not its growth. Growth became possible only when the outer limits of Official Functionalism itself were under attack. And to that extent the paradigm errs less than the human beings responsible for making it work. However, the functional logic itself may be subject to redefinition as a result of our analysis, in that it expects performance and development at variance with the constraints of the environment. Let us go beyond the ILO, then; let us summarize the experience of history and put it alongside the general model of international organizations held appropriate for maximizing integration.

(a) *System and organization.* There appears to be no reason why we should amend the proposition that a given organization may be ineffective with respect to realizing its own program and yet contribute to systemic change. In fact, the ILO tends to confirm this formulation. As postulated, such an organization requires a leadership self-consciously eager to redefine objectives "upward," willing and able to persuade member governments that unintended consequences may be useful to their national objectives, and able to recognize that successful implementation through purposive action is likely to result in stultification. The drafters of the Philadelphia program and of the Morse revaluation certainly acted in consonance with these principles. However, as long as the program remains unrealized, the changes observed are confined to the structure itself, to its prestige, centrality, and task. Eventually, some feedback on the environment is logically required if this prestige and task are not to suffer reduction to the technical, the routine, and the safe. A given organization, a subsystem, cannot be expected to fashion such feedbacks by itself. Consistent contribution to international integration is possible only if other subsystems, and the systemic forces *en gros*, coalesce to permit further struc-

tural growth and impacts on the environment. Our paradigm made no provision for this. It is now amended to do so.

(*b*) *Leadership and ideology.* It was held that the leadership must develop an organizational ideology that will make possible the articulation of
shared objectives culled from a very heterogeneous environment of clients
and supporters whose subgoals must be made consistent with the larger
goals of the leaders. Such an ideology must also bind and fire the organization's staff, and prevent staff members from exclusively identifying themselves with client subgoals. Finally, the ideology must be such as to lend
itself to periodic revaluation that will result in an expansion of the organizational task and a strengthening of organizational powers.

No United Nations agency, with the possible exception of the IBRD,
meets these provisions in fact. The ILO is true to its fellows. That an ideology was articulated was made amply and repetitiously clear; but it soon
proved to be of defensive value only, an instrument to justify survival. Official Functionalism failed to provide a *stable* base of supporters and clients;
it provided no large and reliable coalitions to support the leadership when
revaluations were attempted in 1932, 1947, 1951, and 1955. Official Functionalism united the staff during the first systemic period, during the crises
of the Depression and World War II. In the current systemic period, however, it divided the staff and increased special ties with discrete groups of
clients. In short, it tended toward disintegration. Only the redefinition of
the ideology at the hands of Morse may succeed in re-creating a central
doctrine commanding respect from all. Morse may succeed in persuading
clients to support new central objectives consonant with national perceptions of interest, where his predecessors, relying on a more focused Functionalism, could score no consistent, lasting, or stable successes. Hence our
re-examined paradigm must call attention to the *generality* of ideology.

(*c*) *Experts and political decisions.* Our general organizational propositions asserted that the quality of decisions should be to upgrade common
interests, or at least split the difference, in order to be consistent with integration. This has not been the overwhelming pattern in the ILO; decisions on the basis of the minimum common denominator have been the
usual practice, especially in the representative organs. What, then, can be
said about the role of the expert, whether brought in from the outside or as
a member of the Office, in the process? As predicted, decisions made exclusively by experts in the bureaucratic mode, e.g., with reference to technical assistance work, have been confined to the routine. Further, decisions
made on the basis of voting by instructed delegates have rarely contributed
to task expansion and integration, with the possible exception of certain
decisions of the Governing Body in the field of human rights. By contrast,
decisions referred to *outside* experts, who agree on outcomes but differ

with respect to reasoning patterns, appear to have been more functional than predicted. This is the pattern that prevails in the various committees dealing with forced labor and the enforcement of the Code. Political representatives will not, as a rule, challenge the work of these collegial bodies if their decisions are legitimated by appeal to principles commanding general—if superficial—acceptance. The exception furnished by the position of the Republic of South Africa is extreme and unique. Our paradigm, finally, proved correct in holding the superiority of decisions made by a *mixture* of experts, a combination of the leadership, outside experts, and delegates. Further, this mixture is most successful when the leadership and its officials take the initiative; when their ideas obtain the endorsement of outside experts; and when these ideas are presented as logical alternatives to instructed delegates, many of whom are not only ill-informed and harassed, but called upon to make complex technical decisions in a parliamentary setting that operates under great pressure of time. The limits of the expert in this process will concern us below.

(*d*) *Program and growth.* The ILO, like most of the specialized agencies and many regional organizations, has conspicuously failed to maintain the ideal balance between general goals and subgoals. The subgoals were useful in holding the loyalty of a group of clients in times of trouble. But these clients were trade unions in industrialized and democratic countries; with the diffuse international environment of the current system, their usefulness has become sharply limited. In the future they will not guarantee survival or facilitate programmatic growth. The leadership, *on its own,* must make decisions with respect to programmatic development and seek out a general consensus apart from the formerly favored clients. Although this is the trend in the ILO now, it certainly has not been the consistent practice in the past. Consequently, much of the technical work of the staff was of the routine problem-solving variety, which prevented the marked penetration of the environment with policies and solutions likely to favor transformation. The "irrational" or "manipulated" planning that our paradigm advocates is implicit in the Morse program, and especially in the challenging insertion of the human rights theme into the new economic development doctrine.

In the past, program planning did not generally feature consultation with clients with a view to building *variable* coalitions, composed differently for each issue; currently, such an approach may be crystallizing. Admittedly, the ILO mixed judgment and compromise in preparing past programs, but largely by drawing on the inputs furnished by the favored clients; the current trend is toward a drawing in of additional clients, a permitting of limited compromise after the leadership has made the basic judgmental decisions. In the past, extravagant claims for programmatic uniqueness were made by ILO to a greater extent than by most other international agencies.

These claims came to roost in ideological inflexibility and limits on growth capacity. Again, the current approach to programming is an attempt to cast off the shackles of ideological restraint, while retaining enough of it to infuse the technical with the expansive, the political. In global terms this is a step calculated to increase integration, even though with reference to the pluralistic West such an emphasis may already be beside the point.

This recognition raises, once more, the question of the potential feedback of the new program. Will it meaningfully transform the environment? Will there be a growth in *national* demands for increasing welfare, demands that must be accompanied by an emphasis on individual dignity, by group autonomy, and by a bargaining mentality stressing concrete interests? There is no denying the fact that the industrial-pluralistic-modernizing syndrome of expectations is the most fertile subsoil for effective feedback results; there is also no denying that an intensification of these traits is the condition at once for future organizational success and for systemic transformation. In the absence of such effects, any international organization dedicated to welfare still depends on subgoals to assure its survival; or on autonomous systemic changes to give it a new mandate. *By its own efforts* it cannot hope to change the environment.

A comprehensive attempt to answer this question raises the larger issue of the future of the United Nations and of intergovernmental organization with a global welfare task. It also raises the question of the adequacy of functional analysis in predicting international integration. To these issues I shall turn in the final chapter. For the moment, our task is to refine and revise the paradigmatic model of an international organization in the light of this discussion. Official Functionalism was shown to possess substantial integrative powers as far as the officials of the Organization were concerned. However, functional analysis showed that few such virtues could be consistently found in the minds of supporters and clients. The reasons for this hiatus between the two functionalisms constitute the basic points in the revision of the paradigm.

PLURALISM AND THE LIMITS OF FUNCTIONALISM

This path of analysis leads us to introduce five distinct amendments into the integrative scheme. All hinge on the notion of pluralism and the consequences associated with it. (a) Pluralism must be redefined to allow for its "industrializing" and "post-industrial" variants; (b) pluralism at the national level must be differentiated from its international manifestations; (c) the limits of technocratic expertise must be established; (d) the intensity and scope of the spill-over potential must be fixed; and (e) the scope of unintended consequences from earlier organizational action must be defined.

   (*a*) *Functional integration requires pluralism. But only the pluralism associated with industrialization and democratization seems relevant; post-industrial pluralism may be beside the point.*[5] Thomas and the original Official Functionalists were preoccupied by the kind of pluralism we associate with a society undergoing simultaneous industrialization and democratization. It was a pluralism close to the minds of the revisionist Marxists, a doctrine of attenuated class struggle, envisaging a humanized capitalism and political participation for the working class as the end result. The fruits of capitalist industrialism would be shared by means of social legislation; the workers would successfully penetrate the bourgeois political structure by means of trade unions, labor parties, and the franchise. But the working class was still conceived as outside that structure, albeit knocking on the doors. Class-struggle mentality was taken for granted. The ILO was to derive its strength from the existence of that struggle by utilizing inputs furnished by the working class. It was to reinforce the working class and *universalize* its struggle. It was to infuse societies not yet engaged in industrialization and democratization with the same pluralistic conceptions and institutions. In the long run, then, the whole world would resemble the France and Germany of 1925. And the institutionalization of this kind of pluralism would change the international system by introducing functionally specific welfare demands with a universal environmental base.

We know what actually occurred in the life of the ILO. The outputs of the Organization undoubtedly helped to intensify industrializing pluralism in Europe, and perhaps in North America. At best, though, these activities intensified a process that was already under way for wholly independent reasons. The objectives of the Official Functionalists were clearly achieved in these countries, but not because of the unique contribution of the ILO and certainly without infusing the rest of the world. The principle of tripartite representation and formal group confrontation helped—but did not cause—the institutionalization of this process in the nations of the West. However, by the time our third system took hold, most of the Western nations had left this variety of pluralism behind.

Post-industrial, or post-capitalist, pluralism is of a different order. It operates on the basis of regularized, legitimate, but channeled group conflict. Dichotomous perceptions of "class" may survive among the population, but they are mediated so as to avoid revolt and civil war by means of open bureaucracies, public and private. If there is a "ruling class," it is composed of high civil servants and replaceable political leaders who do not coincide with the "capitalist class" (if such an entity exists at all). Industrial life is shaped more and more on the basis of various kinds of industrial democracy. Industrial conflict has been factored out of total social conflict by means of institutionalized procedures stressing bargaining and conciliation. Man is increasingly preoccupied with extra-industrial concerns: leisure-time pursuits and the status symbols of conspicuous consumption. Social conflict has become so functionally specific that overlapping and bisecting groups dominate, rather than monistically organized trade unions and employer associations. And affluence in industrial production—not to mention chronic agricultural surpluses—makes the welfare state the universal Western type. As Dahrendorf summarizes post-capitalist pluralism:

One of its symptoms consists in the institutional isolation of industry; this in turn involves some disassociation of the scales of wealth and authority. By these and similar factors, the involvement of people in political conflict decreases; individuals, veto groups, and political parties can, so to speak, afford to lose; and if they win, the changes they introduce are piecemeal rather than radical. History is a permanent guest in a free society, not an unwanted intruder whose presence signals revolutionary upheavals.[6]

Does this variety of pluralism still need international organizations like the ILO? Certainly, it does not need the ILO's services as far as the life of its bureaucratized but respectable trade unions and workers is concerned. Nor does it need the technical assistance services or the promotional colloquia, except perhaps when dealing with the arcana of actuarial statistics. At the most, post-industrial Western pluralism needs the ILO in order to universalize the traits of Western society, to feed the tender plant of industrializing pluralism in other parts of the world. Hence the activities relating to freedom of association, anti-discrimination, forced labor, and worker education retain their relevance. In fact, they are crucial.

Yet even this refined version of pluralism hinges on a very risky presupposition. We can rescue the role claimed for pluralism in our functional paradigm only if we assume that industrialization and democratization in Latin America, Asia, and Africa—not to mention the Soviet bloc—will roughly follow the Western historical pattern. We *presuppose* that self-conscious, class-oriented interest groups will arise as a result of the support given by ILO human rights activity. We *expect* that the tripartite principle of representation will stimulate the formation of functionally specific and interest-oriented trade unions and employer associations. We *think* that such groups will simply re-enact the drama played earlier by their European and American counterparts. But we have found very few instances in which this development has actually taken place.* If this presupposition is not matched by the facts that will characterize the environment of the next international system, the pattern of modernization in the non-Western world may nevertheless result in some version of pluralism.

* Perhaps India, Argentina, and Brazil come closest to verifying the expectations of the Official Functionalists on this score.

However, it will not be the kind that supports international integration any more than the now prevalent Western type. Functional integration, in short, cannot be simply and painlessly related to pluralism.

(*b*) *Functional integration requires pluralism. But pluralism at the national level is developing at cross-purposes with pluralism at the international level; congruence between the two is required.* The question then becomes: Is such congruence possible without the universalization of the Western pattern of group conflict?

I shall review the positive as well as the negative answer. On the positive side we find a vision of the United Nations system that projects continued international integration on the basis of tasks alone, without requiring a link with any particular national social structure. The UN is seen as the institutionalization of international pluralism because of the variety of social and political systems it represents. This pluralism begets task expansion, since it enables the evolution of a general consensus on welfare activity to reach a point quite beyond the realm of the national ideologies that furnish the inputs. A pluralism of economic objectives begets common aims in the welfare field, which result in a larger international task and—presumably—in integration, in the sense of standardizing attitudes in the environment. As for the political task of the UN, the maintenance of collective security, the policy-making process here acts as a "school for democracy," in which all the various national actors (with the exception of the Soviet bloc) "learn" to make decisions by parliamentary and conciliatory means. Moreover, the security decisions thus made are functionally specific; they are therefore an improvement over the diffuse and general claims typically associated with new and non-Western nations. In short, with respect to peace as well as welfare, the UN can profit from pluralism to advance integration, even though the *national* pluralistic patterns may and do differ from one another.[7] This trend would be maximized by merely continuing the present welfare activities and adding, in the security field, the functions associated with the International Disarmament Organization and the creation of standing UN emergency forces with temporary supranational powers in small-scale conflicts.

This argument is as fallacious as that which portrays the General Assembly as "democratic" merely because most states are represented and decisions are made by majority vote. It uses the concept of pluralism to connote what is more commonly called "multipolarity." It slurs over the differences in national objectives and political institutions with the tacit assumption that everything will be for the best so long as all the units are bound up together in a global institutional nexus with expanding tasks. Since it says nothing about the transformation of the national setting, it ignores the basic issue that is causing our conceptual troubles: the incapacity of the UN system to shape the environment in line with central policy. A plurality of national objectives is brought into focus in the work of the UN at the very time when the bulk of the member states is becoming less pluralistic in terms of national institutions. This vision illustrates and enshrines the lack of congruence, but it does not transcend it.

A comparison of integrative trends in two regional settings will illustrate further that congruence of *national* pluralistic institutions seems to be a requisite of integration, rather than a mere pluralism at the *central* level. The contrast is between the European Community and the West Indian Federation. First let us note what the two examples have in common.[8] In terms of background factors, we can note the following. Each region was characterized by marked cultural similarities long before the onset of the movement toward integration. Each possessed a growing network of intraregional communication, both physical and vicarious. Common technical services existed in both, though they antedated the launching of the integration movement by only a few years in both instances. The form of government was common to all the members in each case; moreover, in the West Indian case all the units had been part of the same overall polity for three hundred years. Both in Europe and in the West Indies, the integration movement had been sparked by powerful and permanent local interest groups of a functionally specific character, loosely federating regionally in order to advance political integration. Whereas in Europe most of the participating nations were in the post-capitalist pluralist phase, the West Indian islands were on the threshold of the industrializing variety of pluralism. There, the popular movements associated with the process— trade unions and labor parties—furnished the pan-territorial interest group advocating political unity. Finally, it should be mentioned that prior to the attempt to institute representative governing institutions at the center, the work of regional consultation and the running of common services in both cases was in the hands of government bureaucracies, official technocrats outside the arena of political advocacy.

If we recall the seedbed of integration sketched in Chapter 2, we have every right to wonder, after this catalogue of underlying factors, why integration succeeded in Western Europe and—thus far—failed in the Caribbean. Our surprise, however, may be reduced once the immediate structure of rewards and expectations associated with integration is contrasted. This comparison, in turn, must be undertaken as a part of the total developmental sequence of nation, state, and regional aggregate. Differences in sequence correlated with differences in expectations, the capacity to compromise, and the quality of the key acting units. National and regional pluralism in the European case have been congruent; but the opposite seems to have been true in the West Indies.[9]

In Europe, the regional impetus followed the establishment of full-fledged nation-states by at least a century. In Europe, the centralized state had, in most instances, preceded the establishment of a self-conscious nation on its soil. Administrative and governmental monopoly had been achieved before a socially mobilized but functionally differentiated citizenry had evolved, and before the higher stages of industrialization had been attained. The achievement of the post-capitalist syndrome of characteristics coincided with the uniformly experienced trauma of World War II and its aftermath, and with the advance of the Soviet Union. Post-industrial conditions emerged when the national welfare state, based on a mixture of private and public bureaucratic planning, attained final legitimacy, and when industrial plenty reached the higher stages. Economic integration in Western Europe corresponded to the anchoring of the post-capitalist welfare state in a larger regional market, in the possibilities for jointly developing an already advanced industrial structure; in short, it confirmed the post-capitalist social structure. It responded also to the wish for avoiding new wars among the integrating units, and to the desire to reassert European uniqueness vis-à-vis the American and Soviet superpowers, though this theme was of secondary importance. Disenchantment with the nation as the harbinger of the good life was omnipresent, a disenchantment shared by labor, efficient and newer business units, intellectuals, and bureaucrats—as well as by most of the political parties that appealed to these groups.

In the Caribbean, there was neither a pre-existing state nor a nation, nor even island nationalism. The expectations and rewards associated with union were quite nebulous. No world war had left scars of disenchantment, and no foreign threat was on the horizon. Two positive themes were heard: federation was to *create* the non-existing Caribbean nation, and unity was to provide the collective economic strength to fend off victimization by the capricious world economy, an attitude left over from the trauma of the Great Depression. However, the different potentials of the various island economies, and particularly the differences in social structure between Trinidad and Jamaica, soon gave rise to dissonant local developments. The Jamaican economy developed more rapidly than that of the other islands; a specific Jamaican national sentiment developed faster than general West Indian nationalism, partly as a result of the charismatic appeal of Busta-mante to the semi-literate, newly mobilized rural masses. These conflicting trends came to a head in the controversy over the economic planning and financial powers of the federal government. Economic planning was the only *raison d'être* of the federation that commanded general support; but relatively prosperous and nationally aroused Jamaica now feared that she would have to subordinate her economic development to a planning and financial bureaucracy dominated by the other islands, notably Trinidad. Attempts at constitutional compromise were rejected by Jamaica, and the federation collapsed on May 31, 1962.

As indicated by Etzioni, it is a poor strategy to make the reallocation of wealth and resources a regional policy *before* less divisive but potentially integrative functions are exhausted. Reallocation of resources played a subordinate role in the construction of common markets and economic units in Europe. But then the economic differentials were not of such magnitude as to make reallocation a first and central concern. In the West Indies, by contrast, there was nothing to unite the groups other than the expectation of economic reallocation through joint planning.[10] There being few other functions capable of exerting an integrative pull, the leaders of popular and progressive groups who constituted the central actors had to show their capacity for compromise, the quality of "mutual responsiveness" that Deutsch rightly singled out as a key factor in integration.[11] In this they failed.

And they had to fail because the group structure in the islands did not correspond to the statistical bargaining style requisite at the central level. In the islands, the developing interest groups were far from displaying the attributes of mundane functional specificity; in Jamaica, and later in Trinidad, some were also diffuse carriers of general radicalism. Political parties were far more personalistic and subject to charismatic appeal than is appropriate for the pluralistic pattern of intergroup adjustment. Bureaucracies, far from intermingling and consulting continuously with interest groups as in Europe, were austere, neutral, and often alien structures. An emotional pluralism of a pre-industrial nature dominated at the periphery, when the need was for a different kind of pluralism dominating at the center.

The West Indian pattern may well be the scheme of the quasi-pluralism that prevails in much of the non-Western world. But we still cannot decide whether this must of necessity continue to carry disintegrative consequences for the global international system, or whether some variant of the multipolar pattern of "pluralistic" confrontation in the UN remains germane to our problem. We can conclude provisionally that a functional paradigm must take account of the countering trends of pluralism at various levels; and we must therefore admit that functional analysis cannot content itself with the presumed universalization of the Western pluralistic syndrome.

(c) *The expert at the service of international functionalism must be the carrier of scientific and political pluralism, not the prophet who provides total syntheses. This expert must advise the organizational leadership, the quasi-expert manager, who in turn communes with the forces that are dominant in the environment and restrain organizational freedom.* A more elaborate technocratic Utopia, following the path of Saint-Simon, is inconceivable on practical as well as on philosophical grounds.[12] According to an excellent essay by George E. Kelly,

The expert as policy counsellor has been available to societies from earliest times, wearing among other transitory costumes those of magician, tax collector, confessor, constitution-writer, strategist and economic planner. The form has changed with convenience, values on the scale of knowledge, morale and culture; but the function has stayed rather constant. If not always enlisted as a guide to salvation or the millennium, the expert has at least been the confidant of dark secrets or the pathfinder towards some ancillary truth.[13]

All this is certainly applicable to international organizations. But the role explicitly or implicitly claimed for expert management in functional integration demands more precision.

The scientific and experimental mood translated into public service usually has claimed a rational utopian dream as its justification for power. Order, stable progress, knowledge instead of competition among lay power-seekers, have been the watchwords. The possession of knowledge, arcane or merely scientific, has been the expert's badge of admission to the circle of powerful laymen. The layman who accepts this knowledge may usher in Utopia based on reason. But the layman gives up power in order to facilitate the transition. As Saint-Simon put it: "As long as governments protect the learned, in theory and in practice one remains in the old regime. . . . But from the moment the learned protect governments one really begins the new regime."[14] The extreme technocratic mood, thus, finds its Allah in Utopia, its prophet in Saint-Simon, and its first caliphs in the more enterprising leaders of international organizations— such as Jean Monnet.[15] In our era, the content of that Utopia is compounded of a peace freed from the nuclear threat and a global advance toward scientifically ensured mass welfare.

But the modern expert suffers from disabilities with which his predecessors in religion and magic were not afflicted. He has self-doubts, he is immersed in huge bureaucracies, he cannot always communicate with the power-wielders; he is plagued by the suspicion that if he remains a neutral adviser, he is without influence, while a reversal of the emphasis would make him lose his expertise. Furthermore, he often cannot persuade himself that the sum of organization and knowledge equals effective Utopia. To many a specialist in and on the periphery of public life, the limits in the "laws" known to him are sharply and painfully apparent. His knowledge is not certain. If, in addition, he is aware that "organization" alone will not help, that an appreciation of *process* remains central to knowledge itself, he is no longer the technocrat in the pure sense.

Experts in modern society are most influential in crisis situations: "The expert's hold on the reins slackens as the crisis recedes . . . the expert's power is at all times politically revocable, and . . . the expert is concerned purely with the diagnosis and cure of functional disorder and not with commanding the construction of the just society."[16] In fact the knowledge adequate to deal with crisis need not be perfect. It is "crash" knowledge, pressed into service to meet an overpowering need perceived by the politician. Yet let us remember that for every expert there is a counterexpert. Not even a scaled-down self-perception of expertise and a crisis setting are enough to enthrone technocratic dominance. The truth remains that politicians must call the expert—and get rid of him when his advice is unpalatable.

Having evoked the image of the heroic expert and cut it down to size in terms of the contemporary world, let us return to the kinds of experts who actually inhabit international organizations. They may have all the technical attributes of expertise: education, scientific training, professional reputation. They may and do include physicists, epidemiologists, meteorologists, agronomists, management specialists, and lawyers. What matters to us is their position in the *process* of international decision-making. Thus the leader-manager is often himself an expert; he is advised by members of the Secretariat who are also experts. And he is counseled by panels of outside experts responsible to no group or government, as well as by bodies of "instructed" experts, specialists called to advise him but subject to instructions by the appointing governments. Which kind of expert is optimal for integration?

The expert who is tempted to offer final solutions is of little use. Utopian expertise tends to believe that "final problems can be finally solved."[17] The solutions to the problems of the thermonuclear balance of terror that are advanced by some scientists provide an example. This type of expertise, because it ignores the political process, is therefore tempted to resort to totalitarian or other chiliastic remedies in order to capture the power structure. It may, if ever successful, carry on that "oppression exercised in the name of function" of which Simone Weil was afraid. But the expert who appears as judge in the choice among competing expert solutions, who adjudicates with a view toward preserving the society in which choices are to be made, is of equally little relevance. International society has not developed to the point at which this kind of decision has to be made, since its very heterogeneity militates against preservation of any kind of firm consensus. That leaves us with the expert as special crisis counselor, called in when those who wield power perceive a need based on some limited consensus among them.

That is the proper role for the expert in international integration. The consensus may have to be discerned and articulated by the organizational leadership communing with the clients and environmental forces. The basic alternatives may have to be stated by the leaders before being submitted to panels of specialists. The leadership called for here is not that of the "hero in administration" or the philosopher-king; it is the much more mundane variety that is able to appraise the environmental forces and compare them with the trends conducing to peace or welfare. The skill called for is the species of political cunning that is able to persuade different clients with different arguments, to do what seems best calculated to achieve common aims or avoid commonly perceived dangers. This type of leadership will never solve final problems finally, because the act of manipulation will prevent such a total confrontation. Yet the lack of finality will beget the need for more manipulation later.

Such an organizational leadership requires expertise in order to understand the trend of dominant facts and developments. It must surround itself, inside the organization, with a permanent staff that can analyze the past and project aspects of the future without falling victim to highly specialized and subordinate objectives. The very fact that international organizations have little actual power would help to reduce the dominant ambivalence of intellectual experts toward power. In addition, however, such an organizational leadership must rely primarily on instructed experts, specialists with eminence and reputation who are able to appreciate, but not necessarily share, the aims of their political mentors. These experts must remain responsible to the very forces that require persuasion toward organized change, if change is to occur peacefully—national governments. This synthesis remains political. The participating experts do not descend from some scientific and technocratic areopagus to impose their view of the just society. They come from governments and seek to influence governments. But their view of things, if properly exploited by intelligent leadership, can rescue integrative international planning that remains subservient to the facts of international pluralism. These experts, instead of witlessly seeking to transcend the deterministic aspects of our history, represent the very forces in that history which—despite their fixity—permit adjustment.

(d) *The scope and automaticity of the spill-over process depends on the kind and depth of pluralism existing at the national and international levels, just as the role of the expert varies with the complexity of the social and economic issues. The spill-over process at the global welfare level is less pronounced than at the regional level of congruent pluralisms.* By thus scaling down the implication of automaticity in the process of international integration, I am merely making explicit an inevitable inference that follows from our discussion of the types and distributions of pluralism. Furthermore, that very crisis-resolving expert whose image was evoked above is likely to flourish only in a setting in which the consequences of industrial, economic, and scientific *débacle* are experienced by groups with a measure of autonomy and the capacity to influence their official governors. If the process of crisis-counseling is monopolized by experts functioning as part of authoritarian regimes, the chances that their advice will have integrative consequences at the international level are reduced—simply because the number and scope of the pieces of advice will run counter to the law of Requisite Variety.

The spill-over process feeds on industrial complexity, scientific interdependence, and the mass-ingrained preference for butter over guns. The virtues claimed for the spill-over process are encountered in their most concentrated form in the social settings in which the post-capitalist pattern of pluralism prevails. In this kind of setting, the technical requisites of a particular public task, as worked out by the expert, will triumph over a waning ideology. In the setting of UN specialized agencies, however, this situation has so far been approximated only in the realm of telecommunications, meteorology, aircraft safety, and the control of contagious diseases. There, a spill-over into problems of outer space, into new medical techniques, and into ultra-high frequency allocation can be demonstrated. There, unintended consequences of earlier decisions and discoveries lead to task expansion. But these are also the fields quite marginal to the larger issue of system transformation that preoccupies us.

A spill-over process in realms related to political objectives and economic ambitions exists only in much smaller measure in the actual work of global agencies. It can be discovered in the work of the International Bank. We even found traces of it in the work of the ILO. But to expect a continuation and intensification of it with respect to human rights, for example, requires a much more rapid transformation of the environment than can reasonably be expected. The lack of congruence between international and national pluralism is unlikely to feed a dramatic ILO spill-over process. International pluralism will result in a superficially expanded task, new committees, new legal interpretations, and more allegations of violations of Conventions. But the underlying national pluralisms—or lack of them—will continue to make a feedback into national habits problematical.

(e) *Therefore, the incidence of unintended consequences in leading to new powers and tasks is less pronounced than postulated. Such consequences do occur even at the global level of diffuseness and heterogeneity, albeit asymmetrically distributed. But they occur more rarely than at the regional level, where symmetrical heterogeneity tends to prevail.* Symmetrical heterogeneity once more implies a post-industrial pluralism in which roughly corresponding interest groups and parties constitute the acting units.[18] In such a setting, there is a sharp limit on the extent to which leaders and bureaucracies can publicly espouse values that they privately ignore. The hiatus between official proclamation and actual performance is smaller. At the level of international pluralism, however, it is still possible to invoke hallowed phrases and to demand ambitious new programs—only to ignore them in national policy later on. This is particularly true of the fields of public policy most closely geared to economic development that aims at preserving human dignity.

Hence social policies alone cannot be expected to increase organizational legitimacy and authority as long as they evolve in a setting of asymmetry. It is too easy a matter to laud them in Geneva and forget them in Bangkok, Lima, or Brazzaville. The protection of human rights is a slightly different matter, though, because freedom at the national level is more closely linked to the international reputation of a regime. Thus it is possible that those aspects of the human rights field which, because of the nature of current environment, remain unaffected by the uneven distribution of pluralistic traits may demonstrate a capacity for a spill-over process and new unintended consequences.

Forced labor and anti-discrimination measures come to mind. Unintended consequences have already occurred in the field of forced labor; they may well be in the offing with respect to promotional and supervisory powers relating to anti-discrimination in employment. By the same token, however, it is highly unlikely that the areas of equal remuneration and freedom of association will enjoy a spilling over into neighboring economic and social contexts; nor is it likely that they will continue to give rise to unintended consequences in terms of organizational power and influence.

These revisions of the paradigm suggest that functionalism remains of theoretical and analytical importance. They indicate that a functional approach to the issues of integration beyond the nation-state is useful, but hardly exhaustive of all possibilities and certainly no self-sufficient explanation of a set of phenomena. The functional approach remains subject to the assumptions it makes concerning society; pluralism, and interest articulation. It continues to depend for full analytical rigor on a vision of global social processes that approximate those of the industrialized West. Insofar as these processes do not occur elsewhere, the utility of the approach is largely heuristic, a check-list of *potentially* important items which—if established—would possess some theoretical rigor. Functionalism remains confined to outlining possibilities and tendencies. But the empirical relevance of such visions depends, in large measure, on the way in which we project the future of the international system and thus the likely impact of subsystems on future environments. This is the theme of the final chapter.

14. Functionalism, Nationalism, and Historical Sociology

Our survey of international social policy in a nexus of functional integration ended in a paradox. We discovered that the international system changes without the occurrence of a striking feedback at the national level. We found instances of increasing international legitimacy and occasional examples of heightened authority as well. But these developments took place for reasons connected with the changing nature of the environment and the adaptations of the total global system. They could not be related to the effects of the subsystem connected with social policy. All paradoxes, we hope, are only apparent. How are we to explain this one? How can there be integration *without* the emergence of a stronger system based on a more uniform environment?

The United Nations system operates on the basis of compromises among national inputs and regional clusters of demands. To the extent that such inputs are not flatly in mutual contradiction, they can be said to converge, to possess enough in common—despite the wide variety of national motives underlying their enunciation—to allow a central policy for meeting them to be formulated. Sometimes the central policy incorporates a new task for the United Nations, which, itself, calls for new powers and autonomy. In that case an upgrading of common—if only converging—interests takes place. Although this process may go on without the creative intercession of the organizational leadership, it can obviously be helped along by a Dag Hammarskjöld, a Eugene Black, or a David Morse. The typical inputs that give rise to such outputs are demands for action inspired by Cold War and anti-colonial propaganda, activity relating to economic development, measures to stabilize local military tensions not involving the major powers, and steps designed to meet the demands of technological and scientific interdependence.

Compromises among these inputs beget outputs. But where is the origin of the inputs? Common sense suggests that they come from the national sentiments, objectives, governments, and their delegates at the UN; in other words, they are rooted in the national environment. Systems theory, however, suggests that the pattern of convergence is as important as the origin of the demands. Hence the point of origin of the pattern of inter-action might be fixed as the act of clashing in an international forum. Therefore the crucial analytical focus should be the institutionalization of the act of clashing and the learning process presumably associated with it. The UN then becomes a school at which national governments "learn to coexist."

In their own way, both these methods of resolving the paradox are cor-rect. Demands do originate in national settings, and they are often compro-mised in an institutionalized manner. But much still depends on where we place the main emphasis. The World Federalist will stress the second point of origin—to his inevitable disappointment; the Realist will single out the first—only to wind up in deprecating the United Nations. To rely on learning is to assume the supremacy of systemic forces; to rely on the national setting is to treat the developmental patterns of historical sociol-ogy as if they were autonomous and discrete. Our ability to project the future in analytical terms depends in large measure on a correct placing of the emphasis.

This assessment is the purpose of our closing chapter. We must juxta-pose and, if possible, reconcile the environmental and systemic concep-tions of how to continue the process of international integration. We must take as established the inability of existing international institutions con-sistently to transform the environment along functional lines. At the same time we must keep our analytical net open to catch systemic forces that may channel and influence the autonomously evolving environmental cur-rents.

I shall sketch the outlines of the probable future international system in the context of evolving environmental heterogeneity. In a kindred search, Gunnar Myrdal has given us a Functional vision of the future world from a systemic standpoint. His argument will give us a point of departure be-cause the vision appears to me to be in large measure correct. But the systemic emphasis must then be put into the setting of historical sociology, of historically evolved patterns of nationalism that coexist in fact today. These patterns, and the motives of action associated with them, must be regarded as the correctives to the pure systemic approach. We may thus demonstrate how integration can take place in the absence of a uniform pattern of growing pluralism. The system itself may generate compensat-ing forces, impulses which facilitate integration even though the environment is not undergoing any homogenizing process that can be related to international organizations.

GUNNAR MYRDAL AND THE NEW FUNCTIONALIST UTOPIA

When an experienced international official, who is also a distinguished social scientist and national planner, undertakes to reconcile systemic and environmental forces, we are compelled to listen attentively. Myrdal seeks to do just that. He is eager to construct international systemic unity on the basis of admitted environmental diversity, and he attempts to foster international integration thereby. His argument, though more Functional than functional, deserves recapitulation.

Planning for welfare is ubiquitous. Egalitarian norms inspire it, and state intervention is, in fact, universally recognized as the agent for attaining it. But international integration suffers in proportion to the success of national welfare planning. What integrates each nation around the ideal and the processes of successful planning causes global patterns of competition, discrimination, and inequity. Planning for welfare originated in the West and is most highly developed there. It takes place on the basis of informed but continuous bargaining among large social aggregates, prevented by the government and by its own values from victimizing society. Harmony prevails, but "the harmony which is being realized is therefore a 'created harmony,' created by intervention and by planned coordination of interventions. It is the opposite of the natural harmony of the old liberal philosophers and theoreticians."[1] Planning in the West is an unintended adaptation, a "function" of a myriad of specific welfare problems, resolved historically in an ad hoc manner in order to remove grievances that grew out of capitalist society. The successful integration of Western states, therefore, is an unintended consequence from previous chaos, mediated by sporadic and pragmatic planning. Group participation, decentralization, and self-administration come close to making the Western welfare state a Functional Utopia, which is now mature enough, stable and integrated enough, to dispense with irrational nationalism.[2]

Planning in the underdeveloped world is different. It is a deliberate and rational process, designed to achieve welfare by skipping the historical stages traversed by the West and avoiding the totalitarian methods employed by the Soviet Union. Underdeveloped countries, under state auspices, seek to "create harmony" for democratic planning by setting up disciplined voluntary groups to act as partners in the process; they are "planning pluralism." Moreover, the nationalism of the underdeveloped world is as rational as its approach to planning. It is a legitimate device of self-defense against the oversuccessful West.[3]

How is global integration to be rescued in this confrontation between the competing planning postures of the "have" and "have-not" nations? Quite simply by adopting deliberate international welfare planning. Such planning must seek to remove inconsistencies and mutually harmful policies from the national planning processes. International organizations, instead of merely attacking national sovereignty and breaking up nationalism, should draw on what is positive, the common feature underlying all nationalisms: planning for welfare. The Functional logic that leads Myrdal to this prescription bears quoting in full:

The plain fact is this: *When once the national Welfare State has come into existence and built its moorings firmly in the hearts of the peoples who in the democracies of the Western world have the political power, there is no alternative to international disintegration except to begin, by international cooperation and mutual accommodation, to build the Welfare World.* This conclusion from our analysis stands not only, and not primarily, as an expression of a political valuation of what would be desirable, but is presented as a statement of a factual situation. Any other conclusion from our analysis would do violence to logic and to what we know about social reality in the Western countries.[4]

Such planning demands, first and foremost, that the West, which does not need its nationalism, make concessions to Africa, Asia, and Latin America, which do still need their national self-consciousness. Further, Myrdal prefers to base planning on the direct "realism" of idealistic motives than on disagreements and power struggles. He considers the functional logic of indirection as an "opportunistic short-cut." Harmony must be created, not by relying on convergences of hostile strands of inputs, but by getting the West to grant the legitimacy of the present "double standard of [economic] morality."[5] If the West accepts the African, Asian, and Latin American visions of the future welfare world, nationalists on these continents will be able to mature, because they will be accepted as victors in the global planning process.* Only created global harmony can avert an intensified international class struggle.

Myrdal assigns the crucial planning task to international organizations affiliated with the United Nations. Their merit, first of all, consists of their remarkable ability to survive programmatic failure and neglect on the part of governments. Myrdal attributes this resilience to their subgoal-dominant programs and their close ties with specific groups in the member nations. But their ideals are nevertheless held to infuse people and govern-

---

* The analogy that Myrdal develops is compelling. He suggests that the present attitude of the underdeveloped countries toward nationalism and international cooperation is similar to the aggressive and violent behavior of alienated workers in the West before the institutionalization of universal suffrage and collective bargaining. Acceptance into the system removed these immaturities. Acceptance of underdeveloped countries and their aspirations as legitimate would tame nationalism.

ments with an international spirit, and their institutions do furnish the school in which nations learn to cooperate. They will become the instruments of global planning simply because the international system has made them the only reasonable candidates for the job. Myrdal writes:

Today, after having been a participant in, and an observer of, this work for ten years, I am more convinced than ever that we are on the right track and that the efforts must be pursued. And I am not without hope. If a major war is avoided, I believe that the trend will be for the inter-governmental economic organizations to grow in importance. They represent the future form of diplomacy between nations. In another fifteen years' time, I believe that we shall be able to present a very different sort of balance sheet.[6]

Like so many Functionalists, Myrdal is right for the wrong reasons. Environmental forces, channeled by systemic pressures, may very well result in the approach to world economic planning that Myrdal foresees. But they will not do so merely on the basis of the West's yielding to the neutralist inputs. Myrdal's assumptions run counter to the attributes of the contemporary system and cannot, therefore, yield functions consistent with the aim of a welfare world based on simple and direct accommodation by the West.

Myrdal assumes the post-capitalist Western pattern as the norm toward which the underdeveloped world will develop. Rational planning will provide a shortcut for attaining the democratic-pluralistic bargaining state that characterizes the West in this age without ideology.[7] He assumes, further, that this state is not only democratic, but heavily influenced by experts who transcend interest groups. Created harmony implies the successful manipulation of organized selfishness by somebody—the expert. The citizen would be educated to see "his own true interests"; "as his objective knowledge of the national community in which he lives is improved, he will not be misled by the power oligarchy."[8] Created harmony, it appears, requires an immanent general will, which must be made explicit by "education." Such a polity, says Myrdal, is "a state worthy of *consensus sapientium*."[9] In short, the devil of selfishness will be cast out, international economic disintegration will be stopped, and a global welfare-planning consensus can arise on the basis of a purified general will in the West, generously conceding to an immature nationalism in the East the bulk of the outstanding issues.[10]

These assumptions, in my judgment, are not tenable. Myrdal's Functional projection relies on an oversimplified "have" and "have-not" typology of nations. He overlooks the likelihood that divergent national inputs will continue to issue forth from historical political entities that are evolving at *diverse* rates in *several* directions, even though these entities appear concurrently as actors whose aims overlap in the United Nations. The *deus ex machina* who can reconcile environmental with systemic forces here, and rescue the process of integration, can only be that *consensus sapientium* whose acceptance requires an act of faith.

Nevertheless, Myrdal's projection does help to solve the paradox with which we are concerned. He points to interests that *are* shared and that *do* cause convergences in the international forum. He is clearly right in stressing the universal appeal of welfare planning, even if he errs in feeling able to remove the positive thrust from the confrontations of politics. However, by singling out only those aspects of the environment that support the systemic forces, he seeks to "jump history" much as the planner in India or Ghana does. The systemic interaction pattern that he throws into relief is crucial to the continuation of integration in a heterogeneous environment. His analysis gives support to those who seek to present policy-making in international agencies in terms of voting dynamics imputed from the study of national legislatures and party systems.[11] We must give due attention to these forces, even though such an approach skips lightly over the informing motivations of national actors. But we must also put these systemic thrusts into the limiting framework of the actors "in history," rather than rely on some elusive general will to do the job for us.

HISTORICAL SOCIOLOGY
AND THE FUTURE OF NATIONALISM

In the systems of the last century, the "actor in history" has been the nation, and the nationalistically motivated official and citizen who speaks for it. Past interactions between environment and system have been overwhelmingly conditioned by this fact. But not all nationalisms are alike. They differ in the values they profess, the institutions they generate, the processes of social change with which they are associated. The inputs they furnish differ over time and within any one period—the fact that gives each system its peculiar attributes. We are about to sketch an eclectic theory of nationalism that stresses ontology and developmental types. Far from being a digression, this effort is justified by our concern with tracing patterns of similarity and dissimilarity in the inputs fed into the international system, and thus with projecting outputs of an integrative or disintegrative nature. Will the nation of the future be more or less "permeable," more or less susceptible, to external influence?[12] Will there be more or less feedback from the system to the nation? Are there likely to be forces working for increasing or decreasing pluralism at the national level? If increasing pluralism implies increased permeability, will the rate of feedback be accelerated? In short, an appreciation of the types of nationalism is essential to a projection of the future environment and the future system.

The scholarly community has long disagreed on the precise meaning to be given to the notions of "nationalism" and "nation," with the result that discussion has been confused and often ill-focused. I regard the "nation" as a socially mobilized body of individuals, believing themselves to be united by some set of characteristics that differentiate them (in their own minds) from "outsiders," and striving to create or maintain their own state. "Nationalism" is the body of beliefs held by these people as legitimating their search for uniqueness and autonomy; nationalism is the myth of the successful nation. A "national ideology," by contrast, is a body of values and beliefs advocated by some creative minority in an effort to call into being a new nation. If this minority is successful, it will build a nation and create a nationalism; if not, it will be a historical curiosity or an occasional irredentist irritant. The nation is a synthetic *Gemeinschaft*. In the mass setting of modern times, it furnishes the vicarious satisfaction of needs that have previously been met by the warmth of small, traditional, face-to-face social relations. As social life has been transformed by industrialization and social mobilization into something resembling a *Gesellschaft* based on interest calculations, the nation and nationalism continue to provide the integrative cement that gives the appearance of community. On the strength of these definitions, we can now proceed to examine nationalism in terms of the relationship between ideology, myth, institutions, and patterns of social change.[13]

Types of nationalist ideology. Modern history offers several recurring bundles of ideas, aspirations, and values associated with the demand for uniqueness and statehood. The oldest of these is Liberal Nationalism. This ideology regards the nation as a fraternal community whose purpose is the realization of the rights and liberties of *individuals*, thus contributing to the happiness of all. Liberal Nationalism has, of course, been closely related to ideologies of progress, both spiritual and material. It has sometimes given rise to a second variety, Jacobin Nationalism. Jacobin Nationalism dedicates the nation to disseminating the principles of Liberal Nationalism outside its own boundaries. In supreme self-confidence, Jacobin Nationalism amends its Liberal precursor to make it exportable, to bestow it on others still suffering from oppression and exploitation. Jacobin Nationalism thus acquires a mission to liberate others, even to force them to be free. It logically leads to policies and doctrines of imperialism.

Opposed to these two closely related types, we encounter Traditional Nationalism. This ideology stresses the protection of the community against alien doctrines, usually the doctrines exported under the banner of Jacobin Nationalism. Traditional Nationalism seeks to mobilize the people under the banner of an older pattern of life, harking back to feudal days and corporatist ways, tribal values, or the solidarity of a folk society. It emphasizes the rights of discrete groups, classes, guilds, or castes rather than those of individuals. It always creates, or resurrects, a myth of golden ancient days of solidarity under which to organize the newly mobilized masses. Syncretist Nationalism is a variant of this type. Its prophets and advocates seek to protect their people from the new, while also attempting to innovate to the extent of borrowing such novel traits as seem desirable and in tune with the tradition that is to be preserved. Syncretists wish to combine the best of the new and the old. They seek to be adaptive, whereas Traditionalists merely attempt to block.

The individual ceases to be the center of focus in both Traditional and Syncretist Nationalism. He is utterly destroyed in the final variant, Integral Nationalism. In this body of ideas, the nation is an organic whole with a life of its own. The survival of the nation is the supreme goal to which the good of its citizens is rigidly subordinated. Integral Nationalism tends to merge society, economy, and polity into one monolith, whereas Traditional and Syncretist Nationalism sought to limit economy and polity to permit society to flourish.

Where have these types manifested themselves in history? The interplay of Liberal and Jacobin Nationalism is, of course, illustrated by the history of France during the eighteenth and early nineteenth centuries. Liberal Nationalism has flourished in Britain since the seventeenth century, and in most of Western Europe since the nineteenth. Traditional Nationalism is typical of the German and Central-East European polities of the nineteenth and early twentieth centuries; it also flourished in Russia during portions of the nineteenth century. Syncretism is most evident in Japan; it appears, too, in much of modern Indian and Arab thought, and in the ideologies of some new African nations. Integral Nationalism is a manifestation of our century: it arose in Germany, Italy, and the Soviet Union; it can be found today in Indonesia, Ghana, Guinea, and Cuba. But the ideas have been modified. Social change interacts with the evolution of national ideas. Countries have moved from one type to another, and they will continue to do so.

Types of national myths and institutions. Liberal Nationalists took for granted that the kind of state they wished to maintain was the constitutional state. Indeed, Liberal Nationalism as a collective doctrine included the notions of representation, popular participation, and guaranteed rights. The adaptations forced by a transition to Jacobin Nationalism changed the practice rather than the theory of constitutional supremacy. In the name of liberty and constitutional government, guaranteed rights were suppressed and representation curtailed. Jacobin Nationalism, being a doctrine for dealing with national emergencies, foreign invasion, and internal subversion, stressed institutions that enabled the nation to meet these threats. Thus, constitutional dictatorship, terror, manipulation of the masses, and military conscription provided the institutions appropriate for the myth of the "nation in arms in defense of liberty."

The typical institutions of Traditional Nationalism are monarchical. The myth that the Traditional Nationalists wish to have accepted by the nation is loyalty to an ancient body of custom, to order, to stability. The institutions most suited for this purpose are guilds, officially sanctioned castes, and *stand* differences. The monarch may be surrounded by secular and spiritual advisers and *curiae*, but he is in no sense a constitutional monarch. The myth associated with Traditional Nationalism demands the institutionalization of a religious value structure, the subordination of the rights of the individual to those of hereditary and particularistic groups. As for the Syncretist Nationalist, his myth compels him to adapt ancient institutions of kingship and priestly power to the innovations he wishes to introduce. He therefore seeks to institute constitutional monarchies that stress the superior powers of the ruler, to set up special colleges of priests, nobles, or soldiers to advise rulers and administrators on the compatibility of the new with the traditional. He tries to organize the educational system in such a way that the masses are mobilized while new ideas are kept under rigid control. Meiji Japan provides the best example of syncretist institutions; the Russia of Nicholas I illustrates the traditional variant.

Integral Nationalism always implies the authoritarian organization of society, economy, and polity, on the basis (at least in principle) of enforced egalitarianism. The *Volksgemeinschaft* of the Nazis is a case in point. Rigid leadership prevails in theory and in fact, often legitimated on charismatic grounds. Whereas the political institutions of totalitarianism always imply the existence of an Integral Nationalism, the reverse is not necessarily true. As will be shown below, various political systems of an authoritarian nature espouse Integral Nationalism as an official myth without being full-blown totalitarianisms.

Nationalism and social change. We have identified typical nationalist ideologies, myths, and national institutions. We have said little about their evolution, about the origin of nationalist leaders, about the factors that govern their successful appeal to the population. These factors are closely associated with the general pattern of social change of which the evolution of modern nationalism is but a part.

The initial impulse which gives a relatively stable society the push which launches a chain of changes is of secondary importance. Anthropologists disagree about whether this must be one event or a series of discrete happenings that together constitute the critical mass, setting off change. Something happens: the slave trade is imposed, Muslim invaders strike from the North, gunpowder and new money combine to defeat feudal knights and their castles, Commodore Perry sails into Tokyo Bay, Gandhi teaches a new ethic, *conquistadores* begin plantation agriculture through the *encomienda*. What is important for us is that the impulse—whether externally imposed or an autonomous internal development like the capitalism of Europe—disrupts established patterns of communication, undermines existing structures of legitimacy and authority, sows doubt and confusion, causes accepted symbols and values to be questioned. The process of change makes itself felt through new ways of making a living, the movement from country to city, the paying of taxes, subjection to a new code of sacred or secular law. And through these means new patterns of communication between social aggregates are established. Almost invariably, the new patterns extend over a larger territory and encompass more people than they did previously, since the process of change almost invariably includes improved facilities for physical communication. Groups not previously in communication with one another now find themselves neighbors. Probably the most dramatic of all innovative chains having this result is the cluster of events, institutions, and policies associated with modern Western imperialism.

The improvement in physical communication and technology now makes possible the large-scale organization of people who were not previously subject to such discipline, except at the village level. Others are uprooted from the village style of life; they become "socially mobilized." They work for wages, migrate to find jobs, go to school to learn skills, engage in business activities over long distances, serve in the army away from home, learn to read or to listen to the radio. But the socially mobilized are usually dissatisfied. Social change engenders frictions of many kinds, not the least of which is social and economic discrimination. Profiting from the new communications media, this mass of newly mobilized but frustrated individuals now organizes around symbols and values stressing dignity, equality, and *autonomy*—in brief, some kind of nationalism. Those who are at once most dissatisfied and most articulate are the makers of nationalist ideologies, the creative minority of "intellectuals." They create mass movements into which they absorb the—as yet—less mobilized, to whom they appeal through the symbols of whatever nationalist ideology seems to suit local situations and grievances.

Typically, there is not one but a series of competing nationalist ideologies in such a setting. Which will have the attributes to become a successful national myth with its own state? Will the entire administrative unit (whether an independent non-national state or a colony) become a nation, or only some part of it? Or can the dissatisfaction be headed off so as to avoid national consolidation altogether? All these possibilities are real and have historical counterparts. A compelling formula for dealing with them is the "assimilation-mobilization balance" pioneered by Karl Deutsch.*

* Deutsch, *Nationalism and Social Communication*. My treatment of the interaction between patterns of social change and nationalism obviously owes a great deal to Deutsch's concepts. Deutsch relies primarily on linguistic data in demonstrating balances and imbalances in assimilation and communication, notably in Czechoslovakia, Pakistan, and Finland. My treatment assumes that much the same point can be made by using other grounds for differentiation among mobilized groups, such as racial-economic-social factors (as in the case of American Negroes), religion (India, Nigeria), political ideology when identified with socio-economic or racial clusters (Malaysia, Kenya, Sudan).

When the rates of social mobilization are in balance with the rates of the successful absorption of the mobilized into the existing structure of society (assimilation), dissatisfaction can be controlled. When those who become literate, wealthy, self-confident, and critical are offered positions in government, at court, or in society, they will experience few pressures for becoming revolutionaries. When the newly mobilized does not feel that he is the victim of some kind of racial, linguistic, economic, or cultural discrimination, he sees little reason to organize movements of dissent. In short, when the ruling non-national elite is able to assimilate the newly articulate, the frictions that generate nationalism can be controlled. This, however, is very rarely the case. Usually, the rate of mobilization is much faster than the rate of assimilation. If ready grounds exist for differentiating the mobilized but marginal groups from the established power holders (as by language, religion, or race), the seedbed for nationalism is prepared. The mobilization-assimilation imbalance actually accentuates real and imagined social differentiation. This leads to a series of competing "national" loyalties within the same administrative unit.

On the basis of this formulation and of retrospective historical analysis, we can predict *where* national movements will occur and *which types* of ideology they will espouse. When the mobilized but unassimilated are wealthy merchants and industrialists allied with intellectuals, they will demand the liberal-constitutional pattern. When the mobilized are Negro trade unionists chafing under "capitalist" exploitation, they will call for an integral-authoritarian pattern. When the mobilized come from the lower aristocracy and the clergy, they tend to advocate traditional-corporatist institutions and religious sanction. When they come from a variety of social sources and feel themselves under dire attack from external stimuli, all three impulses will be felt, and the compromise may take a syncretist form. But this formulation does not enable us to predict *which type of national myth will ultimately triumph, and whether the administrative unit will remain one or be divided among rival nationalisms.** We can predict the origin and type of frictions, but not the pattern of accommodation or split. The intensity of the communication pattern among the groups and regions will not suffice for purposes of full prediction, even if all the data were available for mapping it, because there is no direct and inevitable causative relationship between the flow of transactions and messages and the political

---

* The case of India illustrates my point. Rival nationalist ideologies clustering around the liberal (Nehru), traditional (Tilak), integral (Bose), and syncretist (Gandhi) variants are plain. Further, religious, cultural, and economic differentiation patterns in various parts of British India combined to produce the Hindu-Muslim split in the 1930's, as well as the linguistic-economic tensions in independent India, leading to the principle of linguistic states. None of these demonstrations, however, enables us to say (1) that the victory of liberal nationalism either was inevitable or is final, (2) that the separation of Pakistan was inevitable, or (3) that the language compromise of the 1950's will either stop further internal "nationalist" dissent or conduce to the break-up of India.

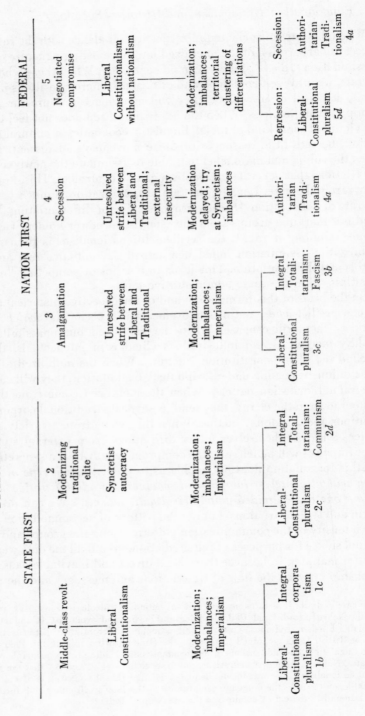

DEVELOPMENTAL TYPES AND THE ONTOLOGY OF NATIONALISM

STATE FIRST

1
Middle-class revolt

Liberal Constitutionalism

Modernization; imbalances; Imperialism

Liberal-Constitutional pluralism
1b

Integral corporatism
1c

2
Modernizing traditional elite

Syncretist autocracy

Modernization; imbalances; Imperialism

Liberal-Constitutional pluralism
2c

Integral Totalitarianism: Communism
2d

NATION FIRST

3
Amalgamation

Unresolved strife between Liberal and Traditional

Modernization; imbalances; Imperialism

Liberal-Constitutional pluralism
3c

Integral Totalitarianism: Fascism
3b

4
Secession

Unresolved strife between Liberal and Traditional; external insecurity

Modernization delayed; try at Syncretism; imbalances

Authoritarian Traditionalism
4d

FEDERAL

5
Negotiated compromise

Liberal Constitutionalism without nationalism

Modernization; imbalances; territorial clustering of differentiations

Secession: Authoritarian Traditionalism
4a

Repression: Liberal-Constitutional pluralism
5d

pattern of cohesion. Nevertheless, there does seem to be a slight historical prejudice in favor of the sanctity of the pre-existing administrative unit. The instances in which the old unit (whether a pre-national state or a colony) survives under different leadership and institutions are far more numerous than the rival cases of fragmentation. Established administrative, legal, and communications channels, even if introduced by a divine-right monarch or a foreign imperialist, do seem to have a special integrative significance.

Exact prediction is not possible; but the sketching of reasonable alternatives is. The spectrum of likely future nationalisms and their associated polities follows from historically and sociologically describable patterns. Historical sociology, it appears, has given us three major developmental "models," each with some less determinate but identifiable "submodels." We shall label them the "state first," "nation first," and "federal" models.

Nationalism and developmental types. The sequence of events, differentiations, and consequences may be summarized in schematic form (see the diagram on p. 470). In the "state first" sequence, the following patterns are historically "typical."

1. The unit is brought under the rule of a single governing elite by force, purchase, or dynastic marriage. The ruler imposes administrative, linguistic, and cultural uniformity as far as the literate and wealthier inhabitants are concerned. An imbalance arises between the ruling elite (nobility, colonial settlers, ethnically alien landowners, etc.) and the newly mobilized population, usually a professionally and commercially sophisticated middle class. As the aspiring class suffers discrimination, it organizes itself around the revolutionary symbols of Liberal Nationalism, captures the state machine, and proceeds to complete the process of social mobilization by instituting constitutional-democratic rule.

1a. Social change, however, does not stop there. Differentiation among groups continues at an uneven rate; skills and aims continue to be developed in diverse clusters, and not all the newly mobilized (or newly alienated) find a niche in the Liberal-Constitutional order.[14] Liberal Nationalists are likely to be fighting Traditionalists, who wish to turn away from rapid change and egalitarianism, industry and urbanism. External imperialism and/or the doctrines of racial-ethnic superiority associated with it become of increasing appeal to deal with fragmentation. No one national myth is firmly established; yet "national" bellicosity is likely to be very high.[15]

1b. Internal dissent may quiet down as assimilation takes up the slack of the alienated-mobilized. Economic growth continues and stills the demands of former Traditionalist Nationalists. Liberal-Constitutional Nationalism then becomes the successful myth, and pluralism the accepted social pattern.[16]

1c. But internal dissent engendered by imbalances and uneven growth rates may not be successfully absorbed. In that case, some approximation to Integral Nationalism with authoritarian institutions is the likely outcome. Instead of the pluralism associated with 1b, we will have a pseudo-pluralism of centrally "coordinated" mass organizations along corporate lines, not only designed to make possible continued planned mobilization, but capable of absorbing some of the Traditional forces previously alienated by the uneven rate of development.[17]

However, there may never have been a successful middle-class revolution at all.* Instead, the pre-national elite, sensing the winds of change and wishing to avert them or restrain them so as to retain control, seeks to make a nation and to modernize on its own initiative. But it seeks to do so without triggering imbalances. Thus

2. A self-reforming autocracy comes into being, based on the traditional ruling elite. It rules an already unified and centrally administered territory.

2a. This elite will espouse and foment a Syncretist Nationalism: modern industry and social cohesion based on vicariously communicated mass values will be fostered; but the institutions will remain authoritarian and religious. In fact, the modernizing state will assume a religious aura.[18] It is likely to stress a "national mission" and to turn to imperialism when this appears relatively costless.

2b. But it is highly unlikely that a modernizing-autocratic elite will succeed indefinitely. Imperialistic wars may result in defeat. Social change may still proceed more rapidly than anticipated and create the

---

* Some students of nationalism object to the inclusion of the post-1945 non-Western national revolutions in any typology of nationalism that uses models derived from European history. They prefer to think of a special "colonial" type that differs from the other types for the following reasons. (a) The basic cultural differences between Europe and Asia or Africa. (b) The fact that the newer nationalisms all owe their origin to their position as victims of what Georges Ballandier calls the "colonial situation," whereas the Western nationalisms arose autonomously. (c) The fact that the new nations are all underdeveloped and happen to combine *two* revolutionary aims in one bundle of institutions and policies: political independence and economic development.

I believe that these reasons, valid though they are in the immediate context, are unduly bound by time and area. Functional and structural similarities elucidating development are present even though the situational context differs. Ideological and institutional similarities are apparent throughout modern history, and they do cut across cultural contexts. All depends on the level of abstraction one wishes to attain. At the lowest level, every event is unique; at the highest all are one. The virtue of historical sociology resides in its ability to attain a middle level of abstraction in which similarities are noted and exploited, while differences are made into the major benchmarks. Further, I believe that we should not be blinded by the political controversy that happens to rage in the present international system. The process of decolonization is not yet complete, and for this reason present-day "colonial" nationalism has a flavor of its own. We are seeking to project the next system in which more standard aspirations will be felt.

very imbalances between assimilated and mobilized that were supposed to be avoided. Internal struggle will ensue, thus intensifying conflicts between reformist Liberal Nationalists, Syncretists, and Integral Nationalists, who see in totalitarian mobilization the only way to satisfaction.

2c. The struggle may result, if development and assimilation are sharply stepped up, in the victory of a Liberal-Constitutional national order.[19]

2d. However, it may result in the firm establishment of a full-blown totalitarian order espousing Integral Nationalism. Whether this, in turn, will reform itself into something else, as the economy and the social system acquire the capacity to satisfy most wants, is not yet clear.[20]

Before proceeding to the next major model, the nation preceding the state, one point must be clarified. Obviously, not all states—even now—are nations in the sense in which we defined a nation. Many countries have not yet reached the stage at which a minority-fostered national ideology has attracted mass support. There are still countries—though their number diminishes year by year—that have not reached the stage either of a middle-class take-over or of autocratic modernization. They are the "oligarchies" we encountered in studying the three international systems that characterize the life of the ILO. One reason why we did not use the typology here described in analyzing the earlier systems was the prevalence of pre-national regimes. The future system is unlikely to be similarly afflicted.

In many historical cases, the sentiment of nationhood came into being as a mass political phenomenon before statehood was achieved by the territory inhabited by the "nationalists." The syndrome of factors may be summarized as follows:

3. A given population is characterized by ethnic, linguistic, or cultural uniformity. But it may live scattered in a number of political units,[21] or be subjugated by another state.[22] Modern professional and industrial skills develop, but are not recognized in time by the rulers, who continue to monopolize positions of wealth and prestige. Imbalances in skills and aspirations occur between two (or more) differentiated groups, so that language, religion, or a sense of past history becomes the unifying symbol of all those who feel that they are the victims of social or economic discrimination on the part of the ruling group, which happens to have a different language and/or religion. A Liberal Nationalist reform movement arises, which demands equality and/or autonomy. It is often not recognized in time, and in frustration its adherents turn to Traditional Nationalism in the search for powerful symbols of difference from their rulers.

3*a*. A nation that lives in scattered states may be unified by an act of force on the part of one unit; this unit will be supported, overtly or covertly, by nationalists in the conquered units. Opposition to the forceful act also exists. The search for a national myth will then stress organic unity. Further, social mobilization will continue, creating imbalances between groups newly differentiated or carried over from the pre-national period. Traditionalists will engage Liberals, and the constitutional order is very much in doubt. Imperialism may be a temporary palliative. The following two alternatives are likely.[23]

3*b*. In the turmoil engendered by competing nationalist ideologies and uneven patterns of development, the totalitarian solution begins to appeal. Integral doctrines and authoritarian institutions begin to arise. Fascism is a likely solution.[24]

3*c*. The nation will develop the capacity for absorbing the newly mobilized and will outlive the Traditionalists. Defeat in war may help. In any event, the Liberal-Constitutional order is confirmed eventually.[25]

If the pattern of unification takes the form of an act of territorial revolt and secession from the former ruler, the chances for the evolution of a Liberal Nationalism are sharply reduced.

4. Revolt or war makes independence possible. It is a precarious independence, however, because a defensive mentality has already been instilled in the nationalists by the frustrations previously experienced at the hands of the former rulers. Furthermore, the process of internal differentiation had not been completed, and the national myth has not had an opportunity to triumph over the competing Liberal and Traditional strains. External insecurity thus gets intertwined with the unresolved tensions of domestic development.

4*a*. Almost invariably, this type of nation eventually develops toward Integral Nationalism, even though many Traditionalist values will survive in it. Its institutions will always be heavily authoritarian. It may continue the process of modernization, but this will be slow and subject to various compromises imposed by the survival of Traditionalism.[26]

There is one evolutionary pattern which, at the outset at least, avoids force altogether. In the "federal" pattern there is, initially, neither a state nor a nation. There are several states that may or may not be infused with nationalism.[27] The unique aspect of this pattern is reliance on a process of rational calculation and negotiation among elites eager to create a new state.

5. Elites representing the various states are persuaded that some common or converging aims can be met more efficiently by political union. Normally, economic considerations predominate. The institutions of the

new federation are always Liberal-Constitutional in inspiration. This is a matter of necessity rather than ideological conviction, since government by persuasion and compromise can take place only in a system of defined powers and rights. The pattern is thus Liberal Nationalist, even though the founding fathers may not be Liberal Nationalists.

5*a*. Union comes about before there is a sense of federal nationhood on a mass basis. Social change continues, and usually begins to create the now familiar imbalances between mobilization, assimilation, skills, and satisfactions. But since this usually occurs *before* there are powerful central symbols, policies, rewards, or convictions, the frustrations and dissatisfactions engendered acquire a territorial referent. The federation is soon in trouble.[28]

5*b*. Civil strife ensues. The ruling elites will resort to Integral Nationalism to tie the union together and supplement it with authoritarian institutions, while continuing a process of mobilization and modernization.[29]

5*c*. The dissident units will resort to Traditional Nationalism to defend their local "way of life" against the encroachments of the central elites. If successful, they will secede and inaugurate a new state on the model of 4 and 4*a*.[30]

5*d*. If the central elites win out, or if some accommodation short of civil war is worked out, the resulting pattern will be the confirmation of Liberal-Constitutionalism with pluralistic institutions and social patterns.

Our task now becomes to relate these developmental alternatives to the types of regimes that can actually be presumed to exist in the next decades. Which of these types, then, are currently in the picture, and how can they be classified in terms of dominant institutions and policies? The answer will give us the international environment of the near future.

THE FUTURE INTERNATIONAL ENVIRONMENT

The process of sorting out actual regimes and polities in terms of these developmental constructs brings us face to face with the paradox that prompted this excursion into the history and sociology of nationalism. First, we must get an impression of the degree of the presumed longevity of the "final" derivatives. Although five were encountered, it is highly unlikely that more than three can be considered as sufficiently viable to last many more years: namely, the liberal-constitutional, integral-corporatist, and integral-totalitarian types. The various combinations of authoritarian institutions legitimated by syncretism or traditionalism are unlikely to withstand the pressures of unresolved internal modernization and mobilization. Further, we shall discover that many actual regimes are located at various intermediate points on the developmental scale; they thus offer little prospect of "settling down" in their present analytical rubric. Their future place must somehow be conjectured. Finally, the question of pluralism and the permeability of the national shell can now be broached in terms of the likelihood of a given regime's future niche. For this purpose we turn once more to the analysis of trade unionism.

We are interested in trade unions and their autonomy, since these groups serve as a sensitive indicator of the prevalence of pluralism and functionally specific group behavior. In many historical cases, the establishment of unions led to the formation of functionally specific employer associations. In most countries, trade-union vigor and autonomy provide a yardstick for judging the existence of a strong pluralism in other contexts, such as service organizations, women's groups, veterans' organizations, and other purely economic groupings.

Hence it proved instructive to draw a spectrum of pluralism and functional specificity, using such recent national studies of trade unionism as were available. These are the attributes of pluralism and functionally specific behavior used: (1) the legal setting, (2) the types of prevalent aims, and (3) the actual autonomy of the unions. Under the first heading, I considered the right to form, maintain, and expand unions without government restriction, the right to strike, and the right to bargain collectively. Under the second heading, data on the objectives and mentality of union bureaucracies were summarized; the extremes range from purely nonpolitical economic bargaining to complete integration into a politically controlled national plan, leaving to the unions only welfare and recreational functions. Under the final heading, I was concerned with union affiliation and/or subordination to political parties, corporations, or government ministries. This analysis yielded eight clusters, which seem to cover all existing combinations:

Group 1. Full freedom; economic objectives and a bargaining mentality; no affiliation with political formations.

Group 2. Full freedom; economic objectives and a bargaining mentality; the maintenance of loose and informal political ties.

Group 3. Full freedom; mixed economic and political objectives, along with a tendency for a revolutionary mentality to take the place of bargaining; maintenance of full and open ties with political parties.

Group 4. Restricted freedom; mixed economic and political aims, the latter often taking precedence; maintenance of full and open ties with political parties.

Group 5. Restricted freedom; mixed economic and political aims; nonpolitical trade unions based on weakness, timidity, and government restrictions.

Group 6. Extremely restricted freedom; it is difficult to speak of economic or political aims, since all union activity is subject either to the inclusion of the union elite in the governing oligarchy or to government toleration; non-political.

Group 7. Extremely restricted freedom; political aims predominate, since these unions are permitted to function only as a part of the official economic modernization plan; a tendency to be a part of the single ruling party.

Group 8. These trade unions are an arm of the state, permitted to function only as part of the total plan for society.

We must now translate our trade union spectrum into the larger developmental types (see Table 33). Thus it seems clear that the countries found in Groups 1, 2, and 3 exhibit most of the characteristics of a *stable* liberal-constitutional pluralism. Internal pressures and earlier imbalances seem to have been resolved sufficiently to make us predict that in the next decade or two no dramatic changes in regime, institutions, or guiding national myth need be expected. It is equally clear that the countries in Group 8 provide a relatively stable basis for projection. Although it is highly likely that the process of "detotalitarianization" will continue in the industrialized states of the communist bloc, we cannot expect a sufficient degree of liberalization to assume the introduction of a meaningful pattern of pluralism. These countries, then, will remain relatively impermeable as far as feedbacks from the international system are concerned, even though the intensity of their Integral Nationalism may well continue to decline in pro-

TABLE 33

TRADE UNIONS, PLURALISM, AND FUNCTIONAL SPECIFICITY:
THE GLOBAL SPECTRUM IN 1963

Freedom to oppose the government				No freedom to oppose the government			
Group 1	Group 2	Group 3	Group 4[a]	Group 5	Group 6	Group 7	Group 8
Canada	Benelux	Chile[a]	Argentina	Lebanon	Burma	Algeria	Soviet
U.S.	Germany	France	Brazil	Malaya	Central	Ghana	bloc
	Israel	Italy	Ceylon	Pakistan	America	Guinea	
	Scandi-	Japan	India	Turkey	Dahomey	Tangan-	
	navia		Indonesia		Ivory	yika	
	U.K.		Mexico		Coast	U.A.R.	
			Morocco		Liberia		
					Libya		
					Thailand		

SOURCE: Based on information culled from Walter Galenson, ed., *Labor in Developing Economics* (Berkeley: University of California Press, 1963), and *Labor and Economic Development* (New York: Wiley, 1959); Bruce H. Millen, *The Political Role of Labor in Developing Countries* (Washington, D.C.: The Brookings Institution, 1963). Additional information was obtained from the on-the-scene surveys of the ILO Freedom of Association group. See its reports on the trade union situation in the United Kingdom (1961), Sweden (1961), Malaya (1962), and Burma (1962). Unlike the earlier reports on the situation in the United States and the Soviet Union, these four reports give merely descriptive detail and refrain from any evaluative statement. In fact, they tend to be quite understanding toward the restrictions on the free trade-union activity described in the cases of Burma and Malaya.

[a] These countries have been included in the broad category "freedom to oppose government," since the restrictive legislation that does exist, and the restraints imposed on full union autonomy, are not used in such a manner as to demand conformity with governments. Lack of full freedom is manifested primarily in restrictions on the right to strike and the preference for compulsory arbitration over collective bargaining.

portion to the solution of internal pressures. A final example of relative stability is presented by the countries in Group 7. They have made their ideological and institutional choice with respect to the next decades. They possess authoritarian institutions, which are linked to official integral ideologies that dictate militant modernization and conformity to doctrine. But they also possess the beginnings of an "official" pluralism in the trend toward more or less compulsory mass organizations of a functionally specific character, which are linked to the ruling party and its program. Since these organizations are more autonomous than their counterparts in communist systems, and continue to possess some leverage in the decision-making process, we consider the countries in this group to fall into the "integral-corporatist" type.

The remaining groups all represent various degrees of instability. They imply lack of permanence as far as our projection is concerned. It is to be assumed that in a decade's time they will have developed in one of two ways: they will have moved either into the more permeable category of national consciousness by maximizing pluralism or into one of the integral rubrics of resistance to integrative forces. Several, however, will just have begun to move into one of the transitional phases that precede an eventual "settling-down" phase.

Thus, a number of countries remain in the pre-national condition of rule by a traditional oligarchy over an unmobilized mass (some Central American countries, Liberia, Libya, several West African nations). One is currently a modernizing autocracy, but already feels the tensions associated with such a regime (Morocco). Others find themselves in an integral-authoritarian phase in which the autocratic government is experimenting with cautious modernization under syncretist and often traditional auspices (Thailand, Burma, Pakistan). The regimes in question are feeling the results of internal differentiations and imbalances and have not yet learned to absorb them. Malaysia finds itself in the very early phases of seeking to accommodate the variegated forces united in a negotiated federation, and has not yet tasted the fruits of drastic internal differentiations in mobilization. Indonesia has not yet completed the transition to what appears to be an integral-corporatist type of regime, although she is well on her way. The syncretist features implicit in the doctrines of "Guided Democracy" and *Mufakat* are still manifest.

Finally, a number of regimes appear to be in various transitional phases approaching a liberal-constitutional-pluralistic final stage. Traditional ideas and forces are still competing with liberal ones, as marked differences in development and political participation subsist between the mobilized urban groups and the pre-modern rural population (Brazil, Mexico, Lebanon, Turkey). Yet the dominant political ideas seem to destine these countries for a secular modernism. The degree of pluralism is already such as to make the totalitarian final solution an unlikely one. India and Ceylon are also characterized by liberal-constitutional institutions, and a Liberal Nationalism prevails; however, the division between articulate city and sleepy village is still marked, as is the strength of traditional and self-consciously syncretist doctrines. Argentina, finally, finds herself closest to the stage in which liberal-constitutionalism is dominant, with mass participation and voluntary-group formation increasing more rapidly than economic modernization.

Where, then, is the weight of our analysis to fall with respect to the future position of these unstable and transitional regimes? Before a semblance of an answer can be hazarded, our grounds for accepting and excluding future "dominant" types of regimes must be set forth. Nothing so firm as a "final" type can be argued; "dominance" is the most our mode of analysis permits us to posit. Yet skepticism regarding the permanence of traditional features was implicit in what was said above. Equally little store was put in various self-conscious efforts at mixing the modern with the traditional in doctrines of syncretism. Our courage is adequate for positing the continuing dominance of liberal-constitutional and integral regimes in the countries in which they are now found; yet how can we be sufficiently audacious to suggest that the efforts of a Sukarno, an Ayub, and a Haile Selassie will not meet with success?

My mode of analyzing and projecting the current spectrum of regimes in underdeveloped countries is heavily influenced by the work of political sociologists applying functional concepts. I am impressed with the pitfalls and difficulties *they* see in the path of the regimes they describe. And I am sufficiently under the spell of historical sociology to make me wish to apply the lessons of unstable regimes in the West to the appraisal of certain polities in Africa, Asia, and Latin America.[31]

According to David Apter, there are three typical regimes, differentiated from one another in their manner of legitimation, the loyalty they exact, the decisional autonomy of the government, and the distribution of authority and of ideological expression. The most dramatically and rigidly innovative of these is the "mobilization system," which is identical with the type we have described as integral-corporatist. Because of its dedication to development and its presumed capacity to subordinate a variety of social forms and impulses to this aim, this type of regime is likely to have a relatively secure future. The likelihood is increased if these regimes do not travel the full road to totalitarianism, which they sometimes approximate. As long as a variety of functionally specific "voluntary" groups exists, and as long as the authority of the single party is mollified by the toleration of some opposition groups, these regimes may retain popularity. An institutionalized and ritualized corporatism may then result, once the current generation of charismatic leaders passes from the scene, thus legitimating in a pseudo-pluralism the drive for modernization.[32] The attraction of this type of polity for other developing nations is too obvious to require comment.

Apter also establishes a "modernizing autocracy," which seeks to innovate so as to maintain traditional patterns of authority intact; indeed, it justifies innovation with reference to the traditional and often succeeds in maintaining its popularity. We have also used this type in our ontology. History, however, shows no case of indefinite success. Sooner or later imbalances occur, mobilized groups are not assimilated, legitimacy is in doubt, and the hitherto creative traditional elite fails in holding the loyalty of the population. At that point, the bifurcation toward the possible liberal or integral forms occurs. Given the constantly rising tide of welfare expectations and the acceleration in technical and popular education, I find it difficult to believe that the Kabaka of Buganda can repeat the feat of the Emperor Meiji for very long.[33] For the same reason, the more easygoing authoritarian regime of contemporary Pakistan, like the similar regimes in Rumania and Poland during the 1930's, cannot be considered anything more than transitional. An integral nationalism is professed toward the outside world, but the ideas and institutions of the country continue to contain traditional and syncretist components. These will get in the way of the deliberate modernization that is being attempted. Syncretism has no hope of survival once the rigors of industrialization are felt by appreciable groups in the population. Given the limited administrative capacity of these countries, it taxes my belief in human adaptability to foresee a continued successful channeling of imbalance.

The dominant types so sharply etched by Apter may also be understood sequentially by adopting the advancement scale suggested by Gino Germani and Kalman Silvert.[34] All polities may be classified on a continuum that slowly changes from the pre-national, traditional, and oligarchical to the current dominant types involving the full and dynamic participation of all citizens in the nation, whether under democratic or totalitarian auspices. The indicators for placing a given regime on the scale comprise the existence of self-conscious upper and middle classes, the degree of ethnic-cultural homogeneity in the population, the degree of individual identification with the nation, the will and ability to participate in politics above the face-to-face level, and the extent of urban-rural discontinuities and geographical imbalances.

In Latin America, at any rate, the normal pattern of development is toward national homogeneity and full participation. At the moment we encounter the following distribution: (*a*) Pre-national oligarchies cautiously usher in such innovation as is perceived useful to the ruling elites; there is almost no middle class, and the bulk of the lower classes remains at the margin of public life.[35] (*b*) Representative democracy with limited participation prevails; there are political parties and free elections, but only the urban, mobilized, articulate middle sector partakes.[36] Cultural and geographical discontinuities continue. (c) Representative democracy with enlarged participation develops from the pressures released by the preceding type, resulting in the absorption of the *urban* lower classes into public life and the radicalization of politics; the rural population still remains outside the nation.[37] This is the crucial stage: it tends to determine whether the liberal-constitutional or one of the two integral dominant types eventually emerges. (d1) If the process of assimilation keeps up with continued mobilization, representative democracy with full participation can be ushered in.[38] (d2) If not, a mobilization system or a communist dictatorship emerges.[39] Clearly, this historical-sociological vision is easily combined with our earlier analysis of the ontology of nation-states and the dominant types of the next few decades.

On the basis of our trade union indicator we concluded that the established pluralistic pattern is relatively stable in Western Europe, North America, and Australasia.[40] We also concluded that the integral-totalitarian pattern is going to be with us for a long time in Eastern Europe. Both dominant national systems will prove receptive to the political and security functions associated with the United Nations. But the very nature of the environment will make the economic and social fuctions of the UN quite irrelevant to the predominant national concerns in both types of polity. These functions will no longer fit the needs of the West, and they will be resisted as irreconcilable with planned objectives in the East.

In Asia and Latin America, the extent of economic development, industrialization, education, and functional specificity in voluntary groups would suggest intensified development toward the liberal-constitutional type already existing in Japan, the Philippines, Argentina, Chile, Uruguay, Costa Rica, and Mexico. Stability in domestic orientation may also be expected in Communist China and the Asian countries in her orbit, though the intensity of integral-totalitarianism will be more marked than in Eastern Europe and much less responsive to international political and security impulses.

The remainder of the world is unstable at present. Some of the transitional countries, such as India and Ceylon, may well continue to approach the liberal-constitutional type *without* giving rise to the kind of pluralism that makes the nation receptive to international impulses. The trade unionists in these countries, for the most part, eschew the Western type of unionism; they prefer support for disciplined and centralized economic planning to either party democracy or interest-group confrontation. In most of Africa and the Middle East, trade unionists perceive themselves as arms of a mobilizing state. They have no wish to oppose the ruling party or doctrine: they want to build "African" or "Arab" Socialism. At best, they are searching for a more functionally specific role for unions and other voluntary organizations *within* the hierarchical structure of the mobilization system, as a party within a party catering to the social, recreational, and educational needs of workers rather than to any autonomous economic role. Some would make unions the managers of cooperatives, others participants in party planning. At best a corporate rather than an independent functional position is envisaged.[41]

In short, the mobilization system is the wave of the future in Africa, in much of Asia, and in Latin America, not Western-style democratic pluralism. Modernizing autocracies and authoritarian-syncretist systems will give way to it. In fact, some of these countries—by supporting the organization of trade unions in order to have corporate partners in a pseudo-pluralistic planning process—are actually undermining their own authority and creating the infrastructure of a future mobilization system.[42] And mobilization systems are very selective with respect to the feedbacks to which they are willing to expose themselves, though more permeable than totalitarianisms.

At the risk of incurring the disaster that befalls so many predictions, I suggest that the distribution of dominant types is likely to be as follows in the coming decade (in number of countries):

	Liberal-constitutional	Integral-totalitarian	Integral-corporatist	Authoritarian-transitional
West and North Europe, N. America, Australasia..	21	–	–	2
East Europe	–	8	–	–
Asia and Middle East	7	5	13	4
Latin America	9	2	7	4
Africa	1	1	33*	1
Total	38	16	53	11

For international organizations, then, the immediate future constitutes the greatest challenge. In order to maximize feedback possibilities, the liberal-constitutional type should be supported by international programs. Hence what the organizations do in countries situated in the unstable and transitional categories on our scale of functional specificity and pluralism is crucial. Simple policies of supporting economic development by technical assistance, basic education, loans, and grants are likely to intensify the pangs of the transition; they will create more mobilized but unassimilated groups and individuals, and thus tilt the balance in favor of one of the integral solutions. Policies, such as the ILO's new emphasis on worker edu-

---

* Includes Nyasaland and Zambia. The total is probably the single most questionable item in the projection. It assumes that almost all current African states will survive and transform their variegated tribal oligarchies into mobilization systems. It is just as probable, however, that many of them will have failed to do so by 1970, and will continue in some transitional pre-national oligarchic pattern.

cation and management skills, that stress the creation of attitudes and competences relating to meaningful participation in a free confrontation among political actors must somehow be geared to the general rate of mobilization, if an ultimate pattern approaching some kind of pluralism is to be achieved. If education runs ahead of actual assimilation into the governing elite, or if the demands of the public outrun the available skills for meeting them, the investment of international organizations will be lost. Instead, impatience and passion will once more outstrip any possibility of pluralistic adjustment, and the environment will continue to change before systemic feedbacks can make themselves felt.

Countries in the transitional categories all struggle with two competing goal conceptions: the drive for development and the desire to maintain the existing polity. Technical assistance and economic aid must be made part of programs that present pluralism to the governing elites as a desirable aspect of national system maintenance. This is probably the greatest challenge to the leaderships of international organizations. *But even if the governing elites are convinced that their competing developmental and system-maintenance goals can be met with a pluralistic formula, the groups so encouraged must be successfully assimilated through planned social as well as economic development.* The task of ideological and human engineering here suggested is so vast as to predict its own failure. And if failure is in store for the immediate pluralistic aspects of international programs, our projection of the future environment is far from fanciful.

THE FUTURE INTERNATIONAL SYSTEM

Before concluding our effort with a sketch of input-output relations, attributes, structures, and functions, certain leading assumptions that have remained implicit had better be made unambiguous. All these projections *must* obviously assume that there will be no major nuclear war. Less obvious but equally important is the assumption *against* any major technological or scientific breakthrough that would conduce to the unilateral advantage of one nation or bloc. It is more than conceivable that science and technology in the next decade will produce an invulnerable anti-missile missile; if not evenly distributed among the major actors, this development would clearly upset the symmetry of the current and any future system. It is also possible that revolutionary meteorological, industrial, and agricultural techniques will be developed, thus changing current expectations and possibilities in the field of economic development and thereby affecting the global economic bargaining pattern. Again, such a development must be symmetrically distributed if our projections are to be valid. Finally, dramatic genetic manipulation may become an actual possibility; the stricture with respect to symmetrical distribution of capabilities applies once more.[43]

The fundamental attribute of the future system may be labeled "hetero-symmetrical multipolarity" with reasonable stability.[44] As far as the balance of thermonuclear strategic weapons is concerned, the present bipolar pattern will continue. Only the United States and the Soviet Union will possess these weapons in the quality and quantity necessary for what Robert Osgood calls a "passive deterrent" capability, which requires the capacity to deliver a credible second strike following an attack on the nation's *home* territory (as distinguished from that of its allies).[45] However, allies of the superpowers, as well as selected neutral states, may well possess less powerful weapons in minor quantity, thus offering a limited "active deterrent" posture of their own, both within and outside the major bipolar military confrontation. Further, conventional military forces will still be important and unevenly distributed. However, the overall distribution of military capabilities of all kinds will be such that (a) the Soviet Union and the United States will occupy a symmetrical position, and (b) the remaining clusters of military strength will be so distributed as to give neither side a decisive edge. This is the essence of "hetero-symmetry."

Multipolarity will be more pronounced than in the present system, since the present regional clusters will increase in number even if some will diminish in cohesion. Multipolarity will obtain, since, in addition to military regional organizations, there will be economic blocs as well as ideological regional entities, notably in Africa. Membership in such regional groupings will be ragged and overlapping. One nation will join a regional grouping for ideological purposes, another for economic reasons, and still another for military ones. Hence hetero-symmetry will exist not merely with respect to military and security questions, but also in the fields of trade, finance, economic planning, and aid, as well as in new functional concerns now on the threshold of our conscious policy-making.

Stability will be more pronounced than in the current system because of the larger possibility for hetero-symmetrical bargains and adjustments. The multiplication of actors will approach an n-person situation in which non-zero-sum outcomes become routine and expected. This is likely even though the new output pattern will operate on a reduced variety of inputs. Hetero-symmetry also implies a heterogeneous pattern of future gains and losses for all acting units, thus reducing the total stake of each in any one situation.

But these attributes are based on a projection of typical inputs provided by the acting units and by the pattern of outputs their confrontation is likely to produce. In Hoffmann's historical sociology, historical systems are differentiated from one another by (a) the nature of the acting units, (b) the aims they follow, and (c) their capacity to carry out these aims. We shall follow this characterization in talking about the future system, while disagreeing with Hoffmann that such a system must be a revolutionary and therefore unstable one. On the contrary, we shall argue that environmental heterogeneity may produce relative system stability.*

In the current system, the acting units comprise many more than the four modal types projected for the future. They range, in nature, from the liberal-constitutional to the communist-totalitarian variety; we believe that the new system will be characterized by fewer types. Further, the number and kind of aims associated with each type will undergo change. In the current system, the Western democracies value their military posture, prefer to contain communism, regard the non-aligned world as a pawn to be kept non-aligned or to be attracted to the West; they yield to anti-colonial demands with this aim in mind, and extend economic assistance for the same reason. The Moscow-oriented communist bloc seems to calculate in essentially similar terms with reference to its aim of achieving supremacy, or at least holding its own. The rest of the world tends toward one or the other side, according to a given elite's perception of its own security and interests, the pace of domestic social mobilization, and the pressures generated by it. Rapidly developing Asian, African, and Latin American countries seek to extract, from both sides, concessions that would also tend to strengthen their independence from both.[46] Less rapidly developing countries, in which traditional elites remain precariously in control or which are ruled by insecure revolutionary elites, tend to show less independence and to identify closely with their protectors.[47] The rapidly developing states stress arms control, the relaxation of Cold War tensions, heavy economic assistance, and a violent anti-colonialism that takes precedence over collective security. The more stagnant tend to stress military protection by the major powers, and generalized collective security under regional or United Nations auspices, as well as economic assistance. Their only reliable link with the more self-conscious neutralists is their equally strong emphasis on anti-colonialism. But in the future system there will be more of the former and fewer of the latter nations. In addition, the colonial issue will probably have ceased to be relevant. Hence the dominant inputs will favor a *détente*,

---

* For Hoffmann's discussion see "International Systems and International Law," *World Politics*, October 1961, pp. 207–10. In a stable system, the objectives, capacities, and character of the actors are by and large compatible (e.g. Europe before the French Revolution and during parts of the nineteenth century) ; in a revolutionary system, they are basically incompatible (e.g. Europe since 1914, and the entire world since 1945). Hoffmann bases these judgments exclusively on environmental considerations. Rosecrance demonstrated that, despite these environmental pressures, the current system is more stable than its predecessor. We must refunnel environmental heterogeneity into systemic relationships, under which the relative degree of unevenness that can be accommodated in the notion of hetero-symmetry can become the dominant criterion of stability.

autonomous military strength for the non-aligned, and increasing economic aid with less and less nationally imposed strings.

With respect to capacity, however, the next system will not differ from the current one as far as the distinctions among types of regimes are concerned. Supreme thermonuclear, technological, scientific, and industrial capacity will still be in the hands of the United States and the Soviet Union. The non-aligned and mobilizing systems in Africa, Asia, and Latin America will not have succeeded in upsetting this relationship, even if they do develop rapidly, because they will still lag behind the present leaders. Developing democracies in Asia and Latin America will be no stronger, relatively, than they now are. The change will occur among the allies of the present leaders, the liberal-constitutional systems in Europe, and the integral-totalitarian ones in Eurasia. They will acquire new capacities, thus weakening the cohesion of the present military blocs and reinforcing the trend toward multipolarity in the military field—though not necessarily in the economic or ideological.

This confrontation of new demands by a larger number of actor nations and more diversified regional associations will alter the output pattern. Both East and West will moderate their demands and expectations in the military realm. Neither will expect to be able to defeat the other in a massive war. Both will seek to confirm the division of the world by means of accommodations, rather than large-scale armed conflict, though such accommodations will involve local wars and procedures for stopping or containing them. Both will experience the necessity for catering to the non-aligned on purely ideological and economic grounds, while keeping them from becoming too strong militarily. The non-aligned, for their part, will find it necessary to keep the *détente* from becoming so complete as to make the flow of economic aid slow down to a trickle. The main outputs of the international system will involve a bargaining pattern for economic aid that confirms national independence. They will also involve ideological issues that both sides can use to continue their spiritual conflict as their military contest abates.

Last and most important, the output pattern will begin to include converging demands that spring from the as yet very unevenly distributed desire to control aspects of future international interdependence: notably in such fields as the control over outer space, telecommunications, new diseases, the resources of the ocean floor, and control of the climate. These objectives will impinge, to some extent, on all nations. They will correspond to aims already experienced actively in some areas; yet the impulse will not necessarily bear any relationship to the present tripolar division and may well cut across the multipolar context that we envisage. The now familiar bargaining pattern involves colonial concessions by the West, economic and military concessions by East and West, and military-ideological concessions by the non-aligned. But the new bargaining may give rise to outputs and organizational tasks that can only be dimly associated with current experience. In fact, it may even contain a suggestion of military and arms control bargaining in which the two superpowers are pitted against the non-aligned bloc, a trend perhaps foreshadowed in the work of the UN's Conference of Eighteen on Disarmament.

A measure of stability, based on systemic pressures involving give-and-take, will prevail despite the absence of any uniform pluralism. It will prevail in the face of the absence of any other generalized homogeneity in the environment. Give-and-take will result from the simple fact that a heterogeneous body of regimes will be compelled to bargain continuously if it wishes to satisfy national demands that call for aid or benevolent neutrality on the part of other regimes. As heretofore, these pressures will be played out primarily in the existing organizations—regional bodies, the United Nations, and specialized agencies, these last playing an increasingly large part as Myrdal's vision becomes reality. But, at this stage, the attentive reader may well suspect that I am falling into the very trap discussed in an earlier chapter: the temptation to use systems analysis in such a fashion as to subordinate the historical and phenomenal material to systems dominance.

The future system I am sketching is no more automatic than its predecessor. It will rest on the aims, hopes, hates, and fears of the actors in the nation-states and international organizations that inhabit it. The system's functions, as in the past, will be the result of that interaction among acting units which produces outputs not entirely in accord with the original inputs, outputs which contain an element of the unintended and which continue to offer the capacity for transforming the system. Actors remain central in this development. Outputs can and do result from what the actors have "learned" about previous interactions: the propaganda losses they may have suffered, the African countries that have slipped out of their control, the monetary discipline they may have imposed on, or spared, a Latin American nation. Actor purposes that turned into functions are often assimilated as lessons, and reappear as purposes at a later stage. We must recognize, however, that the learning may involve disintegrative as well as integrative consequences. Disappointment with the propaganda implications of the freedom of association surveys led the United States to block the continuation of this aspect of the human rights function in the ILO; but the snowballing of the (previously unintended) stress on the abolition of forced labor persuaded the Kennedy Administration to propose to the U.S. Senate the ratification of the forced labor Convention. Thus to the limited extent that there is system feedback, there is learning.

In addition to integrative learning, however, another mechanism keeps the actor predominant in the regulative impact of the hetero-symmetrical multipolar system. Quite apart from the possibilities of feedback—which our ILO study showed to be sharply limited—autonomous changes in the environment produce new convergences of actor aims, which can be meaningfully satisfied only with outputs involving an enlarged functional scope. And hence the system can be regarded as regulative, despite continuing heterogeneity, in those realms of policy in which the actors must delegate authority to an international agency in order to reap the benefits of the outputs.

The question, then, is this: which systemic pressures will conduce to further integration despite hetero-symmetry? Which structures will increase in power over member nations despite the increase in integral regimes? And which rules of law and peaceful adjustment can be expected to flourish? These questions bring us to the consideration of functional law.

INTEGRATION AND INTERNATIONAL LAW

The role of law in the evolution of any political system can best be viewed as a dual one: first, to settle disputes between contending parties in the interest of order and stability; second, to generate new norms, to establish rules for future conduct by which actors can be guided without having to resort to litigation.[48] This dual role is well illustrated by the different institutions familiar to international and municipal law. International law, which lacks courts with generally binding jurisdiction and the capacity for enforcement without consent, stresses various refinements on the arbitral technique. A settlement depends first and foremost on the will of the litigants to submit the case and abide by the judgment. Hence negotiation is never far from the surface, and the purely legal role of settling disputes is supreme. Municipal, especially constitutional, law does have courts with compulsory jurisdiction and enjoys the benefits of bailiffs, marshals, and troops. Hence it may favor the legitimation of orderly change through the authoritative interpretation of legal texts in their political environment. It may cease being wholly "legal" and confined to the parties, in that it reaches for general future guidelines of conduct—provided the judges profess a modicum of judicial activism. However, success in the purely legal realm is a necessary prerequisite to the larger integrative role. As one eminent scholar puts it, "The truth may be that, when courts settle previously unenvisaged questions concerning the most fundamental constitutional rules, they *get* their authority to decide them after the questions have arisen and the decision has been given. Here all that succeeds is success. It is conceivable that the constitutional question at issue may divide society too fundamentally to permit of its disposition by a judicial decision."[49]

Without some certainty that the parties will accept and implement an award, it is idle to speculate on a later norm-creating power of the courts.

Neither the present nor the future international system offers much hope that existing international law and institutions will be able to cross the bridge from arbitration to comprehensive judicial control. Hoffmann divides post-Grotian international law into three categories on the basis of the kind of *stable* historical system in which it developed and which it was designed *by the actors* to support. The most primitive is the law of the political framework; this aims at establishing the ground rules for limiting violence and ordering conflict among sovereign states that are expected indefinitely to espouse opposing aims, which they occasionally uphold with hostile means. To it we owe the notion of the sole legal personality of the state, sovereignty, diplomatic protocol, and much of the law of treaties. Less primitive is the law of reciprocity, which aims at ordering, in greater detail, the normal relations of states, still considered to be separate and autonomous. Here we find most of the commercial law that grew up in the nineteenth century, the law of territorial jurisdiction, and the Hague and Geneva rules of warfare. The purpose of the law was to seal off and confirm the sovereignty of nations, while regulating those areas of contact that would inevitably recur. Finally, there is the law of community, which is concerned with *joint regulation* of those aspects of contact and interdependence which, by definition, can be dealt with only by ignoring national frontiers. This area comprises health, postal communications, telecommunications, and—in contemporary Western Europe—the bulk of economic life.[50]

But the contemporary order is a heterogeneous one. Hoffmann is clearly correct in not expecting a future system to be sufficiently homogeneous to presage the easy institutionalization of the law of community. All three categories are represented in the current order. Since they conflict in emphasis and detail, the result is chaos and the decline of judicial settlement as a technique. Moreover, "much of the present international law, precisely because it reflects a dead system, is obsolete. But changes in the international system have had a second kind of effect on international law: some of the rules which are supposed to be valid today are premature. These are rules which express attempts at imposing a new scheme of world order which purported to draw the lesson from the ultimate failure of the balance-of-power system, but proved to be thoroughly unfit for the present revolutionary world."[51] These premature efforts include two features that Functionalists associated with the ILO cherish particularly: the quasi-federal and the quasi-parliamentary framework for dealing with nation-states, as well as the effort to deal with delicts by governments as if the international legal order were a criminal code operating within an overall constitutional order.* Nevertheless—and this conclusion is crucial for our purposes—the very confusion between the categories, as well as their coexistence and espousal by various types of regimes, has safeguarded an area in which new rules are growing up in an unsystematic and unplanned manner to serve in fields in which the aims of hostile actors do converge. Often this involves much more than reciprocity, and it may begin to resemble the law of community. "Nevertheless, such developments suffice to make contemporary international law look like Janus: it has one face which announces chaos, and one which promises order."[52]

Before exploiting this conclusion in favor of a continuing integrative trend in the future system, we must return to the notions of functional law and existing law. Bridging the gap between arbitration and the generalized creation of new norms involves, first and foremost, judicial institutions with autonomous jurisdictions. What is more, the judges who are expected to engage in generating the new norms must espouse some species of functional jurisprudence in order that the bridge may be built. Functional law stresses the needs of actors, the transpersonality of the task at hand, the informality of procedure, and the avoidance of legal rigidity such as full compliance with detailed texts. It relies on an aura of immanence, which, of course, involves a degree of uniformity in the spontaneous evaluations that the international actors place upon events and needs. In short, it presumes a minimal consensus on what is needed and what is appropriate to meet the need.

When judges are asked to interpret texts and reconcile conflicting legal doctrines and enactments, they can choose between legal formalism and adaptive behavior. Functional jurisprudence assumes that judges will so interpret conflicting doctrines and texts as to stress whatever "need" seems to be overwhelmingly experienced by the society in which they live. They must impute purposes to the texts, purposes that may not have been the operative ones in the minds of the original legislators, purposes that thus become functions in the hands of a judiciary anxious to stay in tune with an evolving society. The consensus on which such acts of interpretation are based must be discovered by the judges themselves.

In any setting other than that of the nation-state that enjoys a stable constitutional order, such an effort contains enormous difficulties. In the world setting, we have neither the judiciary able to do this nor even the consensus for setting it up. But even in the much more homogeneous

* Jenks attempts to justify the human rights "law" of the ILO by stressing the parliamentary and functional group setting in which the norms are written, the approximations to constitutional law that govern the rules regarding interpretation, adjudication, amendment, and reservation, and the weakening of the traditional international rule of "consent" that is implied by all this. In Hoffmann's terms, Jenks parades a body of aspirations drawn from the law of community as if it were an actual operating part of the total system. *International Protection of Trade Union Freedom*, Chapter 27.

regional context of Western Europe, in which the hazards of imputing a consensus are far less perilous, the Court of the European Communities has not seen fit to adhere consistently to functional jurisprudence, though in many decisions it has approximated such a stance. The limits even in the regional context remain sharp. Little effort at generalized norm-creation will be undertaken if the judges suspect that the consensus they discern is not shared by powerful actors, or if the international institutions lack the completeness that will ensure enforcement.[53] If the international law of the current system will not contribute heavily to integration, the limits implicit in a functional law based on judicial institutions can hardly be expected to be of much help in the near future.

The only kind of functional law that can serve our purpose is one without pretense at imposing central institutions *before* the emergence of a consensus on needs. This law would draw its strength from the Janus-faced confusion among types and divergent aims. Within the interstices of the older laws of the political framework and of reciprocity among competing units, the law of community can grow inconspicuously and modestly. It will stress coexistence and conciliation in those functional contexts in which convergences of inputs come to the fore; it will continue to deal with territorial demarcation and the rules of war in the remaining contexts, which will feature the ideological hostilities of the modal regimes of the future. Their national self-assertion will stamp a part of the new system, *but only a part*. The other part is susceptible to the penetration of functional law even while local wars are carried on.

To be sure, it must rest on a consensus. But not the homogeneous agreement on the major values affecting all organized life. The consensus must include those aspects of international relations that can be "learned" by political leaders in each of the typical regimes as a result of institutionalized confrontation. It must count on the convergences of aims that result in central policy adopted in response to a variety of heterogeneous national inputs. In these areas the shibboleths of the law of the political framework —sovereignty and non-intervention—will simply lose their relevance in the minds of the nations.[54] Neither health programs nor telecommunications were always considered matters of joint and transnational concern. Yet both today exhibit not only general norms, but a modest international structure for their administration and further elaboration. There is no inherent reason for thinking that new areas of joint concern cannot develop, or that matters which arouse hostility today may not be converted into areas of joint concern tomorrow.

Whether the field of the international protection of human rights falls into this category is far from clear. In the current systems there is no consensus on need in this field; given the expected hetero-symmetry of the next system, there is equally little ground for believing in such a consensus for the future. Yet an undeniable expansion of international concern and activity in this field has in fact taken place. A functional law is perhaps creeping into the interstices of ideological confrontation, even if that "law" does not have all the qualities claimed for it by the ILO. It is still a law of conciliation and arbitration, in which the wishes of the parties take precedence. It is true that the persons charged with administering it are *attempting* to generalize it—but with little success. In a sense, institutionalization has run ahead of a consensual basis here, even though the institutionalization was itself made possible by hostile confrontations. Structures grew from conflict rather than harmony; but the structures remain very much on the periphery of legal evolution. Yet this type of evolution contains infinitely more promise than the effort to obtain legal uniformity by way of detailed texts in areas *not* experienced as posing a common need, i.e. international labor standards. The law of human rights is much closer to functional law than is the bulk of the International Labor Code. However, its further evolution is completely dependent on the continuation of the input-output pattern that has dominated the United Nations in the current system. With the passage into time of that pattern, the law of human rights may still become the victim of its position in the van of consensus.

OUTPUTS, FUNCTIONS, AND INTEGRATION

In what fields, then, can we expect the functional process of integration to continue, with or without the help of law? Despite hetero-symmetry, we expect both learning and new convergences of separate aims to continue. Despite the absence of strong international influences pushing the evolution of pluralism at the national level—and the resultant international democratic welfare pluralism envisaged by Myrdal—certain new powers may accrue to the United Nations on the basis of newly converging conceptions. *There will be a continued drift toward supranationality*, though no federal millennium is in the offing. Economic planning, local military operations, and ad hoc disarmament will provide the functions.

Economic planning is obviously the chief candidate for integrative functions in the future system. In principle, it is of appeal everywhere, and the intensified practice of international assistance in national and regional development would give us the necessary organizational task to maximize integrative consequences. A closer look, however, will reveal that matters are not so simple, another reason why Myrdal's enthusiasm for this function should not be allowed to be wholly infectious.

The present international structures do a great deal of "planning" in the course of administering aid programs. However, each agency does its own "planning" in the context of its particular task, organizational dynamic, leadership and clientele. The IBRD has evolved a sophisticated technique for judging national development plans, and for scrutinizing the feasibility of national projects, before making loans. It compels underdeveloped countries to consider the interrelations of tax rates, investment incentives, the cost of raw materials, and future markets, and to come up with specific estimates before funds are advanced. The Bank has its loan officers stationed throughout the world as an advance guard of sound financial policy; this makes the recipient countries permeable to centralized financial planning. The IMF has stringent doctrines of short-run financial viability that govern its support programs for national currencies, doctrines that are sometimes enforced over the bitter protest of the recipient governments. International commodity agreements "plan" the flow and the price of primary products, and thus impose a species of centralized direction on agricultural and mineral production and marketing.

The point of concern to us, however, is the fact that although all these efforts involve a drift toward supranationality at the subsystemic level, they do *not* integrate the units that make up the system. These are ad hoc approaches to planning. They do not consistently take into consideration political stability, the rate of social mobilization, the relationship of social mobility to internal demand or world demand. Each agency plans in a restricted context, with relatively little ability (either technical or political), to concern itself with the socio-economic factors of interest to other agencies. The partial and ad hoc character of this planning stands sharply revealed in the dissatisfaction surrounding the first few years of the Alliance for Progress. This effort was self-consciously designed to unite these various contexts in one coherent social and political planning effort. Instead of resulting in one supranational institution, however, responsibility was split among agencies of the U.S. government, the Inter-American Development Bank, the Committee of Nine of the Organization of American States, and the Inter-American Economic and Social Council, which was to act as a general review body. Given considerable diffusion of authority and much dissensus among recipients and donors about what was to be achieved, the main recipient governments still found it preferable to put direct pressure on the U.S. government. One of the main difficulties was lack of agreement about what constituted acceptable criteria of success, and about what should be done, by way of more supranationality, to obtain and meet them.

Such criteria have been proposed and even implemented by certain international agencies, notably the IBRD. They usually involve considerations of efficiency and consistency in the allocation of resources for development. One experienced administrator of aid proposes to unite these contexts by having all national plans based on the following criteria and calculations:

1. The need for outside assistance. This involves (a) establishing a desirable or appropriate rate of development, which can be stated in terms of a specific percentage increase in per-capita income, and (b) the potential ability of a country to contribute to the achievement of this rate, which is reflected to some extent in its absolute level of per-capita income and its past performance in supporting development.

2. A country's own effort with respect to development. This consideration may generally be best satisfied by an examination of where and to what extent a country increases its development effort with outside assistance.

3. A country's ability to use outside assistance, both in terms of physical capacity and maximum returns for outside resources.[55]

But the point remains that these criteria are to be applied within nations and by national officials acting in consultation with international advisers. If successful they would merely increase the viability of each nation; they would result in less permeability and more national self-consciousness.

Precisely the same conclusion could be advanced if we were to assume that the formulation and application of rigorous planning criteria be entrusted wholly to international agencies. In fact, the United Nations Special Fund seeks to approximate that aim. It insists that funds earmarked for its "pre-investment" technical and resource aid be justified in terms of overall economic development planning. A very high premium is put on the requirement that the recipient country match the efforts of the Special Fund personnel in surveying resources, establishing training centers, and seeing the economy as a whole.[56] If successful, these efforts will *not* make the developing countries more penetrable to international influences; on the contrary, they will be in a better position to live up to the ideological pressures associated with integral nationalism. In fact, the Special Fund's approach might be expected to be more palatable to a mobilization system than to a partially mobilized Latin American nation. In short, international economic aid based on coherent rather than ad hoc planning, even if it were to be achieved by a large and powerful UN economic development fund, will not automatically lead to accelerated integration. Even "country programing" as now practiced by the UN family, though an administrative improvement over the earlier ad hoc approach, will make no appreciable difference as far as integration is concerned.

In what sense, then, can economic planning be considered as functional? We predict that requests for economic aid will multiply in the future, and that the two superpowers will feel increasingly compelled to make assistance available through UN channels, thus implying a short-run growth in the powers of international agencies. Such aid will advance international integration only if the problems and challenges remaining after one immediate problem is solved become of greater concern to the actors than the initial development problem. The principle is what Albert Hirschman calls "unbalanced growth." New cooperative and integrating efforts are deliberately induced by stimulating an original decision that will unsettle more than it will solve. It involves the conscious planning of consequences unintended by the national actors, but compelling these elites to undertake new planning later in order to deal with the unintended consequences of their earlier purposes.[57] The implications, of course, would be that the purposes growing out of these consequences could be met only with an increased international task and appropriate supranational institutions. One obvious example—among many possible ones—would be a new power for the FAO to set and change commodity prices in line with minimum earnings considered desirable (and determined earlier by the IBRD) for purposes of supporting a given rate of local investment.

Would such a bundle of guile require the extraordinary manipulatory skills and supreme virtues of the Saint-Simonian expert whose role we downgraded earlier? For perfect consistency and predictable success, we would have to make an assumption in his favor. A public international technocracy would seem required to give institutional reality to Myrdal's vision or to the functional logic. Hence, for the reasons indicated earlier, it is idle to expect the full-fledged evolution of such a body of men or institutions. What is more reasonable, however, is to expect the continuation of a learning process among national elites and international officials. This will make possible the occasional evolution, more accidental than planned, of the kinds of unintended consequences that are bound to flow from the present ad hoc pattern of economic development. But it would be too much to expect such unwilled results consistently to support the trend toward supranational integration.

The same conclusion applies to the field of disarmament. An international function in this field is likely in view of the output pattern that flows from the converging aims of the two superpowers and of the non-aligned. The degree of institutional drift toward supranationality will depend on the degree of international inspection and conciliation built into efforts at disarmament and arms control. A test-ban agreement that excludes underground explosions has no integrating consequences of this sort. But monitoring devices set up to check on such explosions, corps of inspectors to examine denuclearized zones, communications satellites to check on national forays into space, or to determine the existence of orbiting bombs, would have a definite integrating consequence. An agreement for general disarmament, obviously, would have an even greater institutional impact and would push us far toward national permeability in terms of military aims. But even if we assume no such dramatic development, and limit the projection to what the next system makes likely, some ad hoc integrating results remain.

United Nations military operations that are designed to stop or contain local wars fought with conventional weapons fulfill a similar purpose. The command and logistical apparatus built up to support them, and the authority of UN personnel in deploying them, imply an institutional development of some magnitude. The output pattern of the future system will advance these developments further, despite—or, perhaps, because of—the ideological heterogeneity of its regimes. Such developments, though, do not imply the birth of an international army that would take the place of national military establishments. They constitute merely another nibble at the structure of the self-confident national state.

The chances for expanding the human rights function, however, are far cloudier. For reasons already indicated, the legal and political developments that favored the growth of a UN task in this field are closely associated with the output pattern of the current system. The function has not yet acquired the capacity for self-sustained growth in the hands of international institutions able to penetrate the national state. The inputs which favored the confrontations and compromises that gave rise to the function are likely to undergo great change as the Cold War grows less pronounced and decolonization is completed. Integral regimes of the future will have reason to resent and oppose international efforts to make them observe the general human rights standards enshrined in the UN Universal Declaration. The Western democracies will have less reason than before to press them on this matter. Moreover, they will have less compulsion to attack the Soviet bloc in this context. Far more likely, new functions will flow from areas of interdependence that can be considered metapolitical from the outset, such as the exploitation of new natural resources in a global setting dominated by concern over the population explosion.

Heterosymmetry, then, implies the continuation of the present ad hoc pattern of international integration. We have no reason to suppose that the autonomy of subsystems, so marked in the present era, will be less pronounced in the future. Integration must be expected to proceed in line with the forces here outlined, without significant acceleration over the present rate. We have no reason to expect the successful coordination of all such impulses in one system-dominant supranational structure. New agencies will flower or wither in proportion to their ability to meet the purposes of actors, and to upgrade the joint interest by profiting from new convergences of inputs. Integration will come about in the same unplanned and almost accidental fashion that has dominated in the past. The new system will be looser than the one now familiar to us. There will be fewer functions calling for mutual accommodation and therefore less leverage for actors to influence one another, though some of the functions will relate more heavily to world peace and military stability than in the present system. Actors will be more numerous, and their regional blocs less cohesive. But the reduction in inputs implies a lessening of the volume of bargaining and of the integrative compromises possible.

The lesson is clear. Neither Functionalism nor functional analysis can bring international order out of the chaos of national confrontation. Neither a commitment to welfare nor a desire to use the analytical properties of national egotism can build the *civitas dei* or the *civitas maxima*. But functional analysis can tell us in which direction the faint ripples of common concerns are likely to spread. Even chaos becomes bearable when its constituents and their movement are understood.

Appendix

Appendix

The Constitution of the International Labor Organization as Amended to May 20, 1954

PREAMBLE

Whereas universal and lasting peace can be established only if it is based upon social justice;

And whereas conditions of labor exist involving such injustice, hardship and privation to large numbers of people as to produce unrest so great that the peace and harmony of the world are imperilled; and an improvement of those conditions is urgently required: as, for example, by the regulation of the hours of work, including the establishment of a maximum working day and week, the regulation of the labor supply, the prevention of unemployment, the provision of an adequate living wage, the protection of the worker against sickness, disease and injury arising out of his employment, the protection of children, young persons and women, provision for old age and injury, protection of the interests of workers when employed in countries other than their own, recognition of the principle of equal remuneration for work of equal value, recognition of the principle of freedom of association, the organization of vocational and technical education and other measures;

Whereas also the failure of any nation to adopt humane conditions of labor is an obstacle in the way of other nations which desire to improve the conditions in their own countries;

The High Contracting Parties, moved by sentiments of justice and humanity as well as by the desire to secure the permanent peace of the world, and with a view to attaining the objectives set forth in this Preamble, agree to the following Constitution of the International Labor Organization:

CHAPTER I—ORGANIZATION

Art. 1. 1. A permanent organization is hereby established for the promotion of the objects set forth in the Preamble to this Constitution and in the Declaration concerning the aims and purposes of the International Labor Organization adopted at Philadelphia on 10 May 1944, the text of which is annexed to this Constitution.

2. The Members of the International Labor Organization shall be the States which were Members of the Organization on 1 November 1945, and such other States as may become Members in pursuance of the provisions of paragraphs 3 and 4 of this Article.

3. Any original Member of the United Nations and any State admitted to membership of the United Nations by a decision of the General Assembly in accordance with the provisions of the Charter may become a Member of the International Labor Organization by communicating to the Director-General of the International Labor Office its formal acceptance of the obligations of the Constitution of the International Labor Organization.

4. The General Conference of the International Labor Organization may also admit Members to the Organization by a vote concurred in by two-thirds of the delegates attending the session, including two-thirds of the Government delegates present and voting. Such admission shall take effect on the communication to the Director-General of the International Labor Office by the Government of the new Member of its formal acceptance of the obligations of the Constitution of the Organization.

5. No Member of the International Labor Organization may withdraw from the Organization without giving notice of its intention so to do to the Director-General of the International Labor Office. Such notice shall take effect two years after the date of its reception by the Director-General, subject to the Member having at that time fulfilled all financial obligations arising out of its membership. When a Member has ratified any International Labor Convention, such withdrawal shall not affect the continued validity for the period provided for in the Convention of all obligations arising thereunder or relating thereto.

6. In the event of any State having ceased to be a Member of the Organization, its re-admission to membership shall be governed by the provisions of paragraph 3 or paragraph 4 of this Article as the case may be.

Art. 2.   The permanent organization shall consist of:

(a) a General Conference of representatives of the Members;

(b) a Governing Body composed as described in Article 7; and

(c) an International Labor Office controlled by the Governing Body.

Art. 3.   1. The meetings of the General Conference of representatives of the Members shall be held from time to time as occasion may require, and at least once in every year. It shall be composed of four representatives of each of the Members, of whom two shall be Government delegates and the two others shall be delegates representing respectively the employers and the working people of each of the Members.

2. Each delegate may be accompanied by advisers, who shall not exceed two in number for each item on the agenda of the meeting. When questions specially affecting women are to be considered by the Conference, one at least of the advisers should be a woman.

3. Each Member which is responsible for the international relations of non-metropolitan territories may appoint as additional advisers to each of its delegates:

(a) persons nominated by it as representatives of any such territory in regard to matters within the self-governing powers of that territory; and

(b) persons nominated by it to advise its delegates in regard to matters concerning non-self-governing territories.

4. In the case of a territory under the joint authority of two or more Members, persons may be nominated to advise the delegates of such Members.

5. The Members undertake to nominate non-Government delegates and advisers chosen in agreement with the industrial organizations, if such organizations exist, which are most representative of employers or working people as the case may be, in their respective countries.

6. Advisers shall not speak except on a request made by the delegate whom they accompany and by the special authorization of the President of the Conference, and may not vote.

7. A delegate may be notice in writing addressed to the President appoint one of his advisers to act as his deputy, and the adviser, while so acting, shall be allowed to speak and vote.

8. The names of the delegates and their advisers will be communicated to the International Labor Office by the Government of each of the Members.

9. The credentials of delegates and their advisers shall be subject to scrutiny by the Conference, which may, by two-thirds of the votes cast by the delegates present, refuse to admit any delegate or adviser whom it deems not to have been nominated in accordance with this Article.

Art. 4.   1. Every delegate shall be entitled to vote individually on all matters which are taken into consideration by the Conference.

2. If one of the Members fails to nominate one of the non-Government delegates whom it is entitled to nominate, the other non-Government delegate shall be allowed to sit and speak at the Conference, but not to vote.

3. If in accordance with Article 3 the Conference refuses admission to a delegate of one of the Members, the provisions of the present Article shall apply as if that delegate had not been nominated.

Art. 5.   The meetings of the Conference shall, subject to any decisions which may have been taken by the Conference itself at a previous meeting, be held at such place as may be decided by the Governing Body.

Art. 6.   Any change in the seat of the International Labor Office shall be decided by the Conference by a two-thirds majority of the votes cast by the delegates present.

Art. 7.   1. The Governing Body shall consist of forty persons:
Twenty representing Governments,
Ten representing the employers, and
Ten representing the workers.

2. Of the twenty persons representing Governments, ten shall be appointed by the Members of chief industrial importance, and ten shall be appointed by the Members selected for that purpose by the Government delegates to the Conference, excluding the delegates of the ten Members mentioned above.

3. The Governing Body shall as occasion requires determine which are the Members of the Organization of chief industrial importance and shall make rules to ensure that all questions relating to the selection of the Members of chief industrial importance are considered by an impartial committee before being decided by the Governing Body. Any appeal made by a Member from the declaration of the Governing Body as to which are the Members of chief industrial importance shall be decided by the Conference, but an appeal to the Con-

ference shall not suspend the application of the declaration until such time as the Conference decides the appeal.

4. The persons representing the employers and the persons representing the workers shall be elected respectively by the employers' delegates and the workers' delegates to the Conference. Two employers' representatives and two workers' representatives shall belong to non-European States.

5. The period of office of the Governing Body shall be three years. If for any reason the Governing Body elections do not take place on the expiry of this period, the Governing Body shall remain in office until such elections are held.

6. The method of filling vacancies and of appointing substitutes and other similar questions may be decided by the Governing Body subject to the approval of the Conference.

7. The Governing Body shall, from time to time, elect from its number a Chairman and two Vice-Chairmen, of whom one shall be a person representing a Government, one a person representing the employers, and one a person representing the workers.

8. The Governing Body shall regulate its own procedure and shall fix its own times of meeting. A special meeting shall be held if a written request to that effect is made by at least sixteen of the representatives on the Governing Body.

Art. 8. 1. There shall be a Director-General of the International Labor Office, who shall be appointed by the Governing Body, and, subject to the instructions of the Governing Body, shall be responsible for the efficient conduct of the International Labor Office and for such other duties as may be assigned to him.

2. The Director-General or his deputy shall attend all meetings of the Governing Body.

Art. 9. 1. The staff of the International Labor Office shall be appointed by the Director-General under regulations approved by the Governing Body.

2. So far as is possible with due regard to the efficiency of the work of the Office, the Director-General shall select persons of different nationalities.

3. A certain number of these persons shall be women.

4. The responsibilities of the Director-General and the staff shall be exclusively international in character. In the performance of their duties the Director-General and the staff shall not seek or receive instructions from any Government or from any other authority external to the Organization. They shall refrain from any action which might reflect on their position as international officials responsible only to the Organization.

5. Each Member of the Organization undertakes to respect the exclusively international character of the responsibilities of the Director-General and the staff and not to seek to influence them in the discharge of their responsibilities.

Art. 10. 1. The functions of the International Labor Office shall include the collection and distribution of information on all subjects relating to the international adjustment of conditions of industrial life and labor, and particularly the examination of subjects which it is proposed to bring before the Conference with a view to the conclusion of international Conventions, and the conduct of such special investigations as may be ordered by the Conference or by the Governing Body.

2. Subject to such directions as the Governing Body may give, the Office shall

(a) prepare the documents on the various items of the agenda for the meetings of the Conference;

(b) accord to Governments at their request all appropriate assistance within its power in connection with the framing of laws and regulations on the basis of the decisions of the Conference and the improvement of administrative practices and systems of inspection;

(c) carry out the duties required of it by the provisions of this Constitution in connection with the effective observance of Conventions;

(d) edit and issue, in such languages as the Governing Body may think desirable, publications dealing with problems of industry and employment of international interest.

3. Generally, it shall have such other powers and duties as may be assigned to it by the Conference or by the Governing Body.

Art. 11. The Government departments of any of the Members which deal with questions of industry and employment may communicate directly with the Director-General through the representative of their Government on the Governing Body of the International Labor Office or, failing any such representative, through such other qualified official as the Government may nominate for the purpose.

Art. 12. 1. The International Labor Organization shall co-operate within the terms of this Constitution with any general international organization entrusted with the co-ordination of the activities of public international organizations having specialized responsibilities and with public international organizations having specialized responsibilities in related fields.

2. The International Labor Organization may make appropriate arrangements for the representatives of public international organizations to participate without vote in its deliberations.

3. The International Labor Organization may make suitable arrangements for such consultation as it may think desirable with recognized non-governmental international organizations, including international organizations of employers, workers, agriculturists and co-operators.

Art. 13. 1. The International Labor Organization may make such financial and budgetary arrangements with the United Nations as may appear appropriate.

2. Pending the conclusion of such arrangements or if at any time no such arrangements are in force—

(a) each of the Members will pay the traveling and subsistence expenses of its delegates and their advisers and of its representatives attending the meetings of the Conference or the Governing Body, as the case may be;

(b) all other expenses of the International Labor Office and of the meetings of the Conference or Governing Body shall be paid by the Director-General of the International Labor Office out of the general funds of the International Labor Organization;

(c) the arrangements for the approval, allocation and collection of the budget of the International Labor Organization shall be determined by the Conference by a two-thirds majority of the votes cast by the delegates present, and shall provide for the approval of the budget and of the arrangements for the allocation of expenses among the Members of the Organizations by a committee of Government representatives.

3. The expenses of the International Labor Organization shall be borne by the Members in accordance with the arrangements in force in virtue of paragraph 1 or paragraph 2(c) of this Article.

4. A Member of the Organization which is in arrears in the payment of its financial contribution to the Organization shall have no vote in the Conference, in the Governing Body, in any committee, or in the elections of members of the Governing Body, if the amount of its arrears equals or exceeds the amount of the contributions due from it for the preceding two full years: Provided that the Conference may by a two-thirds majority of the votes cast by the delegates present permit such a Member to vote if it is satisfied that the failure to pay is due to conditions beyond the control of the Member.

5. The Director-General of the International Labor Office shall be responsible to the Governing Body for the proper expenditure of the funds of the International Labor Organization.

CHAPTER II—PROCEDURE

Art. 14. 1. The agenda for all meetings of the Conference will be settled by the Governing Body, which shall consider any suggestion as to the agenda that may be made by the Government of any of the Members or by any representative organization recognized for the purpose of Article 3, or by any public international organization.

2. The Governing Body shall make rules to ensure thorough technical preparation and adequate consultation of the Members primarily concerned, by means of a preparatory Conference or otherwise, prior to the adoption of a Convention or Recommendation by the Conference.

Art. 15. 1. The Director-General shall act as the Secretary-General of the Conference, and shall transmit the agenda so as to reach the Members four months before the meeting of the Conference, and, through them, the non-Government delegates when appointed.

2. The reports on each item of the agenda shall be despatched so as to reach the Members in time to permit adequate consideration before the meeting of the Conference. The Governing Body shall make rules for the application of this provision.

Art. 16. 1. Any of the Governments of the Members may formally object to the inclusion of any item or items in the agenda. The grounds for such objection shall be set forth in a statement addressed to the Director-General, who shall circulate it to all the Members of the Organization.

2. Items to which such objection has been made shall not, however, be excluded from the agenda, if at the Conference a majority of two-thirds of the votes cast by the delegates present is in favor of considering them.

3. If the Conference decides (otherwise than under the preceding paragraph) by two-thirds of the votes cast by the delegates present that any subject shall be

considered by the Conference, that subject shall be included in the agenda for the following meeting.

Art. 17. 1. The Conference shall elect a President and three Vice-Presidents. One of the Vice-Presidents shall be a Government delegate, one an employers' delegate and one a workers' delegate. The Conference shall regulate its own procedure and may appoint committees to consider and report on any matter.

2. Except as otherwise expressly provided in this Constitution or by the terms of any Convention or other instrument conferring powers on the Conference or of the financial and budgetary arrangements adopted in virtue of Article 13, all matters shall be decided by a simple majority of the votes cast by the delegates present.

3. The voting is void unless the total number of votes cast is equal to half the number of the delegates attending the Conference.

Art. 18. The Conference may add to any committees which it appoints technical experts without power to vote.

Art. 19. 1. When the Conference has decided on the adoption of proposals with regard to an item in the agenda, it will rest with the Conference to determine whether these proposals should take the form; (a) of an international Convention, or (b) of a Recommendation to meet circumstances where the subject, or aspect of it, dealt with is not considered suitable or appropriate at that time for a Convention.

2. In either case a majority of two-thirds of the votes cast by the delegates present shall be necessary on the final vote for the adoption of the Convention or Recommendation, as the case may be, by the Conference.

3. In framing any Convention or Recommendation of general application the Conference shall have due regard to those countries in which climatic conditions, the imperfect development of industrial organization, or other special circumstances make the industrial conditions substantially different and shall suggest the modifications, if any, which it considers may be required to meet the case of such countries.

4. Two copies of the Convention or Recommendation shall be authenticated by the signatures of the President of the Conference and of the Director-General. Of these copies one shall be deposited in the archives of the International Labor Office and the other with the Secretary-General of the United Nations. The Director-General will communicate a certified copy of the Convention or Recommendation to each of the Members.

5. In the case of a Convention—

(a) the Convention will be communicated to all Members for ratification;

(b) each of the Members undertakes that it will, within the period of one year at most from the closing of the session of the Conference, or if it is impossible owing to exceptional circumstances to do so within the period of one year, then at the earliest practicable moment and in no case later than eighteen months from the closing of the session of the Conference, bring the Convention before the authority or authorities within whose competence the matter lies, for the enactment of legislation or other action;

(c) Members shall inform the Director-General of the International Labor Office of the measures taken in accordance with this Article to bring the Convention before the said competent authority or authorities, with particulars of the authority or authorities regarded as competent, and of the action taken by them;

(d) if the Member obtains the consent of the authority or authorities within whose competence the matter lies, it will communicate the formal ratification of the Convention to the Director-General and will take such action as may be necessary to make effective the provisions of such Convention;

(e) if the Member does not obtain the consent of the authority or authorities within whose competence the matter lies, no further obligation shall rest upon the Member except that it shall report to the Director-General of the International Labor Office, at appropriate intervals as requested by the Governing Body, the position of its law and practice in regard to the matters dealt with in the Convention, showing the extent to which effect has been given, or is proposed to be given, to any of the provisions of the Convention by legislation, administrative action, collective agreement or otherwise, and stating the difficulties which prevent or delay the ratification of such Convention.

6. In the case of a Recommendation—

(a) the Recommendation will be communicated to all Members for their consideration with a view to effect being given to it by national legislation or otherwise;

(b) each of the Members undertakes that it will, within a period of one year at most from the closing of the session of the Conference, or if it is impossible owing to exceptional circumstances to do so within the period of one year, then at the earliest practicable moment and in no case later than eighteen months after the closing of the Conference, bring the Recommendation before the authority or authorities within whose competence the matter lies for the enactment of legislation or other action;

(c) the Members shall inform the Director-General of the International Labor Office of the measures taken in accordance with this Article to bring the Recommendation before the said competent authority or authorities with particulars of the authority or authorities regarded as competent, and of the action taken by them;

(d) apart from bringing the Recommendation before the said competent authority or authorities, no further obligation shall rest upon the Members, except that they shall report to the Director-General of the International Labor Office, at appropriate intervals as requested by the Governing Body, the position of the law and practice in their country in regard to the matter dealt with in the Recommendation, showing the extent to which effect has been given, or is proposed to be given, to the provisions of the Recommendation and such modifications of these provisions as it has been found or may be found necessary to make in adopting or applying them.

7. In the case of a federal State, the following provisions shall apply:

(a) in respect of Conventions and Recommendations which the federal Government regards as appropriate under its constitutional system for federal action, the obligations of the federal State shall be the same as those of Members which are not federal States;

(b) in respect of Conventions and Recommendations which the federal Government regards as appropriate under its constitutional system, in whole or in part, for action by the constituent States, provinces, or cantons rather than for federal action, the federal Government shall—

(i) make, in accordance with its Constitution and the Constitutions of the States, provinces or cantons concerned, effective arrangements for the reference of such Conventions and Recommendations not later than eighteen months from the closing of the session of the Conference to the appropriate federal, State, provincial or cantonal authorities for the enactment of legislation or other action;

(ii) arrange, subject to the concurrence of the State, provincial or cantonal Governments concerned, for periodical consultations between the federal and the State, provincial or cantonal authorities with a view to promoting within the federal State co-ordinated action to give effect to the provisions of such Conventions and Recommendations;

(iii) inform the Director-General of the International Labor Office of the measures taken in accordance with this Article to bring such Conventions and Recommendations before the appropriate federal, State, provincial or cantonal authorities with particulars of the authorities regarded as appropriate and of the action taken by them;

(iv) in respect of each such Convention which it has not ratified, report to the Director-General of the International Labor Office, at appropriate intervals as requested by the Governing Body, the position of the law and practice of the federation and its constituent States, provinces or cantons in regard to the Convention, showing the extent to which effect has been given, or is proposed to be given, to any of the provisions of the Convention by legislation, administrative action, collective agreement, or otherwise;

(v) in respect of each such Recommendation, report to the Director-General of the International Labor Office, at appropriate intervals as requested by the Governing Body, the position of the law and practice of the federation and its constituent States, provinces or cantons in regard to the Recommendation, showing the extent to which effect has been given, or is proposed to be given, to the provisions of the Recommendation and such modifications of these provisions as have been found or may be found necessary in adopting or applying them.

8. In no case shall the adoption of any Convention or Recommendations by the Conference, or the ratification of any Convention by any Member, be deemed to affect any law, award, custom or agreement which ensures more favorable conditions to the workers concerned than those provided for in the Convention or Recommendation.

Art. 20. Any Convention so ratified shall be communicated by the Director-General of the International Labor Office to the Secretary-General of the United Nations for registration in accordance with the provisions of Article 102 of the Charter of the United Nations but shall only be binding upon the Members which ratify it.

Art. 21. 1. If any Convention coming before the Conference for final consideration fails to secure the support of two-thirds of the votes cast by the delegates present, it shall nevertheless be within the right of any of the Members of the Organization to agree to such Convention among themselves.

2. Any Convention so agreed to shall be communicated by the Governments concerned to the Director-General of the International Labor Office and to the Secretary-General of the United Nations for registration in accordance with the provisions of Article 102 of the Charter of the United Nations.

Art. 22. Each of the Members agrees to make an annual report to the International Labor Office on the measures which it has taken to give effect to the provisions of Conventions to which it is a party. These reports shall be made in such form and shall contain such particulars as the Governing Body may request.

Art. 23. 1. The Director-General shall lay before the next meeting of the Conference a summary of the information and reports communicated to him by Members in pursuance of Articles 19 and 22.

2. Each Member shall communicate to the representative organizations recognized for the purpose of Article 3 copies of the information and reports communicated to the Director-General in pursuance of Articles 19 and 22.

Art. 24. In the event of any representation being made to the International Labor Office by an industrial association of employers or of workers that any of the Members has failed to secure in any respect the effective observance within its jurisdiction of any Convention to which it is a party, the Governing Body may communicate this representation to the Government against which it is made, and may invite that Government to make such statement on the subject as it may think fit.

Art. 25. If no statement is received within a reasonable time from the Government in question, or if the statement when received is not deemed to be satisfactory by the Governing Body, the latter shall have the right to publish the representation and the statement, if any, made in reply to it.

Art. 26. 1. Any of the Members shall have the right to file a complaint with the International Labor Office if it is not satisfied that any other Member is securing the effective observance of any Convention which both have ratified in accordance with the foregoing Articles.

2. The Governing Body may, if it thinks fit, before referring such a complaint to a Commission of Enquiry, as hereinafter provided for, communicate with the Government in question in the manner described in Article 24.

3. If the Governing Body does not think it necessary to communicate the complaint to the Government in question, or if when it has made such communication, no statement in reply has been received within a reasonable time which the Governing Body considers to be satisfactory, the Governing Body may appoint a Commission of Enquiry to consider the complaint and to report thereon.

4. The Governing Body may adopt the same procedure either of its own motion or on receipt of a complaint from a delegate to the Conference.

5. When any matter arising out of Articles 25 or 26 is being considered by the Governing Body, the Government in question shall, if not already represented thereon, be entitled to send a representative to take part in the proceedings of the Governing Body while the matter is under consideration. Adequate notice of the date on which the matter will be considered shall be given to the Government in question.

Art. 27.   The Members agree that, in the event of the reference of a complaint to a Commission of Enquiry under Article 26, they will each, whether directly concerned in the complaint or not, place at the disposal of the Commission all the information in their possession which bears upon the subject matter of the complaint.

Art. 28.   When the Commission of Enquiry has fully considered the complaint, it shall prepare a report embodying its findings on all questions of fact relevant to determining the issue between the parties and containing such recommendations as it may think proper as to the steps which should be taken to meet the complaint and the time within which they should be taken.

Art. 29.   1. The Director-General of the International Labor Office shall communicate the report of the Commission of Enquiry to the Governing Body and to each of the Governments concerned in the complaint, and shall cause it to be published.

2. Each of these Governments shall within three months inform the Director-General of the International Labor Office whether or not it accepts the recommendations contained in the report of the Commission; and if not, whether it proposes to refer the complaint to the International Court of Justice.

Art. 30.   In the event of any Member failing to take the action required by paragraphs 5(b), 6(b) or 7(b)(i) of Article 19 with regard to a Convention or Recommendation, any other Member shall be entitled to refer the matter to the Governing Body. In the event of the Governing Body finding that there has been such a failure, it shall report the matter to the Conference.

Art. 31.   The decision of the International Court of Justice in regard to a complaint or matter which has been referred to it in pursuance of Article 29 shall be final.

Art. 32.   The International Court of Justice may affirm, vary or reverse any of the findings or recommendations of the Commission of Enquiry, if any.

Art. 33.   In the event of any Member failing to carry out within the time specified in the recommendations, if any, contained in the report of the Commission of Enquiry, or in the decision of the International Court of Justice, as the case may be, the Governing Body may recommend to the Conference such action as it may deem wise and expedient to secure compliance therewith.

Art. 34.   The defaulting Government may at any time inform the Governing Body that it has taken the steps necessary to comply with the recommendations of the Commission of Enquiry or with those in the decision of the International Court of Justice, as the case may be, and may request it to constitute a Commission of Enquiry to verify its contention. In this case the provisions of Articles 27, 28, 29, 31 and 32 shall apply, and if the report of the Commission of Enquiry or the decision of the International Court of Justice is in favor of the defaulting Government, the Governing Body shall forthwith recommend the discontinuance of any action taken in pursuance of Article 33.

CHAPTER III—GENERAL

Art. 35. 1. The Members undertake that Conventions which they have ratified in accordance with the provisions of this Constitution shall be applied to the non-metropolitan territories for whose international relations they are responsible, including any trust territories for which they are the administering authority, except where the subject matter of the Convention is within the self-governing powers of the territory or the Convention is inapplicable owing to the local conditions or subject to such modifications as may be necessary to adapt the Convention to local conditions.

2. Each Member which ratifies a Convention shall as soon as possible after ratification communicate to the Director-General of the International Labor Office a declaration stating in respect of the territories other than those referred to in paragraphs 4 and 5 below the extent to which it undertakes that the provisions of the Convention shall be applied and giving such particulars as may be prescribed by the Convention.

3. Each Member which has communicated a declaration in virtue of the preceding paragraph may from time to time, in accordance with the terms of the Convention, communicate a further declaration modifying the terms of any former declaration and stating the present position in respect of such territories.

4. Where the subject matter of the Convention is within the self-governing powers of any non-metropolitan territory the Member responsible for the international relations of that territory shall bring the Convention to the notice of the Government of the territory as soon as possible with a view to the enactment of legislation or other action by such Government. Thereafter the Member, in agreement with the Government of the territory may communicate to the Director-General of the International Labor Office a declaration accepting the obligations of the Convention on behalf of such territory.

5. A declaration accepting the obligations of any Convention may be communicated to the Director-General of the International Labor Office—

(a) by two or more Members of the Organization in respect of any territory which is under their joint authority; or

(b) by any international authority responsible for the administration of any territory, in virtue of the Charter of the United Nations or otherwise, in respect of any such territory.

6. Acceptance of the obligations of a Convention in virtue of paragraph 4 or paragraph 5 shall involve the acceptance on behalf of the territory concerned of the obligations stipulated by the terms of the Convention and the obligations under the Constitution of the Organization which apply to ratified Conventions. A declaration of acceptance may specify such modification of the provisions of the Conventions as may be necessary to adapt the Convention to local conditions.

7. Each Member or international authority which has communicated a declaration in virtue of paragraph 4 or paragraph 5 of this Article may from time to time, in accordance with the terms of the Convention, communicate a further declaration modifying the terms of any former declaration or terminating the

acceptance of the obligations of the Convention on behalf of the territory concerned.

8. If the obligations of a Convention are not accepted on behalf of a territory to which paragraph 4 or paragraph 5 of this Article relates, the Member or Members or international authority concerned shall report to the Director-General of the International Labor Office the position of the law and practice of that territory in regard to the matters dealt with in the Convention and the report shall show the extent to which effect has been given, or proposed to be given, to any of the provisions of the Convention by legislation, administrative action, collective agreement or otherwise and shall state the difficulties which prevent or delay the acceptance of such Convention.

Art. 36.   Amendments to this Constitution which are adopted by the Conference by a majority of two-thirds of the votes cast by the delegates present shall take effect when ratified or accepted by two-thirds of the Members of the Organization including five of the ten Members which are represented on the Governing Body as Members of chief industrial importance in accordance with the provisions of paragraph 3 of Article 7 of this Constitution.

Art. 37.   1. Any question or dispute relating to the interpretation of this Constitution or of any subsequent Convention concluded by the Members in pursuance of the provisions of this Constitution shall be referred for decision to the International Court of Justice.

2. Notwithstanding the provisions of paragraph 1 of this Article the Governing Body may make and submit to the Conference for approval rules providing for the appointment of a tribunal for the expeditious determination of any dispute or question relating to the interpretation of a Convention which may be referred thereto by the Governing Body or in accordance with the terms of the Convention. Any applicable judgment or advisory opinion of the International Court of Justice shall be binding upon any tribunal established in virtue of this paragraph. Any award made by such a tribunal shall be circulated to the Members of the Organization and any observations which they may make thereon shall be brought before the Conference.

Art. 38.   1. The International Labor Organization may convene such regional conferences and establish such regional agencies as may be desirable to promote the aims and purposes of the Organization.

2. The powers, functions and procedure of regional conferences shall be governed by rules drawn up by the Governing Body and submitted to the General Conference for confirmation.

CHAPTER IV—MISCELLANEOUS PROVISIONS

Art. 39.   The International Labor Organization shall possess full juridical personality and in particular the capacity—

(a) to contract;

(b) to acquire and dispose of immovable and movable property;

(c) to institute legal proceedings.

Art. 40.   1. The International Labor Organization shall enjoy in the territory of each of its Members such privileges and immunities as are necessary for the fulfillment of its purposes.

2. Delegates to the Conference, members of the Governing Body and the Director-General and officials of the Office shall likewise enjoy such privileges and immunities as are necessary for the independent exercise of their functions in connection with the Organization.

3. Such privileges and immunities shall be defined in a separate agreement to be prepared by the Organization with a view to its acceptance by the Members.

Annex

DECLARATION CONCERNING THE AIMS AND PURPOSES OF THE INTERNATIONAL LABOR ORGANIZATION

The General Conference of the International Labor Organization, meeting in its Twenty-sixth Session in Philadelphia, hereby adopts, this tenth day of May in the year nineteen hundred and forty-four, the present Declaration of the aims and purposes of the International Labor Organization and of the principles which should inspire the policy of its Members.

I

The Conference reaffirms the fundamental principles on which the Organization is based and, in particular, that:

(a) labor is not a commodity;

(b) freedom of expression and of association are essential to sustained progress;

(c) poverty anywhere constitutes a danger to prosperity everywhere;

(d) the war against want requires to be carried on with unrelenting vigor within each nation, and by continuous and concerted international effort in which the representatives of workers and employers, enjoying equal status with those of Governments, join with them in free discussion and democratic decision with a view to the promotion of the common welfare.

II

Believing that experience has fully demonstrated the truth of the statement in the Constitution of the International Labor Organization that lasting peace can be established only if it is based on social justice, the Conference affirms that:

(a) all human beings, irrespective of race, creed or sex, have the right to pursue both their material well-being and their spiritual development in conditions of freedom and dignity, of economic security and equal opportunity;

(b) the attainment of the conditions in which this shall be possible must constitute the central aim of national and international policy;

(c) all national and international policies and measures, in particular those of an economic and financial character, should be judged in this light and accepted only in so far as they may be held to promote and not to hinder the achievement of this fundamental objective;

(d) it is a responsibility of the International Labor Organization to examine and consider all international economic and financial policies and measures in the light of this fundamental objective;

(e) in discharging the tasks entrusted to it the International Labor Organization, having considered all relevant economic and financial factors, may include in its decisions and recommendations any provisions which it considers appropriate.

III

The Conference recognizes the solemn obligation of the International Labor Organization to further among the nations of the world programs which will achieve:

(a) full employment and the raising of standards of living;

(b) the employment of workers in the occupations in which they can have the satisfaction of giving the fullest measure of their skill and attainments and make their greatest contribution to the common well-being;

(c) the provision, as a means to the attainment of this end and under adequate guarantees for all concerned, of facilities for training and the transfer of labor, including migration for employment and settlement;

(d) policies in regard to wages and earnings, hours and other conditions of work calculated to ensure a just share of the fruits of progress to all, and a minimum living wage to all employed and in need of such protection;

(e) the effective recognition of the right of collective bargaining, the co-operation of management and labor in the continuous improvement of productive efficiency, and the collaboration of workers and employers in the preparation and application of social and economic measures;

(f) the extension of social security measures to provide a basic income to all in need of such protection and comprehensive medical care;

(g) adequate protection for the life and health of workers in all occupations;

(h) provision for child welfare and maternity protection;

(i) the provision of adequate nutrition, housing and facilities for recreation and culture;

(j) the assurance of equality of educational and vocational opportunity.

IV

Confident that the fuller and broader utilization of the world's productive resources necessary for the achievement of the objectives set forth in this Declaration can be secured by effective international and national action, including measures to expand production and consumption, to avoid severe economic fluctuations, to promote the economic and social advancement of the less developed regions of the world, to assure greater stability in world prices of primary products, and to promote a high and steady volume of international trade, the Conference pledges the full co-operation of the International Labor Organization with such international bodies as may be entrusted with a share of the responsibility for this great task and for the promotion of the health, education and well-being of all peoples.

V

The Conference affirms that the principles set forth in this Declaration are fully applicable to all peoples everywhere and that, while the manner of their application must be determined with due regard to the stage of social and economic development reached by each people, their progressive application to peoples who are still dependent, as well as to those who have already achieved self-government, is a matter of concern to the whole civilized world.

Notes

Notes

CHAPTER ONE

1. Robert K. Merton, *Social Theory and Social Structure* (Glencoe, Ill.: The Free Press, rev. ed., 1957), p. 23.

2. *Ibid.*, pp. 20–23.

3. See the conclusions of Kingsley Davis on this point: "We find nothing to upset the view that it [functional analysis] is another name for sociological analysis—the interpretation of phenomena in terms of their interconnections with societies as going concerns." "The Myth of Functional Analysis as a Special Method in Sociology and Anthropology," *American Sociological Review*, XXIV (1959), 760. While approving of the kinds of questions asked by functionalists, Davis stringently opposes their reification into a special mode of analysis, precisely because of irremovable verbal complications: "To speak of the *function* of an institution *for* a society or *for* another institution in that society is a way of asking what the institution does within the system to which it is relevant. But, having connotations that are impossible to control, the word is more of a hindrance than a help to communication." *Ibid.*, p. 772 (italics in original).

4. General Electric Company, TEMPO, *International Stability: Problems and Prospects* (Santa Barbara, Calif., R 61 TMP-90, February 1961), pp. 5–6.

5. *Ibid.*, pp. 28–29.

6. The contemporary literature using this mode of demonstration is very large, increasingly so in the field of international relations. For explicitly Parsonian and other demonstrations, see Chapter 3 below.

7. *The Permanent Revolution in Science*, as quoted and analyzed by Paul Meadows, "Models, Systems and Science," *American Sociological Review*, XXII (1957), 3–9.

8. David Mitrany, *International Affairs*, XXIV (1948), 356.

9. *Ibid.*, p. 359. Both these quotations are taken from Harold E. Engle's excellent pioneering analysis of Functionalism, "A Critical Study of the Functionalist Approach to International Organization" (unpublished Ph.D. dissertation, Columbia University, 1957).

10. S. F. Nadel, *The Theory of Social Structure* (London: Cohen and West, 1957), p. 12. The subquote is from Talcott Parsons, *Essays in Sociological Theory* (1949), p. 34.

11. Nadel, *Theory of Social Structure*, p. 1 (italics in original).

12. My summary relies almost exclusively on Engle, though it does not adhere to his sequence and scheme of classification. For a full discussion of the total Functionalist mood and argument—as distinguished from an inappropriate effort to synthesize this approach into a school of thought—see James P. Sewell, "An Evaluation of the Functional Approach to International Organization, with Emphasis on United Nations Programs Financing Economic Development" (unpublished Ph.D. dissertation, University of California, 1962), Chapter 1. Sewell has illustrated the argument very generously, drawing on the pamphlet literature as well as on the major writers.

13. Mitrany, *International Affairs*, XXIV (1948), 359.

14. Mitrany's application of this reasoning is exemplified in International Congress on Mental Health, *Proceedings* (London, 1948), Vol. IV, esp. p. 75.

15. David Mitrany, *A Working Peace System* (London: Royal Institute of International Affairs, 1943), p. 42, as cited by Engle, p. 49.

16. Engle, p. 89. Again, I am here heavily indebted to Engle's trenchant distinctions and analysis.

17. Mitrany, *A Working Peace System*, p. 42.

18. *Ibid.*, p. 41. This point is also strongly brought out by Engle, pp. 72–73.

19. Engle, p. 28.

20. Edgar Saveney, as quoted in Engle, p. 8.

21. Mitrany, *A Working Peace System*, p. 55.

22. The metaphor is not farfetched at all. See Mitrany's exposition in his address to the International Congress of Mental Health and the ideas of some earlier Functionalist writers, as summarized by Engle, pp. 148–49.

23. Engle, p. 58.

24. My treatment is based on Neville M. Goodman, *International Health Organizations and Their Work* (New York–Philadelphia: Blakiston, 1952). In 1885 the British government refused to institute quarantine in Suez, saying that such action "would probably have the result of making the British commerce return to the Cape route, to the great detriment of the Suez Canal" (*ibid.*, p. 61). When, in 1892, a general agreement was worked out for a quarantine at Suez for pilgrims only, the British government tried to get an exemption from the rule for British ships!

25. WHO, *The First Ten Years of the World Health Organization* (Geneva, 1958), pp. 170–71.

26. *Ibid.*, pp. 47 and 54.

27. For evidence of this professionalism and self-limitation, consult the program adopted by the 5th Session of the WHO Executive Board, as ratified by the 4th World Health Assembly, and the cautious attempt at expanding the scope voiced by the 8th Assembly in asking that the program be stretched to study "possibilities of new knowledge and its application to health," including new insecticides and nuclear fission. *Ibid.*, pp. 113–15.

At the 6th Session of the Executive Board it was decided that the World Health Assembly should not merely be a forum of discussion for national public health officials, who would review the Organization's work and make future policy, but should also be "a gathering of public-health workers from all parts of the world who naturally wished to take the opportunity of talking over some of their common problems more thoroughly than the debates in the main committees allowed." As a result, each Assembly devotes some of its time to what is, in effect, a professional meeting given over to some topic of interest to the profession, such as hospital administration, nursing education, or the control of syphilis. *Ibid.*, p. 91.

28. Witness the much-heralded Article 1 of the WHO Constitution: "The objec-

tive of the World Health Organization . . . shall be the attainment by all peoples of the highest possible level of health." My information concerning the obstacles encountered by WHO was obtained from interviews in Geneva and Washington.

29. My treatment relies essentially on the excellent study by Robert Gilpin, *American Scientists and Nuclear Weapons Policy* (Princeton: Princeton University Press, 1962). See especially Chapter 2 for the reasoning summarized above.

30. *Ibid.*, p. 203 (italics in original).

31. "Nuclear Bomb Tests," *Bulletin of the Atomic Scientists*, XIV (1958), 287; quoted in *ibid.*, pp. 215–16. Albert Wohlstetter, in "Scientists, Seers and Strategy," *Foreign Affairs* (April 1963), adduces convincing logic and evidence concerning the false antithesis posed by Rabinowitch, even though the target of his demonstration is Sir Charles Snow.

32. For these and the following details, see Gilpin, Chapter 7.

33. As quoted in *ibid.*, pp. 220–21. Nothing that has happened since changes this conclusion. The Test Ban Agreement of 1963, since it excludes underground explosions, simply sidesteps the "technical" detection issue on which the scientists could not reach agreement.

34. The reference to the "devil theory" and to H. G. Wells may be found in the excellent critique of Functionalism of Inis L. Claude, Jr., on which my treatment relies heavily. See his *Swords into Plowshares* (2d ed., New York: Random House, 1959), p. 379. For Mitrany's formulation, see Int. Cong. of Mental Health, *Proceedings*, IV, 82–83.

35. See Int. Cong. of Mental Health, *Proceedings*, and the discussion in Engle, pp. 11–12.

36. Thus, Hans J. Morgenthau, after agreeing with Mitrany's explanation of how national political communities come about and concurring further that the same sequence of events could apply internationally, nevertheless holds that "the contributions international functional agencies make to the well-being of members of all nations fade into the background. What stands before the eyes of all are the immense political conflicts that divide the great nations. . . . This is not primarily a matter of false emphasis born of ignorance. It is rather the recognition of the undeniable fact that, from a functional point of view, what the national government does or does not do is much more important for the satisfaction of individual wants than what an international functional agency does or does not do." *Politics Among Nations* (3d ed., New York: Knopf, 1960), p. 528.

John H. Herz, while stressing the inadequacy of the sovereign nation-state to defend its territorial integrity under modern technological conditions, denies that factors other than physical power and weapons systems enter into the community-building process. *International Politics in the Atomic Age* (New York: Columbia University Press, 1959), especially Part III.

Werner Levi seems to subscribe to the Functionalist theoretical propositions with even less qualification than Morgenthau. But he still declares that "existing cooperation in this field [international social welfare measures] and the success that the League of Nations and the United Nations have had in it should not create the illusion that the struggle for power among nations can here be overcome. This struggle is still the dominant feature of international relations." *Fundamentals of World Organization* (Minneapolis: University of Minnesota Press, 1950), p. 164.

37. Claude, *Swords into Plowshares*, p. 387.

38. *Political Realism and the Crisis of World Politics* (Princeton: Princeton University Press, 1960), p. 172.

39. *Ibid.*

40. Merton, *Social Theory and Social Structure*, p. 24.

1. For a development of this argument against Functionalism, see Lincoln P. Bloomfield, "The United States, the United Nations and the Creation of Community," *International Organization*, XIV (1960), 505 and 510.

2. See Paul Meadows, "Models, Systems and Science," *American Sociological Review*, XXII (1957), 6.

3. Amitai Etzioni, "A Paradigm for the Study of Political Unification," *World Politics*, XV (1962), 69. Etzioni also identifies this condition as "community." Integration and community, therefore, become synonyms!

4. Bela Balassa, *The Theory of Economic Integration* (Homewood, Ill.: Irwin, 1961), pp. 1–3. Rolf F. Sannwald and Jacques Stohler, *Economic Integration* (Princeton: Princeton University Press, 1959), pp. 42–44.

5. Chauncey D. Leake, "Trends in the World-Wide Dissemination of Knowledge and Their Consequences," mimeographed paper read at the International Relations Conference, Northwestern University, April 8–10, 1959.

6. For abstract definitions of integration and the lists of ranges of transactions, see Karl W. Deutsch, *Political Community at the International Level* (New York: Doubleday, 1954), pp. 33–40, 51–63. For an application of this mode of reasoning to Western European integration, see Karl W. Deutsch, "Towards Western European Integration: An Interim Assessment," *Journal of International Affairs*, XVI (1962), esp. 99–101.

7. Talcott Parsons, *The Social System* (Glencoe, Ill.: The Free Press, 1951), pp. 27 and 36.

8. Merton, *Social Theory and Social Structure*, pp. 30–36.

9. For an example of this line of reasoning and its shortcomings, see Kingsley Davis, "Identification of Fundamental Social Changes Which Condition Inter-Nation Relations," mimeographed paper read at Northwestern Conference, April 8–10, 1959.

10. This conception of integration is elaborated in the context of the study of regional unification and cooperation, provided with indicators appropriate to the setting, and demonstrated empirically in Ernst B. Haas, *The Uniting of Europe* (Stanford, Calif.: Stanford University Press, 1958); "The Challenge of Regionalism," *International Organization*, XII (1958); "International Integration," *ibid.*, XV (1961). In these publications no effort was made to restate the concept more generally so as to compare it with other formulations appropriate to the study of universal organizations.

11. The importance and value of historical sociology are described by Stanley Hoffmann, *Contemporary Theory in International Relations* (Englewood Cliffs: Prentice-Hall, 1960), pp. 171–91. My suggestions and first efforts to apply it to the study of the United Nations, in terms of phases within systems rather than as transitions among systems, are contained in Ernst B. Haas, "Comparative Study of the United Nations," *World Politics*, XII (1960), and "Dynamic Environment and Static System," in M. Kaplan, ed., *The Revolution in World Politics* (New York: Wiley, 1962). For a trenchant discussion of the notion of "social context" in historical sociology and in other contextual approaches—of which ours is one—in relation to the selection and analysis of "case studies" in indicating "typicality," see James J. Heaphey, "Theoretical Aspects of CPAC and IPC Case Studies" (unpublished Ph.D. dissertation, University of California, 1962), Chap. 1, esp. pp. 36–41.

12. As cited in Sheldon S. Wolin, *Politics and Vision* (Boston: Little, Brown, 1960), p. 416.

13. This rejoinder to the Functionalist argument is common currency. It is simply

but effectively presented in the context of a "liberal" ideology of "peace in our time" by Laurence Stapleton, *The Design of Democracy* (New York: Oxford University Press, 1949), Chapter 11. Mitrany answers by suggesting that welfare and security are complementary functions that can be attained simultaneously in the international order.

14. In my treatment of this aspect of Liberalism, I am deeply indebted to the work of Sheldon Wolin, who opened so many eyes to these neglected notions. Wolin, Chapter 10, esp. pp. 304–5, 313, 315, 325, 333, and 339.

15. *Ibid.*, p. 305.

16. *Ibid.*, pp. 313, 339.

17. *Ibid.*, pp. 315, 325.

18. *Ibid.*, p. 333.

19. *Oceana*, as quoted in *ibid.*, p. 390. Mitrany informs me that in 1939 he advanced a similar argument in an unpublished paper for the Foreign Office, in which he suggested that converging national preoccupations with welfare would dominate the post–World War II international scene.

20. Roy C. Macridis, "Interest Groups in Comparative Analysis," *Journal of Politics*, XXIII (1961), 45.

21. Stanley Rothman, "Systematic Political Theory," *American Political Science Review*, LIV (1960), esp. 29–33.

22. For examples of such use, see, above all, Gabriel A. Almond and James S. Coleman, eds., *The Politics of the Developing Areas* (Princeton: Princeton University Press, 1960); Samuel H. Beer *et al.*, *Patterns of Government* (New York: Random House, 1958). See also Gabriel A. Almond, "Comparative Study of Interest Groups," *American Political Science Review*, LII (1958), 270ff and the literature there cited.

23. Almond and Coleman, pp. 33–35, 39–41.

24. Julius Stone, *Quest for Survival* (Cambridge, Mass.: Harvard University Press, 1961), p. 5.

25. Charles de Visscher, *Theory and Reality in Public International Law* (Princeton: Princeton University Press, 1956), pp. 71 and 129. Mitrany is deeply skeptical of this type of evolution because human rights are *not* considered to be among the common interests of nations. See his "Human Rights and International Organisation," *India Quarterly*, Vol. III (1947), No. 2.

26. C. Wilfred Jenks, *The Common Law of Mankind* (London: Stevens, 1958), esp. Chapter 1.

27. W. Friedmann, *Law in a Changing Society* (Berkeley: University of California Press, 1959), pp. 418–19, 460–67. Philip Jessup, along similar lines, has suggested that the growing impact of an interdependent and welfare-oriented economic world has obliterated the traditional distinction between public and private international law, and has *de facto* made subjects of the law such entities as mixed public and private international corporations, private international organizations, and certain types of international interest groups. See his *Transnational Law* (New Haven: Yale University Press, 1956). A reformulation of international law along Parsonian lines was attempted by K. S. Carlston, *Law and Organization in World Society* (Urbana: University of Illinois Press, 1962). While functional in intent, the formulation relies too heavily on a rigid concept of authority to be helpful to our quest.

28. Léon Duguit, *Traité de droit constitutionnel*, I (Paris: Ancienne Librairie Fontemoing, 2d ed., 1921), 100–101. While leaning heavily on Durkheim, Duguit nevertheless manages to reify the notion of "society" as being responsible for the creation and observance of every aspect of law, thus minimizing the role of legisla-

tive and judicial activity in legal evolution. "Social need" becomes a magic formula that is used to explain everything. "Governments are individuals like others, subject like all individuals to the rules of law based on a social and intersocial solidarity; these rules of law prescribe their duties and their acts will be legitimate and will exact obedience not because they emanate from a supposed sovereign personality but when and only when they conform to the rules of law which are imposed upon their authors." *Ibid.*, p. 565.

29. My presentation is based entirely on his *Law Without Force: The Function of Politics in International Law* (Princeton: Princeton University Press, 1941). Niemeyer's work, in turn, is an adaptation of the legal and political philosophy of Hermann Heller. See Heller's *Staatslehre* (Leyden: Sythoff, 1934) and *Die Souveränität* (Berlin and Leipzig: Gruyter, 1927).

30. Niemeyer, pp. 286–87.

31. *Ibid.*, p. 355.

32. *Ibid.*, pp. 105–34, 312–13.

33. Bertrand de Jouvenel, *De la Souveraineté* (Paris: Génin, 1955), pp. 30–32. Pierre Duclos, "La Politification: Trois essais," *Politique* (April-June 1961). These distinctions are discussed with approval in criticizing Functional approaches to European unification in Sidjanski, *Dimensions européennes de la science politique,* pp. 39–41, 177–80.

34. In private communication to me, February 14, 1963 (italics in original).

35. The chief studies consulted on this issue are the following (other than works dealing with the ILO) :

(*a*) *UN specialized agencies.* James P. Sewell, "An Evaluation of the Functional Approach to International Organization, with Emphasis on United Nations Programs Financing Economic Development" (unpublished Ph.D. dissertation, University of California, Berkeley, 1962) ; Walter R. Sharp, *Field Administration in the United Nations System* (New York: Praeger, 1961) ; Robert E. Asher *et al., The United Nations and Promotion of the General Welfare* (Washington, D.C.: Brookings Institution, 1957) ; John G. Stoessinger, "Financing the United Nations," *International Conciliation* (No. 535, November 1961) ; Jacob Schenkman, "The International Civil Aviation Organization" (thesis, Geneva, 1955) ; Eugene R. Black, *Diplomacy of Economic Development* (Cambridge, Mass.: Harvard University Press, 1960; C. Labeyrie-Menahem, *Des Institutions specialisées* (Paris: Pedone, 1953) ; Walter H. C. Laves and Charles A. Thomson. *UNESCO* (Bloomington: Indiana University Press, 1957) ; B. E. Matecki, *Establishment of the International Finance Corporation and United States Policy* (New York: Praeger, 1957) ; J. G. Stoessinger, *The Refugee and the World Community* (Minneapolis: University of Minnesota Press, 1956) ; Louise W. Holborn, *The International Refugee Organization* (New York: Oxford University Press, 1956) ; George A. Codding, Jr., *The International Telecommunications Union* (Leyden: Sythoff, 1952) ; Gove Hambidge, *The Story of FAO* (New York: Van Nostrand, 1955) ; Neville M. Goodman, *International Health Organizations and Their Work* (Philadelphia: Blakiston, 1952) ; World Health Organization. *The First Ten Years of the World Health Organization* (Geneva, 1958) ; Robert Berkov, *The World Health Organization* (Geneva: Droz, 1957) ; Jean Salmon, *Le Rôle des organisations internationales en matière de prêts et d'emprunts* (New York: Praeger, 1958) ; James Morris, *The Road to Huddersfield* (New York: Pantheon, 1963).

(*b*) *UN non-political activities.* David Wightman, *Economic Cooperation in Europe* (New York: Praeger, 1956) ; Wightman, *Toward Economic Cooperation in Asia* (New Haven: Yale University Press, 1963) ; James M. Read, "The United Nations and Refugees," *International Conciliation* (No. 537, March 1962); Leland Goodrich, "New Trends in Narcotics Control," *ibid.* (No. 530, November 1960); Leon Gordenker, *The United Nations and the Peaceful Unification of Korea* (The Hague: Nijhoff, 1959); John G. Hadwen and Johan Kaufmann, *How United Nations Decisions Are Made* (Leyden: Sythoff, 1960); John Edwards, "The United Nations Special Fund" (unpublished M.A. thesis, University of California, 1963).

(*c*) *Western hemisphere.* U.S. Congress, Senate, Committee on Foreign Relations *The Organization of American States* (a study prepared by Northwestern University, 1959); Albert O. Hirschman, ed., *Latin American Issues* (New York: Twentieth Century Fund, 1961); John C. Dreier, *The Organization of American States and the Hemisphere Crisis* (New York: Harper and Row, 1962); John C. Dreier, "The Organization of American States and United States Policy," *International Organization*, Vol. XVII, No. 1 (1963); Robin F. Goldring, "The Inter-American Development Bank" (unpublished M.A. thesis, University of California, 1963); I. L. Claude, Jr., "The OAS, the UN and the United States," *International Conciliation*, No. 547 (March 1964); C. Neale Ronning, *Law and Politics in Inter-American Diplomacy* (New York: Wiley, 1963); Victor L. Urquidi, *Free Trade and Economic Integration in Latin America* (Berkeley: University of California Press, 1962); Eugenio A. Hernandez, S.J., "The Organization of Central American States in Its Historical Perspective" (unpublished Ph.D. dissertation, Harvard University, 1963).

(*d*) *European regional agencies.* Leon N. Lindberg, *Political Dynamics of European Economic Integration* (Stanford, Calif.: Stanford University Press, 1963); Stuart Scheingold, "The Court of the European Communities" (unpublished Ph.D. dissertation, University of California, 1963); Stanley V. Anderson, "The Nordic Council" (*ibid.*, 1962); Jack E. Thomas, "Saceur and Shape: A Study of Peacetime Preparation for Coalition Defense" (*ibid.*, 1959); Walter Yondorff, "Europe of the Six: Dynamics of Integration" (unpublished Ph.D. dissertation, University of Chicago, 1962); William Diebold, Jr., *Trade and Payments in Western Europe* (New York: Harper, 1952); Diebold, *The Schuman Plan* (New York: Praeger, 1959); A. H. Robertson, *The Council of Europe* (2d ed., New York: Praeger, 1961); M. M. Ball, *NATO and the European Union Movement* (New York: Praeger, 1959); Political and Economic Planning, *European Organisations* (London: Allen and Unwin, 1959); Political and Economic Planning, *Occasional Papers* (since 1958); Ernst B. Haas, *The Uniting of Europe* (London: Stevens; Stanford, Calif.: Stanford University Press, 1958); Kenneth Lindsay, ed., *European Assemblies* (London: Stevens, 1960); Walter Hallstein, *United Europe* (Cambridge, Mass.: Harvard University Press, 1962); J. E. Meade, H. H. Liesner, and S. J. Wells, *Case Studies in European Economic Integration* (London: Oxford University Press, 1962); Robert E. Osgood, *NATO: The Entangling Alliance* (Chicago: University of Chicago Press, 1962); Gordon L. Weil, *The European Convention on Human Rights* (Leyden: Sythoff, 1963); George Lichtheim, *The New Europe* (New York: Praeger, 1963); J. G. Polach, *Euratom* (New York: Oceana Publications, 1964); U. W. Kitzinger, *The Politics and Economics of European Integration* (New York: Praeger, 1963); Michael Shanks and John Lambert, *The Common Market: Today and Tomorrow* (New York: Praeger, 1962); Roy Pryce, *The Political Future of the European Community* (London: Marshbank, 1962).

CHAPTER THREE

1. Theorizing that draws its strength from other disciplines is consistently found in *The Journal of Conflict Resolution*, whose motto might be "a peaceful world = a

sane world = a world governed by healthy minds, which results from efforts at understanding this world derived from sciences which produce healthy minds." For scathing attacks on this outlook, see Kenneth N. Waltz, *Man, the State, and War* (New York: Columbia University Press, 1959), Chaps. 2, 3; and International Sociological Association, *The Nature of Conflict* (Paris: UNESCO, 1957), essays by Jessie Bernard and Raymond Aron.

2. For close historical studies of the alleged role of balance-of-power reasoning in specific modern situations, see Richard Rosecrance, *Action and Reaction in World Politics* (Boston: Little, Brown, 1963), and Ernst B. Haas, "Belgium and the Balance of Power" (unpublished Ph.D. dissertation, Columbia University, 1952). For a demonstration of the balance-of-power theory as a futile guide to policy-makers in modern times, i.e., as prescription, see Ernst B. Haas, "The Balance of Power as a Guide to Policy-Making," *Journal of Politics*, Vol. XV, No. 3(1953).

3. This more general level of international systems theory is ably represented by Charles McClelland, "Systems and History in International Relations," *General Systems Yearbook*, Vol. III (1958); "The Function of Theory in International Relations," *Journal of Conflict Resolution*, Vol. IV, No. 3 (1960). Systems theory is presented, in the form of a spectrum of approaches, by the eleven contributors to the October 1961 issue of *World Politics* (Vol. XIV, No. 1), which will furnish much of the material for our analysis. See especially McClelland's own moderate application of his approach to a concrete problem in *ibid.*, pp. 182–204. For other early efforts to apply systems theory to the study of international organizations, see Ernst B. Haas, "The Comparative Study of the United Nations," *World Politics*, Vol. XII, No. 2 (1960); "System and Process in the International Labor Organization," *ibid.*, Vol. XIV, No. 2 (1962); "Dynamic Environment and Static System," in Morton Kaplan, ed., *The Revolution in World Politics* (New York: Wiley, 1962).

4. The systemic generalizations provided by Hoffmann and Haas (in *World Politics*, Vols. XIV and XII, respectively) are of the concrete variety. Systems developed by Morton A. Kaplan, *System and Process in International Politics* (New York: Wiley, 1957), are self-consciously analytic. So are most of the efforts described in the October 1961 issue of *World Politics*.

5. See Chapter 2 for the definition of integration that is here being elaborated in terms of systems theory.

6. Hoffmann, in *World Politics*, XIV (1961), 207–8. It should be noted that the notion of tasks, so crucial to our analysis, is slighted by Hoffmann when he explains transitions between systems, even though he makes it a key element in his definition of a given system.

7. J. David Singer, "The Level-of-Analysis Problem in International Relations," *ibid.*, esp. pp. 88–90.

8. *Ibid.*, p. 91.

9. For Singer's own attempt to build such a bridge, see his "Inter-Nation Influence: A Formal Model," *American Political Science Review*, LVII (1963), 420–30; James N. Rosenau, *Calculated Control as a Unifying Concept in the Study of International Politics and Foreign Policy* (Princeton University, Center of International Studies, February 1963).

10. George Modelski, "Agraria and Industria: Two Models of the International System," *World Politics*, XIV (1961), 120.

11. *Ibid.*, p. 121. Clarity is scarcely enhanced by the fact that Modelski first "assumes," and a sentence later "maintains," that these propositions are true.

12. *Ibid.*, pp. 142–43.

13. *Ibid.*, p. 122.

14. *Ibid.*, p. 139.

15. *Ibid.*, p. 141.

16. The models are set forth in Kaplan, *System and Process in International Politics*. The explanatory modification of the purpose and range of usefulness of these models may be found in Kaplan, "Problems of Theory Building and Theory Confirmation in International Politics," *World Politics*, XIV (1961).

17. *Ibid.*, pp. 16–17.

18. Actually, Kaplan seems to think that the balance of power was a concrete international system. At least, this is strongly implied in his treatment of nineteenth-century international law, which is characterized as the normative order of that system. See Morton A. Kaplan and Nicholas deB. Katzenbach, *The Political Foundations of International Law* (New York: Wiley, 1961).

19. While no claim is made that this system is in any sense a concrete one, it resembles the current international order so strikingly as to pose a strong temptation to use it as a concrete system.

20. *System and Process*, p. 89.

21. *Ibid.*, pp. 116–17.

22. *Ibid.*, pp. 119–20.

23. For more circumspect formulations of "roles" in United Nations discussions, within the bounds of the Loose Bipolar System but reaching different conclusions about how the "roles" are played, see Stanley Hoffmann, "Sisyphus and the Avalanche," *International Organization*, Vol. XI, No. 3 (1957); Hoffmann, "In Search of a Thread: The UN in the Congo Labyrinth," *ibid.*, Vol. XIV, No. 2 (1962); Alfred Grosser, "Suez, Hungary and European Integration," *ibid.*, Vol. XI, No. 3 (1957); Ernst B. Haas, "Types of Collective Security: An Examination of Operational Concepts," *American Political Science Review*, Vol. XLIX, No. 1 (1955); Haas, "Regionalism, Functionalism and Universal International Organization," *World Politics*, Vol. VIII, No. 2 (1956).

24. G. A. Almond and J. S. Coleman, *The Politics of the Developing Areas* (Princeton: Princeton University Press, 1960). The analytical model is developed by Almond in the Introduction, which is entitled "A Functional Approach to Comparative Politics." The concrete systems are described by Coleman in the Conclusion, pp. 532–76. This approach owes a great deal to the work of David Easton, who sought to reduce the American polity to systemic terms. Almond and Coleman, in turn, have been criticized—in my judgment, unnecessarily—for analytically subsuming all developing political systems to a Western-inspired ideal type. It is one of the virtues of functional analysis to call attention to common and recurring "things done" by diverse polities.

25. *Ibid.*, p. 5.

26. Fred W. Riggs, "International Relations as a Prismatic System," *World Politics*, Vol. XIV, No. 1 (1961).

27. *Ibid.*, pp. 154–55.

28. These ideas are developed by Chadwick F. Alger in a deliberate attempt to render useful and synthesize the approaches of Easton, Almond, and Riggs for purposes of international integration studies. See his "Comparison of Intranational and International Politics," *American Political Science Review*, LVII (1963), 406–19.

29. Hoffmann, in *World Politics*, XIV (1961). The attributes and limits of Hoffmann's systems were given above at pp. 53–54.

30. *Ibid.*, pp. 211–15.

31. McClelland, "The Acute International Crisis," *World Politics*, XIV (1961), 198–99.

32. Modelski, in *World Politics*, XIV (1961), 121–22.

33. *Ibid.*, p. 122.

34. *Ibid.*, p. 124.

35. *Ibid.*, p. 123.

36. Kaplan, *System and Process*, pp. 9–12.

37. *Ibid.*, p. 19.

38. Alger, in *American Political Science Review*, LVII (1963), 411–14.

39. The word "structure" in Hoffmann's usage requires one caveat: he uses it as the equivalent of what I call the "environment," reserving words such as "methods," "techniques," and "institutions" for what is usually called "structure" in systems theory.

40. As in this example: "The basic function of international law is to organize the coexistence of the various units." Hoffmann, in *World Politics*, XIV (1961), 212.

41. *Ibid.*, p. 208.

42. For a full exposition of these verbal and contextual meanings, see Ernst B. Haas, "The Balance of Power: Prescription, Concept or Propaganda?," *World Politics*, Vol. V, No. 4 (1953). Descriptive intent must be judged on its factual accuracy; prescriptive intent is dangerous for policy, impossible in action, and irrelevant to serious theory; propagandistic intent is simply irrelevant to theory.

43. The following treatment will rest heavily on Waltz, *Man, the State, and War*, Chapters 6 and 7.

44. *Ibid.*, pp. 184–85.

45. *Ibid.*, p. 204.

46. Rosenau, *International Politics and Foreign Policy*, p. 351.

47. *Ibid.*, p. 364.

48. John H. Herz, "Balance System and Balance Policies in a Nuclear and Bipolar Age," *Journal of International Affairs*, XIV (1960), 35–48. Significantly, this issue is entitled "A New Balance of Power." Arthur Burns contributed an article avoiding the theoretical issue posed by balance-of-power analysis, and limiting himself to a discussion of balancing in factual-descriptive terms. If the word "balance" had been omitted from the discussion, the meaning would have remained the same. *Ibid.*, pp. 61–69.

49. This discussion is based on Glenn H. Snyder, "Balance of Power in the Missile Age," *ibid.*, pp. 21–34. The distinction between deterrence and defense is crucial and perceptive, and is developed by Snyder in *Deterrence and Defense* (Princeton: Princeton University Press, 1961).

50. In *Journal of International Affairs*, XIV (1960), 25–26 (italics in original).

51. Another such formulation is found in the work of George Liska, whose fine sense of the temporal aspects of systems and of their dependence on a multidimensional environment does not prevent him from seeing systems-dominance. See his *International Equilibrium* (Cambridge: Harvard University Press, 1957), and his *Nations in Alliance* (Baltimore: Johns Hopkins Press, 1962).

52. Hoffmann, in *World Politics*, XIV (1961), 218.

53. Compare this explanation of the growth of international law with that provided by Kaplan and Katzenbach, *Political Foundations of International Law*, in which the characteristics of the system rather than the nature of the actors emerge as the crucial explanatory variable.

54. Adda B. Bozeman, using many of the same social and economic considerations in her historical account of international relations adduced by Hoffmann, comes to the opposite conclusion. She claims that the contemporary system of international law and organizations, in effect, represents the universal sway of the European-

western system. Although her argument mistakes the nature of the United Nations and overstates the case considerably, it nevertheless points up the possibility of using this kind of historical demonstration toward a radically different conclusion. *Politics and Culture in International History* (Princeton: Princeton University Press, 1960), pp. 513–22.

55. In a sense we could say that Kaplan's systems are really subsystems within the one I sketched, to the extent that they concern themselves with polarities and military capacity.

56. See above, pp. 61, 66–67.

57. Roger D. Masters, "A Multi-Bloc Model of the International System," *American Political Science Review*, LV (1961), esp. 797.

58. Dorothy Emmet, *Function, Purpose, and Powers* (London: Macmillan, 1958), pp. 293–94 (italics in original).

59. As a minor contribution to semantic confusion, let it be noted that Emmet uses the term "social structure" for what most others call the "social system" (*ibid.*, pp. 24–26). She also uses the concept of the "field" as an aspect of the "structure" selected by the observer to facilitate close attention on the particular relationships that concern him. In so doing, the observer may forgo a description of the social totality and concentrate on what seems to him to be a "strategic" relationship. Emmet advocates "field" studies particularly for international relations. I hope to be true to her intent in using the concept of integration in this sense, and isolating the "field" of systemic relationships hinging on integration as my aspect of the total international system (*ibid.*, pp. 34–38).

60. *Ibid.*, p. 51.

61. For her brilliant destruction of the notions of equilibrium and stability, see *ibid.*, pp. 60–74.

62. Because we are concerned with the transformation of systems, we part company with Emmet at this point. She sums up the virtues of functional analysis thus: "What can be stated in terms of the functional concepts, but not in terms of purposive ones, are the consequences of people's actions which work out in a way which helps maintain a form of society without their being intended to do so" (*ibid.*, p. 96). We would substitute the word "transform" for "maintain," and otherwise accept the formulation.

63. My largest debt is to Robert K. Merton's *Social Theory and Social Structure*, Part I. What follows is greatly influenced by Merton's famous paradigm of functional analysis, *ibid.*, pp. 50–54.

64. A very similar argument is advanced by Talcott Parsons, even though the implication is one of deterministic progress toward world community, the determinism flowing naturally from the system itself. Parsons holds that the fact of the Cold War and the bipolarization of physical power establishes the fact of an ongoing world community, a rudimentary system of order. Why? Because the mere prevalence of ideological conflict presupposes a common frame of reference. This he finds in the universal preoccupation with gaining or safeguarding the fruits of industrialism and of the socio-political equality associated with it. If the notion of violent revolution could be banished from the non-Western world, the millennium of world community would be within our grasp. "Polarization and the Problem of International Order," *Berkeley Journal of Sociology*, VI (1961), 115–34.

65. The superiority of historical systems is clearly demonstrated by Hoffmann's discussion of the nature of international law in the current "revolutionary system." Because the current system is characterized by a whole series of specifiable and identifiable heterogeneities, certain rules of law are "obsolete" in the sense that they

merely command verbal attachment and are a residue from the preceding system. Certain other rules of law, however, are "premature" in that they herald a new system which is not yet feasible because of the environmental heterogeneities. Yet this coexistence of laws has been "functional" in the sense of yielding a body of practical task-oriented rules on which nations can agree despite heterogeneity, e.g., in technical assistance, space, Antarctica, etc. In *World Politics*, XIV (1961), 229.

66. For two pioneering efforts to generalize about international relations on the basis of manipulating large bodies of statistical data in preference to the clinical-historical approach, see Hayward R. Alker, Jr., "Dimensions of Voting in the United Nations" (unpublished Ph.D. dissertation, Yale University, 1963), and Rudolph J. Rummel, "Dimensions of Conflict Behavior Within and Between Nations" (unpublished Ph.D. dissertation, Northwestern University, 1963). Despite the large number of indicators used and the complexity of the factor analysis undertaken, neither study presents findings unfamiliar to the clinical-historical tradition.

67. Merton, p. 51 (my italics).

68. Our disagreement with Merton's distinction between latent and manifest functions can be illustrated from the examples he adduces. Merton cites Veblen's treatment of conspicuous consumption as a latent function of the social-economic system being analyzed (*ibid.*, pp. 68–70). This must mean that whatever the overt purposes of the consumers, and whatever the manifest functions in terms of their eventual recognition of the unintended consequences, the "real" function remained unrecognized—"costliness = mark of higher social status"—by the American capitalist. It may be that the Fricks, Huntingtons, Vanderbilts, and Goulds were not aware of this Veblenian equation; but I doubt it. Even if we were to assume their lack of awareness, the concept of latent functions is not likely to help us in an analysis of the international system. In contrast with the myriad behavior patterns and social roles in a broad social context, in international relations we are dealing with the specific and finite demands of government. While the units being analyzed are more complex, their inputs into the system—paradoxically—are analytically simpler than the task Veblen set himself. Is it not likely that the actors will sooner or later grow aware of the unintended consequences of earlier purposes? Statesmen may be dolts, but they are not robots.

Merton uses an extended example of bossism in American urban politics to illustrate the same thesis. He puts the problem in this way: "Proceeding from the functional view, therefore, that we should *ordinarily* (not invariably) expect persistent social patterns and social structures to perform positive functions *which are at the time not adequately fulfilled by other existing patterns and structures*, the thought occurs that perhaps this publicly maligned organization is, *under present conditions*, satisfying basic latent functions" (*ibid.*, pp. 71–72, italics in original).

In terms of the manifest functions, the machine is dysfunctional for the polity because it encourages corruption and defeats the purpose of the official political structures. But it may satisfy the latent functions of underprivileged groups in the polity, who, because of ignorance, illiteracy, poverty, recent immigrant status, etc., have no opportunity to obtain redress of their demands from the official structures. Legitimate and illicit business obtain from the machine "protection" not otherwise available. Bossism then provides the informal structures for meeting these latent functions. "Put in more generalized terms," says Merton, "*the functional deficiencies of the official structure generate an alternative (unofficial) structure to fulfill existing needs somewhat more effectively*. Whatever its specific historical origins, the political machine persists as an apparatus for satisfying otherwise unfulfilled needs of diverse groups in the population" (*ibid.*, p. 73, italics in original).

In the first place, let us note that the meaning of "function'" has now shifted away from "unintended consequences" to "need." Which is the latent function? The way in which the machine meets the needs of certain urban groups, or the needs themselves? Is bossism a structure that arose to meet the latent function, or the function itself? The treatment begs the question. In our paradigm it would appear as a structure. But the real problem still hinges on the issue of latency. Although bossism may have arisen as an unintended consequence, surely it did not remain unrecognized for long by politicians, the underprivileged, the racketeers, the reformers, the observers. I am not disputing Merton's argument that the machine fulfilled the positive function of meeting some of the needs of the groups studied; nor am I quarreling with his contention that functional analysis sensitizes the observer to recognizing this kind of indirect benefit from structure which, on the surface, appears to be reprehensible morally and dysfunctional for the total system. But I am disputing the adequacy of a formulation that holds these features to be both unintended *and* unrecognized by the participants, leaving the observer as the only one detached enough to be aware of the total context. Indeed, the likelihood of their recognition leads me to postulate the hiatus between the functional and dysfunctional consequences of actor purposes in international systems.

69. Merton, p. 54. The essay by Parsons, cited above, clearly does contain an unavowed ideological bias in favor of an integrated world order. "The subordination of 'parochial' interests to those of a more extensive system" is deduced as systemically desirable, even though it is also clearly the author's wish that gives rise to the shape of the system he sketches. Parsons, p. 120.

CHAPTER FOUR

1. The heterogeneity of theory, and the patent capacity of recognized and leading students of the field to entertain quite distinct notions of how one approaches theory, are demonstrated in Mason Haire, ed., *Modern Organization Theory* (New York: Wiley, 1959), a work that contains a number of fascinating essays and furnishes a spectrum of current thought. I have drawn on it liberally in the pages that follow.

2. Dwight Waldo, "Organization Theory: An Elephantine Problem," *Public Administration Review*, XXI (1961), 211.

3. *Ibid.*, p. 216 (italics in original). Consider E. Wight Bakke's definition of "organization," also commented on by Waldo, as given in Haire, p. 50: "A social organization is a continuing system of differentiated and coordinated human activities utilizing, transforming, and welding together a specific set of human, material, capital, ideational, and natural resources into a unique problem-solving whole whose function is to satisfy particular human needs in interaction with systems of human activities and resources in its particular environment."

Almost each term requires additional definition, and when that has been done, the species so circumscribed becomes almost coterminous with any human collectivity, whether we call it system, bureaucracy, society, state, or whatever. Bakke also provides an exhaustive scheme for studying and interrelating each of these components of an "organization." I am reminded, in perusing this effort, of Richard C. Snyder's approach to decision-making: rather than explaining any one thing, Snyder's total effort is a check-list of "things" any self-respecting social scientist *should* study and ponder if he wishes to achieve a systematic view of a phenomenon, without specifying priorities, strategies, or assumptions we could safely make initially. Bakke's and Snyder's efforts, then, are impressive as taxonomies but not as explanations, and hence not very useful in our context. For a succinct statement of Snyder's approach, see his "A Decision-Making Approach to the Study of Political Phenomena," in Roland Young, *Approaches to the Study of Politics* (Evanston: Northwestern University Press, 1958), pp. 3–37.

4. See the discussion of administration by Norton E. Long, "The Administrative Organization as a Political System," in Sidney Mailick and Edward H. Van Ness, eds., *Concepts and Issues in Administrative Behavior* (Englewood Cliffs: Prentice-Hall, 1962), pp. 120–21.

5. This four-fold scheme is borrowed from R. M. Cyert and J. G. March, "Organizational Objectives," Haire, p. 78. The authors treat these headings as "subsystems" of a "model" appropriate for all organizations. "Model" here seems to mean the same as "system"; and even though each subsystem is treated autonomously for purposes of simulation on the computer, the assumption of dependence on the total system is retained. I make no such claims here. These headings are merely suggestive empirically and logically in giving us a way of talking intelligibly about organizational behavior; they are in no sense autonomous and in no way merely aspects of an analytical system. They are real processes in agencies made up of reasoning and reasonably intelligent officials, all too aware of their own concreteness.

6. For an exhaustive statement of the motivational-organic approach to the study of organizations, see Rensis Likert, in Haire, pp. 184–214.

7. Anatol Rapoport describes a small-group experiment whose major characteristics parallel certain problems of international organizations quite well, especially in terms of the patterns of cooperation and conflict that are thought to arise in problem-solving. But it is doubtful that a theory of international integration can learn from this analogy any more than it can from the "games" played by teams of individuals simulating governments and international organizations in the "interpersonal" approach to international relations featured by Harold Guetzkow. For Rapoport's experiment, see "A Logical Task as a Research Tool in Organization Theory," Haire, pp. 91ff.

8. Three "models of bureaucracy" are presented in James G. March and Herbert A. Simon, *Organizations* (New York: Wiley, 1958), pp. 36–47. Internal efficiency is the overriding criterion of organization here too, even though the basic analogy is mechanical rather than organic. The effort, it should be noted, does not result in "models" that meet the more rigorous mathematical-predictive requirements. Further, efficiency is equated with organizational self-maintenance, or the survival of the unit in isolation from the environment in which it is—one would assume—located. Useful as such a formulation may be for theorizing about bureaucracy, it helps very little when one seeks relationships *between* environment and organization, and hopes to discover something about integration of organization with clients or subjects.

9. Dwight Waldo, *The Administrative State* (New York: Ronald Press, 1948), pp. 198–205.

10. Haire, pp. 304–5.

11. "Survival" models of organizations are discussed in these works: Talcott Parsons, "Suggestions for a Sociological Approach to the Theory of Organizations," *Administrative Science Quarterly* (June 1956 and September 1956), pp. 63–85, 225–39; Chester I. Barnard, *The Functions of the Executive* (Cambridge: Harvard University Press, 1947); Amitai Etzioni, "Two Approaches to Organizational Analysis," *Administrative Science Quarterly*, Vol. V (1960). The link to systems theory is explicitly argued by William G. Scott, "Organization Theory: An Overview and an Appraisal," *Journal of the Academy of Management* (April 1961).

12. Barnard, pp. 3–7, 14–15, 88–89, 98–99.

13. *Ibid.*, pp. 56–57.

14. Etzioni, pp. 267–69.

15. Etzioni (p. 260) really ignores the goals and objectives of organizations on the ground that such goals "are not meant to be realized." The founders of the World Health Organization or the International Labor Organization would, no doubt, be fascinated to learn this about themselves!

16. Joseph P. Chamberlain, "International Organization," as reprinted in *International Organization* (New York: Carnegie Endowment for International Peace, 1955), p. 87. Chamberlain's essay is a famous statement of the Functionalist rationale and a more direct application of it to actual international agencies than attempted by Mitrany. It was originally published in 1942. In the volume cited, Philip C. Jessup, Adolf Lande, and Oliver J. Lissitzyn examine "Functional" developments since 1942 and come to the conclusion that Chamberlain's formulation retains its entire validity. *Ibid.*, p. 83.

17. *Ibid.*, p. 91.

18. Victor A. Thompson, *Modern Organization* (New York: Knopf, 1961), p. 9.

19. The Chicago Housing Authority study was published by Martin Meyerson and E. C. Banfield as *Politics, Planning and the Public Interest* (Glencoe, Ill.: The Free Press, 1955). My treatment here has used and adapted Banfield's own summary, "Ends and Means in Planning," in Mailick and Van Ness, pp. 78–79.

For most international agencies, Banfield's sardonic statement of the role of formal objectives may be accepted provisionally: "The end-system of an organization is rarely, if ever, a clear and coherent picture of a desirable future toward which action is to be directed. Usually, a set of vague platitudes and pious cant is used to justify the existence of the organization in the eyes of its members and of outsiders. The stated ends are propaganda, not criteria for guiding action." *Ibid.*, pp. 77–78.

20. Herbert A. Simon, *Administrative Behavior* (New York: Macmillan, 1957), p. xxiv.

21. The following discussion is heavily indebted to Selznick's *Leadership in Administration* (Evanston: Row, Peterson, 1957), which—while accepting the political constraints on organizational action posited by Banfield—strives for a theory of organization that can help explain systemic change.

22. *Ibid.*, p. 138 (italics in original). Selznick also conceives of his "institutions" in quasi-organismic terms, as "social organisms" or "natural communities." I have no wish to push the notion that far.

23. *Ibid.*, p. 14.

24. *Ibid.*, p. 16. I prefer this formulation of the notion of "commitment" (or "engagement," as European students of international life are likely to put it) to Selznick's emphasis on "need," which suggests an organic and bio-psychological approach I am anxious to avoid in view of my own emphasis on perceptions of interest. See Selznick, pp. 17, 74, 89, 143.

25. Barnard, pp. 75–76. I shy away from the consistent adoption of the electromagnetic metaphor, tempting though it is, because Barnard claims that "the hypothesis we follow is that all of the phenomena concerned are usefully explained if we adopt it, and that existing knowledge and experience are consistent with that assumption."

26. Gunnar Myrdal, *Realities and Illusions in Regard to Inter-Governmental Organizations* (London: Oxford University Press, 1955), pp. 4–5.

27. *Ibid.*, p. 25.

28. For a discussion and admirable critique of the Weberian model, see Peter M. Blau, *Bureaucracy in Modern Society* (New York: Random House, 1956), and Blau, "Critical Remarks on Weber's Theory of Authority," *American Political Science Review*, LVII (1963), esp. 306–8, 311–15.

29. For an elaboration of the democratic model of bureaucracy, see Thompson, *Modern Organization*, pp. 74–77. Thompson would give the specialist full powers by stripping the central administrator of charismatic and dramaturgic qualities. He stresses the importance of experts and interest groups because he feels that the hierarchical or monocratic organizational model is both unreal and undesirable. Competent specialists cooperating freely are held to make for effective organizations. I would counter this emphasis by suggesting that the deliberate scrapping of the Weberian conception condemns the leadership of an international organization to the subversion of central goals in favor of exclusive catering to the external special interests of clients who are acting in coalition with appropriate specialists on the staff.

30. Barnard, p. 163.

31. Selznick, pp. 104–7.

32. *Ibid.*, p. 112.

33. *Ibid.*, pp. 121–22, 127.

34. *Ibid.*, p. 145 (italics in original).

35. "Critical" and "routine" decisions are discussed by Selznick, pp. 38–42, and also very acutely by William R. Dill, "Administrative Decision-Making," in Mailick and Van Ness, pp. 42–43.

36. Selznick, pp. 65–68.

37. This manner of viewing interest politics is inspired by what Robert A. Dahl and Charles E. Lindblom have called "polyarchy" and "bargaining." See their *Politics, Economics, and Welfare* (New York: Harper, 1953).

38. A purely administrative emphasis, by way of contrast, is given to the issue of coalition formation by the formulation adopted by March and Cyert (in Haire, pp. 88–89). They wish to be able to predict optimal choices for potential coalition partners, and hence they want to give quantitative values to group demands. However, quite apart from the feasibility of quantifying demands, the source of the demands is sought *inside* the organization, and the environment as a source of inputs is again neglected.

39. Barnard, pp. 281–84. The personal qualities requisite for this type of leadership are truly heroic. The executive must be a master of the "science of cooperation, a true adept who substitutes creative decisions based on management science for the slap-dash procedures of the ordinary, short-run political process." *Ibid.*, pp. 291–93. The heroic dimension is clearly implicit when Barnard describes the quality of "mind" required of the major executive as including "logical reasoning processes [which are] increasingly necessary but are disadvantageous if not in subordination to highly developed intuitional processes." *Ibid.*, p. 320.

40. Such an emphasis is demonstrated as flowing from the experience summed up in the case program in public administration, and is formally argued in a very convincing manner in Heaphey, "Theoretical Aspects of CPAC and IPC Case Studies," esp. pp. 80–82.

41. The notion of "weakness" is used as Gandhi used it in contrasting non-violent direct action with *satyagraha*. One involves merely non-violent group action to remedy a specific injustice; the other includes a commitment to a positive general program of perfection, of personal and collective search for "truth." "Weakness" thus means not only relative distance from official power, but also a spiritual imperfection. For an excellent discussion of these issues, as well as for an analysis of nine types of "non-violence," see Gene Sharp, "The Meanings of Non-Violence: A Typology (revised)," *Journal of Conflict Resolution*, III (March 1959), esp. pp. 56–58.

42. James D. Thompson and Arthur Tuden, "Strategies, Structures and Processes of Organizational Decision," in Administrative Science Center, University of Pittsburgh, *Comparative Studies in Administration* (Pittsburgh: University of Pittsburgh Press, 1959). The matrix represents a fusion and slight rewording of the separate diagrams appearing in Thompson and Tuden, pp. 198 and 204. The authors are concerned with developing operational sociological models of organizational decision-making, instead of being concerned with efficiency models aimed at maximizing benefits in an economic sense, or with psychological models oriented toward describing satisfactory participation of individuals. They are interested in decisions made on behalf of organizations by a group with power and authority to decide. Decisions are choices among alternative outcomes of action. They want to correlate types of decisions with types of issues that arise, i.e., types of situations representing a choice among alternatives (pp. 195–97). In a slightly different (and forced) manner, they also identify causation with "means," and preferences with "ends" (p. 197).

43. This point is elaborated by Thomas E. Phipps, Jr., "Resolving 'Hopeless' Conflicts," *Journal of Conflict Resolution*, V (September 1961), 274–78.

44. For insight into the relevance of *satyagraha* to bureaucratic decision-making, I am deeply indebted to Joan V. Bondurant's fine treatment in *Conquest of Violence* (Princeton: Princeton University Press, 1958), esp. pp. 214–32.

45. See Indian Council of World Affairs, *India and the United Nations* (New York: Manhattan Publishing Co., 1957), and Ross N. Berkes and Mohinder S. Bedi, *The Diplomacy of India* (Stanford, Calif.: Stanford University Press, 1958).

46. E. Foda, *The Projected Arab Court of Justice* (The Hague: Nijhoff, 1957), pp. 54–55, 128–29. The appeal to *solh* has been used on a number of recent occasions in disputes among Islamic states, involving, however, the services of a mediator, who apparently appointed himself or was chosen by the opposing governments. Foda argues that the doctrine of *solh* remains central to the Arab efforts to create a system of compulsory legal settlement among themselves.

47. *Ibid.*, p. 130.

48. Naess, p. 151 (italics mine).

49. March and Simon (pp. 129–31), disregarding the variable impact of organizational objectives and environmental forces, seek to reduce all intrabureaucratic conflict resolution to computational and compromise modes. This formulation hinders our effort.

Robert Presthus, however, offers an oligarchical model of organization, in which the forces isolated by me as crucial are well described. *The Organizational Society* (New York: Knopf, 1962), pp. 56–58. Emphasis on the actual and natural predominance of oligarchy is a major reason for avoiding the temptation of stating an organizational model that sanctifies and legitimates the technocratic element. Reliance on the Functionalist concept of administration by technocrats imbued with a vision of the general welfare, a means of conflict resolution that would take the place of politically dominated selfishness, could be easily combined with Barnard's vision of the "scientific" task of the executive and Selznick's treatment of bureaucratic leadership. The result would be an organizational model that would not only maximize international integration, but also present an ethical alternative to politics. My commitment to an interest calculus, and to the reality of the constraints of the international system, precludes the use of such a model.

50. For a fuller exposition with a variety of examples from the European regional context, see Ernst B. Haas, "International Integration," *International Organization*, XV (1961), 367–68.

51. As cited in Metcalf and Urwick, eds., *Dynamic Administration* (New York: Harper, 1940), p. 32. In this context, of course, it makes eminent sense to speak of the "integrative function of conflict." Conflict, far from necessarily tearing apart the fabric of organizational consensus, actually facilitates the facing of issues, the collective examination of separate and joint objectives, and thereby gives the leading elements an opportunity for revaluing the overall trend of objectives. Conflict is then the occasion for growth and a new consensus. For a sensitive development of this theme, see R. C. North, H. E. Koch, and D. A. Zinnes, "The Integrative Functions of Conflict," *Journal of Conflict Resolution*, IV (September 1960), 355ff.

52. Charles E. Osgood, "Suggestions for Winning the Real War with Communism," *ibid.*, III (December 1959), 321. The dissonance principle was developed by Leon Festinger, *A Theory of Cognitive Dissonance* (Stanford, Calif.: Stanford University Press, 1957).

53. For psychological attempts to apply the dissonance principle to conflict resolution in the international system, see Robert P. Abelson, "Modes of Resolution of Belief Dilemmas," *Journal of Conflict Resolution*, IV (September 1960), 343ff. Also Irving L. Janis, "Decisional Conflicts: A Theoretical Analysis," *ibid.*, III (March 1959), esp. 20–21.

54. These limitations on the neatness of the scheme are discussed by Thompson and Tuden themselves (pp. 205–8). It may well be that the Soviet and United States decision to carry on difficult disarmament negotiations was spurred by the necessarily divided judgment in each government concerning the impact of scientific advances on military security. In other words, considerable doubt about the nature of the "relevant facts" at the national level may have caused a judgmental decision to limit uncertainty by international agreement.

55. This argument is well developed by Blau (pp. 106–7) with reference to bureaucratic discipline in a democratic national society.

56. In Mailick and Van Ness, pp. 71–73.

57. March and Simon, p. 196.

58. *Ibid.*, pp. 156–58. March and Simon admit that depoliticized programming that is firmly tied to well-understood subgoals is likely to interfere with innovation. Administrative steps involving novel program items tend to depend on the needs of organizational units. Interunit jealousy and insecurity could interfere with adaptation. Hence they advocate that the top leadership retain programmatic innovation as its special mission. *Ibid.*, p. 197, and Mailick and Van Ness, p. 68.

59. William R. Dill, "The Impact of the Environment," in Mailick and Van Ness, p. 104.

60. Cyert and March, in Haire, pp. 78–79, 85–88.

61. For a telling demonstration of the differential effect of the Iron Law on German and American trade unions, see Blau, pp. 95–96.

62. My classification of groups follows Almond and Coleman, *The Politics of the Developing Areas*, pp. 33–55.

63. For evidence supporting this argument, drawn from the experience of the United Nations, see Haas, "Dynamic Environment and Static System: Revolutionary Regimes in the United Nations," in Kaplan, ed., *The Revolution in World Politics* (New York: Wiley, 1962).

64. Myrdal, *Realities and Illusions in Regard to Inter-Governmental Organizations*, p. 13; also pp. 6–7. Myrdal is quite right in arguing that for purposes of maintaining a minimal attachment to certain common objectives during the Cold War, the veto provision in the United Nations Charter was—and is—essential.

65. In order to comprehend our criteria of success under more general rubrics, it

would be tempting to have recourse to typologies of organizations developed by sociologists. Such typologies are offered in two recent studies, neither of which, however, concerns itself with public administrative agencies at the national or international levels. Hence the types were found to elucidate and classify very little of what appears to us as crucial in the life of international organizations.

Etzioni classifies all organizations in terms of their power-compliance patterns, a choice that would appear highly relevant to the international setting. Organizations exercise power on the basis of coercion, economic assets, or normative values. Each form of control has its own proper form of compliance, yielding organizations that are primarily coercive, utilitarian, or normative in their impact on the environment. *A Comparative Analysis of Complex Organizations* (New York, 1961). Now international organizations, at best, would be of the normative type. But are they? In view of our discussion of the heterogeneity and intractability of the environment, a normative appeal to the clients and members would have to be a very selective process, summed up better in the descriptive terms of a functional, partial, and constantly changing consensus than in normative appeals and compliances.

Blau and Scott establish a typology based on the principle of *cui bono*: who benefits from the activities of the organization. They distinguish four types of beneficiaries: members and participants (mutual-benefit associations), owners and managers (business concerns), clients (service organizations), and the public at large (commonweal organizations). International organizations would be of the mutual-benefit variety; but they do not behave in terms of the canons for such organizations established by the authors! On the other hand, it is significant that the canons of behavior and the recurrent problems associated with service organizations seem to apply to international agencies. Blau and Scott, *Formal Organizations* (San Francisco: Chandler, 1962), pp. 42–81. This finding encourages me to retain my more limited scheme of classification, rather than seek to subsume international organizations under more general typologies that do not "fit" very well.

66. My treatment relies on David Wightman, *Economic Cooperation in Europe* (London: Stevens, 1956), esp. Chapters 1, 2, 14, 15, 17, 18.

67. Julian Huxley, *UNESCO: Its Purposes and Its Philosophy*, UNESCO doc. C/6, Sept. 15, 1946. See also Charles S. Ascher, "The Development of UNESCO's Program," *International Organization*, Vol. IV, No. 1 (February 1950), for a vivid analysis of this phase in the organization's history. For a leadership doctrine friendly to subgoal domination, see the statement by the former Director-General of UNESCO Luther H. Evans in "Some Management Problems of UNESCO," *ibid.*, XVII (1963), 76–90.

68. Food and Agriculture Organization, *So Bold an Aim* (Rome, 1955), pp. 26–42. Gove Hambidge, *The Story of FAO* (Princeton: Van Nostrand, 1955), pp. 50–60. The Bruce-Orr-McDougall ideology was eloquently expressed in the preamble of the FAO Constitution, but the delegates were not in sufficient agreement to include it in the operative portions of that document. The British government, for its part, saw fit to include Orr only as a technical adviser to its delegation.

69. Brock Chisholm, *Prescription for Survival* (New York: Columbia University Press, 1957), p. 3. Note also that the Constitution of WHO defines health as a "state of complete physical, mental and social well-being." My treatment of Chisholm is based on the work cited, his lectures delivered at the University of North Carolina, March 1959, and the Asilomar Conference of the Mental Health Society of Northern California, September 10, 1954.

70. Chisholm said: "I think *the next appropriate step* is a good phrase to keep in mind. We try to do this in the WHO because everywhere there are visionaries and a

visionary is fine—if he sees the bridge to his vision. But if he tries to jump to his vision without a bridge, he is in trouble. So we always try to think about what is the next appropriate step . . . what we do today and tomorrow, in order to be able to implement this in ten, twenty, or fifty years from now." Lecture at the University of North Carolina, p. 36, italics in original.

71. Chisholm, however, would argue that this restrained approach is consistent with the third canon because it lays the necessary foundation for the systemic-attitudinal changes he wants. In order to agree, I would have to accept his ideology as an accurate prognosis for systemic change, which I do not. For my judgment concerning the WHO mental health program, see WHO, *The First Ten Years*, pp. 324–33. Chisholm's programmatic skill, however, is also evident in his ability to abide by certain crucial environmental constraints (e.g., appeasing the United States medical profession when the U.S. contributed 40 per cent of the WHO budget) and to ignore others as irrelevant to the subgoals that he selected (e.g., the early U.S. demand that WHO control the international trade in new and untried pharmaceuticals, which was opposed by most underdeveloped countries; and his neglect to persuade the Soviet bloc nations to remain in WHO when Moscow decided that it wanted medical supplies, not advice on treatment). For details, see Charles E. Allen, "World Health and World Politics," *International Organization*, IV (1950), 37, 38, 40–42.

72. The following treatment of Hammarskjöld's thoughts rests on three major statements by him: the Copenhagen speech of May 1, 1959, the Oxford University speech of May 30, 1961, and the Introduction to the Annual Report of the Secretary-General to the General Assembly, June 15, 1961—considered by himself to be his political testament. The last item is reprinted as "Two Differing Concepts of United Nations Assayed," in *International Organization*, XV (1961), 549–63. For a treatment of the ideology in the practical setting of the Congo Crisis, see Stanley Hoffmann, "In Search of a Thread: The UN in the Congo Labyrinth," *ibid.*, XVI (1962), 331–61. See also Richard I. Miller, *Dag Hammarskjöld and Crisis Diplomacy* (New York: Oceana Publications, 1962). For more general discussions of "strong" secretaries-general, with ample references to Hammarskjöld, see A. L. Burns and N. Heathcote, *Peace-Keeping by U.N. Forces from Suez to the Congo* (New York: Praeger, 1963); Jean Siotis, *Essai sur le Secrétariat International* (Geneva: Librairie Droz, 1963); Sidney D. Bailey, *The Secretariat of the United Nations* (New York: Carnegie Endowment for International Peace, 1962).

CHAPTER FIVE

1. See Chapter 3.

2. These indicators are described in greater detail, as well as being contrasted with similar suggestions by Karl W. Deutsch and James S. Coleman, in Ernst B. Haas, "System and Process in the International Labor Organization," *World Politics*, Vol. XIV, No. 2 (January 1962). See also Karl W. Deutsch, "Toward an Inventory of Basic Trends and Patterns in Comparative and International Politics," *American Political Science Review*, Vol. LIV, No. 1 (March 1960), and Almond and Coleman, *Politics of the Developing Areas*, pp. 561–76.

3. Compare my treatment of this point with that of Robert V. Presthus, in "Authority in Organization," Mailick and Van Ness, *Concepts and Issues in Administrative Behavior*, pp. 135–36. He confines the use of the term to the process whereby the leaders of the organization gain and retain the respect of their staff, i.e., contribute to organizational efficiency. Again, such a restricted use of the term emphasizes internal organizational relationships at the expense of dependence on the

environment and is therefore not readily applicable to the study of international organizations.

CHAPTER SIX

1. The formal mandate issued by the Supreme Allied Council directed that "a Commission, composed of two representatives apiece from the five Great Powers represented at the Peace Conference, be appointed to inquire into the conditions of employment from the international aspect, and to consider the international means necessary to secure common action in a permanent agency to continue such inquiry in cooperation with and under the direction of the League of Nations." Cited in Francis G. Wilson, *Labor in the League System* (Stanford, Calif.: Stanford University Press, 1934), pp. 34–35. The most complete source on the origin of the ILO is James T. Shotwell, ed., *The Origins of the International Labor Organization* (New York, 1934, 2 vols.). Most of the important members of the Labor Commission have written autobiographies or monographs on the early history of the ILO that enable us to reconstruct the story without difficulty. This material is analyzed, with complete identification of sources, by Léon-Eli Troclet, *Législation sociale internationale* (Brussels: Les Editions de la Librairie Encyclopédique, 1952), I, 75–96, 287–309. The American role in these negotiations is treated well by John B. Tipton, *Participation of the United States in the International Labor Organization* (Urbana: University of Illinois, Institute of Labor and Industrial Relations, 1959), pp. 15–26.

2. See Troclet, pp. 86–87, for a systematic comparison of the Preamble with Art. 427 of the Treaty of Versailles.

3. Discussion in the Commission was dominated by the American, British, French, Italian, and Belgian representatives. G. N. Barnes (U.K.) and E. Vandervelde (Belgium), though holding ministerial positions, were co-opted trade unionists; Gompers and Léon Jouhaux served as American and French representatives in their capacity as trade union leaders. But even though the other delegates were all national officials, the following had deep understanding of labor questions and a commitment to the Functional mode of thought: Harold Butler (U.K.), A. Fontaine (France), Mayor des Planches (Italy), E. Mahaim (Belgium). See Troclet, p. 296, for the full composition of the Commission.

4. The officials in question were Harold Butler and Edward J. Phelan, later Directors of ILO, and both almost continuously concerned with ILO matters from the Peace Conference on. For the pre-1919 official British reasoning, see Bernard Béguin, "ILO and the Tripartite System," *International Conciliation*, No. 523 (May 1959), pp. 405–10.

5. Edward J. Phelan, *Yes and Albert Thomas* (New York: Columbia University Press, 1949), pp. 12–18, 23–35, 258–59. In 1920, Butler was chosen Deputy-Director of ILO, and Phelan chief assistant to Thomas. The Governing Body during the formative years of the Organization included among its members most of the dominant personalities who had also served as members of the Commission on International Labor Legislation, notably Sir Malcolm Delevingne (U.K., government), Jouhaux (France, worker), Fontaine (France, government), Mahaim (Belgium, government).

6. Albert Thomas, *International Social Policy* (Geneva: International Labor Office, 1948), pp. 133, 139, 148–50. The neatness of the argument is somewhat disturbed by the occasional emphasis on a reverse causation: i.e., social justice was unobtainable *unless* expectations of peace freed governments to devote themselves to it. See *ibid.*, p. 132.

7. Phelan, p. 240.

8. *Ibid.*

9. E.g., Thomas, pp. 24, 72–73.

10. *Ibid.*, pp. 10, 16, 18, 22–23, 28–31, 35, 45. Phelan, 38–42, 242–47, 248–51, 260–61.

11. Thomas, pp. 36, 42–44, 69, 71. One very important function of the Office's social and economic research was to substitute craftsmanlike, professional treatment of questions of social reform for a simple and sentimental humanitarianism.

12. The figures were compiled on the basis of the characteristics of member states attending International Labor Conferences, rather than total membership. This choice was dictated by the fact that all those who regularly influenced the work of the ILO were also in attendance. For a full explanation of these figures, see E. B. Haas, "System and Process in the International Labor Organization," *World Politics,* XIV (1962), 324.

13. The number of ratifications in 1934, when the Organization had a membership of 49, was as follows:

Hours of Work (Industry), No. 1, 1919	20
Minimum Age (Industry), No. 5, 1919	26
Minimum Age (Agriculture), No. 10, 1921	17
Right of Association (Agriculture), No. 11, 1921	27
Weekly Rest (Industry), No. 14, 1921	24
Forced Labor, No. 29, 1930	16
Minimum Age (Non-Industrial Employment), No. 33, 1932	3

14. M. R. K. Burge, "Some Aspects of Administration in the International Labor Organisation," *Public Administration,* XXIII (1945), 22–23, 26.

15. Troclet, pp. 454–62, 464–67.

16. These cases are analyzed in detail by C. Wilfred Jenks, "La Compétence de l'Organization Internationale du Travail: Examen de quatre avis consultatifs rendus par la Cour Permanente de Justice internationale," *Revue de Droit International et de Legislation Comparée,* Nos. 1 and 3 (1937), esp. pp. 19–21, 26, 49, 51, 57, and 63.

17. *Competence of the ILO in Questions of Agricultural Labor,* PCIJ, Series B, No. 2, 1922. ILO, *Official Bulletin,* VI, 343–55.

18. *Competence of the ILO in the Examination of Problems Relating to Agricultural Production,* PCIJ, Series B, No. 3, 1922. ILO, *Official Bulletin,* VI, 383–87. The Court sought to limit the continuum presented by Thomas by arguing that "the examination even of the means of organizing production and for the development of production seen from the economic viewpoint are outside the sphere of activity which Part XIII of the Treaty assigns to the International Labor Organization." The particular case that gave rise to the litigation involved a survey of agricultural unemployment. Perhaps, because the distinction drawn by the Court is not capable of ready administrative application, Jenks optimistically concluded that the Opinion enlarges ILO competence. Jenks, pp. 26 and 63.

19. *Competence of the ILO to Regulate Incidentally the Personal Work of the Employer,* PCIJ, Series B, No. 13, 1926. ILO, *Official Bulletin,* XI, 300–315. Functionalists will be interested to learn that this case was argued before the Court exclusively by counsel for interest groups, and that Albert Thomas appeared personally before the Court to plead for the ILO in all four cases.

20. *Interpretation of the 1919 Convention Concerning the Employment of Women During the Night,* PCIJ, Series A/B, No. 50, 1932.

21. Haas, in *World Politics,* XIV (1962), 324. By 1939, these figures had changed

again because of the withdrawal of several totalitarian states from the ILO; in that year we have a democratic membership of 42 per cent, an oligarchical of 47 per cent, and a totalitarian of only 11 per cent.

22. By 1939, the withdrawal pattern had resulted in the shrinking of the membership with corporatist economic institutions from 15 per cent in 1935 to 2 per cent.

23. Francis G. Wilson, writing in 1933, all but predicted that the juxtaposition of these environmental pressures would result in just such a program. Wilson, pp. 6–9, 282–85.

24. Thomas, pp. 85–90, 112–13, 118–19, 123, 126. He went so far as to advocate a species of globally planned economy that would include comprehensive commodity regulation. Even though none of these demands then bore fruit and never accrued to the benefit of the ILO, they were of course taken up after 1945 in the context of United Nations discussions and in the programs of several other specialized agencies.

25. U.S. membership was solicited by Director Harold Butler in a letter to Secretary of Labor Frances Perkins, who then persuaded Franklin D. Roosevelt that American participation would complement internationally the domestic aspects of the National Industrial Recovery Act, especially the introduction of the 40-hour week. The AFL also supported this step. For Perkins's reasoning, see Tipton, pp. 64, 42–43. American membership was secured by joint congressional resolution, adopted unanimously in the Senate, and by a vote of 233 to 109 in the House, after a very brief debate. *Ibid.*, p. 45.

26. It was during this period that the United States ratified five maritime Conventions and exerted itself mightily for the completion of Conventions 47 (Forty-Hour Week) and 61 (Reduction of Hours of Work, Textiles). These two constitute examples of the most unsuccessful standardizing efforts in terms of ratifications. The Senate declined to ratify Convention 61, as well as several less important ones.

27. Tipton, p. 51. Winant was among the first Americans to be added to the Office staff in 1934, becoming an Assistant-Director, only to be recalled soon to Washington to head the newly created Social Security Board. His experience in Geneva, however, was probably important in that the United States social security legislation then being enacted reflected in good measure the standards previously set by ILO Conventions.

28. See *ibid.*, pp. 53–54, 65, for appropriate statements by Perkins and Roosevelt. The AFL, at this time, was ready to endow the ILO with formal peace-keeping functions. American employer delegates during this period were all chosen from the "progressive" industrial community, whose outlook was later represented by the Committee for Economic Development, and therefore agreed with the government. It might be noted, incidentally, that these American employers were out of step with their European counterparts and did not vote or consult with them regularly in the Employer Group.

29. *Ibid.*, p. 57.

30. N. N. Kaul, *India and the ILO* (New Delhi: Metropolitan Book Co., 1956), pp. 46–64.

31. Burge, p. 26. What is implicit in the policy demands of the directors was made explicit during this period by one of the key younger ILO officials, C. Wilfred Jenks. He argued that the ILO legislative process is the best approximation to regular peaceful change at the international level because that process makes possible advances in areas of common and converging interests in an overall world-setting of conflict and opposition. This, in true Functionalist terms, is an indirect approach to peace and world community, held to be infinitely superior to the direct political approach, which always founders on the very factors that caused the League to fail

at the time this argument was advanced. Tripartism and common mundane interests would lead to a constant, if slow, expansion of the international program and task, and thus into immanent community. See his "The International Labour Organization and Peaceful Change," *New Commonwealth Quarterly*, Vol. IV, No. 4 (March 1939).

32. The decisions and resolutions of the Governing Body and its Unemployment Committee can be found in ILO, *Official Bulletin*, Dec. 31, 1930, p. 147; May 31, 1931, p. 27; Feb. 1, 1932, pp. 22–25; June 15, 1932, pp. 101–3; Aug. 1, 1932, pp. 157–58; Mar. 31, 1933, pp. 7–8; Dec. 31, 1934, p. 115. The major studies done by the Office in line with the determination of Thomas and Butler to make the ILO task encompass international measures for overcoming the Depression were published as International Labor Office, *Studies and Reports*, Series B (Economic Conditions) and C (Employment and Unemployment), between 1931 and 1936. The chief monographs deal with national countercyclical policy measures, the type of international public works that could be launched and the techniques for launching them, investment policies and employment, the organization of employment exchanges, and the social consequences of unemployment.

33. ILO, *Official Bulletin*, May 15, 1932, pp. 87–88.

34. *Ibid.*, Mar. 31, 1933, p. 14; Dec. 31, 1934, p. 115; Apr. 30, 1935, p. 37; Apr. 15, 1936, pp. 9–11; July 20, 1936, pp. 82–83.

35. See *ibid.*, Aug. 15, 1937, pp. 85–89, for the texts of these Recommendations.

36. See *ibid.*, Dec. 27, 1939, p. 105, for the quotation. Other Governing Body discussions are summarized at Dec. 31, 1937, pp. 176–77; Apr. 10, 1938, p. 22; Dec. 31, 1938, p. 107; July 31, 1939, p. 28.

37. For examples of controls exercised by the Governing Body during these years and of reluctance to have too much independent research, see Wilson, pp. 298–306, 313–18.

38. Recruiting of Indigenous Workers (No. 50, 1936); Contracts of Employment, Indigenous Workers (No. 64, 1939); Penal Sanctions, Indigenous Workers (No. 65, 1939). These Conventions were ratified by the major colonial powers at the end of World War II.

39. Unemployment Provision (No. 44, 1934); Forty-Hour Week (No. 47, 1935); Holidays with Pay (No. 52, 1936). None of these Conventions was widely ratified at the time. In 1962, the figures were as follows: No. 44 obtained 10 ratifications; No. 47, 4 ratifications; and No. 52, 34 ratifications.

40. Philadelphia Declaration, as printed in U.S. Congress, Senate, Committee on Foreign Relations, *A Decade of American Foreign Policy* (81st Congress, 1st Session, Doc. 123, Washington, D.C., 1950), pp. 25–26.

41. *Ibid.*, p. 26.

42. Tipton, p. 70 (my italics). It was the United States that took the initiative at the Philadelphia Conference in "selling" the Office program to the delegates, and in initiating negotiations between the ILO and the United Nations designed to assure the continued autonomy of the ILO. Britain wanted to have the ILO singled out by name in the UN Charter as the major international planning agency, a suggestion foiled by the Soviet Union's stubborn opposition to the ILO and its unwillingness to have anything to do with it. *Ibid.*, pp. 74–77.

43. International Labor Conference, 26th Session, 1944, *Report 1*, "Future Policy, Programme and Status of the International Labour Organization," pp. 75–77; hereafter cited as "Future Policy." The work of Industrial Committees is discussed in Chapter 10.

44. *Ibid.* At the same time, C. W. Jenks proposed on behalf of the Office that in the

future more consideration should be given to the universal standardization of wages, hours, and working conditions by having ILO member states incorporate the content of ILO conventions into collective agreements, thus avoiding the necessity of ratification and new legislation. He also suggested a variety of legal devices whereby this might be done in various countries. This suggestion was treated with great reserve at the Philadelphia Conference. See Jenks, "The Application of International Labour Conventions by Means of Collective Agreements," *Zeitschrift für Ausländisches Oeffentliches Recht und Völkerrecht*, XIX (1958), 197–224.

45. Haas, in *World Politics*, XIV (1962), 324.

46. The central document summarizing the Office doctrine that led to the Philadelphia Declaration is "Future Policy." It is largely the work of Phelan and Jenks.

47. *Ibid.*, pp. 1–4.

48. *Ibid.*, p. 20. The document also contains a lengthy catalogue of inter-Allied meetings at which the ILO was represented, a step apparently felt necessary to buttress the argument that the Organization was competent to deal with all kinds of economic questions. It also contains a very petulant complaint that the ILO had not been invited to participate in the meetings resulting in the creation of the Food and Agriculture Organization. *Ibid.*, p. 30. The ILO took the "scrutinizing" function so seriously, before it was even granted by the membership, that it chided the nascent International Bank for not taking higher living standards, poverty, and full employment policies into account in its criteria for lending. *Ibid.*, pp. 32–33.

49. *Ibid.*, pp. 40–41.

50. A survey of remarks made by delegates at the 26th Conference indicates that a great many did not share the Office's exalted vision of what was implied by "scrutiny" over all international economic and financial policies. The following delegates all urged caution or restraint in this respect, calling attention to the specialized competence of the ILO, and warning that the most that could be expected was close and cooperative relations of a consultative nature with the many new agencies being created: government delegates (U.S., France, Sweden, Netherlands, India, Belgium, Canada); employer delegate (U.K.); worker delegate (Belgium). The following delegates, by contrast, expressed themselves in favor of an ambitious interpretation of the "scrutiny" function: government delegates (Chile, Mexico, Czechoslovakia, U.K.); worker delegates (Cuba, Netherlands).

However, see the much more guarded United States and British statements on this point in the meetings of the Committee on Constitutional Questions of the Governing Body, January 18–25, 1945. By this time the delegates of the major powers felt bound by the Dumbarton Oaks draft of the United Nations Charter, which had not been completed at the time of the Philadelphia Conference. International Labor Office, *Official Bulletin* (Dec. 10, 1945), "Discussion and Proposals concerning the Constitution . . . at the 26th Session," pp. 171–88, 225–68. This issue of the *Official Bulletin* is entitled "Constitutional Questions," and hereafter is cited as such.

Yet the commentary on the Declaration published by two senior members of the U.S. delegation immediately after the adjournment of the Conference clearly indicates a sense of restraint with respect to a new and autonomous ILO task. See Carter Goodrich and John Gambs, "Results of International Labor Conference, April–May 1944," *Monthly Labor Review* (July 1944), pp. 2–6.

51. Herman Finer, *The United Nations Economic and Social Council* (Boston: World Peace Foundation, 1946). Finer served as assistant to Phelan, 1942–44.

52. *Ibid.*, p. 10.

53. *Ibid.*, p. 79 (my italics).

54. The argument as stated by Finer is an eloquent reaffirmation of the Function-

alist creed: "No economy can break itself loose from established expectations without breaking itself, as it is a part of a whole to which each part contributes. This new
factor, new, not because there was no social policy in individual countries in the nineteenth and early twentieth centuries, but because of the highly organized form it
takes and the resolute temper of the masses, makes more acute the need for international economic collaboration." *Ibid.*, p. 19.

55. *Ibid.*, pp. 22–23. True to the Functional perspective, Finer does *not* argue that
international understanding directly contributes to peace. He merely suggests that
task-oriented cooperation in a narrower sense would be facilitated by such understanding. Note, however, that Mitrany reverses the argument by suggesting that
understanding develops spontaneously from task-oriented cooperation. Finer's different emphasis possibly grew out of his experience with such tasks.

56. *Ibid.*, pp. 25–33. For a full enumeration of specific tasks to be discharged by
the ILO individually or in cooperation with other agencies (always safeguarding the
right of the ILO to review *all* international social and economic policies), see "Future Policy," pp. 48–63. Additional new demands for an expanded task include an
internationally guaranteed work week and year, jurisdiction over all phases of social
security, comprehensive controls over minimum social policy standards in dependent
territories, an international fair wage clause to specify conditions of employment and
welfare services for workers employed on projects financed by the International
Bank (!), and an international minimum wage. Less spectacular but equally unrealistic demands called for more comprehensive international codes dealing with
industrial disputes, minimum social standards to be applied in rebuilding war-devastated factories and worker housing, model safety codes in various industries, model
industrial health codes, employment opportunities for women, and the general improvement of the lot of agricultural workers.

57. "Constitutional Questions," p. 142.

58. *Ibid.*

59. *Ibid.*, p. 143 (italics mine). Not unnaturally, the Opinion cited with great approval McCullough v. Maryland and Missouri v. Holland as judicial endorsements of
the "dynamic or functional approach."

60. *Ibid.*, pp. 119–20.

61. The Office's attitude toward constitutional revision comes very close to meeting
the desiderata of Niemeyer's functional jurisprudence, discussed in Chapter 2. It is
faithful to the stress on automaticity and the evolution of norms from a substratum
of problem-solving postures. It differs from functional jurisprudence in that the Office wished to have things both ways: the *origin* of new norms might be left to automatic forces; but once the norms have been established, their substantive *application*
must remain subject to the procedural rules of positive law.

62. The constitutional articles in question include numbers 1, 7, 9, 10, and 13. The
Office submitted specific recommendations with respect to them to the Governing
Body and the Conference. "Constitutional Questions," pp. 450–52. Also Troclet, pp.
309–30.

63. See the discussion relative to the amendment of Article 36 of the Constitution
in "Constitutional Questions," pp. 453–54, 462, 463, 493–501. This point was one of
the very few that was not settled definitively prior to the consideration by the 29th
Session of the Conference (1946) of the completed new draft Constitution. On that
occasion the opponents of the big-power veto made one last unsuccessful effort to
have it deleted. C. W. Jenks at this time proposed, on behalf of the Office, an ingenious scheme to obviate a cumbersome amendment procedure for the ILO Constitution. He wanted to have changes in the Constitution incorporated into a general

peace settlement and thus to be automatically ratified by the belligerents of World War II.

64. This point is discussed in detail in Chapters 8 and 11. It refers to the amendment of Articles 28, 29, 30, 32, 33, and 34 of the Constitution.

65. "Constitutional Questions," pp. 314–49. For a complete treatment of the difficult negotiations between the ILO and the nascent United Nations, and of the results in terms of ILO constitutional revision and the formal agreement with the United Nations, see John H. E. Fried, "Relations Between the United Nations and the International Labor Organization," *American Political Science Review*, XLI (1947), 963–77.

66. This point is discussed in detail in Chapter 8.

67. Panama and Uruguay, for example, asked for technical assistance concerning the application, rather than the preparation, of labor legislation. The non-Western attitude concerning the issue of representation is symbolized by the Indian effort to amend the Constitution so as to expand mandatory non-Western membership on the Governing Body and the Office. *Report of the Conference Delegation on Constitutional Questions*, International Labor Conference, 29th Session (Montreal, 1946), Report II (1), p. 162. The United States delegation, in general, was opposed to all the more ambitious suggestions.

68. *Ibid.*, pp. 73–78, 159. The new obligations also included a provision for stimulating the growth of trade unions and employer associations in dependent territories, and for including their representatives in the delegations of the metropolitan country to the ILO (new Article 3). The unsuccessful Indian position was argued on the floor of the 29th Conference, supported by Cuba. International Labor Conference, 29th Session, *Record of Proceedings*, pp. 214–16.

69. The only exception to this finding is Phelan's claim that the Office *on its own* initiated, in 1944, the procedure of requiring periodic reports from member states on the application of Recommendations. The Office formally requested the Conference to continue this procedure in 1945. "Constitutional Questions," pp. 311 and 412.

70. *Ibid.*, pp. 181, 189, 371, 460, 583.

71. New Zealand suggested that member states be enabled to ratify Conventions when their national legislation met the text in general, though departing from it in technical detail. Turkey wanted the right to ratify Conventions in part or subject to reservations. Denmark insisted that Conventions should be ratified only *after* national legislation had met their content in every particular. *Ibid.*, pp. 154, 165, 168.

72. The more cynical interpretation is given substance by the introduction on the part of Sir John Forbes Watson of his famous "tables," since 1945 reprinted in every issue of the *Proceedings* of the Conference, which show quite clearly which governments do not ratify Conventions they support. Sir John quite consistently stressed this argument during these two years, apparently in order to deflate the claims of the Office concerning the sweep of the Conventions.

73. "Constitutional Questions," pp. 464–66. Forbes Watson, in subsequent discussion, used this text as the basis for his efforts to revise Article 19. *Ibid.*, pp. 468–73. The final revisions reflect, in good measure, the suggestions of the Conference Committee on Conventions. The details of these rules are treated in Chapter 9. In the deliberations of this Committee, Forbes Watson also urged that member states be compelled to report annually on their reasons for not ratifying Conventions, and to resubmit to the competent authorities texts initially declined. The United States opposed both suggestions. On the other hand, the United States gladly agreed to the suggestion—later incorporated into the amended Constitution—that all member states submit periodic reports on the degree of implementation of the International

Code irrespective of formal ratification. The American delegation felt that because of the high level of American labor standards such reports would take the wind out of the sails of the Forbes Watson argument.

74. *Ibid.*, pp. 167–69, 172–73. The Canadian proposal was no doubt prompted by constitutional difficulties experienced by the Dominion government in persuading provincial regimes to abide by ILO Conventions ratified by Ottawa. At first, all American delegates opposed the Canadian suggestion.

75. *Ibid.*, p. 410. He also suggested—and had the suggestion struck out by the Committee on the Application of Conventions—that federal states consider amending their constitutions so as to enable them to carry out ILO obligations!

76. Conventions 68 through 76. With the exception of Convention 76, these texts in turn dealt with very specific aspects of catering, pensions, certification, paid vacations, accommodations aboard ship, and medical examinations. Convention 76 attempted to deal with the more ambitious topic of wages, hours, and manning; it is among the four that never entered into force. Convention 75 was subsequently revised as Accommodation of Crews Convention (No. 92, 1949), and entered into force.

77. Conventions 82 through 86. Discussed in greater detail in Chapter 9.

78. Convention 77, Medical Examinations of Young Persons (Industry); Convention 78, Medical Examinations of Young Persons (Non-Industrial Occupations); Convention 79, Night Work of Young Persons (Non-Industrial Occupations); Convention 89, Night Work, Women (Revised); Convention 90, Night Work, Young Persons, Industry (Revised).

79. Convention 80 deals with formal adaptation to the 1946 Constitution, and Convention 88 deals with Employment Services. This could be considered as implementing the Philadelphia full employment doctrine.

80. Convention 81, Labor Inspection; Convention 87, Freedom of Association and Protection of the Right to Organize.

81. Kaul, *India and the ILO*. But he also notes that Indian government delegates easily and consistently identified with the ILO program because it corresponded so closely with the domestic program of the Congress Party.

82. The "official" ideology is well summarized in Anon., "The International Labour Organization Since the War," *International Labour Review*, February 1953, pp. 109–55. For Phelan's insistence on this point, see his "The Contribution of the International Labor Organization to Peace," *ibid.*, June 1949, p. 612. Director-General Morse's endorsement of these views is much more muted and marks the beginning of a different type of ideological emphasis. For a full statement of his early views, see "Report of the Director-General to the International Labor Conference," 1951, p. 1.

83. Jenks, *The Common Law of Mankind*, p. 166. See also pp. 163ff and 205–7.

CHAPTER SEVEN

1. The Committee had been created by the Governing Body in 1940, but had not met during the war. The two meetings in question took place in January-February 1947 and July 1948. They were attended by fourteen European governments interested in emigration, as well as by China, India, and Egypt. Among governments interested in attracting migrants, there were eleven Latin American delegations, Australia, New Zealand, Canada, and the United States. *International Labour Review*, Jan.–Feb. 1947, pp. 98–108; July 1948, pp. 47–53. Also see ILO, *Studies and Reports* (New Series), No. 10, 1948.

2. *International Labour Review,* July 1948, p. 52. ILO, *Studies and Reports,* pp. 153–57.

3. The plan and the work of the Naples Conference that buried it are summarized in "The ILO and Migration Problems," *International Labour Review,* February 1952, pp. 163–83.

4. For an examination of United States policy at the Naples Conference, see Robert E. Asher *et al., The United Nations and Promotion of the General Welfare* (Washington, D.C.: The Brookings Institution, 1957), pp. 524–25.

5. ILO, *Report of the Director-General to the International Labour Conference, 1949,* p. 3; henceforward cited as *Report,* with the appropriate date.

6. *Report, 1951,* p. 41.

7. *Report, 1950,* p. 3.

8. *Report, 1953,* pp. 55–57; also *Report, 1952,* p. 44.

9. *Report, 1952,* pp. 33–38. *Report, 1956,* pp. 59–68. *Report, 1958,* pp. 57–61.

10. *Report, 1958,* p. 39. *Report, 1953,* pp. 65, 70. *Report, 1950,* p. 81.

11. *Report, 1956,* Chapter 2.

12. *Report, 1958,* p. 26.

13. *Ibid.,* pp. 28–29 (italics in original).

14. See his *Report, 1957.* Part I of the *Report* is devoted entirely to this subject. Emphasis on the motivation and role of youth is to be found in *Report, 1960,* Pt. I, "Youth and Work." Morse's reply to the discussion following the presentation of the Report is particularly rich in comments illustrating our theme. Int. Labor Conference, *Provisional Record,* 44th Session (Geneva, 1960) pp. 448–54.

15. For a detailed development of this argument, see "Reply of the Director-General to the Discussion of his Report," Int. Labor Conference, 43d Session, June 24, 1959, *Record of Proceedings,* pp. 560–66.

16. *Report, 1958.* See also *Report, 1957,* Pt. II, pp. 51–56.

17. *Report, 1958,* p. 68. See also *Report, 1960,* Pt. II, pp. 70–74.

18. *Report, 1959,* Pt. II, p. 68 (italics mine).

19. David A. Morse, "The International Labor Organization in a Changing World," *The Annals,* March 1957, p. 33.

20. *Ibid.,* pp. 34 and 37–38 (italics mine). See *International Labour Review,* Sept. 1958, pp. 229–30, for Morse's desire to downgrade Conventions and Recommendations.

21. "Reply of the Director-General," 43d Session of the Int. Labor Conference, *Record of Proceedings,* p. 564. It should be noted that the downgrading of Conventions and law in the ideology of the Office has had a certain effect, apparently, on the Functional doctrine of C. W. Jenks, the ILO official most closely identified with the older approach. Impressed with the work of the European supranational communities, Jenks has begun to advocate the gradual introduction of the same procedure in United Nations agencies. But, true to his Functionalist convictions, he stresses recognized areas of economic interdependence as the logical starting points. Thus he suggests that there already exists a common substantive law of economic responsibility with respect to full employment policies and to trade practices that are considered generally harmful. The source of this substantive law is found in the various constitutional texts of international organizations and in national legislation. But supranationality is essentially a procedural phenomenon. Jenks finds a procedural basis for his common economic law in the almost universal recognition of the principle of conciliation in bringing hostile parties together before they become litigants. The international counterpart to the principle of conciliation is the constitutionally recog-

nized obligation to *consult continually* in international organizations with respect to the consequences of national economic policies. On this very fragile legal reed, Jenks then builds his case for the extension of functional law through the ILO. *The Common Law of Mankind*, pp. 155–63, 192–96, 231–32, 297–99.

22. *Report, 1951*, p. 2.

23. This survey follows the Organization's own soul-searching program analysis presented as "Appraisal of the ILO Programme, 1959–1964," *Official Bulletin*, Vol. XLIII, No. 1 (1960), hereafter referred to as "Appraisal." The appraisal was undertaken in response to a request of the Economic and Social Council voted in July 1958. Similar appraisals were made by FAO, IAEA, WMO, WHO, and UNESCO.

24. *Ibid.*, p. 3.

25. The number of ratifications in 1962 for the seven revised texts, the eight new texts, and the ten human rights texts are as follows:

Convention 91, Paid Vacations, Seafarers 9
Convention 92, Accommodations of Crews 13
Convention 93, Wages, Hours of Work, and Manning (Sea), 1949....... 4
Convention 94, Labor Clauses (Public Contracts) 26
Convention 95, Protection of Wages 52
Convention 96, Fee-charging Employment Agencies 24
Convention 97, Migration for Employment 15
Convention 98, Right to Organize and Collective Bargaining 57
Convention 99, Minimum Wage-Fixing Machinery (Agriculture) 20
Convention 100, Equal Remuneration 38
Convention 101, Holidays with Pay (Agriculture) 25
Convention 102, Social Security (Minimum Standards) 13
Convention 103, Maternity Protection 8
Convention 104, Abolition of Penal Sanctions (Indigenous Workers) 10
Convention 105, Abolition of Forced Labor 57
Convention 106, Weekly Rest (Commerce and Offices) 19
Convention 107, Indigenous and Tribal Populations 15
Convention 108, Seafarers' Identity Documents 6
Convention 109, Wages, Hours of Work, and Manning (Sea), 1958 3
Convention 110, Plantations 5
Convention 111, Discrimination (Employment and Occupation) 36
Convention 112, Minimum Age (Fishermen) 13
Convention 113, Medical Examinations (Fishermen) 8
Convention 114, Fishermen's Articles of Agreement 8
Convention 115, Radiation Protection 4

26. *Ibid.*, pp. 9 and 15.

27. *Ibid.*, pp. 28–30. For Belgian satisfaction concerning Conventions 104, 105, and 107, in no small part motivated by resentment against the new nations that repudiated the *mission civilisatrice*, see F. Van Langenhove, "La Protection internationale des Populations aborigènes" (Brussels, n.d.).

28. "Appraisal," pp. 12, 16, 27, 29, 33. In fact, Morse tried to downgrade the quasi-judicial aspect of the complaint procedure in favor of conciliation by experts and systematic fact-finding unrelated to specific complaints, thus minimizing confrontations between the ILO and individual member governments. The effort was defeated by the Governing Body, even though the fact-finding procedure was used for four years. See Doc. GB 138/2/7, March 1958.

29. "Appraisal," p. 36.

30. *Ibid.*, pp. 4–6, 8, 18–20, 25, 31–34.

31. *Ibid.*, p. 10.

32. The Center is located in Turin in the Palace of Labor, which was donated to the ILO by the Italian government and designed by Pier Luigi Nervi. Financing posed an initial problem because of opposition in the ILO to heavy new outlays; the problem, however, was solved by depending on voluntary contributions from governments, international organizations, and private bodies. The Center expects to be able to train 2,000 technicians and managers per year, attending for periods from 14 to 22 weeks. ILO, *The Turin International Centre for Advanced Technical and Vocational Training* (Geneva, 1963).

33. "Appraisal," p. 7.

34. *Ibid.*, p. 11.

35. *Ibid.*, pp. 11, 17–18, 22–23, 24–26, 36.

36. Governing Body, 140th Session, 18–21, November 1958, "Report of the Director-General, First Supplementary Report," *Proposals Relating to an ILO Management Development Programme* (Doc GB 140/18/7, mimeo.).

37. The Cole Report is published as "Improving Labour-Management Cooperation," *International Labour Review*, May 1956, pp. 483–500. It is sympathetically summarized by C. W. Jenks, *The International Protection of Trade Union Freedom* (London: Stevens, 1957), pp. 208–11.

38. ILO, "Meeting of Experts on Industrial and Human Relations," *Report* (Geneva, 2–11 July 1956, Doc. M.I.H.R./9/1956, mimeo.).

39. Governing Body, 140th Session, Nov. 18–21, 1958, "Action to be Taken on the Resolutions Adopted by the 42nd Session of the International Labour Conference," (Doc. GB 140/5/3, pp. 9–11, mimeo.). *Ibid.*, "Proposals Concerning Bipartite Technical Meeting on Labour-Management Relations Inside Undertakings" (Doc. GB 140/17/10, mimeo.).

40. The Institute is governed by a Council composed of the Director-General, six persons designated by the Governing Body from among its own members (which also has the right to approve the curriculum), five outstanding experts also designated by the Governing Body, and the *conseiller d'état* in charge of education of the Canton of Geneva. The tripartite principle is to be observed in selecting the six Governing Body members. Although the Institute is administered by a single Director, he is assisted by a Consultative Commission made up of experts selected by ILO, UNESCO, the UN, and the University of Geneva, as well as experts selected by the Council. The teaching staff will consist of members of the Office. The Institute is financed through an endowment based on special contributions made by governments, foundations, and private donors. See International Labour Office, *Institut International d'Etudes Sociales: Etablissement par le Conseil d'administration du Bureau international du Travail* (Geneva, 1960).

41. International Institute for Labour Studies, Second Study Course, Sept. 16–Dec. 6, 1963, *Draft Programme*, Doc. SC.2/MA/5 (mimeo.).

42. *Report, 1963*. I am using the somewhat abbreviated text published as ILO, *Social and Labour Aspects of Economic Development* (Geneva, 1963), pp. 3–7.

43. *Ibid.*, pp. 10–20.

44. *Ibid.*, p. 27.

45. *Ibid.*, pp. 41–42.

46. *Ibid.*, pp. 44–60. A first step in this direction was the setting up of a trade union training center in Africa.

47. *Ibid.*, pp. 61–72.

48. *Ibid.*, pp. 75–80.

CHAPTER EIGHT

1. This is the judgment of Harold Butler, participant in the Paris negotiations and second Director of the ILO. See his treatment in Shotwell, *The Origins of the International Labor Organization*, I, 316.

2. For details, see *ibid.*, pp. 316–19. The Belgian efforts had the full support of the French and British employer delegates.

3. The Soviet Union ceased to be a member of the ILO in 1940 as an automatic consequence, under the 1919 Constitution, of its expulsion from the League of Nations following the attack on Finland.

4. Ruth B. Russell and Jeannette E. Muther, *A History of the United Nations Charter* (Washington, D.C.: The Brookings Institution, 1958), pp. 798–802.

5. "Constitutional Questions," pp. 463, 475. Britain's sensitivity to the French position on Soviet membership caused her to withdraw her insistence at the San Francisco UN Conference to have the ILO singled out by name in the Charter. This was also the United States position.

6. *Ibid.*, p. 564. The Jouhaux statement is in *ibid.*, p. 569.

7. The cases, among others, involved the unsuccessful challenges of the Greek worker (1946), the Spanish worker (1956), and all communist workers (1954—the year during which most East European states rejoined the ILO). The Argentine worker (1945) and the Venezuelan delegate (1950) were successfully excluded. The entire Hungarian delegation was refused admission after the events of 1956. While it is true that the ILO rejected the Rumanian application for admission on the grounds that freedom of association did not exist, no similar bars were put in the way of the applications of Morocco, Sudan, and Tunisia at roughly the same time. Rumania subsequently became a member by virtue of its admission to the UN. For a detailed discussion of the credentials controversy, see Jenks, *International Protection of Trade Union Freedom*, pp. 90–93, 104–37.

8. *Ibid.*, pp. 491–92.

9. Harold K. Jacobson, "The USSR and ILO," *International Organization*, XIV (1960), 408–9.

10. For the pre-1948 period, see Tipton, pp. 78–79.

11. It should be noted that the Catholic Church apparently considers the ILO as an especially appropriate vehicle for the realization of Christian social doctrine. See J. M. Joblin, S.J., "The Papal Encyclical 'Mater et Magistra,' " *International Labour Review*, September 1961.

12. The world membership claimed by each of the major international trade union federations is as follows:

WFTU, 119,506,000 (*International Labour Review*, August 1962, p. 186). Over 90 per cent of the total is found in communist countries.

ICFTU, 57,000,000 (*International Labour Review*, January 1963, p. 76). Perhaps 85 per cent of the total is confined to Western-industrialized countries.

ICCTU, 5,200,000 (*ICCTU Directory*, July 15, 1959). The great bulk of the total is Western European, with France, Belgium, and the Netherlands accounting for about 40 per cent.

13. In 1960, thirty-six national employer federations belonged to the IOE, including among the non-North Atlantic affiliates employers from Brazil, Argentina, Chile, Uruguay, India, Japan, Egypt, Iran, and Liberia. Just after World War II, most West European commercial employers split from the IOE and set up the International Council of Commercial Employers. They complained that the IOE was preoccupied with industrial problems and did not take the interests of salaried em-

ployees sufficiently seriously. In addition, the dissenters were far more interested in cooperating with the ILO, as opposed to the consistently critical attitude of the IOE. The Commercial Employers are now primarily interested in European economic integration problems and rarely concern themselves with the ILO.

14. The bulk of the employer delegates opposed the Franco-Belgian thesis on revised tripartism because the very principle of nationalized industries was anathema. The American employer threatened withdrawal from the ILO if the formula were accepted.

15. The formula is described below. See Jacobson, pp. 409–12. In contrast to the workers and most governments, the employers continued their efforts to exclude the Hungarian delegation even after 1958. Furthermore, the complexity of the ILO committee system allows the free employers to arrange matters so that the communist employers are altogether excluded from participating in Employer Group discussions of substantive issues.

16. There are some exceptions to this statement. The International Chamber of Commerce has consistently defended a series of demands flowing from the doctrine of "modern capitalism" (akin to the ideology of the U.S. Committee for Economic Development). The International Federation of Shipowners has a distinct position to defend in terms of concrete common economic interests (see Chapter 10).

17. As recently as 1955 the European employers voted against certain recommendations for increasing labor productivity adopted by a European Regional ILO Conference because the program called for trade union participation in the planning and execution. In 1959 the British employers' federation, apparently adjusting to new times, formally adopted a "progressive" attitude and incidentally appointed a new ILO representative sympathetic to the new approach. In 1960 the employers from underdeveloped countries formed a coalition to defeat the Waline leadership in the Group, whereupon Waline agreed to tone down the free employers' unflinching opposition to the participation of communist employers in the life of the Group, a step that resulted, for the first time since 1954, in the functioning of the entire Employer Group for purposes of deciding assignments to committees.

18. Pierre Waline, "Labor Relations With or Without Freedom," *Revue des Deux Mondes*, October 1, 1961. The translation was circulated in mimeographed form by Waline, the quoted passage appearing on p. 12. See also Waline, "Coexistence pacifique ou combative?," *ibid.*, August 1, 1960. Waline, while still stressing that communist employers are appointed by the state, also recognized their "technical competence and abilities as managers of their undertakings" in the 1961 statement.

19. The six "preferred" non-governmental organizations are the International Cooperative Alliance, the International Federation of Agricultural Producers, the ICFTU, ICCTU, WFTU, and the IOE.

20. A partial list of non-governmental organizations committed to programs that make it desirable for them to have access to ILO policy-making would comprise the following groups. Not all of them are now on the ILO's "special list."

a. Trade union federations other than the major world bodies. Most of these participate actively in ILO Industrial Committees and other specialized meetings: twelve International Trade Secretariats (friendly to ICFTU); International Confederation of Arab Trade Unions (independent); All-African Trade Union Federation (independent but friendly to WFTU); International Federation of Employees and Technicians (independent); International Confederation of Civil Service Technicians (independent).

b. Organizations of administrators created, subsidized, and housed by the ILO in order to support ILO Conventions at the national level: International Social Security Institute; International Association for Social Progress.

c. Employer organizations: International Council of Commercial Employers; International Union of Handicraft, Small and Medium Enterprises; World Medical Association.

d. Women's organizations interested in achieving non-discriminatory status for women employees and workers: St. Joan's League; World Alliance of Christian Women's Unions; International Council of Women; International Federation of Business and Professional Women; International Federation of University Women.

e. Social service organizations whose programs parallel or complement that of the ILO: League of Red Cross Societies; World Veterans Federation; World Union ORT; International Catholic Union for Social Service.

f. Organizations interested in the international protection of human rights: International League for the Rights of Man; International Commission Against Concentration Camp Practices; Anti-Slavery Society; World Jewish Congress; Women's International League for Peace and Freedom.

21. See, for instance, International Federation of Agricultural Producers, *Proceedings of the 11th General Conference* (New Delhi, 1959), pp. 9, 30–32. *World Agriculture* (January 1960), pp. 33–36. For information on resolutions adopted since 1934 by the International Federation of Business and Professional Women, I am indebted to Miss Sylvia A. Meyer of the Federation's Geneva office. For information on the World Veterans Federation, see *World Veteran*, August-September 1960. The work of the ICA is reported in detail in the monthly *Review of International Cooperation* (London).

22. For a discussion of the special position of governments by one of the most distinguished theorists of tripartism, see Jenks, *Trade Union Freedom*, p. 80. It should also be remembered, however, that in four cases on which the PCIJ was asked for an advisory opinion relating to ILO norms the Court asked to hear representatives of international industrial associations.

23. In countries of major industrial importance, the ILO maintains branch offices. In such countries the ILO representative acts as the national correspondent, thus preserving an unambiguous line of authority to Geneva.

24. The only result of these efforts was the creation of the International Association of Labor Inspectors, originally composed of members of national ILO delegations who happened to occupy such positions. Since 1923, these men have occasionally met during the annual Conference to discuss matters of professional interest to them. Efforts to strengthen the Association and to give it an ILO mandate have failed. See Jean Zarras, *Le Contrôle de l'application des conventions internationales du travail* (Paris: Librairie du Recueil Sirey, 1937), pp. 352–54.

25. See Jacobson, pp. 410–11. Béguin, "ILO and the Tripartite System," pp. 443–48.

26. See Chapter 4 above.

27. Such conferences are convened very frequently with reference to the revision of Conventions, or to the advisability of drafting Conventions in new fields. The ILO commonly convenes them at the regional level too. Several such meetings were held in the preparation of the Morse promotional program.

28. For statistics on regional clusters, see Haas, in *World Politics*, XIV (1962), 347–50.

29. "Constitutional Questions," pp. 304, 353, 358, 361, 362, 365, 562, 583.

30. The Office proposals are published under the title "Proposed Instrument for the Amendment of the Constitution of the International Labor Organization," in *ibid.*, pp. 449–56. See especially Articles 9 and 11 of the Office text.

31. *Ibid.*, p. 453, Art. 10 of the Office text.

32. "Report of The Conference Delegation on Constitutional Questions," International Labor Conference, 29th Session, Montreal, *Report II (1), Constitutional Questions* (1946), pp. 54–55.

33. *Ibid.*, p. 56.

34. *Ibid.* (my italics).

35. One example must suffice. In 1958 the Office called a bipartite advisory conference of the air transport industry to discuss standardization of hours and working conditions, national differences in which were a crucial item in a very lively international competitive picture and—of course—had a definite impact on air safety. Even though the Office had prepared the conference with a careful exposé by experts of these implications, the workers and airlines were unable to agree on anything. In 1960 the Office called a tripartite conference for the same purpose, hoping that the governments would break the deadlock. These hopes were disappointed because governments, in their capacity as owners of airline-members of the International Air Transport Association, took the same position as the private members of the Association. It remains to be seen whether a common dedication to cartel-like practices will triumph over competition and thus beget agreement on labor standards.

36. The preparation of the major Social Security Convention (No. 102, 1952) provides an example. The Workers demanded an instrument covering all types of social security, with a maximum scale of benefits. The Employers called for a much more permissive text, which made allowances for differences in economic development and the efforts of other international organizations, and they held out for separate agreements for each type of coverage, including private social security schemes. The issue was resolved by adopting a text which (1) covered all types, (2) contained minimum scales of benefits, and (3) could be ratified in part. *International Labour Review*, August-September 1951, pp. 139–40; *ibid.*, October 1952, pp. 290ff.

37. See Chapter 3 above.

38. Resolution 350 (XII), UN Economic and Social Council, 12th Session, *Official Records*, Supplement No. 1. For further details, see Moses Moskowitz, *Human Rights and World Order* (New York: Oceana Publications, 1958), pp. 43–47.

39. This additional evidence referred to affidavits alleging mistreatment that certain governments and voluntary organizations submitted on behalf of refugees and former inmates of labor camps. The Committee was composed of Sir Ramaswami Mudaliar (a senior Indian civil servant), Paal Berg (former President of the Norwegian Supreme Court), and Enrique Garcia Sayan (former foreign minister of Peru), all serving in their personal capacity. Mudaliar and Berg were concurrently members of the ILO's Committee of Experts on the Application of Conventions. The definition of forced labor included in the Committee's mandate was taken from the 1930 ILO Convention (No. 29), but it was to be applied to national practices *irrespective* of whether that Convention had been ratified. The Ad Hoc Committee heard and dismissed charges against the United States as being outside the mandate it had been given by the ECOSOC. It did, however, mildly criticize American vagrancy laws.

40. Resolution 524 (XVII) and Resolution 607 (XXI), Economic and Social Council, *Official Records*, 17th (1954) and 21st (1956) Sessions.

41. *Minutes of the 129th Session of the Governing Body* (Geneva, May 24–June 1, 1955), pp. 48–49.

42. "Report of the ILO Committee on Forced Labour," International Labor Office, *Minutes of the 135th Session of the Governing Body* (Geneva, May 31 and June 1, 1957), pp. 51–81. See especially paragraphs 16, 17, and 28 for the mandate and

procedure of the Committee, which was composed of Paul Ruegger (former Swiss diplomat and President of the International Committee of the Red Cross), Cesar Charlone (Uruguayan judge), and T. P. P. Goonetilleke (Ceylonese judge). Ruegger later became a member of the ILO Committee of Experts on the Application of Conventions.

43. *Ibid.*, paras. 492–510.

44. *Minutes of the 137th Session of the Governing Body* (Geneva, October 29–November 1, 1957). In many respects, however, the basic objections entertained by Western governments anxious not to exacerbate Cold War tensions were restated in 1957. As in 1955, the British and Canadian government delegates initially opposed renewing the Committee's mandate, and they were now joined by the Belgian government. Myrddin-Evans even used the arguments adduced by Arutiunian in 1955. Nevertheless, the bulk of the other governments again joined a united Worker and Employer Group coalition to force the matter to a head, and Britain eventually associated herself with them. The final vote was 35 to 3 with one abstention. Since this was not a roll-call, the identity of all opponents could not be ascertained.

45. "Report of the ILO Committee on Forced Labor," International Labor Office, *Minutes of the 142nd Session of the Governing Body* (Geneva, May-June 1959), pp. 74–84. The Committee noted that the few allegations received all came from voluntary groups; and since they lacked sufficient official and internal corroboration, they did not provide a sufficient basis for action.

46. *Ibid.*, para. 91 (italics mine). At this stage it must be a matter of conjecture whether the effort of the ILO to use the forced labor machinery against the new African states will result in further intensification of the trend, or in its atrophy.

47. For a discussion of the Joint Maritime Commission, see Chapter 10.

48. International Labor Office, *Conditions in Ships Flying the Panama Flag* (Geneva, 1950), p. 86.

49. See Tables 3 and 4, Chapter 9. Since Panama was not party to any ILO Conventions, the complaints launched by the ITF and the investigation ordered by the ILO did not technically fall under the "representation" procedure of the ILO Constitution, even though the measures taken do not differ significantly from that procedure.

50. ILO, *Freedom of Association and Conditions of Work in Venezuela* (Geneva, 1950). The sharp condemnation of the Venezuelan government and the mission's suggestions for remedial action are found on pp. 173–85. Venezuela, in 1950, was party to nineteen ILO conventions. In 1962 the figure was the same.

51. Apparently, one of the strongest motives in the new attitude of aggressive self-confidence was the desire to rebut the charges contained in the report of the Ad Hoc Committee on Forced Labor. For evidence on the Soviet decision, see Robert I. Hislop, "The United States and the Soviet Union in the International Labor Organization" (unpublished Ph.D. dissertation, University of Colorado, 1961), pp. 228–29.

52. The following discussion is based on interviews, as well as on the studies of Jacobson, in *International Organization*, Vol. XIV, and Alfred P. Fernbach, *Soviet Coexistence Strategy* (Washington, D.C.: Public Affairs Press, 1960). In 1955, Alvin Rubinstein interpreted the Soviet return to Geneva as merely a Cold War gambit, designed to destroy the ILO and likely to succeed. The argument demonstrates the danger of reasoning purely on the basis of national doctrine and policy, and of ignoring the possible feedback power of international institutions. See his "The USSR and the ILO," *The Russian Review*, Vol. XIV, No. 1 (January 1955).

53. Hislop, pp. 224–25. The text of the Soviet letter requesting these terms is reproduced in *Current Digest of the Soviet Press*, V, 10.

54. Fernbach, pp. 45–46.

55. International Labor Office, *The Trade Union Situation in the U.S.S.R.* (Geneva, 1960), p. 8. The following material is taken from this Report.

56. The Report often mentions "collective agreements" negotiated by the unions, but apparently this refers to wage and bonus schemes agreed to jointly in the discussions between the AUCCTU and the State planning agencies, *not* to modes of accommodation resembling collective bargaining. See *ibid.*, pp. 98–103. The ILO leadership recognizes that there is no collective bargaining in the USSR. See *Report, 1961*, p. 103.

57. International Labor Office, *The Trade Union Situation in the U.S.S.R.*, p. 136.

58. For similar evaluations of the impact of the Soviet Union on the ILO and the ILO effect on the client, see Jacobson, pp. 421, 426–27; Fernbach, pp. 56–60.

59. See Tipton, pp. 71–72, 84–85.

60. *Ibid.*, pp. 86–93.

61. *Ibid.*, pp. 98–104. For evidence that, for the AFL, the forced labor issue was purely a Cold War propaganda gimmick, see *The American Federationist*, as cited in Hislop, p. 234.

62. The Committee was headed by Joseph E. Johnson, President of the Carnegie Endowment for International Peace, and additionally consisted of three professors of labor relations and economics as well as one business executive. Its report, entitled "The United States and the International Labor Organization," was reprinted in *The Annals*, March 1957, pp. 182–95. The Committee held hearings and consulted with a variety of interested American groups.

63. International Labor Office, *The Trade Union Situation in the United States* (Geneva, 1960), p. 9. This is the Mission's Report, and the following summary is based on it.

64. *Ibid.*, p. 144 (italics mine). This conclusion, coupled with the tolerant treatment accorded the Soviet Union, was responsible for the American workers' pressing for the abolition of the surveys. For details, see Chapter 11.

65. *Ibid.*, p. 145. The Report is very critical of American employer practices that seek to influence union elections for recognition purposes and of general public relations activities designed to question the legitimacy of certain union practices. Management efforts to praise its own associational ideology while attacking labor's is felt by ILO to be inconsistent with freedom of association!

66. For evidence on United States performance with respect to ILO human rights standards, see Chapter 11.

67. On this topic, see particularly Walter R. Sharp, *Field Administration in the United Nations System* (New York: Praeger, 1960), and C. Hart Schaaf, "The Role of the Resident Representative of the UN Technical Assistance Board," *International Organization*, Vol. XIV, No. 4 (Autumn 1960). These activities and powers are essentially irrelevant to the issue of international integration, because the very success of the technical assistance and planning operations in initially weak and disorganized countries makes the continued exercise of these powers both unnecessary and onerous to the recipients.

68. For many interesting details on the ILO productivity program, see International Labor Office, *ILO Productivity Missions to Underdeveloped Countries* (Geneva, 1957). Also printed in *International Labour Review*, July and August 1957. Much the same conclusions could of course be stated in connection with the ILO technical assistance program in the field of rural cooperation and vocational training.

69. It is for this reason that the Soviet Union first opposed the labor-management relations program, considering it a camouflaged means for perpetuating capitalism. As an example of the type of program here described, the case of a joint employer-worker industrial relations mission to Bolivia may be mentioned. The mission was

composed of Socialist and Catholic Belgians. Its job was to persuade Bolivian trade unionists to substitute collective bargaining in good faith for political demonstrations and general strikes, an effort that required something akin to group therapy. For information on the role of ILO missions in Bolivia, see Carter Goodrich, "Bolivia and Technical Assistance," *Foreign Affairs*, April 1954; Robert J. Alexander, *The Bolivian National Revolution* (New Brunswick: Rutgers University Press, 1958), Chap. 13; Richard W. Patch, "Bolivia: Decision or Debacle," *American Universities Field Staff* (Latin America, RWP–3–'59, April 18, 1959).

70. See Kaul, *India and the ILO*, pp. 89–100. India adopted at the national and state levels its own tripartite consultative structure for the consideration of labor legislation modeled exactly on that of the ILO.

71. Francis G. Wilson argued as early as 1934 that organizational survival in a changing world environment depended on a *de facto* revision of the tripartite formula. He suggested that the purist pluralist doctrine of representation be quietly abandoned, and that worker and employer delegates coming from different national settings be admitted *sine die*. He suggested further that the principles of labor economics be consistently introduced into ILO deliberations and be used to bring about an apluralist consensus. Wilson, *Labor in the League System*, p. 23.

72. Jenks, *Trade Union Freedom*, pp. 519, 522, 562.

CHAPTER NINE

1. For examples of each of these arguments and their influence on early ILO efforts to supervise the implementation of Conventions, see Zarras, *Le Contrôle de l'application des conventions internationales du travail*, pp. 58–71. The variety of legal practices and doctrines, as they relate to ratification, revision, denunciation, reservation, delay in application, and applicability to new member states, is treated exhaustively in Léon-Eli Troclet, *Législation Sociale Internationale* (Brussels: Les Editions de la Librairie Encyclopédique, 1952), I, 513–70.

An informed United States commentary holds that there "is not even a moral obligation to treat ILO Conventions" as if they were draft treaties initialed by plenipotentiaries; i.e., the President is under no obligation to submit them to the Senate. Johnson Report, p. 186. The actual practice of the United States confirms the Johnson dictum. ILO Conventions and Recommendations are forwarded to state governors without comment. They are also sent to the Senate without comment, unless the President wishes the instrument to be ratified, in which case such a preference is communicated. With the exception of the maritime Conventions ratified during the 1930's and in 1953, a favorable recommendation was given to the Senate only in connection with the Freedom of Association Convention (No. 87, 1947), Convention 63 (Statistics of Wages and Hours) and Convention 88 (Employment Services); and when opposition developed in the Senate the President did not press his views. This policy is, of course, in keeping with the general American official indifference to the ILO's standard-setting task. Note, moreover, that in 1919 the French and Italian delegates to the conference drafting the ILO Constitution demanded full legislative effect for labor Conventions, thus denying the need for national ratification. The British and American delegations strongly opposed this view as "unrealistic."

2. Troclet, pp. 490–94. Additional devices for introducing "flexibility" into the norms include the use of optional parts, optional annexes, and alternative parts.

3. Compare Art. 19, para. 9, of the unrevised Constitution with Art. 19, para. 7, of the revised Constitution. Among federal states, India and Australia have taken these provisions seriously.

4. These Conventions are often referred to by the ILO as "human rights" instru-

ments. They are as follows: Right of Association, Agriculture, 1921 (No. 11);
Forced Labor, 1930 (No. 29); Labor Inspection, 1947 (No. 81); Social Policy
(Non-Metropolitan Territories), 1947 (No. 82); Labor Standards (Non-Metropolitan Territories, 1947 (No. 83); Right of Association (Non-Metropolitan Territories), 1947 (No. 84); Labor Inspectorates (Non-Metropolitan Territories), 1947
(No. 85); Freedom of Association and Protection of the Right to Organize, 1947
(No. 87); Right to Organize and Collective Bargaining, 1949 (No. 98); Equal Remuneration, 1951 (No. 100); Social Security (Minimum Standards), 1952 (No.
102); Abolition of Forced Labor, 1957 (No. 105); and Discrimination (Employment and Occupation), 1958 (No. 111).

5. For a summary of the discussion in 1919 and 1946, see Troclet, pp. 637–39.

6. See, for example, the discussion in connection with the Recommendations on
Minimum Age (Coal Mines) and Protection of Workers' Health. *International
Labour Review*, December 1953, p. 26.

ANNUAL REPORTS OF ILO MEMBER STATES ON RATIFIED CONVENTIONS

Period	Reports requested	Reports received at the date requested		Reports received in time for the session of the Committee[a]		Reports received in time for the session of the Conference	
		Number	%	Number	%	Number	%
1931–32	447	—	—	406	90.8	423	94.6
1932–33	522	—	—	435	83.3	453	86.7
1933–34	601	—	—	508	84.5	544	90.5
1934–35	630	—	—	584	92.7	620	98.4
1935–36	662	—	—	577	87.2	604	91.2
1936–37	702	—	—	580	82.6	634	90.3
1937–38	748	—	—	616	82.4	635	84.9
1938–39	766	—	—	588	76.8	—b	—
1943–44	583	—	—	251	43.1	314	53.9
1944–45	725	—	—	351	48.4	523	72.2
1945–46	731	—	—	370	50.6	578	79.1
1946–47	763	—	—	581	76.1	666	87.3
1947–48	799	—	—	521	65.2	648	81.1
1948–49	806	134c	16.6	666	82.6	695	86.2
1949–50	831	253	30.4	597	71.8	666	80.1
1950–51	907	288	31.7	705	77.7	761	83.9
1951–52	981	268	27.3	743	75.7	826	84.2
1952–53	1,026	212	20.6	840	81.8	917	89.3
1953–54	1,175	268	22.8	1,077	91.7	1,119	95.2
1954–55	1,234	283	22.9	1,063	86.1	1,170	94.8
1955–56	1,333	332	24.9	1,234	92.5	1,283	96.2
1956–57	1,418	210	14.7	1,295	91.3	1,349	95.1
1957–58	1,558	340	21.8	1,484	95.2	1,509	96.8
1958–59	995d	200	20.4	864	86.8	902	90.6
1959–60	1,100d	256	23.2	838	76.1	963	87.4
1960–61	1,362d	243	18.1	1,090	80.0	—	—

SOURCE: International Labor Office, *Report of the Committee of Experts on the Application of Conventions and
Recommendations* (Geneva, 1962), p. 140. Published as Report III (Part IV) of the annual International Labor
Conference. Hereafter cited as *RCE* (with appropriate date).

a Generally, the session of the Committee of Experts opens at the end of March or the beginning of April. It
has, however, opened as early as February 29 in 1932, and as late as July 23 in 1945; the date limit for the receipt of reports has accordingly varied.

b The Conference did not meet in 1940.

c First year for which this figure is available.

d As a result of a decision by the Governing Body, detailed reports were requested on only certain ratified
Conventions.

7. See the discussion of the Collective Agreements Recommendation. *Ibid.*, September 1951, p. 146.

8. See the discussion in connection with the preparation of the Equal Remuneration Convention. *Ibid.*, September 1951, p. 154. The governments involved were Australia, Denmark, India, Sweden, and the United Kingdom. Moreover, most of these governments opposed the text on the merits.

9. Advisory opinions delivered by the Permanent Court of International Justice and International Court of Justice are, of course, binding on the ILO—as distinguished from the member governments. To perpetuate the illusion that we are here dealing with a genuine codex, the Office has published a document that lists separately the provisions contained in single Conventions, resolutions, and Recommendations, and classes them under general subject matter rubrics, thus making them look like a true code. See International Labor Office, *The International Labour Code*, Vol. I (Geneva, 1951).

10. For statistics of annual reports on ratified Conventions, see table on p. 557.

11. See Art. 35, para. 8, of the ILO Constitution.

12. For Conventions, see Art. 19, para. 5 (c), and for Recommendations, see Art. 19, para. 6 (c), of the Constitution. The cumulative record of members in meeting this obligation is summarized thus by the ILO:

NUMBER OF STATES WHICH HAVE COMMUNICATED, WITHIN THE PRESCRIBED TIME LIMITS, INFORMATION INDICATING THAT CONVENTIONS AND RECOMMENDATIONS HAVE BEEN SUBMITTED TO THE COMPETENT AUTHORITIES

Session[a]	Number of decisions submitted			Total members of Organization
	All	Some	None[b]	
31st Session, 1948	16	7	37	60
32nd Session, 1949	17	2	42	61
33rd Session, 1950	21	—[c]	42	63
34th Session, 1951	25	4	35	64
35th Session, 1952	25	3	38	66
36th Session, 1953	28	1	37	66
37th Session, 1954	29	—[c]	40	69
38th Session, 1955	24	4	41	69
39th Session, 1956	38	1	37	76
40th Session, 1957	38	13	26	77
41st Session, 1958	33	3	43	79
42nd Session, 1958	36	6	37	79
43rd Session, 1959	34	8	38	80
44th Session, 1960	39	1	43	83

SOURCE: *RCE, 1962*, p. 186 (slightly altered).
   a Except for the 41st Session (April–May), all sessions of the Conference were held in June.
   b Includes cases in which no information has been supplied by the government.
   c At this session the Conference adopted one Recommendation only.

13. For Conventions, see Art. 19, para. 5(e) and 7(b) (iv). For Recommendations, see Art. 19, para. 6(d) and 7(b) (v).

14. See Zarras, pp. 158–60, 177–78. Wilson, *Labor in the League System*, p. 232. It is tempting to speculate that the Irish initiative may have been motivated by the desire to find an institutional mechanism to embarrass Britain over the state of labor legislation in Northern Ireland; if so, Britain reacted in such a manner as to accelerate the process of ILO institutional growth at her own expense.

15. This right was almost never used by governments, with the exception of the French Popular Front's attempt in 1937 to "sell" its progressive colonial labor policy to the ILO. Zarras, p. 167.

16. For these evolutionary details during the pre-World-War-II period, see Wilson, pp. 233–38; Zarras, p. 167.

17. Zarras, p. 173. The Committee's practice of demanding supplementary information from its respondents, i.e., information in excess of what the reports contain, was initiated by the Committee itself and never effectively challenged.

18. Composition of the Committee of Experts:

1927–40	Nationality	1946–62[b]	1927–40	Profession	1946–62[b]
	Argentina	1	7	Professor of Law	13
	Barbados	1			
1	Belgium	1	2	Professor (other)	3
	Brazil	1			
1	Bulgaria		4	Civil Servant	8
	China[a]	2	1	Judge	3
1	Czechoslovakia		2	Politician	3
	Denmark	1	1	Engineer	0
1	Finland		2	Unknown	0
2	France	2			
1	Germany	2	19	Total	30
1	Hungary				
1	India	3			
2	Italy	1			
	Jamaica[a]	1			
1	Japan				
	Lebanon	1			
	Netherlands	2			
	Norway	1			
	Pakistan	1			
	Peru	1			
2	Poland	1			
	Portugal	1			
	Senegal	1			
1	Switzerland	2			
3	U.K.	1			
	U.S.	2			
1	Uruguay				
19	Total	30			

Source: International Labor Office, *Official Bulletin*, Mar. 30, 1927, p. 80; Oct. 5, 1928, p. 146; May 15, 1929, p. 26; May 31, 1934, p. 8; July 20, 1936, p. 96; Mar. 31, 1937, p. 26; July 15, 1937, p. 56; Dec. 31, 1937, p. 180; Apr. 30, 1939, p. 8; Dec. 27, 1939, p. 114. The composition since 1946 is given at the opening of the annual *Report* of the Committee of Experts.
[a] These experts never actually exercised their duties.
[b] In 1963, three new members were added, one each of Soviet, Japanese, and Nigerian nationality.

19. For the pre-war experience, see Zarras, pp. 166–67. The first six years of the Committee's work were evaluated by one of its members; see Arnold D. McNair, "The Committee of Experts on Article 408," *British Yearbook of International Law* (1933), pp. 143–45. A sensitive and full-scale evaluation by another veteran Committee member confirms my treatment; see Baron F. M. van Asbeck, "Une Commission d'Experts," *Symbolae Verzijl* (The Hague, 1958), pp. 9–21. Van Asbeck puts great emphasis on the continuity in membership and the complete independence of the Experts; to these two factors he attributes the Committee's ability to persist in morally compelling governments to make available ever more complete information and, if necessary, to justify themselves before the Conference. Members of the Office participate in the sense of furnishing factual information when called upon. They do not, on their own initiative, participate in plenary sessions of the Committee.

20. "One member of the Committee, Mr. Gubinski, stated that he could not associate himself with the Committee's observations regarding the . . . Freedom of Association Convention . . . since in his opinion account should be taken of the economic and social system existing in these countries." *RCE, 1961*, p. 60.

21. *RCE, 1962,* pp. 14–15.

22. As quoted in Zarras, p. 175. Retranslated from the French.

23. See, for example, *International Labour Review,* Oct.-Nov., 1953, pp. 356–69.

24. These data are based on an unpublished study. It must be stressed that the infractions noted did not usually comprise instances of national practice but were confined to legal conformity. Provisional data, including the work of the Committee's 1963–64 session, suggest an even more favorable picture, with full action taken in 33 per cent of cases calling for critical comment, partial action in 30 per cent, no action in 35 per cent, and denunciations in 2 per cent.

Seventy-eight member states were at various times singled out for critical comment. Twenty-five member states had perfect records of compliance; but of these, 7 had ratified only four Conventions (or fewer), and 16 had only recently joined the ILO. Countries outstanding for not heeding the criticism of the Committee are Argentina, Colombia, Uruguay, Afghanistan, China, Philippines, and Czechoslovakia. Countries with a strong record of remedying infractions of the Code called to their attention are Morocco, Haiti, India, Austria, Belgium, France, Greece, Finland, Italy, Spain, Poland, and Yugoslavia. Finally, countries showing a tendency to take remedial action for certain kinds of Conventions but to be obdurate with respect to others are Nicaragua, Bulgaria, Hungary, and Romania.

25. Zarras, pp. 179–80. Wilson and Zarras agree, for the pre-war period, in considering the Conference Committee the chief force in making the supervisory system a success. They also credit the Committee with providing the power behind the early efforts to extract a wider mandate for the Experts from the Governing Body.

26. For pre-war evidence along this line, see Zarras, p. 173, and Wilson, pp. 239–40. The founder of the Committee, Professor O'Rahilly, noted in 1932 that "the Committee is competent to conduct an inquiry on the territory of sovereign states composing the Conference with respect to internal administrative acts. If, fifteen years ago, we had proposed such a method nobody would have believed it possible." Zarras, p. 188. For the post-war period, similar judgments from delegates can be found in *International Labour Review,* December 1953, p. 464, and December 1957, p. 239.

27. It is revealing that when Bulgaria proposed in 1935 that the Conference investigate the reasons for non-ratification and the actual implementation of Conventions, this proposal received the support of the employers. All these efforts were sidestepped by the Governing Body prior to the constitutional reforms of 1946. Zarras, p. 212.

28. The most extreme such pre-war instance was the threat expressed by the Committee in 1932 to ask the Governing Body for sanctions against Cuba, when that state appeared particularly delinquent in carrying out ratified Conventions. The threat was withdrawn after the Cuban government delegate presented elaborate public justifications and promises. Zarras, pp. 182–84, 187.

29. For one of many examples of these objections to ratification, see the discussion in *RCE, 1960,* p. 117, with particular reference to the protection of children and young workers, a relatively non-controversial area.

30. States whose performance markedly improved after being singled out by the Committee of Experts are Albania, Argentina, Belgium, Bulgaria, the Dominican Republic, France, Hungary, Iceland, Luxembourg, the Netherlands, New Zealand, Philippines, Turkey, United States, and Viet Nam.

31. The perennial delinquents are Afghanistan, Australia, Bolivia, Brazil, Burma, Chile, China, Colombia, Costa Rica, Cuba, Czechoslovakia, Ecuador, Ethiopia, Greece, Guatemala, Guinea, Haiti, Indonesia, Iran, Iraq, Israel, Italy, Jordan, Lebanon, Liberia, Libya, Malaya, Mexico, Nicaragua, Pakistan, Panama, Paraguay,

Peru, Poland, Portugal, El Salvador, Sudan, Thailand, United Arab Republic, Uruguay, and Venezuela.

32. This tactic backfires occasionally. The West German Bundestag approved the ratification of Conventions 29, 87, 98, and 100, even though the government had not submitted the texts and had opposed their adoption by Germany.

33. See *RCE, 1953,* pp. 50–54, for a list of specific acts of omission attributed to governments, and an enumeration of 33 states that had failed to abide by Art. 23.

34. *Report of the Committee on the Application of Conventions and Recommendations,* 46th Session (Geneva, 1962), p. iii. The history of debate in the Conference regarding the nature and desirability of the blacklist is recapitulated in *ibid.,* 43rd Session (1959), pp. ii–iv. Blacklisting was re-emphasized as a necessary means to put pressure on delinquent member states by the Worker Group, following a decision of the Governing Body in May 1959 to modify the obligation for annual reports on ratified Conventions under Art. 22 of the Constitution. The Governing Body, with the very reluctant concurrence of the Worker Group, decided to ease the work of the Committee of Experts, then being overwhelmed by the bulk of reports, by requiring a general report on all ratified Conventions every year, but detailed reports on specific Conventions only every alternate year. This decision was accepted by the Workers only on the understanding that the rigor of supervision would increase. Their concern for the blacklist then grew out of the fear that the new procedure would undermine the Code. During the debate of the Conference in 1959, the Soviet-bloc countries protested and voted against the Governing Body decision as undermining the supervisory procedure! Another government member protested against the blacklist by suggesting that it would militate against further ratification of Conventions. But the criteria regarding blacklisting set forth above were reaffirmed at that time.

35. Even though the list seems to be getting longer every year, the Conference Committee also noted in 1962 that there was a sharp increase in the instances of national compliance with the observations of the Committee of Experts, i.e., the cases in question did not reach the blacklist. "Whereas the Committee of Experts' report had averaged some 30 instances of this kind during each of the past three or four years, an exceptionally high figure of 80 cases had been reached this year." *Ibid.,* 46th Session, p. iv.

36. The case of conditions on ships of Panamanian registry should be recalled in this context (see Chapter 8). Even though Panama had not ratified the relevant maritime Conventions at the time the dispute arose, and did not ratify them subsequently, the government reacted to international pressure mobilized by the ILO and the International Transport Workers Federation by making a good many of the changes suggested as a result of the ILO inquiry.

37. The Conventions in question were the following: Maternity Protection, 1919 (No. 3); Night Work, Women, 1919 (No. 4); Minimum Age (Industry), 1919 (No. 5); Night Work, Young Persons (Industry), 1919 (No. 6); Right of Association (Agriculture), 1921 (No. 11); White Lead (Painting), 1921 (No. 13); Weekly Rest (Industry), 1921 (No. 14); Workmen's Compensation (Accidents), 1925 (No. 17); Equality of Treatment (Accident Compensation), 1925 (No. 19); Minimum Wage-Fixing Machinery, 1928 (No. 26); Forced Labor, 1930 (No. 29); Minimum Age (Non-Industrial Employment), 1932 (No. 33); Night Work, Women (revised), 1934 (No. 41); Recruiting of Indigenous Workers, 1936 (No. 50); Contracts of Employment (Indigenous Workers), 1939 (No. 64); Penal Sanctions (Indigenous Workers), 1939 (No. 65).

In addition, several minor maritime Conventions were also widely accepted. British and French acceptances were much more extensive than those of other colonial powers. Conventions 50, 64, and 65 were generally accepted in British but not in French possessions. Conventions 4, 5, 6, 11, and 14 were more widely accepted in French than in British territories. For a statement of the British position on the modesty of intentions in 1943, see *RCE, 1948,* p. 35.

38. The Conventions in question were the following: Social Policy (Non-Metropolitan Territories), 1947 (No. 82); Labor Standards (Non-Metropolitan Territories), 1947 (No. 83); Right of Association (Non-Metropolitan Territories), 1947 (No. 84); Labor Inspectorates (Non-Metropolitan Territories), 1947 (No. 85); Contracts of Employment (Indigenous Workers), 1947 (No. 86).

The most extensive of these Conventions is No. 82. It not only establishes certain principles of social policy, e.g., equal remuneration, non-discrimination, social planning with efforts not to disrupt traditional society unduly, and the protection of wages against employer abuse, but also requires voluntary associations to be consulted and to participate in public planning. It was, however, ratified only by Belgium, France, New Zealand, and Britain.

39. The Committee of Experts noted in 1961: "The number of declarations communicated during this period [since 1955] is 1,089, representing an average of more than 180 declarations a year. By virtue of these declarations, various Conventions became applicable without modification to 417 territories and, subject to modifications, to 64 territories. . . . The total number of formal communications made since 1922 under article 35 of the ILO Constitution . . . is 3,223. In 1,941 cases, these were communications to make a Convention applicable to a given territory." *RCE, 1961,* p. 323.

40. Freedom of Association and Protection of the Right to Organize, 1948 (No. 87); Protection of Wages, 1949 (No. 95); Right to Organize and Collective Bargaining, 1949 (No. 98); Minimum Wage-Fixing Machinery (Agriculture), 1951 (No. 99); Abolition of Penal Sanctions (Indigenous Workers), 1955 (No. 104); Abolition of Forced Labor, 1957 (No. 105); Indigenous and Tribal Populations, 1957 (No. 107); Plantations, 1958 (No. 110); Discrimination (Employment and Occupation), 1958 (No. 111). The French government accepted only Conventions 87 and 95 for its territories, while the British government tended to accept 98 and 105, in addition.

41. *RCE, 1962,* p. 10. The constitutional controversy is discussed in International Labor Conference, *Report of the Committee on the Application of Conventions,* 44th Session (Geneva, 1960), p. v. On the same occasion, the Employer Group recommended that territories about to become independent should be given technical assistance by the Office in preparing annual reports, since adequately trained administrative personnel seems to be unavailable in many cases.

42. *RCE, 1961,* pp. 324–25.

43. *Ibid.,* pp. 312–20.

44. For an official statement of this formula, see Francis Wolf, "Les Conventions internationales du travail et la succession d'états," *Annuaire Français de Droit International,* 1961, pp. 742–51.

45. Social Policy (Basic Aims and Standards) Convention, No. 117, 1962.

46. The more important exceptions, i.e. denunciations of texts previously accepted *without* modification, are these: Rwanda, Convention 27; Trinidad and Tobago, Convention 64; Malaya, Convention 86; Uganda, Conventions 15, 16, 58.

47. *RCE, 1961,* pp. 326–27. The Committee, of course, was referring obliquely to the doctrine of *investissement humain* as professed in parts of West Africa. In the rest of its condemnations, it was addressing itself to practices in Africa in which trade unions and employers are subordinated to the demands of the single party of which they are a part. See also *RCE, 1962,* pp. 214–16.

48. *RCE, 1961*, pp. 327–30. The Committee strongly suggested that the new nations ratify the earlier ILO Conventions.

49. This is true of several Central American states, Ghana, and Thailand. The Office is assisting in the writing of a Central American maritime labor code. In these cases the pressure for lower standards was also exerted by the shipowners' associations in industrialized countries.

50. The comprehensive social security Convention (No. 102, 1952), despite the fact that its various sections can be ratified piecemeal, has been accepted by only five underdeveloped countries: Greece, Mexico, Peru, Senegal, and Yugoslavia (as of June 1963). Symptomatic of this questionable legitimacy is the fact that the International Labor Conference adopted the Convention over heavy opposition. Thirty-two negative and 22 abstaining votes were cast, a much higher percentage of opposition than is usually true of votes on Conventions.

51. Jef Rens, "Latin America and the ILO—Forty Years of Collaboration, 1919–1959," *International Labour Review*, July 1959, p. 20. Other information on social security can be found in *Lasting Peace the ILO Way*, pp. 68–69, and Stuart Maclure, *If You Wish Peace, Cultivate Justice* (Geneva: 1960, World Federation of United Nations Associations), pp. 28–29. The ILO also seeks to further the application of social security standards by sponsoring and financing two unofficial international associations of national social security administrators, the International Social Security Association and the Inter-American Conference on Social Security.

52. For details see Troclet, pp. 275–80.

53. *RCE, 1958*, p. 37; *RCE, 1959*, p. 51; *RCE, 1960*, pp. 48–49; *RCE, 1962*, p. 114.

54. Also Argentina in connection with Convention 96: *RCE, 1953. RCE, 1959*, p. 51; *RCE, 1962*, p. 113.

55. *RCE, 1959*, pp. 42, 45; *RCE, 1962*, p. 29.

56. *RCE, 1961*, p. 104. In addition, there have been some instances in which governments requested and received technical assistance in the drafting of comprehensive national labor codes, e.g. in Colombia, Taiwan, El Salvador, Iran, and the Somali Republic.

57. Esther Bloss, *Labor Legislation in Czechoslovakia* (New York: Columbia University Press, 1938); Alexandre Berenstein, "Influence of ILO Conventions on Swiss Legislation," *International Labour Review*, June 1958. pp. 495ff.

58. In order to meet this objection, an unsuccessful effort was made to persuade the major interested countries to ratify the mining Conventions simultaneously. Bloss, pp. 190–91, 202–3.

59. Luisa Riva-Sanseverino, "Influence of ILO Conventions on Italian Legislation," *International Labour Review*, June 1961, pp. 579ff. Nicolas Valticos, "The Influence of ILO Conventions on Greek Legislation," *ibid.*, June 1955, pp. 594ff.

60. Certain special problems should be noted in the case of Italy. Neither national legislation nor ratification of Conventions necessarily implies faithful application of rules in fact, though this has been the aim of Italian administration since 1945. Italy is not applying the Employment Services Convention (1948) to the letter because she permits workers greater representation on the public supervisory committee than the parity with employers demanded by the Convention, and admonitions by the ILO have been ignored. The 48-Hour Week Convention (1919) was ratified on condition that Italy's major European competitors in international trade accept it; since most of them did not ratify it, the Convention remains unapplied in law (though not in fact). Even though the Collective Bargaining Convention has been ratified, it remains peripheral in Italy, since free collective bargaining is not the standard technique for arriving at labor contracts. Agriculture

presents a special problem here, since not even the provisions of Article 39 of the Italian Constitution are applied in protecting agricultural labor. Riva-Sanseverino, pp. 582, 586, 597.

It should also be noted that during the Fascist period, Italian delegates generally supported demands that the functions of the ILO be expanded, since they saw the relevance of the ILO program to the corporatist-nationalist commitment to intensified industrialization linked to social reform.

61. Valticos, p. 613.

62. Anon., "The Influence of International Labour Conventions on Nigerian Labour Legislation," *International Labour Review*, July 1960, pp. 26–43.

63. My treatment relies on N. N. Kaul, *India and the ILO*, and V. K. R. Menon, "Influence of International Labour Conventions on Indian Labour Legislation," *International Labour Review*, June 1956, pp. 552ff.

64. Kaul, p. 38.

65. Menon, pp. 567–69. Similar tripartite organizations were introduced in Burma and Malaya.

66. Anon., "International Labour Standards and Asian Countries," *International Labour Review*, April 1961, pp. 306ff. See also ILO Constitution, Art. 19, para. 3. The International Labor Conference, as of 1961, had authorized 12 special clauses allowing for exceptions and exclusions for Asian countries.

67. Thirty Conventions were singled out as "priority instruments": namely the major Conventions governing minimum age, maximum hours, social security, and forced labor of the pre-1940 era; later Conventions revising these instruments upward; the human rights Conventions of the 1940's; and the Conventions covering Equal Remuneration (1951), Indigenous and Tribal Populations (1957), and Discrimination (1958). Twelve Asian member states thus *could* have deposited 360 ratifications, but only 82 were actually deposited, or 23 per cent.

Current Asian self-consciousness regarding separate regional needs contrasts sharply with the first phase of the ILO's history. The fathers of the ILO Constitution, in effect, regarded their Organization as a European regional grouping, not taking seriously the beginnings of industrialization outside Europe and North America. Japan, a charter member of the ILO, could not accept this proto-patronizing attitude as a matter of national pride; yet, given the cost structure of her industries, she could not accept the logic of the International Labor Code either. Her solution was to deny the need for special regional exemptions from the Code but to demand that all ILO instruments be merely recommendations! Wilson, *Labor in the League System*, pp. 10–11.

The evolution of doctrines of "regionalism" within the presumptively universal context of standard setting is summarized in Troclet, pp. 425–41. Troclet, who often represented the Belgian government in ILO organs, seems to approve of regionalization.

68. See Anon., in *International Labour Review*, April 1961, pp. 312–15, for *examples* of such cases, which in the aggregate do not constitute *evidence* of any kind of trend. In more cautious language the anonymous author shares my pessimistic judgment. *Ibid.*, pp. 318–21.

69. It would be fascinating to undertake a case study of the influence of the ILO in the progress of labor legislation in Bulgaria. Both the royal and the communist governments of Bulgaria were in the forefront of nations ratifying Conventions; Bulgaria, in 1963, tied with France as the member state with the most ratifications to its credit (73). Bulgaria has not appeared regularly on the blacklist. The Code appears to be a legitimate means of introducing reforms during industrialization under two very disparate types of regime. Why?

70. Wilson, p. 281. For the argument concerning the false issue posed by the notion of international competition, see *ibid.*, pp. 292–97. In view of the admitted fact that the trade unionists were themselves concerned over the damage that "unfair" international competition could do to the introduction of welfare legislation, the notion of competition was perhaps not as extrinsic to the success of the humanitarian aim as Wilson claims.

71. Wilson's argument remains of central importance on analytical grounds, even though the neat distinction between humanitarian and anti-competitive motives cannot be sustained empirically. In any event, Wilson himself cites evidence that the drafters of the ILO Constitution did not perceive the doctrinal issue in dichotomous terms. See *ibid*, pp. 282–85.

72. For statistical evidence supporting this argument, see Haas, in *World Politics*, XIV (1962), 330–32.

73. Troclet, pp. 642–44.

74. For such examples, see E. A. Landy, "The Effective Application of International Labour Standards," *International Labour Review*, Oct.-Nov. 1953, pp. 355–59. The difficulty confronting the Committee of Experts as well as the analyst seeking to generalize the work of the Committee stands revealed in these examples. With respect to the application of the Labor Inspection Convention (No. 81, 1947) by non-ratifying states, the Committee noted that inspectorates exist in 51 countries, but that "there are wide differences in the degree of organization and in the functioning of the services." The Committee, though gratified by the wide diffusion of inspectorates, is by no means certain that all, or even most, function satisfactorily. *RCE, 1957*, pp. 160–61. Yet the evaluation had to be scored as indicating uniform application. In evaluating the application of the Right to Organize Convention (No. 98, 1949), the Committee found that "the extent to which each provision of the Convention is applied . . . varies according to the form of protection contemplated: protection of the right to organize, or protection of the right to bargain collectively." The Committee then found that the right to bargain collectively is observed generally, but that wide variation exists with respect to freedom to organize. In a mere 12 of the non-ratifying states is the Convention applied in full. *RCE, 1956*, p. 142. Even though the Committee expressed itself with cautious optimism about general application, I scored the findings as *not* indicating uniform application.

75. See *RCE, 1947*, Appendix III, pp. 26–29.

76. *International Labour Review*, February 1953, p. 141.

77. International Labour Office, *Official Bulletin*, vol. 39, No. 9 (1956), "Report of the Committee on the Freedom of Employers' and Workers' Organizations." This report was drawn up on the basis of information furnished or checked by governments and is buttressed by seventy national monographs. It constitutes the most massive impartial survey on the subject ever undertaken. For a summary, see C. W. Jenks, *The International Protection of Trade Union Freedom* (London: Stevens, 1957), pp. 488–90.

78. *Ibid.*, p. 488.

79. My treatment relies entirely on Roberto Vernengo, "Freedom of Association and Industrial Relations in Latin America," *International Labour Review*, May and June 1956, pp. 451–82, 592–618. The numerical incidence of variety, of course, refers to the year of Vernengo's survey. There is no reason to suppose greater uniformity today in view of shifts in the nature of Latin American regimes, both to the right and to the left.

80. For the Swiss statement, see *International Labour Review*, September 1958,

p. 231. An Italian endorsement of the same position is also expressed there. For the Soviet and Brazilian statements see *ibid.*, September 1959, pp. 211–12.

81. *Ibid.*, September 1959, p. 212. For Swiss, British, and Malayan governmental opinion, see *ibid.*, September 1958, pp. 230–31. For similar Australian and Yugoslav governmental opinions, see *ibid.*, September 1960, p. 232.

82. *Ibid.*, September 1960, pp. 234–35.

83. All but one of these Conventions deal with social security coverage. For details, see Jenks, *The Common Law of Mankind*, pp. 226–28. All these Conventions provide for a continuing ILO role in supervising and perfecting their implementation. Jenks regards this development as further legitimating the standard-setting task of the ILO, rather than derogating from it.

84. For details, see Anon., "The European Social Charter and International Labour Standards," *International Labour Review*, Nov.-Dec. 1961, especially pp. 475–77.

85. For details, see Zarras, pp. 123–25, 352–54. Before the creation of the ILO, the idea of international inspection was always opposed by the strongest industrial states; even though Britain mellowed in its opposition after 1906 and seemed prepared to undertake some modest steps in that direction, Germany and Belgium remained opposed. The most recent (unsuccessful) proposal for a stronger ILO role in inspection was made in the International Labor Conference by Georges Scelle. Troclet, pp. 601–2.

CHAPTER TEN

1. For details on the Philadelphia discussions, see Chapter 6.

2. For these and many of the following details, see John Price, "Industrial Committees of the ILO," *International Labour Review*, January 1952, pp. 1–43.

3. *Ibid.*, pp. 7–8.

4. *Ibid.*, pp. 35–36.

5. *Ibid.*, pp. 9-10.

6. *Ibid.*, pp. 6–7. Similarly, the Governing Body avoided the recurrent issue of workers and employers "representing" nationalized industries.

7. ILO, *Official Bulletin*, Vol. XXXII, No. 1 (June 15, 1949), "Document for the Guidance of Industrial Committees," para. 7, p. 37.

8. *Ibid.*, para. 8.

9. *Ibid.*, p. 40.

10. *Ibid.*, paras. 13, 14, 15, p. 39.

11. Standing Orders adopted at the 104th Session of the Governing Body (Geneva, March 1948), Arts. 6, 14, 18, 25.

12. *Official Bulletin*, Dec. 15, 1949, p. 280. While this formula is less permissive than the procedure previously used, it still fell short of the request formulated by the Iron and Steel Committee in 1950 under which governments were to call bipartite national meetings to implement conclusions of Industrial Committees. Apparently this request had encountered lively opposition within the Iron and Steel Committee itself. International Labor Office, Iron and Steel Committee (4th Session), *Report I* (Geneva, 1952), p. 69.

13. International Labor Organization, *Standing Orders for Industrial Committees* (Geneva, 1955), Art. 15. *Ibid.*, 1962 (mimeo.). Art 14 of both documents tightens the powers of the Director-General in deferring consideration of a request by an Industrial Committee, if such a request implies cooperative or overlapping work on the part of several international organizations. This arrangement was made necessary because the UN Economic Commission for Europe and the Organization

for European Economic Cooperation also maintained industrial committees whose mandate was very similar to the ILO's committees. Further, there was a considerable amount of overlap among the delegates attending meetings of the three parallel sets of committees, despite the fact that ECE and OEEC bodies were not formally tripartite.

14. *Ibid.*, 1962, Art. 6, para. 3. Actually, the revision of the Standing Orders merely formalized a procedure in use for some time previously. *Official Bulletin*, Dec. 15, 1954, p. 186.

15. *Standing Orders*, 1962, Art. 21 bis. Also see Arts. 20, 22 bis, and 25, which incorporate the new Working Parties into the general rules governing subcommittees.

16. International Labor Office, Governing Body, 140th Session (Geneva, November 1958), Doc. GB 140/15/28 (mimeo.), pp. 4–5. *Ibid.*, 143rd Session (Geneva, November 1959), Doc. GB 143/I.C./D.2/1 and the supplementary material referred to therein. It might be added that the 1955 Standing Orders also liberalized the procedure for admitting non-governmental organizations with consultative status in the ILO as non-voting participants in sessions. The Industrial Committees vary in size from 16 to 26 member countries.

17. Unless otherwise indicated, this assessment is drawn from John Price, "The Industrial Committees of the International Labour Organization" (mimeo. in English, but published in the *Rassegna del Lavoro*, April-May 1958, in Italian).

18. "Appraisal," p. 12.

19. International Labor Office, Governing Body, Doc. GB 143/I.C./D.2 (2) /4 (Geneva, November 1959), mimeo. The countries were Australia, Belgium, Czechoslovakia, France, Germany, Greece, India, Iran, Italy, Mexico, Pakistan, Yugoslavia.

20. *Ibid.* Cuba, Ecuador, Honduras.

21. *Ibid.* Hungary, Poland, Ukraine.

22. For examples of lobbying by the ITS's, see International Labor Office, Governing Body, 140th Session, Doc. GB 140/15/28 (Geneva, November 1958), pp. 6–7, 12, 15, 16–17. Requests included demands for freedom of association for civil servants, protection from the effects of automation for transport workers, and the establishment of new Committees for hotel and culinary workers and for mines other than collieries. When the Governing Body considered the membership question, the International Transportworkers Federation lobbied for the retention of Industrial Committees. Requests for studies of the impact on labor of the European Common Market have also been made.

23. Price, in *International Labour Review*, January 1952, p. 22.

24. For an example, see the discussion of the Panamanian ships' case, Chapter 8, pp. 226–27, above. The investigation of Panamanian ships was carried out by the Office personnel servicing the JMC. However, during the discussion between the Panamanian government and the Governing Body over the terms of the official report, the ITF was not consulted. Since the Panamanian government was remiss in living up to the terms of the report, such enforcement as is possible is "delegated" to the ITF. For this purpose the unions were given the list of unsatisfactory conditions on each ship visited, and were encouraged to insist on their removal before seamen were permitted to sign on.

25. Haas, in *World Politics*, XIV (1962), 332, Table 2c. Of twenty-four Conventions adopted since 1920, only Britain, France, the Netherlands, and Norway—among important maritime countries—ratified more than nine.

26. Ghana and Thailand are beginning to ratify the older Conventions. The Office is giving technical assistance to several Central American states that are trying to

write maritime labor codes. Existing Conventions serve as the basis for the Office services. For additional evidence on the indirect impact of unratified Conventions, see *International Labour Review*, February 1953, pp. 138–40.

27. International Labor Office, Governing Body, Doc. GB 117/6/5, 117th Session (Geneva, November 1951).

28. The material that follows was obtained by analyzing and coding these ILO reports, all prepared by the Office:

a. Coal Mines. Coal Mines Committee, 1st Session (1945) in *Official Bulletin* (Sept. 15, 1945), *Report I*, 2nd Session (1947), 3rd Session (1949), 4th Session (1951), 5th Session (1953), 6th Session (1956), 7th Session (1959).

b. Petroleum. Petroleum Committee, 1st Session (1947) in *Official Bulletin* (Sept. 15, 1947), *Report I*, 2nd Session (1948), 3rd Session (1950), 4th Session (1952), 5th Session (1955 and 1956), 6th Session (1960).

c. Textiles. Textiles Committee, 1st Session (1946) in *Official Bulletin* (Sept. 15, 1947) *Report I*, 2nd Session (1948), 3rd Session, (1950), 4th Session (1953), 5th Session (1955), 6th Session (1958).

d. Metal Trades. Metal Trades Committee, 1st Session (1946) in *Official Bulletin* (Sept. 15, 1947), *Report I*, 2nd Session (1947), 3rd Session (1949), 4th Session (1952), 5th Session (1954), 6th Session (1957).

e. Inland Transport. Inland Transport Committee, 1st Session (1945) in *Official Bulletin* (Sept. 15, 1947), *Report I*, 2nd Session (1947), 3rd Session (1949), 4th Session (1951), 5th Session (1954), 6th Session (1957), 7th Session (1961).

f. Chemicals. Chemical Industries Committee, 1st Session (1948), in *Official Bulletin* (June 15, 1949), *Report I*, 2nd Session (1950), 3rd Session (1952), 4th Session (1955), 5th Session (1958).

g. Building Trades. Building, Civil Engineering, and Public Works Committee, 1st Session (1946) in *Official Bulletin* (Sept. 15, 1947), *Report I*, 2nd Session (1949), 3rd Session (1951), 4th Session (1953), 5th Session (1956), 6th Session (1959).

h. Salaried Employees. Advisory Committee on Salaried Employees and Professional Workers, *Report I*, 1st Session (1949), 2nd Session (1952), 3rd Session (1954), 4th Session (1957), 5th Session (1960).

i. Plantations. Committee on Work on Plantations, 1st Session (1950) in *Official Bulletin* (Dec. 20, 1950), *Report I*, 2nd Session (1953), 3rd Session (1955), 4th Session (1961).

j. Iron and Steel. Iron and Steel Committee, 1st Session (1946) in *Official Bulletin* (Sept. 15, 1947), *Report I*, 2nd Session (1947), 3rd Session (1949), 4th Session (1952), 5th Session (1954), 6th Session (1957).

29. For evidence on the widespread confusion among member states concerning their "obligations," see Price, in *International Labour Review*, pp. 18–20, 35.

30. Let us recall that both Turkey and Austria rank among the highest "special performers."

31. Only five of the faithfully reporting countries are underdeveloped (Burma, Ceylon, the Dominican Republic, Pakistan, the Philippines). All the others are industrialized or industrializing; of these, all but the Soviet Union and Yugoslavia are democracies. Again, let us recall from the earlier indices that Ceylon and the Philippines are especially interested in and mindful of the work of the Committees.

32. Tunisia's score is a statistical fluke that is due to the small number of reports for which the government could be held responsible. The figures for Indonesia, Cuba, the Dominican Republic, and Iran reflect positive reports submitted to Geneva, which might perhaps be taken with some reserve.

33. Burma and Turkey, during the period under review, hovered between democracy and rule by military-revolutionary oligarchy. The point of interest is that the advent of reforming-revolutionary oligarchical leadership often implied *increased* receptivity to internationally approved measures for industrial improvement.

34. Chemical Industries Committee, Res. IV-2 (Nos. 22, 23), "Classification and Labelling of Dangerous Substances," *Official Bulletin*, XXXVIII (1955), No. 135.

35. Res. I-4 (No. 17), "Vocational Training in the Construction Industry," *Report I, Record of the Second Session* (1949), p. 150.

36. Committee on Coal Mines, Res. I-1, "The Mineworkers Charter," *Report I*, Second Session (1947), p. 4.

37. Res. II-1, 2, 3, "Manpower," *ibid.*, pp. 173ff.

38. For example, see Textile Committee, "Resolution Concerning Vocational Training," *Official Bulletin*, June 15, 1949, p. 10.

39. For example, see Building, Civil Engineering, and Public Works Committee, Res. No. 53, "Safety in the Construction Industry," *Official Bulletin*, XXXIX (1956), 421.

40. For example, see Advisory Committee on Salaried Employees and Professional Workers, Res. No. 12, "Hygiene in Shops and Offices," *ibid.*, No. 3 (1952), p. 105.

41. For example, see Advisory Committee on Salaried Employees and Professional Workers, Res. No. 26, "Unemployment," *Official Bulletin*, No. 3 (1954), p. 70. Building, Civil Engineering, and Public Works Committee, Res. A-6, "Stabilization of Employment in the Construction Industry," *ibid.*, Sept. 15, 1947, p. 243.

42. For example, see Iron and Steel Committee, Res. No. 25, "Technological Improvements and Their Effect on Employment," *Report I* (1949). Chemical Industries, Res. IV-1, "Productivity in the Chemical Industries," *Official Bulletin*, XXXVIII (1955), 133.

43. Metal Trades Committee, Res. No. 26, "Minimum Income Security," *ibid.*, Sept. 15, 1948, p. 122. Res. No. 30, "Systems of Wage Calculation in the Metal Trades," *ibid.*, Dec. 15, 1949, p. 261.

44. For example, see Inland Transport Committee, Res. No. 9, "Industrial Relations in Inland Transport," *ibid.*, Sept. 15, 1948, p. 90.

45. For example, see Coal Mines Committee, Res. V-2 (No. 39), "Social Welfare Facilities and Services," *ibid.*, Dec. 20, 1953, pp. 147–49. Committee on Plantations, Res. No. 7, "Education and Training of Workers," *ibid.*, Dec. 20, 1950, pp. 177–78.

46. Metal Trades Committee, Res. I-12, "Government Expenditure on Capital Goods, Consumers' Goods and Services," *Official Bulletin*, Sept. 15, 1947, p. 119. Coal Mines Committee, Res. VI-4, "Social Consequences of Fuel and Power Consumption," *ibid.*, XXXIX (1956), 387. Inland Transport Committee, Res. No. 10, "Employment in Inland Transport," *ibid.*, Sept. 15, 1948, p. 93. Building, Civil Engineering, and Public Works Committee, Res. No. 55, "National Housing Programs and Full Employment," *ibid.*, XXXIX (1956), 424.

47. Iron and Steel Committee, Res. Nos. 18, 24, "Guaranteed Weekly Wage," *Report II* (1949). Textiles Committee, Res. No. 9, "Guaranteed Adequate Minimum Weekly Wage," *Official Bulletin*, Sept. 15, 1947, p. 127. Building, Civil Engineering, and Public Works Committee, Res. No. 6, "General Conditions of Work," *ibid.*, September 1947, p. 137.

48. Petroleum Committee, Res. No. 38, "Principles and Methods Used in the Petroleum Industry in Determining Wages," *ibid.*, Dec. 20, 1952, p. 174; Res. No. 21, "Regulation of Wages on Plantations," *ibid.*, Aug. 20, 1953, p. 30.

49. Committee on Work on Plantations, Res. No. 3, "Hours of Work, Weekly Rest

and Holidays," *ibid.*, Dec. 20, 1950, p. 173. Textile Committee, Res. No. 7, "Need for Increased Production," *ibid.*, Sept. 15, 1947, p. 127.

50. Textile Committee, Memorandum 27, "Disparities in Textile Wages Between the Various Countries," *Official Bulletin*, Dec. 20, 1950, p. 159; Res. No. 29, "Raw Materials in the Textile Industry," *ibid.*, p. 162; Res. No. 33, "International Trade and Social Standards," *ibid.*, June 1, 1953, p. 6.

51. Coal Mines Committee, Res. I-4, "International Economic Agreement," *General Report*, 1947, p. 13.

52. Arthur M. Ross, "Prosperity and British Industrial Relations," *Industrial Relations*, II (1963), 82 (italics in original). Additional material with respect to the thesis here argued will be found in these studies by Ross: "Prosperity and Labor Relations in Western Europe: Italy and France," *Industrial and Labor Relations Review*, Vol. XVI, No. 1 (1962) ; "The New Industrial Relations in Britain," *Labor Law Journal* (July 1962) ; "Prosperity and Labor Relations in Europe: The Case of West Germany," *The Quarterly Journal of Economics*, Vol. LXXVI, No. 3 (1962). For American patterns in collective bargaining, see Arnold R. Weber, ed., *The Structure of Collective Bargaining* (Chicago, Ill.: The Free Press, 1961). For patterns in underdeveloped countries, see W. Galenson, ed., *Labor and Economic Development* (New York: Wiley, 1959), and *Labor in Developing Economies* (Berkeley: University of California Press, 1963).

53. Ibid., p. 63.

CHAPTER ELEVEN

1. C. W. Jenks, *Human Rights and International Labour Standards* (London: Stevens, 1960), pp. 3–5.

2. *Ibid.*, pp. 8–9. Jenks, *Trade Union Freedom*, pp. 479–81.

3. Jenks, *Human Rights*, pp. 131–32.

4. *Ibid.*, pp. 132–33.

5. *Ibid.*, pp. 140–41.

6. *Ibid.*, pp. 59–60.

7. *Ibid.*, pp. 13–14.

8. Jenks fully recognizes the importance of this argument and uses it in defense of ILO measures to protect freedom of association, even though his concern is not identical with the present analytical focus. *Ibid.*, p. 68.

9. *Ibid.*, p. 9. In 1958 the Conference adopted, unanimously, a resolution proclaiming the attachment of the ILO to the rule of law, and such fundamental freedoms as freedom of opinion, expression, peaceful assembly, and freedom from arbitrary arrest or exile. However, such declarations are rhetorical unless translated into firm texts and sustained programs—which these were not.

10. Such an indicator is provided by the ILO in the form of the so-called Forbes Watson Tables, annually appended to the report of the Conference Committee on the Application of Conventions and Recommendations. These tables compare the votes of governments on such texts with their record of ratifications—and come to the inevitable conclusion that governments commonly vote for new standards that they do not intend to apply. As Troclet commented, "these documents could have constituted a useful tool if they had not been transformed into an 'honor roll' of member states and if their author had not wanted to draw conclusions from them which their statistical elements do not permit." Troclet. *Législation sociale internationale*, p. 617. Forbes Watson. of course, wished to demonstrate that the international labor standards system does not work well because of the uneven incidence

of ratifications. But he confined his demonstration to gross ratifications, not taking into account the applicability of the text to a given economy, the presence and participation of the delinquent governments in the earlier phases of preparation, or the desire of governments to support standards demanded by others but not considered applicable by the supporter. Finally, the Forbes Watson method has nothing to offer on the more vital issue of implementation of ratified Conventions. For a full discussion of the various weaknesses of the Forbes Watson Tables, see *ibid.*, pp. 618–27.

11. Jenks, *Human Rights*, p. 153.

12. *Ibid.*, p. 154. For a balanced treatment of the issue of the international protection for human rights, merging my concern with jurisprudential considerations of rhetorical, natural, and positive law, see Maurice Cranston, *What Are Human Rights?* (New York: Basic Books, 1962).

13. Jenks, *Trade Union Freedom*, p. 62.

14. *Ibid.*, pp. 516–17, 547–50, and 523ff. Elsewhere Jenks argues that just as at the international level the ILO represents the best judgment of mankind, at the federal level, in the national politics of such states as the United States, Australia, and India, the central government represents the best national judgment, which must always supersede the (restrictive) judgment of the constituent units. *Human Rights*, p. 142.

15. *Ibid.*, pp. 138–39. The one instance in which the special role of tripartism is clear beyond doubt is the drafting of the European Social Charter (described in Chapter 9). The participation of worker and employer delegations was directly responsible for the introduction of a number of substantive changes. Note, however, that the success of tripartism is here associated with a homogeneous pluralistic environment.

16. For details see Chapter 9 above.

17. For a full list of such cognate but overspecialized texts, see the complete and authoritative summary of Nicolas Valticos, "Les Droits de l'homme et l'organisation internationale du travail," *Mélanges Séfériadès* (Athens, 1960), pp. 101–3.

18. Convention 81 (labor inspection) has been included, even though it is an instrumental rather than a substantive human rights text, because the national enforcement of internationally accepted substantive rights is not possible without the concurrent existence of adequate administrative machinery. The existence of such machinery is in itself an indicator of organizational legitimacy and authority. The Right of Association (Agriculture) Convention of 1921 (No. 11) was excluded because its operative clauses are made dependent on conditions of association for industry, and because the impact of the Convention is doubtful. The Forced Labor Convention of 1930 (No. 29) was omitted because it primarily abolished forced labor for *private* purposes, whereas the later text included all forms of forced labor. See Valticos, pp. 105–8.

Jenks singles out the following Recommendations as particularly important for the protection of human rights, though he says nothing on their implementation: Collective Agreements (1951), suggesting collective bargaining machinery and the extension of agreements to uncovered sectors; Voluntary Conciliation and Arbitration (1951); Cooperation at the Level of the Undertaking (1952), suggesting various items of consultative machinery and works councils; Discrimination (Employment and Occupation), elaborating on the corresponding Convention (1958).

19. See Chapter 8 above.

20. The importance of the UN in the work of the ILO is not confined to initiating

new tasks. The ILO has a regular follow-up procedure for reporting to the ECOSOC on progress concerning human rights efforts that had their origin in UN resolutions. See, for example, "Report on the Application of the International Labour Convention (No. 100) and Recommendation (No. 90) concerning Equal Remuneration for Men and Women Workers for Work of Equal Value," UN Doc. E/CN.6/231, Dec. 14, 1953, and "Equal Pay for Equal Work," UN Doc. E/CN.6/359, 1960. The Office provides material for inclusion in the UN's *Yearbook on Human Rights* and furnishes background information, on request, to the UN Commission on Human Rights. Such information summarizes cases of progress noted by the Committee of Experts, thus making available for UN consumption the material covered by the Committee's *Reports*. It should be added that "human rights" are here given their most extensive meaning, since these reports include as "progress on human rights" any improvement in member state performance with respect to almost all ILO Conventions. For the 1954–56 period, see UN Doc. E/CN.4/758/Add 1. Similar triennial reports were prepared for the periods 1957–59 and 1960–62.

21. The phrases "national extraction" and "social origin" need a word of comment. The latter evidently refers to the practice in communist countries of discriminating against persons of "bourgeois" background. The former, according to a ruling of the Committee of Experts in 1963, means "national origin" rather than "nationality." In other words, the Convention does not bar discrimination in the employment of aliens. *RCE, 1963*, pp. 183–84.

22. Ad hoc missions to deal with "complaints" were sent to Hungary (1920), Venezuela (1949), India and Pakistan (1949), Panama (1950), Iran (1950), and the Suez Canal Zone (1951–52). The "complaints" involved allegations voiced in the ILO but outside the formal "complaint procedure" specified in the Constitution.

23. Let us recall that the McNair inquiry was undertaken initially to sidestep the dispute over the credentials of communist employers. See Chapter 8. The results of the first inquiry were published as *Freedom of Association*, International Labor Office, Studies and Reports, Series A, Nos. 28–32, 5 vols. (Geneva, 1927–30), and the McNair Committee's findings as "Report of the Committee on the Freedom of Employers' and Workers' Organisations," *Official Bulletin*, Vol. XXXIX, No. 9 (1956).

24. See Chapter 8.

25. For an excellent summary of the discussion in 1919, see Wilson, *Labor in the League System*, pp. 220–24. What follows is a summary of Articles 409–20 of the 1919 Constitution.

26. Art. 414, para. 2, of the 1919 Constitution.

27. Wilson, p. 222, n. 7.

28. Art. 33, 1946 Constitution. A similar power is granted to the Governing Body and the Conference in the event that a state complains of another's failure to submit ILO texts to competent national authorities. See Art. 30, 1946 Constitution. Under the old Constitution this power had been vested in the PCIJ.

29. The reports on the United States and the Soviet Union are discussed in Chapter 8. The other reports will be considered in a different context in Chapter 13. A similar importance, so far potential rather than real, may be attached to resolutions adopted by various technical and regional ILO bodies. At the Inter-American ILO Conference of 1952, for instance, the Latin American delegates wanted to create a special western-hemisphere system of protection for freedom of association, which was opposed by the United States as duplicating the procedure available at Geneva. Instead, the conference adopted a strongly worded resolution calling on governments

to make use of the ILO Fact-Finding and Conciliation Commission. Jenks, *Trade Union Freedom*, p. 190.

30. Wilson, pp. 16–22.

31. The procedure of the Commission is described in detail in Troclet, pp. 679–86.

32. Jenks, *Trade Union Freedom*, p. 6.

33. International Labor Conference, 44th Session, *Record of Proceedings* (Geneva, 1960), pp. 417–26. South Africa abstained on the final vote.

34. Governing Body, 154th Session (Geneva, March 5–8, 1963), "Report of the Committee on Discrimination," Doc. GB 154/4/29, p. 3. See also *ibid.*, Doc. GB 154/P.V.3, pp. 8–10.

35. Members of the United Nations are automatically entitled to become members of all specialized agencies. The question of whether they can be legally expelled from them without first being removed from the United Nations remains moot.

36. The United States delegation voted with the Africans most of the time; however, only the American worker delegate joined in the various walkouts. Nevertheless, many Western delegates, including workers, appealed to the Africans to observe constitutional rules.

37. Governing Body, Draft Minutes of the 156th Session, Geneva, June 28–29, 1963, Doc. GB 156-1400, Annex I. The governments of Australia, Canada, the United States, and the United Kingdom voted against the resolution barring South Africa from ILO meetings other than the Conference.

38. When the Governing Body refused to consider the appeal by the Spanish trade unions, Léon Jouhaux warned the delegates that the workers would be compelled to leave the ILO because the recognition of lack of jurisdiction over Spain tended to negate the basic concept of Official Functionalism. When similar charges were pressed against Italy in 1925 by the Dutch worker delegate on the Governing Body, the issue was avoided once more. Zarras, *Le Contrôle de l'application des conventions internationales du travail*, pp. 229–30.

39. Zarras, pp. 249–57; Wilson, pp. 225–26.

40. Troclet, p. 666. Even though the Convention in question subordinated agricultural trade union rights to national law governing industrial unions, the ILO did not have to capitulate quite so readily. At one stage in the proceedings, members of the Governing Body grew restless because the complaining union had not replied to a request for additional information. The Estonian representative, when questioned about possible further acts of repression, affirmed that the trade union official involved had just been elected to Parliament!

41. See the Panamanian and Venezuelan cases discussed in Chapter 8.

42. *Ibid.*, p. 512. Thomas, for his part, seems to have preferred this "friendly" and "non-contentious" approach to the formal procedure that would have punctuated organizational authority. In 1932 the Cuban government came close to being subjected to the complaint procedure, when the Labor Conference strongly criticized it for not applying ratified Conventions. Hurried assurances by the Cuban delegate that improvements would be undertaken sufficed to stop the effort. Zarras, p. 275.

43. Troclet, pp. 667–69.

44. *Ibid.*, p. 672.

45. Wilson, pp. 227–28.

46. Wilson, pp. 228–29; Troclet, pp. 658–59. Among the conditions of receivability, we find that the allegation must cite a ratified Convention and introduce some evidence that this Convention is not being applied.

47. In the Venezuelan case, the Governing Body insisted on its right to publish

the report anyway, but the text was accompanied by another document setting forth the observations of the Venezuelan government. Negotiated reports were published in all the other instances of ad hoc missions of inquiry. Jenks, *Trade Union Freedom*, p. 178.

48. Zarras, pp. 262–64.

49. Troclet, pp. 670–71. Jenks's judgment concerning the obsolescence of the representation procedure is more flattering to the authority of the ILO. He argues that the very formality of the procedure militates against its continued use, since equally effective but more informal means for achieving the same purposes have flowered with the growth of the annual reporting *cum* debate process under Articles 19 and 22 of the Constitution. Jenks, *Trade Union Freedom*, pp. 495–97. For my judgment concerning this process, see Chapter 9 above.

50. International Labor Office, *Official Bulletin*, Vol. XLV, No. 2, April 1962 (Suppl. II), "Report of the Commission Appointed Under Article 26 of the Constitution . . . to Examine the Complaint Filed by . . . Ghana Concerning the Observance by the Government of Portugal of the Abolition of Forced Labour Convention, 1957 (No. 105)," p. 1. The following material is based entirely on this document and on interviews.

51. At that time, Messrs. George Lodge (U.S.), Pierre Waline (France), and Jean Möri (Switzerland).

52. *Ibid.*, pp. 4–5.

53. *Ibid.*, p. 122. The documents and statements exchanged by the parties during this phase are given on pp. 117–41.

54. *Ibid.*, p. 124.

55. *Ibid.*, pp. 5–6. Ruegger, a former Swiss diplomat, was also chairman of the International Committee of the Red Cross, chairman of the ILO Committee on Forced Labor, and most recently a member of the Committee of Experts on the Application of Conventions. Armand-Ugon is a former president of the Supreme Court of Uruguay and a member of the ICJ. Forster is the president of the Senegalese Supreme Court and also a member of the Committee of Experts. The appointments were by unanimous vote; no Soviet objection was heard.

56. *Ibid.*, pp. 10–21, 228.

57. *Ibid.*, p. 24 (my italics).

58. *Ibid.*, p. 234.

59. *Ibid.*

60. *Ibid.*, p. 241. In addition, Portugal has since adopted a new rural labor code for its overseas territories.

61. *Ibid.*, p. 243.

62. The Commission's Report recognizes the role of the Office in the repeated grateful references to the advice and assistance given the International Labor Standards Division, and in particular by C. Wilfred Jenks. *Ibid.*, pp. 6 and 247. Also, the Office availed itself of the preferences of the Portuguese Ministry of Labor, which apparently had been anxious to make reforms in Africa for some time, but had been opposed by other ministries.

63. *Ibid.*, pp. 226–27, 232.

64. *Ibid.*, pp. 242–43.

65. *Ibid.*, p. 245.

66. *Ibid.*, p. 247.

67. Governing Body, 151st Session (Geneva, Mar. 6–9, 1962), Doc. GB 151/P.V.2.

68. Goonetilleke (Ceylon) previously served as member of the ILO Committee on Forced Labor; Castrén (Finland) is a newcomer to the small family of experts

used on ILO committees of this type; he is a professor of law, and a member of the UN International Law Commission, the Permanent Court of Arbitration, and several international arbitration tribunals.

69. "Report of the Commission Appointed under Article 26 of the Constitution . . . to Examine the Complaint by the Government of Portugal concerning the Observance by the Government of Liberia of the Forced Labour Convention, 1930 (No. 29)," *Official Bulletin*, Vol. XLVI, No. 2 (1963), Suppl. II, pp. 171–73, 176–79.

70. *Ibid.*, 175–76, 179–81.

71. *Ibid.*, p. 181. It may be mentioned, incidentally, that the sole Liberian trade union—the Congress of Industrial Organizations—is headed by William V. S. Tubman, Jr., the son of the long-time President of the Republic.

72. *Ibid.*, pp. 165–66, 177.

73. *Ibid.*, p. 169.

74. *Ibid.*, p. 177.

75. Statement of Edward R. Moore, Liberian agent, July 3, 1962. *Ibid.*, p. 28 (italics mine). See also his statement on July 2, 1962, *ibid.*, pp. 25–26.

76. *Ibid.*, p. 169.

77. *Ibid.*, p. 156. For the reasoning of the Ghana-Portugal Commission, see note 66 above. A *prima facie* case was thought to exist because of the material previously presented by the Committee of Experts.

78. *Ibid.*, pp. 32–33, 36–37.

79. *Ibid.*, pp. 8–9, 171.

80. The Committee of Experts "would like to stress particularly that . . . the examination which it was called upon to undertake this year could in all respects be no more than a preliminary one." *RCE, 1963*, p. 178. The Committee went on to explain that most of the member states did not fully respond to the Office questionnaire and had not yet "fully grasped" the meaning of the Convention. Hence the Committee's "evaluation" confined itself to discussing whether certain examples of national legislation and practice could be considered compatible with the Convention.

81. The sources used for scoring governmental responses were as follows:

Conv. 81.—ILO, International Labor Conference, 30th Session, Geneva, 1947, Report IV: *The Organization of Labour Inspection in Industrial and Commercial Undertakings* (Montreal, 1946). ILO, International Labor Conference, 30th Session, Geneva, 1947, Report IV Supplement: *The Organization of Labour Inspection in Industrial and Commercial Undertakings* (Geneva, 1947).

Conv. 87.—ILO, International Labor Conference, 31st Session, San Francisco, 1948, Report VII: *Freedom of Association and Protection of the Right to Organise* (Geneva, 1948). ILO, ILC, 31st Session, San Francisco, 1948, Report VII Supplement: *Freedom of Association and Protection of the Right to Organise* (Geneva, 1958).

Conv. 98.—ILO, International Labor Conference, 32nd Session, Geneva, 1949, Report IV (2): *Application of the Principles of the Right to Organise and to Bargain Collectively* (Geneva, 1949).

Conv. 100.—ILO, International Labor Conference, 34th Session, Geneva, 1951, Report VII (2): *Equal Remuneration for Men and Women Workers for Work of Equal Value* (Geneva, 1951). ILO, International Labor Conference, 33rd Session, Geneva, 1950, Report V (2): *Equal Remuneration for Men and Women Workers for Work of Equal Value* (Geneva, 1950).

Conv. 105.—ILO, International Labor Conference, 39th Session, Geneva, 1956, Report VI (2): *Forced Labour* (Geneva, 1956). ILO, International Labor Conference, 40th Session, Geneva, 1957, Report IV (2) : *Forced Labour* (Geneva, 1957).

Conv. 111.—ILO, International Labor Conference, 42nd Session, Geneva, 1958, Report IV (1) : *Discrimination in the Field of Employment and Occupation* (Geneva, 1957) ; *ibid.*, Report IV (2) (Geneva, 1958).

82. The sources used for coding the vote were as follows:

Conv. 81.—ILC, 30th Session, 19th Sitting, Geneva, 1947, *Record of Proceedings* (Geneva 1948), p. 310.

Conv. 87.—ILC, 31st Session, 18th Sitting, San Francisco, 1948, *Record of Proceedings* (Geneva 1950), p. 268.

Conv. 98.—ILC, 32nd Session, 22nd Sitting, Geneva, 1949, *Record of Proceedings* (Geneva 1951), p. 352.

Conv. 100.—ILC, 34th Session, 25th Sitting, Geneva, 1951, *Record of Proceedings* (Geneva 1952), p. 447.

Conv. 105.—ILC, 40th Session, 27th Sitting, Geneva, 1957, *Record of Proceedings* (Geneva 1958), p. 444.

Conv. 111.—ILC, 41st Session, 30th Sitting, Geneva, 1958, *Record of Proceedings* (Geneva 1959), p. 479.

83. The source used for coding ratification was International Labor Office, *Chart of Ratifications,* 1962.

84. The sources used for coding conduct with respect to implementation were as follows:

Conv. 81.—International Labor Conference, 34th Session, Geneva, 1951, Report III (Part IV), *Report of the Committee of Experts on the Application of Conventions and Recommendations,* pp. 48–51. *Ibid.*, 40th Session, Geneva, 1957, pp. 153–61.

Conv. 87.—Ibid., pp. 161–73. *Ibid.*, 43rd Session, Geneva, 1959, pp. 101–29.

Conv. 98.—Ibid., 39th Session, Geneva, 1956, pp. 135–43. *Ibid.*, 43rd Session, Geneva, 1959, pp. 101–29.

Conv. 100.—Ibid., 39th Session, Geneva, 1956, pp. 148–56.

Conv. 105.—Ibid., 46th Session, Geneva, 1962, pp. 193–289.

Conv. 111.—Ibid., 47th Session, Geneva, 1963, pp. 173–258.

85. Even though the performance data with respect to Convention 111 are incomplete, it is useful to introduce some of them here. First, 27 states did not respond to the Office preliminary questionnaire, voted for the text, and then failed to ratify it (as of 1962). This list includes all types of regimes and doctrines, and permits of no patterned interpretation. Fourteen states did not respond to the Office preliminary questionnaire, voted for the Convention, and then promptly ratified it. This list includes the following revolutionary regimes: Bulgaria, Ghana, Hungary, Iraq, Tunisia, the Soviet Union, and the Ukraine. It should be pointed out once more that ratification exposes the state concerned not only to the procedure of Article 22 of the Constitution, but also to the possibility of complaints being submitted. Further, Convention 111 bars not only racial discrimination (which could be considered as directed against the Western democracies), but discrimination based on social origin or political belief, i.e., situations in which the practice of communist and other revolutionary regimes is far from clean. The same conclusion emerges from the list of the 11 countries that supported the drafting of the text, voted for it, and then ratified it; this list includes not only many democracies, but also Byelorussia, Poland, the U.A.R., and Yugoslavia. A further group of 7 countries supported the drafting of the Convention, voted for it, has not yet ratified, but is likely to do so on the basis of past performance; this group includes Romania in addition to several democracies.

Another group of countries consistently opposed the Convention. Fourteen countries did not reply to the questionnaire, abstained or were absent on the vote, and have not ratified. This group, too, includes several revolutionary regimes: Burma, Bolivia, Indonesia. Whether opposition is due to principle or to administrative inefficiency and inertia is not clear. Finally, the United States and Britain opposed the drafting of the text, voted for it, but have not ratified it.

86. *RCE, 1956*, pp. 142–43.

87. *RCE, 1957*, p. 172. A more direct indicator of authority would be provided by the practice of governments to apply fully Conventions they had initially opposed, a condition not really met in the conduct of the revolutionary regimes here surveyed. Actually only two such cases were encountered: Yugoslavia's applying Convention 105 and Luxembourg's implementation of Convention 100.

CHAPTER TWELVE

1. Jenks, *Trade Union Freedom*, p. 186. The final decision to set up the Commission was made at the February 1950 session of the Governing Body.

2. For the procedural rules governing ECOSOC discretion regarding the forwarding of complaints, see *ibid.*, p. 184. Although the Body was to refer allegations against governments that were not members of the ILO to the ECOSOC, a number of such cases were in fact considered by the Body. *Ibid.*, pp. 185–87. By interpreting the rules to suit its purposes, the ILO has managed to preserve a monopoly on dealing with trade union rights in the UN family.

3. *Ibid.*, p. 185.

4. The consent requirement that accompanies the on-site surveys of freedom of association previously discussed also aroused the ICFTU's opposition. The free unions preferred surveys for which the Office did not require previous diplomatic negotiation, and they promise themselves little from the procedure actually used. The U.S. Worker delegate (Delaney), who first proposed the surveys to the Governing Body, did so without ICFTU authorization.

5. Jenks, p. 188.

6. Early in 1964, the Governing Body decided to ask the Japanese government's consent to dispatch the Conciliation Commission to Japan; thus, after thirteen years of disuse, the machinery was called into life by the acceptance, on the part of Japan, of its authority.

7. *Official Bulletin*, summaries of the 117th Session of the Governing Body, pp. 45–50, 66–67, 77, 88–89; 118th Session, p. 60; 120th Session, p. 60; 126th Session, p. 13; 136th Session, pp. 12–13; 146th Session, pp. 12–13; 149th Session, p. 37.

8. Paul Ramadier served as Chairman of the Committee during his entire 10-year tenure.

9. Roberto Ago assumed the chairmanship of the Committee upon Ramadier's retirement.

10. For Waline's commitment to the ILO doctrine and his ideology concerning international labor issues—all consistent with the expansion of the ILO task into the human rights field—see Chapter 8 above.

11. 136th Session of the Governing Body, June 28, 1957, *Official Bulletin*, pp. 12–13. The Czech representative associated himself with this position.

12. Case No. 58 (Poland), 11th and 22nd Reports of the Committee.

13. Case No. 148 (Poland), 22nd Report.

14. The distinction is well elaborated by Jenks, p. 423. He also notes that in a

large number of cases the Committee felt that general repressive measures did affect trade unions and therefore should be considered on their merits.

15. The following cases were excluded from the study:

(*a*) Cases about which no information had been released by the ILO at the time of this study, because they were still in the earliest stages of the procedure and had not been fully considered by the Committee: Nos. 201, 218, 241, 242, 264, 273, 277, 278, 280, 281, 285, 287, 288, 292, 296, 298, 299, 300, 302, 303, 305, 307, 308, 309.

(*b*) Cases docketed but never considered by the Committee because the state complained against was not a member of the ILO: No. 36 (Saudi Arabia), No. 123 (East Germany).

(*c*) Cases so vaguely drawn and indiscriminately directed against several governments simultaneously that no detailed analysis was possible: No. 39 (Peru and Bolivia), No. 226 (Haiti, Nicaragua, Paraguay), No. 304 (Greece, Portugal, Spain, South Africa, Iran).

(*d*) Cases substantially identical with an earlier complaint lodged against the same state and disposed of by the Committee by reference to the earlier case. Normally the Office joins such complaints to cases already docketed. I have done the same with these cases even though, for some reason, separate numbers were assigned to them: No. 43 (Chile, joined with No. 10), No. 95 (U.S., joined with No. 71), No. 119 (South Africa, joined with No. 63), No. 122 (Venezuela, joined with No. 72), No. 141 (Chile, joined with No. 134), No. 154 (Chile, joined with No. 153), No. 162 (U.K., joined with No. 96), No. 164 (U.S., joined with No. 138), No. 203 (Hungary, joined with No. 160).

Since our survey stopped in the spring of 1963 at Case No. 310, this gives us a total of 272 cases for tabulation.

16. It may be, though it cannot be demonstrated, that this conclusion would have to be adjusted if the precise nature of the growing number of "indeterminate" charges were known.

17. On the tricky question of the burden of proof and the presumption of innocence, in a setting in which governments are presumed merely to be cooperating voluntarily for the greater glory of the principle of freedom of association, see Jenks, pp. 467–68.

18. These limitations on the receivability of charges were defined as follows by the Committee: "In future allegations shall be receivable only if they are submitted by a national organization directly interested in the matter, an international organization of employers or workers having consultative status with the ILO, or another international organization of employers or workers where the allegations relate to matters directly affecting its affiliated organizations." *Official Bulletin*, Vol. XLIII, No. 3 (1960), p. 79.

19. Case No. 329 (Cuba) in 1963.

20. Decisions to file charges are made in Brussels in all cases involving the ICFTU, or national unions acting on its instructions, on the basis of information received from the local unions. The ICFTU may approach the Office for further details if the case is too sketchy, and if additional information is available in Geneva. Conversely, if additional information becomes available as the Committee gets ready to write its report, the ICFTU will communicate it to Geneva. Occasionally, the ICFTU will call to the attention of the Office abuses in certain countries that the Confederation would like to eliminate without resorting to the complaint procedure, encouraging the Office to eliminate the practices through informal communication with the government concerned. The same procedure is followed, in principle, in relations with other complainants.

21. Case No. 179 (Japan), discussed in greater detail on pp. 421–22 below.

22. Jenks, p. 196.

23. *1st Report* of the Committee, para. 31.

24. This reassertion of the Committee's power occurred at the same time as the professed attachment to conciliation rather than adjudication. In Case No. 2 (Venezuela) and Case No. 3 (Dominican Republic), the respective governments had indicated their refusal to admit the Fact-Finding and Conciliation Commission before the Committee had even recommended such a step to the Governing Body. See *1st Report* of the Committee.

25. *29th Report, Official Bulletin*, Vol. XLIII, No. 3, 1960, para. 6. One wonders how "personal" a "personal part" must be.

26. For details, see Jenks, pp. 178–79, 190. Costa Rica and Libya invited ILO visits in connection with complaints against them. The request was addressed to. Japan.

27. For example, Cases Nos. 1 (Peru), 20 (Lebanon), 30 (U.K.-Malaya), 49 (Pakistan), 65 (Cuba), 55 and 66 (Greece).

28. For example, Cases Nos. 16 (France-Morocco), 17 and 61 (France-Tunisia), 156 (France-Algeria), 38, 24, and 59 (U.K.-Cyprus).

29. For example, Cases Nos. 5, 47 (India), 29 (U.K.-Kenya), 50 (Turkey).

30. Cases Nos. 109, 131 (Guatemala) and 167 (Jordan).

31. Jenks, pp. 235–37, 510. For certain colonial purposes, ILO practice also includes Convention 84 (Right of Association, Non-Metropolitan Territories, even though the norms defined in that text are less demanding than in the other two Conventions.

32. *Ibid.*, p. 63.

33. *Ibid.*, p. 447.

34. Sweeping anti-communist legislation impinging on trade unions has been upheld in the following countries: Chile, Switzerland, South Africa, United States, the Netherlands, Malaya, India, United Kingdom, Greece.

35. Cases Nos. 233 (Congo-Brazzaville), 290 (Congo-Léopoldville), 235 (Cameroun), 289 (Senegal). However, in all these instances the Committee also asked the defendant governments "to review" their legislation.

36. Cases Nos. 221 (U.K.-Aden), 251 (U.K.-Southern Rhodesia), 313 (Dahomey).

37. Cases Nos. 168 (Paraguay), 191 (Sudan), 202 (Thailand). Note also that in Case No. 239 (Costa Rica), a democratic but economically underdeveloped country was admonished to cease interfering with the right of plantation workers to organize.

38. Case No. 274 (Libya).

39. Cases Nos. 167 (Jordan), 260 (Iraq), 265 (Iran).

40. Cases Nos. 185, 224, 240, and 295. Three of these resulted in requests to the Greek government to change its conduct, and one is still pending. In addition, however, note that in Case No. 198 the General-Secretary of the Athens Printers' Association, though allegedly summoned by the police to recant his opinions and being maltreated upon refusing to do so, received no support from the Committee on the grounds that it could not be shown that trade union rights had been infringed.

41. Efforts to limit the right to form federations and to affiliate were rejected in 1948. It was then proposed to make such a right subject to the unions' remaining completely autonomous of the federations and to the insistence that internationals should have the same objectives as national centers.

42. The legal stumbling block here, of course, is the provision in Convention 87 that associations must obey "the law of the land," and that law happens to include most of the activities which have subsequently become political exceptions to the

rules. Anticipating such a possibility, the Worker Group successfully insisted on the inclusion of the modifying phrase "the law of the land shall not be such as to impair, nor shall it be so applied as to impair, the guarantees provided for in this Convention." During the 1948 Conference, it was urged that this meant the preservation of the independence of the judiciary in passing on permissible suppressions of associations. Jenks (p. 28) comments that the ensemble means "reasonable discretion" for states in subjecting associations to national law, subject to international review.

43. Cases Nos. 169 (Turkey), 183 (South Africa), 232 (Morocco).

44. Cases Nos. 179 (Japan), 194 (U.K.-Singapore), 229 and 261 (South Africa).

45. Cases Nos. 192, 199, 216, 221 (Argentina).

46. When Convention 87 was drafted, an unsuccessful effort was made by a few employers to exempt employers' organizations from the scope of freedom of association. However, it was agreed that trusts and cartels were outside its scope.

47. In 1948, efforts to amend the prohibition of a state's power to dissolve an association were defeated overwhelmingly. The amendment had urged "illegal activity" as sufficient grounds for administrative dissolution.

48. Cases Nos. 143 (Spain), 266 (Portugal).

49. The more celebrated cases involving ILO condemnation of communist trade union policy are the following (in varying degrees of severity): Case No. 14 (Czechoslovakia), Cases Nos. 19 and 158 (Hungary), Cases Nos. 58 and 148 (Poland), Cases Nos. 111 and 155 (U.S.S.R.). For a full discussion, see Jenks, Chapter 21.

50. Jenks, pp. 191–95, 504.

51. This is especially true in cases submitted only for propaganda reasons, in which the ICFTU makes little effort to check with its national affiliate on whether there has been a follow-up. It is also true of cases in which the decision was hortatory and platitudinous in tone. It might be added that after 1958 the ICFTU lost its interest in attacking Soviet-bloc countries, apparently because of the lack of commitment to Cold War gambits on the part of African and Asian affiliates.

52. A few examples of this type of implementation may be cited. Anti-union legislation introduced into the Costa Rican legislature may have been tabled as a result of a complaint (Case No. 108). British authorities in Honduras and the Dutch in the West Indies dropped restrictions on trade unions as a result of complaints that did not reach the stage of requests for changes in conduct (Cases Nos. 73, 133). National legislation to control communism was amended in order to eliminate dangers of anti-union discrimination as a result of ILO suggestions "to review" (Cases Nos. 5, 47, India; 30, U.K.-Malaya). The Mexican government, when threatened with a complaint that never had to be submitted, recognized a pilots' union which it had sought to bar. Greece (Case No. 18) commuted several death sentences as a result of an ILO hearing.

53. In addition, the complaints were supported by the ICFTU and three of its affiliated Trade Secretariats. All information regarding this case (No. 179) is taken from the 32nd, 41st, 47th, 48th, 54th, 58th, 60th, 64th and 66th *Reports* of the Committee.

54. The government's position was based on the Public Corporation and National Enterprise Labor Relations Law (Section 4.3) and the Local Public Enterprise Labor Relations Law (Section 5.3). Japan had ratified Convention 98.

55. Jenks, p. 196.

56. Ibid., p. 67.

57. *Ibid.*, p. 68.

58. *Ibid.*, pp. 528–29.

59. *Ibid.*, pp. 180, 481.
60. Jenks, *Human Rights*, p. 62.
61. Jenks, *Trade Union Freedom*, p. 490.

CHAPTER THIRTEEN

1. Rosecrance, p. 231.
2. *Ibid.*, p. 232.
3. I have used these four phases in my analysis of the impact of revolutionary regimes on the UN, in Kaplan, *The Revolution in World Politics*, pp. 267–309. There, my concern was to show the relatively stable nature of the structures in the face of considerable environmental dynamism, primarily with respect to the collective security function.
4. Even major powers are subject to these forces. Witness the slow and unobtrusive way in which the United States has accommodated itself—and thus recognized organizational authority—in fields in which it had frankly opposed changed procedures in 1944–45. The following constitutional changes were all opposed by the United States when they were suggested in 1945, but had become informal reality by 1963: acceptance of employer delegates from socialized or mixed economies; representation for international organizations of employers and workers; fuller representation for agricultural workers and salaried employees; extraction of explanations from governments for reasons of non-ratification of Conventions; permission to ratify Conventions by stages; establishment of some international control to ensure the enforcement of ratified Conventions, and the use of national labor inspectorates for that purpose; and publicity for the reasons advanced for not ratifying Conventions. For a complete list of these suggestions, see *Official Bulletin*, December 10, 1945, pp. 415–17. For information regarding the position of the United States at that time, I am indebted to Professor Carter Goodrich.
5. These distinctions and the discussion that follows from them are inspired by the contemporary sociological literature on what is variously called "post-industrial," "post-bourgeois," "post-capitalist," or "post-ideological" society. All these terms have been used to refer to essentially the same phenomena. See, for example, Ralf Dahrendorf, *Class and Class Conflict in Industrial Society* (Stanford, Calif.: Stanford University Press, 1959); S. M. Lipset, *Political Man* (Garden City, N.Y.: Doubleday, 1960); Raymond Aron, *L'Opium des Intellectuels* (Paris: Calman-Lévy, 1955); Daniel Bell, *The End of Ideology* (Glencoe, Ill.: The Free Press, 1960); George Lichtheim, *The New Europe* (New York: Praeger, 1963).
6. Dahrendorf, p. 318.
7. The argument I am summarizing is taken from Commission to Study the Organization of Peace, *The United Nations, Regional Arrangements and the Free World* (16th Report, New York, July 1963), and particularly from the paper by Marion H. McVitty and Howard Taubenfeld, pp. 24–31. This treatment of the "democratic" and "pluralistic" character of the UN is based on a notion of consensus on aims and values. It should be sharply differentiated from a kindred approach that stresses the *analytical* (as opposed to value) attributes of domestic systems, and suggests their use for the study of consensus formation in the UN, a consensus then derivable from systemic interaction rather than manifest actor motives. This problem will concern us in the final chapter. For an exposition of this approach, see Bruce M. Russett, "Toward a Model of Competitive International Politics," *Journal of Politics*, II (1963), 226–47, as well as Chadwick F. Alger, "Comparison of Intra-

national and International Politics," *American Political Science Review*, LVII (1963), 406–19.

8. For the literature on the Western European process, see the items cited in Chapter 2. For the West Indian case I have relied on J. H. Proctor, Jr., "The Functional Approach to Political Union: Lessons from the Effort to Federate the British Caribbean Territories," *International Organization*, Vol. 10, No. 1 (February 1956), and especially Hugh W. Springer, *Reflections on the Failure of the First West Indian Federation* (Harvard University Center for International Affairs, Occasional Papers No. 4. July 1962).

9. I am aware of the temptation to attribute the failure of the first West Indian Federation to strong personal rivalries. The conflict in Jamaica—the least cooperative as well as the most powerful unit—between Sir Alexander Bustamante and Norman Manley comes to mind, as well as the conflict between these Jamaicans, on the one hand, and Sir Grantley Adams of Barbados and Eric Williams of Trinidad, on the other. Let us note, then, that all these men are at the trade union - labor - radical modernizing end of the pluralistic spectrum. Let us note further that the *conditions* of modernization are far from uniform in the islands. It follows—unless Carlyle is to be considered an irresistible master—that personal differences fit into the larger picture of structural variety with different functional consequences and resultant disintegration.

10. Amitai Etzioni, "European Unification: A Strategy of Change," *World Politics*, XVI (October 1963), 43–46.

11. Karl W. Deutsch, *Political Community at the International Level* (Garden City, N.Y.: Doubleday, 1954), pp. 37–38, 51–53, 57–58.

12. My treatment is greatly influenced by George E. Kelly's essay, "The Expert as Historical Actor," *Daedalus* (Summer 1963), pp. 529 ff.

13. *Ibid.*, p. 529.

14. As quoted in *ibid.*, p. 540.

15. Monnet's practical and intellectual debt to Saint-Simon has sometimes been exposed. I think the purity of the lineage can be exaggerated, though the connection is far from fanciful. Monnet's most powerful intellectual sources were probably purely pragmatic experiences in economic planning, national and international. Hence his technocratic stance, in practice, has usually been tempered with a political acumen conspicuously lacking in the Positivist technocrat. The Eurocrats of Brussels personify the pluralistic and politically sensitive expert I am about to extol.

16. Kelly, p. 545.

17. *Ibid.*, p. 543.

18. Obviously, this bald statement of the distribution of traits and relationships does not claim that there are no differences in pluralism within Western Europe, or among countries that share membership in the post-capitalist syndrome. For evidence on such differences, see Gabriel A. Almond and Sidney Verba, *The Civic Culture: Political Attitudes and Democracy in Five Nations* (Princeton, N.J.: Princeton University Press, 1963).

CHAPTER FOURTEEN

1. Gunnar Myrdal, *Beyond the Welfare State* (New Haven: Yale University Press, 1960), p. 80.

2. *Ibid.*, pp. 95–100.

3. *Ibid.*, pp. 132–35, 218–23.

4. *Ibid.*, p. 176 (italics in original).

5. *Ibid.*, pp. 196, 205.

6. *Ibid.*, p. 282; also pp. 275–81.

7. *Ibid.*, p. 264.

8. *Ibid.*, p. 111.

9. *Ibid.*, p. 96.

10. *Ibid.*, pp. 286–87.

11. For efforts at such projections using the work of Downs, Dahl, Stokes, Mac-Rae, and others, see Bruce M. Russett, "Toward a Model of Competitive International Politics," *Journal of Politics*, Vol. II (1963).

12. The concept of "permeability" is borrowed from John H. Herz. See his "Rise and Demise of the Territorial State," *World Politics*, Vol. IX, No. 4 (1957).

13. The historical as well as the analytical literature on nationalism is gargantuan. I shall list merely those works that have impressed me as seminal, and to which I owe much of the treatment that follows. Salo W. Baron, *Modern Nationalism and Religion* (New York: Harper, 1947); Karl W. Deutsch, *Nationalism and Social Communication* (New York: Wiley, 1953); Rupert Emerson, *From Empire to Nation* (Cambridge: Harvard University Press, 1960); C. J. H. Hayes, *The Historical Evolution of Modern Nationalism* (New York: Macmillan, 1948); Friedrich O. Hertz, *Nationality in History and Politics* (London: Kegan Paul, 1944); John H. Kautsky, *Political Change in Underdeveloped Countries: Nationalism and Communism* (New York: Wiley, 1962); Hans Kohn, *The Idea of Nationalism* (New York: Macmillan, 1943).

14. Actually, a relatively brief period of aggressive external Jacobin Nationalism may intervene. This did, in fact, happen in France, but it seems unsafe to generalize about it. Indonesia and Ghana, however, are showing very much the same tendencies now.

15. Britain, France, and Holland during the second half of the nineteenth century; Argentina since 1945; Brazil since 1950.

16. This is the general situation in Western Europe since 1945.

17. Ghana, Indonesia, perhaps Burma since 1960; Egypt since 1952.

18. Russia, 1825–1905; Meiji Japan; Buganda.

19. Japan since 1945.

20. Soviet Union, China.

21. Germany, 1815–70; Italy, 1815–60; Israel.

22. Poland, 1830–1918; Serbia during most of the nineteenth century; Czechoslovakia; Pakistan.

23. Germany and Italy between 1870 and 1920. For a brilliant exposition of Fascism as a "transitional" system which owed its development to unresolved imbalances and differentiations in industrializing society, see Ernst Nolde, *Der Faschismus in seiner Epoche* (Munich: Piper Verlag, 1963).

24. Pakistan after 1958; Germany and Italy during the interwar period.

25. Germany and Italy since 1945.

26. This has been the dominant pattern in Eastern Europe and the Balkans. Czechoslovakia is a deviant case because Liberal-Constitutionalism actually developed successfully until the communist take-over. Norway is another deviant.

27. In the instances of the United States, Canada, Nigeria, and the West Indies, there was little—if any—"nationalism" at the level of the federating states, though there were local attachments of a different sort. But in the case of Western Europe (since 1955), there was clearly nationalism at the level of the participating states, though there is precious little of it at the all-European level.

Clearly, I am not using "federal" in the constitutional sense of the term. Not every

constitutionally federal state represents the "federal" pattern of nationalist development, as is borne out by India, Mexico, and Yugoslavia.

28. Central American Federation, 1821–39; Gran Colombia between 1810 and
1825; West Indian Federation. Perhaps Malaysia will soon illustrate the same trend.

29. United States, 1861–76.

30. Confederate States of America, Swiss Sonderbund, various movements in
Quebec. Nigeria may reverse the pattern because the (currently) dominant elite is
also the Traditional-Authoritarian group, whereas the dissidents are the modern-
izers.

31. With respect to African governments, my greatest debt is to David E. Apter,
whose mode of analysis and categories I shamelessly exploited. See his "System,
Process and the Politics of Economic Development," in W. Moore and B. Hoselitz,
eds., *Industrialization and Society* (The Hague: Mouton, 1963). For a most impressive and persuasive analysis and projection of historical and current Latin-American
regimes, see Gino Germani and Kalman Silvert, "Politics, Social Structure and Military Intervention in Latin America," *European Journal of Sociology*, II (1961),
62–81.

32. I am indebted to David Apter for this projection. For his discussion of the
flexibility of mobilization systems, see *ibid.*, pp. 147–48, and his *Ghana in Transition* (New York: Atheneum, 1963).

33. David E. Apter, *The Political Kingdom in Uganda* (Princeton: Princeton University Press, 1961). Apter also uses a "reconciliation system" as a residual category
to connote any polity that values accommodation and consent over central direction.
But "rapid economic growth is possible in a reconciliation system if and only if there
is extensive self-discipline, popular participation, and great civic devotion. These
preconditions occur only very rarely in new nations." Apter, in Moore and Hoselitz,
p. 150.

34. Germani and Silvert, p. 64. The two most primitive of the six positions on the
continuum they suggest are not relevant to our projection.

35. All of Latin America today except the countries named in notes 36, 37, 38,
and 39.

36. Contemporary Colombia.

37. Brazil since Vargas; Chile; Mexico.

38. Uruguay and Costa Rica have attained this stage. Argentina may be on the
threshold.

39. Cuba has attained this stage. Venezuela is somewhere between the previous
stage and the fatal choice between the two dominant types.

40. See also the final section of Chapter 10, and the literature on post-capitalist
society there cited. We should add that the traditional negotiating function of trade
unions will probably decline in the West with the growth of extra-union factory
organs and national planning.

41. For illustrations of these arguments, see the material in Millen, pp. 35, 47, 70–
74, 98, 107–11, 112 ff. Also Tom Mboya, *Freedom and After* (Boston: Little, Brown,
1963).

42. Such has been Ayub's policy in Pakistan, using ILO advice in the process.
Galenson, *Labor in Developing Economies*, pp. 67–69. If the modernization process
were able to absorb the trade unionists thus "mobilized" into the governing elite,
no imbalance need be anticipated. In view of the general stagnation of Pakistan,
however, this is unlikely.

43. See U.S. Senate, Committee on Foreign Relations, 86th Cong., 1st Sess., *Possible Nonmilitary Scientific Developments and Their Potential Impact on Foreign*

Policy Problems of the United States, prepared by the Stanford Research Institute (Washington: GPO, 1959).

44. The term, as well as the reasoning associated with it, owes a great deal to the work of Wolfram Hanrieder, who stimulated my own work enormously. See his "International System and Foreign Policy: The Foreign Policy Goals of the Federal Republic of Germany (unpublished Ph.D. dissertation, University of California, Berkeley, 1963), pp. 215–37.

45. Robert E. Osgood, "Stabilizing the Military Environment," *American Political Science Review,* Vol. LV, No. 1 (1961).

46. For example, United Arab Republic, Guinea, Brazil, Mexico, Indonesia.

47. For example, Peru, Colombia, Congo (Léopoldville), Chad, Thailand, Iran, Cuba, North Korea.

48. My understanding and discussion of functional law are greatly indebted to Stuart A. Scheingold's studies of the judicial process in the European Communities. See his "Law and Politics in Western European Integration" (unpublished Ph.D. dissertation, University of California, Berkeley, 1963).

49. H. L. A. Hart, *The Concept of Law* (Oxford: Oxford University Press, 1961), p. 149 (italics in original).

50. Hoffmann, in *World Politics,* October 1961, pp. 212–13.

51. *Ibid.,* p. 227.

52. Hoffmann, p. 229.

53. For a detailed examination on the possibilities and limits on functional jurisprudence in Western Europe, see Scheingold, Chapters 15 and 16.

54. Two jurisprudential instances may be cited which, if consistently acted upon, would *not* advance this trend. One is the mixture of neo-naturalism and policy-oriented law that would seek to standardize as rules the major principles of military coexistence *and* the ideological commitment to the Western social pattern. See Myres S. McDougal and Florentino P. Feliciano, *Law and Minimum World Public Order* (New Haven: Yale University Press, 1961), and Richard A. Falk, *Law, Morality and War in the Contemporary World* (New York: Praeger, 1963). The other is provided by the Functionalism of Jenks. He is still enough of the traditional international lawyer to attempt to combine the functional notion of transterritorial "need" with a rigid textual procedure stressing open, public, and understandable processes and the satisfaction of the parties that standards of fairness have been observed. Yet, at the same time, he also insists that such procedure be supported by aroused public opinion! He can hardly expect to have it both ways, either in the current or in the future system. Jenks, *Trade Union Freedom,* pp. 530–31, 559–61.

In this connection, see also the rather puzzling treatment of functional law as applied to international voluntary groups in J. J. Lador-Lederer, *International Non-Governmental Organizations and Economic Entities* (Leyden: Sythoff, 1963). The author attempts to demonstrate a trend toward the dominance of the functional perspective over traditional legal notions, resting heavily on the argument of the need for international pluralism. But his survey of some 1,500 NGO's leads him to believe that they are "mere pressure groups" that would not actually meet the need.

55. Gustav F. Papanek, "Framing a Development Program," *International Conciliation,* No. 527 (March 1960), pp. 365–66. Papanek allows for the possibility that in any one country these considerations may be in conflict, and that not all need be satisfied in every case.

56. See John B. Edwards, "The Politics of the United Nations Special Fund" (unpublished M.A. thesis, University of California, Berkeley, 1963). Papanek proposed a private international foundation to make available a core of trained, apolitical, and

interchangeable economic development planners, who would be seconded to developing countries on request. Their impact would not substantially help international integration. See his *A Plan for Planning* (Harvard University, Center for International Affairs, Occasional Paper No. 1, 1961).

57. Hirschman proposed this concept and the policies connected with it in order to stimulate creative decision-making among elites in underdeveloped countries, who, in the past, have been psychologically or culturally unable to plan energetically with a view toward general social consequences. The specific socio-economic policies involved do not concern us here. What matters is the principle of planning implied. See his *The Strategy of Economic Development* (New Haven: Yale University Press, 1958) and historical examples of this kind of planning in *Journeys Toward Progress: Studies of Economic Policy-Making in Latin America* (New York: Twentieth Century Fund, 1963).

Even though Hirschman did not apply this concept to international economic planning, it remains within the bounds of possibility that the Inter-American Committee of the Alliance for Progress, created by the OAS in January 1964, will come to carry out such a function. The Committee is composed of experts broadly "representing" economic approaches rather than specific countries. It has the power to assess and stimulate economic planning in Latin America, as well as passing on United States measures supporting Latin American development. Even though the purpose of the Committee is to make the United States more responsive to Latin American economic development aspirations, it remains to be seen whether this effect will be achieved.

Index

Index

Adaptation and redefinition of goals, 48, 94–96, 97, 101, 111, 126–28, 131–33, 410, 443
Ad Hoc Committee on Forced Labor, 222–25, 257, 351
Ago formula, 211, 229
Alliance for Progress, 493
Almond, Gabriel A., 37, 59–60, 65–66
American Federation of Labor: opposition to ILO, 141, 142; participation in ILO, 198, 199, 221, 346, 541
Apter, David, 479–80
Argentina, and freedom of association, 420
Authority: and human rights, 340, 361, 366–67, 369–70, 370–80, 441; and international integration, 99–100, 131–32, 188–89, 276, 409, 431, 457f; of Committee on Freedom of Association, 403, 407, 415–23; of ILO, 195, 284, 380, 413, 425, 441f, 457; of Industrial Committees, 295, 307–32, 441; of international labor standards, 259–69, 276, 434–35
Autonomy, organizational, 88, 100–101, 119, 188; of Committee of Experts, 256–57; of ILO, 135, 162, 252–59, 431, 435–36, 438–39, 441, 443

Balance of power, 4–5, 52, 68–76
Banfield, E. C., 96, 114, 533
Barnard, Chester, 91, 96, 100, 103
Belgium: and international collective agreements, 293; and revision of ILO constitution, 163f, 295
Bevin, Ernest, and Industrial Committees, 293
Blacklisting in ILO, 253–54, 265–69
Building Trades Committee, 299f, 316, 321, 326f, 330f
Bureaucracy, 96, 98–100. *See also* Organization
Burns, Arthur Lee, 71–73
Butler, Harold, 143, 151f, 257, 435, 539

Center for Advanced Technical and Vocational Training, 184
Chemical Industries Committee, 317, 327, 330–31
Chile, and bakers' complaint, 356, 361
Chisholm, Brock, 122–23
Civil liberties, and freedom of association, 407–14
Claude, Inis L., 23, 521
Coal Mines Committee, 299, 316, 321, 325, 327, 332
Cognitive dissonance, 112
Collective bargaining, international, 292, 332–34. *See also* Industrial Committees; Joint Maritime Commission
Committee of Experts, 251–59, 263, 345, 367, 379–80
Communist countries: and human rights Conventions, 376, 378f; and Committee of Experts, 256, 259; and Committee on Freedom of Association, 384–85, 387, 395, 403, 416; and Industrial Committees, 302f, 334; and ILO, 212, 219, 224, 243, 317, 378, 440 (*see also* ILO and impact of Cold War); and labor standards, 262, 268, 272
Conference Committee, 251–59
Conflict: and decision-making, 103–13; and Functionalism, 20–21, 346, 424; and organizational growth, 93–96, 101, 110, 115, 127. *See also* Decision-making
Congress of Industrial Organizations (CIO), 199
Consensus, 38–40; accidental, 38, 79; based on converging interests, 33–34, 38–40, 134; and human rights, 339, 424–25; and international organization, 103, 110–11, 115–16, 244, 410, 454ff, 488–92 *passim*; in Committee on Freedom of Association, 383–85, 424; in Employer Group, 202–6; in Government Group, 209–12; in Indus-